CQ's State Fact Finder 1998

Rankings Across America

Kendra A. Hovey

Harold A. Hovey

Congressional Quarterly Inc.
Washington, D.C.

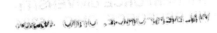

Printed in the United States of America

ISBN 1-56802-383-9 (cloth)
ISBN 1-56802-384-7 (paper)
ISSN 1079-7149

Contents

Detailed Contents of Subject Rankings

Government

Federal Impacts

Taxes

Revenues and Finances

Education

Health

Crime and Law Enforcement

Transportation

Welfare

Introduction

CQ's State Fact Finder is an important information source and analytical tool for any person interested in developments in America's fifty states and the District of Columbia. The series is a valuable reference source for anyone looking to uncover trends in the states, whether a policy expert seeking detailed data or an individual wishing to learn more about today's social, political, and economic currents.

The nation's economy, our population, and government actions are constantly changing. These changes affect states differently. So it is important that information be as up-to-date as possible. To meet this need, Congressional Quarterly is publishing *State Fact Finder* every year. This 1998 book is the fourth edition.

State Fact Finder 1998 reflects these changes with new data for more than 90 percent of the statistics covered in the 1997 edition. It is likely that about 90 percent of the statistics in this edition will be different by the time the 1999 edition is issued early in 1999. Readers can make sure they will receive the next edition as soon as it is published by establishing a standing order with Congressional Quarterly Press.

Many users will want to use the successive volumes of *State Fact Finder* as a valuable tool for identifying trends over time. The tables and statistical concepts in this book are closely comparable to those found in the first edition (1993). They are so comparable in the 1996, 1997, and 1998 editions that readers will be able to use them for statistical analyses of changes at the state level.

About This Book

The book was prepared by experts who work constantly with data comparing states to analyze state policy options and to compare states in ways important to policymakers, such as the success of their efforts to promote economic development and the costs and apparent results of their decisions. As a result, this book differs considerably from ordinary compilations of statistics in several important ways.

First, *State Fact Finder* includes many statistics that are not included in standard statistical reports of government agencies, and thus don't appear in compilations of statistics which rely solely on such published reports. For example, many of the tables in the health and welfare sections comparing state programs for low-income people are based on unpublished statistics maintained by agencies that administer these programs. Also, there are tables such as B-28, the Index of State Economic Momentum, and G-21, a comparison of state spending needs, which reflect original research by State Policy Research.

Second, information from other sources is converted to a basis that makes comparisons meaningful. For example, information on the headquarters of the largest companies in America in Table B-16 includes the number of companies in each state in relation to population as well as the total number of companies.

Third, each table provides a ranking of the states. This makes it easy for readers to see how the state or states that interest them relate to neighboring states and to other states throughout the nation.

Fourth, the volume begins with an essay (*Finding What Information Users Want to Know*), in which the authors guide readers through the use of the information. This section helps readers understand the scope of information available to them.

Finally, *State Fact Finder* offers carefully documented source notes that follow the tables in each section. These notes list the origins of the statistics in each table and guide readers to additional sources where more information on the same topic can be obtained.

About the Publisher

This book was first published by Congressional Quarterly in 1993 as part of CQ's fifty-year tradition of providing comprehensive, reliable, and focused information about national public policy issues in America. This effort has broadened in recent years to include developments and trends in the states through books such as *State Fact Finder* and the creation of *Governing*, a magazine covering all aspects of state government.

About the Authors

State Policy Research is known to state government experts everywhere as one of the most reliable and knowledgeable organizations dealing with state-level information. State Policy Research publishes the periodicals *State Policy Reports* and *State Budget & Tax News* and for a decade published *States in Profile*, which has now merged into *State Fact Finder*. The organization also provides the tables which appear in *Governing* magazine's annual *State and Local Sourcebook*.

Information Development

Any data book is by definition a work in progress. What is useful one year may be less helpful the next, as new information needs arise. For these and many other reasons, the editors welcome reaction from readers, suggestions for additional information or changes in presentation, and, of course, any corrections or clarifications that come to the readers' attention. These should be sent to Kendra Hovey at State Policy Research, 221 West Lakeview Ave., Columbus, Ohio 43202. She can be reached by phone at 614-262-9229 or by fax at 614-268-2669.

Finding Information Users Want to Know

Readers differ in their preferences on many things—from what they value in a place to live to the amount of state government spending they consider appropriate. They will not agree on such subjects as where they should move or which state is governed best.

In this section, rather than impose personal values as though they were facts by ranking some states as the "best place" to live or do business, the authors have provided guideposts on how to use the tables so that readers can obtain the information they need. Using a question-and-answer format, this section leads readers to groups of tables that can be consulted together to deal with the broad questions, such as which state might have the best schools or the best business opportunities.

The section is divided into three parts, each based on particular types of decisions people use state statistics to make. The first covers personal and family decisions, such as job opportunities. The second focuses on business decisions, such as where to locate a new plant. The third provides information about the government to assist people in their roles as voters and in influencing public policy.

Subject Rankings

This section forms the heart of the book. It is organized in twelve subject areas that are challenging policy makers throughout the country: population, economies, geography, government, federal impacts, taxes, revenues and finances, education, health, crime, transportation, and welfare. States are listed alphabetically in each table. The information also is presented in rankings that allow a reader to see how each state compares with the others.

Source Notes

The source notes that follow each section are designed to be used in tandem with the subject rankings to understand the specific usefulness of, and any caveats about, the data. The sources for all the statistics in the book are documented so that the calculations can be replicated or expanded upon by those who need more detail than space allows here. These source notes allow the reader to locate other information sources that may be useful.

State Rankings

The state rankings section provides the reader with a composite view of each state. In this section, the editors bring together the rankings for each state of most of the data included in the volume. This compilation gives readers a quick summary of their states' positions in each subject area.

Index

The index guides the reader to topics presented in the various sections of the book.

Introduction to the Data

Rankings: There is nothing magical about rankings, though *State Fact Finder* generally follows the convention of most statisticians by ranking from highest to lowest. Most rankings can be interpreted similarly by reversing them. For example, a table showing tax burdens from highest to lowest can be reversed to show tax burdens from lowest to highest by ranking the fiftieth state first, the forty-ninth state second, and so on.

Data Accuracy: The statistics in this volume vary greatly in their accuracy. Some, such as the land area of states or the number of state legislators, can be measured precisely. Other data, such as birth rates or finances of local governments, are estimates. The source notes generally explain how the data were developed or direct readers to the statistical providers, who usually have available detailed technical papers on their methods.

In preparing this report, the editors worked with data as presented by the statistical source. In presenting the data in tables, figures were rounded to a manageable number of digits (such as by expressing financial data as $24.5 million rather than $24,515,078). As a result, the rankings that are based on detailed data will show one state ranked above another even though they are apparently tied in the data published in the table.

Junk Data: Many special interest groups have strong opinions about appropriate policies for governments. They translate these opinions into rankings of which states are "best" for the subject of their interest, such as protecting the environment, providing mental health, or keeping a favorable climate for business. Sometimes the resulting statistics themselves are unreliable. Sometimes they combine individually reliable statistics into measures that simply reflect the policy preferences of those who rank the composite results. Such reports are generally not included in *State Fact Finder*, but the editors are familiar with them and are willing to help *State Fact Finder* readers deal with them.

Time Periods: The tables all deal with the specific time periods indicated in the headings. These are normally calendar years. In the case of fiscal data, the time period is fiscal years that end in the year shown.

District of Columbia: The District of Columbia has a unique status in any statistical compilation. It is not a state in the sense that it has no voting representatives in Congress and is counted as a city, not a state, in all Census Bureau statistics on government finances. However, the Census Bureau does include its residents within the total population of the United States. Federal agencies and private data-gathering organizations differ in how they treat the District, Puerto Rico, the Virgin Islands, and other entities in their statistics.

State Fact Finder presents information for the District of Columbia in each table but does not include it in the state rankings. State Policy Research has consistently avoided including the District for two reasons. First, users of rankings find this inclusion cumbersome to explain, often having to resort to particular explanations of rankings (such as a state being ranked fifth, fourth among states and also behind the District of Columbia). Second, the District is economically and demographically a central city with fiscal and other attributes of most central cities (high taxes, high crime rates, large percentages of population in poverty and receiving government benefits, and so forth). When ranked along with states, the District often ranks first or last in the tables, distorting other rankings.

Finding What Information Users Want To Know

Most people look at state statistics to answer specific questions related to a decision they need to make but often discover that the statistics they seek do not appear in the reference books they consult. Alternatively, they find some comparisons that seem to be relevant but wonder if they are.

State Fact Finder continues a feature not found in other compilations of data about states. Besides finding tables, readers can consult this section to find a list of frequently asked questions. Under each question they will find information about which statistics in this book should be helpful in trying to find answers, as well as road maps to other statistics that might be useful. Readers sometimes will be informed that the statistics they seek are not available anywhere and why.

This section is divided into three parts, each based on particular types of decisions people use state statistics to make. The first covers personal and family decisions, such as finding the states with the best job opportunities, the best health care, and even the best chances for finding a spouse. The second covers business decisions, such as where to locate a new business or where to find the most productive workers. This section is also useful for investors. The third contains information about government to assist people in their roles as voters and in influencing public policy.

About Personal Decisions on Where to Live or Visit

1 Where is the best place to find a job?

As a general rule, people find it easier to get a job, higher pay, better opportunities for advancement, and better opportunities for building professional practices if they locate in rapidly expanding economies. If they go to places in economic decline they will find few job opportunities and stiff competition to get the positions that do exist.

To find states with rapidly expanding economies, look at measures of recent economic growth, particularly the Index of State Economic Momentum (B-28), population growth (A-3), job growth (B-29, B-30), and projections of future population growth (A-4). The Index (B-28) is especially useful because it summarizes the three elements of economic growth important to job-seekers: population growth, income growth, and increases in the number of jobs.

Growth rates are particularly important if you seek jobs that are inherently related to growth, such as jobs in the construction industry. Because the need for construction relates to *changes* in the need for homes and buildings, there are massive differences between fast- and slow-growing states. For example, in 1996 there were 23 new homes being built for every 1,000 residents of Nevada but only 2 for every 1,000 residents of New York (B-20).

When a state is classified as rapidly growing, this does not necessarily mean that all local areas in the state are growing. For example, the fast growth in Nevada is concentrated in the Las Vegas area. Growth in the Pacific Northwest is occurring along the Pacific Coast between Seattle and Portland, but there are few job opportunities in the eastern parts of Oregon and Washington. To find which areas are growing and in what types of industries and jobs, you can consult local sources, such as state economic development departments, local chambers of commerce, or even friends familiar with the area. For nationwide statistics on growth in metropolitan areas, you can get information on recent job growth from the Bureau of Labor Statistics. Somewhat less current statistics on income and other economic factors are available from the Department of Commerce, including detailed books on major counties called *County Business Patterns*.

2 Where will tax burdens be least for me and my family?

The tables in the Taxes section (F) are good guides to average tax burdens. Table F-1 shows what share of personal income goes to state and local taxes in each state. Tables F-6, F-9, and F-13 do this for each of the major taxes: property, sales, and personal income. The range among states is very large. For example, New York governments take 15.5 percent of income in state and local taxes, while governments in Alabama take only 9.4 percent.

The taxes you actually pay will depend on your circumstances, such as how much property you plan to own in relation to your income. You can see the major differences on Tables F-16 and F-23. For example, Florida and Texas have tax systems that wealthy retirees will like— no income, inheritance, or estate taxes. Young couples without much income will pay heavy sales taxes and find that renters do not share in special property tax breaks for homeowners. For them, states like Oregon, which have no sales tax but steep income taxes, might be a better deal.

The state and local taxes you pay will be a combination of state government taxes, which are uniform throughout entire states, and local taxes. These vary greatly from place to place within a state. There are about 50,000 local governments in the United States with the power to set tax rates and there are 50 states—an average of about 1,000 different local governments in each state.

Depending on where you decide to live, you may find you are paying property taxes that are the sum of individual taxes levied by a county; a municipality or township; a school district; perhaps a second school district, such as a community college or vocational district; and hosts of special districts, such as road districts, transit districts, mosquito control districts, and levee districts—to mention just a few of the possibilities. Local governments in many states also levy sales taxes and a few states have significant local income taxes, such as the steep income taxes of New York City and Philadelphia. All these taxes are reflected in the state averages.

Because of these differences, what you pay will depend on where you live even though state government taxes are uniform throughout each state. To find local areas with low taxes within a state, look for places that have large business sources of tax revenues combined with small numbers of people to serve. In most metropolitan areas, there are suburbs with concentrations of office buildings, shopping centers, and businesses that have much lower property taxes than surrounding areas. Realtors in metropolitan regions will be able to identify them. For property taxes, check the county government where you want to locate. The county officials who collect property taxes will have rate information for each local area.

Most state tax departments, with offices in state capitals and major cities, publish free booklets describing all their state taxes and tax rates.

3 Which state has the best public schools?

To compare how well students do, consider the first five tables in the Education section. Use Tables H-1 and H-2 for overall comparisons, H-3 for students not going to college right away, and H-4 and H-5 for the college preparation programs. You can also use the tables to compare states on measures of what they spend per student (H-15), what they pay teachers (H-16), class sizes (H-9), and more.

Except in Hawaii, all schools are local. Expect to find immense variations within areas in every state; these are as important as the variations from state to state. All state education departments, located in state capitals, keep statistics for each school district on spending and number of teachers and pupils. Some states issue "report cards" comparing district performance measures, such as how students do on standardized tests. You can use these or research locally such indicators as percentage of graduates that go on to college, percentages winning National Merit Scholarships and other awards, and local reputations for good schools.

How well students do depends heavily on how much help and motivation they get at home, not just on what happens at school. Much of the difference among states is caused by differences in the students, not in the schools. This is true for districts within a state as well.

One key is getting a child into the right school, not just the right school district. Some of the best specialized programs, and some of the worst schools, are found in central cities.

If you want to send children to private schools, do not expect much help from government. Many states are considering "voucher" plans that would help with tuition, but such plans are only available now in Ohio and Wisconsin, where they mostly serve poor, inner-city children. Iowa and Minnesota provide limited income tax breaks if you pay private school tuition.

4 Which state is best for children?

Throughout *State Fact Finder* you will find many tables comparing states on aspects of life important to children, including health, education, crime, and economic opportunity. If you crave even more comparisons, detailed ones are available from the Children's Defense Fund (25 E Street NW, Washington, D.C. 20001, 202-628-8787) and from the Annie E. Casey Foundation (One Lafayette Place, Greenwich, CT 06830, 203-661-2773) in the annual *Kids Count Data Book*.

Children grow up in small worlds, such as school buildings and neighborhoods, so do not expect to rely totally on facts about states, metropolitan areas, or even individual cities and counties for information important to your child's life. Where your child is within one of these areas is often much more important than which area the child is in. State differences are important in such fields as the quality of education and the possibilities for getting a job.

5 Which is the best state for retirement?

Most people retire within twenty miles of where they lived when they stopped working. For them, finding the right place is more a matter of finding the right house or apartment in the right community rather than finding the right state. If you are thinking about retirement in another state, *State Fact Finder* can be helpful, but you will need to go beyond it to make an informed decision.

Do not start with statistics comparing places, unless your overriding concern is minimizing the taxes you will pay. Start with your own preferences. Decide first on how far you are willing to be from your family and old friends and on key climate issues, such as whether you want to avoid ice and snow and whether you will like places that do not have changing seasons of the year. Most people will be able to narrow their choices considerably this way before they look at statistics.

If you are willing to take the time to look systematically at what is important to you about a place, take a "preference inventory" such as the one found in *Retirement Places Rated* by David Savageneau. It will force you to consider whether being able to get a part time job, see and hear a symphony orchestra, follow a professional sports team, and other items are important to you.

In the tables in *State Fact Finder*, you will see systematic differences among the states in such characteristics as income and education levels of residents, living costs, crime, and taxes.

There are many books designed to help with retirement decisions. A library or good bookstore should be able to recommend some reference book choices. Some describe places to live and provide information on investments, Medicare, and estate planning. *The Only Retirement Guide You'll Ever Need* by Kathryn and Ross Petras (1991) is an example. Some deal only with places to retire, often with different emphases, such as health (*The 50 Healthiest Places to Live and Retire in the United States* by Normal D. Ford, 1991) or specialized retirement areas (*Retirement Places Rated*, which covers Kauai, Hawaii, and Hilton Head, South Carolina, but not New York City or any place in Ohio or Illinois).

The American Association of Retired Persons is a good source for a variety of publications on retirement, including specialized guides on state taxes. One topic of particular interest to retirees is what percentage of income from Social Security is taxed by each state.

6 Which state universities are best?

State Fact Finder contains some important statistics that are relevant to selecting among state university systems. Look for them in Tables H-19 to H-24. State statistics alone cannot pick a university to attend because state systems include everything from community colleges to medical schools. California even has systems within systems. They vary from the University of California, with campuses at Berkeley and elsewhere, which contains some of the finest institutions in the country; to California State University, which enjoys less of a national reputation but has some outstanding specialized programs; to community colleges with diverse and varying strengths and weaknesses.

Students attend schools, not states. Consult guides and ratings on individual schools that contain information on the numbers of students, types of curriculum, costs, and attempted assessments of the quality of students and faculty.

7 Which state has the best cultural attractions and recreation?

Recreational opportunities cannot be adequately measured by statistics. Attempts to do so often are misleading. For example, you will find by far the best ratio of park land to people in Alaska, but much of the state is covered by glaciers that are not fit for hiking or camping. Some fine experiences—the "big sky" of Montana, the bustle of the streets of New York, and the beauty of fall foliage in New England—are not specific places and do not count attendance.

There are fairly good statistics about how many people participate in various sports in each state. Table C-6 is an example. See the notes to this table at the end of the chapter for how to obtain specific information on other sports. Most sports have specialized equipment stores, magazines, and guidebooks that are superior to state statistics for making personal recreational choices. For example, just because there are more golfers and courses per capita in one state than another does not mean you will not find more than enough courses and players to make foursomes in the lower ranked states.

Cultural opportunities are listed in the many guidebooks and specialized magazines published in nearly every possible field of interest. Government spending on the arts, shown in Table C-8, is not a useful indicator of the extent or quality of arts in each state. States spend, on average, about $1 per year per capita funding the arts—amounts that are dwarfed by sales revenues, admissions, and donations.

8 Where is the best place to invest in property?

Nearly everyone interested in owning real estate has heard the old saw about the three keys to real estate investment: location, location, and location. This applies to states and metropolitan areas within states. For example, statistics in Table B-21 from the Office of Federal Housing Enterprise Oversight show that in the three years from 1992 to 1997, the average house in Utah appreciated by 73.8 percent while the average house in Hawaii lost 9.9 percent of its value. Of course, how much your investment will lose or appreciate depends on the property you buy, whether you pay the right price, and local market conditions.

It is hard to pick a winner in a field of losers and hard to pick a loser in a field of winners. You want to pick the right state (and metropolitan area in that state) for your investment.

Real estate prices depend on supply and demand. Supply does not go down much in poor markets—who would tear down a house or office building just because values were dropping? Supply responds to increased demand in good markets, but prices rise because new construction usually costs more than established buildings, prices of lots and construction labor tend to rise, and the most desirable locations generally already have buildings on them.

The best strategy for real estate investment is to pick an area with an expanding economy, where lots of new jobs are being created. Look at the answer to Question 1 (where to find a job) for tips on using *State Fact Finder* to identify those places.

9 Can picking the right states help pick winners in stocks and bonds?

Few economists or investment professionals would suggest picking which company's stocks to buy based on the states in which their headquarters or plants are found. The important questions are how good are the products and how well are they marketed. Some successful companies operate from unlikely places. For example, computer-maker Gateway is based in farm country in South Dakota and apparel seller L. L. Bean is based in rural Maine.

For making things, being in a fast-growing economy is bad news, not good news. In fast-growing economies, it is harder to get and keep good workers, their pay is often higher, and transportation facilities are often congested. Only look for strong state and regional economies when looking for regionally oriented companies that sell products, such as new homes and fast food, directly to consumers.

Most people who buy tax-exempt bonds do so through mutual funds or rely heavily on bond-rating agencies, such as Standard & Poor's and Moody's. Those professional investors rely heavily on the kinds of economic, population, and government statistics used in *State Fact Finder* and analyses of recent fiscal developments presented in publications like State Policy Research's *State Budget & Tax News* and *State Policy Reports*. People who buy individual bonds or buy mutual funds of tax-exempt bonds issued from a single state, like those that invest solely in the bonds of New York or California, can use these same statistics.

10 Which state government will interfere least with my freedom?

People occasionally say they would like to live where government interferes less with their daily lives. Government intrusiveness cannot easily be compared because governments often restrict the freedom of some citizens to enhance that of others. The ultimate example is capital punishment, which is the most intrusive concept imaginable for the person being punished but is used in the name of increasing freedom from fear and crime for everyone else. State policies are not necessarily consistent on intrusiveness issues. For example, the states that are most likely to allow you to own weapons without restriction are least likely to let you grow marijuana on your own property for personal consumption.

Some elements of government intrusiveness can be measured. One is taxes, measured by the many comparisons in the Taxes section (F). *State Policy Reports* designed an experimental comparison of tax intrusiveness (Vol. 12, Issue 24, December 1994), giving extra weight to property taxes and counting only taxes paid by households, not businesses. With a national average set at 100, it showed variation from 142 in most intrusive New York to 32 in least intrusive Alaska.

Another way to look at intrusiveness is the ratio of state and local government employees to population (D-13). If you find local governments closer to citizens and less intrusive than state governments, look at measures of differences in state and local roles as indicated by public employees (D-15) and revenue raising (D-16).

11 Where are taxes likely to go up/down in the future?

Tax rates are set by state legislatures and local bodies (school boards, city councils, county commissions, etc.). Predicting where taxes will be raised or lowered would appear to be a matter of forecasting the views of those who now serve or will subsequently be elected to these bodies. The economic and population statistics in *State Fact Finder* provide some excellent clues to future tax rates, as does common sense thinking about why some states have higher taxes than others.

Right now, the states with the lowest taxes on people who live there are the states that get lots of their money from other sources—tourists, oil and gas, and gaming casinos, for example. States amply endowed with these—such as Alaska, Nevada, Texas, and Wyoming—have been able to keep taxes low while still offering extensive government services. Some states have been able to keep taxes on their residents relatively low because they have been able to draw new residents who pay substantial taxes but do not have children in public schools, which is the biggest single cause of state and local spending. Fast-growing states of the Southwest and Florida have been the best examples.

These same states will be under the strongest pressures to raise tax levels in the future. As more people come to them, the amount that their unique resources contribute to revenues *per resident* drops. Furthermore, as time passes, their populations become more like the national averages. For example, the childless young people who flocked to Florida in large numbers to work at tourist attractions and to provide health care and other services to retirees are having children in large numbers. Florida has to pay for putting nearly 100,000 additional students in its classrooms every year. California and Texas face similar pressures.

12 Which states have the least/most pollution?

State Fact Finder presents summary statistics on air and water pollution and hazardous waste (C-10 to C-14). More important, the notes to the tables provide leads to where to get more details on local areas. State averages are misleading for people seeking to decide where to live or visit. For example, western cities, like Denver and Salt Lake City, have some of the worst air pollution problems in the nation, but away from urban areas the air in these states is about as pure as you will find. An average for California that lumps downtown Los Angeles with the forests of northern California and the state's deserts will not give an accurate picture of any of these places.

13 Where do I find the best health care?

Because much more money is spent in gathering them, state-by-state statistics on health and health care (section I) are quite comprehensive compared with statistics in other fields. The statistics cover (1) health of average people in a state's population, (2) apparent availability of care, (3) cost of care, and (4) government programs, which are generally oriented to poor people. These statistics suggest strong concentrations of health professionals in northeastern states.

People worried about whether they can find adequate health care for themselves and their family need not be guided by these statistics. Most people are limited to amounts their insurance will pay. Because insurers will not pay for long-distance travel and hotel bills except in rare cases, the doctors capable of performing all types of operations have been locating in the areas across the country where paying patients are found. One result is the development of top-flight facilities across the country, such as the University of Iowa hospital, which serves as a specialized facility for patients throughout that state, and the medical complex around Birmingham, Alabama. There is no reason for anyone to avoid an entire state because of concerns about health care, unless they have a very specialized medical problem. The main limits on health care are primarily those that people accept by their decisions on where to locate within a state. People who seek near-wilderness isolation by buying ranches in Colorado or locating on small islands off the Atlantic Ocean must accept the consequences of their isolation on the availability of health care.

14 Where will I be safest from crime?

State statistics, and even city statistics, on crime are not much help in looking for a safe place to live. In every state, crime is most prevalent in the low-income areas of central cities. Violent crimes are most prevalent in these areas after dark. Reported crime statistics overstate crime risks for people who do not spend evenings in low-income central city areas. A high crime rate for an entire state says more about the percentage of a state's population living in these areas than about safety in that state's suburban, small town, and rural areas as compared with similar areas in other states.

City and state crime rates are also misleading when used to consider which places are safe to visit on business or recreational trips. All statistics, like crime rates and per capita amounts, that relate a category to population use night-time population—the number of people whose regular beds are in a city or state. States such as Florida, Hawaii, and Nevada have many visitors for vacations and conventions. Cities have day-time commuters and business and vacation travelers. Crime rates in cities and these states are much lower for people at risk than when expressed in relation to the number of people who regularly sleep there.

15 Where is the best place to look for a mate?

People looking for an opposite sex partner can reasonably expect better opportunities in locations where they are outnumbered by persons of the opposite sex (A-13). However, aggregate statistics can be misleading for people under fifty-five looking for a partner about their own age. Because women live longer than men, the states with predominately older populations (A-6) also tend to have high ratios of women to men. Careful research by several women on the Federal Reserve Bank of Boston's research staff found the worst sex ratios (from the standpoint of women seeking men) in older northeastern cities and the states with a high percentage of jobs in health care, government, and financial services, which are disproportionately filled by women. The best ratios, again from the perspective of women seeking men, were in booming western states where economic growth draws large numbers of young men to occupations such as mining and construction.

16 Where can I find the lowest living costs?

State Fact Finder includes the best information in use on comparative living costs (B-8), but the data must be used with care. For reasons appearing in the table notes, these measures are not likely to be accurate for what they try to measure—average living costs—and more accurate data are not likely to be available. Also, there are substantial variations within states. All costs, except state and local taxes, are about the same in midsize cities and rural areas throughout the nation. The major differences are taxes (see section F) and costs related to economic growth (see section B). In booming communities and states, housing prices soar, wage rates tend to be higher, and ample and growing sales discourage everyone from doctors to corner store owners from engaging in price wars. In depressed communities and slow-growth states (for example, West Virginia and older industrial communities such as Syracuse, and St. Louis), the reverse factors are reducing housing costs, wages, and prices.

Different people buy different things, so the costs they experience will differ from averages, often by wide margins. Business travelers experience enormous price differences in what they buy—downtown hotel rooms, rental cars, and meals at restaurants catering to expense-account travelers. Highly paid executives with downtown jobs will find large differentials, particularly if they hope to live within fifteen minutes commuting time of their work. The largest differentials are associated with the size of metropolitan areas, not with states. New York, Chicago, and Los Angeles are expensive places for these people, but Rochester, Joliet, and Fresno are not.

Most people will not see such large differences in living costs. Much of what they buy—cars, furniture, alcoholic beverages and soft drinks, packaged foods, motion pictures and videotapes, books, sports equipment, clothing, and more—is produced long distances away. The prices generally reflect only minor differences in shipping costs among states, except Alaska and Hawaii where prices are higher. A large part of the housing costs will depend on mortgage rates, which are nearly uniform nationwide. Most will select homes far enough away from congested central cities so that older home prices cannot get too far out of line with what it costs to build new houses, which is about the same nationwide.

About Business Decisions on Where to Locate and Expand

1 Where is the best place to locate a business?

State Fact Finder provides useful statistics for some kinds of business but not all. Businesses that depend on local customers—from doctors' offices to fast-food franchises—will usually do better in rapidly growing areas. To use *State Fact Finder* to identify these areas, see Question 1 in the previous section. Some local businesses have specialized markets, appealing primarily to clearly defined groups, such as children or the retired. To identify where such populations are large and growing, study the tables in the sections on population and the economy.

Sophisticated investors in consumer-oriented businesses, like franchises, often do extensive market research before committing their money. The same is true for companies deciding how and where to market consumer products, from cars to shampoo. The serious researchers are generally looking at geographic detail not found in sources like *State Fact Finder*—zip codes and even streets and Census tracts, rather than states or metropolitan areas. They rely on their own publications, most notably *American Demographics*. Many private companies specialize in providing such information and in the computer software to use it. They advertise in such publications.

Some businesses, such as manufacturing companies, can separate where they produce products from where their consumers are located. Their business often limits their location choices. Mining and oil production companies need to be on top of their raw materials. Manufacturing needs an ample supply of labor and may have special transportation requirements, such as access to a rail line or deep-water port.

Among locations that satisfy manufacturers' needs, the factors that help determine what is the best location mostly relate to costs—labor costs, state and local taxes, electricity prices, and transportation costs. Every firm, indeed every plant, is different in where it gets supplies, where its customers are located, how much and what kind of energy it uses, and the relative use of labor and machinery. This means the best place to locate depends on the match between the needs of a particular firm and the attractions of a potential plant site.

State Fact Finder contains much useful information to compare business locations. The Population (A) and Economics (B) sections provide information about potential markets for selling products and hiring workers. The Government (D) section offers information about how states are governed. The Taxes (F) and Revenues (G) sections cover factors associated with each state's tax burdens. Elements of government-provided services that are important to business are discussed in the Education (H) and Transportation (K) sections.

In establishing a business oriented to local economic growth, the important question is what growth *will be,* not what growth was. Most statistics show what it *was.* As the warning about mutual funds goes, "past performance is no guarantee of future results." So, too, for state economic growth.

Future growth will depend on many factors, such as changes in oil prices, federal spending (particularly defense), and how well particular firms and industries (and thus the places where they are located) do in the marketplace. To make predictions on future growth, you can review trend statistics (A-2, B-29, and E-2) or look at the composite Index of State Economic Momentum (B-28). Forecasts can be purchased from firms specializing in forecasting or obtained inexpensively from the Department of Commerce (14th Street and Constitution Avenue N.W., Washington, D.C. 20230).

2 Which state has the most productive workers?

In their industrial development ads in business magazines, some states try to convince firms to locate within their borders because their workers are more productive. Productivity in this context is an elusive concept. Many experts are not even sure that national figures about changes in worker productivity are right, much less state-by-state numbers on the same subject.

Employers' ideas of a productive worker may vary from situation to situation. For example, software design and advertising place a premium on creativity and originality, so employees that work irregular hours still may be considered highly productive. An assembly line, however, will not work unless all the workers show up at the same time. Having lots of formal schooling may make engineers productive, but experience may be better for those who repair plumbing or who fish for a living.

State Fact Finder has many statistics on factors employers may consider to be signs of productivity, particularly in the Education (H) and Health (I) sections. *State Fact Finder* also includes the statistics usually used to calculate productivity in states (B-7), but such data are misleading for the reasons explained in the notes to the table.

3 Which states have the lowest labor costs?

Most comparisons among states regarding labor costs are based on average annual pay (B-5), as well as annual averages in retailing (B-10) and manufacturing (B-9). However, they will not necessarily be correct for hiring new workers in a particular occupation in a particular location within a state. The wages that must be paid to get competent workers in such a situation will depend upon the supply of labor and the demand for it in that local labor market. Firms looking for low-wage workers should do just the opposite of workers looking for high-paying firms, as discussed in Question 1 of the Personal Decisions section.

The really important statistic is how much work an employer gets from a worker in relation to a dollar paid. That statistic is elusive because productivity per worker is hard to calculate accurately (see Question 2, above). For a sophisticated attempt to calculate this unit labor cost in relation to productivity, see the research presented by Regional Financial Associates (West Chester, Pa.), including *The High Costs of High Costs* (1995).

4 Where will my business pay the least taxes?

State taxes on business are a complex web of interlocking provisions made even more complex because many local governments have separate taxes on business. These combinations have different impacts on different types of business, depending on such factors as how profitable they are; how capital-intensive they are; whether they qualify for state and local economic development incentives; and whether they are organized as proprietorships, partnerships, S (small business) corporations, or C (regular) corporations. There is no substitute for learning the tax rules for the states and localities where you might operate and applying them to the expected characteristics (payroll, profits, etc.) of the business you plan to start or move. These calculations are so complicated that a major consulting industry has developed to make them.

State Fact Finder provides some good indicators of the possible results of these calculations. Start with the overall levels of taxes (F-1 to F-3). If these are high, you will pay them somewhere—if not in taxes on your firm, then in taxes on your salary, your house, and what your firm pays for utility services. Next, look at the burdens of the specific taxes important to your operations. If you will have high investments in property (plant and equipment), see Tables F-6 to F-8. If you are concerned about payroll taxes, see Tables F-13 to F-16. If you are concerned about taxes on your sales, see Tables F-9 to F-12.

If yours is a local service business, such as a bakery or retail store, you do not have to worry much about state taxes on your business. Unless you are near a border with another state, your competitors will be paying the same taxes as you. This may not be true with local taxes, so you have to check them specifically. If yours is a small business, you may not be as worried about some taxes, particularly corporate income and franchise taxes, as large firms. You may be more concerned with certain taxes on individuals, such as income and estate taxes, as shown in Tables F-16 and F-23.

If yours is a nationally oriented business, such as manufacturing, you may be in for some pleasant and unpleasant surprises about taxes on your business. Some states with high overall tax levels, such as New York, are very competitive in taxes on manufacturing. Some states with low taxes on households, particularly those with no taxes on personal incomes, have relatively high taxes on firms. For multistate firms, opening a plant in one state affects corporate income taxes in all the states because of the way corporate income is apportioned among states for tax purposes. For samples of calculations of corporate taxes of different industries in many states, see studies that the accounting firm of KPMG Peat Marwick has prepared for states studying their "tax competitiveness." Recent studies have been made for Kentucky, New York, and North Carolina.

5 Which states provide the best incentives to locate in them?

The amounts and types of assistance available from state and local governments in tax breaks, grants, and loans for locating in their jurisdiction depend on the type of business. If your business inherently serves local customers—an auto dealership, restaurant, retail store, or repair business, for example—expect no significant help from these governments. Your new business is not going to increase the wealth or income of the area you serve but rather just move it from those already there and competing for the same business you want. You may get some technical assistance and even loans, but mostly from state and local agencies administering federal small business money. If you pick the right state and right local government within that state, you may get some tax breaks because local communities compete for tax base with other local communities.

If your business will draw money from out-of-state, your business (large or small) will likely be offered major incentives from just about any state. There are so many incentives and the number is growing so fast that a directories of them, such as the one published by the Urban Institute in 1991, are obsolete the day they are released. Do not try to use national directories of these. Even if you do you will miss the deals that states might be willing to tailor to fit your business. Nearly every community of any size and all states employ "developers"—economic development professionals whose mission is to draw employers to their community or state by providing information and administering incentives. These people are eager to provide you with details about sites, taxes, worker availability, and state and local incentives. Look for state agencies with *development* in their titles and find local agencies through county or city governments or chambers of commerce.

6 Which states have the lowest utility rates?

Statistics comparing state averages of electric rates for various consumers appear in Tables B-34. They are indicative of rate differentials for other fuels as well. In general, the farther you locate from the sources of inexpensive energy (the gas fields of the Southwest and hydroelectric sites), the more expensive energy will be. Taxes make a big difference in what you pay for energy. So do state policies that determine how the total bill is divided between household, commercial, and industrial uses, as Table B-34 dramatically illustrates. There are price variations within states among users of differing quantities and among types of industrial service (such as cheaper rates for those who will close their plants on high-use days). Many concessions are made to firms newly locating in an area or who demonstrate they can obtain service from a competitor utility. There is no substitute for checking the prices the local utilities charge.

7 Which states regulate business the least?

There is no statistical way to compare state and local regulation of business across the board because there are so many different ways government regulation touches business operations. There is also great variation in policies among states and local areas. Many of the regulatory differences are not systematic. For example, some southern states have less stringent regulation of workplace conditions while imposing more stringent regulation on how corporations are governed.

8 Where is the transportation system best?

The interstate transportation systems—road, rail, air, and even barge lines—form an interconnected network that reaches every state in some way. Once your products or raw materials reach this network, service is close to uniform until they leave it. For businesses with large shipping requirements, the key aspect is how easily you can connect with the national networks used by your particular business. This varies with geography, not state lines, and is critically dependent on exactly where your site is located relative to rail and other transportation access points. As every driver knows, the quality and capacity of roads depends on exactly which roads you use.

However, there are systematic differences among states. These appear most dramatically in measures of maintenance and construction, the condition of bridges (K-3), and highway pavement (K-2).

9 Which states have pro-business attitudes?

Like the rest of us, business owners and managers have differing needs and differing views of appropriate public policies. For example, a company engaged in a low-technology, labor-intensive activity such as poultry processing is not much concerned with the education of its workers but is highly concerned with pollution control costs, state labor regulations, and taxes. A company engaged in high-tech competition for improved designs of computer chips or software is not as affected by such state regulation or even taxes; it is highly sensitive to how well educated employees are and whether governments offer strong university systems and cultural and recreational opportunities. Thus, a state with relatively high taxes that is accustomed to paying for top-flight schools and state universities will appear anti-business to some business leaders and pro-business to others.

The phrase *business climate* was widely used in the 1980s in discussions of state policies for economic development, regulation, labor laws, and taxes. The statistics were developed by the Grant Thornton accounting firm, based on opinions of which characteristics were important to those manufacturing firms that participated in state manufacturing associations. The state rankings much favored southeastern states with low taxes, low wages, and little business regulation. The influence of these ratings on state policies encouraged the development of counter-statistics, particularly the annual *Development Report Card for the States,* published by the Corporation for Enterprise Development (777 North Capitol Street NE, Suite 410, Washington DC 20002, 202-408-9788), whose sponsors include many unions. As the name implies, the *Report Card* gives letter grades, not aggregate rankings, to reflect the complexity and controversy associated with deciding which state policies are pro-business and which are successful in causing state economic

development. The state grades are nearly a flip-flop from the business climate rankings. In this evaluation, southeastern states tend to have the lowest grades.

The availability of these more sophisticated measures discouraged use of the old business climate rankings, which are no longer published. The term *business climate* has been appropriated by the publishers of the business-oriented quarterly *Site Selection.* Its ranking procedure, associated with the number of new jobs primarily in manufacturing, inherently favors large states over less populous ones. Using the test of which states are drawing the most new work, see Table B-30, which shows growth in manufacturing jobs. Using the test of where firms locate their headquarters, see Tables B-16 and B-17.

10 Which states are the best places to sell business-to-business?

Many companies do not sell to consumers; they sell goods and services to other businesses. Finding firms that might want to buy office supplies, parts, maintenance services, and other business-to-business offerings is different from finding individual consumers (which is discussed in Question 1). The statistics needed for finding business customers are too specialized for this book but exist in abundance from government sources. The Bureau of Labor Statistics in the Department of Labor keeps up-to-date statistics on the number of jobs in each state, with breakdowns by major industry. The Commerce Department keeps detailed data and publishes them on a county level in *County Business Patterns.* The Commerce Department also does major surveys of industries, such as the Census of Manufacturing and the Census of Retail Trade.

State governments have even more detailed information, though some do a better job than others in keeping it current and making it available in usable form. The state agencies that administer Unemployment Compensation (UC)—typically called the Department of Labor or Employment Services Administration—know details on all private firms because they collect UC payroll taxes from them every quarter. Corporations, from mom-and-pop stores to General Motors, are chartered by states and often need some kind of permit to operate in states where they are not chartered. Secretaries of state are the keepers of these records. Many state economic development departments have detailed statistics on businesses operating in the state, and some publish directories.

About Government and Public Policy

1 Which state is the best managed?

No one has ever found a way to use statistics to determine which states, or for that matter which private companies, are best managed. Bottom-line results—good schools, low taxes, and high and growing business profits—count. But some companies and states face greater challenges than others in achieving them because of circumstances beyond the control of their managers. There are awards for well-managed companies and governments, but these are like civic awards. Who gets them depends on who is on the selection committees, the criteria those particular people think are important, and their personal knowledge of the award candidates.

Somewhat more objective measures of state financial management are available. Bond rating agencies, such as Moody's, assess credit risks (G-15) much like a bank would determine how much to loan a family seeking a mortgage. Like personal credit ratings, these concern only the likelihood that loans will be repaid, not whether the borrower is competent, efficient, or doing the right things.

States can also be compared in financial management practices, such as whether they conform to generally accepted accounting principles and whether they use performance-oriented budgeting. Most experts believe these practices improve the quality of state decisions. These comparisons can be found in Table G-20. For a more detailed discussion of these and comparisons of such state practices as balanced budget requirements, governors' item-veto powers, and use of stabilization or "rainy day" funds, see *State Policy Reports* (Vol. 13, Issue 5, March 1995).

2 Which state has the fairest tax system?

Fairness in taxes depends entirely on one's perspective about who should bear what share of tax burdens—a specific example of the old maxim, "Where you stand depends on where you sit." The data needed to form opinions are found in Tables F-6 through F-22 in the Taxes section. Included are tables on progressivity of taxes; relative reliance on sales, income, and other tax bases; and tax burdens on high- and low-income households.

A large group of experts and state officials—including governors, legislators, and tax commissioners—have jointly published a study about the elements of good tax systems. *Financing State Government in the 1990s* is available from the National Conference of State Legislatures in Denver or the National Governors' Association in Washington, D.C. The study advocates keeping rates of all taxes as low as possible, given the money to be raised, by avoiding lots of special exemptions and balancing reliance on property, income, and sales tax. Look for balance in percentage of three-tax revenue in Tables F-8, F-11, and F-15.

3 Which states keep the share of taxes paid by business low?

Economists argue that all taxes must reduce some person's income in order to make it available for government. They do not believe that legal abstractions, such as corporations and partnerships, bear the burden of any taxes. Instead, the tax burdens find their way into prices paid by customers, lower wages paid to workers, lower prices paid to suppliers, and lower profits credited to stockholders.

Many people do not agree with this. Public opinion polls usually show that voters would rather see taxes on corporations than taxes they *know* they pay, such as sales taxes and personal income taxes. While many business leaders do not agree with the economists' outlook, others believe it but want

to protect everyone involved—stockholders, suppliers, workers, and customers—by avoiding taxes on their business. As a result there is a lot of interest in comparing how states distribute tax burdens between businesses and people.

Good data to make such comparisons will never exist because the people who might gather the information, the tax collectors, do not care about it. Most collect the same property tax on houses and stores whether they are owned by occupants, individual landlords, or a corporate landlord. When someone buys a pad of paper and pays sales tax no one asks if they are buying it for grocery lists or for a business project. The family farm is both a business and a home, but most states do not divide the value between the two or make the tax lower or higher if the family is organized as a sole proprietorship, partnership, or corporation.

Consequently, comparisons of states on the share of taxes paid by businesses inherently involve guesswork and arbitrary distinctions, such as calling all severance taxes business taxes and all farm taxes people taxes. The most recent comparison was published in *State Policy Reports* in September 1997. It found business paid the lowest share of state and local taxes in Maryland (25.6 percent) and the highest in Alaska (88.4 percent). These data deliberately are not included in *State Fact Finder*.

4 Which state has the highest taxes?

The three standard measures of tax burdens are found in the first three tables of the Taxes section (F-1, F-2, and F-3). None of them is as good as the other tables in this section for considering what taxes are likely to be on an individual household or business. For those answers, see the answers to Question 2 in the Personal Decisions section and Question 4 in the Business Decisions section.

5 Which state has the best education policies?

People disagree about the best policies in education and other public policy fields. To answer questions like these, there are sporadic publications of evaluations of aggregate policies that rank states, but these simply reflect the policy preferences of the interest group issuing them. The scores and rankings are useful to those who share their biases, misleading to those who do not. *State Fact Finder* provides statistics on education (section H) and lets you decide which ones are most important to you.

6 Which states help the poor the most?

There is much disagreement about what is truly helpful to the poor. For example, some people believe providing welfare cash helps, but others argue that this hurts in the long run because it discourages working and hinders the opportunity to rise out of poverty. *State Fact Finder* has many tables on programs for the poor, including food stamps (L-3), welfare (L-2, L-9, L-15, and L-16), Medicaid (I-12, I-13, I-16, I-17, and I-18), and school aid for the disadvantaged (H-12), as well as on tax policies affecting low income households (L-11). If you want to look further into this question, consult the Center for Budget and Policy Priorities (820 1st Street NE, Suite 510, Washington D.C.

20002, 202-408-1080). This group has analyzed which states are most generous to the poor in their spending and how regressive state and local tax policies are—that is, whether they take away in taxes a larger percentage of the purchasing power of the poor than of the rich.

7 Which states have the best roads?

Comparing state policies on a topic such as education does not work well because different people have different ideas about what constitutes good or bad policy. However, for some services, such as providing well-maintained roads, people generally agree on what is good and bad. Even when people can agree on desirable results (for example, how children should perform on standard reading tests), it is difficult to judge states on these outcomes because so much of the result is determined by factors governments do not control. Because state and local governments maintain their own roads, few extraneous factors are involved.

Highways provide a good example of how services can be compared (see Tables K-2 and K-3). Truckers run their own surveys, which can be found in the special interest magazine *Overdrive*.

8 Overall, which states use tax dollars in the most cost-effective manner?

For conceptual reasons, this question cannot be answered. Conceptual problems arise because people do not agree on what governments should do and how they should do it. For example, most people would agree that administrative costs for welfare should be kept at a minimum so all available money can be devoted to real work. Most people would agree that it is bad for society if large numbers of people are allowed to cheat their governments and most would also agree that welfare recipients should be encouraged to find jobs. These beliefs produce contradictory results when applied to available data, such as costs per case of administering welfare (L-17) and collecting child support (L-13). These costs are lowest if a state does little counseling and does not spend much money checking for fraud. Another example of a conceptual problem is the size of elementary school classes (H-9); some people think really small classes are ideal for all schools, while others believe small classes result in unnecessary spending.

Conceptual problems are not unique to governments. How can a company effectively measure whether its public relations or shareholder relations departments are cost-effective?

Even if conceptual problems could be solved, there are enormous difficulties in collecting the relevant data. For many functions, we do not have good measures of effectiveness. Do you know an effective police officer when you meet one, or an effective state university professor, or an effective state legislator? If you do, can you think how you would apply your effectiveness tests to every police officer, state university professor, or legislator in the nation? Often good measures of costs are not available either, at least not ones that are related closely to particular services or outputs of government. This problem is not unique to government. What

percentage of the cost of a steer goes with the beef and what percentage with the leather?

Most attempts to measure the cost-effectiveness of government are experimental, usually confined to activities that can be measured fairly easily, such as gathering refuse, maintaining highways, and collecting bills. For more information, see the many useful books by Harry Hatry, published by the Urban Institute (2100 M Street NW, Washington D.C. 20037, 202-833-7200)

9 Which states have the best government institutions?

Beauty is clearly in the eye of the beholder when it comes to deciding how governments ought to be organized, their policies established, and their leaders selected. Some people have strong preferences on these matters, which are from time to time reflected in comparisons oriented to showing the states with the "best" practices.

For the past thirty years, experts have advocated and states have moved to organizing the executive branches of state government in ways that strengthen the power of governors. These moves include (1) strengthening the veto power, including "line-item" vetoes; (2) reducing the number of executive officials (comptrollers, education superintendents, and insurance commissioners, etc.) selected by elections rather than appointed; (3) increasing the governor's role in preparing and administering budgets; and (4) extending governor's terms by converting two-year terms to four-year terms and allowing governors to run for reelection. Information on these developments and classifications of which states have which practices appear in the Government section (D).

For decades state legislatures were criticized as citadels of corrupt power removed from popular control and unresponsive to the needs of citizens. One major change came with a Supreme Court decision on reapportionment, requiring "one man (or woman), one vote." Now the U.S. Senate is the only governing body in the nation where voting power is not proportional to population. The National Conference of State Legislatures and some business groups and foundations have sponsored research on "modern" legislatures emphasizing (1) longer annual sessions, (2) more staff, and (3) higher legislative pay and expenses. Three such measures of the results appear in Tables D-5, D-8, and D-9.

These ideas have come under considerable criticism recently. Some people saw more staffing and full-time legislators making the field a career as a move toward professionalizing the legislature; others saw this as a recipe for making bureaucrats out of legislators, creating "full-time politicians," and pulling legislators out of touch with the people they represent. One result has been a move to limit the number of terms legislators can serve (D-8), in effect encouraging turnover (D-7).

Surveys show that large numbers of Americans think corruption is common among elected officials at the state and federal level. There is no statistical way to compare ethics, but laws on conflict of interest and disclosure of personal financial information can be compared. The National Conference of State Legislatures does this, with the organization Common Cause providing a kind of watchdog role.

There is no prevailing doctrine on whether "bigger is better" for business and government. Sometimes the fashion is consolidation—forming conglomerates for business and merging regional governments to reduce the roughly 80,000 different state and local governments. Sometimes the emphasis is decentralization and local control, with spin-offs for business and special districts (for example, downtown revitalization areas, police service districts) and decentralized control of neighborhood schools within large school systems. One way to look at differing state policy is to compare the ratio of governments to people (D-4). Another approach is to examine the percentage of local government spending that local officials do not have to finance with their own taxes (D-16).

10 Overall, which states have the best policies?

For some people, picking the best policy is simple: the best state is the one with the lowest taxes, or the one that spends the most on schools or taking care of the poor, or is active in some other area of interest to the person making the judgment. For most people, this question is too general to be answered meaningfully because opinions differ so markedly on "best." Even for a particular person, one state may combine "good" policies on one subject with "bad" policies on another.

One thing is clear: State officials have to play the hands they are dealt, balancing the needs of their population and the tax base available for revenue to meet those needs. Needs appear in the form of children to be educated (H-10), poor people potentially eligible for services (A-11), and more. Tax bases are apparent from economic differences, as shown in the Economies section (B). State differences are summarized in Table G-21 for spending needs and Table F-3 for tax bases.

By comparing these statistics, some conclusions are pretty obvious. For example, compared with most states, it is easy for Connecticut officials to look good, as the state has both low taxes and high spending in relation to what it does, such as spending per school pupil. The state has a rich tax base and a comparatively small percentage of people needing service. Mississippi faces the exact opposite situation.

11 All things considered, which state is run the best?

Readers are advised not to pay attention to magazine rankings purporting to show which state governments are best, or which states are governed the best by the combination of state and local officials responsible for their policies. You can get a pretty good idea that there is something slippery about these just by comparing results. For example, in the mid-1990s, two financial magazines, *Worth* and *Financial World*, published rankings. One said Wyoming was best and Alaska was second. The other ranked Wyoming forty-third and put Alaska next to last.

The rankings for cities and metropolitan areas are no better than those for states. For a good discussion of the pitfalls involved in such rankings, see "Why Nice Cities Finish Last" in *Governing* magazine (September 1995).

If you must rank states on something, pick some areas where they compete for the same prize, such as jobs (B-29); where residents are judged by the same test (H-3); or where the same objective criteria are being applied, such as tax levels (F-1).

There is widespread agreement on what constitutes a valuable football player or an outstanding actress. This is not true for governments. Many people think those that govern best govern least, but others are looking for good schools, good roads, and quick responses from police and fire departments.

Subject Rankings

Population

State	Population 1996 (000)	Percent of national total 1996 %	Rank by %
Alabama	4,273	1.6	23
Alaska	607	0.2	48
Arizona	4,428	1.7	21
Arkansas	2,510	0.9	33
California	31,878	12.0	1
Colorado	3,823	1.4	25
Connecticut	3,274	1.2	28
Delaware	725	0.3	46
Florida	14,400	5.4	4
Georgia	7,353	2.8	10
Hawaii	1,184	0.4	41
Idaho	1,189	0.4	40
Illinois	11,847	4.5	6
Indiana	5,841	2.2	14
Iowa	2,852	1.1	30
Kansas	2,572	1.0	32
Kentucky	3,884	1.5	24
Louisiana	4,351	1.6	22
Maine	1,243	0.5	39
Maryland	5,072	1.9	19
Massachusetts	6,092	2.3	13
Michigan	9,594	3.6	8
Minnesota	4,658	1.8	20
Mississippi	2,716	1.0	31
Missouri	5,359	2.0	16
Montana	879	0.3	44
Nebraska	1,652	0.6	37
Nevada	1,603	0.6	38
New Hampshire	1,162	0.4	42
New Jersey	7,988	3.0	9
New Mexico	1,713	0.6	36
New York	18,185	6.9	3
North Carolina	7,323	2.8	11
North Dakota	644	0.2	47
Ohio	11,173	4.2	7
Oklahoma	3,301	1.2	27
Oregon	3,204	1.2	29
Pennsylvania	12,056	4.5	5
Rhode Island	990	0.4	43
South Carolina	3,699	1.4	26
South Dakota	732	0.3	45
Tennessee	5,320	2.0	17
Texas	19,128	7.2	2
Utah	2,000	0.8	34
Vermont	589	0.2	49
Virginia	6,675	2.5	12
Washington	5,533	2.1	15
West Virginia	1,826	0.7	35
Wisconsin	5,160	1.9	18
Wyoming	481	0.2	50
50 States	264,741	99.8	
DC	543	0.2	
United States	265,284	100.0	

By %

1. California
2. Texas
3. New York
4. Florida
5. Pennsylvania
6. Illinois
7. Ohio
8. Michigan
9. New Jersey
10. Georgia
11. North Carolina
12. Virginia
13. Massachusetts
14. Indiana
15. Washington
16. Missouri
17. Tennessee
18. Wisconsin
19. Maryland
20. Minnesota
21. Arizona
22. Louisiana
23. Alabama
24. Kentucky
25. Colorado
26. South Carolina
27. Oklahoma
28. Connecticut
29. Oregon
30. Iowa
31. Mississippi
32. Kansas
33. Arkansas
34. Utah
35. West Virginia
36. New Mexico
37. Nebraska
38. Nevada
39. Maine
40. Idaho
41. Hawaii
42. New Hampshire
43. Rhode Island
44. Montana
45. South Dakota
46. Delaware
47. North Dakota
48. Alaska
49. Vermont
50. Wyoming

State	Population 1995 (000)	Percent change in population 1995-1996 %	Rank by % change	By %
Alabama	4,246	0.6	32	1. Nevada
Alaska	603	0.7	25	2. Arizona
Arizona	4,305	2.9	2	3. Utah
Arkansas	2,485	1.0	17	4. Georgia
California	31,565	1.0	18	5. Colorado
Colorado	3,748	2.0	5	6. Idaho
Connecticut	3,271	0.1	46	7. Oregon
Delaware	717	1.1	15	8. Texas
Florida	14,184	1.5	11	9. North Carolina
Georgia	7,209	2.0	4	10. Washington
Hawaii	1,179	0.4	38	11. Florida
Idaho	1,166	2.0	6	12. New Mexico
Illinois	11,790	0.5	35	13. Tennessee
Indiana	5,797	0.8	24	14. New Hampshire
Iowa	2,843	0.3	44	15. Delaware
Kansas	2,564	0.3	42	16. Montana
Kentucky	3,857	0.7	29	17. Arkansas
Louisiana	4,338	0.3	45	18. California
Maine	1,239	0.4	39	19. Minnesota
Maryland	5,039	0.6	31	20. Virginia
Massachusetts	6,071	0.4	40	21. South Carolina
Michigan	9,538	0.6	33	22. Oklahoma
Minnesota	4,615	0.9	19	23. Nebraska
Mississippi	2,696	0.7	27	24. Indiana
Missouri	5,319	0.7	26	25. Alaska
Montana	870	1.0	16	26. Missouri
Nebraska	1,639	0.8	23	27. Mississippi
Nevada	1,533	4.5	1	28. Wisconsin
New Hampshire	1,148	1.2	14	29. Kentucky
New Jersey	7,950	0.5	34	30. Vermont
New Mexico	1,690	1.4	12	31. Maryland
New York	18,191	0.0	48	32. Alabama
North Carolina	7,202	1.7	9	33. Michigan
North Dakota	642	0.3	43	34. New Jersey
Ohio	11,134	0.3	41	35. Illinois
Oklahoma	3,275	0.8	22	36. Wyoming
Oregon	3,149	1.7	7	37. South Dakota
Pennsylvania	12,060	0.0	49	38. Hawaii
Rhode Island	992	-0.1	50	39. Maine
South Carolina	3,667	0.9	21	40. Massachusetts
South Dakota	730	0.4	37	41. Ohio
Tennessee	5,247	1.4	13	42. Kansas
Texas	18,801	1.7	8	43. North Dakota
Utah	1,958	2.2	3	44. Iowa
Vermont	585	0.7	30	45. Louisiana
Virginia	6,615	0.9	20	46. Connecticut
Washington	5,448	1.6	10	47. West Virginia
West Virginia	1,825	0.0	47	48. New York
Wisconsin	5,122	0.7	28	49. Pennsylvania
Wyoming	479	0.5	36	50. Rhode Island
50 States	262,335	0.9		
DC	555	-2.0		
United States	262,890	0.9		

State	Population 1981 (000)	Percent change in population 1981-1996 %	Rank by % change	Rank in order By
Alabama	3,929	8.8	28	1. Nevada
Alaska	416	45.9	3	2. Arizona
Arizona	2,807	57.8	2	3. Alaska
Arkansas	2,301	9.1	27	4. Florida
California	24,265	31.4	7	5. Georgia
Colorado	2,984	28.1	11	6. Utah
Connecticut	3,123	4.8	38	7. California
Delaware	598	21.2	16	8. Washington
Florida	10,196	41.2	4	9. Texas
Georgia	5,571	32.0	5	10. New Mexico
Hawaii	980	20.8	17	11. Colorado
Idaho	965	23.2	13	12. New Hampshire
Illinois	11,476	3.2	44	13. Idaho
Indiana	5,490	6.4	33	14. North Carolina
Iowa	2,918	-2.3	47	15. Virginia
Kansas	2,390	7.6	31	16. Delaware
Kentucky	3,677	5.6	37	17. Hawaii
Louisiana	4,300	1.2	46	18. Oregon
Maine	1,133	9.7	25	19. Maryland
Maryland	4,257	19.1	19	20. South Carolina
Massachusetts	5,755	5.9	35	21. Tennessee
Michigan	9,211	4.2	40	22. Vermont
Minnesota	4,113	13.2	23	23. Minnesota
Mississippi	2,545	6.7	32	24. Montana
Missouri	4,940	8.5	29	25. Maine
Montana	796	10.5	24	26. Wisconsin
Nebraska	1,583	4.4	39	27. Arkansas
Nevada	845	89.7	1	28. Alabama
New Hampshire	937	24.1	12	29. Missouri
New Jersey	7,407	7.8	30	30. New Jersey
New Mexico	1,335	28.3	10	31. Kansas
New York	17,561	3.6	42	32. Mississippi
North Carolina	5,957	22.9	14	33. Indiana
North Dakota	661	-2.6	49	34. Oklahoma
Ohio	10,797	3.5	43	35. Massachusetts
Oklahoma	3,106	6.3	34	36. South Dakota
Oregon	2,672	19.9	18	37. Kentucky
Pennsylvania	11,880	1.5	45	38. Connecticut
Rhode Island	952	4.0	41	39. Nebraska
South Carolina	3,186	16.1	20	40. Michigan
South Dakota	692	5.8	36	41. Rhode Island
Tennessee	4,639	14.7	21	42. New York
Texas	14,765	29.6	9	43. Ohio
Utah	1,516	32.0	6	44. Illinois
Vermont	517	13.9	22	45. Pennsylvania
Virginia	5,444	22.6	15	46. Louisiana
Washington	4,237	30.6	8	47. Iowa
West Virginia	1,961	-6.9	50	48. Wyoming
Wisconsin	4,727	9.2	26	49. North Dakota
Wyoming	494	-2.6	48	50. West Virginia
50 States	229,007	15.6		
DC	633	-14.2		
United States	229,637	15.5		

State	Projected population 2005 (000)	Percent change in population 1996-2005 %	Rank by % change	Rank in order By %
Alabama	4,631	8.4	25	1. Nevada
Alaska	700	15.3	8	2. Idaho
Arizona	5,230	18.1	4	3. Utah
Arkansas	2,750	9.6	22	4. Arizona
California	34,441	8.0	26	5. Wyoming
Colorado	4,468	16.9	7	6. New Mexico
Connecticut	3,317	1.3	48	7. Colorado
Delaware	800	10.4	19	8. Alaska
Florida	16,279	13.0	13	9. Georgia
Georgia	8,413	14.4	9	10. Montana
Hawaii	1,342	13.4	11	11. Hawaii
Idaho	1,480	24.4	2	12. Washington
Illinois	12,266	3.5	41	13. Florida
Indiana	6,215	6.4	33	14. Oregon
Iowa	2,941	3.1	43	15. North Carolina
Kansas	2,761	7.3	29	16. Texas
Kentucky	4,098	5.5	36	17. Tennessee
Louisiana	4,535	4.2	39	18. South Dakota
Maine	1,285	3.4	42	19. Delaware
Maryland	5,467	7.8	27	20. New Hampshire
Massachusetts	6,310	3.6	40	21. Virginia
Michigan	9,763	1.8	47	22. Arkansas
Minnesota	5,005	7.5	28	23. South Carolina
Mississippi	2,908	7.1	30	24. Vermont
Missouri	5,718	6.7	31	25. Alabama
Montana	1,006	14.4	10	26. California
Nebraska	1,761	6.6	32	27. Maryland
Nevada	2,070	29.1	1	28. Minnesota
New Hampshire	1,281	10.2	20	29. Kansas
New Jersey	8,392	5.1	38	30. Mississippi
New Mexico	2,016	17.7	6	31. Missouri
New York	18,250	0.4	50	32. Nebraska
North Carolina	8,227	12.3	15	33. Indiana
North Dakota	677	5.2	37	34. Wisconsin
Ohio	11,428	2.3	44	35. Oklahoma
Oklahoma	3,491	5.8	35	36. Kentucky
Oregon	3,613	12.8	14	37. North Dakota
Pennsylvania	12,281	1.9	46	38. New Jersey
Rhode Island	1,012	2.2	45	39. Louisiana
South Carolina	4,033	9.0	23	40. Massachusetts
South Dakota	810	10.6	18	41. Illinois
Tennessee	5,966	12.2	17	42. Maine
Texas	21,487	12.3	16	43. Iowa
Utah	2,411	20.5	3	44. Ohio
Vermont	638	8.4	24	45. Rhode Island
Virginia	7,324	9.7	21	46. Pennsylvania
Washington	6,258	13.1	12	47. Michigan
West Virginia	1,849	1.3	49	48. Connecticut
Wisconsin	5,479	6.2	34	49. West Virginia
Wyoming	568	18.0	5	50. New York
50 States	285,451	7.8		
DC	529	-2.6		
United States	285,981	7.8		

State	Estimated 2000 population (000)	Rank
Alabama	4,451	22
Alaska	653	48
Arizona	4,798	21
Arkansas	2,631	33
California	32,521	1
Colorado	4,168	24
Connecticut	3,284	29
Delaware	768	46
Florida	15,233	4
Georgia	7,875	10
Hawaii	1,257	41
Idaho	1,347	39
Illinois	12,051	6
Indiana	6,045	14
Iowa	2,900	30
Kansas	2,668	32
Kentucky	3,995	25
Louisiana	4,425	23
Maine	1,259	40
Maryland	5,275	19
Massachusetts	6,199	13
Michigan	9,679	8
Minnesota	4,830	20
Mississippi	2,816	31
Missouri	5,540	17
Montana	950	44
Nebraska	1,705	38
Nevada	1,871	35
New Hampshire	1,224	42
New Jersey	8,178	9
New Mexico	1,860	36
New York	18,146	3
North Carolina	7,777	11
North Dakota	662	47
Ohio	11,319	7
Oklahoma	3,373	28
Oregon	3,397	27
Pennsylvania	12,202	5
Rhode Island	998	43
South Carolina	3,858	26
South Dakota	777	45
Tennessee	5,657	16
Texas	20,119	2
Utah	2,207	34
Vermont	617	49
Virginia	6,997	12
Washington	5,858	15
West Virginia	1,841	37
Wisconsin	5,326	18
Wyoming	525	50
50 States	274,112	
DC	523	
United States	274,634	

Rank in order

By population

1. California
2. Texas
3. New York
4. Florida
5. Pennsylvania
6. Illinois
7. Ohio
8. Michigan
9. New Jersey
10. Georgia
11. North Carolina
12. Virginia
13. Massachusetts
14. Indiana
15. Washington
16. Tennessee
17. Missouri
18. Wisconsin
19. Maryland
20. Minnesota
21. Arizona
22. Alabama
23. Louisiana
24. Colorado
25. Kentucky
26. South Carolina
27. Oregon
28. Oklahoma
29. Connecticut
30. Iowa
31. Mississippi
32. Kansas
33. Arkansas
34. Utah
35. Nevada
36. New Mexico
37. West Virginia
38. Nebraska
39. Idaho
40. Maine
41. Hawaii
42. New Hampshire
43. Rhode Island
44. Montana
45. South Dakota
46. Delaware
47. North Dakota
48. Alaska
49. Vermont
50. Wyoming

State	Population 65 and over (000)	Percent 65 and over %	Rank by %
Alabama	557	13.0	23
Alaska	31	5.2	50
Arizona	586	13.2	21
Arkansas	362	14.4	7
California	3,516	11.0	45
Colorado	385	10.1	47
Connecticut	470	14.3	9
Delaware	93	12.8	25
Florida	2,657	18.5	1
Georgia	730	9.9	48
Hawaii	153	12.9	24
Idaho	135	11.4	41
Illinois	1,486	12.5	29
Indiana	735	12.6	27
Iowa	433	15.2	5
Kansas	352	13.7	15
Kentucky	489	12.6	26
Louisiana	497	11.4	39
Maine	173	13.9	11
Maryland	578	11.4	40
Massachusetts	859	14.1	10
Michigan	1,193	12.4	31
Minnesota	577	12.4	32
Mississippi	333	12.3	33
Missouri	742	13.8	12
Montana	116	13.2	22
Nebraska	229	13.8	13
Nevada	183	11.4	38
New Hampshire	140	12.0	36
New Jersey	1,100	13.8	14
New Mexico	189	11.0	44
New York	2,434	13.4	19
North Carolina	917	12.5	30
North Dakota	93	14.5	6
Ohio	1,497	13.4	18
Oklahoma	445	13.5	16
Oregon	430	13.4	17
Pennsylvania	1,912	15.9	2
Rhode Island	156	15.8	3
South Carolina	447	12.1	35
South Dakota	105	14.4	8
Tennessee	667	12.5	28
Texas	1,951	10.2	46
Utah	175	8.8	49
Vermont	71	12.1	34
Virginia	747	11.2	43
Washington	641	11.6	37
West Virginia	278	15.2	4
Wisconsin	686	13.3	20
Wyoming	54	11.2	42
50 States	33,785	12.8	
DC	75	13.9	
United States	33,861	12.8	

Rank in order

By %

1. Florida
2. Pennsylvania
3. Rhode Island
4. West Virginia
5. Iowa
6. North Dakota
7. Arkansas
8. South Dakota
9. Connecticut
10. Massachusetts
11. Maine
12. Missouri
13. Nebraska
14. New Jersey
15. Kansas
16. Oklahoma
17. Oregon
18. Ohio
19. New York
20. Wisconsin
21. Arizona
22. Montana
23. Alabama
24. Hawaii
25. Delaware
26. Kentucky
27. Indiana
28. Tennessee
29. Illinois
30. North Carolina
31. Michigan
32. Minnesota
33. Mississippi
34. Vermont
35. South Carolina
36. New Hampshire
37. Washington
38. Nevada
39. Louisiana
40. Maryland
41. Idaho
42. Wyoming
43. Virginia
44. New Mexico
45. California
46. Texas
47. Colorado
48. Georgia
49. Utah
50. Alaska

State	Population 17 and under (000)	Percent of population 17 and under %	Rank by %	Rank in order By %
Alabama	1,076	25.2	35	1. Utah
Alaska	184	30.4	2	2. Alaska
Arizona	1,150	26.0	25	3. Idaho
Arkansas	659	26.3	19	4. New Mexico
California	8,866	27.8	9	5. Texas
Colorado	998	26.1	21	6. Louisiana
Connecticut	798	24.4	43	7. South Dakota
Delaware	176	24.3	44	8. Mississippi
Florida	3,423	23.8	47	9. California
Georgia	1,952	26.6	16	10. Wyoming
Hawaii	307	25.9	27	11. Minnesota
Idaho	349	29.3	3	12. Nebraska
Illinois	3,156	26.6	15	13. Kansas
Indiana	1,499	25.7	28	14. Oklahoma
Iowa	719	25.2	34	15. Illinois
Kansas	687	26.7	13	16. Georgia
Kentucky	969	24.9	38	17. Montana
Louisiana	1,233	28.4	6	18. Michigan
Maine	300	24.1	45	19. Arkansas
Maryland	1,286	25.4	31	20. North Dakota
Massachusetts	1,422	23.3	49	21. Colorado
Michigan	2,537	26.4	18	22. Wisconsin
Minnesota	1,247	26.8	11	23. Missouri
Mississippi	756	27.8	8	24. Nevada
Missouri	1,394	26.0	23	25. Arizona
Montana	233	26.5	17	26. Washington
Nebraska	442	26.8	12	27. Hawaii
Nevada	417	26.0	24	28. Indiana
New Hampshire	296	25.5	30	29. Ohio
New Jersey	1,987	24.9	40	30. New Hampshire
New Mexico	501	29.3	4	31. Maryland
New York	4,541	25.0	37	32. South Carolina
North Carolina	1,834	25.0	36	33. Oregon
North Dakota	169	26.2	20	34. Iowa
Ohio	2,848	25.5	29	35. Alabama
Oklahoma	881	26.7	14	36. North Carolina
Oregon	808	25.2	33	37. New York
Pennsylvania	2,895	24.0	46	38. Kentucky
Rhode Island	235	23.8	48	39. Vermont
South Carolina	938	25.4	32	40. New Jersey
South Dakota	204	27.9	7	41. Tennessee
Tennessee	1,322	24.9	41	42. Virginia
Texas	5,452	28.5	5	43. Connecticut
Utah	679	33.9	1	44. Delaware
Vermont	147	24.9	39	45. Maine
Virginia	1,632	24.4	42	46. Pennsylvania
Washington	1,437	26.0	26	47. Florida
West Virginia	422	23.1	50	48. Rhode Island
Wisconsin	1,343	26.0	22	49. Massachusetts
Wyoming	133	27.7	10	50. West Virginia
50 States	68,939	26.0		
DC	110	20.2		
United States	69,048	26.0		

State	Median age 1996	Rank		By #
Alabama	35	24		1. West Virginia
Alaska	32	49		2. Florida
Arizona	34	39		3. Pennsylvania
Arkansas	35	16		4. Maine
California	33	47		5. Montana
Colorado	35	22		6. Oregon
Connecticut	36	7		7. Connecticut
Delaware	35	22		8. Iowa
Florida	38	2		9. New Jersey
Georgia	33	42		10. Rhode Island
Hawaii	35	18		11. Vermont
Idaho	33	44		12. Massachusetts
Illinois	34	41		13. New York
Indiana	35	31		13. Ohio
Iowa	36	8		13. Tennessee
Kansas	35	33		16. Arkansas
Kentucky	35	18		16. Missouri
Louisiana	33	44		18. Hawaii
Maine	37	4		18. Kentucky
Maryland	35	24		18. New Hampshire
Massachusetts	36	12		18. Wisconsin
Michigan	35	35		22. Colorado
Minnesota	35	35		22. Delaware
Mississippi	33	46		24. Alabama
Missouri	35	16		24. Maryland
Montana	37	5		24. Nebraska
Nebraska	35	24		24. North Dakota
Nevada	35	31		24. Oklahoma
New Hampshire	35	18		24. Washington
New Jersey	36	9		24. Wyoming
New Mexico	33	42		31. Indiana
New York	35	13		31. Nevada
North Carolina	35	34		33. Kansas
North Dakota	35	24		34. North Carolina
Ohio	35	13		35. Michigan
Oklahoma	35	24		35. Minnesota
Oregon	36	6		37. South Dakota
Pennsylvania	37	3		37. Virginia
Rhode Island	36	10		39. Arizona
South Carolina	34	39		39. South Carolina
South Dakota	35	37		41. Illinois
Tennessee	35	13		42. Georgia
Texas	33	48		42. New Mexico
Utah	27	50		44. Idaho
Vermont	36	11		44. Louisiana
Virginia	35	37		46. Mississippi
Washington	35	24		47. California
West Virginia	38	1		48. Texas
Wisconsin	35	18		49. Alaska
Wyoming	35	24		50. Utah
50 States	n/a			
DC	36			
United States	35			

State	African American population (000)	Percent of total population %	Rank by %	Rank in order By %
Alabama	1,078.9	25.6	6	1. Mississippi
Alaska	25.4	4.2	32	2. Louisiana
Arizona	138.6	3.4	34	3. South Carolina
Arkansas	389.1	15.9	12	4. Georgia
California	2,415.1	7.7	24	5. Maryland
Colorado	157.7	4.3	31	6. Alabama
Connecticut	294.9	9.0	21	7. North Carolina
Delaware	129.4	18.2	9	8. Virginia
Florida	2,025.5	14.5	14	9. Delaware
Georgia	1,966.2	27.9	4	10. New York
Hawaii	28.8	2.4	38	11. Tennessee
Idaho	5.1	0.4	47	12. Arkansas
Illinois	1,794.6	15.3	13	13. Illinois
Indiana	464.4	8.1	22	14. Florida
Iowa	54.1	1.9	40	15. Michigan
Kansas	154.3	6.0	27	16. New Jersey
Kentucky	272.0	7.1	25	17. Texas
Louisiana	1,364.1	31.6	2	18. Ohio
Maine	4.8	0.4	49	19. Missouri
Maryland	1,320.2	26.4	5	20. Pennsylvania
Massachusetts	364.3	6.0	28	21. Connecticut
Michigan	1,363.7	14.4	15	22. Indiana
Minnesota	121.7	2.7	37	23. Oklahoma
Mississippi	958.1	35.9	1	24. California
Missouri	581.8	11.0	19	25. Kentucky
Montana	2.8	0.3	50	26. Nevada
Nebraska	62.2	3.8	33	27. Kansas
Nevada	103.2	7.1	26	28. Massachusetts
New Hampshire	7.1	0.6	44	29. Wisconsin
New Jersey	1,134.3	14.4	16	30. Rhode Island
New Mexico	40.2	2.4	39	31. Colorado
New York	3,179.4	17.5	10	32. Alaska
North Carolina	1,568.0	22.2	7	33. Nebraska
North Dakota	3.7	0.6	45	34. Arizona
Ohio	1,234.6	11.1	18	35. Washington
Oklahoma	251.0	7.7	23	36. West Virginia
Oregon	54.9	1.8	41	37. Minnesota
Pennsylvania	1,156.8	9.6	20	38. Hawaii
Rhode Island	47.3	4.7	30	39. New Mexico
South Carolina	1,102.2	30.1	3	40. Iowa
South Dakota	3.5	0.5	46	41. Oregon
Tennessee	838.7	16.2	11	42. Utah
Texas	2,235.3	12.2	17	43. Wyoming
Utah	15.4	0.8	42	44. New Hampshire
Vermont	2.3	0.4	48	45. North Dakota
Virginia	1,276.9	19.5	8	46. South Dakota
Washington	176.1	3.3	35	47. Idaho
West Virginia	57.7	3.2	36	48. Vermont
Wisconsin	275.6	5.4	29	49. Maine
Wyoming	3.7	0.8	43	50. Montana
50 States	32,305.6	12.4		
DC	364.0	64.2		
United States	32,669.6	12.5		

State	Hispanic population	Percent of total population %	Rank by %	By %
Alabama	30.9	0.7	45	1. New Mexico
Alaska	21.7	3.6	21	2. California
Arizona	823.6	20.2	4	3. Texas
Arkansas	26.6	1.1	40	4. Arizona
California	8,939.2	28.4	2	5. New York
Colorado	492.1	13.5	6	6. Colorado
Connecticut	239.1	7.3	12	7. Florida
Delaware	19.3	2.7	26	8. Nevada
Florida	1,872.0	13.4	7	9. New Jersey
Georgia	140.3	2.0	32	10. Illinois
Hawaii	97.4	8.3	11	11. Hawaii
Idaho	65.9	5.8	13	12. Connecticut
Illinois	1,050.5	8.9	10	13. Idaho
Indiana	115.3	2.0	31	14. Rhode Island
Iowa	43.2	1.5	35	15. Wyoming
Kansas	108.7	4.3	20	16. Massachusetts
Kentucky	26.0	0.7	47	17. Utah
Louisiana	101.5	2.4	28	18. Washington
Maine	7.2	0.6	49	19. Oregon
Maryland	162.6	3.3	22	20. Kansas
Massachusetts	338.7	5.6	16	21. Alaska
Michigan	226.7	2.4	27	22. Maryland
Minnesota	71.5	1.6	34	23. Oklahoma
Mississippi	19.1	0.7	46	24. Virginia
Missouri	71.2	1.3	38	25. Nebraska
Montana	14.6	1.7	33	26. Delaware
Nebraska	48.4	3.0	25	27. Michigan
Nevada	175.6	12.1	8	28. Louisiana
New Hampshire	13.1	1.2	39	29. Pennsylvania
New Jersey	868.0	11.0	9	30. Wisconsin
New Mexico	645.8	39.1	1	31. Indiana
New York	2,498.5	13.7	5	32. Georgia
North Carolina	95.6	1.4	37	33. Montana
North Dakota	5.2	0.8	44	34. Minnesota
Ohio	157.2	1.4	36	35. Iowa
Oklahoma	101.6	3.1	23	36. Ohio
Oregon	141.9	4.6	19	37. North Carolina
Pennsylvania	269.8	2.2	29	38. Missouri
Rhode Island	57.6	5.8	14	39. New Hampshire
South Carolina	36.3	1.0	41	40. Arkansas
South Dakota	6.4	0.9	42	41. South Carolina
Tennessee	43.3	0.8	43	42. South Dakota
Texas	5,022.3	27.3	3	43. Tennessee
Utah	104.7	5.5	17	44. North Dakota
Vermont	3.9	0.7	48	45. Alabama
Virginia	196.5	3.0	24	46. Mississippi
Washington	268.9	5.0	18	47. Kentucky
West Virginia	9.5	0.5	50	48. Vermont
Wisconsin	111.5	2.2	30	49. Maine
Wyoming	27.4	5.8	15	50. West Virginia
50 States	26,033.7	10.0		
DC	39.1	6.9		
United States	26,072.9	10.0		

State	Total population in poverty (000)	Percent of population in poverty %	Rank by %
Alabama	595	14.0	16
Alaska	54	8.2	46
Arizona	980	20.5	3
Arkansas	449	17.2	6
California	5,472	16.9	9
Colorado	412	10.6	36
Connecticut	392	11.7	29
Delaware	63	8.6	45
Florida	2,037	14.2	15
Georgia	1,097	14.8	14
Hawaii	142	12.1	22
Idaho	140	11.9	24
Illinois	1,429	12.1	22
Indiana	428	7.5	49
Iowa	279	9.6	41
Kansas	287	11.2	31
Kentucky	658	17.0	7
Louisiana	873	20.5	3
Maine	135	11.2	31
Maryland	522	10.3	37
Massachusetts	622	10.1	39
Michigan	1,068	11.2	31
Minnesota	458	9.8	40
Mississippi	575	20.6	2
Missouri	500	9.5	42
Montana	155	17.0	7
Nebraska	169	10.2	38
Nevada	133	8.1	47
New Hampshire	73	6.4	50
New Jersey	726	9.2	43
New Mexico	472	25.5	1
New York	3,058	16.7	10
North Carolina	885	12.2	21
North Dakota	69	11.0	34
Ohio	1,424	12.7	18
Oklahoma	556	16.6	11
Oregon	382	11.8	27
Pennsylvania	1,374	11.6	30
Rhode Island	104	11.0	34
South Carolina	482	13.0	17
South Dakota	82	11.8	27
Tennessee	878	15.9	13
Texas	3,180	16.6	11
Utah	153	7.7	48
Vermont	74	12.6	19
Virginia	795	12.3	20
Washington	666	11.9	24
West Virginia	323	18.5	5
Wisconsin	460	8.8	44
Wyoming	58	11.9	24
50 States	36,398	n/a	
DC	130	24.1	
United States	36,529	13.7	

Rank in order

By %

1. New Mexico
2. Mississippi
3. Arizona
3. Louisiana
5. West Virginia
6. Arkansas
7. Kentucky
7. Montana
9. California
10. New York
11. Oklahoma
11. Texas
13. Tennessee
14. Georgia
15. Florida
16. Alabama
17. South Carolina
18. Ohio
19. Vermont
20. Virginia
21. North Carolina
22. Hawaii
22. Illinois
24. Idaho
24. Washington
24. Wyoming
27. Oregon
27. South Dakota
29. Connecticut
30. Pennsylvania
31. Kansas
31. Maine
31. Michigan
34. North Dakota
34. Rhode Island
36. Colorado
37. Maryland
38. Nebraska
39. Massachusetts
40. Minnesota
41. Iowa
42. Missouri
43. New Jersey
44. Wisconsin
45. Delaware
46. Alaska
47. Nevada
48. Utah
49. Indiana
50. New Hampshire

State	Number of persons under 18 in poverty (000)	Percent in poverty %	Rank by %
Alabama	244	22.0	16
Alaska	25	10.6	47
Arizona	449	31.7	3
Arkansas	173	23.2	13
California	2,312	25.5	8
Colorado	127	12.5	42
Connecticut	207	22.7	14
Delaware	27	14.3	36
Florida	734	22.2	15
Georgia	414	21.3	17
Hawaii	50	17.0	27
Idaho	57	17.3	26
Illinois	605	18.6	22
Indiana	126	9.2	50
Iowa	101	12.3	44
Kansas	100	13.5	39
Kentucky	250	24.9	10
Louisiana	368	31.8	2
Maine	42	16.4	30
Maryland	219	16.6	29
Massachusetts	226	14.7	35
Michigan	454	17.7	23
Minnesota	178	13.2	40
Mississippi	247	29.6	4
Missouri	169	12.0	45
Montana	69	26.9	5
Nebraska	70	15.1	32
Nevada	45	11.4	46
New Hampshire	26	9.5	49
New Jersey	266	14.2	37
New Mexico	211	34.2	1
New York	1,204	25.1	9
North Carolina	337	18.8	20
North Dakota	21	13.0	41
Ohio	563	18.8	20
Oklahoma	247	26.4	7
Oregon	161	20.1	18
Pennsylvania	461	15.7	31
Rhode Island	30	15.0	33
South Carolina	184	19.4	19
South Dakota	25	13.9	38
Tennessee	353	23.7	12
Texas	1,350	24.4	11
Utah	62	9.6	48
Vermont	27	17.7	23
Virginia	257	17.7	23
Washington	252	16.8	28
West Virginia	92	26.7	6
Wisconsin	179	12.5	42
Wyoming	20	14.8	34
50 States	14,416	n/a	
DC	47	38.6	
United States	14,463	20.5	

Rank in order

By %

1. New Mexico
2. Louisiana
3. Arizona
4. Mississippi
5. Montana
6. West Virginia
7. Oklahoma
8. California
9. New York
10. Kentucky
11. Texas
12. Tennessee
13. Arkansas
14. Connecticut
15. Florida
16. Alabama
17. Georgia
18. Oregon
19. South Carolina
20. North Carolina
20. Ohio
22. Illinois
23. Michigan
23. Vermont
23. Virginia
26. Idaho
27. Hawaii
28. Washington
29. Maryland
30. Maine
31. Pennsylvania
32. Nebraska
33. Rhode Island
34. Wyoming
35. Massachusetts
36. Delaware
37. New Jersey
38. South Dakota
39. Kansas
40. Minnesota
41. North Dakota
42. Colorado
42. Wisconsin
44. Iowa
45. Missouri
46. Nevada
47. Alaska
48. Utah
49. New Hampshire
50. Indiana

State	Female population (000)	Percent of population %	Rank by %	Rank in order By %
Alabama	2,219	51.9	2	1. Mississippi
Alaska	288	47.4	50	2. Alabama
Arizona	2,235	50.5	39	3. Rhode Island
Arkansas	1,296	51.6	11	4. Pennsylvania
California	15,914	49.9	46	5. New York
Colorado	1,926	50.4	40	6. Louisiana
Connecticut	1,683	51.4	18	7. West Virginia
Delaware	372	51.3	23	8. Massachusetts
Florida	7,406	51.4	15	9. South Carolina
Georgia	3,770	51.3	20	10. Tennessee
Hawaii	586	49.5	48	11. Arkansas
Idaho	595	50.0	45	12. Ohio
Illinois	6,062	51.2	25	13. Missouri
Indiana	2,994	51.3	22	14. New Jersey
Iowa	1,462	51.3	21	15. Florida
Kansas	1,306	50.8	31	16. Kentucky
Kentucky	1,997	51.4	16	17. North Carolina
Louisiana	2,253	51.8	6	18. Connecticut
Maine	636	51.2	26	19. Maryland
Maryland	2,602	51.3	19	20. Georgia
Massachusetts	3,152	51.7	8	21. Iowa
Michigan	4,917	51.3	24	22. Indiana
Minnesota	2,360	50.7	35	23. Delaware
Mississippi	1,412	52.0	1	24. Michigan
Missouri	2,761	51.5	13	25. Illinois
Montana	441	50.2	43	26. Maine
Nebraska	843	51.0	28	27. Oklahoma
Nevada	786	49.0	49	28. Nebraska
New Hampshire	590	50.8	32	29. Virginia
New Jersey	4,112	51.5	14	30. Wisconsin
New Mexico	868	50.6	36	31. Kansas
New York	9,424	51.8	5	32. New Hampshire
North Carolina	3,764	51.4	17	33. Vermont
North Dakota	322	50.1	44	34. South Dakota
Ohio	5,764	51.6	12	35. Minnesota
Oklahoma	1,686	51.1	27	36. New Mexico
Oregon	1,620	50.6	38	37. Texas
Pennsylvania	6,252	51.9	4	38. Oregon
Rhode Island	514	51.9	3	39. Arizona
South Carolina	1,912	51.7	9	40. Colorado
South Dakota	371	50.7	34	41. Washington
Tennessee	2,747	51.6	10	42. Utah
Texas	9,677	50.6	37	43. Montana
Utah	1,004	50.2	42	44. North Dakota
Vermont	299	50.7	33	45. Idaho
Virginia	3,404	51.0	29	46. California
Washington	2,777	50.2	41	47. Wyoming
West Virginia	945	51.7	7	48. Hawaii
Wisconsin	2,621	50.8	30	49. Nevada
Wyoming	239	49.7	47	50. Alaska
50 States	135,185	51.1		
DC	289	53.2		
United States	135,474	51.1		

State	Births per 1,000 population	Rank
Alabama	14.4	19
Alaska	16.7	5
Arizona	18.0	2
Arkansas	14.5	17
California	16.9	4
Colorado	14.6	16
Connecticut	13.5	37
Delaware	14.1	25
Florida	13.2	38
Georgia	15.6	9
Hawaii	15.5	11
Idaho	16.0	7
Illinois	15.6	9
Indiana	14.3	21
Iowa	13.0	41
Kansas	15.4	12
Kentucky	13.6	35
Louisiana	15.2	14
Maine	11.1	50
Maryland	13.7	31
Massachusetts	13.2	38
Michigan	14.3	21
Minnesota	13.7	31
Mississippi	15.3	13
Missouri	13.8	29
Montana	12.2	47
Nebraska	14.1	25
Nevada	16.2	6
New Hampshire	12.5	45
New Jersey	14.3	21
New Mexico	15.9	8
New York	14.9	15
North Carolina	14.4	19
North Dakota	13.0	41
Ohio	13.7	31
Oklahoma	14.0	27
Oregon	13.6	35
Pennsylvania	12.4	46
Rhode Island	12.6	44
South Carolina	13.7	31
South Dakota	14.3	21
Tennessee	13.9	28
Texas	17.1	3
Utah	20.7	1
Vermont	11.5	48
Virginia	13.8	29
Washington	14.5	17
West Virginia	11.3	49
Wisconsin	13.0	41
Wyoming	13.1	40
50 States	n/a	
DC	15.3	
United States	14.8	

Rank in order

By rate

1. Utah
2. Arizona
3. Texas
4. California
5. Alaska
6. Nevada
7. Idaho
8. New Mexico
9. Georgia
10. Illinois
11. Hawaii
12. Kansas
13. Mississippi
14. Louisiana
15. New York
16. Colorado
17. Arkansas
18. Washington
19. Alabama
20. North Carolina
21. Indiana
22. Michigan
23. New Jersey
24. South Dakota
25. Delaware
26. Nebraska
27. Oklahoma
28. Tennessee
29. Missouri
30. Virginia
31. Maryland
32. Minnesota
33. Ohio
34. South Carolina
35. Kentucky
36. Oregon
37. Connecticut
38. Florida
39. Massachusetts
40. Wyoming
41. Iowa
42. North Dakota
43. Wisconsin
44. Rhode Island
45. New Hampshire
46. Pennsylvania
47. Montana
48. Vermont
49. West Virginia
50. Maine

A-15 DEATH RATES (AGE-ADJUSTED), 1996

State	Deaths per 100,000 population	Rank
Alabama	580.8	4
Alaska	473.7	28
Arizona	506.6	18
Arkansas	549.3	8
California	461.9	31
Colorado	435.9	43
Connecticut	443.9	38
Delaware	527.1	14
Florida	478.9	25
Georgia	561.3	5
Hawaii	389.1	50
Idaho	431.5	45
Illinois	511.2	17
Indiana	527.2	13
Iowa	430.0	46
Kansas	466.8	29
Kentucky	547.7	10
Louisiana	600.9	2
Maine	435.2	44
Maryland	516.8	16
Massachusetts	441.6	40
Michigan	503.9	21
Minnesota	411.9	48
Mississippi	604.8	1
Missouri	517.8	15
Montana	455.4	33
Nebraska	447.0	37
Nevada	551.1	7
New Hampshire	449.6	34
New Jersey	475.1	26
New Mexico	474.0	27
New York	483.9	24
North Carolina	537.6	11
North Dakota	419.7	47
Ohio	505.4	19
Oklahoma	536.6	12
Oregon	465.2	30
Pennsylvania	504.0	20
Rhode Island	437.4	42
South Carolina	588.5	3
South Dakota	448.7	36
Tennessee	560.2	6
Texas	486.9	23
Utah	407.1	49
Vermont	449.3	35
Virginia	493.8	22
Washington	441.3	41
West Virginia	547.8	9
Wisconsin	442.0	39
Wyoming	456.6	32
50 States	n/a	
DC	771.7	
United States	493.6	

Rank in order

By rate

1. Mississippi
2. Louisiana
3. South Carolina
4. Alabama
5. Georgia
6. Tennessee
7. Nevada
8. Arkansas
9. West Virginia
10. Kentucky
11. North Carolina
12. Oklahoma
13. Indiana
14. Delaware
15. Missouri
16. Maryland
17. Illinois
18. Arizona
19. Ohio
20. Pennsylvania
21. Michigan
22. Virginia
23. Texas
24. New York
25. Florida
26. New Jersey
27. New Mexico
28. Alaska
29. Kansas
30. Oregon
31. California
32. Wyoming
33. Montana
34. New Hampshire
35. Vermont
36. South Dakota
37. Nebraska
38. Connecticut
39. Wisconsin
40. Massachusetts
41. Washington
42. Rhode Island
43. Colorado
44. Maine
45. Idaho
46. Iowa
47. North Dakota
48. Minnesota
49. Utah
50. Hawaii

State	Persons per square mile	Rank
Alabama	84	25
Alaska	1	50
Arizona	39	37
Arkansas	48	34
California	204	12
Colorado	37	38
Connecticut	676	4
Delaware	371	7
Florida	267	10
Georgia	127	20
Hawaii	184	13
Idaho	14	44
Illinois	213	11
Indiana	163	16
Iowa	51	33
Kansas	31	40
Kentucky	98	23
Louisiana	100	22
Maine	40	36
Maryland	519	5
Massachusetts	777	3
Michigan	169	14
Minnesota	59	31
Mississippi	58	32
Missouri	78	27
Montana	6	48
Nebraska	21	42
Nevada	15	43
New Hampshire	130	18
New Jersey	1,077	1
New Mexico	14	45
New York	385	6
North Carolina	150	17
North Dakota	9	47
Ohio	273	8
Oklahoma	48	35
Oregon	33	39
Pennsylvania	269	9
Rhode Island	948	2
South Carolina	123	21
South Dakota	10	46
Tennessee	129	19
Texas	73	29
Utah	24	41
Vermont	64	30
Virginia	169	15
Washington	83	26
West Virginia	76	28
Wisconsin	95	24
Wyoming	5	49
50 States	75	
DC	8,847	
United States	75	

Rank in order

By density

1. New Jersey
2. Rhode Island
3. Massachusetts
4. Connecticut
5. Maryland
6. New York
7. Delaware
8. Ohio
9. Pennsylvania
10. Florida
11. Illinois
12. California
13. Hawaii
14. Michigan
15. Virginia
16. Indiana
17. North Carolina
18. New Hampshire
19. Tennessee
20. Georgia
21. South Carolina
22. Louisiana
23. Kentucky
24. Wisconsin
25. Alabama
26. Washington
27. Missouri
28. West Virginia
29. Texas
30. Vermont
31. Minnesota
32. Mississippi
33. Iowa
34. Arkansas
35. Oklahoma
36. Maine
37. Arizona
38. Colorado
39. Oregon
40. Kansas
41. Utah
42. Nebraska
43. Nevada
44. Idaho
45. New Mexico
46. South Dakota
47. North Dakota
48. Montana
49. Wyoming
50. Alaska

A-17 ILLEGAL IMMIGRANT POPULATION, 1996

State	Illegal immigrant population #	Percent of illegal immigrant population %	Percent of total population %	Rank by number of immigrants
Alabama	4,000	0.1	0.1	39
Alaska	3,700	0.1	0.6	40
Arizona	115,000	2.3	2.6	7
Arkansas	5,400	0.1	0.2	37
California	2,000,000	40.0	6.3	1
Colorado	45,000	0.9	1.2	11
Connecticut	29,000	0.6	0.9	18
Delaware	2,500	0.1	0.3	44
Florida	350,000	7.0	2.4	4
Georgia	32,000	0.6	0.4	17
Hawaii	9,000	0.2	0.8	31
Idaho	16,000	0.3	1.3	25
Illinois	290,000	5.8	2.4	5
Indiana	14,000	0.3	0.2	28
Iowa	6,400	0.1	0.2	35
Kansas	20,000	0.4	0.8	24
Kentucky	6,000	0.1	0.2	36
Louisiana	22,000	0.4	0.5	21
Maine	3,300	0.1	0.3	42
Maryland	44,000	0.9	0.9	12
Massachusetts	85,000	1.7	1.4	8
Michigan	37,000	0.7	0.4	13
Minnesota	7,200	0.1	0.2	34
Mississippi	3,700	0.1	0.1	41
Missouri	16,000	0.3	0.3	25
Montana	1,200	0.0	0.1	48
Nebraska	7,600	0.2	0.5	33
Nevada	24,000	0.5	1.5	19
New Hampshire	2,000	0.0	0.2	45
New Jersey	135,000	2.7	1.7	6
New Mexico	37,000	0.7	2.2	13
New York	540,000	10.8	3.0	3
North Carolina	22,000	0.4	0.3	21
North Dakota	800	0.0	0.1	49
Ohio	23,000	0.5	0.2	20
Oklahoma	21,000	0.4	0.6	23
Oregon	33,000	0.7	1.0	16
Pennsylvania	37,000	0.7	0.3	13
Rhode Island	12,000	0.2	1.2	30
South Carolina	4,800	0.1	0.1	38
South Dakota	800	0.0	0.1	49
Tennessee	13,000	0.3	0.2	29
Texas	700,000	14.0	3.7	2
Utah	15,000	0.3	0.7	27
Vermont	2,700	0.1	0.5	43
Virginia	55,000	1.1	0.8	9
Washington	52,000	1.0	0.9	10
West Virginia	2,000	0.0	0.1	45
Wisconsin	7,700	0.2	0.1	32
Wyoming	1,700	0.0	0.4	47
50 States	4,916,500	98.3	1.9	
DC	30,000	0.6	5.5	
United States	5,000,000	100.0	1.9	

Rank in order

By #

1. California
2. Texas
3. New York
4. Florida
5. Illinois
6. New Jersey
7. Arizona
8. Massachusetts
9. Virginia
10. Washington
11. Colorado
12. Maryland
13. Michigan
13. New Mexico
13. Pennsylvania
16. Oregon
17. Georgia
18. Connecticut
19. Nevada
20. Ohio
21. Louisiana
21. North Carolina
23. Oklahoma
24. Kansas
25. Idaho
25. Missouri
27. Utah
28. Indiana
29. Tennessee
30. Rhode Island
31. Hawaii
32. Wisconsin
33. Nebraska
34. Minnesota
35. Iowa
36. Kentucky
37. Arkansas
38. South Carolina
39. Alabama
40. Alaska
41. Mississippi
42. Maine
43. Vermont
44. Delaware
45. New Hampshire
45. West Virginia
47. Wyoming
48. Montana
49. North Dakota
49. South Dakota

Source Notes for Population (Section A)

A-1 Population and Percent Distribution, 1996: The U.S. population is counted every ten years by the U.S. Census Bureau. The last such count was in 1990. For all other years, the Census Bureau prepares estimates for July 1 of each year. The 1996 estimates were posted on the Internet and are available on the Census web page (http://www.census.gov) as *Estimates of the Population of States, Annual Time Series, July 1, 1990 to July 1, 1996.* Outside experts and the Census Bureau agree that the 1990 Census probably undercounted the nation's population by approximately five million people. This undercount was concentrated in low-income areas in major cities. The understatement of population is greatest for these communities and the states that contain them. Because population estimates are used to determine representation in Congress and how much state and local governments get from federal aid programs, some states and cities have gone to court seeking to force the federal government to use more correct estimates. The Census Bureau successfully resisted this because, while it agrees the official count is inaccurate, it did not know what data might be substituted for that count.

A-2 Percent Change in Population, 1995-1996: When the Census Bureau makes its annual estimates of population each year, it often changes the estimates for previous years. For example, the population changes shown are calculated from the 1996 and 1995 population estimates made in early 1997 (see Table A-1), not those made in early 1996.

A-3 Percent Change in Population, 1981-1996: The 1981 Census estimates are based on the 1980 Census, reflecting the count as of July 1, 1981.

A-4 Projected Population 2005 and Projected Population Change, 1996-2005: The population projections for 2005 were made by the U.S. Bureau of the Census and are available on their web site (http://www.census.gov) as "Projections of the Total Population of States: 1995 to 2025." See Table A-1 for the 1996 population numbers used to calculate the projected change over time. Many private market research and economic forecasting firms also make population projections. The projections reflect recent trends, so Western states are predicted to gain population rapidly while the slowest growth appears in the Northeast and Midwest. Projections for short periods are quite reliable because they are based on events that are predictable for large groups, such as the percentage of persons who will die each year and the percentage of women of childbearing age who will have babies. Over longer periods, more guesswork is involved. Major economic shifts can be caused by changes in defense spending, fluctuations in oil and gas prices, and success

or failure of particular firms or industries. Those shifts affect migration of workers and ultimately where they have children and die.

A-5 Projected Population for the Year 2000: These estimates, from the Census Bureau (see notes to Table A-4), show minor changes in the population ranking of states when compared with the 1996 estimates shown in Table A-1. If the estimates prove accurate, some southern and western states will gain seats in the House of Representatives when it is reapportioned after the Census taken in the year 2000.

A-6 Population 65 And Over and as Percent of Population, 1996: These Census Bureau estimates are available on the Census web page (see notes to Table A-1) and are consistent with Census Bureau Release CB97-64, issued April 21, 1997. Two kinds of states have the largest percentage of elderly citizens. First, there are states, like Florida and Arkansas, that draw large numbers of retirees from other states. Second, there are states with slow population growth, such as Pennsylvania, that lose many of their working-age younger people through migration to other states.

A-7 Population Age 17 and Under and as Percent of Population, 1996: These estimates, from the same source as Table A-6, show the flip side of the high concentrations of elderly citizens shown in Table A-6. The highest ranking states, typified by Utah, have a large percentage of adults of childbearing age and high birth rates.

A-8 Median Age, 1996: In each state, half the population was older than the age shown, while half was younger. This statistic, from the same source as Table A-6, is a way to capture age differences among states in a single number for each state. The rankings are based on unrounded numbers.

A-9 African American Population and Percent of Population, 1994: Census takers ask citizens to identify their race. Nearly every respondent does this, using the Census Bureau categories, but not everyone classifies the same way the Census Bureau does. For example, "Hispanic" is not considered a race, so Hispanics are asked to classify themselves as "black" or "white." Regardless of how they classify themselves, most Americans are of mixed races, but this category is not recognized in the federal statistics. The 1994 estimates come from the Census Bureau web page (see notes to Table A-1). They were made available on September 3, 1996 as *Estimates of the Population of States by race and Hispanic origin, July 1, 1994.* Estimates for other federally recognized racial groups are available from the Census Bureau. The "undercount" (see notes to Table A-1) means that statistics probably undercount African Americans and Hispanics.

A-10 Hispanic Population and Percent of Population, 1994: See notes to Table A-9. While the Census theoretically accounts for every resident in the country, illegal immigrants (many of whom are Hispanic) have an understandable fear of being identified by any government agency. Therefore, the count of this group is probably not very accurate.

A-11 Population in Poverty, 1996: The federal government has a uniform definition of the income families need to avoid poverty. The amount considered necessary varies with family size but not with rural or urban location or from state to state. The income used to calculate whether households are living in poverty does not include the value of non-cash benefits, such as free medical care, provided to the poor under government programs. The estimates shown are from a Census Bureau tabulation (Table 25: "Poverty Status By State And Ten Large Metropolitan Areas In 1996") provided to *State Fact Finder* on September 30, 1997. They are based in part on monthly household surveys of a small sample of the nation's population, not a full count. They reflect possible sampling errors, particularly for less populous states.

A-12 Number and Rate of Children in Poverty, 1996: These Census Bureau statistics, provided by fax on October 16, 1997, are subject to the same caveats as similar data for persons of all ages in Table A-11. The percentage of children in poverty exceeds the percentage of all persons in poverty because households with children are often headed by a parent or parents in their early earning years and the income needed to avoid the poverty standard is higher for families with children than adults without children. Children not related to heads of households, such as foster children, are not included in this count.

A-13 Female Population, 1996: More than half of newly born children are male, but women tend to outlive men. The result is about equal numbers of each in the population as a whole, but disproportionate numbers of women in states with more aged population (see Table A-8). These data come from the same source as Table A-6.

A-14 Birth Rates, 1996: These data show that 14.8 children are born each year for every 1000 people. The birth rate is nearly 65.7 per 1000 when only women of childbearing age are considered. The data come from the National Center for Health Statistics publication, *Monthly Vital Statistics Report* (Vol. 46, No.1(S)2, September 11, 1997). See notes to Table A-15 below.

A-15 Death Rates (age-adjusted), 1996: Raw death rates like raw birth rates (births related to population) are highly sensitive to the age distribution of a state's population. A state with large numbers of older persons will tend to have lower raw birth rates and higher death rates. The National Center for Health Statistics makes special calculations adjusting deaths for age and births for the numbers of women of childbearing age (called fertility rates). *State Fact Finder* illustrates both approaches by using raw rates for births (Table A-14) and adjusted rates for deaths. Data showing fertility rates for births and raw rates for deaths are available from the source cited in the notes to Table A-14. This source also provides technical notes indicating exactly how adjustments are made. This table is indicating that, on average, people living in Mississippi die sooner than those in Hawaii.

A-16 Population Density, 1996: Although the Census Bureau only reports population density for Census years, the land area of states does not change. *State Fact Finder* calculated this table by taking the land area estimate from the 1990 Census (p. 360 of the *United States Summary)* and relating it to the 1996 population. The result is a rough measure of urban-rural characteristics of each state and is often cited as a proxy for possible crowding. However, in many states much of the land area is unusable for settlement because of lack of water, extraordinary low or high elevation, and other factors. Consequently, much of the population of a low-density state may in fact be densely packed in a few small areas.

A-17 Illegal Immigrant Population, 1996: Counting illegal immigrants, many of whom fear being counted, is inherently difficult. These estimates come from an Immigration and Naturalization Service press release titled, *Estimates of the Unauthorized Immigrant Population Residing in the United States: October 1996.* While the estimates may not be accurate, they are useful in illustrating the large differences among states.

Economies

State	Personal income $(millions)	Rank
Alabama	85,698	25
Alaska	14,907	47
Arizona	92,942	23
Arkansas	47,506	32
California	801,532	1
Colorado	95,889	22
Connecticut	108,688	21
Delaware	20,021	44
Florida	347,092	4
Georgia	166,984	11
Hawaii	29,782	40
Idaho	23,237	43
Illinois	315,091	5
Indiana	131,063	16
Iowa	64,336	29
Kansas	59,883	31
Kentucky	76,461	26
Louisiana	86,246	24
Maine	25,893	41
Maryland	138,052	14
Massachusetts	179,355	10
Michigan	238,032	9
Minnesota	119,145	19
Mississippi	47,452	33
Missouri	122,522	17
Montana	16,749	45
Nebraska	38,075	36
Nevada	40,802	34
New Hampshire	30,829	39
New Jersey	248,052	8
New Mexico	32,160	38
New York	523,403	2
North Carolina	161,179	13
North Dakota	13,328	48
Ohio	262,972	7
Oklahoma	63,872	30
Oregon	72,623	28
Pennsylvania	297,402	6
Rhode Island	24,523	42
South Carolina	73,067	27
South Dakota	15,758	46
Tennessee	115,778	20
Texas	421,676	3
Utah	38,321	35
Vermont	13,023	49
Virginia	166,385	12
Washington	137,425	15
West Virginia	33,675	37
Wisconsin	120,063	18
Wyoming	10,228	50
50 States	6,409,177	
DC	18,975	
United States	6,428,129	

Rank in order

By $

1. California
2. New York
3. Texas
4. Florida
5. Illinois
6. Pennsylvania
7. Ohio
8. New Jersey
9. Michigan
10. Massachusetts
11. Georgia
12. Virginia
13. North Carolina
14. Maryland
15. Washington
16. Indiana
17. Missouri
18. Wisconsin
19. Minnesota
20. Tennessee
21. Connecticut
22. Colorado
23. Arizona
24. Louisiana
25. Alabama
26. Kentucky
27. South Carolina
28. Oregon
29. Iowa
30. Oklahoma
31. Kansas
32. Arkansas
33. Mississippi
34. Nevada
35. Utah
36. Nebraska
37. West Virginia
38. New Mexico
39. New Hampshire
40. Hawaii
41. Maine
42. Rhode Island
43. Idaho
44. Delaware
45. Montana
46. South Dakota
47. Alaska
48. North Dakota
49. Vermont
50. Wyoming

State	Gross state product $(millions)	Per capita $	Rank by per capita
Alabama	88,661	21,034	45
Alaska	22,720	37,778	1
Arizona	94,093	22,997	35
Arkansas	50,575	20,602	46
California	875,697	27,922	11
Colorado	99,767	27,239	13
Connecticut	110,449	33,745	3
Delaware	26,697	37,717	2
Florida	317,829	22,759	38
Georgia	183,042	25,915	18
Hawaii	36,718	31,312	7
Idaho	24,185	21,282	42
Illinois	332,853	28,366	10
Indiana	138,190	24,033	30
Iowa	68,298	24,113	29
Kansas	61,758	24,219	28
Kentucky	86,485	22,606	39
Louisiana	101,101	23,432	34
Maine	26,069	21,057	44
Maryland	132,703	26,543	16
Massachusetts	186,199	30,817	8
Michigan	240,390	25,341	22
Minnesota	124,641	27,260	12
Mississippi	50,587	18,960	50
Missouri	128,216	24,306	27
Montana	16,862	19,687	48
Nebraska	41,357	25,442	21
Nevada	43,958	30,025	9
New Hampshire	29,393	25,889	19
New Jersey	254,945	32,248	5
New Mexico	37,832	22,801	37
New York	570,994	31,379	6
North Carolina	181,521	25,643	20
North Dakota	13,494	21,094	43
Ohio	274,844	24,768	23
Oklahoma	66,189	20,343	47
Oregon	74,366	24,033	31
Pennsylvania	294,431	24,417	26
Rhode Island	23,867	23,960	32
South Carolina	79,925	21,940	40
South Dakota	17,250	23,820	33
Tennessee	126,539	24,452	25
Texas	479,774	26,027	17
Utah	41,657	21,815	41
Vermont	13,282	22,874	36
Virginia	177,708	27,132	14
Washington	143,867	26,886	15
West Virginia	34,654	19,018	49
Wisconsin	125,321	24,648	24
Wyoming	15,660	32,915	4
50 States	6,787,613	26,126	
DC	48,028	84,553	
United States	6,835,641	26,253	

By per capita

1. Alaska
2. Delaware
3. Connecticut
4. Wyoming
5. New Jersey
6. New York
7. Hawaii
8. Massachusetts
9. Nevada
10. Illinois
11. California
12. Minnesota
13. Colorado
14. Virginia
15. Washington
16. Maryland
17. Texas
18. Georgia
19. New Hampshire
20. North Carolina
21. Nebraska
22. Michigan
23. Ohio
24. Wisconsin
25. Tennessee
26. Pennsylvania
27. Missouri
28. Kansas
29. Iowa
30. Indiana
31. Oregon
32. Rhode Island
33. South Dakota
34. Louisiana
35. Arizona
36. Vermont
37. New Mexico
38. Florida
39. Kentucky
40. South Carolina
41. Utah
42. Idaho
43. North Dakota
44. Maine
45. Alabama
46. Arkansas
47. Oklahoma
48. Montana
49. West Virginia
50. Mississippi

State	Per capita personal income $	Rank	By $
Alabama	20,055	39	1. Connecticut
Alaska	24,558	19	2. New Jersey
Arizona	20,989	36	3. Massachusetts
Arkansas	18,928	47	4. New York
California	25,144	12	5. Delaware
Colorado	25,084	13	6. Maryland
Connecticut	33,189	1	7. Illinois
Delaware	27,622	5	8. New Hampshire
Florida	24,104	20	9. Minnesota
Georgia	22,709	26	10. Nevada
Hawaii	25,159	11	11. Hawaii
Idaho	19,539	43	12. California
Illinois	26,598	7	13. Colorado
Indiana	22,440	29	14. Virginia
Iowa	22,560	28	15. Washington
Kansas	23,281	22	16. Michigan
Kentucky	19,687	42	17. Rhode Island
Louisiana	19,824	40	18. Pennsylvania
Maine	20,826	37	19. Alaska
Maryland	27,221	6	20. Florida
Massachusetts	29,439	3	21. Ohio
Michigan	24,810	16	22. Kansas
Minnesota	25,580	9	23. Wisconsin
Mississippi	17,471	50	24. Nebraska
Missouri	22,864	25	25. Missouri
Montana	19,047	46	26. Georgia
Nebraska	23,047	24	27. Oregon
Nevada	25,451	10	28. Iowa
New Hampshire	26,520	8	29. Indiana
New Jersey	31,053	2	30. Vermont
New Mexico	18,770	48	31. Texas
New York	28,782	4	32. North Carolina
North Carolina	22,010	32	33. Tennessee
North Dakota	20,710	38	34. South Dakota
Ohio	23,537	21	35. Wyoming
Oklahoma	19,350	44	36. Arizona
Oregon	22,668	27	37. Maine
Pennsylvania	24,668	18	38. North Dakota
Rhode Island	24,765	17	39. Alabama
South Carolina	19,755	41	40. Louisiana
South Dakota	21,516	34	41. South Carolina
Tennessee	21,764	33	42. Kentucky
Texas	22,045	31	43. Idaho
Utah	19,156	45	44. Oklahoma
Vermont	22,124	30	45. Utah
Virginia	24,925	14	46. Montana
Washington	24,838	15	47. Arkansas
West Virginia	18,444	49	48. New Mexico
Wisconsin	23,269	23	49. West Virginia
Wyoming	21,245	35	50. Mississippi
50 States	n/a		
DC	34,932		
United States	24,231		

State	Wages & salaries $(millions)	As percent of personal income %	Rank by %	By %
Alabama	48,023	56.0	26	1. Utah
Alaska	9,263	62.1	2	2. Alaska
Arizona	52,852	56.9	23	3. Nevada
Arkansas	25,100	52.8	39	4. Georgia
California	440,733	55.0	28	5. Minnesota
Colorado	57,156	59.6	8	6. Delaware
Connecticut	59,748	55.0	29	7. North Carolina
Delaware	12,023	60.1	6	8. Colorado
Florida	169,945	49.0	48	9. Massachusetts
Georgia	101,849	61.0	4	10. Michigan
Hawaii	16,974	57.0	22	11. South Carolina
Idaho	12,314	53.0	36	12. Tennessee
Illinois	183,064	58.1	13	13. Illinois
Indiana	75,975	58.0	15	14. Virginia
Iowa	33,704	52.4	40	15. Indiana
Kansas	31,954	53.4	33	16. New York
Kentucky	42,874	56.1	25	17. Ohio
Louisiana	46,160	53.5	32	18. Texas
Maine	13,464	52.0	43	19. Wisconsin
Maryland	71,080	51.5	44	20. Missouri
Massachusetts	106,103	59.2	9	21. Oregon
Michigan	140,103	58.9	10	22. Hawaii
Minnesota	72,115	60.5	5	23. Arizona
Mississippi	25,156	53.0	35	24. Washington
Missouri	70,380	57.4	20	25. Kentucky
Montana	8,137	48.6	49	26. Alabama
Nebraska	20,856	54.8	30	27. New Mexico
Nevada	25,129	61.6	3	28. California
New Hampshire	15,613	50.6	46	29. Connecticut
New Jersey	132,778	53.5	31	30. Nebraska
New Mexico	17,718	55.1	27	31. New Jersey
New York	301,994	57.7	16	32. Louisiana
North Carolina	96,213	59.7	7	33. Kansas
North Dakota	6,931	52.0	42	34. Vermont
Ohio	151,419	57.6	17	35. Mississippi
Oklahoma	33,446	52.4	41	36. Idaho
Oregon	41,472	57.1	21	37. Pennsylvania
Pennsylvania	157,308	52.9	37	38. Wyoming
Rhode Island	12,497	51.0	45	39. Arkansas
South Carolina	42,771	58.5	11	40. Iowa
South Dakota	7,489	47.5	50	41. Oklahoma
Tennessee	67,713	58.5	12	42. North Dakota
Texas	242,440	57.5	18	43. Maine
Utah	24,594	64.2	1	44. Maryland
Vermont	6,949	53.4	34	45. Rhode Island
Virginia	96,599	58.1	14	46. New Hampshire
Washington	77,232	56.2	24	47. West Virginia
West Virginia	16,879	50.1	47	48. Florida
Wisconsin	68,985	57.5	19	49. Montana
Wyoming	5,405	52.8	38	50. South Dakota
50 States	3,596,680	56.1		
DC	29,414	155.0		
United States	3,626,094	56.4		

State	Average annual pay $	Rank
Alabama	24,592	32
Alaska	30,548	9
Arizona	25,923	26
Arkansas	21,832	46
California	31,183	6
Colorado	28,182	15
Connecticut	36,439	2
Delaware	30,592	8
Florida	25,045	30
Georgia	27,611	17
Hawaii	26,371	24
Idaho	23,047	41
Illinois	31,130	7
Indiana	26,379	23
Iowa	23,160	40
Kansas	24,574	33
Kentucky	24,130	34
Louisiana	24,732	31
Maine	23,288	39
Maryland	28,945	10
Massachusetts	33,765	4
Michigan	31,406	5
Minnesota	28,554	11
Mississippi	21,461	47
Missouri	26,551	21
Montana	20,082	50
Nebraska	22,823	43
Nevada	26,931	20
New Hampshire	27,648	16
New Jersey	35,351	3
New Mexico	22,604	44
New York	36,714	1
North Carolina	25,168	29
North Dakota	20,754	48
Ohio	27,448	18
Oklahoma	22,901	42
Oregon	26,434	22
Pennsylvania	28,369	13
Rhode Island	26,129	25
South Carolina	23,637	38
South Dakota	20,111	49
Tennessee	25,724	27
Texas	28,421	12
Utah	24,103	35
Vermont	24,040	36
Virginia	27,315	19
Washington	28,217	14
West Virginia	23,724	37
Wisconsin	25,505	28
Wyoming	22,264	45
50 States	n/a	
DC	40,195	
United States	28,581	

Rank in order

By $

1. New York
2. Connecticut
3. New Jersey
4. Massachusetts
5. Michigan
6. California
7. Illinois
8. Delaware
9. Alaska
10. Maryland
11. Minnesota
12. Texas
13. Pennsylvania
14. Washington
15. Colorado
16. New Hampshire
17. Georgia
18. Ohio
19. Virginia
20. Nevada
21. Missouri
22. Oregon
23. Indiana
24. Hawaii
25. Rhode Island
26. Arizona
27. Tennessee
28. Wisconsin
29. North Carolina
30. Florida
31. Louisiana
32. Alabama
33. Kansas
34. Kentucky
35. Utah
36. Vermont
37. West Virginia
38. South Carolina
39. Maine
40. Iowa
41. Idaho
42. Oklahoma
43. Nebraska
44. New Mexico
45. Wyoming
46. Arkansas
47. Mississippi
48. North Dakota
49. South Dakota
50. Montana

B-6 AVERAGE HOURLY EARNINGS, 1997

State	Average hourly earnings $	Rank		Rank in order By $
Alabama	11.81	38		1. Michigan
Alaska	12.24	33		2. Washington
Arizona	11.66	40		3. Ohio
Arkansas	10.71	47		4. Delaware
California	13.15	24		5. Indiana
Colorado	13.35	17		6. Connecticut
Connecticut	14.32	6		7. Wyoming
Delaware	14.87	4		8. Maryland
Florida	10.74	46		9. New Jersey
Georgia	11.47	41		10. Louisiana
Hawaii	13.10	26		11. Nevada
Idaho	12.20	34		12. Pennsylvania
Illinois	13.33	19		13. Wisconsin
Indiana	14.58	5		14. Minnesota
Iowa	13.42	15		15. Iowa
Kansas	13.41	16		16. Kansas
Kentucky	13.22	22		17. Colorado
Louisiana	14.09	10		18. Massachusetts
Maine	12.92	28		19. Illinois
Maryland	14.24	8		19. Oregon
Massachusetts	13.34	18		21. Montana
Michigan	16.84	1		22. Kentucky
Minnesota	13.55	14		23. New York
Mississippi	10.34	49		24. California
Missouri	12.96	27		25. West Virginia
Montana	13.25	21		26. Hawaii
Nebraska	12.04	36		27. Missouri
Nevada	13.88	11		28. Maine
New Hampshire	12.42	32		29. Vermont
New Jersey	14.14	9		30. Utah
New Mexico	11.40	42		31. Virginia
New York	13.17	23		32. New Hampshire
North Carolina	11.33	43		33. Alaska
North Dakota	11.04	45		34. Idaho
Ohio	15.02	3		35. Texas
Oklahoma	12.01	37		36. Nebraska
Oregon	13.33	19		37. Oklahoma
Pennsylvania	13.62	12		38. Alabama
Rhode Island	11.19	44		39. Tennessee
South Carolina	10.35	48		40. Arizona
South Dakota	9.95	50		41. Georgia
Tennessee	11.78	39		42. New Mexico
Texas	12.06	35		43. North Carolina
Utah	12.65	30		44. Rhode Island
Vermont	12.76	29		45. North Dakota
Virginia	12.44	31		46. Florida
Washington	15.03	2		47. Arkansas
West Virginia	13.14	25		48. South Carolina
Wisconsin	13.58	13		49. Mississippi
Wyoming	14.29	7		50. South Dakota
50 States	n/a			
DC	13.94			
United States	13.09			

State	Value added $(millions)	Per capita $	Rank by per capita		By per capita
Alabama	29,079	6,848	22		1. Indiana
Alaska	1,459	2,421	45		2. North Carolina
Arizona	20,912	4,857	40		3. Wisconsin
Arkansas	18,640	7,502	14		4. Ohio
California	178,358	5,650	32		5. Iowa
Colorado	18,943	5,055	36		6. Michigan
Connecticut	24,988	7,640	12		7. Kentucky
Delaware	5,666	7,902	11		8. South Carolina
Florida	37,934	2,674	50		9. Tennessee
Georgia	50,220	6,967	19		10. Illinois
Hawaii	1,489	1,262	49		11. Delaware
Idaho	7,932	6,802	23		12. Connecticut
Illinois	93,763	7,952	10		13. New Hampshire
Indiana	60,992	10,521	1		14. Arkansas
Iowa	26,215	9,221	5		15. Missouri
Kansas	17,743	6,921	20		16. Minnesota
Kentucky	33,632	8,720	7		17. Pennsylvania
Louisiana	30,405	7,009	18		18. Louisiana
Maine	7,030	5,676	31		19. Georgia
Maryland	17,148	3,403	43		20. Kansas
Massachusetts	41,901	6,902	21		21. Massachusetts
Michigan	87,398	9,163	6		22. Alabama
Minnesota	32,553	7,054	16		23. Idaho
Mississippi	17,443	6,469	24		24. Mississippi
Missouri	39,737	7,470	15		25. Oregon
Montana	1,779	2,044	47		26. New Jersey
Nebraska	9,361	5,710	30		27. Virginia
Nevada	2,991	1,951	48		28. Texas
New Hampshire	8,659	7,541	13		29. Vermont
New Jersey	48,260	6,071	26		30. Nebraska
New Mexico	8,358	4,946	37		31. Maine
New York	89,924	4,943	38		32. California
North Carolina	73,919	10,263	2		33. Rhode Island
North Dakota	1,559	2,431	44		34. South Dakota
Ohio	103,713	9,315	4		35. Washington
Oklahoma	14,622	4,465	42		36. Colorado
Oregon	19,677	6,249	25		37. New Mexico
Pennsylvania	84,582	7,013	17		38. New York
Rhode Island	5,426	5,472	33		39. West Virginia
South Carolina	31,467	8,581	8		40. Arizona
South Dakota	3,927	5,384	34		41. Utah
Tennessee	43,126	8,220	9		42. Oklahoma
Texas	112,425	5,980	28		43. Maryland
Utah	9,498	4,850	41		44. North Dakota
Vermont	3,445	5,891	29		45. Alaska
Virginia	40,134	6,067	27		46. Wyoming
Washington	28,150	5,167	35		47. Montana
West Virginia	8,948	4,902	39		48. Nevada
Wisconsin	50,989	9,955	3		49. Hawaii
Wyoming	1,030	2,149	46		50. Florida
50 States	1,707,544	6,509			
DC	1,636	2,951			
United States	1,709,180	6,502			

Rank in order

B-8 COST OF LIVING, 1996

State	Cost of living index	Rank
Alabama	93.0	39
Alaska	113.7	3
Arizona	99.8	17
Arkansas	91.1	48
California	101.1	14
Colorado	99.6	19
Connecticut	112.4	6
Delaware	103.6	12
Florida	94.8	30
Georgia	91.9	45
Hawaii	127.3	1
Idaho	95.2	29
Illinois	99.9	16
Indiana	96.5	24
Iowa	93.9	34
Kansas	93.8	35
Kentucky	91.8	46
Louisiana	93.2	38
Maine	105.2	9
Maryland	98.3	20
Massachusetts	113.2	5
Michigan	94.6	31
Minnesota	94.6	31
Mississippi	90.3	50
Missouri	93.5	37
Montana	95.5	27
Nebraska	94.3	33
Nevada	100.1	15
New Hampshire	108.3	8
New Jersey	114.0	2
New Mexico	97.4	23
New York	113.4	4
North Carolina	92.3	44
North Dakota	93.6	36
Ohio	98.0	21
Oklahoma	92.4	43
Oregon	97.8	22
Pennsylvania	105.0	10
Rhode Island	110.8	7
South Carolina	92.5	42
South Dakota	92.6	41
Tennessee	93.0	39
Texas	91.5	47
Utah	99.7	18
Vermont	104.0	11
Virginia	95.8	26
Washington	102.0	13
West Virginia	90.8	49
Wisconsin	95.5	27
Wyoming	95.9	25
50 States	n/a	
DC	105.2	
United States	100.0	

By index

1. Hawaii
2. New Jersey
3. Alaska
4. New York
5. Massachusetts
6. Connecticut
7. Rhode Island
8. New Hampshire
9. Maine
10. Pennsylvania
11. Vermont
12. Delaware
13. Washington
14. California
15. Nevada
16. Illinois
17. Arizona
18. Utah
19. Colorado
20. Maryland
21. Ohio
22. Oregon
23. New Mexico
24. Indiana
25. Wyoming
26. Virginia
27. Montana
27. Wisconsin
29. Idaho
30. Florida
31. Michigan
31. Minnesota
33. Nebraska
34. Iowa
35. Kansas
36. North Dakota
37. Missouri
38. Louisiana
39. Alabama
39. Tennessee
41. South Dakota
42. South Carolina
43. Oklahoma
44. North Carolina
45. Georgia
46. Kentucky
47. Texas
48. Arkansas
49. West Virginia
50. Mississippi

State	Average annual pay in manufacturing $	Rank
Alabama	28,705	45
Alaska	29,205	42
Arizona	37,168	13
Arkansas	24,811	49
California	39,810	7
Colorado	37,080	14
Connecticut	47,045	2
Delaware	50,692	1
Florida	31,946	28
Georgia	30,595	34
Hawaii	29,884	38
Idaho	32,274	26
Illinois	38,343	10
Indiana	36,328	16
Iowa	31,707	30
Kansas	32,967	25
Kentucky	31,631	31
Louisiana	35,137	19
Maine	30,521	35
Maryland	38,074	11
Massachusetts	42,635	5
Michigan	46,739	3
Minnesota	37,250	12
Mississippi	24,334	50
Missouri	34,315	21
Montana	26,856	46
Nebraska	28,857	44
Nevada	31,905	29
New Hampshire	36,378	15
New Jersey	44,126	4
New Mexico	29,630	40
New York	41,843	6
North Carolina	29,110	43
North Dakota	26,569	47
Ohio	38,356	9
Oklahoma	29,740	39
Oregon	34,870	20
Pennsylvania	36,328	17
Rhode Island	31,250	32
South Carolina	30,085	37
South Dakota	24,882	48
Tennessee	30,790	33
Texas	36,163	18
Utah	30,196	36
Vermont	33,019	24
Virginia	31,999	27
Washington	39,086	8
West Virginia	33,678	22
Wisconsin	33,464	23
Wyoming	29,486	41
50 States	n/a	
DC	52,970	
United States	36,235	

State	Average annual pay in retailing $	Rank
Alabama	13,663	36
Alaska	18,325	2
Arizona	16,075	11
Arkansas	13,828	33
California	17,276	5
Colorado	15,528	16
Connecticut	17,806	3
Delaware	14,993	19
Florida	15,621	14
Georgia	14,848	20
Hawaii	16,849	8
Idaho	13,783	34
Illinois	15,668	13
Indiana	13,394	38
Iowa	12,422	45
Kansas	13,396	37
Kentucky	13,190	39
Louisiana	13,168	40
Maine	14,126	29
Maryland	16,365	9
Massachusetts	16,853	7
Michigan	14,560	23
Minnesota	14,497	25
Mississippi	12,747	43
Missouri	14,243	27
Montana	12,382	46
Nebraska	12,627	44
Nevada	17,574	4
New Hampshire	15,535	15
New Jersey	18,366	1
New Mexico	13,884	32
New York	16,890	6
North Carolina	14,352	26
North Dakota	11,859	50
Ohio	14,126	30
Oklahoma	13,012	41
Oregon	15,857	12
Pennsylvania	14,515	24
Rhode Island	14,665	22
South Carolina	13,725	35
South Dakota	11,942	49
Tennessee	15,018	18
Texas	15,341	17
Utah	14,237	28
Vermont	13,998	31
Virginia	14,746	21
Washington	16,083	10
West Virginia	12,295	48
Wisconsin	12,916	42
Wyoming	12,372	47
50 States	n/a	
DC	16,260	
United States	15,215	

By $

1. New Jersey
2. Alaska
3. Connecticut
4. Nevada
5. California
6. New York
7. Massachusetts
8. Hawaii
9. Maryland
10. Washington
11. Arizona
12. Oregon
13. Illinois
14. Florida
15. New Hampshire
16. Colorado
17. Texas
18. Tennessee
19. Delaware
20. Georgia
21. Virginia
22. Rhode Island
23. Michigan
24. Pennsylvania
25. Minnesota
26. North Carolina
27. Missouri
28. Utah
29. Maine
30. Ohio
31. Vermont
32. New Mexico
33. Arkansas
34. Idaho
35. South Carolina
36. Alabama
37. Kansas
38. Indiana
39. Kentucky
40. Louisiana
41. Oklahoma
42. Wisconsin
43. Mississippi
44. Nebraska
45. Iowa
46. Montana
47. Wyoming
48. West Virginia
49. South Dakota
50. North Dakota

State	Labor force (000)	Labor force as percent of population %	Rank by %	By %
Alabama	2,107	49.3	44	1. Minnesota
Alaska	323	53.2	21	2. Wisconsin
Arizona	2,279	51.5	33	3. Colorado
Arkansas	1,247	49.7	41	4. New Hampshire
California	15,862	49.8	40	5. Nevada
Colorado	2,166	56.7	3	6. Iowa
Connecticut	1,747	53.3	19	7. Vermont
Delaware	391	54.0	12	8. Nebraska
Florida	7,142	49.6	43	9. Maryland
Georgia	3,867	52.6	25	10. Kansas
Hawaii	597	50.4	38	11. North Dakota
Idaho	641	53.9	13	12. Delaware
Illinois	6,142	51.8	32	13. Idaho
Indiana	3,119	53.4	18	14. Washington
Iowa	1,600	56.1	6	15. Maine
Kansas	1,392	54.1	10	16. Wyoming
Kentucky	1,928	49.6	42	17. South Dakota
Louisiana	2,005	46.1	49	18. Indiana
Maine	668	53.7	15	19. Connecticut
Maryland	2,776	54.7	9	20. Oregon
Massachusetts	3,234	53.1	23	21. Alaska
Michigan	4,858	50.6	37	22. Missouri
Minnesota	2,667	57.3	1	23. Massachusetts
Mississippi	1,274	46.9	48	24. Virginia
Missouri	2,850	53.2	22	25. Georgia
Montana	461	52.4	27	26. Utah
Nebraska	922	55.8	8	27. Montana
Nevada	902	56.2	5	28. Tennessee
New Hampshire	656	56.4	4	29. New Jersey
New Jersey	4,156	52.0	29	30. North Carolina
New Mexico	825	48.1	47	31. Texas
New York	8,776	48.3	46	32. Illinois
North Carolina	3,809	52.0	30	33. Arizona
North Dakota	348	54.0	11	34. South Carolina
Ohio	5,730	51.3	35	35. Ohio
Oklahoma	1,602	48.5	45	36. Rhode Island
Oregon	1,706	53.3	20	37. Michigan
Pennsylvania	6,009	49.8	39	38. Hawaii
Rhode Island	504	50.9	36	39. Pennsylvania
South Carolina	1,904	51.5	34	40. California
South Dakota	392	53.5	17	41. Arkansas
Tennessee	2,773	52.1	28	42. Kentucky
Texas	9,933	51.9	31	43. Florida
Utah	1,050	52.5	26	44. Alabama
Vermont	329	56.0	7	45. Oklahoma
Virginia	3,533	52.9	24	46. New York
Washington	2,980	53.9	14	47. New Mexico
West Virginia	807	44.2	50	48. Mississippi
Wisconsin	2,931	56.8	2	49. Louisiana
Wyoming	258	53.6	16	50. West Virginia
50 States	136,179	51.4		
DC	257	47.3		
United States	136,436	51.4		

State	Unemployed (000)	Unemployment rate %	Rank by %
Alabama	99	4.7	24
Alaska	23	7.2	1
Arizona	94	4.1	33
Arkansas	68	5.5	9
California	973	6.1	7
Colorado	66	3.1	44
Connecticut	83	4.8	21
Delaware	17	4.3	30
Florida	329	4.6	26
Georgia	168	4.3	29
Hawaii	37	6.2	6
Idaho	32	4.9	19
Illinois	284	4.6	25
Indiana	99	3.2	42
Iowa	42	2.6	48
Kansas	54	3.9	34
Kentucky	101	5.3	15
Louisiana	127	6.3	5
Maine	34	5.0	17
Maryland	131	4.7	23
Massachusetts	125	3.9	35
Michigan	186	3.8	36
Minnesota	82	3.1	43
Mississippi	64	5.0	18
Missouri	102	3.6	41
Montana	23	5.1	16
Nebraska	22	2.4	50
Nevada	40	4.4	28
New Hampshire	20	3.0	46
New Jersey	223	5.4	12
New Mexico	53	6.4	4
New York	561	6.4	3
North Carolina	142	3.7	40
North Dakota	9	2.6	49
Ohio	240	4.2	32
Oklahoma	60	3.8	39
Oregon	90	5.3	14
Pennsylvania	317	5.3	13
Rhode Island	28	5.5	8
South Carolina	87	4.6	27
South Dakota	11	2.7	47
Tennessee	152	5.5	10
Texas	540	5.4	11
Utah	31	3.0	45
Vermont	13	3.8	37
Virginia	148	4.2	31
Washington	141	4.7	22
West Virginia	54	6.7	2
Wisconsin	111	3.8	38
Wyoming	13	4.9	20
50 States	6,546	4.8	
DC	19	7.4	
United States	6,565	4.8	

By %

1. Alaska
2. West Virginia
3. New York
4. New Mexico
5. Louisiana
6. Hawaii
7. California
8. Rhode Island
9. Arkansas
10. Tennessee
11. Texas
12. New Jersey
13. Pennsylvania
14. Oregon
15. Kentucky
16. Montana
17. Maine
18. Mississippi
19. Idaho
20. Wyoming
21. Connecticut
22. Washington
23. Maryland
24. Alabama
25. Illinois
26. Florida
27. South Carolina
28. Nevada
29. Georgia
30. Delaware
31. Virginia
32. Ohio
33. Arizona
34. Kansas
35. Massachusetts
36. Michigan
37. Vermont
38. Wisconsin
39. Oklahoma
40. North Carolina
41. Missouri
42. Indiana
43. Minnesota
44. Colorado
45. Utah
46. New Hampshire
47. South Dakota
48. Iowa
49. North Dakota
50. Nebraska

State	Employed (000)	Employment rate %	Rank by %	By %
Alabama	2,009	95.3	27	1. Nebraska
Alaska	300	92.8	50	2. North Dakota
Arizona	2,185	95.9	18	3. Iowa
Arkansas	1,179	94.5	42	4. South Dakota
California	14,890	93.9	44	5. New Hampshire
Colorado	2,100	96.9	7	6. Utah
Connecticut	1,663	95.2	30	7. Colorado
Delaware	374	95.7	21	8. Minnesota
Florida	6,814	95.4	25	9. Indiana
Georgia	3,699	95.7	22	10. Missouri
Hawaii	560	93.8	45	11. North Carolina
Idaho	610	95.1	32	12. Oklahoma
Illinois	5,857	95.4	26	13. Wisconsin
Indiana	3,020	96.8	9	14. Vermont
Iowa	1,558	97.4	3	15. Michigan
Kansas	1,338	96.1	17	16. Massachusetts
Kentucky	1,827	94.7	36	17. Kansas
Louisiana	1,878	93.7	46	18. Arizona
Maine	634	95.0	34	19. Ohio
Maryland	2,645	95.3	28	20. Virginia
Massachusetts	3,110	96.1	16	21. Delaware
Michigan	4,672	96.2	15	22. Georgia
Minnesota	2,585	96.9	8	23. Nevada
Mississippi	1,211	95.0	33	24. South Carolina
Missouri	2,748	96.4	10	25. Florida
Montana	437	94.9	35	26. Illinois
Nebraska	900	97.6	1	27. Alabama
Nevada	862	95.6	23	28. Maryland
New Hampshire	636	97.0	5	29. Washington
New Jersey	3,934	94.6	39	30. Connecticut
New Mexico	772	93.6	47	31. Wyoming
New York	8,216	93.6	48	32. Idaho
North Carolina	3,667	96.3	11	33. Mississippi
North Dakota	339	97.4	2	34. Maine
Ohio	5,490	95.8	19	35. Montana
Oklahoma	1,542	96.2	12	36. Kentucky
Oregon	1,616	94.7	37	37. Oregon
Pennsylvania	5,692	94.7	38	38. Pennsylvania
Rhode Island	476	94.5	43	39. New Jersey
South Carolina	1,817	95.4	24	40. Texas
South Dakota	381	97.3	4	41. Tennessee
Tennessee	2,621	94.5	41	42. Arkansas
Texas	9,393	94.6	40	43. Rhode Island
Utah	1,019	97.0	6	44. California
Vermont	317	96.2	14	45. Hawaii
Virginia	3,385	95.8	20	46. Louisiana
Washington	2,839	95.3	29	47. New Mexico
West Virginia	753	93.3	49	48. New York
Wisconsin	2,820	96.2	13	49. West Virginia
Wyoming	246	95.1	31	50. Alaska
50 States	129,633	95.2		
DC	238	92.6		
United States	129,871	95.2		

State	Government employment (000)	Percent of total employment %	Rank by %	Rank in order By %
Alabama	342	18.6	17	1. Alaska
Alaska	73	27.6	1	2. Wyoming
Arizona	319	16.2	30	3. New Mexico
Arkansas	181	16.6	25	4. North Dakota
California	2,149	16.3	27	5. Montana
Colorado	312	16.1	31	6. Hawaii
Connecticut	229	14.1	43	7. Mississippi
Delaware	53	13.7	45	8. South Dakota
Florida	938	14.6	38	9. Oklahoma
Georgia	573	15.9	33	10. Idaho
Hawaii	111	21.0	6	11. Louisiana
Idaho	100	19.8	10	12. West Virginia
Illinois	815	14.2	42	13. Maryland
Indiana	387	13.6	47	14. Virginia
Iowa	231	16.4	26	15. Kansas
Kansas	237	18.7	15	16. Washington
Kentucky	295	17.2	21	17. Alabama
Louisiana	361	19.6	11	18. South Carolina
Maine	93	16.9	23	19. Nebraska
Maryland	423	18.8	13	20. Texas
Massachusetts	402	12.9	49	21. Kentucky
Michigan	635	14.4	40	22. New York
Minnesota	388	15.6	35	23. Maine
Mississippi	231	20.9	7	24. Utah
Missouri	415	16.0	32	25. Arkansas
Montana	77	21.1	5	26. Iowa
Nebraska	152	17.8	19	27. California
Nevada	108	12.0	50	28. Oregon
New Hampshire	81	14.0	44	29. Vermont
New Jersey	565	15.2	36	30. Arizona
New Mexico	176	24.9	3	31. Colorado
New York	1,377	17.2	22	32. Missouri
North Carolina	577	15.9	34	33. Georgia
North Dakota	70	22.2	4	34. North Carolina
Ohio	764	14.3	41	35. Minnesota
Oklahoma	275	19.8	9	36. New Jersey
Oregon	250	16.3	28	37. Tennessee
Pennsylvania	733	13.5	48	38. Florida
Rhode Island	61	13.6	46	39. Wisconsin
South Carolina	304	17.8	18	40. Michigan
South Dakota	71	20.0	8	41. Ohio
Tennessee	383	15.0	37	42. Illinois
Texas	1,471	17.4	20	43. Connecticut
Utah	168	16.9	24	44. New Hampshire
Vermont	45	16.2	29	45. Delaware
Virginia	602	18.7	14	46. Rhode Island
Washington	467	18.6	16	47. Indiana
West Virginia	139	19.6	12	48. Pennsylvania
Wisconsin	382	14.4	39	49. Massachusetts
Wyoming	58	26.3	2	50. Nevada
50 States	19,647	16.2		
DC	232	37.6		
United States	19,880	16.3		

B-15 MANUFACTURING EMPLOYMENT, 1997

State	Manufacturing employment (000)	Percent of total employment %	Rank by %
Alabama	378	20.5	8
Alaska	15	5.6	47
Arizona	206	10.4	39
Arkansas	251	22.9	3
California	1,898	14.4	28
Colorado	198	10.2	41
Connecticut	276	17.0	17
Delaware	58	15.0	25
Florida	495	7.7	42
Georgia	587	16.3	20
Hawaii	16	3.1	50
Idaho	73	14.5	27
Illinois	978	17.0	18
Indiana	668	23.5	1
Iowa	249	17.7	14
Kansas	204	16.1	21
Kentucky	316	18.4	12
Louisiana	190	10.4	40
Maine	87	15.9	23
Maryland	173	7.7	43
Massachusetts	448	14.4	29
Michigan	953	21.7	6
Minnesota	435	17.5	15
Mississippi	243	22.0	5
Missouri	405	15.6	24
Montana	24	6.6	46
Nebraska	116	13.6	31
Nevada	40	4.4	49
New Hampshire	108	18.6	11
New Jersey	482	13.0	33
New Mexico	47	6.6	45
New York	919	11.5	38
North Carolina	843	23.2	2
North Dakota	23	7.3	44
Ohio	1,076	20.1	10
Oklahoma	179	12.8	34
Oregon	245	16.0	22
Pennsylvania	930	17.1	16
Rhode Island	81	18.2	13
South Carolina	359	21.0	7
South Dakota	50	14.1	30
Tennessee	514	20.1	9
Texas	1,070	12.6	35
Utah	131	13.2	32
Vermont	47	16.7	19
Virginia	396	12.3	36
Washington	371	14.7	26
West Virginia	82	11.5	37
Wisconsin	603	22.8	4
Wyoming	11	5.0	48
50 States	18,546	15.3	
DC	14	2.2	
United States	18,560	15.2	

Rank in order

By %

1. Indiana
2. North Carolina
3. Arkansas
4. Wisconsin
5. Mississippi
6. Michigan
7. South Carolina
8. Alabama
9. Tennessee
10. Ohio
11. New Hampshire
12. Kentucky
13. Rhode Island
14. Iowa
15. Minnesota
16. Pennsylvania
17. Connecticut
18. Illinois
19. Vermont
20. Georgia
21. Kansas
22. Oregon
23. Maine
24. Missouri
25. Delaware
26. Washington
27. Idaho
28. California
29. Massachusetts
30. South Dakota
31. Nebraska
32. Utah
33. New Jersey
34. Oklahoma
35. Texas
36. Virginia
37. West Virginia
38. New York
39. Arizona
40. Louisiana
41. Colorado
42. Florida
43. Maryland
44. North Dakota
45. New Mexico
46. Montana
47. Alaska
48. Wyoming
49. Nevada
50. Hawaii

State	B-16 FORTUNE 500 COMPANIES, 1997 Number of Fortune 500 companies	Fortune 500 companies per million populaton	Rank by per million
Alabama	4	0.9	31
Alaska	0	n/a	n/a
Arizona	2	0.5	38
Arkansas	5	2.0	15
California	58	1.8	18
Colorado	3	0.8	34
Connecticut	22	6.7	1
Delaware	3	4.1	2
Florida	13	0.9	32
Georgia	13	1.8	19
Hawaii	0	n/a	n/a
Idaho	3	2.5	13
Illinois	39	3.3	5
Indiana	6	1.0	28
Iowa	2	0.7	37
Kansas	2	0.8	35
Kentucky	5	1.3	25
Louisiana	1	0.2	41
Maine	2	1.6	20
Maryland	6	1.2	27
Massachusetts	16	2.6	10
Michigan	14	1.5	22
Minnesota	15	3.2	6
Mississippi	1	0.4	39
Missouri	14	2.6	11
Montana	0	n/a	n/a
Nebraska	6	3.6	3
Nevada	0	n/a	n/a
New Hampshire	1	0.9	33
New Jersey	23	2.9	8
New Mexico	0	n/a	n/a
New York	61	3.4	4
North Carolina	7	1.0	30
North Dakota	0	n/a	n/a
Ohio	29	2.6	12
Oklahoma	4	1.2	26
Oregon	6	1.9	17
Pennsylvania	32	2.7	9
Rhode Island	3	3.0	7
South Carolina	1	0.3	40
South Dakota	1	1.4	24
Tennessee	4	0.8	36
Texas	36	1.9	16
Utah	2	1.0	29
Vermont	0	n/a	n/a
Virginia	16	2.4	14
Washington	8	1.4	23
West Virginia	0	n/a	n/a
Wisconsin	8	1.6	21
Wyoming	0	n/a	n/a
50 States	497	1.9	
DC	3	5.5	
United States	500	1.9	

Rank in order

By per million

1. Connecticut
2. Delaware
3. Nebraska
4. New York
5. Illinois
6. Minnesota
7. Rhode Island
8. New Jersey
9. Pennsylvania
10. Massachusetts
11. Missouri
12. Ohio
13. Idaho
14. Virginia
15. Arkansas
16. Texas
17. Oregon
18. California
19. Georgia
20. Maine
21. Wisconsin
22. Michigan
23. Washington
24. South Dakota
25. Kentucky
26. Oklahoma
27. Maryland
28. Indiana
29. Utah
30. North Carolina
31. Alabama
32. Florida
33. New Hampshire
34. Colorado
35. Kansas
36. Tennessee
37. Iowa
38. Arizona
39. Mississippi
40. South Carolina
41. Louisiana

State	Forbes 500 companies #	Forbes 500 companies per million companies	Rank by per million	By per million
Alabama	12	2.8	17	1. Connecticut
Alaska			n/a	2. Delaware
Arizona	4	0.9	42	3. Minnesota
Arkansas	6	2.4	23	4. Illinois
California	90	2.8	16	5. New York
Colorado	10	2.6	18	6. Missouri
Connecticut	32	9.8	1	7. Ohio
Delaware	5	6.9	2	8. Virginia
Florida	20	1.4	37	9. Nebraska
Georgia	16	2.2	24	10. New Jersey
Hawaii	3	2.5	19	11. Massachusetts
Idaho	3	2.5	20	12. Pennsylvania
Illinois	58	4.9	4	13. Texas
Indiana	12	2.1	27	14. Rhode Island
Iowa	5	1.8	33	15. Wisconsin
Kansas	2	0.8	43	16. California
Kentucky	6	1.5	35	17. Alabama
Louisiana	5	1.1	40	18. Colorado
Maine	3	2.4	22	19. Hawaii
Maryland	11	2.2	25	20. Idaho
Massachusetts	22	3.6	11	21. Utah
Michigan	19	2.0	30	22. Maine
Minnesota	23	4.9	3	23. Arkansas
Mississippi	4	1.5	36	24. Georgia
Missouri	24	4.5	6	25. Maryland
Montana			n/a	26. Tennessee
Nebraska	6	3.6	9	27. Indiana
Nevada	2	1.2	39	28. North Carolina
New Hampshire	2	1.7	34	29. Washington
New Jersey	29	3.6	10	30. Michigan
New Mexico			n/a	31. Oregon
New York	85	4.7	5	32. Oklahoma
North Carolina	15	2.0	28	33. Iowa
North Dakota			n/a	34. New Hampshire
Ohio	50	4.5	7	35. Kentucky
Oklahoma	6	1.8	32	36. Mississippi
Oregon	6	1.9	31	37. Florida
Pennsylvania	42	3.5	12	38. South Dakota
Rhode Island	3	3.0	14	39. Nevada
South Carolina	4	1.1	41	40. Louisiana
South Dakota	1	1.4	38	41. South Carolina
Tennessee	11	2.1	26	42. Arizona
Texas	59	3.1	13	43. Kansas
Utah	5	2.5	21	44. West Virginia
Vermont			n/a	
Virginia	27	4.0	8	
Washington	11	2.0	29	
West Virginia	1	0.5	44	
Wisconsin	15	2.9	15	
Wyoming			n/a	
50 States	775	2.9		
DC	9	16.6		
United States	784	3.0		

B-18 TOURISM SPENDING, 1994

State	Tourism spending $(millions)	Share of U.S. total %	Per capita $	Rank by per capita		By per capita
Alabama	3,845	1.1	911	42		1. Nevada
Alaska	1,164	0.3	1,931	5		2. Hawaii
Arizona	5,867	1.7	1,438	12		3. Wyoming
Arkansas	2,928	0.9	1,194	28		4. Florida
California	43,982	12.9	1,400	16		5. Alaska
Colorado	6,396	1.9	1,747	7		6. Vermont
Connecticut	3,472	1.0	1,060	36		7. Colorado
Delaware	879	0.3	1,242	26		8. New Mexico
Florida	29,050	8.6	2,081	4		9. Montana
Georgia	9,795	2.9	1,388	17		10. Utah
Hawaii	6,179	1.8	5,244	2		11. Virginia
Idaho	1,536	0.5	1,354	18		12. Arizona
Illinois	14,883	4.4	1,266	24		13. New Jersey
Indiana	4,423	1.3	769	49		14. South Carolina
Iowa	2,963	0.9	1,047	38		15. Tennessee
Kansas	2,503	0.7	981	41		16. California
Kentucky	3,791	1.1	990	40		17. Georgia
Louisiana	5,548	1.6	1,285	21		18. Idaho
Maine	1,475	0.4	1,190	30		19. New Hampshire
Maryland	5,411	1.6	1,082	35		20. North Dakota
Massachusetts	7,679	2.3	1,271	23		21. Louisiana
Michigan	7,943	2.3	837	46		22. Oregon
Minnesota	4,639	1.4	1,016	39		23. Massachusetts
Mississippi	2,970	0.9	1,112	34		24. Illinois
Missouri	6,560	1.9	1,243	25		25. Missouri
Montana	1,446	0.4	1,689	9		26. Delaware
Nebraska	1,868	0.6	1,150	31		27. North Carolina
Nevada	14,485	4.3	9,907	1		28. Arkansas
New Hampshire	1,503	0.4	1,323	19		29. South Dakota
New Jersey	11,187	3.3	1,416	13		30. Maine
New Mexico	2,837	0.8	1,714	8		31. Nebraska
New York	20,713	6.1	1,141	33		32. Texas
North Carolina	8,512	2.5	1,204	27		33. New York
North Dakota	833	0.2	1,303	20		34. Mississippi
Ohio	9,126	2.7	822	47		35. Maryland
Oklahoma	2,790	0.8	857	45		36. Connecticut
Oregon	3,938	1.2	1,276	22		37. Washington
Pennsylvania	10,589	3.1	878	44		38. Iowa
Rhode Island	737	0.2	741	50		39. Minnesota
South Carolina	5,130	1.5	1,408	14		40. Kentucky
South Dakota	861	0.3	1,190	29		41. Kansas
Tennessee	7,262	2.1	1,403	15		42. Alabama
Texas	21,157	6.2	1,149	32		43. Wisconsin
Utah	2,846	0.8	1,491	10		44. Pennsylvania
Vermont	1,041	0.3	1,794	6		45. Oklahoma
Virginia	9,479	2.8	1,447	11		46. Michigan
Washington	5,590	1.6	1,047	37		47. Ohio
West Virginia	1,421	0.4	779	48		48. West Virginia
Wisconsin	4,588	1.4	903	43		49. Indiana
Wyoming	1,130	0.3	2,373	3		50. Rhode Island
50 States	336,945	99.0	1,297			
DC	3,083	0.9	5,438			
United States	340,028	100.0	1,306			

State	Exports $(millions)	Exports per capita $	Rank by per capita	By per capita
Alabama	5,170	1,210	33	1. Vermont
Alaska	2,879	4,743	4	2. Louisiana
Arizona	10,503	2,372	10	3. Washington
Arkansas	2,003	798	44	4. Alaska
California	93,418	2,930	6	5. Texas
Colorado	4,883	1,277	31	6. California
Connecticut	6,100	1,863	18	7. Michigan
Delaware	1,594	2,200	11	8. Oregon
Florida	20,744	1,441	29	9. Massachusetts
Georgia	10,982	1,493	27	10. Arizona
Hawaii	284	240	50	11. Delaware
Idaho	1,571	1,321	30	12. North Carolina
Illinois	24,176	2,041	13	13. Illinois
Indiana	10,984	1,881	17	14. Ohio
Iowa	4,400	1,543	25	15. Minnesota
Kansas	3,784	1,471	28	16. New York
Kentucky	6,385	1,644	23	17. Indiana
Louisiana	21,667	4,980	2	18. Connecticut
Maine	1,380	1,110	37	19. Wisconsin
Maryland	5,019	990	41	20. Virginia
Massachusetts	14,524	2,384	9	21. South Carolina
Michigan	27,553	2,872	7	22. Utah
Minnesota	8,993	1,931	15	23. Kentucky
Mississippi	2,623	966	42	24. New Jersey
Missouri	5,404	1,008	39	25. Iowa
Montana	440	500	49	26. Tennessee
Nebraska	1,907	1,154	36	27. Georgia
Nevada	1,268	791	45	28. Kansas
New Hampshire	1,481	1,274	32	29. Florida
New Jersey	13,119	1,642	24	30. Idaho
New Mexico	931	543	48	31. Colorado
New York	34,230	1,882	16	32. New Hampshire
North Carolina	15,734	2,149	12	33. Alabama
North Dakota	707	1,098	38	34. Pennsylvania
Ohio	22,677	2,030	14	35. West Virginia
Oklahoma	2,365	716	46	36. Nebraska
Oregon	8,948	2,793	8	37. Maine
Pennsylvania	14,364	1,191	34	38. North Dakota
Rhode Island	919	928	43	39. Missouri
South Carolina	6,698	1,811	21	40. Wyoming
South Dakota	443	605	47	41. Maryland
Tennessee	8,094	1,522	26	42. Mississippi
Texas	66,862	3,495	5	43. Rhode Island
Utah	3,296	1,648	22	44. Arkansas
Vermont	3,302	5,610	1	45. Nevada
Virginia	12,215	1,830	20	46. Oklahoma
Washington	26,482	4,786	3	47. South Dakota
West Virginia	2,169	1,188	35	48. New Mexico
Wisconsin	9,504	1,842	19	49. Montana
Wyoming	481	998	40	50. Hawaii
50 States	555,655	2,099		
DC	305	561		
United States	624,767	2,355		

B-20 HOUSING PERMITS, 1996

State	Housing permits (000)	Permits per 10,000 population	Rank by per 10,000
Alabama	19.9	46.5	27
Alaska	2.6	43.5	31
Arizona	53.7	121.3	2
Arkansas	11.1	44.4	29
California	92.1	28.9	45
Colorado	41.1	107.6	4
Connecticut	8.5	26.1	47
Delaware	4.4	60.3	18
Florida	125.0	86.8	8
Georgia	74.9	101.8	5
Hawaii	3.9	33.2	40
Idaho	10.8	90.5	7
Illinois	49.6	41.9	34
Indiana	37.2	63.7	15
Iowa	12.0	42.2	33
Kansas	14.7	57.1	21
Kentucky	18.8	48.4	26
Louisiana	18.0	41.4	35
Maine	4.7	37.7	37
Maryland	25.1	49.5	24
Massachusetts	17.3	28.4	46
Michigan	52.4	54.6	22
Minnesota	27.0	58.1	20
Mississippi	10.4	38.2	36
Missouri	26.3	49.1	25
Montana	2.7	30.5	43
Nebraska	10.1	61.1	17
Nevada	37.2	232.3	1
New Hampshire	4.9	42.4	32
New Jersey	24.2	30.3	44
New Mexico	10.2	59.4	19
New York	34.9	19.2	50
North Carolina	67.0	91.5	6
North Dakota	2.3	36.1	38
Ohio	49.3	44.1	30
Oklahoma	10.6	32.2	41
Oregon	27.8	86.8	9
Pennsylvania	37.9	31.4	42
Rhode Island	2.5	24.8	48
South Carolina	29.4	79.5	10
South Dakota	3.7	49.8	23
Tennessee	40.5	76.2	11
Texas	118.8	62.1	16
Utah	23.5	117.4	3
Vermont	2.1	35.2	39
Virginia	45.9	68.8	13
Washington	39.6	71.6	12
West Virginia	3.6	19.8	49
Wisconsin	33.3	64.5	14
Wyoming	2.2	45.5	28
50 States	1,425.7	53.9	
DC	0.0	0.0	
United States	1,425.6	53.7	

Rank in order

By per 10,000

1. Nevada
2. Arizona
3. Utah
4. Colorado
5. Georgia
6. North Carolina
7. Idaho
8. Florida
9. Oregon
10. South Carolina
11. Tennessee
12. Washington
13. Virginia
14. Wisconsin
15. Indiana
16. Texas
17. Nebraska
18. Delaware
19. New Mexico
20. Minnesota
21. Kansas
22. Michigan
23. South Dakota
24. Maryland
25. Missouri
26. Kentucky
27. Alabama
28. Wyoming
29. Arkansas
30. Ohio
31. Alaska
32. New Hampshire
33. Iowa
34. Illinois
35. Louisiana
36. Mississippi
37. Maine
38. North Dakota
39. Vermont
40. Hawaii
41. Oklahoma
42. Pennsylvania
43. Montana
44. New Jersey
45. California
46. Massachusetts
47. Connecticut
48. Rhode Island
49. West Virginia
50. New York

State	Change in price %	Rank
Alabama	23.8	25
Alaska	18.4	33
Arizona	27.2	20
Arkansas	26.5	22
California	-8.7	49
Colorado	50.6	3
Connecticut	-2.1	48
Delaware	3.1	46
Florida	14.5	35
Georgia	22.0	29
Hawaii	-9.9	50
Idaho	39.6	6
Illinois	21.9	30
Indiana	28.0	17
Iowa	29.7	13
Kansas	28.6	15
Kentucky	27.9	18
Louisiana	29.5	14
Maine	5.2	42
Maryland	5.1	43
Massachusetts	12.6	37
Michigan	35.9	9
Minnesota	26.6	21
Mississippi	23.4	26
Missouri	23.4	26
Montana	47.2	4
Nebraska	33.8	11
Nevada	15.7	34
New Hampshire	4.5	44
New Jersey	6.3	40
New Mexico	36.7	8
New York	3.3	45
North Carolina	25.0	23
North Dakota	24.8	24
Ohio	28.4	16
Oklahoma	21.8	31
Oregon	55.3	2
Pennsylvania	8.4	39
Rhode Island	-1.8	47
South Carolina	20.8	32
South Dakota	37.0	7
Tennessee	29.9	12
Texas	14.4	36
Utah	73.8	1
Vermont	6.1	41
Virginia	9.1	38
Washington	23.1	28
West Virginia	27.4	19
Wisconsin	35.1	10
Wyoming	42.4	5
50 States	n/a	
DC	-0.6	
United States	16.5	

Rank in order

By %

1. Utah
2. Oregon
3. Colorado
4. Montana
5. Wyoming
6. Idaho
7. South Dakota
8. New Mexico
9. Michigan
10. Wisconsin
11. Nebraska
12. Tennessee
13. Iowa
14. Louisiana
15. Kansas
16. Ohio
17. Indiana
18. Kentucky
19. West Virginia
20. Arizona
21. Minnesota
22. Arkansas
23. North Carolina
24. North Dakota
25. Alabama
26. Mississippi
26. Missouri
28. Washington
29. Georgia
30. Illinois
31. Oklahoma
32. South Carolina
33. Alaska
34. Nevada
35. Florida
36. Texas
37. Massachusetts
38. Virginia
39. Pennsylvania
40. New Jersey
41. Vermont
42. Maine
43. Maryland
44. New Hampshire
45. New York
46. Delaware
47. Rhode Island
48. Connecticut
49. California
50. Hawaii

State	Net farm income $(000)	Net farm income per capita $	Rank by total income
Alabama	1,074,115	251	17
Alaska	10,328	17	49
Arizona	721,619	163	24
Arkansas	2,101,176	837	9
California	5,662,985	178	1
Colorado	843,535	221	22
Connecticut	153,730	47	39
Delaware	138,075	190	41
Florida	1,769,062	123	10
Georgia	2,233,736	304	8
Hawaii	n/a	n/a	n/a
Idaho	818,438	688	23
Illinois	2,255,272	190	6
Indiana	1,240,962	212	15
Iowa	3,969,022	1,392	2
Kansas	1,728,549	672	11
Kentucky	1,045,863	269	18
Louisiana	700,944	161	25
Maine	86,846	70	43
Maryland	372,622	73	34
Massachusetts	141,852	23	40
Michigan	375,895	39	33
Minnesota	2,242,923	482	7
Mississippi	963,672	355	20
Missouri	1,194,572	223	16
Montana	334,898	381	36
Nebraska	3,075,464	1,862	4
Nevada	56,109	35	45
New Hampshire	43,302	37	46
New Jersey	260,597	33	37
New Mexico	363,356	212	35
New York	462,487	25	31
North Carolina	3,374,008	461	3
North Dakota	964,049	1,498	19
Ohio	1,327,718	119	14
Oklahoma	551,396	167	29
Oregon	618,721	193	26
Pennsylvania	945,911	78	21
Rhode Island	36,979	37	47
South Carolina	492,747	133	30
South Dakota	1,331,947	1,819	13
Tennessee	386,142	73	32
Texas	2,573,495	135	5
Utah	213,677	107	38
Vermont	132,808	226	42
Virginia	567,940	85	27
Washington	1,599,341	289	12
West Virginia	10,332	6	48
Wisconsin	560,396	109	28
Wyoming	66,755	139	44
50 States	52,194,364	197	
DC	n/a	n/a	
United States	52,194,363	197	

By total income

1. California
2. Iowa
3. North Carolina
4. Nebraska
5. Texas
6. Illinois
7. Minnesota
8. Georgia
9. Arkansas
10. Florida
11. Kansas
12. Washington
13. South Dakota
14. Ohio
15. Indiana
16. Missouri
17. Alabama
18. Kentucky
19. North Dakota
20. Mississippi
21. Pennsylvania
22. Colorado
23. Idaho
24. Arizona
25. Louisiana
26. Oregon
27. Virginia
28. Wisconsin
29. Oklahoma
30. South Carolina
31. New York
32. Tennessee
33. Michigan
34. Maryland
35. New Mexico
36. Montana
37. New Jersey
38. Utah
39. Connecticut
40. Massachusetts
41. Delaware
42. Vermont
43. Maine
44. Wyoming
45. Nevada
46. New Hampshire
47. Rhode Island
48. West Virginia
49. Alaska

State	Total assets $(millions)	Per capita assets $	Rank by per capita	By per capita
Alabama	65,191	15,256	25	1. Delaware
Alaska	6,059	9,982	46	2. New York
Arizona	48,567	10,968	45	3. South Dakota
Arkansas	34,036	13,561	34	4. Massachusetts
California	665,255	20,869	12	5. North Carolina
Colorado	43,532	11,388	43	6. Illinois
Connecticut	50,469	15,414	23	7. Hawaii
Delaware	117,328	161,867	1	8. Pennsylvania
Florida	177,514	12,327	38	9. Nebraska
Georgia	152,915	20,796	13	10. Nevada
Hawaii	28,635	24,191	7	11. North Dakota
Idaho	7,165	6,025	50	12. California
Illinois	296,933	25,065	6	13. Georgia
Indiana	81,867	14,017	32	14. Ohio
Iowa	48,421	16,979	20	15. Missouri
Kansas	36,393	14,149	31	16. Utah
Kentucky	59,721	15,377	24	17. Wyoming
Louisiana	51,925	11,935	41	18. Wisconsin
Maine	16,586	13,340	35	19. New Hampshire
Maryland	48,720	9,606	48	20. Iowa
Massachusetts	207,364	34,037	4	21. Minnesota
Michigan	138,655	14,452	30	22. Virginia
Minnesota	78,217	16,793	21	23. Connecticut
Mississippi	31,164	11,474	42	24. Kentucky
Missouri	103,647	19,342	15	25. Alabama
Montana	10,497	11,937	40	26. Tennessee
Nebraska	36,501	22,094	9	27. New Jersey
Nevada	35,178	21,943	10	28. Washington
New Hampshire	19,996	17,201	19	29. Vermont
New Jersey	118,653	14,854	27	30. Michigan
New Mexico	16,971	9,905	47	31. Kansas
New York	1,153,514	63,433	2	32. Indiana
North Carolina	199,157	27,197	5	33. Texas
North Dakota	14,113	21,930	11	34. Arkansas
Ohio	224,613	20,104	14	35. Maine
Oklahoma	42,338	12,826	36	36. Oklahoma
Oregon	36,438	11,374	44	37. West Virginia
Pennsylvania	288,889	23,962	8	38. Florida
Rhode Island	12,020	12,139	39	39. Rhode Island
South Carolina	34,074	9,212	49	40. Montana
South Dakota	30,179	41,205	3	41. Louisiana
Tennessee	79,891	15,018	26	42. Mississippi
Texas	267,452	13,982	33	43. Colorado
Utah	36,562	18,276	16	44. Oregon
Vermont	8,579	14,574	29	45. Arizona
Virginia	105,365	15,784	22	46. Alaska
Washington	81,381	14,708	28	47. New Mexico
West Virginia	23,374	12,802	37	48. Maryland
Wisconsin	90,871	17,611	18	49. South Carolina
Wyoming	8,524	17,707	17	50. Idaho
50 States	5,571,409	21,045		
DC	3,672	6,760		
United States	5,606,535	21,134		

State	Bankruptcy petitions	Petitions per 1,000 residents	Rank by per 1000	By per 1,000
Alabama	32,710	7.7	3	1. Tennessee
Alaska	1,274	2.1	50	2. Georgia
Arizona	21,725	4.9	17	3. Alabama
Arkansas	13,895	5.5	9	4. Nevada
California	192,405	6.0	6	5. Mississippi
Colorado	17,068	4.5	23	6. California
Connecticut	12,030	3.7	31	7. Oklahoma
Delaware	2,221	3.1	42	8. Virginia
Florida	62,990	4.4	24	9. Arkansas
Georgia	57,534	7.8	2	10. Washington
Hawaii	3,489	2.9	43	11. Oregon
Idaho	5,713	4.8	19	12. Indiana
Illinois	57,446	4.8	18	13. Maryland
Indiana	31,574	5.4	12	14. Kentucky
Iowa	9,154	3.2	40	15. Utah
Kansas	11,753	4.6	22	16. Louisiana
Kentucky	19,683	5.1	14	17. Arizona
Louisiana	21,487	4.9	16	18. Illinois
Maine	3,313	2.7	48	19. Idaho
Maryland	26,739	5.3	13	20. Rhode Island
Massachusetts	18,911	3.1	41	21. New Jersey
Michigan	33,855	3.5	33	22. Kansas
Minnesota	19,238	4.1	27	23. Colorado
Mississippi	17,135	6.3	5	24. Florida
Missouri	23,075	4.3	25	25. Missouri
Montana	2,993	3.4	36	26. Ohio
Nebraska	5,477	3.3	37	27. Minnesota
Nevada	11,387	7.1	4	28. Wyoming
New Hampshire	4,033	3.5	34	29. New Mexico
New Jersey	36,608	4.6	21	30. West Virginia
New Mexico	6,370	3.7	29	31. Connecticut
New York	65,824	3.6	32	32. New York
North Carolina	23,702	3.2	39	33. Michigan
North Dakota	1,809	2.8	46	34. New Hampshire
Ohio	47,200	4.2	26	35. Texas
Oklahoma	19,635	5.9	7	36. Montana
Oregon	17,493	5.5	11	37. Nebraska
Pennsylvania	35,195	2.9	44	38. Wisconsin
Rhode Island	4,687	4.7	20	39. North Carolina
South Carolina	10,330	2.8	47	40. Iowa
South Dakota	2,064	2.8	45	41. Massachusetts
Tennessee	50,409	9.5	1	42. Delaware
Texas	65,839	3.4	35	43. Hawaii
Utah	9,940	5.0	15	44. Pennsylvania
Vermont	1,502	2.6	49	45. South Dakota
Virginia	38,554	5.8	8	46. North Dakota
Washington	30,244	5.5	10	47. South Carolina
West Virginia	6,764	3.7	30	48. Maine
Wisconsin	16,847	3.3	38	49. Vermont
Wyoming	1,825	3.8	28	50. Alaska
50 States	1,233,148	4.7		
DC	2,105	3.9		
United States	1,247,065	4.7		

B-25 PATENTS ISSUED, FY 1996

State	Patents issued	Patents per 100,000 population	Rank by per 100,000	By per 100,000
Alabama	317	7.4	46	1. Delaware
Alaska	52	8.6	45	2. Connecticut
Arizona	1,109	25.0	20	3. Vermont
Arkansas	160	6.4	49	4. Minnesota
California	11,293	35.4	8	5. Massachusetts
Colorado	1,275	33.4	10	6. New Jersey
Connecticut	1,692	51.7	2	7. New Hampshire
Delaware	468	64.6	1	8. California
Florida	2,458	17.1	26	9. Michigan
Georgia	1,077	14.6	30	10. Colorado
Hawaii	105	8.9	44	11. Illinois
Idaho	357	30.0	13	12. New York
Illinois	3,643	30.8	11	13. Idaho
Indiana	1,357	23.2	22	14. Utah
Iowa	474	16.6	27	15. Rhode Island
Kansas	335	13.0	37	16. Oregon
Kentucky	361	9.3	43	17. Wisconsin
Louisiana	421	9.7	41	18. Ohio
Maine	122	9.8	40	19. Pennsylvania
Maryland	1,114	22.0	24	20. Arizona
Massachusetts	2,580	42.3	5	21. Washington
Michigan	3,271	34.1	9	22. Indiana
Minnesota	1,993	42.8	4	23. Texas
Mississippi	162	6.0	50	24. Maryland
Missouri	778	14.5	31	25. North Carolina
Montana	131	14.9	29	26. Florida
Nebraska	176	10.7	39	27. Iowa
Nevada	209	13.0	36	28. Oklahoma
New Hampshire	458	39.4	7	29. Montana
New Jersey	3,217	40.3	6	30. Georgia
New Mexico	243	14.2	34	31. Missouri
New York	5,501	30.3	12	32. South Carolina
North Carolina	1,373	18.7	25	33. Virginia
North Dakota	62	9.6	42	34. New Mexico
Ohio	3,061	27.4	18	35. Tennessee
Oklahoma	522	15.8	28	36. Nevada
Oregon	920	28.7	16	37. Kansas
Pennsylvania	3,120	25.9	19	38. Wyoming
Rhode Island	289	29.2	15	39. Nebraska
South Carolina	528	14.3	32	40. Maine
South Dakota	52	7.1	48	41. Louisiana
Tennessee	706	13.3	35	42. North Dakota
Texas	4,348	22.7	23	43. Kentucky
Utah	585	29.2	14	44. Hawaii
Vermont	259	44.0	3	45. Alaska
Virginia	950	14.2	33	46. Alabama
Washington	1,298	23.5	21	47. West Virginia
West Virginia	134	7.3	47	48. South Dakota
Wisconsin	1,469	28.5	17	49. Arkansas
Wyoming	52	10.8	38	50. Mississippi
50 States	66,637	25.2		
DC	37	6.8		
United States	66,716	25.1		

State	WC weekly benefit $	Rank
Alabama	458	27
Alaska	700	4
Arizona	323	48
Arkansas	348	46
California	490	24
Colorado	468	26
Connecticut	678	5
Delaware	372	43
Florida	479	25
Georgia	300	49
Hawaii	501	19
Idaho	390	39
Illinois	781	2
Indiana	428	35
Iowa	873	1
Kansas	338	47
Kentucky	447	30
Louisiana	349	45
Maine	441	33
Maryland	553	10
Massachusetts	631	7
Michigan	553	10
Minnesota	615	9
Mississippi	271	50
Missouri	513	15
Montana	384	41
Nebraska	427	36
Nevada	492	22
New Hampshire	756	3
New Jersey	496	20
New Mexico	363	44
New York	400	38
North Carolina	512	16
North Dakota	387	40
Ohio	521	13
Oklahoma	426	37
Oregon	519	14
Pennsylvania	542	12
Rhode Island	503	18
South Carolina	451	29
South Dakota	375	42
Tennessee	453	28
Texas	491	23
Utah	446	31
Vermont	674	6
Virginia	496	20
Washington	627	8
West Virginia	445	32
Wisconsin	509	17
Wyoming	434	34
50 States	n/a	
DC	749	
United States	n/a	

Rank in order

By $

1. Iowa
2. Illinois
3. New Hampshire
4. Alaska
5. Connecticut
6. Vermont
7. Massachusetts
8. Washington
9. Minnesota
10. Maryland
10. Michigan
12. Pennsylvania
13. Ohio
14. Oregon
15. Missouri
16. North Carolina
17. Wisconsin
18. Rhode Island
19. Hawaii
20. New Jersey
20. Virginia
22. Nevada
23. Texas
24. California
25. Florida
26. Colorado
27. Alabama
28. Tennessee
29. South Carolina
30. Kentucky
31. Utah
32. West Virginia
33. Maine
34. Wyoming
35. Indiana
36. Nebraska
37. Oklahoma
38. New York
39. Idaho
40. North Dakota
41. Montana
42. South Dakota
43. Delaware
44. New Mexico
45. Louisiana
46. Arkansas
47. Kansas
48. Arizona
49. Georgia
50. Mississippi

State	Average weekly UC benefit $	Rank
Alabama	142	48
Alaska	172	32
Arizona	151	46
Arkansas	170	35
California	152	45
Colorado	208	11
Connecticut	222	7
Delaware	224	6
Florida	178	27
Georgia	166	37
Hawaii	270	1
Idaho	182	25
Illinois	213	9
Indiana	187	24
Iowa	200	17
Kansas	202	16
Kentucky	171	34
Louisiana	128	50
Maine	171	33
Maryland	195	19
Massachusetts	254	3
Michigan	205	13
Minnesota	234	4
Mississippi	141	49
Missouri	154	43
Montana	165	38
Nebraska	161	40
Nevada	194	20
New Hampshire	153	44
New Jersey	255	2
New Mexico	157	41
New York	206	12
North Carolina	193	21
North Dakota	175	30
Ohio	202	15
Oklahoma	175	29
Oregon	191	22
Pennsylvania	219	8
Rhode Island	228	5
South Carolina	165	39
South Dakota	150	47
Tennessee	155	42
Texas	189	23
Utah	198	18
Vermont	168	36
Virginia	173	31
Washington	210	10
West Virginia	176	28
Wisconsin	202	14
Wyoming	181	26
50 States	n/a	
DC	236	
United States	189	

B-27 AVERAGE UNEMPLOYMENT COMPENSATION BENEFIT, 1996

Rank in order

By $

1. Hawaii
2. New Jersey
3. Massachusetts
4. Minnesota
5. Rhode Island
6. Delaware
7. Connecticut
8. Pennsylvania
9. Illinois
10. Washington
11. Colorado
12. New York
13. Michigan
14. Wisconsin
15. Ohio
16. Kansas
17. Iowa
18. Utah
19. Maryland
20. Nevada
21. North Carolina
22. Oregon
23. Texas
24. Indiana
25. Idaho
26. Wyoming
27. Florida
28. West Virginia
29. Oklahoma
30. North Dakota
31. Virginia
32. Alaska
33. Maine
34. Kentucky
35. Arkansas
36. Vermont
37. Georgia
38. Montana
39. South Carolina
40. Nebraska
41. New Mexico
42. Tennessee
43. Missouri
44. New Hampshire
45. California
46. Arizona
47. South Dakota
48. Alabama
49. Mississippi
50. Louisiana

B-28 INDEX OF STATE ECONOMIC MOMENTUM, SEPTEMBER 1997

State	Index of state economic momentum September 1997	Rank
Alabama	-0.53	38
Alaska	-1.96	50
Arizona	1.10	5
Arkansas	-0.15	28
California	0.41	12
Colorado	0.80	7
Connecticut	-0.30	30
Delaware	0.70	8
Florida	0.43	11
Georgia	0.20	16
Hawaii	-1.72	49
Idaho	-0.01	21
Illinois	-0.68	40
Indiana	-0.44	35
Iowa	-0.52	37
Kansas	0.27	14
Kentucky	0.26	15
Louisiana	-0.61	39
Maine	-0.10	25
Maryland	-0.23	29
Massachusetts	0.50	10
Michigan	-0.34	32
Minnesota	0.06	20
Mississippi	-0.81	44
Missouri	-0.43	34
Montana	-0.10	26
Nebraska	0.07	19
Nevada	3.41	1
New Hampshire	0.39	13
New Jersey	-0.33	31
New Mexico	-0.68	41
New York	-0.82	45
North Carolina	0.83	6
North Dakota	-0.04	22
Ohio	-0.87	46
Oklahoma	0.12	17
Oregon	1.45	3
Pennsylvania	-0.37	33
Rhode Island	-0.77	43
South Carolina	-0.13	27
South Dakota	-0.06	24
Tennessee	-0.05	23
Texas	0.63	9
Utah	2.20	2
Vermont	-0.88	47
Virginia	0.09	18
Washington	1.24	4
West Virginia	-0.70	42
Wisconsin	-0.48	36
Wyoming	-1.17	48
50 States	n/a	
DC	n/a	
United States	0.00	

By Index

1. Nevada
2. Utah
3. Oregon
4. Washington
5. Arizona
6. North Carolina
7. Colorado
8. Delaware
9. Texas
10. Massachusetts
11. Florida
12. California
13. New Hampshire
14. Kansas
15. Kentucky
16. Georgia
17. Oklahoma
18. Virginia
19. Nebraska
20. Minnesota
21. Idaho
22. North Dakota
23. Tennessee
24. South Dakota
25. Maine
26. Montana
27. South Carolina
28. Arkansas
29. Maryland
30. Connecticut
31. New Jersey
32. Michigan
33. Pennsylvania
34. Missouri
35. Indiana
36. Wisconsin
37. Iowa
38. Alabama
39. Louisiana
40. Illinois
41. New Mexico
42. West Virginia
43. Rhode Island
44. Mississippi
45. New York
46. Ohio
47. Vermont
48. Wyoming
49. Hawaii
50. Alaska

State	Employment change June 1996-1997	Percent change in employment %	Rank by % change	Rank in order By %
Alabama	16.3	0.9	42	1. Nevada
Alaska	0.4	0.1	48	2. Arizona
Arizona	79.6	4.3	2	3. Utah
Arkansas	8.9	0.8	43	4. Washington
California	345.8	2.7	8	5. Oregon
Colorado	32.9	1.7	22	6. Florida
Connecticut	27.6	1.7	21	7. Kansas
Delaware	8.2	2.1	15	8. California
Florida	222.4	3.6	6	9. North Dakota
Georgia	44.2	1.2	33	10. Oklahoma
Hawaii	-2.4	-0.5	50	11. Texas
Idaho	7.8	1.6	25	12. Virginia
Illinois	51.9	0.9	41	13. Massachusetts
Indiana	30.7	1.1	36	14. Minnesota
Iowa	22.2	1.6	24	15. Delaware
Kansas	34.1	2.8	7	16. Pennsylvania
Kentucky	34.7	2.1	17	17. Kentucky
Louisiana	19.2	1.1	37	18. North Carolina
Maine	7.5	1.4	30	19. Missouri
Maryland	32.0	1.4	28	20. Wisconsin
Massachusetts	67.3	2.2	13	21. Connecticut
Michigan	58.1	1.3	31	22. Colorado
Minnesota	52.5	2.1	14	23. New Mexico
Mississippi	1.7	0.2	47	24. Iowa
Missouri	48.6	1.9	19	25. Idaho
Montana	3.5	1.0	39	26. Nebraska
Nebraska	13.1	1.6	26	27. West Virginia
Nevada	54.7	6.5	1	28. Maryland
New Hampshire	7.5	1.3	32	29. New Jersey
New Jersey	52.0	1.4	29	30. Maine
New Mexico	11.1	1.6	23	31. Michigan
New York	81.2	1.0	38	32. New Hampshire
North Carolina	72.3	2.0	18	33. Georgia
North Dakota	8.4	2.7	9	34. Vermont
Ohio	49.1	0.9	40	35. South Dakota
Oklahoma	35.9	2.6	10	36. Indiana
Oregon	55.1	3.7	5	37. Louisiana
Pennsylvania	112.8	2.1	16	38. New York
Rhode Island	1.4	0.3	46	39. Montana
South Carolina	12.1	0.7	45	40. Ohio
South Dakota	3.9	1.1	35	41. Illinois
Tennessee	19.9	0.8	44	42. Alabama
Texas	211.0	2.6	11	43. Arkansas
Utah	40.7	4.2	3	44. Tennessee
Vermont	3.4	1.2	34	45. South Carolina
Virginia	69.7	2.2	12	46. Rhode Island
Washington	94.4	3.9	4	47. Mississippi
West Virginia	10.5	1.5	27	48. Alaska
Wisconsin	47.6	1.8	20	49. Wyoming
Wyoming	0.1	0.0	49	50. Hawaii
50 States	2,323.6	1.9		
DC	-5.7	-0.9		
United States	2,317.9	1.9		

B-30 MANUFACTURING EMPLOYMENT CHANGE, 1996-1997

State	Manufacturing employment change July 1996-1997 (000)	Percent change in manufacturing employment %	Rank by %		Rank in order By %
Alabama	-4.9	-1.3	46		1. North Dakota
Alaska	-0.9	-3.6	50		2. Washington
Arizona	6.9	3.5	6		3. South Dakota
Arkansas	-2.1	-0.8	42		4. Oregon
California	36.5	1.9	13		5. Kansas
Colorado	1.8	0.9	20		6. Arizona
Connecticut	-0.1	0.0	31		7. Nevada
Delaware	-0.3	-0.5	37		8. New Hampshire
Florida	2.9	0.6	23		9. New Mexico
Georgia	2.2	0.4	27		10. Kentucky
Hawaii	-0.2	-1.2	44		11. Nebraska
Idaho	0.9	1.2	19		12. Oklahoma
Illinois	5.9	0.6	22		13. California
Indiana	2.4	0.4	28		14. Iowa
Iowa	4.6	1.9	14		15. Vermont
Kansas	7.7	3.9	5		16. Minnesota
Kentucky	6.3	2.0	10		17. Texas
Louisiana	0.8	0.4	24		18. Utah
Maine	-0.3	-0.3	35		19. Idaho
Maryland	-1.9	-1.1	43		20. Colorado
Massachusetts	3.6	0.8	21		21. Massachusetts
Michigan	-7.0	-0.7	40		22. Illinois
Minnesota	6.3	1.5	16		23. Florida
Mississippi	-3.9	-1.6	47		24. Louisiana
Missouri	-5.0	-1.2	45		25. Montana
Montana	0.1	0.4	25		26. Wisconsin
Nebraska	2.3	2.0	11		27. Georgia
Nevada	1.3	3.4	7		28. Indiana
New Hampshire	2.9	2.8	8		29. Pennsylvania
New Jersey	-2.9	-0.6	39		30. Wyoming
New Mexico	1.0	2.2	9		31. Connecticut
New York	-5.4	-0.6	38		32. Rhode Island
North Carolina	-2.5	-0.3	34		33. West Virginia
North Dakota	1.8	8.5	1		34. North Carolina
Ohio	-20.7	-1.9	49		35. Maine
Oklahoma	3.5	2.0	12		36. Virginia
Oregon	11.7	4.9	4		37. Delaware
Pennsylvania	0.7	0.1	29		38. New York
Rhode Island	-0.1	-0.1	32		39. New Jersey
South Carolina	-5.8	-1.6	48		40. Michigan
South Dakota	2.4	5.0	3		41. Tennessee
Tennessee	-4.1	-0.8	41		42. Arkansas
Texas	13.3	1.3	17		43. Maryland
Utah	1.6	1.2	18		44. Hawaii
Vermont	0.7	1.5	15		45. Missouri
Virginia	-1.9	-0.5	36		46. Alabama
Washington	26.3	7.6	2		47. Mississippi
West Virginia	-0.2	-0.2	33		48. South Carolina
Wisconsin	2.3	0.4	26		49. Ohio
Wyoming	0.0	0.0	30		50. Alaska
50 States	90.5	0.5			
DC	0.5	3.8			
United States	91.0	0.5			

State	Home ownership rates %	Rank
Alabama	71.0	14
Alaska	62.9	41
Arizona	62.0	42
Arkansas	66.6	34
California	55.0	47
Colorado	64.5	38
Connecticut	69.0	20
Delaware	71.5	12
Florida	40.4	50
Georgia	67.1	30
Hawaii	69.3	18
Idaho	50.6	49
Illinois	71.4	13
Indiana	68.2	25
Iowa	74.2	4
Kansas	72.8	9
Kentucky	67.5	29
Louisiana	73.2	6
Maine	64.9	36
Maryland	76.5	1
Massachusetts	66.9	32
Michigan	61.7	44
Minnesota	73.3	5
Mississippi	75.4	2
Missouri	73.0	7
Montana	70.2	17
Nebraska	68.6	22
Nevada	66.8	33
New Hampshire	61.1	45
New Jersey	65.0	35
New Mexico	64.6	37
New York	67.1	30
North Carolina	52.7	48
North Dakota	70.4	15
Ohio	68.2	25
Oklahoma	69.2	19
Oregon	68.4	24
Pennsylvania	63.1	39
Rhode Island	71.7	11
South Carolina	56.6	46
South Dakota	72.9	8
Tennessee	67.8	28
Texas	68.8	21
Utah	61.8	43
Vermont	72.7	10
Virginia	70.3	16
Washington	68.5	23
West Virginia	63.1	39
Wisconsin	74.3	3
Wyoming	68.2	25
50 States	68.0	
DC	39.2	
United States	64.7	

Rank in order

By %

1. Maryland
2. Mississippi
3. Wisconsin
4. Iowa
5. Minnesota
6. Louisiana
7. Missouri
8. South Dakota
9. Kansas
10. Vermont
11. Rhode Island
12. Delaware
13. Illinois
14. Alabama
15. North Dakota
16. Virginia
17. Montana
18. Hawaii
19. Oklahoma
20. Connecticut
21. Texas
22. Nebraska
23. Washington
24. Oregon
25. Indiana
25. Ohio
25. Wyoming
28. Tennessee
29. Kentucky
30. Georgia
30. New York
32. Massachusetts
33. Nevada
34. Arkansas
35. New Jersey
36. Maine
37. New Mexico
38. Colorado
39. Pennsylvania
39. West Virginia
41. Alaska
42. Arizona
43. Utah
44. Michigan
45. New Hampshire
46. South Carolina
47. California
48. North Carolina
49. Idaho
50. Florida

State	Gambling gross revenue $(millions)	Per capita gambling revenue $	Rank by total revenue
Alabama	64	15	40
Alaska	58	96	42
Arizona	220	50	31
Arkansas	56	22	43
California	2,393	75	4
Colorado	654	171	19
Connecticut	407	124	26
Delaware	284	392	27
Florida	1,511	105	9
Georgia	861	117	14
Hawaii	n/a	n/a	n/a
Idaho	49	41	44
Illinois	2,312	195	5
Indiana	789	135	16
Iowa	774	271	17
Kansas	128	50	36
Kentucky	501	129	21
Louisiana	2,071	476	6
Maine	95	76	37
Maryland	739	146	18
Massachusetts	1,122	184	12
Michigan	866	90	13
Minnesota	417	90	25
Mississippi	1,894	697	7
Missouri	831	155	15
Montana	249	283	28
Nebraska	137	83	34
Nevada	7,453	4649	1
New Hampshire	136	117	35
New Jersey	4,861	609	2
New Mexico	64	38	39
New York	2,431	134	3
North Carolina	8	1	46
North Dakota	67	104	38
Ohio	1,347	121	10
Oklahoma	61	19	41
Oregon	540	169	20
Pennsylvania	1,141	95	11
Rhode Island	194	196	32
South Carolina	419	113	24
South Dakota	241	329	30
Tennessee	n/a	n/a	n/a
Texas	1,822	95	8
Utah	n/a	n/a	n/a
Vermont	35	59	45
Virginia	489	73	22
Washington	481	87	23
West Virginia	185	102	33
Wisconsin	247	48	29
Wyoming	8	16	47
50 States	41,712	158	
DC	118	217	
United States	41,830	158	

Rank in order

By total

1. Nevada
2. New Jersey
3. New York
4. California
5. Illinois
6. Louisiana
7. Mississippi
8. Texas
9. Florida
10. Ohio
11. Pennsylvania
12. Massachusetts
13. Michigan
14. Georgia
15. Missouri
16. Indiana
17. Iowa
18. Maryland
19. Colorado
20. Oregon
21. Kentucky
22. Virginia
23. Washington
24. South Carolina
25. Minnesota
26. Connecticut
27. Delaware
28. Montana
29. Wisconsin
30. South Dakota
31. Arizona
32. Rhode Island
33. West Virginia
34. Nebraska
35. New Hampshire
36. Kansas
37. Maine
38. North Dakota
39. New Mexico
40. Alabama
41. Oklahoma
42. Alaska
43. Arkansas
44. Idaho
45. Vermont
46. North Carolina
47. Wyoming

State	Average annual Kwh use per residential customer	Rank
Alabama	13,652	3
Alaska	8,175	36
Arizona	10,983	23
Arkansas	11,440	19
California	6,260	47
Colorado	7,368	42
Connecticut	8,075	37
Delaware	10,220	26
Florida	13,244	7
Georgia	12,141	15
Hawaii	7,433	40
Idaho	13,345	6
Illinois	8,416	35
Indiana	11,309	20
Iowa	9,854	28
Kansas	9,633	30
Kentucky	12,734	11
Louisiana	14,069	2
Maine	6,054	50
Maryland	12,002	16
Massachusetts	6,637	44
Michigan	7,428	41
Minnesota	9,034	32
Mississippi	13,177	9
Missouri	11,106	21
Montana	9,754	29
Nebraska	11,084	22
Nevada	10,809	24
New Hampshire	6,628	45
New Jersey	7,478	39
New Mexico	6,343	46
New York	6,166	48
North Carolina	12,531	13
North Dakota	12,251	14
Ohio	9,918	27
Oklahoma	11,446	18
Oregon	12,564	12
Pennsylvania	8,867	33
Rhode Island	6,164	49
South Carolina	13,581	5
South Dakota	10,793	25
Tennessee	14,379	1
Texas	13,059	10
Utah	7,874	38
Vermont	7,272	43
Virginia	13,226	8
Washington	13,594	4
West Virginia	11,624	17
Wisconsin	8,723	34
Wyoming	9,351	31
50 States	n/a	
DC	8,362	
United States	10,042	

Rank in order

By kwh

1. Tennessee
2. Louisiana
3. Alabama
4. Washington
5. South Carolina
6. Idaho
7. Florida
8. Virginia
9. Mississippi
10. Texas
11. Kentucky
12. Oregon
13. North Carolina
14. North Dakota
15. Georgia
16. Maryland
17. West Virginia
18. Oklahoma
19. Arkansas
20. Indiana
21. Missouri
22. Nebraska
23. Arizona
24. Nevada
25. South Dakota
26. Delaware
27. Ohio
28. Iowa
29. Montana
30. Kansas
31. Wyoming
32. Minnesota
33. Pennsylvania
34. Wisconsin
35. Illinois
36. Alaska
37. Connecticut
38. Utah
39. New Jersey
40. Hawaii
41. Michigan
42. Colorado
43. Vermont
44. Massachusetts
45. New Hampshire
46. New Mexico
47. California
48. New York
49. Rhode Island
50. Maine

B-34 AVERAGE REVENUE PER KILOWATT HOUR, 1995

State	Average revenue cents per kwh industrial	Average revenue cents per kwh residential	Residential as percent of industrial %	Rank by residential as percent of industrial %
Alabama	4.1	6.7	165.7	27
Alaska	8.3	11.2	134.5	47
Arizona	5.3	9.1	173.2	21
Arkansas	4.5	8.0	176.9	19
California	7.4	11.6	157.5	37
Colorado	4.5	7.4	163.9	30
Connecticut	8.0	12.0	150.1	40
Delaware	4.7	9.1	192.6	8
Florida	5.2	7.8	151.6	39
Georgia	4.5	7.8	173.8	20
Hawaii	9.3	13.3	143.7	42
Idaho	2.8	5.3	189.7	10
Illinois	5.3	10.4	196.4	6
Indiana	4.2	6.7	161.6	32
Iowa	3.9	8.2	209.1	2
Kansas	4.8	7.9	164.3	28
Kentucky	2.9	5.6	191.5	9
Louisiana	4.0	7.3	182.9	16
Maine	6.6	12.5	188.7	11
Maryland	4.2	8.4	199.3	5
Massachusetts	8.4	11.3	133.6	48
Michigan	5.2	8.3	161.9	31
Minnesota	4.3	7.2	166.7	25
Mississippi	4.4	7.0	157.4	38
Missouri	4.5	7.3	159.9	34
Montana	3.4	6.1	177.0	18
Nebraska	3.8	6.4	165.9	26
Nevada	5.1	7.1	140.8	44
New Hampshire	9.6	13.5	141.2	43
New Jersey	8.2	12.0	147.0	41
New Mexico	4.4	9.0	203.4	4
New York	5.5	13.9	253.6	1
North Carolina	4.9	8.1	167.6	23
North Dakota	4.5	6.2	138.4	45
Ohio	4.2	8.6	206.2	3
Oklahoma	3.7	6.8	182.8	17
Oregon	3.5	5.5	158.2	36
Pennsylvania	5.9	9.7	164.2	29
Rhode Island	8.9	11.5	129.3	50
South Carolina	4.0	7.5	188.5	12
South Dakota	4.4	7.1	159.8	35
Tennessee	4.5	5.9	131.0	49
Texas	4.0	7.7	193.5	7
Utah	3.7	6.9	186.3	14
Vermont	7.6	10.5	137.7	46
Virginia	4.2	7.8	188.5	13
Washington	3.0	4.9	166.8	24
West Virginia	4.0	6.5	161.3	33
Wisconsin	3.8	7.0	184.4	15
Wyoming	3.6	6.1	171.5	22
50 States	n/a	n/a	n/a	
DC	4.4	7.6	174.8	
United States	4.7	8.4	180.3	

By %

1. New York
2. Iowa
3. Ohio
4. New Mexico
5. Maryland
6. Illinois
7. Texas
8. Delaware
9. Kentucky
10. Idaho
11. Maine
12. South Carolina
13. Virginia
14. Utah
15. Wisconsin
16. Louisiana
17. Oklahoma
18. Montana
19. Arkansas
20. Georgia
21. Arizona
22. Wyoming
23. North Carolina
24. Washington
25. Minnesota
26. Nebraska
27. Alabama
28. Kansas
29. Pennsylvania
30. Colorado
31. Michigan
32. Indiana
33. West Virginia
34. Missouri
35. South Dakota
36. Oregon
37. California
38. Mississippi
39. Florida
40. Connecticut
41. New Jersey
42. Hawaii
43. New Hampshire
44. Nevada
45. North Dakota
46. Vermont
47. Alaska
48. Massachusetts
49. Tennessee
50. Rhode Island

State	New companies	Companies per 1,000 employees	Rank by per 1,000
Alabama	10,965	5.5	32
Alaska	1,984	6.8	20
Arizona	13,920	6.6	22
Arkansas	7,344	6.3	24
California	138,726	9.6	7
Colorado	20,317	10.1	2
Connecticut	9,457	5.8	30
Delaware	3,461	9.5	8
Florida	49,870	7.6	12
Georgia	26,440	7.4	13
Hawaii	3,992	7.2	15
Idaho	5,242	8.9	10
Illinois	28,064	4.9	44
Indiana	14,260	4.8	45
Iowa	6,014	3.9	50
Kansas	6,693	5.2	39
Kentucky	9,133	5.2	41
Louisiana	10,087	5.4	34
Maine	4,461	7.0	18
Maryland	13,895	5.2	38
Massachusetts	16,635	5.5	33
Michigan	24,387	5.3	37
Minnesota	13,557	5.4	35
Mississippi	6,180	5.2	40
Missouri	14,763	5.3	36
Montana	4,144	9.8	4
Nebraska	3,945	4.5	49
Nevada	8,043	10.1	3
New Hampshire	4,961	8.3	11
New Jersey	27,315	7.1	16
New Mexico	4,975	6.8	21
New York	56,771	7.0	19
North Carolina	21,857	6.0	26
North Dakota	1,668	5.0	42
Ohio	25,795	4.8	46
Oklahoma	9,003	6.0	28
Oregon	14,995	9.3	9
Pennsylvania	25,433	4.5	47
Rhode Island	3,416	7.3	14
South Carolina	10,856	6.2	25
South Dakota	1,835	4.9	43
Tennessee	15,617	6.0	27
Texas	54,031	5.9	29
Utah	9,433	9.8	5
Vermont	2,186	7.1	17
Virginia	20,960	6.5	23
Washington	31,295	11.6	1
West Virginia	4,207	5.6	31
Wisconsin	12,766	4.5	48
Wyoming	2,365	9.7	6
50 States	837,719	6.6	
DC	4,087	16.4	
United States	847,168	6.7	

Rank in order

By per 1,000

1. Washington
2. Colorado
3. Nevada
4. Montana
5. Utah
6. Wyoming
7. California
8. Delaware
9. Oregon
10. Idaho
11. New Hampshire
12. Florida
13. Georgia
14. Rhode Island
15. Hawaii
16. New Jersey
17. Vermont
18. Maine
19. New York
20. Alaska
21. New Mexico
22. Arizona
23. Virginia
24. Arkansas
25. South Carolina
26. North Carolina
27. Tennessee
28. Oklahoma
29. Texas
30. Connecticut
31. West Virginia
32. Alabama
33. Massachusetts
34. Louisiana
35. Minnesota
36. Missouri
37. Michigan
38. Maryland
39. Kansas
40. Mississippi
41. Kentucky
42. North Dakota
43. South Dakota
44. Illinois
45. Indiana
46. Ohio
47. Pennsylvania
48. Wisconsin
49. Nebraska
50. Iowa

Source Notes for Economies (Section B)

B-1 Personal Income, 1996: These data reflect income of residents of each state, including pensions, dividends, interest, and rent as well as amount received from employers as wages and salaries. These estimates are made by the Department of Commerce each quarter. The calendar year 1996 estimates in the table were provided in a Department of Commerce Press Release dated April 28, 1997.

B-2 Gross State Product, Total And Per Capita, 1994: The gross state product is the state counterpart of the gross national product (now called the gross domestic product). This is the single best measure of the size of a state's economy. It is the sum of all the value of production of goods and services. While estimates of national data are released on a current basis, state-by-state estimates are made by the Department of Commerce only with a substantial lag. These 1994 data appeared in a Department of Commerce press release dated June 3, 1997.

B-3 Per Capita Personal Income, 1996: These data, from the same source as Table B-1, reflect personal income in relation to population. They are a common measure of the relative affluence of each state. The data are also used to determine what percentage the federal government pays of each state's Medicaid costs.

B-4 Personal Income from Wages and Salaries, 1996: These data show the portion of personal income that comes from wages and salaries. The data on origins of personal income are published by the Department of Commerce Bureau of Economic Analysis and provided to *State Fact Finder* on October 10, 1997. The percentages, calculated for *State Fact Finder*, indicate relative reliance of states' economies on current work, as distinct from investments and government payments.

B-5 Average Annual Pay, 1996: These data reflect the average pay of workers in each state. They are prepared by the Department of Labor. They were released September 11, 1997 as *Average Annual Pay by State and Industry, 1996* (USDL 97-315).

B-6 Average Hourly Earnings, 1997: These data are often used to compare wage costs of the states. They are prepared by the Department of Labor monthly and released in the publication *Employment and Earnings*. These January 1997 data appeared in the March 1997 edition. These data only cover production workers, excluding service and retailing employees as well as government employees.

B-7 Value Added in Manufacturing, 1995: This table measures the value that is added by manufacturing operations in each state. Value added is calculated by subtracting the value of inputs to production from the value of the outputs. For example, the value of manufacturing a car is the value of the car minus the value of

components, such as engines, purchased to manufacture it. These data are from the Census Bureau's *1995 Annual Survey of Manufacturers (M95(AS)-3)* issued April, 1997. Value added per worker can be calculated from this report. This per worker statistic is sometimes used to compare the productivity of state work forces but is a misleading statistic because capital investments in machinery make massive contributions to adding values in highly automated operations such as chemical manufacturing.

B-8 Cost of Living, 1996: The federal government has not attempted to produce measures that compare living costs since the 1980s and, even then, provided the data only for selected large metropolitan areas, not states. Some researchers periodically try to produce such indices, but they are of doubtful statistical validity. The one shown is used in the 1997 report *The Federal Budget and the States, Fiscal Year 1996* published jointly by the offices of Senator Daniel Patrick Moynihan (D-N.Y.) and the John F. Kennedy School of Government at Harvard.

B-9 Average Annual Pay in Manufacturing, 1996: This is the manufacturing component of the data described for Table B-5, from the same source. States with many jobs in high-wage industries, like chemical or vehicle manufacturing, rank highest.

B-10 Average Annual Pay in Retailing, 1996: This is the retailing component of the data described for Table B-5, from the same source. Because most retailing jobs are entry-level positions requiring little experience or formal training, these data are a good measure of the costs of obtaining new workers in the states.

B-11 Labor Force, 1997: About 136 million people, 51% of Americans, are either working or looking for work but not working (unemployed). These two groups make up the labor force. The rest of the population isn't in the labor force because they are retired, too young to work, disabled, or have opted not to work. This group includes "discouraged workers" who indicate that they would like to work but have given up hope of finding a job.

The labor force data are available on the web site of the Bureau of Labor Statistics (http://www.bls.gov). They are available in their monthly publication *Metropolitan Area Employment and Unemployment* which appeared in August 1997 with estimates for July. The data are seasonally adjusted to make month-to-month comparisons possible despite fluctuations associated with time of the year such as hiring by retail stores for the December holiday season and summertime hiring of students. The 1996 population estimates come from the Census Bureau (see Table A-1). Labor force as a percentage of population varies among states because of differences in the percentage of population at working age and the percentage of people who want to work, the labor force participation rate.

B-12 Unemployed and Unemployment Rate, 1997: The estimates of persons unemployed and the unemployment rate (percentage of labor force unemployed) are from the same source as Table B-11.

B-13 Employment and Employment Rate, 1997: The Bureau of Labor Statistics faces a perpetual dilemma in presenting statistics on employment and unemployment. It must make national unemployment estimates based on a survey of households in which people are asked whether they are looking for work. This *household survey* also provides the national estimate of the people who are employed. But the sample is too small to provide reliable estimates of employment for less populous states. To provide estimates for those states, the Bureau obtains monthly reports from employers, called the *establishment survey*. The national totals from the two different surveys often diverge by hundreds of thousands of workers. {Periodically, the Bureau "benchmarks" the totals and revises past estimates to make them consistent.}

To make the matter even more complicated, the Bureau attempts in various complex ways to use the results of one survey to guide estimating procedures for the other. How this is done is explained in detail in various technical publications available from the Bureau. The net effect harmonizes the results of the two approaches better for large states than small ones. For example, the employment in Wyoming implicit in the Bureau's estimates is the labor force (Table B-11) minus the unemployed (Table B-12) is 245,600 but the employment published in a different table in the report (see notes to Table B-11) is 222,100. For Table B-13, *State Fact Finder* uses the implicit estimate so that employment plus unemployment sum to the labor force for each state. The employment rate is the relationship between the employment shown and the labor force on Table B-11.

Because *State Fact Finder* contains many tables relying on employment data for individual states, it uses the best employment estimates available, those from the establishment survey, in Table B-14 and other tables showing state-by-state details of employment.

B-14 Government Employment, 1997: This table uses seasonally adjusted data from the establishment survey (see notes to Table B-13 on differences between the household and establishment surveys) as reported in tables in the Bureau of Labor Statistics publication *Metropolitan Area Employment and Unemployment* (USDL 97-294) which appeared in August 1997 with estimates for July. The employment reported on this table includes federal, state, and local employees.

These Bureau of Labor Statistics data on government employment covering 1997 are much more current than data provided by the Census Bureau. The latest Census Bureau data, published in 1997, cover information on October 1995 payrolls. But the Census Bureau data are used often in *State Fact Finder* because the Bureau of Labor Statistics data do not include such details as how much employees are paid and the type of service (e.g., education, transportation) they provide.

B-15 Manufacturing Employment, 1997: These data are comparable to those shown in Table B-14, but cover manufacturing.

B-16 Fortune 500 Companies, 1997: Two major business magazines—*Fortune* and *Forbes*—provide annual listings of the largest companies in America, using somewhat different criteria. This table reflects the list as published in *Fortune* (April 28, 1997). Because large states tend to have the most large companies, the rankings are based on a calculation of the representation of these companies' headquarters in each state in relation to population of that state.

B-17 Forbes 500 Companies, 1997: This table is the counterpart of Table B-16. This listing was published in *Forbes* magazine (April 21, 1997). Because *Forbes* uses four separate criteria for its listings, 785 American companies are included in the 500 list. Previous editions of *State Fact Finder* have included the *Business Week* 1000 listing, but as of Summer 1997 *Business Week* has discontinued its annual listing.

B-18 Tourism Spending, 1994: The travel industry is a major factor in the economies of all states and a dominant factor in a few. However, data on it are elusive. Many trips combine business and pleasure, so separating tourism from business is difficult. Other trips combine an activity, such as coming home for Christmas, with a tourist activity, such as visiting a museum. Restaurants and gift shops do not normally know whether their customers are tourists or local customers. Consequently, estimates of tourism spending have more guesswork than most of the statistics in *State Fact Finder*. The 1994 data shown in the table are estimates provided on August 13, 1996 by the Travel Industry Association of America. As of November 1997 they were the most up-to-date numbers.

B-19 Exports, 1996: National estimates of exports are made quarterly by the Department of Commerce to develop estimates of gross domestic product and balance of payments with other nations. Relatively current estimates by state are also made by the Commerce Department but are of doubtful reliability because of data-gathering limitations and conceptual problems. For example, does a shipment from a New York port of a product from an Ohio plant of items made from components from Ohio and Mississippi contained in boxes produced in South Carolina constitute an export from New York, Ohio, or where? The data shown come from the Census Bureau's Foreign Trade Division in a fax dated July 29, 1997.

B-20 Housing Permits, 1996: No state-by-state system exists to report completion of single-family houses and apartment and condominium units, but there are good data on the issuance of permits for such construction. Although some builders obtain permits and then don't build, permits are expensive so most permits are followed by construction. The data shown were compiled by the National Association of Home Builders and published in *Housing Economics, May, 1997.* The relationship to population shows which states have rapidly growing populations and which are more stagnant.

B-21 Percent Change in Home Prices, 1992-1997: Most people are interested in changes in housing prices because of the implications for a specific existing home—usually the one they own. The data often cited in the media, which come from realtors' sales records, come from averages of homes sold. As a result, they include large percentages of new (and typically larger, better equipped, and more expensive) homes in fast-growing states than in other states. A preferable way to measure price changes is to examine prices for successive sales of the same homes. This has recently become possible with improvements in computing capacity and the increasing importance of secondary mortgage lenders, who buy massive numbers of mortgages from banks and other lenders. The data in the table reflect this approach. The information comes from the Second Quarter 1997 issue of *House Price Index* published by the Office of Federal Housing Enterprise Oversight.

B-22 Net Farm Income, 1996: These data reflect the net income derived from farming—the value of farm sales minus the cost of production. They are estimates made by the Department of Agriculture and are available on their website (http://www.econ.ag.gov). The *State Fact Finder* calculation of per capita amounts provides a basis for comparing the importance of agriculture to the economies of each state.

B-23 Financial Institution Assets, 1996: This table shows total assets of banks, trust companies and savings institutions. These data, from the Federal Deposit Insurance Corporation's *Statistics on Banking: 1996,* provide a good measure of the importance of banking in each state. However, they provide no indication of the wealth of individuals in a state as deposits flow freely across state lines. States that have successfully tried to draw financial institutions, like Delaware and South Dakota, show large per capita amounts, as do regional banking centers, such as the Boston banks that serve customers throughout New England.

B-24 Bankruptcy Filings by Individuals and Businesses, 1997: These data show how new bankruptcy cases (mostly individuals rather than businesses) were distributed among the states. These data cover the twelve month period ending March 31, 1997 and come from the Administrative Office of the U.S. Courts in a news release dated June 9, 1997.

B-25 Patents Issued, FY 1996: The U.S. Patent Office issued over 66,000 new patents in 1996 to residents (both corporations and individuals) in the states shown. When related to population, this statistic is often used to compare states in the degree to which they are on the forefront of new technology. The data were provided to *State Fact Finder* in a fax dated August 28, 1997 from the United Stated Patent And Trademark Office, Office of Public Affairs. Because patent applications are often made by or for companies, headquarters of companies (e.g. DuPont in Delaware, 3-M in Minnesota) affect the results.

B-26 Workers' Compensation Temporary Disability Payments, 1997: All states maintain a program that provides compensation for workers who are injured on the job. These programs differ massively from state to state in how much money is paid for certain injuries, how hard it is to prove disability and its relationship to the job, and how employers are forced to pay program costs. These differences, set by state policy, are not captured by aggregate statistics on Workers' Compensation costs because some industries (like construction and logging) are inherently more hazardous than others (like banking), so state-by-state costs will vary with the mix of industries. This table compares one major dimension of benefit generosity/parsimony, the maximum payment per month to a worker who is temporarily unable to work because of a job-related injury. The data come from the Department of Labor publication dated January 1997, *State Workers' Compensation Laws.*

B-27 Average Unemployment Compensation Benefit, 1996: All states maintain a federally supervised program of Unemployment Compensation. States have wide discretion in determining how large unemployment compensation payments will be, how long they will last, and how costs are distributed among employers. This table, from a computer run furnished by the Department of Labor, Unemployment Insurance Service on August 27, 1997 shows the average weekly benefit paid in each state.

B-28 Index of State Economic Momentum, September 1997: Each quarter *State Policy Reports* publishes its Index of State Economic Momentum as a way to compare the recent economic performance of each state in relation to the national average. A state growing at the national average rate would show an Index of 0.0 while one growing roughly 1 percent faster would show an Index of 1.0.

Negative numbers show states lagging behind national average growth. The index combines (with equal weights) the most recent known one-year changes in (1) employment, (2) personal income, and (3) population.

B-29 Employment Change, 1996-1997: This table uses Department of Labor data from June of 1996 and 1997 (not seasonally adjusted) to show the change in the number of jobs in each state. The data, from the August 1997 edition of *State and Metropolitan Area Unemployment and Unemployment*, are one component of the momentum index shown in Table B-28.

B-30 Manufacturing Employment Change, 1996-1997: This table uses Department of Labor (see source for Table B-29) data from July 1996 to July 1997 (not seasonally adjusted) to show the states experiencing job loss and those experiencing job growth in manufacturing These data are released monthly and revised often, but differences in state economic performance tend to persist from month to month.

B-31 Home Ownership, 1996: These data show the percentage of households living in homes they own. The data come from the *Housing Vacancy Survey* available on the Census web site (http://www.census.gov). These are estimates based on Census surveys. Because of the relatively small samples, the margin of error for less populous states is relatively large.

B-32 Gambling, 1996: Legal gambling establishments in the United States grossed nearly $42 million in 1996—$158 per person, including people who do not gamble at all. The distribution of these revenues among the states is shown in the table, reflecting estimates made in *International Gaming & Wagering Business* (August 1997).

These statistics dealing with the revenues of gaming establishments provide one indication of the amount of gambling activity. However, they should not be confused with amounts bet. While gamblers lose, on average, about 55 cents for every dollar spent on state lotteries and 20 cents for every dollar at horse tracks, they only lose about 2 cents of what they bet at casino table games and about 5 cents at slot machines. So, the same dollar is, in effect, bet many times before it is lost. *Gaming & Wagering* has much more detailed estimates of gambling by state and type of gambling, as well as information on gambling taxes and revenues of gambling establishments.

B-33 Average Annual Electricity Use Per Residential Customer, 1995: These data from the Edison Electric Institute's *Statistical Yearbook of the Electric Utility Industry 1995* show differences in electricity use among the states. The results are heavily influenced by the relative importance of heating and air conditioning and the mix of fuels used for heating.

B-34 Average Revenue Per Kilowatt Hour, 1995: These data also come from the Edison Electric Institute (see source for Table B-33), which maintains additional details on other years, types of consumers, and more. The data have many uses. The revenue per kilowatt hour permits comparisons among states of electricity costs for households and businesses. The residential rate as a percentage of industrial rate is a useful indicator of the extent to which state regulatory policy (which controls rate charged by private companies) is tilted toward providing low industrial rates to stimulate economic development or low residential rates to keep prices low for voter/consumers at the potential expense of loss of industry. Based on costs of service, industrial users should pay less because they are cheaper per kilowatt to bill and often agree to have service curtailed when there is a shortage of power.

B-35 New Companies, 1996: These data show the number of companies that applied for new account numbers from state employment services. These data were made available to *State Fact Finder* by Tom Stengle of the U.S. Department of Labor Unemployment Insurance Service in a fax dated September 2, 1997. *State Fact Finder* then related these numbers to the total number of workers in each state. These employment numbers are annual averages and come from the Census Report *State and Regional Unemployment, 1996 Annual Averages* (USDL 97-88).

Geography

State	Land area square mile	Rank	By sq. mile
Alabama	50,750	28	1. Alaska
Alaska	570,373	1	2. Texas
Arizona	113,642	6	3. California
Arkansas	52,075	27	4. Montana
California	155,973	3	5. New Mexico
Colorado	103,728	8	6. Arizona
Connecticut	4,845	48	7. Nevada
Delaware	1,954	49	8. Colorado
Florida	53,997	26	9. Wyoming
Georgia	57,919	21	10. Oregon
Hawaii	6,423	47	11. Utah
Idaho	82,751	12	12. Idaho
Illinois	55,593	24	13. Kansas
Indiana	35,870	38	14. Minnesota
Iowa	55,875	23	15. Nebraska
Kansas	81,823	13	16. South Dakota
Kentucky	39,732	36	17. North Dakota
Louisiana	43,566	33	18. Missouri
Maine	30,864	39	19. Oklahoma
Maryland	9,775	42	20. Washington
Massachusetts	7,838	45	21. Georgia
Michigan	56,809	22	22. Michigan
Minnesota	79,616	14	23. Iowa
Mississippi	46,914	31	24. Illinois
Missouri	68,898	18	25. Wisconsin
Montana	145,556	4	26. Florida
Nebraska	76,877	15	27. Arkansas
Nevada	109,805	7	28. Alabama
New Hampshire	8,969	44	29. North Carolina
New Jersey	7,419	46	30. New York
New Mexico	121,364	5	31. Mississippi
New York	47,224	30	32. Pennsylvania
North Carolina	48,718	29	33. Louisiana
North Dakota	68,994	17	34. Tennessee
Ohio	40,953	35	35. Ohio
Oklahoma	68,678	19	36. Kentucky
Oregon	96,002	10	37. Virginia
Pennsylvania	44,820	32	38. Indiana
Rhode Island	1,045	50	39. Maine
South Carolina	30,111	40	40. South Carolina
South Dakota	75,896	16	41. West Virginia
Tennessee	41,219	34	42. Maryland
Texas	261,914	2	43. Vermont
Utah	82,768	11	44. New Hampshire
Vermont	9,249	43	45. Massachusetts
Virginia	39,598	37	46. New Jersey
Washington	66,581	20	47. Hawaii
West Virginia	24,087	41	48. Connecticut
Wisconsin	54,314	25	49. Delaware
Wyoming	97,104	9	50. Rhode Island
50 States	3,536,868		
DC	61		
United States	3,536,338		

State	Total acres of federally owned land (000)	Percent of land federally owned %	Rank by total acres
Alabama	1,075	3.3	27
Alaska	248,021	67.9	1
Arizona	34,308	47.2	4
Arkansas	2,762	8.2	18
California	44,707	44.6	3
Colorado	24,154	36.3	11
Connecticut	6	0.2	49
Delaware	27	2.2	48
Florida	3,114	9.0	16
Georgia	1,488	4.0	24
Hawaii	634	15.5	36
Idaho	32,614	61.6	6
Illinois	961	2.7	30
Indiana	401	1.7	39
Iowa	336	0.9	42
Kansas	422	0.8	38
Kentucky	1,080	4.2	26
Louisiana	745	2.6	31
Maine	155	0.8	45
Maryland	187	3.0	44
Massachusetts	66	1.3	47
Michigan	4,589	12.6	14
Minnesota	5,367	10.5	13
Mississippi	1,306	4.3	25
Missouri	2,096	4.7	20
Montana	26,142	28.0	9
Nebraska	710	1.4	34
Nevada	58,265	82.9	2
New Hampshire	734	12.7	32
New Jersey	149	3.1	46
New Mexico	25,203	32.4	10
New York	209	0.7	43
North Carolina	1,970	6.3	21
North Dakota	1,879	4.2	22
Ohio	342	1.3	41
Oklahoma	705	1.6	35
Oregon	32,291	52.4	7
Pennsylvania	608	2.1	37
Rhode Island	2	0.3	50
South Carolina	722	3.7	33
South Dakota	2,806	5.7	17
Tennessee	994	3.7	29
Texas	2,245	1.3	19
Utah	33,661	63.9	5
Vermont	358	6.0	40
Virginia	1,597	6.3	23
Washington	12,080	28.3	12
West Virginia	1,028	6.7	28
Wisconsin	3,537	10.1	15
Wyoming	30,477	48.9	8
50 States	649,335	n/a	
DC	10	26.1	
United States	649,346	28.6	

Rank in order

By total acres

1. Alaska
2. Nevada
3. California
4. Arizona
5. Utah
6. Idaho
7. Oregon
8. Wyoming
9. Montana
10. New Mexico
11. Colorado
12. Washington
13. Minnesota
14. Michigan
15. Wisconsin
16. Florida
17. South Dakota
18. Arkansas
19. Texas
20. Missouri
21. North Carolina
22. North Dakota
23. Virginia
24. Georgia
25. Mississippi
26. Kentucky
27. Alabama
28. West Virginia
29. Tennessee
30. Illinois
31. Louisiana
32. New Hampshire
33. South Carolina
34. Nebraska
35. Oklahoma
36. Hawaii
37. Pennsylvania
38. Kansas
39. Indiana
40. Vermont
41. Ohio
42. Iowa
43. New York
44. Maryland
45. Maine
46. New Jersey
47. Massachusetts
48. Delaware
49. Connecticut
50. Rhode Island

State	State park acreage (000)	Acreage per 1,000 population	Rank by total acreage	Rank in order By total
Alabama	49,710	11.7	40	1. Alaska
Alaska	3,242,223	5380.9	1	2. California
Arizona	46,400	10.8	41	3. Texas
Arkansas	50,904	20.5	39	4. Florida
California	1,334,362	42.3	2	5. Illinois
Colorado	337,233	90.0	6	6. Colorado
Connecticut	176,221	53.9	18	7. Kansas
Delaware	15,528	21.7	49	8. New Jersey
Florida	437,473	30.8	4	9. Massachusetts
Georgia	66,129	9.2	34	10. Pennsylvania
Hawaii	24,615	20.9	45	11. Michigan
Idaho	41,848	35.9	43	12. New York
Illinois	419,197	35.6	5	13. Washington
Indiana	59,292	10.2	37	14. Maryland
Iowa	62,330	21.9	36	15. Minnesota
Kansas	324,177	126.5	7	16. Ohio
Kentucky	42,748	11.1	42	17. West Virginia
Louisiana	39,007	9.0	44	18. Connecticut
Maine	91,898	74.2	31	19. New Hampshire
Maryland	247,445	49.1	14	20. Nevada
Massachusetts	315,352	51.9	9	21. North Carolina
Michigan	265,391	27.8	11	22. Tennessee
Minnesota	245,074	53.1	15	23. Missouri
Mississippi	22,687	8.4	46	24. Nebraska
Missouri	133,632	25.1	23	25. Wisconsin
Montana	52,469	60.3	38	26. New Mexico
Nebraska	133,367	81.4	24	27. Wyoming
Nevada	148,578	96.9	20	28. Utah
New Hampshire	153,520	133.7	19	29. South Dakota
New Jersey	321,145	40.4	8	30. Oregon
New Mexico	120,193	71.1	26	31. Maine
New York	260,793	14.3	12	32. South Carolina
North Carolina	140,041	19.4	21	33. Oklahoma
North Dakota	19,959	31.1	47	34. Georgia
Ohio	204,274	18.3	16	35. Vermont
Oklahoma	71,635	21.9	33	36. Iowa
Oregon	92,277	29.3	30	37. Indiana
Pennsylvania	282,500	23.4	10	38. Montana
Rhode Island	8,748	8.8	50	39. Arkansas
South Carolina	81,557	22.2	32	40. Alabama
South Dakota	92,710	127.1	29	41. Arizona
Tennessee	133,920	25.5	22	42. Kentucky
Texas	519,154	27.6	3	43. Idaho
Utah	97,753	49.9	28	44. Louisiana
Vermont	64,101	109.6	35	45. Hawaii
Virginia	15,683	2.4	48	46. Mississippi
Washington	255,094	46.8	13	47. North Dakota
West Virginia	198,765	108.9	17	48. Virginia
Wisconsin	128,097	25.0	25	49. Delaware
Wyoming	119,866	250.1	27	50. Rhode Island
50 States	11,807,076	45.0		
DC	0	0.0		
United States	11,807,076	44.9		

State	State park total visitors (000)	Visitors per capita	Rank by per capita
Alabama	6,213	1.5	43
Alaska	4,299	7.1	5
Arizona	2,180	0.5	49
Arkansas	7,491	3.0	20
California	64,314	2.0	34
Colorado	10,949	2.9	22
Connecticut	7,993	2.4	28
Delaware	3,246	4.5	11
Florida	11,798	0.8	47
Georgia	15,880	2.2	31
Hawaii	19,000	16.1	1
Idaho	2,675	2.3	29
Illinois	40,027	3.4	17
Indiana	10,700	1.8	36
Iowa	12,185	4.3	13
Kansas	6,708	2.6	26
Kentucky	8,530	2.2	30
Louisiana	1,435	0.3	50
Maine	2,008	1.6	41
Maryland	10,985	2.2	32
Massachusetts	18,238	3.0	21
Michigan	24,292	2.5	27
Minnesota	8,065	1.7	37
Mississippi	4,263	1.6	42
Missouri	16,058	3.0	19
Montana	1,837	2.1	33
Nebraska	9,023	5.5	8
Nevada	2,874	1.9	35
New Hampshire	1,178	1.0	46
New Jersey	13,574	1.7	38
New Mexico	4,649	2.8	24
New York	64,406	3.5	15
North Carolina	11,974	1.7	39
North Dakota	1,043	1.6	40
Ohio	62,284	5.6	7
Oklahoma	15,615	4.8	10
Oregon	41,265	13.1	2
Pennsylvania	36,541	3.0	18
Rhode Island	3,372	3.4	16
South Carolina	10,565	2.9	23
South Dakota	7,712	10.6	3
Tennessee	29,656	5.7	6
Texas	24,249	1.3	45
Utah	7,059	3.6	14
Vermont	828	1.4	44
Virginia	4,573	0.7	48
Washington	47,186	8.7	4
West Virginia	9,082	5.0	9
Wisconsin	13,420	2.6	25
Wyoming	2,108	4.4	12
50 States	n/a	n/a	
DC	0	0.0	
United States	745,602	2.8	

By per capita

1. Hawaii
2. Oregon
3. South Dakota
4. Washington
5. Alaska
6. Tennessee
7. Ohio
8. Nebraska
9. West Virginia
10. Oklahoma
11. Delaware
12. Wyoming
13. Iowa
14. Utah
15. New York
16. Rhode Island
17. Illinois
18. Pennsylvania
19. Missouri
20. Arkansas
21. Massachusetts
22. Colorado
23. South Carolina
24. New Mexico
25. Wisconsin
26. Kansas
27. Michigan
28. Connecticut
29. Idaho
30. Kentucky
31. Georgia
32. Maryland
33. Montana
34. California
35. Nevada
36. Indiana
37. Minnesota
38. New Jersey
39. North Carolina
40. North Dakota
41. Maine
42. Mississippi
43. Alabama
44. Vermont
45. Texas
46. New Hampshire
47. Florida
48. Virginia
49. Arizona
50. Louisiana

State	Percent reporting not to be physically active %	Rank
Alabama	45.8	1
Alaska	26.0	28
Arizona	23.7	34
Arkansas	34.5	11
California	21.9	39
Colorado	17.9	49
Connecticut	21.8	40
Delaware	35.5	10
Florida	27.4	26
Georgia	34.1	12
Hawaii	21.3	43
Idaho	21.8	40
Illinois	33.4	15
Indiana	29.5	24
Iowa	32.7	16
Kansas	33.9	13
Kentucky	45.7	2
Louisiana	33.5	14
Maine	41.0	5
Maryland	31.1	19
Massachusetts	24.4	31
Michigan	23.4	36
Minnesota	22.0	38
Mississippi	38.3	7
Missouri	31.0	20
Montana	20.7	46
Nebraska	24.1	32
Nevada	21.6	42
New Hampshire	26.1	27
New Jersey	30.5	21
New Mexico	19.7	47
New York	36.9	9
North Carolina	43.0	4
North Dakota	32.0	17
Ohio	38.0	8
Oklahoma	30.0	22
Oregon	20.8	45
Pennsylvania	25.8	29
Rhode Island	n/a	n/a
South Carolina	31.7	18
South Dakota	30.0	22
Tennessee	39.8	6
Texas	28.3	25
Utah	22.2	37
Vermont	24.0	33
Virginia	23.7	34
Washington	18.3	48
West Virginia	44.1	3
Wisconsin	25.7	30
Wyoming	21.0	44
50 States	n/a	
DC	49.3	
United States	28.9	

Rank in order

By %

1. Alabama
2. Kentucky
3. West Virginia
4. North Carolina
5. Maine
6. Tennessee
7. Mississippi
8. Ohio
9. New York
10. Delaware
11. Arkansas
12. Georgia
13. Kansas
14. Louisiana
15. Illinois
16. Iowa
17. North Dakota
18. South Carolina
19. Maryland
20. Missouri
21. New Jersey
22. Oklahoma
22. South Dakota
24. Indiana
25. Texas
26. Florida
27. New Hampshire
28. Alaska
29. Pennsylvania
30. Wisconsin
31. Massachusetts
32. Nebraska
33. Vermont
34. Arizona
34. Virginia
36. Michigan
37. Utah
38. Minnesota
39. California
40. Connecticut
40. Idaho
42. Nevada
43. Hawaii
44. Wyoming
45. Oregon
46. Montana
47. New Mexico
48. Washington
49. Colorado

State	Hunters with firearms (000)	Percent of population %	Rank by %	By %
Alabama	432	10.1	14	1. Montana
Alaska	n/a	n/a	n/a	2. Wyoming
Arizona	310	7.0	38	3. West Virginia
Arkansas	365	14.5	6	4. Wisconsin
California	707	2.2	44	5. Idaho
Colorado	262	6.9	34	6. Arkansas
Connecticut	80	2.4	45	7. South Dakota
Delaware	18	2.5	41	8. Maine
Florida	436	3.0	42	9. Oregon
Georgia	489	6.7	28	10. North Dakota
Hawaii	n/a	n/a	n/a	11. Minnesota
Idaho	192	16.1	5	12. Mississippi
Illinois	548	4.6	39	13. Nebraska
Indiana	345	5.9	30	14. Alabama
Iowa	310	10.9	21	15. Vermont
Kansas	161	6.3	31	16. Utah
Kentucky	304	7.8	24	17. Pennsylvania
Louisiana	474	10.9	20	18. Missouri
Maine	148	11.9	8	19. Michigan
Maryland	168	3.3	40	20. Louisiana
Massachusetts	131	2.2	47	21. Iowa
Michigan	867	9.0	19	22. North Carolina
Minnesota	525	11.3	11	23. South Carolina
Mississippi	378	13.9	12	24. Kentucky
Missouri	560	10.5	18	25. Oklahoma
Montana	318	36.2	1	26. Tennessee
Nebraska	171	10.4	13	27. New Mexico
Nevada	64	4.0	37	28. Georgia
New Hampshire	55	4.7	46	29. Texas
New Jersey	246	3.1	43	30. Indiana
New Mexico	76	4.4	27	31. Kansas
New York	899	4.9	33	32. Virginia
North Carolina	553	7.6	22	33. New York
North Dakota	92	14.3	10	34. Colorado
Ohio	556	5.0	35	35. Ohio
Oklahoma	249	7.5	25	36. Washington
Oregon	405	12.6	9	37. Nevada
Pennsylvania	1,253	10.4	17	38. Arizona
Rhode Island	n/a	n/a	n/a	39. Illinois
South Carolina	217	5.9	23	40. Maryland
South Dakota	122	16.7	7	41. Delaware
Tennessee	482	9.1	26	42. Florida
Texas	1,397	7.3	29	43. New Jersey
Utah	290	14.5	16	44. California
Vermont	76	12.9	15	45. Connecticut
Virginia	413	6.2	32	46. New Hampshire
Washington	350	6.3	36	47. Massachusetts
West Virginia	411	22.5	3	
Wisconsin	702	13.6	4	
Wyoming	124	25.8	2	
50 States	17,731	6.7		
DC	n/a	n/a		
United States	17,752	6.7		

State	Registered boats (000)	Registered boats per 1,000 population	Rank by total #	Rank in order By total #
Alabama	261	61.2	17	1. Michigan
Alaska	27	44.4	48	2. California
Arizona	150	33.9	29	3. Minnesota
Arkansas	178	71.0	27	4. Florida
California	881	27.6	2	5. Texas
Colorado	95	24.9	34	6. Wisconsin
Connecticut	98	30.0	33	7. New York
Delaware	43	59.1	44	8. South Carolina
Florida	749	52.0	4	9. Ohio
Georgia	303	41.2	15	10. Illinois
Hawaii	15	12.8	50	11. Pennsylvania
Idaho	81	67.8	36	12. North Carolina
Illinois	366	30.9	10	12. Louisiana
Indiana	204	34.9	22	14. Missouri
Iowa	201	70.6	23	15. Georgia
Kansas	100	38.9	32	16. Tennessee
Kentucky	157	40.3	28	17. Alabama
Louisiana	321	73.8	12	18. Washington
Maine	116	93.2	31	19. Mississippi
Maryland	194	38.3	25	20. Virginia
Massachusetts	137	22.6	30	21. Oklahoma
Michigan	946	98.6	1	22. Indiana
Minnesota	759	162.9	3	23. Iowa
Mississippi	244	89.9	19	24. Oregon
Missouri	307	57.3	14	25. Maryland
Montana	46	52.8	43	26. New Jersey
Nebraska	70	42.6	38	27. Arkansas
Nevada	55	34.6	40	28. Kentucky
New Hampshire	88	75.6	35	29. Arizona
New Jersey	183	22.9	26	30. Massachusetts
New Mexico	56	32.5	39	31. Maine
New York	458	25.2	7	32. Kansas
North Carolina	321	43.9	12	33. Connecticut
North Dakota	38	59.0	46	34. Colorado
Ohio	398	35.7	9	35. New Hampshire
Oklahoma	221	66.9	21	36. Idaho
Oregon	195	60.9	24	37. Utah
Pennsylvania	335	27.8	11	38. Nebraska
Rhode Island	32	32.8	47	39. New Mexico
South Carolina	416	112.5	8	40. Nevada
South Dakota	47	63.6	42	41. West Virginia
Tennessee	298	56.0	16	42. South Dakota
Texas	611	32.0	5	43. Montana
Utah	72	35.8	37	44. Delaware
Vermont	39	66.1	45	45. Vermont
Virginia	229	34.3	20	46. North Dakota
Washington	246	44.5	18	47. Rhode Island
West Virginia	52	28.7	41	48. Alaska
Wisconsin	543	105.3	6	49. Wyoming
Wyoming	24	50.0	49	50. Hawaii
50 States	12,011	45.4		
DC	1	2.2		
United States	12,057	45.5		

State	State spending for the arts $(000)	Per capita in pennies	Rank by per capita
Alabama	3,008	70	24
Alaska	457	75	22
Arizona	2,547	58	31
Arkansas	1,287	51	36
California	12,432	39	46
Colorado	1,835	48	40
Connecticut	3,676	112	12
Delaware	2,316	319	2
Florida	27,300	190	5
Georgia	4,421	60	30
Hawaii	6,430	543	1
Idaho	809	68	27
Illinois	7,502	63	28
Indiana	3,003	51	35
Iowa	1,430	50	37
Kansas	1,346	52	34
Kentucky	3,392	87	19
Louisiana	4,136	95	17
Maine	525	42	42
Maryland	7,726	152	8
Massachusetts	14,647	240	3
Michigan	21,730	226	4
Minnesota	6,936	149	9
Mississippi	1,533	56	32
Missouri	10,016	187	6
Montana	121	14	50
Nebraska	1,282	78	20
Nevada	648	40	44
New Hampshire	483	42	43
New Jersey	11,657	146	10
New Mexico	1,823	106	14
New York	32,375	178	7
North Carolina	5,421	74	23
North Dakota	288	45	41
Ohio	11,867	106	15
Oklahoma	3,036	92	18
Oregon	1,142	36	48
Pennsylvania	9,100	75	21
Rhode Island	620	63	29
South Carolina	3,604	97	16
South Dakota	396	54	33
Tennessee	2,631	49	38
Texas	3,324	17	49
Utah	2,562	128	11
Vermont	410	70	25
Virginia	2,669	40	45
Washington	2,025	37	47
West Virginia	2,000	110	13
Wisconsin	2,552	49	39
Wyoming	332	69	26
50 States	252,807	95	
DC	1,724	317	
United States	271,898	102	

By per capita

1. Hawaii
2. Delaware
3. Massachusetts
4. Michigan
5. Florida
6. Missouri
7. New York
8. Maryland
9. Minnesota
10. New Jersey
11. Utah
12. Connecticut
13. West Virginia
14. New Mexico
15. Ohio
16. South Carolina
17. Louisiana
18. Oklahoma
19. Kentucky
20. Nebraska
21. Pennsylvania
22. Alaska
23. North Carolina
24. Alabama
25. Vermont
26. Wyoming
27. Idaho
28. Illinois
29. Rhode Island
30. Georgia
31. Arizona
32. Mississippi
33. South Dakota
34. Kansas
35. Indiana
36. Arkansas
37. Iowa
38. Tennessee
39. Wisconsin
40. Colorado
41. North Dakota
42. Maine
43. New Hampshire
44. Nevada
45. Virginia
46. California
47. Washington
48. Oregon
49. Texas
50. Montana

State	Energy consumption (trillion BTUs)	BTUs per capita	Rank by per capita	By per capita
Alabama	1,933	455,301	7	1. Alaska
Alaska	686	1,139,002	1	2. Louisiana
Arizona	1,059	245,969	45	3. Wyoming
Arkansas	998	401,608	14	4. Texas
California	7,577	240,041	47	5. North Dakota
Colorado	1,075	286,907	39	6. Kentucky
Connecticut	786	240,404	46	7. Alabama
Delaware	264	368,180	21	8. West Virginia
Florida	3,519	248,066	42	9. Indiana
Georgia	2,512	348,483	26	10. Montana
Hawaii	255	216,079	49	11. Oklahoma
Idaho	456	391,215	17	12. Maine
Illinois	3,804	322,661	34	13. Kansas
Indiana	2,592	447,149	9	14. Arkansas
Iowa	1,067	375,404	20	15. Washington
Kansas	1,041	405,911	13	16. Mississippi
Kentucky	1,770	459,024	6	17. Idaho
Louisiana	3,814	879,100	2	18. South Carolina
Maine	513	414,429	12	19. Tennessee
Maryland	1,312	260,354	40	20. Iowa
Massachusetts	1,494	246,052	44	21. Delaware
Michigan	3,157	330,994	30	22. Ohio
Minnesota	1,622	351,514	24	23. Nebraska
Mississippi	1,059	392,703	16	24. Minnesota
Missouri	1,663	312,595	37	25. Nevada
Montana	379	435,342	10	26. Georgia
Nebraska	580	354,011	23	27. Wisconsin
Nevada	537	350,315	25	28. New Mexico
New Hampshire	285	247,770	43	29. Oregon
New Jersey	2,543	319,882	36	30. Michigan
New Mexico	575	340,267	28	31. Utah
New York	3,913	215,134	50	32. North Carolina
North Carolina	2,328	323,242	32	33. South Dakota
North Dakota	350	545,747	5	34. Illinois
Ohio	4,038	362,672	22	35. Pennsylvania
Oklahoma	1,360	415,162	11	36. New Jersey
Oregon	1,048	332,883	29	37. Missouri
Pennsylvania	3,886	322,189	35	38. Virginia
Rhode Island	235	237,067	48	39. Colorado
South Carolina	1,401	381,974	18	40. Maryland
South Dakota	236	323,235	33	41. Vermont
Tennessee	1,975	376,464	19	42. Florida
Texas	10,512	559,081	4	43. New Hampshire
Utah	638	325,995	31	44. Massachusetts
Vermont	150	256,337	41	45. Arizona
Virginia	2,056	310,798	38	46. Connecticut
Washington	2,159	396,239	15	47. California
West Virginia	819	448,649	8	48. Rhode Island
Wisconsin	1,749	341,481	27	49. Hawaii
Wyoming	405	845,590	3	50. New York
50 States	90,185	343,777		
DC	178	320,633		
United States	90,547	344,431		

State	Toxic chemical release in pounds (000)	Per capita release in pounds	Rank by per capita
Alabama	102,765	24.2	4
Alaska	6,960	11.6	15
Arizona	35,833	8.3	22
Arkansas	34,682	14.0	11
California	42,727	1.4	46
Colorado	4,575	1.2	48
Connecticut	8,764	2.7	39
Delaware	4,510	6.3	31
Florida	83,973	5.9	33
Georgia	55,524	7.7	26
Hawaii	470	0.4	50
Idaho	8,188	7.0	28
Illinois	99,753	8.5	21
Indiana	79,778	13.8	12
Iowa	34,765	12.2	13
Kansas	22,816	8.9	20
Kentucky	41,925	10.9	18
Louisiana	172,259	39.7	2
Maine	10,168	8.2	23
Maryland	13,322	2.6	40
Massachusetts	8,141	1.3	47
Michigan	75,264	7.9	25
Minnesota	22,460	4.9	34
Mississippi	56,755	21.1	7
Missouri	49,647	9.3	19
Montana	43,892	50.4	1
Nebraska	10,958	6.7	30
Nevada	3,559	2.3	42
New Hampshire	2,563	2.2	43
New Jersey	14,645	1.8	45
New Mexico	18,706	11.1	16
New York	36,573	2.0	44
North Carolina	86,160	12.0	14
North Dakota	2,562	4.0	37
Ohio	121,871	10.9	17
Oklahoma	24,953	7.6	27
Oregon	21,195	6.7	29
Pennsylvania	54,260	4.5	36
Rhode Island	2,783	2.8	38
South Carolina	54,339	14.8	10
South Dakota	1,913	2.6	41
Tennessee	111,183	21.2	6
Texas	283,932	15.1	8
Utah	76,322	39.0	3
Vermont	553	0.9	49
Virginia	52,913	8.0	24
Washington	26,451	4.9	35
West Virginia	27,357	15.0	9
Wisconsin	31,178	6.1	32
Wyoming	11,003	23.0	5
50 States	2,197,850	8.4	
DC	30	0.1	
United States	2,208,749	8.4	

Rank in order

By per capita

1. Montana
2. Louisiana
3. Utah
4. Alabama
5. Wyoming
6. Tennessee
7. Mississippi
8. Texas
9. West Virginia
10. South Carolina
11. Arkansas
12. Indiana
13. Iowa
14. North Carolina
15. Alaska
16. New Mexico
17. Ohio
18. Kentucky
19. Missouri
20. Kansas
21. Illinois
22. Arizona
23. Maine
24. Virginia
25. Michigan
26. Georgia
27. Oklahoma
28. Idaho
29. Oregon
30. Nebraska
31. Delaware
32. Wisconsin
33. Florida
34. Minnesota
35. Washington
36. Pennsylvania
37. North Dakota
38. Rhode Island
39. Connecticut
40. Maryland
41. South Dakota
42. Nevada
43. New Hampshire
44. New York
45. New Jersey
46. California
47. Massachusetts
48. Colorado
49. Vermont
50. Hawaii

C-11 HAZARDOUS WASTE SITES, 1997

State	Hazardous waste sites	Rank
Alabama	13	30
Alaska	7	43
Arizona	10	37
Arkansas	12	31
California	94	3
Colorado	17	22
Connecticut	15	28
Delaware	18	19
Florida	54	6
Georgia	16	24
Hawaii	4	45
Idaho	10	37
Illinois	41	8
Indiana	31	11
Iowa	17	22
Kansas	11	34
Kentucky	16	24
Louisiana	18	19
Maine	12	31
Maryland	16	24
Massachusetts	30	12
Michigan	74	5
Minnesota	30	12
Mississippi	3	46
Missouri	22	18
Montana	9	41
Nebraska	10	37
Nevada	1	49
New Hampshire	18	19
New Jersey	106	1
New Mexico	10	37
New York	79	4
North Carolina	23	17
North Dakota	0	50
Ohio	38	10
Oklahoma	11	34
Oregon	11	34
Pennsylvania	102	2
Rhode Island	12	31
South Carolina	26	15
South Dakota	2	48
Tennessee	15	28
Texas	28	14
Utah	16	24
Vermont	8	42
Virginia	25	16
Washington	50	7
West Virginia	7	43
Wisconsin	40	9
Wyoming	3	46
50 States	1,241	
DC	n/a	
United States	1,255	

Rank in order

By #

1. New Jersey
2. Pennsylvania
3. California
4. New York
5. Michigan
6. Florida
7. Washington
8. Illinois
9. Wisconsin
10. Ohio
11. Indiana
12. Massachusetts
12. Minnesota
14. Texas
15. South Carolina
16. Virginia
17. North Carolina
18. Missouri
19. Delaware
19. Louisiana
19. New Hampshire
22. Colorado
22. Iowa
24. Georgia
24. Kentucky
24. Maryland
24. Utah
28. Connecticut
28. Tennessee
30. Alabama
31. Arkansas
31. Maine
31. Rhode Island
34. Kansas
34. Oklahoma
34. Oregon
37. Arizona
37. Idaho
37. Nebraska
37. New Mexico
41. Montana
42. Vermont
43. Alaska
43. West Virginia
45. Hawaii
46. Mississippi
46. Wyoming
48. South Dakota
49. Nevada
50. North Dakota

C-12 MILES OF POLLUTED RIVERS AND STREAMS, 1994

State	Polluted miles #	Percent of river & stream miles polluted %	Rank by %	By %
Alabama	4,888	36.1	29	1. Kansas
Alaska	2,889	71.3	12	2. Hawaii
Arizona	3,745	66.6	16	3. Oklahoma
Arkansas	4,050	55.8	23	4. Washington
California	8,500	72.2	10	5. Delaware
Colorado	3,897	11.1	44	6. Mississippi
Connecticut	301	33.7	32	7. South Dakota
Delaware	644	87.0	5	8. New Mexico
Florida	4,128	34.7	31	9. Montana
Georgia	4,025	64.5	18	10. California
Hawaii	30	93.8	2	11. Nebraska
Idaho	n/a	n/a	n/a	12. Alaska
Illinois	7,257	51.3	24	13. West Virginia
Indiana	1,479	20.2	40	14. Massachusetts
Iowa	3,281	57.4	21	15. Wyoming
Kansas	16,700	99.2	1	16. Arizona
Kentucky	3,813	25.0	37	17. Nevada
Louisiana	3,995	43.6	26	18. Georgia
Maine	423	1.3	49	19. Ohio
Maryland	1,866	31.1	35	20. Minnesota
Massachusetts	974	68.4	14	21. Iowa
Michigan	1,416	6.9	46	22. Oregon
Minnesota	2,025	58.8	20	23. Arkansas
Mississippi	7,692	85.5	6	24. Illinois
Missouri	9,794	46.6	25	25. Missouri
Montana	13,962	79.0	9	26. Louisiana
Nebraska	6,109	71.5	11	27. South Carolina
Nevada	891	66.0	17	28. Utah
New Hampshire	170	1.6	48	29. Alabama
New Jersey	516	31.9	34	30. Tennessee
New Mexico	3,256	83.5	8	31. Florida
New York	4,785	9.1	45	32. Connecticut
North Carolina	9,379	27.2	36	33. Texas
North Dakota	1,600	22.5	39	34. New Jersey
Ohio	4,904	58.8	19	35. Maryland
Oklahoma	6,471	91.9	3	36. North Carolina
Oregon	16,457	56.5	22	37. Kentucky
Pennsylvania	4,607	18.5	43	38. Rhode Island
Rhode Island	154	23.1	38	39. North Dakota
South Carolina	10,534	40.0	27	40. Indiana
South Dakota	3,077	85.4	7	41. Vermont
Tennessee	3,818	35.0	30	42. Wisconsin
Texas	4,831	33.6	33	43. Pennsylvania
Utah	2,271	39.7	28	44. Colorado
Vermont	1,010	19.2	41	45. New York
Virginia	2,322	6.7	47	46. Michigan
Washington	6,651	89.5	4	47. Virginia
West Virginia	4,410	69.2	13	48. New Hampshire
Wisconsin	4,022	18.9	42	49. Maine
Wyoming	4,086	67.1	15	
50 States	218,105	35.8		
DC	37	100.0		
United States	224,236	36.4		

C-13 SURFACE WATER POLLUTION DISCHARGES, FY 1996

State	Surface water discharge %	Rank		By %
Alabama	18.5	6		1. Utah
Alaska	1.3	44		2. Michigan
Arizona	10.3	17		3. Rhode Island
Arkansas	14.4	9		4. Missouri
California	1.3	45		5. Florida
Colorado	0.9	46		6. Alabama
Connecticut	13.3	10		7. Nebraska
Delaware	6.7	30		8. Minnesota
Florida	20.5	5		9. Arkansas
Georgia	1.7	43		10. Connecticut
Hawaii	3.7	36		11. Indiana
Idaho	2.9	40		12. West Virginia
Illinois	7.0	29		13. Iowa
Indiana	12.9	11		14. Ohio
Iowa	12.0	13		15. Texas
Kansas	n/a	n/a		16. Louisiana
Kentucky	0.1	47		17. Arizona
Louisiana	10.3	16		18. Nevada
Maine	7.1	28		19. Oklahoma
Maryland	2.2	42		20. Mississippi
Massachusetts	9.1	21		21. Massachusetts
Michigan	31.3	2		22. South Carolina
Minnesota	16.5	8		23. Virginia
Mississippi	9.2	20		24. New York
Missouri	28.0	4		25. New Hampshire
Montana	2.2	41		26. Pennsylvania
Nebraska	17.9	7		27. North Carolina
Nevada	10.0	18		28. Maine
New Hampshire	7.3	25		29. Illinois
New Jersey	5.7	32		30. Delaware
New Mexico	6.3	31		31. New Mexico
New York	7.4	24		32. New Jersey
North Carolina	7.2	27		33. Oregon
North Dakota	0.0	48		34. Tennessee
Ohio	11.8	14		35. Wisconsin
Oklahoma	9.8	19		36. Hawaii
Oregon	5.6	33		37. Wyoming
Pennsylvania	7.2	26		38. South Dakota
Rhode Island	29.6	3		39. Washington
South Carolina	8.0	22		40. Idaho
South Dakota	3.3	38		41. Montana
Tennessee	5.2	34		42. Maryland
Texas	11.2	15		43. Georgia
Utah	35.1	1		44. Alaska
Vermont	0.0	48		45. California
Virginia	7.5	23		46. Colorado
Washington	3.3	39		47. Kentucky
West Virginia	12.1	12		48. North Dakota
Wisconsin	5.2	35		48. Vermont
Wyoming	3.5	37		
50 States	n/a			
DC	n/a			
United States	n/a			

C-14 AIR POLLUTION EMISSIONS, 1995

State	Emissions in short tons (000)	Per capita	Rank by total emissions
Alabama	4,982	1.2	14
Alaska	834	1.4	44
Arizona	2,932	0.7	27
Arkansas	2,376	1.0	34
California	13,916	0.4	2
Colorado	2,742	0.7	31
Connecticut	1,300	0.4	41
Delaware	557	0.8	47
Florida	8,857	0.6	3
Georgia	6,810	0.9	8
Hawaii	409	0.3	49
Idaho	1,791	1.5	37
Illinois	7,504	0.6	6
Indiana	6,578	1.1	9
Iowa	2,768	1.0	30
Kansas	3,102	1.2	25
Kentucky	3,807	1.0	19
Louisiana	5,219	1.2	13
Maine	794	0.6	45
Maryland	2,583	0.5	33
Massachusetts	2,712	0.4	32
Michigan	6,088	0.6	10
Minnesota	3,778	0.8	21
Mississippi	3,628	1.3	22
Missouri	5,523	1.0	12
Montana	2,325	2.7	35
Nebraska	1,891	1.2	36
Nevada	993	0.6	43
New Hampshire	640	0.6	46
New Jersey	3,260	0.4	24
New Mexico	2,799	1.7	29
New York	6,926	0.4	7
North Carolina	5,597	0.8	11
North Dakota	1,582	2.5	40
Ohio	8,447	0.8	4
Oklahoma	4,851	1.5	15
Oregon	2,923	0.9	28
Pennsylvania	7,528	0.6	5
Rhode Island	369	0.4	50
South Carolina	3,370	0.9	23
South Dakota	1,054	1.4	42
Tennessee	4,781	0.9	16
Texas	17,760	0.9	1
Utah	1,611	0.8	39
Vermont	422	0.7	48
Virginia	4,255	0.6	17
Washington	4,203	0.8	18
West Virginia	2,936	1.6	26
Wisconsin	3,795	0.7	20
Wyoming	1,613	3.4	38
50 States	197,521	0.8	
DC	174	0.3	
United States	197,698	0.8	

Rank in order

By total

1. Texas
2. California
3. Florida
4. Ohio
5. Pennsylvania
6. Illinois
7. New York
8. Georgia
9. Indiana
10. Michigan
11. North Carolina
12. Missouri
13. Louisiana
14. Alabama
15. Oklahoma
16. Tennessee
17. Virginia
18. Washington
19. Kentucky
20. Wisconsin
21. Minnesota
22. Mississippi
23. South Carolina
24. New Jersey
25. Kansas
26. West Virginia
27. Arizona
28. Oregon
29. New Mexico
30. Iowa
31. Colorado
32. Massachusetts
33. Maryland
34. Arkansas
35. Montana
36. Nebraska
37. Idaho
38. Wyoming
39. Utah
40. North Dakota
41. Connecticut
42. South Dakota
43. Nevada
44. Alaska
45. Maine
46. New Hampshire
47. Delaware
48. Vermont
49. Hawaii
50. Rhode Island

Source Notes for Geography (Section C)

C-1 Total Land Area, 1990: This statistic comes from the geography division of the Bureau of the Census and appears in various 1990 Census reports including the *Statistical Abstract of the United States*. It can be combined with population statistics to calculate the population "density" of each state (see Table A-16).

C-2 Land Owned by Federal Government, 1991: The federal government owns land for its buildings, military installations, and other facilities in every state, but these holdings are not major factors in the land use patterns of most states. The federal government also owns massive areas as part of the National Park Service and the Forest Service, and public lands managed by the U.S. Department of the Interior, primarily arid lands in Western states. These federal land holdings, measured in land area—not land usefulness—are more than half of the land in some states. The data are maintained by the individual federal agencies that own the land and the data appear in the *Statistical Abstract of the United States*.

C-3 State Park Acreage, FY 1995: These statistics show the acres of state parks and the number of acres of state parks per 1,000 people. The data are for the year ending June 30, 1995 and come from the National Association of State Park Directors (904-893-4959) by fax dated August, 28, 1997. The ratio was calculated by *State Fact Finder*.

C-4 State Park Visitors, FY 1995: State park agencies make estimates of the number of visitors to state parks maintained by the National Association of State Park Directors (See source for Table C-3). *State Fact Finder* related these visits to population using Census data. The data can be viewed as indicating that the average person visits a state park about 2.8 times a year.

C-5 Percent of Population Not Physically Active, 1994: There are few reliable data on a state level on the participation of citizens in various forms of recreational activities, as no one maintains records of who hikes, plays tennis, or fishes except when they use facilities requiring admission. These data from a survey of the Centers for Disease Control and Prevention appeared in the *Morbidity and Mortality Weekly Report* released August 8, 1996.

C-6 Hunters with Firearms, 1996: These data show the sharp differences among states in the use of firearms for hunting—statistics highly relevant to debates over use and control of firearms. Note that participants in hunting in a particular state may not be residents of that state. Estimates by state are made by the National Sporting Goods Association (Mt. Prospect, Illinois 60056) for all major recreation activities.

C-7 Registered Boats, 1996: All states require registration of motorboats and some require registration of other boats, such as canoes and sailboats. These data, collected from state authorities by the U.S. Coast Guard, show the number of registered boats and the relationship between the number of boats and population. The data come from the Consumer Affairs and Analysis Branch of the U.S. Coast Guard and were provided to *State Fact Finder* in a fax dated October 24, 1997.

C-8 State Spending for the Arts, FY 1997: The federal government subsidizes arts programs in the states and encourages states to do the same. This table measures state support in fiscal 1997 using data collected by the National Assembly of State Arts Agencies, as published in their report, *Legislative Appropriations Survey, Annual Survey, FY 97 Update*.

C-9 Energy Consumption Total and Per Capita, 1995: At the time of the "energy crisis" of the 1970s, the federal government established a Department of Energy (DOE) and a vast data collection mechanism covering production and consumption of all forms of energy, including coal, oil, gas, and nuclear power. This table from the Energy Information Administration (EIA) of the DOE shows total energy consumption and relates it to the population of each state.

These data show consumption by all users, including businesses, by the state where energy is used, not necessarily where it was produced. States with relatively small populations and intensive energy use for mining and petrochemical manufacturing show the largest use. The EIA has detailed data by state on sources of energy and use in categories, such as residential and industrial. For those users interested in comparisons over time, the 1995 as well as the 1994 data (which was published in the 1997 edition of *State Fact Finder)* are not comparable to previously released data for earlier years. As of the release of the 1994 data, the EIA has included renewable energy sources (wood and waste are examples) in energy consumption compilations. The EIA has revised 90-93 data to also include renewable energy. These numbers appear in the EIA's *State Energy Data Report 1994*. Data on 1995 energy consumption come from the EIA in a preliminary release provided especially to *State Fact Finder* in a fax dated December 8, 1997 and will be included in their *State Energy Data Report 1995* due in early 1998.

C-10 Toxic Chemical Release, 1995: The U.S. Environmental Protection Administration requires detailed reporting of what it defines as "toxic" chemical releases into the atmosphere. These data, from the *1995 Toxics Release Inventory*, are frequently cited by the media as indicators of health risks and air pollution in particular states. They are of little value for this purpose. The effects of releases in a particular state often are not felt in that state because they are carried to an adjacent state or the oceans. High totals are generally associated with a few plants, whose owners argue that their releases are not hazardous to health.

C-11 Hazardous Waste Sites, 1997: This table shows the number of sites the Environmental Protection Administration has designated for cleanup under the Superfund program. The program and the designations are highly controversial, but the data are often cited as indicators of the relative prevalence of hazardous waste problems in particular states. The data are from an April 1997 EPA publication, *Background Information: National Priorities List, Proposed Rule and Final Rule*.

C-12 Miles of Polluted Rivers and Streams, 1994: Under federal water pollution laws, each state reports to the Environmental Protection Agency on the status of its rivers, specifically whether they are safe for fishing (and eating the catch) and swimming. Because this assessment includes the total river-miles assessed and the number of miles not suitable for such uses, State Policy Research could make the arithmetic calculation of the percentage of river miles polluted, which is used to rank states in the table. The data come from the EPA's *National Water Quality Inventory: 1994 Report to Congress*. The report is updated every two years, the next release is due in December 1997.

This table and other available measures of the pollution of rivers are not particularly useful for many purposes. Any compilation of river-miles includes many stretches in remote locations that are of little use for swimming or fishing because of inaccessibility, low flows, few fish, and insufficient depth for swimming. There is no statistic that allows comparing states on a basis more reflective of the extent to which pollution prevents safe fishing and swimming in relation to the fishing and swimming that would occur if there were no pollution at all.

C-13 Surface Water Pollution Discharges, FY 1996: This statistic, prepared by the Environmental Protection Agency and compiled by the Corporation for Enterprise Development (Washington, DC) for its *1997 Development Report Card for the States*, provides a measure of pollution discharged into surface waters, such as lakes and streams, without compliance with established water quality standards. These numbers differ from previous years because the Corporation for Enterprise Development used single fourth quarter rather than annual statistics.

C-14 Air Pollution Emissions, 1995: Despite many years and millions of dollars put into efforts to measure air pollution on a state-by-state basis, no satisfactory way has been found to develop a summary measure. There are many problems. Air pollution affects people where they breathe, so for some purposes the relevant measure is what's in the ambient air but there is little interest in measuring air quality in places with few or no people like mountains and deserts. So, such measures focus on metropolitan areas, not states. Within each state, there are dramatic differences in pollution levels associated with such factors as proximity to prevailing winds and pollution sources and elevation.

Air pollution can only be controlled where it originates, so measurement related to enforcement concentrates on place of origin which is often not the same as the state where people are affected. Airborne pollutants don't recognize state lines, so the relevant concept is airsheds not states.

State Fact Finder developed this table primarily to lead users to the vast quantities of data available. The table reflects added estimates of short tons of pollution emissions in each state for five pollutants — carbon monoxide, nitrogen oxide, volatile organic compounds, sulfur dioxide, and particulate matter. The per capita calculation is provided only as a subject of possible interest. The ranking based on total tons of emissions is not a proxy for the seriousness of air pollution to the residents of the states listed and not a recognized measure of how effectively states control pollution.

The data on each pollutant by state and major causes (e.g., transportation, farming, utility operation) come from *National Air Pollutant Emission Trends, 1990-1995*. This publication from the EPA Office of Air Quality Planning and Standards also contains considerable other information useful to readers interested in comparing air pollution emissions of the various states.

Government

D-1 MEMBERS OF THE UNITED STATES HOUSE, 1998

State	House members #	Rank		By #
Alabama	7	21		1. California
Alaska	1	44		2. New York
Arizona	6	23		3. Texas
Arkansas	4	32		4. Florida
California	52	1		5. Pennsylvania
Colorado	6	23		6. Illinois
Connecticut	6	23		7. Ohio
Delaware	1	44		8. Michigan
Florida	23	4		9. New Jersey
Georgia	11	11		10. North Carolina
Hawaii	2	38		11. Georgia
Idaho	2	38		12. Virginia
Illinois	20	6		13. Indiana
Indiana	10	13		14. Massachusetts
Iowa	5	29		15. Missouri
Kansas	4	32		16. Tennessee
Kentucky	6	23		17. Washington
Louisiana	7	21		18. Wisconsin
Maine	2	38		19. Maryland
Maryland	8	19		20. Minnesota
Massachusetts	10	13		21. Alabama
Michigan	16	8		22. Louisiana
Minnesota	8	19		23. Arizona
Mississippi	5	29		24. Colorado
Missouri	9	15		25. Connecticut
Montana	1	44		26. Kentucky
Nebraska	3	34		27. Oklahoma
Nevada	2	38		28. South Carolina
New Hampshire	2	38		29. Iowa
New Jersey	13	9		30. Mississippi
New Mexico	3	34		31. Oregon
New York	31	2		32. Arkansas
North Carolina	12	10		33. Kansas
North Dakota	1	44		34. Nebraska
Ohio	19	7		35. New Mexico
Oklahoma	6	23		36. Utah
Oregon	5	29		37. West Virginia
Pennsylvania	21	5		38. Hawaii
Rhode Island	2	38		39. Idaho
South Carolina	6	23		40. Maine
South Dakota	1	44		41. Nevada
Tennessee	9	15		42. New Hampshire
Texas	30	3		43. Rhode Island
Utah	3	34		44. Alaska
Vermont	1	44		45. Delaware
Virginia	11	11		46. Montana
Washington	9	15		47. North Dakota
West Virginia	3	34		48. South Dakota
Wisconsin	9	15		49. Vermont
Wyoming	1	44		50. Wyoming
50 States	435			
DC	n/a			
United States	435			

State	Senate members	House members	Total members	Rank by total members		Rank in order By total
Alabama	35	105	140	28		1. New Hampshire
Alaska	20	40	60	49		2. Pennsylvania
Arizona	30	60	90	43		3. Georgia
Arkansas	35	100	135	31		4. New York
California	40	80	120	36		5. Minnesota
Colorado	35	65	100	42		6. Massachusetts
Connecticut	36	151	187	9		7. Missouri
Delaware	21	41	62	48		8. Maryland
Florida	40	120	160	18		9. Connecticut
Georgia	56	180	236	3		10. Maine
Hawaii	25	51	76	46		11. Texas
Idaho	35	70	105	39		12. Vermont
Illinois	59	118	177	13		13. Illinois
Indiana	50	100	150	19		14. Mississippi
Iowa	50	100	150	19		15. North Carolina
Kansas	40	125	165	17		15. South Carolina
Kentucky	38	100	138	30		17. Kansas
Louisiana	39	105	144	27		18. Florida
Maine	35	151	186	10		19. Indiana
Maryland	47	141	188	8		19. Iowa
Massachusetts	40	160	200	6		19. Montana
Michigan	38	110	148	24		19. Rhode Island
Minnesota	67	134	201	5		23. Oklahoma
Mississippi	52	122	174	14		24. Michigan
Missouri	34	163	197	7		25. North Dakota
Montana	50	100	150	19		25. Washington
Nebraska	49	n/a	49	50		27. Louisiana
Nevada	21	42	63	47		28. Alabama
New Hampshire	24	400	424	1		28. Virginia
New Jersey	40	80	120	36		30. Kentucky
New Mexico	42	70	112	38		31. Arkansas
New York	61	150	211	4		32. West Virginia
North Carolina	50	120	170	15		33. Ohio
North Dakota	49	98	147	25		33. Tennessee
Ohio	33	99	132	33		33. Wisconsin
Oklahoma	48	101	149	23		36. California
Oregon	30	60	90	43		36. New Jersey
Pennsylvania	50	203	253	2		38. New Mexico
Rhode Island	50	100	150	19		39. Idaho
South Carolina	46	124	170	15		40. South Dakota
South Dakota	35	70	105	40		41. Utah
Tennessee	33	99	132	33		42. Colorado
Texas	31	150	181	11		43. Arizona
Utah	29	75	104	41		43. Oregon
Vermont	30	150	180	12		43. Wyoming
Virginia	40	100	140	28		46. Hawaii
Washington	49	98	147	25		47. Nevada
West Virginia	34	100	134	32		48. Delaware
Wisconsin	33	99	132	33		49. Alaska
Wyoming	30	60	90	43		50. Nebraska
50 States	1,984	5,440	7,424			
DC	n/a	n/a	n/a			
United States	1,984	5,440	7,424			

D-3 LEGISLATORS PER MILLION POPULATION, 1998

State	Legislators per million population	Rank
Alabama	33	30
Alaska	99	9
Arizona	20	42
Arkansas	54	18
California	4	50
Colorado	26	35
Connecticut	57	17
Delaware	86	11
Florida	11	48
Georgia	32	31
Hawaii	64	14
Idaho	88	10
Illinois	15	45
Indiana	26	36
Iowa	53	19
Kansas	64	15
Kentucky	36	27
Louisiana	33	28
Maine	150	7
Maryland	37	25
Massachusetts	33	29
Michigan	15	43
Minnesota	43	23
Mississippi	64	16
Missouri	37	26
Montana	171	5
Nebraska	30	32
Nevada	39	24
New Hampshire	365	1
New Jersey	15	44
New Mexico	65	13
New York	12	47
North Carolina	23	39
North Dakota	228	3
Ohio	12	46
Oklahoma	45	22
Oregon	28	33
Pennsylvania	21	40
Rhode Island	151	6
South Carolina	46	21
South Dakota	143	8
Tennessee	25	38
Texas	9	49
Utah	52	20
Vermont	306	2
Virginia	21	41
Washington	27	34
West Virginia	73	12
Wisconsin	26	37
Wyoming	187	4
50 States	28	
DC	n/a	
United States	28	

By per million

1. New Hampshire
2. Vermont
3. North Dakota
4. Wyoming
5. Montana
6. Rhode Island
7. Maine
8. South Dakota
9. Alaska
10. Idaho
11. Delaware
12. West Virginia
13. New Mexico
14. Hawaii
15. Kansas
16. Mississippi
17. Connecticut
18. Arkansas
19. Iowa
20. Utah
21. South Carolina
22. Oklahoma
23. Minnesota
24. Nevada
25. Maryland
26. Missouri
27. Kentucky
28. Louisiana
29. Massachusetts
30. Alabama
31. Georgia
32. Nebraska
33. Oregon
34. Washington
35. Colorado
36. Indiana
37. Wisconsin
38. Tennessee
39. North Carolina
40. Pennsylvania
41. Virginia
42. Arizona
43. Michigan
44. New Jersey
45. Illinois
46. Ohio
47. New York
48. Florida
49. Texas
50. California

D-4 UNITS OF GOVERNMENT, 1992

State	Government units #	Units per 10,000 population	Rank per 10,000	By per 10,000
Alabama	1,122	2.7	32	1. North Dakota
Alaska	175	3.0	29	2. South Dakota
Arizona	591	1.5	41	3. Nebraska
Arkansas	1,447	6.0	13	4. Montana
California	4,393	1.4	42	5. Kansas
Colorado	1,761	5.1	18	6. Vermont
Connecticut	564	1.7	39	7. Wyoming
Delaware	276	4.0	22	8. Idaho
Florida	1,014	0.8	48	9. Minnesota
Georgia	1,298	1.9	36	10. Iowa
Hawaii	21	0.2	50	11. Maine
Idaho	1,087	10.2	8	12. Missouri
Illinois	6,723	5.8	14	13. Arkansas
Indiana	2,899	5.1	17	14. Illinois
Iowa	1,881	6.7	10	15. Oklahoma
Kansas	3,892	15.4	5	16. Wisconsin
Kentucky	1,321	3.5	24	17. Indiana
Louisiana	459	1.1	46	18. Colorado
Maine	797	6.5	11	19. Oregon
Maryland	402	0.8	47	20. New Hampshire
Massachusetts	844	1.4	43	21. Pennsylvania
Michigan	2,722	2.9	30	22. Delaware
Minnesota	3,580	8.0	9	23. West Virginia
Mississippi	870	3.3	27	24. Kentucky
Missouri	3,310	6.4	12	25. Utah
Montana	1,276	15.5	4	26. Washington
Nebraska	2,924	18.2	3	27. Mississippi
Nevada	208	1.6	40	28. Ohio
New Hampshire	528	4.8	20	29. Alaska
New Jersey	1,513	1.9	34	30. Michigan
New Mexico	342	2.2	33	31. Texas
New York	3,299	1.8	38	32. Alabama
North Carolina	938	1.4	44	33. New Mexico
North Dakota	2,765	43.5	1	34. New Jersey
Ohio	3,524	3.2	28	35. South Carolina
Oklahoma	1,795	5.6	15	36. Georgia
Oregon	1,451	4.9	19	37. Tennessee
Pennsylvania	5,159	4.3	21	38. New York
Rhode Island	126	1.3	45	39. Connecticut
South Carolina	698	1.9	35	40. Nevada
South Dakota	1,786	25.1	2	41. Arizona
Tennessee	924	1.8	37	42. California
Texas	4,792	2.7	31	43. Massachusetts
Utah	627	3.5	25	44. North Carolina
Vermont	682	12.0	6	45. Rhode Island
Virginia	455	0.7	49	46. Louisiana
Washington	1,761	3.4	26	47. Maryland
West Virginia	692	3.8	23	48. Florida
Wisconsin	2,739	5.5	16	49. Virginia
Wyoming	550	11.8	7	50. Hawaii
50 States	85,004	3.3		
DC	2			
United States	85,006			

State	Salary $	Per diem during session $	Rank by salary
Alabama	1,050	2,280/month	46
Alaska	24,012	168/day	18
Arizona	15,000	35/day	25
Arkansas	12,500	95/day	29
California	75,600	110/day	1
Colorado	17,500	45/day	21
Connecticut	16,760	0	23
Delaware	27,000	6,500/year	15
Florida	24,912	102/day	17
Georgia	11,348	59/day	33
Hawaii	32,000	80/day	10
Idaho	12,360	75/day	30
Illinois	47,039	82/day	5
Indiana	11,600	109/day	32
Iowa	20,120	86/day	19
Kansas	5,997	80/day	42
Kentucky	10,270	88/day	36
Louisiana	16,800	75/day	22
Maine	10,500	38/day	34
Maryland	29,700	116/day	12
Massachusetts	46,410	50/day	6
Michigan	51,895	8925/year	4
Minnesota	29,657	56/day	13
Mississippi	10,000	94/day	38
Missouri	26,803	35/day	16
Montana	58.5/day	70/day	n/a
Nebraska	12,000	30-83/day	31
Nevada	7,800	federal rate	40
New Hampshire	100	0	47
New Jersey	35,000	0	9
New Mexico	0	163/day	48
New York	57,500	89-130/day	2
North Carolina	13,951	104/day	27
North Dakota	111/day	900/month	n/a
Ohio	42,426	0	7
Oklahoma	32,000	35/day	10
Oregon	13,104	87/day	28
Pennsylvania	57,367	108/day	3
Rhode Island	10,250	0	37
South Carolina	10,400	88/day	35
South Dakota	4,267	75/day	44
Tennessee	16,500	120/day	24
Texas	7,200	95/day	41
Utah	4,500	35/day	43
Vermont	8,889	82/day	39
Virginia	18,000	102/day	20
Washington	28,800	79/day	14
West Virginia	15,000	85/day	25
Wisconsin	39,211	75/day	8
Wyoming	3,250	80/day	45
50 States	20,487		
DC	n/a		
United States	20,487		

Rank in order

By salary

1. California
2. New York
3. Pennsylvania
4. Michigan
5. Illinois
6. Massachusetts
7. Ohio
8. Wisconsin
9. New Jersey
10. Hawaii
10. Oklahoma
12. Maryland
13. Minnesota
14. Washington
15. Delaware
16. Missouri
17. Florida
18. Alaska
19. Iowa
20. Virginia
21. Colorado
22. Louisiana
23. Connecticut
24. Tennessee
25. Arizona
25. West Virginia
27. North Carolina
28. Oregon
29. Arkansas
30. Idaho
31. Nebraska
32. Indiana
33. Georgia
34. Maine
35. South Carolina
36. Kentucky
37. Rhode Island
38. Mississippi
39. Vermont
40. Nevada
41. Texas
42. Kansas
43. Utah
44. South Dakota
45. Wyoming
46. Alabama
47. New Hampshire
48. New Mexico

D-6 PERCENTAGE OF LEGISLATORS WHO ARE FEMALE, 1997

State	Percent of female legislators %	Rank	By %
Alabama	4.3	50	1. Washington
Alaska	13.3	43	2. Arizona
Arizona	37.8	2	3. Colorado
Arkansas	17.0	35	4. Nevada
California	22.5	24	5. Vermont
Colorado	35.0	3	6. New Hampshire
Connecticut	28.9	10	7. Minnesota
Delaware	25.8	15	8. Maryland
Florida	23.1	21	9. Kansas
Georgia	16.5	36	10. Connecticut
Hawaii	17.1	32	11. New Mexico
Idaho	23.8	18	12. Nebraska
Illinois	26.0	13	13. Illinois
Indiana	18.7	28	13. Rhode Island
Iowa	21.3	26	15. Delaware
Kansas	29.7	9	15. Maine
Kentucky	9.4	49	17. Oregon
Louisiana	11.1	47	18. Idaho
Maine	25.8	15	19. Wisconsin
Maryland	29.8	8	20. Montana
Massachusetts	23.0	22	21. Florida
Michigan	23.0	22	22. Massachusetts
Minnesota	30.3	7	22. Michigan
Mississippi	12.1	46	24. California
Missouri	21.3	26	25. Ohio
Montana	23.3	20	26. Iowa
Nebraska	26.5	12	26. Missouri
Nevada	33.3	4	28. Indiana
New Hampshire	30.9	6	29. New York
New Jersey	15.8	38	30. Texas
New Mexico	26.8	11	31. Wyoming
New York	18.5	29	32. Hawaii
North Carolina	17.1	32	32. North Carolina
North Dakota	16.3	37	32. South Dakota
Ohio	22.0	25	35. Arkansas
Oklahoma	10.1	48	36. Georgia
Oregon	25.6	17	37. North Dakota
Pennsylvania	12.3	45	38. New Jersey
Rhode Island	26.0	13	39. Utah
South Carolina	12.9	44	40. Virginia
South Dakota	17.1	32	41. West Virginia
Tennessee	13.6	42	42. Tennessee
Texas	18.2	30	43. Alaska
Utah	15.4	39	44. South Carolina
Vermont	32.2	5	45. Pennsylvania
Virginia	15.0	40	46. Mississippi
Washington	39.5	1	47. Louisiana
West Virginia	14.9	41	48. Oklahoma
Wisconsin	23.5	19	49. Kentucky
Wyoming	17.8	31	50. Alabama
50 States	n/a		
DC	n/a		
United States	21.5		

State	Percentage of new legislators %	Rank	By %
Alabama	0	49	1. Maine
Alaska	27	12	2. California
Arizona	34	4	3. South Dakota
Arkansas	20	23	4. Arizona
California	40	2	5. Oregon
Colorado	27	12	6. Idaho
Connecticut	11	46	6. Louisiana
Delaware	6	48	6. New Mexico
Florida	12	42	9. New Hampshire
Georgia	19	24	10. Kansas
Hawaii	17	30	10. Vermont
Idaho	31	6	12. Alaska
Illinois	15	38	12. Colorado
Indiana	15	38	12. Wyoming
Iowa	23	19	15. Kentucky
Kansas	28	10	15. Utah
Kentucky	25	15	15. West Virginia
Louisiana	31	6	18. Nevada
Maine	42	1	19. Iowa
Maryland	0	49	19. Washington
Massachusetts	18	26	21. South Carolina
Michigan	16	36	22. North Carolina
Minnesota	19	24	23. Arkansas
Mississippi	18	26	24. Georgia
Missouri	16	36	24. Minnesota
Montana	17	30	26. Massachusetts
Nebraska	12	42	26. Mississippi
Nevada	24	18	26. North Dakota
New Hampshire	30	9	26. Tennessee
New Jersey	17	30	30. Hawaii
New Mexico	31	6	30. Montana
New York	14	40	30. New Jersey
North Carolina	21	22	30. Ohio
North Dakota	18	26	30. Rhode Island
Ohio	17	30	30. Texas
Oklahoma	14	40	36. Michigan
Oregon	32	5	36. Missouri
Pennsylvania	12	42	38. Illinois
Rhode Island	17	30	38. Indiana
South Carolina	22	21	40. New York
South Dakota	36	3	40. Oklahoma
Tennessee	18	26	42. Florida
Texas	17	30	42. Nebraska
Utah	25	15	42. Pennsylvania
Vermont	28	10	42. Virginia
Virginia	12	42	46. Connecticut
Washington	23	19	46. Wisconsin
West Virginia	25	15	48. Delaware
Wisconsin	11	46	49. Alabama
Wyoming	27	12	49. Maryland
50 States	20		
DC	n/a		
United States	20		

State	Term limits Governor	Term limits House	Term limits Senate	Rank by House members		Rank in order By House
Alabama				n/a		1. Louisiana
Alaska				n/a		1. Nevada
Arizona	8	8	8	6		1. Oklahoma
Arkansas	8	6	8	16		1. Utah
California	8	6	8	16		1. Wyoming
Colorado		8	8	6		6. Arizona
Connecticut				n/a		6. Colorado
Delaware				n/a		6. Florida
Florida	8	8	8	6		6. Idaho
Georgia				n/a		6. Maine
Hawaii				n/a		6. Massachusetts
Idaho	8	8	8	6		6. Missouri
Illinois				n/a		6. Montana
Indiana				n/a		6. Ohio
Iowa				n/a		6. South Dakota
Kansas				n/a		16. Arkansas
Kentucky				n/a		16. California
Louisiana		12	12	1		16. Michigan
Maine	8	8	8	6		16. Oregon
Maryland				n/a		16. Washington
Massachusetts	8	8	8	6		
Michigan	8	6	8	16		
Minnesota				n/a		
Mississippi				n/a		
Missouri		8	8	6		
Montana	8	8	8	6		
Nebraska				n/a		
Nevada	8	12	12	1		
New Hampshire				n/a		
New Jersey				n/a		
New Mexico				n/a		
New York				n/a		
North Carolina				n/a		
North Dakota				n/a		
Ohio	8	8	8	6		
Oklahoma		12	12	1		
Oregon	8	6	8	16		
Pennsylvania				n/a		
Rhode Island				n/a		
South Carolina				n/a		
South Dakota	8	8	8	6		
Tennessee				n/a		
Texas				n/a		
Utah	12	12	12	1		
Vermont				n/a		
Virginia				n/a		
Washington	8	6	8	16		
West Virginia				n/a		
Wisconsin				n/a		
Wyoming	8	12	12	1		
50 States						
DC						
United States						

State	Legislative length in calendar days	Rank
Alabama	105.0	13
Alaska	120.0	9
Arizona	100.0	16
Arkansas	no regular session	n/a
California	239.0	2
Colorado	120.0	9
Connecticut	92.0	20
Delaware	169.0	4
Florida	60.0	29
Georgia	63.0	26
Hawaii	107.0	12
Idaho	72.0	25
Illinois	no limit	n/a
Indiana	63.0	26
Iowa	102.0	14
Kansas	90.0	21
Kentucky	100.0	16
Louisiana	45.0	34
Maine	99.0	18
Maryland	90.0	21
Massachusetts	no limit	n/a
Michigan	no limit	n/a
Minnesota	78.0	24
Mississippi	90.0	21
Missouri	129.0	7
Montana	no regular session	n/a
Nebraska	99.0	18
Nevada	no regular session	n/a
New Hampshire	138.0	6
New Jersey	no limit	n/a
New Mexico	31.0	36
New York	no limit	n/a
North Carolina	51.0	33
North Dakota	no regular session	n/a
Ohio	no limit	n/a
Oklahoma	117.0	11
Oregon	no regular session	n/a
Pennsylvania	329.0	1
Rhode Island	191.0	3
South Carolina	143.0	5
South Dakota	62.0	28
Tennessee	101.0	15
Texas	no regular session	n/a
Utah	45.0	34
Vermont	122.0	8
Virginia	60.0	29
Washington	60.0	29
West Virginia	60.0	29
Wisconsin	no limit	n/a
Wyoming	26.0	37
50 States	n/a	
DC	n/a	
United States	n/a	

By #

1. Pennsylvania
2. California
3. Rhode Island
4. Delaware
5. South Carolina
6. New Hampshire
7. Missouri
8. Vermont
9. Alaska
9. Colorado
11. Oklahoma
12. Hawaii
13. Alabama
14. Iowa
15. Tennessee
16. Arizona
16. Kentucky
18. Maine
18. Nebraska
20. Connecticut
21. Kansas
21. Maryland
21. Mississippi
24. Minnesota
25. Idaho
26. Georgia
26. Indiana
28. South Dakota
29. Florida
29. Virginia
29. Washington
29. West Virginia
33. North Carolina
34. Louisiana
34. Utah
36. New Mexico
37. Wyoming

D-10 PARTY CONTROL OF STATE LEGISLATURES, 1998

State	Number of Democrats in combined houses	Number of Republicans in combined houses	Legis-lative control	Percent of members Democratic	Rank by percent Democratic members
Alabama	92	48	D	65.7	10
Alaska	21	39	R	35.0	43
Arizona	34	56	R	37.8	40
Arkansas	113	21	D	83.7	1
California	65	53	D	54.2	19
Colorado	39	61	R	39.0	38
Connecticut	115	72	D	61.5	11
Delaware	26	36	S	41.9	36
Florida	72	88	R	45.0	33
Georgia	134	101	D	56.8	17
Hawaii	62	14	D	81.6	3
Idaho	16	89	R	15.2	49
Illinois	88	89	S	49.7	27
Indiana	69	81	S	46.0	30
Iowa	68	82	R	45.3	31
Kansas	61	104	R	37.0	41
Kentucky	84	54	D	60.9	12
Louisiana	102	42	D	70.8	6
Maine	99	84	D	53.2	22
Maryland	130	56	D	69.1	7
Massachusetts	163	36	D	81.5	4
Michigan	74	73	S	50.0	26
Minnesota	111	88	D	55.2	18
Mississippi	118	53	D	67.8	8
Missouri	105	91	D	53.3	21
Montana	51	99	R	34.0	44
Nebraska	n/a	n/a	Unicameral	n/a	n/a
Nevada	34	29	S	54.0	20
New Hampshire	155	262	R	36.6	42
New Jersey	47	73	R	39.2	37
New Mexico	67	45	D	59.8	14
New York	123	87	S	58.3	15
North Carolina	89	81	S	52.4	24
North Dakota	45	99	R	30.6	46
Ohio	51	81	R	38.6	39
Oklahoma	98	51	D	65.8	9
Oregon	39	51	R	43.3	35
Pennsylvania	119	133	R	47.0	29
Rhode Island	125	25	D	83.3	2
South Carolina	77	91	S	45.3	32
South Dakota	35	70	R	33.3	45
Tennessee	79	53	D	59.8	13
Texas	96	85	S	53.0	23
Utah	29	75	R	27.9	48
Vermont	104	71	D	57.8	16
Virginia	71	67	D	50.7	25
Washington	64	83	R	43.5	34
West Virginia	99	35	D	73.9	5
Wisconsin	64	67	S	48.5	28
Wyoming	26	64	R	28.9	47
50 States	3,848	3,488	21D, 18R, 10S	51.8	
DC	0	0	n/a	n/a	
United States	3,848	3,488	21D, 18R, 10S	51.8	

Rank in order

By %

1. Arkansas
2. Rhode Island
3. Hawaii
4. Massachusetts
5. West Virginia
6. Louisiana
7. Maryland
8. Mississippi
9. Oklahoma
10. Alabama
11. Connecticut
12. Kentucky
13. Tennessee
14. New Mexico
15. New York
16. Vermont
17. Georgia
18. Minnesota
19. California
20. Nevada
21. Missouri
22. Maine
23. Texas
24. North Carolina
25. Virginia
26. Michigan
27. Illinois
28. Wisconsin
29. Pennsylvania
30. Indiana
31. Iowa
32. South Carolina
33. Florida
34. Washington
35. Oregon
36. Delaware
37. New Jersey
38. Colorado
39. Ohio
40. Arizona
41. Kansas
42. New Hampshire
43. Alaska
44. Montana
45. South Dakota
46. North Dakota
47. Wyoming
48. Utah
49. Idaho

State	Rating	Rank
Alabama	2.8	42
Alaska	3.7	14
Arizona	3.4	26
Arkansas	3.4	26
California	3.2	32
Colorado	3.2	32
Connecticut	3.8	8
Delaware	3.3	28
Florida	3.3	28
Georgia	3.1	38
Hawaii	4.1	1
Idaho	3.7	14
Illinois	3.8	8
Indiana	2.8	42
Iowa	3.8	8
Kansas	3.7	14
Kentucky	3.5	24
Louisiana	2.7	45
Maine	3.1	38
Maryland	4.1	1
Massachusetts	3.2	32
Michigan	3.8	8
Minnesota	3.6	21
Mississippi	3.2	32
Missouri	3.6	21
Montana	3.5	24
Nebraska	3.7	14
Nevada	2.8	42
New Hampshire	3.2	32
New Jersey	4.0	5
New Mexico	3.2	32
New York	4.1	1
North Carolina	2.3	50
North Dakota	3.8	8
Ohio	4.0	5
Oklahoma	2.7	45
Oregon	3.3	28
Pennsylvania	4.1	1
Rhode Island	3.0	41
South Carolina	2.7	45
South Dakota	3.8	8
Tennessee	3.7	14
Texas	2.5	49
Utah	3.7	14
Vermont	2.6	48
Virginia	3.3	28
Washington	3.1	38
West Virginia	4.0	5
Wisconsin	3.7	14
Wyoming	3.6	21
50 States	n/a	
DC	n/a	
United States	3.4	

Rank in order

By rating

1. Hawaii
1. Maryland
1. New York
1. Pennsylvania
5. New Jersey
5. Ohio
5. West Virginia
8. Connecticut
8. Illinois
8. Iowa
8. Michigan
8. North Dakota
8. South Dakota
14. Alaska
14. Idaho
14. Kansas
14. Nebraska
14. Tennessee
14. Utah
14. Wisconsin
21. Minnesota
21. Missouri
21. Wyoming
24. Kentucky
24. Montana
26. Arizona
26. Arkansas
28. Delaware
28. Florida
28. Oregon
28. Virginia
32. California
32. Colorado
32. Massachusetts
32. Mississippi
32. New Hampshire
32. New Mexico
38. Georgia
38. Maine
38. Washington
41. Rhode Island
42. Alabama
42. Indiana
42. Nevada
45. Louisiana
45. Oklahoma
45. South Carolina
48. Vermont
49. Texas
50. North Carolina

D-12 NUMBER OF STATEWIDE ELECTED OFFICIALS, 1997

State	Elected officials	Rank
Alabama	7	13
Alaska	2	45
Arizona	5	30
Arkansas	5	30
California	8	7
Colorado	5	30
Connecticut	6	18
Delaware	6	18
Florida	8	7
Georgia	9	3
Hawaii	2	45
Idaho	8	7
Illinois	7	13
Indiana	8	7
Iowa	7	13
Kansas	6	18
Kentucky	6	18
Louisiana	8	7
Maine	1	48
Maryland	5	30
Massachusetts	6	18
Michigan	4	41
Minnesota	5	30
Mississippi	9	3
Missouri	5	30
Montana	5	30
Nebraska	5	30
Nevada	6	18
New Hampshire	1	48
New Jersey	1	48
New Mexico	6	18
New York	4	41
North Carolina	10	2
North Dakota	11	1
Ohio	6	18
Oklahoma	9	3
Oregon	6	18
Pennsylvania	5	30
Rhode Island	5	30
South Carolina	9	3
South Dakota	6	18
Tennessee	2	45
Texas	5	30
Utah	4	41
Vermont	7	13
Virginia	3	44
Washington	8	7
West Virginia	6	18
Wisconsin	6	18
Wyoming	7	13
50 States	n/a	
DC	n/a	
United States	n/a	

Rank in order

By

1. North Dakota
2. North Carolina
3. Georgia
3. Mississippi
3. Oklahoma
3. South Carolina
7. California
7. Florida
7. Idaho
7. Indiana
7. Louisiana
7. Washington
13. Alabama
13. Illinois
13. Iowa
13. Vermont
13. Wyoming
18. Connecticut
18. Delaware
18. Kansas
18. Kentucky
18. Massachusetts
18. Nevada
18. New Mexico
18. Ohio
18. Oregon
18. South Dakota
18. West Virginia
18. Wisconsin
30. Arizona
30. Arkansas
30. Colorado
30. Maryland
30. Minnesota
30. Missouri
30. Montana
30. Nebraska
30. Pennsylvania
30. Rhode Island
30. Texas
41. Michigan
41. New York
41. Utah
44. Virginia
45. Alaska
45. Hawaii
45. Tennessee
48. Maine
48. New Hampshire
48. New Jersey

D-13 STATE AND LOCAL GOVERNMENT EMPLOYEES, 1995

State	Government employees	Per 10,000 population	Rank by per 10,000
Alabama	246,118	580	17
Alaska	45,621	757	2
Arizona	218,806	508	39
Arkansas	138,019	555	22
California	1,479,629	469	49
Colorado	204,934	547	27
Connecticut	164,807	504	40
Delaware	41,279	576	19
Florida	708,937	500	42
Georgia	448,092	622	8
Hawaii	65,458	555	23
Idaho	67,090	575	20
Illinois	584,754	496	44
Indiana	305,747	527	32
Iowa	169,403	596	14
Kansas	166,097	648	4
Kentucky	206,035	534	30
Louisiana	263,576	608	10
Maine	66,441	536	28
Maryland	252,816	502	41
Massachusetts	301,600	497	43
Michigan	464,454	487	46
Minnesota	268,609	582	16
Mississippi	172,368	639	7
Missouri	271,522	510	37
Montana	56,316	647	5
Nebraska	105,876	646	6
Nevada	73,480	479	48
New Hampshire	55,268	481	47
New Jersey	437,174	550	24
New Mexico	110,699	655	3
New York	1,113,591	612	9
North Carolina	395,200	549	25
North Dakota	38,299	597	13
Ohio	567,185	509	38
Oklahoma	196,252	599	11
Oregon	166,089	527	31
Pennsylvania	521,411	432	50
Rhode Island	48,700	491	45
South Carolina	213,785	583	15
South Dakota	40,725	558	21
Tennessee	272,878	520	33
Texas	1,126,242	599	12
Utah	104,794	535	29
Vermont	33,874	579	18
Virginia	362,702	548	26
Washington	283,163	520	34
West Virginia	94,247	516	36
Wisconsin	265,601	519	35
Wyoming	37,937	792	1
50 States	14,043,700	535	
DC	46,831	845	
United States	14,090,531	536	

Rank in order

By per 10,000

1. Wyoming
2. Alaska
3. New Mexico
4. Kansas
5. Montana
6. Nebraska
7. Mississippi
8. Georgia
9. New York
10. Louisiana
11. Oklahoma
12. Texas
13. North Dakota
14. Iowa
15. South Carolina
16. Minnesota
17. Alabama
18. Vermont
19. Delaware
20. Idaho
21. South Dakota
22. Arkansas
23. Hawaii
24. New Jersey
25. North Carolina
26. Virginia
27. Colorado
28. Maine
29. Utah
30. Kentucky
31. Oregon
32. Indiana
33. Tennessee
34. Washington
35. Wisconsin
36. West Virginia
37. Missouri
38. Ohio
39. Arizona
40. Connecticut
41. Maryland
42. Florida
43. Massachusetts
44. Illinois
45. Rhode Island
46. Michigan
47. New Hampshire
48. Nevada
49. California
50. Pennsylvania

State	Average salary $	Rank	By $
Alabama	25,333	45	1. Alaska
Alaska	44,698	1	2. New Jersey
Arizona	30,189	21	3. California
Arkansas	23,398	49	4. New York
California	39,998	3	5. Connecticut
Colorado	32,007	18	6. Rhode Island
Connecticut	39,539	5	7. Washington
Delaware	31,897	20	8. Michigan
Florida	29,247	23	9. Maryland
Georgia	26,122	38	10. Nevada
Hawaii	32,136	17	11. Massachusetts
Idaho	26,077	39	12. Illinois
Illinois	34,076	12	13. Pennsylvania
Indiana	28,229	27	14. Wisconsin
Iowa	29,034	25	15. Oregon
Kansas	26,859	35	16. Minnesota
Kentucky	28,704	26	17. Hawaii
Louisiana	23,823	48	18. Colorado
Maine	28,003	29	19. Ohio
Maryland	35,131	9	20. Delaware
Massachusetts	34,378	11	21. Arizona
Michigan	36,351	8	22. New Hampshire
Minnesota	32,283	16	23. Florida
Mississippi	23,332	50	24. Virginia
Missouri	26,343	37	25. Iowa
Montana	27,265	33	26. Kentucky
Nebraska	27,299	32	27. Indiana
Nevada	34,649	10	28. Utah
New Hampshire	30,137	22	29. Maine
New Jersey	40,895	2	30. Vermont
New Mexico	25,792	43	31. North Carolina
New York	39,963	4	32. Nebraska
North Carolina	27,643	31	33. Montana
North Dakota	27,124	34	34. North Dakota
Ohio	31,951	19	35. Kansas
Oklahoma	24,120	47	36. Texas
Oregon	33,036	15	37. Missouri
Pennsylvania	34,076	13	38. Georgia
Rhode Island	36,951	6	39. Idaho
South Carolina	25,958	41	40. Tennessee
South Dakota	24,448	46	41. South Carolina
Tennessee	26,063	40	42. Wyoming
Texas	26,744	36	43. New Mexico
Utah	28,103	28	44. West Virginia
Vermont	27,817	30	45. Alabama
Virginia	29,198	24	46. South Dakota
Washington	36,668	7	47. Oklahoma
West Virginia	25,715	44	48. Louisiana
Wisconsin	33,642	14	49. Arkansas
Wyoming	25,914	42	50. Mississippi
50 States	32,091		
DC	40,395		
United States	32,118		

D-15 LOCAL EMPLOYMENT, 1995

State	Local employees #	Local share of state & local employees %	Rank by %
Alabama	165,125	67.1	33
Alaska	23,561	51.6	48
Arizona	160,643	73.4	9
Arkansas	90,429	65.5	36
California	1,141,207	77.1	1
Colorado	147,575	72.0	13
Connecticut	101,732	61.7	43
Delaware	19,268	46.7	49
Florida	534,220	75.4	6
Georgia	333,314	74.4	8
Hawaii	14,087	21.5	50
Idaho	46,220	68.9	26
Illinois	444,216	76.0	4
Indiana	217,188	71.0	18
Iowa	116,123	68.5	28
Kansas	118,165	71.1	17
Kentucky	132,577	64.3	39
Louisiana	170,733	64.8	38
Maine	45,109	67.9	32
Maryland	171,852	68.0	30
Massachusetts	219,838	72.9	11
Michigan	323,707	69.7	23
Minnesota	195,935	72.9	10
Mississippi	122,160	70.9	20
Missouri	192,220	70.8	22
Montana	38,238	67.9	31
Nebraska	76,267	72.0	12
Nevada	52,871	72.0	14
New Hampshire	38,415	69.5	24
New Jersey	312,168	71.4	15
New Mexico	68,271	61.7	44
New York	856,096	76.9	2
North Carolina	280,508	71.0	19
North Dakota	21,806	56.9	47
Ohio	424,605	74.9	7
Oklahoma	128,709	65.6	35
Oregon	113,946	68.6	27
Pennsylvania	369,461	70.9	21
Rhode Island	28,553	58.6	46
South Carolina	135,667	63.5	40
South Dakota	26,590	65.3	37
Tennessee	188,471	69.1	25
Texas	858,155	76.2	3
Utah	62,791	59.9	45
Vermont	21,244	62.7	42
Virginia	246,935	68.1	29
Washington	187,628	66.3	34
West Virginia	59,687	63.3	41
Wisconsin	201,123	75.7	5
Wyoming	27,074	71.4	16
50 States	10,072,483	71.7	
DC	46,831	100.0	
United States	10,119,314	71.8	

By %

1. California
2. New York
3. Texas
4. Illinois
5. Wisconsin
6. Florida
7. Ohio
8. Georgia
9. Arizona
10. Minnesota
11. Massachusetts
12. Nebraska
13. Colorado
14. Nevada
15. New Jersey
16. Wyoming
17. Kansas
18. Indiana
19. North Carolina
20. Mississippi
21. Pennsylvania
22. Missouri
23. Michigan
24. New Hampshire
25. Tennessee
26. Idaho
27. Oregon
28. Iowa
29. Virginia
30. Maryland
31. Montana
32. Maine
33. Alabama
34. Washington
35. Oklahoma
36. Arkansas
37. South Dakota
38. Louisiana
39. Kentucky
40. South Carolina
41. West Virginia
42. Vermont
43. Connecticut
44. New Mexico
45. Utah
46. Rhode Island
47. North Dakota
48. Alaska
49. Delaware
50. Hawaii

State	Local spending raised by local government %	Rank		Rank in order By %
Alabama	60.3	33		1. New Hampshire
Alaska	60.8	31		2. Vermont
Arizona	57.3	39		3. Georgia
Arkansas	53.7	47		4. Illinois
California	54.9	45		5. Florida
Colorado	64.4	27		6. Hawaii
Connecticut	67.9	13		7. Texas
Delaware	50.4	49		8. Maryland
Florida	73.1	5		9. South Dakota
Georgia	74.6	3		10. Nebraska
Hawaii	73.1	6		11. New Jersey
Idaho	59.9	34		12. Tennessee
Illinois	73.2	4		13. Connecticut
Indiana	65.0	26		14. Rhode Island
Iowa	65.0	24		15. New York
Kansas	65.1	22		16. Missouri
Kentucky	55.4	43		17. South Carolina
Louisiana	66.0	21		18. Maine
Maine	67.2	18		19. Massachusetts
Maryland	72.0	8		20. Michigan
Massachusetts	66.9	19		21. Louisiana
Michigan	66.5	20		22. Kansas
Minnesota	56.6	42		23. Pennsylvania
Mississippi	57.4	38		24. Iowa
Missouri	67.4	16		25. Virginia
Montana	54.5	46		26. Indiana
Nebraska	70.6	10		27. Colorado
Nevada	53.0	48		28. Ohio
New Hampshire	93.7	1		29. Oregon
New Jersey	69.4	11		30. Wyoming
New Mexico	46.1	50		31. Alaska
New York	67.7	15		32. Utah
North Carolina	57.2	40		33. Alabama
North Dakota	59.8	35		34. Idaho
Ohio	63.6	28		35. North Dakota
Oklahoma	58.8	37		36. Washington
Oregon	63.1	29		37. Oklahoma
Pennsylvania	65.1	23		38. Mississippi
Rhode Island	67.9	14		39. Arizona
South Carolina	67.3	17		40. North Carolina
South Dakota	70.8	9		41. Wisconsin
Tennessee	68.5	12		42. Minnesota
Texas	72.3	7		43. Kentucky
Utah	60.4	32		44. West Virginia
Vermont	74.9	2		45. California
Virginia	65.0	25		46. Montana
Washington	59.2	36		47. Arkansas
West Virginia	55.1	44		48. Nevada
Wisconsin	56.6	41		49. Delaware
Wyoming	61.5	30		50. New Mexico
50 States	64.5			
DC	66.9			
United States	64.5			

State	% registered voters	Rank
Alabama	77	20
Alaska	98	1
Arizona	72	34
Arkansas	73	33
California	62	45
Colorado	80	15
Connecticut	80	15
Delaware	77	20
Florida	75	29
Georgia	71	36
Hawaii	62	45
Idaho	76	23
Illinois	76	23
Indiana	80	15
Iowa	81	12
Kansas	76	23
Kentucky	82	8
Louisiana	81	12
Maine	n/a	n/a
Maryland	68	39
Massachusetts	76	23
Michigan	94	2
Minnesota	80	15
Mississippi	88	4
Missouri	84	7
Montana	91	3
Nebraska	85	6
Nevada	66	42
New Hampshire	82	8
New Jersey	72	34
New Mexico	69	37
New York	75	29
North Carolina	76	23
North Dakota	n/a	n/a
Ohio	82	8
Oklahoma	n/a	n/a
Oregon	82	8
Pennsylvania	74	32
Rhode Island	80	15
South Carolina	65	43
South Dakota	87	5
Tennessee	76	23
Texas	77	20
Utah	81	12
Vermont	n/a	n/a
Virginia	65	43
Washington	75	29
West Virginia	69	37
Wisconsin	68	39
Wyoming	68	39
50 States	n/a	
DC	83	
United States	n/a	

Rank in order

By %

1. Alaska
2. Michigan
3. Montana
4. Mississippi
5. South Dakota
6. Nebraska
7. Missouri
8. Kentucky
8. New Hampshire
8. Ohio
8. Oregon
12. Iowa
12. Louisiana
12. Utah
15. Colorado
15. Connecticut
15. Indiana
15. Minnesota
15. Rhode Island
20. Alabama
20. Delaware
20. Texas
23. Idaho
23. Illinois
23. Kansas
23. Massachusetts
23. North Carolina
23. Tennessee
29. Florida
29. New York
29. Washington
32. Pennsylvania
33. Arkansas
34. Arizona
34. New Jersey
36. Georgia
37. New Mexico
37. West Virginia
39. Maryland
39. Wisconsin
39. Wyoming
42. Nevada
43. South Carolina
43. Virginia
45. California
45. Hawaii

State	Percent voting %	Rank
Alabama	45.8	27
Alaska	59.1	6
Arizona	41.6	38
Arkansas	41.6	38
California	45.0	30
Colorado	46.4	23
Connecticut	51.3	14
Delaware	41.2	40
Florida	42.3	37
Georgia	35.4	47
Hawaii	46.0	26
Idaho	50.7	15
Illinois	42.8	35
Indiana	38.7	44
Iowa	52.5	11
Kansas	50.5	17
Kentucky	34.5	48
Louisiana	34.2	49
Maine	58.2	8
Maryland	46.2	25
Massachusetts	51.6	13
Michigan	52.2	12
Minnesota	58.4	7
Mississippi	44.3	32
Missouri	54.5	9
Montana	60.7	5
Nebraska	54.3	10
Nevada	40.1	43
New Hampshire	41.2	40
New Jersey	40.3	42
New Mexico	46.8	20
New York	44.6	31
North Carolina	35.7	46
North Dakota	61.1	3
Ohio	46.6	22
Oklahoma	46.8	20
Oregon	60.9	4
Pennsylvania	42.7	36
Rhode Island	50.6	16
South Carolina	45.2	29
South Dakota	63.9	1
Tennessee	43.0	34
Texas	37.6	45
Utah	44.1	33
Vermont	48.8	19
Virginia	45.7	28
Washington	46.3	24
West Virginia	33.9	50
Wisconsin	49.6	18
Wyoming	63.5	2
50 States	47.2	
DC	55.6	
United States	44.6	

Rank in order

By %

1. South Dakota
2. Wyoming
3. North Dakota
4. Oregon
5. Montana
6. Alaska
7. Minnesota
8. Maine
9. Missouri
10. Nebraska
11. Iowa
12. Michigan
13. Massachusetts
14. Connecticut
15. Idaho
16. Rhode Island
17. Kansas
18. Wisconsin
19. Vermont
20. New Mexico
20. Oklahoma
22. Ohio
23. Colorado
24. Washington
25. Maryland
26. Hawaii
27. Alabama
28. Virginia
29. South Carolina
30. California
31. New York
32. Mississippi
33. Utah
34. Tennessee
35. Illinois
36. Pennsylvania
37. Florida
38. Arizona
38. Arkansas
40. Delaware
40. New Hampshire
42. New Jersey
43. Nevada
44. Indiana
45. Texas
46. North Carolina
47. Georgia
48. Kentucky
49. Louisiana
50. West Virginia

State	Number of initiatives #	Initiatives approved by voters #	Rank by number of initiatives
Alabama	2	2	16
Alaska	0	n/a	n/a
Arizona	4	4	7
Arkansas	3	2	11
California	12	6	2
Colorado	8	4	3
Connecticut	0	n/a	n/a
Delaware	0	n/a	n/a
Florida	4	3	7
Georgia	0	n/a	n/a
Hawaii	0	n/a	n/a
Idaho	4	1	7
Illinois	0	n/a	n/a
Indiana	0	n/a	n/a
Iowa	0	n/a	n/a
Kansas	0	n/a	n/a
Kentucky	0	n/a	n/a
Louisiana	0	n/a	n/a
Maine	3	2	11
Maryland	0	n/a	n/a
Massachusetts	1	1	18
Michigan	3	1	11
Minnesota	0	n/a	n/a
Mississippi	0	n/a	n/a
Missouri	3	2	11
Montana	5	2	4
Nebraska	4	1	7
Nevada	5	4	4
New Hampshire	0	n/a	n/a
New Jersey	0	n/a	n/a
New Mexico	0	n/a	n/a
New York	0	n/a	n/a
North Carolina	0	n/a	n/a
North Dakota	3	1	11
Ohio	1	0	18
Oklahoma	0	n/a	n/a
Oregon	17	4	1
Pennsylvania	0	n/a	n/a
Rhode Island	0	n/a	n/a
South Carolina	0	n/a	n/a
South Dakota	1	1	18
Tennessee	0	n/a	n/a
Texas	0	n/a	n/a
Utah	0	n/a	n/a
Vermont	0	n/a	n/a
Virginia	0	n/a	n/a
Washington	5	1	4
West Virginia	0	n/a	n/a
Wisconsin	0	n/a	n/a
Wyoming	2	2	16
50 States	90	44	
DC	0	n/a	
United States	90	44	

Rank in order

By #

1. Oregon
2. California
3. Colorado
4. Montana
4. Nevada
4. Washington
7. Arizona
7. Florida
7. Idaho
7. Nebraska
11. Arkansas
11. Maine
11. Michigan
11. Missouri
11. North Dakota
16. Alabama
16. Wyoming
18. Massachusetts
18. Ohio
18. South Dakota

Source Notes for Government (Section D)

D-1 Members of the U.S. House, 1998: Each state is allocated two senators and representation in the House of Representatives based on population, as determined by the Census, which is taken in every year ending in zero (for example, 1990 and 2000). The data in the table list the number of House seats as of 1998. This allocation will prevail for the remainder of the decade.

D-2 Members of State Legislatures, 1998: Like the Congress, state legislatures—except Nebraska's one-House legislature—have an upper and lower house, generally called senates and assemblies. These data come from the organization of legislators nationwide, the National Conference of State Legislatures.

D-3 Legislators Per Million Population, 1998: Some small population states, like New Hampshire, have large legislatures. Some large states, like California, have relatively small ones. This table highlights the differences by relating the number of legislators (see Table D-2) to the most recent population estimates (see Table A-1).

D-4 Units of Government, 1992: There are more than 80,000 units of government in the United States, including counties, cities, towns, townships, school districts, and special districts that provide water, maintain sewage systems, build and maintain roads, control mosquitoes, and more. There are so many that they are only counted every five years in the Census Bureau's Census of Governments, the most recent of which was in 1992. The next official count will be for the year 1997. It is expected to be released by the Census sometime in 1998.

D-5 State Legislator Compensation, 1997: These data show the major sources of cash compensation of legislators, annual salaries and per diem amounts. The data are drawn from Table 1 of the National Conference of State Legislatures' extensive compilation *Compensation and Benefits for State Legislators*. Though this compilation is biannual, Table 1 concerning salaries and per diem is updated yearly. Two states, Montana and North Dakota are not included in the rankings because the payment rate is daily and there was no regularly scheduled session in 1997.

Comparisons of legislative pay from state-to-state are nearly impossible. Some states pay their legislators like most employers pay their employees—a regular salary plus reimbursement of employment-related travel expenses while on official business away from the normal place of work. In addition, because most legislators live in their districts, they are paid expenses when staying overnight in the state capitol. Some states compensate legislators at a per diem rate, often adding an expense allowance that can exceed expenses actually incurred. Additionally, some legislatures provide extra pay for committee chairpersons and legislative leaders.

Pensions for legislative service are nonexistent or negligible in some states, while pension and other benefits, such as employer-paid health care, are an important part of legislative compensation in other states.

D-6 Percentage of Legislators Who Are Female, 1997: The percentage of legislators who are women passed 20 percent in 1993 from less than 10 percent in the 1970s and less than 5 percent in the 1960s. The percentages for each state were calculated by the Center for the American Woman and Politics, Eagleton Institute of Politics, at Rutgers University. The Center provided the statistics to *State Fact Finder* in a fax dated October 24, 1997.

D-7 Turnover in Legislatures, 1994-1996: This table, from a fax dated December 2, 1996 from the National Conference of State Legislatures, shows the percentage of new state legislators taking office after the 1995 and 1996 elections. Nationwide about 80 percent of legislators in the 1997 sessions were in their second or subsequent terms. This percentage is likely to drop as limits on legislative terms take effect in an increasing number of states.

D-8 Term Limits, 1997: This table, from the National Conference of State Legislatures web page (http://www.ncsl.org), shows the maximum number of consecutive years governors and legislators can serve. The states shown with no limits allow elected officials to serve as long as voters approve. The states are ranked, with many ties, somewhat arbitrarily. Those with the longest allowable terms for members of their lower house are ranked highest.

D-9 Legislative Session Length, 1998: Many states have constitutional limits on the length of time the legislature meets in its regular sessions. Those shown in the table are calendar days (for example, a sixty-day limit would be about two months) Many of the states with short sessions exercise the option of having special sessions called by the legislative leadership or governor. These data are available on the web site of the National Conference of State Legislatures (see source for Table D-8).

It is difficult to compare the varying practices of the states. For instance, states listed as having no regular session in 1998 meet biannually, meeting in 1997 and 1999.

D-10 Party Control of State Legislatures, 1998: These data, developed by the National Conference of State Legislatures shortly after the 1997 election, show the party affiliation of legislators taking office in 1998. The states are ranked by the percentage of Democrats (reading top to bottom) or Republicans (bottom to top) in the combined legislative houses. S represents a split in party control.

D-11 Governor's Power Rating, 1997: This table presents the results of a special study by Dr. Thad Beyle of the University of North Carolina (Chapel Hill), published in *North Carolina Focus* published by the North Carolina Center For Public Policy Research, Inc. (Raleigh, NC). The ranking is based on six measures of power—tenure, appointment power, the number of other statewide elected officials, budget power, veto power, and party control.

D-12 Number of Statewide Elected Officials, 1997: The federal pattern of holding nationwide elections for only the chief executive and running mate (president and vice president) is not followed by the states. States often elect the attorneys general, secretaries of state, comptrollers, treasurers, and auditors. The count in the table, from the Council of State Governments *The Book of the States 1996-97*, excludes judges, who are also elected in many states. *The Book of the States* is a biannual publication. The 1998-1999 edition should be available by mid-year 1998.

D-13 State and Local Government Employees, 1995: These statistics, from the Census Bureau's count of public employees available on the Census web site (http://www.census.gov), express the full-time equivalent of part-time workers plus full-time workers in state and local governments and relate the totals to population.

D-14 Average Salaries of State and Local Government Employees, 1995: These statistics, from the same source as Table D-13, show annual average state and local government salaries, which were obtained by comparing compensation in October 1995 with employees in 1995 and multiplying by twelve.

D-15 Local Employment, 1995: The count of local employees identified is substantially larger than the number of state employees. The table shows the percentage of local employees. See Table D-13 for the source of these data.

D-16 Local Spending Accountability, FY 1994: Since 1970 there has been a massive growth in both federal and state aid to local governments. As a result, local officials finance over one-third of what they spend with money they do not raise by their own local taxes and fees. Critics say this encourages government spending to be excessive because the elected officials who spend the money do not have to account to taxpayers for raising it. The Wisconsin Taxpayers Association has dubbed this difference "the accountability gap." The table shows a measure of this gap, as calculated by State Policy Research using data from the Census Bureau (See Source Note to Table F-1 for important details).

The numbers reflect the percentage of their spending local officials raised. New Hampshire ranks first by this measure because it has uniquely low state taxes (with no state sales or income tax) and only minor state aid programs by comparison with other states.

D-17 Percent of Eligible Voters Registered, November 1996: These statistics, dated November 1, 1996 reflect pre-election counts. They were furnished to *State Fact Finder* by the National Association of State Election Directors in a fax dated November 4, 1996. These data show the percentage of persons presumably eligible to vote in each state, based on the voting age population in relation to the number who have complied with that state's requirements to vote (that is, becoming and staying registered as voters). State-by-state data on 1997 registered voters will become available sometime in 1998.

D-18 Percent of Population Voting in November 1994: Not all persons legally old enough to vote actually do so. The table shows the percentage who actually voted in the elections of November 1994. It comes from a Census Bureau tabulation available on the Internet (http://www.census.gov).

D-19 Statewide Initiatives, 1996: In most states, voters select candidates to make policy for them as legislators but never vote directly on policy except when changes in the state constitution are being made. Some states allow "direct democracy," including allowing voters to put up a measure for popular vote by collecting a minimum number of signatures (voter initiatives). This tabulation shows the number of such initiatives on state ballots in 1996. The numbers reflect (1) whether initiatives are permitted in the state; (2) the difficulty of putting measures on the ballot, as affected by the number for signatures required and other factors in the constitutions of each state; and (3) voter interest in making state policy by this direct democracy approach. These statistics were compiled by the Public Affairs Research Institute of New Jersey, Inc. in Princeton, New Jersey.

Federal Impacts

State	Total federal spending $(millions)	Per capita federal spending $	Rank by per capita	By per capita
Alabama	23,409	5,478	14	1. Virginia
Alaska	4,341	7,151	3	2. Maryland
Arizona	21,819	4,927	29	3. Alaska
Arkansas	12,076	4,811	30	4. New Mexico
California	157,446	4,939	28	5. Hawaii
Colorado	20,009	5,234	20	6. Missouri
Connecticut	17,915	5,472	16	7. Massachusetts
Delaware	3,363	4,639	36	8. Rhode Island
Florida	79,166	5,498	13	9. Montana
Georgia	34,731	4,723	33	10. Mississippi
Hawaii	8,016	6,771	5	11. North Dakota
Idaho	5,476	4,606	38	12. West Virginia
Illinois	51,229	4,324	44	13. Florida
Indiana	24,215	4,146	46	14. Alabama
Iowa	13,408	4,701	35	15. Maine
Kansas	12,347	4,800	32	16. Connecticut
Kentucky	19,618	5,051	26	17. Pennsylvania
Louisiana	22,117	5,083	24	18. South Dakota
Maine	6,808	5,477	15	19. Washington
Maryland	37,040	7,303	2	20. Colorado
Massachusetts	36,456	5,984	7	21. Wyoming
Michigan	39,286	4,095	48	22. New York
Minnesota	18,857	4,048	49	23. Tennessee
Mississippi	15,184	5,591	10	24. Louisiana
Missouri	35,094	6,549	6	25. Oklahoma
Montana	4,973	5,658	9	26. Kentucky
Nebraska	7,595	4,598	39	27. South Carolina
Nevada	7,428	4,634	37	28. California
New Hampshire	5,001	4,304	45	29. Arizona
New Jersey	38,346	4,800	31	30. Arkansas
New Mexico	12,073	7,048	4	31. New Jersey
New York	94,667	5,206	22	32. Kansas
North Carolina	32,771	4,475	42	33. Georgia
North Dakota	3,570	5,544	11	34. Vermont
Ohio	50,143	4,488	41	35. Iowa
Oklahoma	16,685	5,055	25	36. Delaware
Oregon	14,173	4,423	43	37. Nevada
Pennsylvania	64,166	5,322	17	38. Idaho
Rhode Island	5,658	5,715	8	39. Nebraska
South Carolina	18,401	4,975	27	40. Texas
South Dakota	3,872	5,290	18	41. Ohio
Tennessee	27,557	5,180	23	42. North Carolina
Texas	86,493	4,522	40	43. Oregon
Utah	8,193	4,097	47	44. Illinois
Vermont	2,775	4,711	34	45. New Hampshire
Virginia	50,301	7,536	1	46. Indiana
Washington	29,246	5,286	19	47. Utah
West Virginia	10,059	5,509	12	48. Michigan
Wisconsin	19,958	3,868	50	49. Minnesota
Wyoming	2,515	5,228	21	50. Wisconsin
50 States	1,336,045	5,047		
DC	22,475	41,391		
United States	1,394,057	5,180		

E-2 INCREASE IN TOTAL FEDERAL SPENDING, FY 1991-1996

State	Total federal spending FY 1991 $(millions)	% increase in federal spending %	Rank by %	Rank in order By %
Alabama	18,464	26.8	29	1. Nevada
Alaska	3,655	18.8	44	2. Georgia
Arizona	15,491	40.8	5	3. Vermont
Arkansas	9,053	33.4	14	4. North Carolina
California	127,684	23.3	36	5. Arizona
Colorado	16,474	21.5	42	6. Florida
Connecticut	16,460	8.8	50	7. Delaware
Delaware	2,435	38.1	7	8. Louisiana
Florida	56,276	40.7	6	9. Washington
Georgia	23,739	46.3	2	10. Oregon
Hawaii	6,162	30.1	19	11. Mississippi
Idaho	4,287	27.7	28	12. West Virginia
Illinois	40,767	25.7	30	13. Texas
Indiana	18,806	28.8	26	14. Arkansas
Iowa	10,306	30.1	18	15. Missouri
Kansas	10,519	17.4	46	16. Montana
Kentucky	15,231	28.8	25	17. Tennessee
Louisiana	16,270	35.9	8	18. Iowa
Maine	5,601	21.5	41	19. Hawaii
Maryland	29,507	25.5	31	20. Virginia
Massachusetts	31,449	15.9	47	21. Pennsylvania
Michigan	31,565	24.5	33	22. New Mexico
Minnesota	16,366	15.2	48	23. New Hampshire
Mississippi	11,240	35.1	11	24. Wyoming
Missouri	26,410	32.9	15	25. Kentucky
Montana	3,743	32.9	16	26. Indiana
Nebraska	6,419	18.3	45	27. Oklahoma
Nevada	4,922	50.9	1	28. Idaho
New Hampshire	3,874	29.1	23	29. Alabama
New Jersey	30,862	24.2	34	30. Illinois
New Mexico	9,338	29.3	22	31. Maryland
New York	76,790	23.3	37	32. South Dakota
North Carolina	23,243	41.0	4	33. Michigan
North Dakota	3,253	9.7	49	34. New Jersey
Ohio	41,414	21.1	43	35. South Carolina
Oklahoma	12,973	28.6	27	36. California
Oregon	10,457	35.5	10	37. New York
Pennsylvania	49,463	29.7	21	38. Rhode Island
Rhode Island	4,604	22.9	38	39. Wisconsin
South Carolina	14,907	23.4	35	40. Utah
South Dakota	3,106	24.7	32	41. Maine
Tennessee	20,890	31.9	17	42. Colorado
Texas	64,472	34.2	13	43. Ohio
Utah	6,694	22.4	40	44. Alaska
Vermont	1,930	43.8	3	45. Nebraska
Virginia	38,674	30.1	20	46. Kansas
Washington	21,529	35.8	9	47. Massachusetts
West Virginia	7,465	34.7	12	48. Minnesota
Wisconsin	16,246	22.8	39	49. North Dakota
Wyoming	1,951	28.9	24	50. Connecticut
50 States	1,043,436	28.0		
DC	19,105	17.6		
United States	1,096,493	27.1		

E-3 FEDERAL SPENDING ON GRANTS, TOTAL AND PER CAPITA, FY 1996

State	Federal grants to state & local government $(millions)	Per capita federal grants to state & local government $	Rank by per capita	By per capita
Alabama	3,325	778	28	1. Alaska
Alaska	1,051	1,731	1	2. Wyoming
Arizona	3,095	699	42	3. New York
Arkansas	2,131	849	19	4. Rhode Island
California	26,413	829	22	5. South Dakota
Colorado	2,410	630	46	6. West Virginia
Connecticut	3,080	941	16	7. North Dakota
Delaware	600	828	23	8. New Mexico
Florida	8,442	586	48	9. Massachusetts
Georgia	5,359	729	37	10. Maine
Hawaii	1,126	951	15	11. Montana
Idaho	887	746	34	12. Louisiana
Illinois	9,229	779	27	13. Vermont
Indiana	3,657	626	47	14. Mississippi
Iowa	2,030	712	41	15. Hawaii
Kansas	1,700	661	45	16. Connecticut
Kentucky	3,355	864	18	17. Oregon
Louisiana	4,734	1,088	12	18. Kentucky
Maine	1,389	1,117	10	19. Arkansas
Maryland	3,544	699	43	20. Tennessee
Massachusetts	6,813	1,118	9	21. Pennsylvania
Michigan	7,194	750	33	22. California
Minnesota	3,535	759	31	23. Delaware
Mississippi	2,754	1,014	14	24. South Carolina
Missouri	4,091	763	30	25. New Jersey
Montana	964	1,097	11	26. Ohio
Nebraska	1,232	746	35	27. Illinois
Nevada	876	547	49	28. Alabama
New Hampshire	890	766	29	29. New Hampshire
New Jersey	6,506	814	25	30. Missouri
New Mexico	1,942	1,134	8	31. Minnesota
New York	24,560	1,351	3	32. Washington
North Carolina	5,227	714	39	33. Michigan
North Dakota	734	1,140	7	34. Idaho
Ohio	8,776	785	26	35. Nebraska
Oklahoma	2,435	738	36	36. Oklahoma
Oregon	2,797	873	17	37. Georgia
Pennsylvania	10,117	839	21	38. Utah
Rhode Island	1,176	1,188	4	39. North Carolina
South Carolina	3,032	820	24	40. Wisconsin
South Dakota	867	1,184	5	41. Iowa
Tennessee	4,476	841	20	42. Arizona
Texas	13,297	695	44	43. Maryland
Utah	1,446	723	38	44. Texas
Vermont	641	1,088	13	45. Kansas
Virginia	3,403	510	50	46. Colorado
Washington	4,152	750	32	47. Indiana
West Virginia	2,088	1,144	6	48. Florida
Wisconsin	3,679	713	40	49. Nevada
Wyoming	708	1,473	2	50. Virginia
50 States	217,965	823		
DC	2,578	4,747		
United States	227,542	845		

E-4 FEDERAL SPENDING ON PROCUREMENT, TOTAL AND PER CAPITA, FY 1996

State	Total spending on procurement $(millions)	Per capita procurement spending $	Rank by per capita	By per capita
Alabama	2,937	687	19	1. Virginia
Alaska	804	1,324	5	2. New Mexico
Arizona	3,485	787	16	3. Missouri
Arkansas	453	180	50	4. Maryland
California	27,724	870	10	5. Alaska
Colorado	4,656	1,218	6	6. Colorado
Connecticut	3,123	954	8	7. Massachusetts
Delaware	154	212	48	8. Connecticut
Florida	8,126	564	23	9. Nevada
Georgia	4,741	645	21	10. California
Hawaii	1,027	868	11	11. Hawaii
Idaho	945	795	15	12. Mississippi
Illinois	3,165	267	45	13. Washington
Indiana	2,090	358	34	14. Tennessee
Iowa	778	273	44	15. Idaho
Kansas	1,110	431	30	16. Arizona
Kentucky	2,005	516	25	17. Maine
Louisiana	2,086	480	27	18. Texas
Maine	907	730	17	19. Alabama
Maryland	8,522	1,680	4	20. South Carolina
Massachusetts	6,081	998	7	21. Georgia
Michigan	2,189	228	46	22. New Hampshire
Minnesota	1,535	329	38	23. Florida
Mississippi	2,326	856	12	24. Utah
Missouri	10,594	1,977	3	25. Kentucky
Montana	263	299	42	26. Vermont
Nebraska	585	354	35	27. Louisiana
Nevada	1,407	878	9	28. New Jersey
New Hampshire	672	578	22	29. Pennsylvania
New Jersey	3,750	470	28	30. Kansas
New Mexico	3,676	2,146	2	31. Rhode Island
New York	6,320	348	36	32. Ohio
North Carolina	2,293	313	41	33. Oklahoma
North Dakota	210	326	39	34. Indiana
Ohio	4,583	410	32	35. Nebraska
Oklahoma	1,205	365	33	36. New York
Oregon	610	191	49	37. South Dakota
Pennsylvania	5,531	459	29	38. Minnesota
Rhode Island	423	427	31	39. North Dakota
South Carolina	2,505	677	20	40. Wyoming
South Dakota	249	340	37	41. North Carolina
Tennessee	4,317	812	14	42. Montana
Texas	13,840	724	18	43. West Virginia
Utah	1,072	536	24	44. Iowa
Vermont	295	501	26	45. Illinois
Virginia	14,529	2,177	1	46. Michigan
Washington	4,603	832	13	47. Wisconsin
West Virginia	514	281	43	48. Delaware
Wisconsin	1,162	225	47	49. Oregon
Wyoming	153	318	40	50. Arkansas
50 States	176,330	666		
DC	4,580	8,434		
United States	200,543	745		

State	Total federal payment to individuals $(millions)	Per capita federal payments to individuals $	Rank by per capita	Rank in order By per capita
Alabama	13,616	3,187	5	1. Florida
Alaska	1,021	1,682	50	2. West Virginia
Arizona	12,269	2,771	23	3. Pennsylvania
Arkansas	7,984	3,181	6	4. Rhode Island
California	80,432	2,523	39	5. Alabama
Colorado	8,814	2,305	47	6. Arkansas
Connecticut	9,692	2,960	12	7. Massachusetts
Delaware	2,096	2,892	17	8. Mississippi
Florida	53,349	3,705	1	9. Oklahoma
Georgia	17,933	2,439	44	10. New Jersey
Hawaii	3,238	2,734	27	11. New York
Idaho	2,865	2,410	45	12. Connecticut
Illinois	31,744	2,679	32	13. Maine
Indiana	15,096	2,585	36	14. Missouri
Iowa	7,687	2,695	29	15. Tennessee
Kansas	7,054	2,742	26	16. Kentucky
Kentucky	11,289	2,907	16	17. Delaware
Louisiana	12,575	2,890	18	18. Louisiana
Maine	3,654	2,940	13	19. Maryland
Maryland	14,491	2,857	19	20. South Carolina
Massachusetts	18,731	3,075	7	21. Ohio
Michigan	26,183	2,729	28	22. Virginia
Minnesota	10,694	2,296	48	23. Arizona
Mississippi	8,191	3,016	8	24. Montana
Missouri	15,667	2,924	14	25. Oregon
Montana	2,416	2,748	24	26. Kansas
Nebraska	4,216	2,552	38	27. Hawaii
Nevada	4,201	2,621	34	28. Michigan
New Hampshire	2,842	2,446	43	29. Iowa
New Jersey	23,889	2,991	10	30. South Dakota
New Mexico	4,429	2,586	35	31. Washington
New York	54,035	2,971	11	32. Illinois
North Carolina	19,453	2,656	33	33. North Carolina
North Dakota	1,656	2,572	37	34. Nevada
Ohio	31,166	2,789	21	35. New Mexico
Oklahoma	9,880	2,993	9	36. Indiana
Oregon	8,798	2,746	25	37. North Dakota
Pennsylvania	40,973	3,399	3	38. Nebraska
Rhode Island	3,266	3,299	4	39. California
South Carolina	10,336	2,794	20	40. Vermont
South Dakota	1,971	2,693	30	41. Wisconsin
Tennessee	15,497	2,913	15	42. Wyoming
Texas	45,723	2,390	46	43. New Hampshire
Utah	3,919	1,959	49	44. Georgia
Vermont	1,485	2,522	40	45. Idaho
Virginia	18,562	2,781	22	46. Texas
Washington	14,838	2,682	31	47. Colorado
West Virginia	6,407	3,509	2	48. Minnesota
Wisconsin	12,925	2,505	41	49. Utah
Wyoming	1,195	2,483	42	50. Alaska
50 States	740,443	2,797		
DC	2,596	4,781		
United States	749,273	859		

E-6 FEDERAL SPENDING ON SOCIAL SECURITY AND MEDICARE, FY 1996

State	Total Social Security and Medicare spending $(millions)	Per capita spending $	Rank by per capita
Alabama	9,228	2,160	12
Alaska	500	823	50
Arizona	8,677	1,960	26
Arkansas	5,566	2,218	9
California	54,757	1,718	40
Colorado	5,851	1,531	48
Connecticut	7,810	2,385	5
Delaware	1,510	2,083	16
Florida	39,881	2,770	1
Georgia	12,076	1,642	42
Hawaii	1,918	1,621	45
Idaho	1,946	1,637	43
Illinois	24,127	2,037	23
Indiana	12,019	2,058	20
Iowa	6,140	2,153	13
Kansas	5,308	2,064	18
Kentucky	7,951	2,047	22
Louisiana	8,959	2,059	19
Maine	2,551	2,052	21
Maryland	9,094	1,793	36
Massachusetts	14,403	2,364	6
Michigan	20,875	2,176	11
Minnesota	8,177	1,755	38
Mississippi	5,449	2,006	24
Missouri	11,858	2,213	10
Montana	1,665	1,893	32
Nebraska	3,134	1,897	30
Nevada	2,864	1,787	37
New Hampshire	2,156	1,855	35
New Jersey	18,253	2,285	7
New Mexico	2,712	1,583	47
New York	40,997	2,254	8
North Carolina	13,881	1,896	31
North Dakota	1,241	1,929	28
Ohio	23,694	2,121	14
Oklahoma	6,823	2,067	17
Oregon	6,251	1,951	27
Pennsylvania	31,430	2,607	2
Rhode Island	2,385	2,409	4
South Carolina	6,980	1,887	33
South Dakota	1,406	1,920	29
Tennessee	11,118	2,090	15
Texas	30,709	1,605	46
Utah	2,512	1,256	49
Vermont	1,104	1,876	34
Virginia	10,916	1,635	44
Washington	9,585	1,732	39
West Virginia	4,524	2,478	3
Wisconsin	10,278	1,992	25
Wyoming	820	1,703	41
50 States	534,072	2,017	
DC	1,084	1,995	
United States	539,473	2,034	

Rank in order

By per capita

1. Florida
2. Pennsylvania
3. West Virginia
4. Rhode Island
5. Connecticut
6. Massachusetts
7. New Jersey
8. New York
9. Arkansas
10. Missouri
11. Michigan
12. Alabama
13. Iowa
14. Ohio
15. Tennessee
16. Delaware
17. Oklahoma
18. Kansas
19. Louisiana
20. Indiana
21. Maine
22. Kentucky
23. Illinois
24. Mississippi
25. Wisconsin
26. Arizona
27. Oregon
28. North Dakota
29. South Dakota
30. Nebraska
31. North Carolina
32. Montana
33. South Carolina
34. Vermont
35. New Hampshire
36. Maryland
37. Nevada
38. Minnesota
39. Washington
40. California
41. Wyoming
42. Georgia
43. Idaho
44. Virginia
45. Hawaii
46. Texas
47. New Mexico
48. Colorado
49. Utah
50. Alaska

State	Social Security amounts paid $(000)	Number of recipients (000)	SS average monthly benefit $	Rank by average benefit	Rank in order By $
Alabama	458,190	776	591	45	1. Connecticut
Alaska	27,500	45	618	37	2. New Jersey
Arizona	465,250	703	662	19	3. New York
Arkansas	292,450	503	581	48	4. Michigan
California	2,643,080	3,984	664	18	5. Illinois
Colorado	312,870	495	632	31	6. Delaware
Connecticut	413,090	566	729	1	7. Washington
Delaware	83,190	122	684	6	8. Pennsylvania
Florida	1,975,670	2,984	662	20	9. Indiana
Georgia	609,800	1,010	604	42	10. Wisconsin
Hawaii	107,600	166	648	24	11. Nevada
Idaho	112,900	178	635	30	12. Kansas
Illinois	1,267,510	1,829	693	5	13. Oregon
Indiana	654,980	962	681	9	14. New Hampshire
Iowa	353,930	540	656	22	15. Massachusetts
Kansas	290,820	434	670	12	16. Rhode Island
Kentucky	416,850	712	586	47	17. Ohio
Louisiana	404,990	702	577	49	18. California
Maine	142,570	237	601	43	19. Arizona
Maryland	449,350	679	662	21	20. Florida
Massachusetts	698,640	1,049	666	15	21. Maryland
Michigan	1,108,320	1,594	695	4	22. Iowa
Minnesota	461,280	713	647	25	23. Wyoming
Mississippi	271,830	495	550	50	24. Hawaii
Missouri	617,780	968	638	28	25. Minnesota
Montana	95,210	152	628	32	26. Nebraska
Nebraska	182,090	282	647	26	27. Utah
Nevada	153,970	229	673	11	28. Missouri
New Hampshire	124,260	186	667	14	29. Vermont
New Jersey	954,760	1,310	729	2	30. Idaho
New Mexico	151,430	258	586	46	31. Colorado
New York	2,078,100	2,972	699	3	32. Montana
North Carolina	758,050	1,232	615	38	33. West Virginia
North Dakota	70,090	116	607	40	34. Virginia
Ohio	1,270,580	1,913	664	17	35. Texas
Oklahoma	355,830	575	619	36	36. Oklahoma
Oregon	364,280	544	669	13	37. Alaska
Pennsylvania	1,591,710	2,332	682	8	38. North Carolina
Rhode Island	126,420	190	666	16	39. South Carolina
South Carolina	380,170	625	608	39	40. North Dakota
South Dakota	80,640	136	595	44	41. Tennessee
Tennessee	559,520	926	604	41	42. Georgia
Texas	1,526,700	2,461	620	35	43. Maine
Utah	144,370	224	643	27	44. South Dakota
Vermont	62,700	98	637	29	45. Alabama
Virginia	591,550	949	623	34	46. New Mexico
Washington	541,270	793	682	7	47. Kentucky
West Virginia	239,600	384	623	33	48. Arkansas
Wisconsin	595,600	884	674	10	49. Louisiana
Wyoming	46,550	71	653	23	50. Mississippi
50 States	27,685,890	42,285	655		
DC	44,370	78	565		
United States	28,143,360	43,380	649		

E-7 SOCIAL SECURITY BENEFITS PAID, 1995

State	Total federal spending on wages & salaries $(millions)	Per capita spending on wages & salaries $	Rank by per capita		Rank in order By per capita
Alabama	2,898	678	15		1. Alaska
Alaska	1,327	2,187	1		2. Hawaii
Arizona	2,523	570	26		3. Virginia
Arkansas	1,037	413	42		4. Maryland
California	18,038	566	28		5. North Dakota
Colorado	3,235	846	7		6. New Mexico
Connecticut	1,418	433	41		7. Colorado
Delaware	411	567	27		8. Washington
Florida	7,660	532	29		9. Oklahoma
Georgia	5,904	803	11		10. Wyoming
Hawaii	2,409	2,034	2		11. Georgia
Idaho	630	530	31		12. Utah
Illinois	5,440	459	36		13. South Dakota
Indiana	1,970	337	47		14. Montana
Iowa	944	331	48		15. Alabama
Kansas	1,700	661	17		16. North Carolina
Kentucky	2,442	629	19		17. Kansas
Louisiana	2,084	479	33		18. Rhode Island
Maine	722	581	24		19. Kentucky
Maryland	7,324	1,444	4		20. Nebraska
Massachusetts	2,857	469	34		21. South Carolina
Michigan	2,778	290	49		22. Missouri
Minnesota	1,655	355	46		23. Texas
Mississippi	1,571	579	25		24. Maine
Missouri	3,185	594	22		25. Mississippi
Montana	632	719	14		26. Arizona
Nebraska	1,031	624	20		27. Delaware
Nevada	850	530	30		28. California
New Hampshire	448	386	45		29. Florida
New Jersey	3,556	445	39		30. Nevada
New Mexico	1,686	984	6		31. Idaho
New York	7,157	394	44		32. Tennessee
North Carolina	4,898	669	16		33. Louisiana
North Dakota	644	999	5		34. Massachusetts
Ohio	4,612	413	43		35. Pennsylvania
Oklahoma	2,721	824	9		36. Illinois
Oregon	1,410	440	40		37. Vermont
Pennsylvania	5,625	467	35		38. West Virginia
Rhode Island	634	640	18		39. New Jersey
South Carolina	2,203	596	21		40. Oregon
South Dakota	534	730	13		41. Connecticut
Tennessee	2,702	508	32		42. Arkansas
Texas	11,249	588	23		43. Ohio
Utah	1,478	739	12		44. New York
Vermont	270	458	37		45. New Hampshire
Virginia	12,322	1,846	3		46. Minnesota
Washington	4,574	827	8		47. Indiana
West Virginia	815	446	38		48. Iowa
Wisconsin	1,377	267	50		49. Michigan
Wyoming	395	822	10		50. Wisconsin
50 States	155,985	589			
DC	11,304	20,818			
United States	169,731	631			

E-9 FEDERAL GRANT SPENDING PER DOLLAR OF STATE TAX REVENUE, FY 1996

E-10 STATE & LOCAL GENERAL REVENUE FROM FEDERAL GOV'T, FY 1994

State	Total general revenue from federal gov't $(millions)	Percent of revenue from federal gov't	Rank by %
Alabama	3,300	22.6	14
Alaska	1,003	15.0	46
Arizona	2,825	19.0	31
Arkansas	2,001	25.4	8
California	30,471	21.6	18
Colorado	2,455	16.7	42
Connecticut	2,832	16.9	41
Delaware	529	15.3	45
Florida	8,127	14.9	47
Georgia	4,922	18.3	35
Hawaii	1,212	19.3	28
Idaho	766	18.8	32
Illinois	8,061	17.4	39
Indiana	4,371	19.6	27
Iowa	2,183	18.6	33
Kansas	1,793	17.4	38
Kentucky	3,076	22.8	13
Louisiana	5,035	28.9	1
Maine	1,176	23.1	11
Maryland	3,325	15.9	44
Massachusetts	5,701	19.8	25
Michigan	7,539	18.3	34
Minnesota	3,612	16.4	43
Mississippi	2,610	28.0	4
Missouri	3,893	22.3	16
Montana	894	26.0	7
Nebraska	1,180	18.0	36
Nevada	805	14.0	48
New Hampshire	950	21.3	19
New Jersey	5,241	13.3	50
New Mexico	1,446	20.4	23
New York	22,462	19.8	26
North Carolina	5,296	20.5	22
North Dakota	717	26.2	6
Ohio	8,905	20.8	20
Oklahoma	2,111	19.2	29
Oregon	3,050	22.5	15
Pennsylvania	9,578	20.0	24
Rhode Island	1,079	24.4	10
South Carolina	2,926	21.7	17
South Dakota	710	26.8	5
Tennessee	3,997	23.0	12
Texas	12,580	19.0	30
Utah	1,459	20.7	21
Vermont	634	25.2	9
Virginia	3,259	13.9	49
Washington	4,158	17.5	37
West Virginia	1,994	28.6	2
Wisconsin	3,808	17.2	40
Wyoming	822	28.1	3
50 States	212,878	19.4	
DC	2,567	45.6	
United States	215,445	19.6	

Rank in order

By %

1. Louisiana
2. West Virginia
3. Wyoming
4. Mississippi
5. South Dakota
6. North Dakota
7. Montana
8. Arkansas
9. Vermont
10. Rhode Island
11. Maine
12. Tennessee
13. Kentucky
14. Alabama
15. Oregon
16. Missouri
17. South Carolina
18. California
19. New Hampshire
20. Ohio
21. Utah
22. North Carolina
23. New Mexico
24. Pennsylvania
25. Massachusetts
26. New York
27. Indiana
28. Hawaii
29. Oklahoma
30. Texas
31. Arizona
32. Idaho
33. Iowa
34. Michigan
35. Georgia
36. Nebraska
37. Washington
38. Kansas
39. Illinois
40. Wisconsin
41. Connecticut
42. Colorado
43. Minnesota
44. Maryland
45. Delaware
46. Alaska
47. Florida
48. Nevada
49. Virginia
50. New Jersey

E-11 FEDERAL TAX BURDEN, TOTAL AND PER CAPITA, FY 1997

State	Federal tax burden total $(millions)	Federal tax burden per capita $	Rank by per capita	Rank in order By per capita
Alabama	19,105	4,471	38	1. Connecticut
Alaska	3,743	6,166	8	2. New Jersey
Arizona	20,621	4,657	35	3. Massachusetts
Arkansas	10,252	4,085	48	4. New York
California	181,267	5,686	17	5. Illinois
Colorado	22,377	5,854	12	6. Maryland
Connecticut	27,262	8,326	1	7. New Hampshire
Delaware	4,455	6,146	9	8. Alaska
Florida	81,496	5,659	19	9. Delaware
Georgia	37,355	5,080	28	10. Nevada
Hawaii	6,536	5,522	20	11. Washington
Idaho	5,177	4,353	41	12. Colorado
Illinois	76,004	6,416	5	13. Michigan
Indiana	30,329	5,193	26	14. Virginia
Iowa	13,709	4,807	34	15. Minnesota
Kansas	13,445	5,227	24	16. Rhode Island
Kentucky	16,748	4,312	43	17. California
Louisiana	18,467	4,245	44	18. Pennsylvania
Maine	5,718	4,599	36	19. Florida
Maryland	32,463	6,401	6	20. Hawaii
Massachusetts	42,192	6,925	3	21. Wyoming
Michigan	55,873	5,824	13	22. Ohio
Minnesota	26,824	5,759	15	23. Wisconsin
Mississippi	10,045	3,698	50	24. Kansas
Missouri	27,568	5,145	27	25. Oregon
Montana	3,817	4,341	42	26. Indiana
Nebraska	8,273	5,008	29	27. Missouri
Nevada	9,810	6,119	10	28. Georgia
New Hampshire	7,294	6,275	7	29. Nebraska
New Jersey	60,278	7,546	2	30. Texas
New Mexico	7,170	4,185	47	31. Vermont
New York	119,531	6,573	4	32. Tennessee
North Carolina	35,681	4,873	33	33. North Carolina
North Dakota	2,874	4,466	39	34. Iowa
Ohio	59,200	5,299	22	35. Arizona
Oklahoma	13,841	4,193	46	36. Maine
Oregon	16,679	5,206	25	37. South Dakota
Pennsylvania	68,433	5,676	18	38. Alabama
Rhode Island	5,698	5,754	16	39. North Dakota
South Carolina	16,181	4,375	40	40. South Carolina
South Dakota	3,315	4,526	37	41. Idaho
Tennessee	26,213	4,928	32	42. Montana
Texas	95,295	4,982	30	43. Kentucky
Utah	8,418	4,208	45	44. Louisiana
Vermont	2,913	4,949	31	45. Utah
Virginia	38,523	5,771	14	46. Oklahoma
Washington	32,753	5,920	11	47. New Mexico
West Virginia	7,164	3,924	49	48. Arkansas
Wisconsin	27,272	5,285	23	49. West Virginia
Wyoming	2,583	5,366	21	50. Mississippi
50 States	1,468,240	5,546		
DC	4,359	8,024		
United States	1,472,596	5,551		

State	Spending per $ of taxes paid $	Rank
Alabama	1.33	8
Alaska	1.26	16
Arizona	1.15	19
Arkansas	1.28	13
California	0.94	36
Colorado	0.97	34
Connecticut	0.71	49
Delaware	0.82	42
Florida	1.05	25
Georgia	1.01	29
Hawaii	1.33	8
Idaho	1.15	19
Illinois	0.73	48
Indiana	0.87	40
Iowa	1.06	24
Kansas	1.00	30
Kentucky	1.27	14
Louisiana	1.30	11
Maine	1.29	12
Maryland	1.24	17
Massachusetts	0.94	36
Michigan	0.76	45
Minnesota	0.76	45
Mississippi	1.64	2
Missouri	1.38	6
Montana	1.41	5
Nebraska	1.00	30
Nevada	0.82	42
New Hampshire	0.74	47
New Jersey	0.69	50
New Mexico	1.83	1
New York	0.86	41
North Carolina	1.00	30
North Dakota	1.35	7
Ohio	0.92	38
Oklahoma	1.31	10
Oregon	0.92	38
Pennsylvania	1.02	28
Rhode Island	1.08	22
South Carolina	1.23	18
South Dakota	1.27	14
Tennessee	1.14	21
Texas	0.98	33
Utah	1.08	22
Vermont	1.03	27
Virginia	1.42	4
Washington	0.97	34
West Virginia	1.52	3
Wisconsin	0.79	44
Wyoming	1.05	25
50 States	n/a	
DC	5.59	
United States	1.00	

By $

1. New Mexico
2. Mississippi
3. West Virginia
4. Virginia
5. Montana
6. Missouri
7. North Dakota
8. Alabama
8. Hawaii
10. Oklahoma
11. Louisiana
12. Maine
13. Arkansas
14. Kentucky
14. South Dakota
16. Alaska
17. Maryland
18. South Carolina
19. Arizona
19. Idaho
21. Tennessee
22. Rhode Island
22. Utah
24. Iowa
25. Florida
25. Wyoming
27. Vermont
28. Pennsylvania
29. Georgia
30. Kansas
30. Nebraska
30. North Carolina
33. Texas
34. Colorado
34. Washington
36. California
36. Massachusetts
38. Ohio
38. Oregon
40. Indiana
41. New York
42. Delaware
42. Nevada
44. Wisconsin
45. Michigan
45. Minnesota
47. New Hampshire
48. Illinois
49. Connecticut
50. New Jersey

State	Charges returned %	Rank
Alabama	67	36
Alaska	415	1
Arizona	66	38
Arkansas	77	28
California	69	34
Colorado	81	26
Connecticut	162	6
Delaware	122	11
Florida	68	35
Georgia	61	48
Hawaii	206	2
Idaho	107	15
Illinois	86	23
Indiana	67	36
Iowa	83	24
Kansas	83	24
Kentucky	63	44
Louisiana	62	46
Maine	104	17
Maryland	73	30
Massachusetts	163	5
Michigan	62	46
Minnesota	92	20
Mississippi	65	42
Missouri	66	38
Montana	156	8
Nebraska	77	28
Nevada	95	19
New Hampshire	106	16
New Jersey	81	26
New Mexico	90	22
New York	115	14
North Carolina	66	38
North Dakota	158	7
Ohio	72	32
Oklahoma	66	38
Oregon	117	13
Pennsylvania	91	21
Rhode Island	177	3
South Carolina	63	44
South Dakota	165	4
Tennessee	60	49
Texas	59	50
Utah	72	32
Vermont	140	9
Virginia	64	43
Washington	101	18
West Virginia	120	12
Wisconsin	73	30
Wyoming	123	10
50 States	n/a	
DC	301	
United States	80	

By %

1. Alaska
2. Hawaii
3. Rhode Island
4. South Dakota
5. Massachusetts
6. Connecticut
7. North Dakota
8. Montana
9. Vermont
10. Wyoming
11. Delaware
12. West Virginia
13. Oregon
14. New York
15. Idaho
16. New Hampshire
17. Maine
18. Washington
19. Nevada
20. Minnesota
21. Pennsylvania
22. New Mexico
23. Illinois
24. Iowa
24. Kansas
26. Colorado
26. New Jersey
28. Arkansas
28. Nebraska
30. Maryland
30. Wisconsin
32. Ohio
32. Utah
34. California
35. Florida
36. Alabama
36. Indiana
38. Arizona
38. Missouri
38. North Carolina
38. Oklahoma
42. Mississippi
43. Virginia
44. Kentucky
44. South Carolina
46. Louisiana
46. Michigan
48. Georgia
49. Tennessee
50. Texas

State	Federal grants to state & local governments $(millions)	Terms of trade, ratio of federal grants to federal taxes paid	Rank by ratio
Alabama	3,325	1.13	18
Alaska	1,051	1.82	2
Arizona	3,095	0.97	25
Arkansas	2,131	1.35	12
California	26,413	0.94	32
Colorado	2,410	0.70	47
Connecticut	3,080	0.73	44
Delaware	600	0.87	36
Florida	8,442	0.67	48
Georgia	5,359	0.93	33
Hawaii	1,126	1.11	19
Idaho	887	1.11	21
Illinois	9,229	0.79	42
Indiana	3,657	0.78	43
Iowa	2,030	0.96	29
Kansas	1,700	0.82	40
Kentucky	3,355	1.30	15
Louisiana	4,734	1.66	7
Maine	1,389	1.57	10
Maryland	3,544	0.71	45
Massachusetts	6,813	1.05	24
Michigan	7,194	0.83	38
Minnesota	3,535	0.85	37
Mississippi	2,754	1.77	3
Missouri	4,091	0.96	27
Montana	964	1.63	9
Nebraska	1,232	0.96	26
Nevada	876	0.58	49
New Hampshire	890	0.79	41
New Jersey	6,506	0.70	46
New Mexico	1,942	1.75	5
New York	24,560	1.33	14
North Carolina	5,227	0.95	31
North Dakota	734	1.65	8
Ohio	8,776	0.96	28
Oklahoma	2,435	1.14	17
Oregon	2,797	1.09	23
Pennsylvania	10,117	0.96	30
Rhode Island	1,176	1.34	13
South Carolina	3,032	1.21	16
South Dakota	867	1.69	6
Tennessee	4,476	1.11	22
Texas	13,297	0.90	34
Utah	1,446	1.11	20
Vermont	641	1.42	11
Virginia	3,403	0.57	50
Washington	4,152	0.82	39
West Virginia	2,088	1.89	1
Wisconsin	3,679	0.87	35
Wyoming	708	1.77	4
50 States	217,965	0.96	
DC	2,578	3.83	
United States	227,542	1.00	

Rank in order

By ratio

1. West Virginia
2. Alaska
3. Mississippi
4. Wyoming
5. New Mexico
6. South Dakota
7. Louisiana
8. North Dakota
9. Montana
10. Maine
11. Vermont
12. Arkansas
13. Rhode Island
14. New York
15. Kentucky
16. South Carolina
17. Oklahoma
18. Alabama
19. Hawaii
20. Utah
21. Idaho
22. Tennessee
23. Oregon
24. Massachusetts
25. Arizona
26. Nebraska
27. Missouri
28. Ohio
29. Iowa
30. Pennsylvania
31. North Carolina
32. California
33. Georgia
34. Texas
35. Wisconsin
36. Delaware
37. Minnesota
38. Michigan
39. Washington
40. Kansas
41. New Hampshire
42. Illinois
43. Indiana
44. Connecticut
45. Maryland
46. New Jersey
47. Colorado
48. Florida
49. Nevada
50. Virginia

State	Federal tax liability $(millions)	Federal tax liability per capita $	Rank by per capita
Alabama	7,631	1,797	37
Alaska	1,676	2,781	7
Arizona	8,546	1,985	33
Arkansas	3,869	1,557	48
California	74,372	2,356	17
Colorado	9,758	2,604	10
Connecticut	13,168	4,026	1
Delaware	1,813	2,528	12
Florida	34,968	2,465	14
Georgia	15,692	2,177	23
Hawaii	2,511	2,129	28
Idaho	2,034	1,745	41
Illinois	33,575	2,848	5
Indiana	12,612	2,176	24
Iowa	5,323	1,872	35
Kansas	5,480	2,137	27
Kentucky	6,444	1,671	44
Louisiana	7,338	1,692	43
Maine	2,139	1,727	42
Maryland	13,587	2,696	9
Massachusetts	18,688	3,078	3
Michigan	23,775	2,493	13
Minnesota	11,308	2,450	16
Mississippi	3,734	1,385	50
Missouri	11,010	2,070	30
Montana	1,382	1,587	46
Nebraska	3,364	2,052	31
Nevada	4,581	2,987	4
New Hampshire	3,120	2,717	8
New Jersey	26,965	3,392	2
New Mexico	2,690	1,592	45
New York	50,650	2,784	6
North Carolina	14,461	2,008	32
North Dakota	1,121	1,747	40
Ohio	24,270	2,180	22
Oklahoma	5,164	1,577	47
Oregon	6,640	2,109	29
Pennsylvania	27,790	2,304	18
Rhode Island	2,183	2,201	21
South Carolina	6,426	1,752	39
South Dakota	1,344	1,842	36
Tennessee	11,226	2,140	26
Texas	40,823	2,171	25
Utah	3,510	1,792	38
Vermont	1,128	1,928	34
Virginia	16,228	2,453	15
Washington	14,048	2,579	11
West Virginia	2,631	1,442	49
Wisconsin	11,277	2,202	20
Wyoming	1,065	2,223	19
50 States	615,138	2,345	
DC	1,738	3,133	
United States	620,972	2,362	

Rank in order

By per capita

1. Connecticut
2. New Jersey
3. Massachusetts
4. Nevada
5. Illinois
6. New York
7. Alaska
8. New Hampshire
9. Maryland
10. Colorado
11. Washington
12. Delaware
13. Michigan
14. Florida
15. Virginia
16. Minnesota
17. California
18. Pennsylvania
19. Wyoming
20. Wisconsin
21. Rhode Island
22. Ohio
23. Georgia
24. Indiana
25. Texas
26. Tennessee
27. Kansas
28. Hawaii
29. Oregon
30. Missouri
31. Nebraska
32. North Carolina
33. Arizona
34. Vermont
35. Iowa
36. South Dakota
37. Alabama
38. Utah
39. South Carolina
40. North Dakota
41. Idaho
42. Maine
43. Louisiana
44. Kentucky
45. New Mexico
46. Montana
47. Oklahoma
48. Arkansas
49. West Virginia
50. Mississippi

State	Federal share of welfare and Medicaid %	Rank
Alabama	69.5	10
Alaska	50.0	40
Arizona	65.5	14
Arkansas	73.3	2
California	50.2	39
Colorado	52.3	36
Connecticut	50.0	40
Delaware	50.0	40
Florida	55.8	31
Georgia	61.5	22
Hawaii	50.0	40
Idaho	68.0	12
Illinois	50.0	40
Indiana	61.6	21
Iowa	62.9	19
Kansas	58.9	30
Kentucky	70.1	8
Louisiana	71.4	6
Maine	63.7	18
Maryland	50.0	40
Massachusetts	50.0	40
Michigan	55.2	32
Minnesota	53.6	34
Mississippi	77.2	1
Missouri	60.0	25
Montana	69.0	11
Nebraska	59.1	28
Nevada	50.0	40
New Hampshire	50.0	40
New Jersey	50.0	40
New Mexico	72.7	3
New York	50.0	40
North Carolina	63.9	17
North Dakota	67.7	13
Ohio	59.3	27
Oklahoma	70.0	9
Oregon	60.5	24
Pennsylvania	52.9	35
Rhode Island	53.9	33
South Carolina	70.4	7
South Dakota	64.9	15
Tennessee	64.6	16
Texas	62.6	20
Utah	72.3	5
Vermont	61.1	23
Virginia	51.5	37
Washington	50.5	38
West Virginia	72.6	4
Wisconsin	59.0	29
Wyoming	59.9	26
50 States	n/a	
DC	50.0	
United States	n/a	

Rank in order

By %

1. Mississippi
2. Arkansas
3. New Mexico
4. West Virginia
5. Utah
6. Louisiana
7. South Carolina
8. Kentucky
9. Oklahoma
10. Alabama
11. Montana
12. Idaho
13. North Dakota
14. Arizona
15. South Dakota
16. Tennessee
17. North Carolina
18. Maine
19. Iowa
20. Texas
21. Indiana
22. Georgia
23. Vermont
24. Oregon
25. Missouri
26. Wyoming
27. Ohio
28. Nebraska
29. Wisconsin
30. Kansas
31. Florida
32. Michigan
33. Rhode Island
34. Minnesota
35. Pennsylvania
36. Colorado
37. Virginia
38. Washington
39. California
40. Alaska
40. Connecticut
40. Delaware
40. Hawaii
40. Illinois
40. Maryland
40. Massachusetts
40. Nevada
40. New Hampshire
40. New Jersey
40. New York

Source Notes for Federal Impacts (Section E)

E-1 Federal Spending Total and Per Capita, FY 1996: The federal government affects state economies and state finances through its massive spending, accounting for nearly one-quarter of all economic activity in the United States. The primary components of that spending are grants to state and local governments; payments to individuals, such as Social Security; wages and salaries of federal employees; and purchases of goods and services, such as weapons for the Defense Department. Details of where these funds are spent are compiled by federal agencies and summarized by the Census Bureau in *Federal Expenditures by State*. Many tables in this section reflect the latest version of this report, covering federal spending in fiscal 1996, which for the federal government ended in September 1996.

This table reflects total federal spending of almost $1.4 trillion, along with the results of dividing each state's total by its population to permit meaningful comparisons among states. The federal figures exclude certain forms of federal spending that cannot reasonably be associated with particular states, primarily interest on the federal debt and money spent in other countries.

E-2 Increase in Total Federal Spending, FY 1991-1996: This table uses the Census reports for federal fiscal years 1991 and 1996 to show the percentage change in total federal spending in each state over a five-year period. The data come from the federal report described in the notes to Table E-1.

E-3 Federal Spending on Grants, Total and Per Capita, FY 1996: This table reflects the federal spending for grants that help state and local governments finance welfare, Medicaid, highway construction, and other activities. The data come from the federal report described in the notes to Table E-1.

E-4 Federal Spending on Procurement, Total and Per Capita, FY 1996: This table reflects the federal spending for purchases ranging from tanks and space shuttles to gasoline for federal vehicles. The data come from the federal report described in the notes to Table E-1.

E-5 Federal Spending on Payments to Individuals, Total and Per Capita, FY 1996: This table reflects the federal spending for payments to individuals. The primary components are Social Security pensions, Medicare payments to health care providers, pensions for retired federal workers, and Food Stamps. The data come from the federal report described in the notes to Table E-1.

E-6 Federal Spending on Social Security and Medicare, Total and Per Capita, FY 1996: This table reflects the federal spending for Social Security pensions and Medicare payments to health care providers. This spending is a part of the total covered by Table E-5. The per capita amounts suggest the massive impact that this flow of funds has among states. While revenues from payroll taxes are concentrated in states that are showing strong economic growth, states with slower growth (primarily those in the Northeast) receive large portions of personal income from these retirement-related federal payments and private pensions. The data come from the federal report described in the notes to Table E-1.

E-7 Social Security Benefits Paid, 1995: This table provides another perspective on Social Security payments, using tabulations for December 1995 payments prepared by the Social Security Administration (provided by fax from Carolyn Cheeyum in the SSA Press Office). This agency can provide additional details on benefits paid in each state, such as the amounts paid to retired workers, to deceased workers' beneficiaries, and to workers and their families based on disability. Besides the amounts paid and number of recipient households, the table shows the average benefit per household. This amount is appreciably higher in states where salaries have been high (such as in the Northeast) than where they have been low (such as in the South).

E-8 Federal Spending on Employee Wages and Salaries, Total and Per Capita, FY 1996: This table reflects the federal spending on payments for salaries of civilian and military federal employees. The largest amounts are found in states with major federal installations, such as military bases. Because the Postal Service is included and some agencies, such as the Department of Agriculture, operate in every state, even states without major installations show substantial federal spending. The data come from the federal report described in the notes to Table E-1.

E-9 Federal Grant Spending Per Dollar of State Tax Revenue, FY 1996: Most federal grant spending is now concentrated on state administered programs, such as welfare and Medicaid. The amounts are substantial when compared with the amount that states raise from state taxes, as shown by the table, which relates the amounts provided by federal grants to the amounts states raised from taxes. The data for fiscal 1996 are from "State Government Finances" available on the Census Bureau website (http://www.census.gov) and were retrieved by

State Fact Finder on September 29, 1997. The corresponding data for 1996 for local governments are not yet available.

E-10 State and Local General Revenue from Federal Government, FY 1994:
These data, covering both state and local government, show the amount of federal aid contributing to "general revenue" as defined by the Census Bureau in its annual survey of government finances. It excludes certain trust funds, such as Unemployment Insurance, but includes others, such as those used for highway construction. The data are calculated from the Census Bureau's *State And Local Government Finance Estimates, by State* for FY 1994, available on the Census Bureau website (http://www.census.gov).

E-11 Federal Tax Burden, Total and Per Capita, FY 1997:
This table shows where the burdens of federal taxes fell in federal fiscal year 1997. The data come from the Tax Foundation's *Special Report* (July 97, No. 70), which uses formulas to spread the burden of certain taxes, such as the corporate income tax, among states and actual data from federal tax collectors to show the sources of major tax revenues, such as those from personal income and payroll taxes.

E-12 Federal Spending Per Dollar of Taxes Paid, FY 1996:
These data relate how much taxpayers in each state pay in federal taxes to the amounts the federal government spends in each state. The information comes from calculations by the Tax Foundation using allocations of tax burdens (see Table E-11) and the Census Bureau report on federal spending (see Table E-1). Many states get more than a dollar back in federal spending for every dollar sent to the federal government in taxes. This occurs primarily in states where federal installations and/or purchasing is concentrated. Because a substantial portion of federal spending is financed by borrowing (deficit spending), the nationwide total would show more money returned as spending than paid as taxes, so the Tax Foundation adjusted spending to eliminate the deficit-financed portion.

E-13 Highway Charges Returned to States, FY 1996:
Federal spending for highways is financed by special user charges, such as federal taxes on gasoline and diesel fuel. Some states, such as Alaska and Hawaii, receive much more federal highway aid than federal user charges collected in their states. Others, which highway officials call "donor states," usually receive less than a dollar of aid from every dollar in federal highway taxes collected within their boundaries. Some states — Massachusetts is an example in the table — will appear as donee states because of large Interstate projects underway in a particular period. Which states should "donate" how much is a subject of perpetual controversy in the Congress. The controversy spawns many different ways to measure the federal redistribution of highway revenues.

The statistics were prepared by the Federal Highway Administration as "Comparison of Highway Trust Fund Receipts Attributable To The States And Federal-Aid Apportionments And Allocations From The Fund, Highway Account Only, Fiscal Years 1996." In FY 1996, federal collections of highway user charges were about $22 billion while allocations of spending authority to states were only about $17.6 billion, so only 80% of federal revenues were allocated for highway purposes. State officials and highway users are critical of the federal government for not allocating all of the highway taxes collected. Federal spending for highways is financed by special "user charges," such as federal taxes on gasoline and diesel fuel. This table is parallel to Table E-12 but covers only highway spending. It was developed by the Federal Highway Administration in its *1996 Highway Statistics.*

E-14 Terms of Trade with the Federal Government, 1996:
This table was developed by State Policy Research to show the relationship between amounts paid by taxpayers in each state to the federal grants to state and local government financed by their federal taxes. The table shows federal grants, identical to the amounts shown in Table E-3. Because all grants, even those paid currently out of money the federal government raises by borrowing, are ultimately paid for by taxpayers, the total federal tax revenue to pay for grants was stipulated as equal to the grants for the fifty states and the District of Columbia. To determine how this tax burden to pay for grants was distributed among states, the total tax burden for grants was allocated based on the percentage of all federal taxes paid by citizens and corporations in each state, using the Tax Foundation's logic (also used to prepare Table E-11). The result is that the sum of grants and of taxes are identical for the fifty states plus the District of Columbia.

However, the amounts are by no means equal for individual states. States with relatively high personal incomes (and thus federal tax liabilities) but low grants will show ratios below one. Conceptually, for example, 0.95 can be considered as getting 95 cents back in grants for every dollar in federal taxes paid, or a 95 percent return. Conversely, states with lower incomes and high grants will show a ratio above one.

E-15 Federal Personal Income Taxes, 1995: This table shows how much households in each state were required to pay in federal income taxes on their income during 1995, as reported in tax returns filed in early 1996. The data are from the Internal Revenue Service as reported in the *SOI Bulletin* (Spring 1997).

E-16 Federal Share of Welfare and Medicaid, 1997: The federal grants to states for Medicaid are based on multiplying the total costs of these programs by the federal cost-sharing percentages shown in the table. The formula used to determine each state's share provides the largest federal shares for the states with the lowest per capita incomes. A special rule overrides the calculation for more affluent states, so no state has less than 50 percent of these costs paid by the federal government. The percentages were published in Federal Funds Information for States' *Issue Brief 97-8*, released September 22, 1997.

Federal welfare reform legislation, enacted in 1996, was partially implemented at the option of the states during late 1996 and early 1997. Effective in October of 1997, the block grants established under the legislation became fully effective. They are based on federal spending patterns from FY 1994 which reflected federal cost sharing percentages similar to those shown on the table. However, under the block grants, the federal government no longer shares in additional welfare costs with matching money.

Taxes

State	State & local taxes $(millions)	State & local taxes as % of personal income %	Rank by %	Rank in order By %
Alabama	6,755	9.4	50	1. New York
Alaska	1,954	14.2	2	2. Alaska
Arizona	8,873	12.4	12	3. Hawaii
Arkansas	4,118	10.6	43	4. Wisconsin
California	75,571	11.1	35	5. New Mexico
Colorado	8,207	10.7	42	6. Wyoming
Connecticut	11,269	12.3	16	7. Vermont
Delaware	1,761	11.6	41	8. Minnesota
Florida	30,499	10.8	40	9. Maine
Georgia	14,923	11.2	31	10. Iowa
Hawaii	3,756	13.7	3	11. Michigan
Idaho	2,220	11.5	21	12. Arizona
Illinois	29,080	11.0	34	13. Utah
Indiana	12,189	11.1	33	14. Washington
Iowa	6,497	12.6	10	15. North Dakota
Kansas	5,900	11.7	20	16. Connecticut
Kentucky	7,386	11.5	23	17. Oregon
Louisiana	7,422	10.4	45	18. New Jersey
Maine	2,915	12.5	9	19. Nebraska
Maryland	13,301	11.2	30	20. Kansas
Massachusetts	17,126	11.6	27	21. Idaho
Michigan	24,235	12.4	11	22. Rhode Island
Minnesota	12,481	13.1	8	23. Kentucky
Mississippi	4,413	11.4	26	24. West Virginia
Missouri	9,844	9.6	48	25. Montana
Montana	1,671	11.4	25	26. Mississippi
Nebraska	3,717	11.7	19	27. Massachusetts
Nevada	3,430	10.9	29	28. North Carolina
New Hampshire	2,490	10.0	47	29. Nevada
New Jersey	25,422	12.1	18	30. Maryland
New Mexico	3,477	13.2	5	31. Georgia
New York	70,029	15.5	1	32. Ohio
North Carolina	14,919	11.5	28	33. Indiana
North Dakota	1,295	11.9	15	34. Illinois
Ohio	24,473	11.2	32	35. California
Oklahoma	6,015	10.9	37	36. Pennsylvania
Oregon	6,993	11.9	17	37. Oklahoma
Pennsylvania	28,226	11.0	36	38. South Carolina
Rhode Island	2,491	11.7	22	39. Texas
South Carolina	6,598	10.8	38	40. Florida
South Dakota	1,311	10.2	44	41. Delaware
Tennessee	9,103	9.7	49	42. Colorado
Texas	37,248	10.8	39	43. Arkansas
Utah	3,663	12.2	13	44. South Dakota
Vermont	1,440	12.9	7	45. Louisiana
Virginia	14,162	10.1	46	46. Virginia
Washington	13,873	12.1	14	47. New Hampshire
West Virginia	3,351	11.4	24	48. Missouri
Wisconsin	13,715	13.7	4	49. Tennessee
Wyoming	1,196	12.9	6	50. Alabama
50 States	623,003	11.7		
DC	2,523	14.6		
United States	625,527	11.7		

State	State & local taxes per capita $	State taxes per capita $	Local taxes per capita $	Rank by state & local per capita	Rank in order By state & local
Alabama	1,602	1,131	472	50	1. New York
Alaska	3,225	2,047	1,178	3	2. Connecticut
Arizona	2,177	1,388	789	29	3. Alaska
Arkansas	1,679	1,295	384	48	4. New Jersey
California	2,404	1,581	823	17	5. Hawaii
Colorado	2,245	1,138	1,107	25	6. Massachusetts
Connecticut	3,441	2,088	1,353	2	7. Minnesota
Delaware	2,494	2,045	449	14	8. Wisconsin
Florida	2,186	1,276	910	28	9. Maryland
Georgia	2,115	1,245	870	32	10. Washington
Hawaii	3,185	2,539	646	5	11. Michigan
Idaho	1,959	1,420	539	37	12. Wyoming
Illinois	2,474	1,324	1,150	16	13. Rhode Island
Indiana	2,119	1,300	819	31	14. Delaware
Iowa	2,297	1,460	837	22	15. Vermont
Kansas	2,310	1,439	871	21	16. Illinois
Kentucky	1,930	1,488	442	39	17. California
Louisiana	1,720	1,016	704	47	18. Maine
Maine	2,351	1,423	928	18	19. Nevada
Maryland	2,657	1,515	1,142	9	20. Pennsylvania
Massachusetts	2,835	1,824	1,011	6	21. Kansas
Michigan	2,552	1,511	1,041	11	22. Iowa
Minnesota	2,733	1,894	839	7	23. Nebraska
Mississippi	1,653	1,246	407	49	24. Oregon
Missouri	1,852	1,112	740	41	25. Colorado
Montana	1,952	1,356	596	38	26. Ohio
Nebraska	2,290	1,321	969	23	27. New Hampshire
Nevada	2,354	1,634	720	19	28. Florida
New Hampshire	2,190	736	1,453	27	29. Arizona
New Jersey	3,216	1,707	1,509	4	30. Virginia
New Mexico	2,102	1,653	450	34	31. Indiana
New York	3,854	1,832	2,022	1	32. Georgia
North Carolina	2,110	1,488	622	33	33. North Carolina
North Dakota	2,030	1,387	643	35	34. New Mexico
Ohio	2,204	1,278	926	26	35. North Dakota
Oklahoma	1,846	1,309	538	42	36. Texas
Oregon	2,266	1,309	957	24	37. Idaho
Pennsylvania	2,342	1,422	920	20	38. Montana
Rhode Island	2,498	1,440	1,058	13	39. Kentucky
South Carolina	1,801	1,229	572	44	40. Utah
South Dakota	1,819	914	905	45	41. Missouri
Tennessee	1,759	1,108	651	46	42. Oklahoma
Texas	2,027	1,060	967	36	43. West Virginia
Utah	1,920	1,266	654	40	44. South Carolina
Vermont	2,482	1,435	1,047	15	45. South Dakota
Virginia	2,162	1,227	935	30	46. Tennessee
Washington	2,596	1,822	774	10	47. Louisiana
West Virginia	1,839	1,402	438	43	48. Arkansas
Wisconsin	2,699	1,658	1,040	8	49. Mississippi
Wyoming	2,513	1,553	960	12	50. Alabama
50 States	2,398	1,437	961		
DC	4,427	n/a	4,427		
United States	2,403	1,434	969		

State	Tax effort %	Rank
Alabama	81	46
Alaska	119	2
Arizona	103	8
Arkansas	82	44
California	95	24
Colorado	86	39
Connecticut	99	17
Delaware	80	48
Florida	86	39
Georgia	95	24
Hawaii	95	24
Idaho	94	28
Illinois	100	13
Indiana	93	30
Iowa	100	13
Kansas	100	13
Kentucky	100	13
Louisiana	89	36
Maine	102	10
Maryland	103	8
Massachusetts	101	12
Michigan	107	7
Minnesota	112	5
Mississippi	92	32
Missouri	85	41
Montana	78	49
Nebraska	99	17
Nevada	73	50
New Hampshire	84	42
New Jersey	112	5
New Mexico	96	22
New York	156	1
North Carolina	87	37
North Dakota	92	32
Ohio	96	22
Oklahoma	93	30
Oregon	97	20
Pennsylvania	95	24
Rhode Island	115	4
South Carolina	90	35
South Dakota	83	43
Tennessee	82	44
Texas	87	37
Utah	94	28
Vermont	97	20
Virginia	91	34
Washington	99	17
West Virginia	102	10
Wisconsin	118	3
Wyoming	81	46
50 States	n/a	
DC	157	
United States	100	

By %

1. New York
2. Alaska
3. Wisconsin
4. Rhode Island
5. Minnesota
5. New Jersey
7. Michigan
8. Arizona
8. Maryland
10. Maine
10. West Virginia
12. Massachusetts
13. Illinois
13. Iowa
13. Kansas
13. Kentucky
17. Connecticut
17. Nebraska
17. Washington
20. Oregon
20. Vermont
22. New Mexico
22. Ohio
24. California
24. Georgia
24. Hawaii
24. Pennsylvania
28. Idaho
28. Utah
30. Indiana
30. Oklahoma
32. Mississippi
32. North Dakota
34. Virginia
35. South Carolina
36. Louisiana
37. North Carolina
37. Texas
39. Colorado
39. Florida
41. Missouri
42. New Hampshire
43. South Dakota
44. Arkansas
44. Tennessee
46. Alabama
46. Wyoming
48. Delaware
49. Montana
50. Nevada

State	Tax capacity %	Rank
Alabama	81	47
Alaska	178	1
Arizona	94	25
Arkansas	78	48
California	115	9
Colorado	109	11
Connecticut	130	4
Delaware	125	6
Florida	103	15
Georgia	91	31
Hawaii	146	2
Idaho	82	44
Illinois	102	18
Indiana	90	35
Iowa	93	27
Kansas	93	27
Kentucky	83	42
Louisiana	89	37
Maine	95	23
Maryland	106	13
Massachusetts	117	8
Michigan	94	25
Minnesota	101	19
Mississippi	68	50
Missouri	91	31
Montana	91	31
Nebraska	95	23
Nevada	128	5
New Hampshire	110	10
New Jersey	119	7
New Mexico	87	39
New York	103	15
North Carolina	93	27
North Dakota	91	31
Ohio	93	27
Oklahoma	87	39
Oregon	100	20
Pennsylvania	96	22
Rhode Island	89	37
South Carolina	83	42
South Dakota	86	41
Tennessee	82	44
Texas	97	21
Utah	82	44
Vermont	105	14
Virginia	103	15
Washington	108	12
West Virginia	77	49
Wisconsin	90	35
Wyoming	134	3
50 States	n/a	
DC	123	
United States	100	

By %

1. Alaska
2. Hawaii
3. Wyoming
4. Connecticut
5. Nevada
6. Delaware
7. New Jersey
8. Massachusetts
9. California
10. New Hampshire
11. Colorado
12. Washington
13. Maryland
14. Vermont
15. Florida
15. New York
15. Virginia
18. Illinois
19. Minnesota
20. Oregon
21. Texas
22. Pennsylvania
23. Maine
23. Nebraska
25. Arizona
25. Michigan
27. Iowa
27. Kansas
27. North Carolina
27. Ohio
31. Georgia
31. Missouri
31. Montana
31. North Dakota
35. Indiana
35. Wisconsin
37. Louisiana
37. Rhode Island
39. New Mexico
39. Oklahoma
41. South Dakota
42. Kentucky
42. South Carolina
44. Idaho
44. Tennessee
44. Utah
47. Alabama
48. Arkansas
49. West Virginia
50. Mississippi

State	% change in state & local taxes %	% change in state & local taxes per capita %	% change in state & local taxes as % of pers. inc. %	Rank by % change in state & local taxes
Alabama	32.4	29.4	-4.3	34
Alaska	-5.5	-17.2	-30.6	50
Arizona	35.6	17.8	-2.8	26
Arkansas	43.7	40.8	5.9	8
California	24.6	15.4	-5.2	47
Colorado	38.2	25.1	-4.3	19
Connecticut	38.9	37.5	8.8	17
Delaware	30.1	23.7	-18.1	40
Florida	47.1	33.5	3.9	5
Georgia	42.3	29.6	1.4	10
Hawaii	39.8	32.5	-6.5	15
Idaho	56.8	39.9	2.8	2
Illinois	33.4	32.6	1.5	29
Indiana	37.5	33.8	10.3	20
Iowa	30.3	30.7	3.3	39
Kansas	36.7	34.7	4.9	24
Kentucky	42.7	39.1	4.7	9
Louisiana	19.3	21.2	-12.3	49
Maine	22.2	20.6	-3.2	48
Maryland	28.2	20.4	-4.0	41
Massachusetts	25.9	23.3	1.2	45
Michigan	31.3	28.3	0.9	36
Minnesota	32.7	26.3	-2.7	32
Mississippi	42.2	39.6	5.6	11
Missouri	30.7	27.8	0.8	37
Montana	32.9	25.1	-7.1	31
Nebraska	37.2	36.0	2.0	22
Nevada	72.3	30.7	2.7	1
New Hampshire	39.6	36.1	15.3	16
New Jersey	35.1	32.2	5.7	28
New Mexico	46.6	35.0	3.3	6
New York	27.8	26.1	-3.4	42
North Carolina	44.4	34.1	0.7	7
North Dakota	33.1	37.4	4.9	30
Ohio	32.5	30.3	-0.4	33
Oklahoma	26.6	25.4	-2.6	43
Oregon	37.3	25.1	-4.6	21
Pennsylvania	35.2	35.0	0.8	27
Rhode Island	31.3	31.5	1.2	35
South Carolina	30.4	25.7	-6.0	38
South Dakota	38.6	36.8	-1.1	18
Tennessee	40.3	33.9	-1.4	12
Texas	40.2	29.2	-2.0	13
Utah	48.8	33.0	0.5	4
Vermont	37.0	33.8	4.2	23
Virginia	26.2	17.5	-6.2	44
Washington	52.6	35.8	0.9	3
West Virginia	36.2	38.8	1.4	25
Wisconsin	39.8	33.8	3.5	14
Wyoming	24.9	24.7	-14.7	46
50 States	33.6	27.3	-0.9	
DC	12.5	19.6	-15.7	
United States	33.5	27.3	-1.1	

F-5 CHANGE IN STATE AND LOCAL TAXES, FY 1989-1994

Rank in order

By % change

1. Nevada
2. Idaho
3. Washington
4. Utah
5. Florida
6. New Mexico
7. North Carolina
8. Arkansas
9. Kentucky
10. Georgia
11. Mississippi
12. Tennessee
13. Texas
14. Wisconsin
15. Hawaii
16. New Hampshire
17. Connecticut
18. South Dakota
19. Colorado
20. Indiana
21. Oregon
22. Nebraska
23. Vermont
24. Kansas
25. West Virginia
26. Arizona
27. Pennsylvania
28. New Jersey
29. Illinois
30. North Dakota
31. Montana
32. Minnesota
33. Ohio
34. Alabama
35. Rhode Island
36. Michigan
37. Missouri
38. South Carolina
39. Iowa
40. Delaware
41. Maryland
42. New York
43. Oklahoma
44. Virginia
45. Massachusetts
46. Wyoming
47. California
48. Maine
49. Louisiana
50. Alaska

F-6 PROPERTY TAXES, TOTAL & AS % OF PERSONAL INCOME, FY 1994

State	Property taxes $(millions)	Property taxes as % of personal income %	Rank by %	By %
Alabama	826	1.15	50	1. New Hampshire
Alaska	645	4.68	11	2. Vermont
Arizona	2,726	3.82	22	3. New Jersey
Arkansas	623	1.61	48	4. Maine
California	20,652	3.02	36	5. Wisconsin
Colorado	2,653	3.46	27	6. Michigan
Connecticut	4,379	4.78	12	7. New York
Delaware	262	1.72	49	8. Wyoming
Florida	11,000	3.88	21	9. Rhode Island
Georgia	4,405	3.32	28	10. Montana
Hawaii	625	2.28	40	11. Alaska
Idaho	581	3.01	35	12. Connecticut
Illinois	11,204	4.25	16	13. Nebraska
Indiana	4,253	3.89	20	14. Iowa
Iowa	2,237	4.34	14	15. Oregon
Kansas	1,852	3.68	24	16. Illinois
Kentucky	1,219	1.90	44	17. South Dakota
Louisiana	1,288	1.81	46	18. Texas
Maine	1,172	5.03	4	19. Massachusetts
Maryland	3,618	3.05	34	20. Indiana
Massachusetts	5,949	4.04	19	21. Florida
Michigan	9,961	5.12	6	22. Arizona
Minnesota	3,649	3.84	23	23. Minnesota
Mississippi	1,038	2.67	37	24. Kansas
Missouri	2,304	2.25	41	25. Washington
Montana	714	4.89	10	26. North Dakota
Nebraska	1,370	4.31	13	27. Colorado
Nevada	749	2.37	39	28. Georgia
New Hampshire	1,640	6.57	1	29. Ohio
New Jersey	11,724	5.57	3	30. Pennsylvania
New Mexico	435	1.65	47	31. Utah
New York	22,639	5.02	7	32. Virginia
North Carolina	3,270	2.52	38	33. South Carolina
North Dakota	373	3.43	26	34. Maryland
Ohio	6,978	3.21	29	35. Idaho
Oklahoma	985	1.79	45	36. California
Oregon	2,519	4.27	15	37. Mississippi
Pennsylvania	8,084	3.16	30	38. North Carolina
Rhode Island	1,049	4.95	9	39. Nevada
South Carolina	1,887	3.08	33	40. Hawaii
South Dakota	523	4.07	17	41. Missouri
Tennessee	2,072	2.21	43	42. West Virginia
Texas	13,882	4.02	18	43. Tennessee
Utah	938	3.12	31	44. Kentucky
Vermont	610	5.45	2	45. Oklahoma
Virginia	4,390	3.14	32	46. Louisiana
Washington	4,169	3.64	25	47. New Mexico
West Virginia	655	2.23	42	48. Arkansas
Wisconsin	5,107	5.11	5	49. Delaware
Wyoming	447	4.82	8	50. Alabama
50 States	196,329	3.67		
DC	811	4.70		
United States	197,140	3.68		

State	Property tax per capita	Rank		Rank in order By per capita
Alabama	196	50		1. New Jersey
Alaska	1,064	5		2. New Hampshire
Arizona	669	29		3. Connecticut
Arkansas	254	49		4. New York
California	657	30		5. Alaska
Colorado	726	24		6. Rhode Island
Connecticut	1,337	3		7. Vermont
Delaware	371	43		8. Michigan
Florida	788	19		9. Wisconsin
Georgia	624	32		10. Massachusetts
Hawaii	530	34		11. Illinois
Idaho	513	37		12. Maine
Illinois	953	11		13. Wyoming
Indiana	739	22		14. Nebraska
Iowa	791	18		15. Montana
Kansas	725	23		16. Oregon
Kentucky	319	45		17. Minnesota
Louisiana	298	47		18. Iowa
Maine	945	12		19. Florida
Maryland	723	25		20. Washington
Massachusetts	985	10		21. Texas
Michigan	1,049	8		22. Indiana
Minnesota	799	17		23. Kansas
Mississippi	389	42		24. Colorado
Missouri	433	40		25. Maryland
Montana	834	15		26. South Dakota
Nebraska	844	14		27. Pennsylvania
Nevada	514	36		28. Virginia
New Hampshire	1,442	2		29. Arizona
New Jersey	1,483	1		30. California
New Mexico	263	48		31. Ohio
New York	1,246	4		32. Georgia
North Carolina	463	39		33. North Dakota
North Dakota	585	33		34. Hawaii
Ohio	629	31		35. South Carolina
Oklahoma	302	46		36. Nevada
Oregon	816	16		37. Idaho
Pennsylvania	671	27		38. Utah
Rhode Island	1,052	6		39. North Carolina
South Carolina	515	35		40. Missouri
South Dakota	725	26		41. Tennessee
Tennessee	400	41		42. Mississippi
Texas	755	21		43. Delaware
Utah	491	38		44. West Virginia
Vermont	1,052	7		45. Kentucky
Virginia	670	28		46. Oklahoma
Washington	780	20		47. Louisiana
West Virginia	359	44		48. New Mexico
Wisconsin	1,005	9		49. Arkansas
Wyoming	940	13		50. Alabama
50 States	756			
DC	1,423			
United States	757			

State	Property tax as percent of three-tax revenues %	Rank	By %
Alabama	14.3	50	1. New Hampshire
Alaska	75.1	2	2. Alaska
Arizona	33.6	27	3. Wyoming
Arkansas	16.9	48	4. Montana
California	31.4	32	5. New Jersey
Colorado	34.8	25	6. Michigan
Connecticut	44.1	10	7. Vermont
Delaware	25.0	41	8. South Dakota
Florida	41.4	15	9. Rhode Island
Georgia	32.2	31	10. Connecticut
Hawaii	17.7	47	11. Maine
Idaho	30.3	34	12. Oregon
Illinois	42.5	14	13. Texas
Indiana	38.5	19	14. Illinois
Iowa	38.5	20	15. Florida
Kansas	35.5	23	16. Wisconsin
Kentucky	19.6	46	17. Nebraska
Louisiana	20.6	44	18. Massachusetts
Maine	43.7	11	19. Indiana
Maryland	30.1	35	20. Iowa
Massachusetts	39.0	18	21. New York
Michigan	47.5	6	22. North Dakota
Minnesota	33.1	29	23. Kansas
Mississippi	26.2	38	24. Pennsylvania
Missouri	26.0	39	25. Colorado
Montana	54.8	4	26. Virginia
Nebraska	40.5	17	27. Arizona
Nevada	25.7	40	28. Washington
New Hampshire	75.9	1	29. Minnesota
New Jersey	50.6	5	30. South Carolina
New Mexico	15.3	49	31. Georgia
New York	36.9	21	32. California
North Carolina	24.7	42	33. Ohio
North Dakota	36.0	22	34. Idaho
Ohio	31.4	33	35. Maryland
Oklahoma	20.0	45	36. Utah
Oregon	43.7	12	37. Tennessee
Pennsylvania	34.9	24	38. Mississippi
Rhode Island	45.6	9	39. Missouri
South Carolina	32.4	30	40. Nevada
South Dakota	45.9	8	41. Delaware
Tennessee	26.6	37	42. North Carolina
Texas	42.6	13	43. West Virginia
Utah	27.7	36	44. Louisiana
Vermont	47.0	7	45. Oklahoma
Virginia	34.8	26	46. Kentucky
Washington	33.1	28	47. Hawaii
West Virginia	23.9	43	48. Arkansas
Wisconsin	40.7	16	49. New Mexico
Wyoming	57.2	3	50. Alabama
50 States	35.9		
DC	35.8		
United States	35.9		

State	State & local sales taxes $(millions)	State & local taxes as % of personal income %	Rank by %	Rank in order By %
Alabama	3,503	4.89	15	1. Washington
Alaska	214	1.56	48	2. Hawaii
Arizona	3,969	5.57	7	3. Nevada
Arkansas	2,093	5.40	11	4. New Mexico
California	27,573	4.04	27	5. Mississippi
Colorado	3,037	3.97	31	6. Tennessee
Connecticut	3,314	3.62	37	7. Arizona
Delaware	213	1.40	49	8. Louisiana
Florida	15,544	5.49	9	9. Florida
Georgia	5,708	4.30	21	10. Texas
Hawaii	1,935	7.07	2	11. Arkansas
Idaho	770	4.00	26	12. Utah
Illinois	10,103	3.83	32	13. North Dakota
Indiana	3,391	3.10	43	14. South Dakota
Iowa	2,042	3.96	28	15. Alabama
Kansas	2,171	4.32	20	16. West Virginia
Kentucky	2,860	4.45	18	17. Oklahoma
Louisiana	3,975	5.58	8	18. Kentucky
Maine	892	3.83	29	19. North Carolina
Maryland	3,506	2.95	44	20. Kansas
Massachusetts	3,596	2.44	45	21. Georgia
Michigan	6,136	3.15	42	22. Nebraska
Minnesota	3,930	4.14	25	23. New York
Mississippi	2,285	5.88	5	24. Missouri
Missouri	4,174	4.08	24	25. Minnesota
Montana	243	1.66	47	26. Idaho
Nebraska	1,300	4.09	22	27. California
Nevada	2,164	6.85	3	28. Iowa
New Hampshire	485	1.94	46	29. Maine
New Jersey	6,968	3.31	39	30. South Carolina
New Mexico	1,825	6.91	4	31. Colorado
New York	18,639	4.13	23	32. Illinois
North Carolina	5,698	4.39	19	33. Wisconsin
North Dakota	527	4.85	13	34. Wyoming
Ohio	7,953	3.65	36	35. Vermont
Oklahoma	2,624	4.77	17	36. Ohio
Oregon	668	1.13	50	37. Connecticut
Pennsylvania	8,378	3.27	40	38. Rhode Island
Rhode Island	723	3.41	38	39. New Jersey
South Carolina	2,409	3.93	30	40. Pennsylvania
South Dakota	617	4.80	14	41. Virginia
Tennessee	5,619	5.98	6	42. Michigan
Texas	18,729	5.43	10	43. Indiana
Utah	1,519	5.06	12	44. Maryland
Vermont	403	3.60	35	45. Massachusetts
Virginia	4,418	3.16	41	46. New Hampshire
Washington	8,410	7.35	1	47. Montana
West Virginia	1,419	4.83	16	48. Alaska
Wisconsin	3,815	3.82	33	49. Delaware
Wyoming	335	3.61	34	50. Oregon
50 States	222,822	4.17		
DC	805	4.67		
United States	223,628	4.17		

State	Sales taxes per capita $	Rank
Alabama	831	20
Alaska	354	47
Arizona	974	10
Arkansas	853	17
California	877	13
Colorado	831	21
Connecticut	1,012	9
Delaware	301	48
Florida	1,114	4
Georgia	809	23
Hawaii	1,642	1
Idaho	680	40
Illinois	860	14
Indiana	590	45
Iowa	722	33
Kansas	850	19
Kentucky	747	31
Louisiana	921	11
Maine	719	34
Maryland	700	37
Massachusetts	595	44
Michigan	646	43
Minnesota	860	15
Mississippi	856	16
Missouri	785	28
Montana	284	49
Nebraska	801	26
Nevada	1,486	3
New Hampshire	426	46
New Jersey	882	12
New Mexico	1,104	5
New York	1,026	7
North Carolina	806	25
North Dakota	826	22
Ohio	716	35
Oklahoma	806	24
Oregon	216	50
Pennsylvania	695	38
Rhode Island	725	32
South Carolina	657	42
South Dakota	856	18
Tennessee	1,086	6
Texas	1,019	8
Utah	796	27
Vermont	694	39
Virginia	674	41
Washington	1,574	2
West Virginia	779	29
Wisconsin	751	30
Wyoming	703	36
50 States	858	
DC	1,413	
United States	859	

1. Hawaii
2. Washington
3. Nevada
4. Florida
5. New Mexico
6. Tennessee
7. New York
8. Texas
9. Connecticut
10. Arizona
11. Louisiana
12. New Jersey
13. California
14. Illinois
15. Minnesota
16. Mississippi
17. Arkansas
18. South Dakota
19. Kansas
20. Alabama
21. Colorado
22. North Dakota
23. Georgia
24. Oklahoma
25. North Carolina
26. Nebraska
27. Utah
28. Missouri
29. West Virginia
30. Wisconsin
31. Kentucky
32. Rhode Island
33. Iowa
34. Maine
35. Ohio
36. Wyoming
37. Maryland
38. Pennsylvania
39. Vermont
40. Idaho
41. Virginia
42. South Carolina
43. Michigan
44. Massachusetts
45. Indiana
46. New Hampshire
47. Alaska
48. Delaware
49. Montana
50. Oregon

F-11 SALES TAX REVENUE AS % OF THREE-TAX REVENUES, FY 1994			Rank in order
State	Sales taxes as percent of three-tax revenues %	**Rank**	**By %**
Alabama	60.8	6	1. Nevada
Alaska	24.9	45	2. Tennessee
Arizona	49.0	16	3. Washington
Arkansas	57.0	10	4. New Mexico
California	41.9	22	5. Louisiana
Colorado	39.9	27	6. Alabama
Connecticut	33.4	35	7. Florida
Delaware	20.3	48	8. Mississippi
Florida	58.6	7	9. Texas
Georgia	41.7	23	10. Arkansas
Hawaii	54.9	11	11. Hawaii
Idaho	40.2	26	12. South Dakota
Illinois	38.3	29	13. Oklahoma
Indiana	30.7	39	14. West Virginia
Iowa	35.2	33	15. North Dakota
Kansas	41.6	24	16. Arizona
Kentucky	45.9	18	17. Missouri
Louisiana	63.7	5	18. Kentucky
Maine	33.3	36	19. Utah
Maryland	29.1	44	20. North Carolina
Massachusetts	23.6	46	21. Wyoming
Michigan	29.3	43	22. California
Minnesota	35.6	32	23. Georgia
Mississippi	57.7	8	24. Kansas
Missouri	47.1	17	25. South Carolina
Montana	18.6	49	26. Idaho
Nebraska	38.4	28	27. Colorado
Nevada	74.3	1	28. Nebraska
New Hampshire	22.4	47	29. Illinois
New Jersey	30.0	42	30. Pennsylvania
New Mexico	64.3	4	31. Ohio
New York	30.4	41	32. Minnesota
North Carolina	43.0	20	33. Iowa
North Dakota	50.8	15	34. Virginia
Ohio	35.7	31	35. Connecticut
Oklahoma	53.3	13	36. Maine
Oregon	11.6	50	37. Rhode Island
Pennsylvania	36.2	30	38. Vermont
Rhode Island	31.4	37	39. Indiana
South Carolina	41.3	25	40. Wisconsin
South Dakota	54.1	12	41. New York
Tennessee	72.1	2	42. New Jersey
Texas	57.4	9	43. Michigan
Utah	44.9	19	44. Maryland
Vermont	31.0	38	45. Alaska
Virginia	35.0	34	46. Massachusetts
Washington	66.9	3	47. New Hampshire
West Virginia	51.7	14	48. Delaware
Wisconsin	30.4	40	49. Montana
Wyoming	42.8	21	50. Oregon
50 States	40.7		
DC	35.5		
United States	40.7		

State	Services subject to sales tax	Rank
Alabama	32	28
Alaska	1	49
Arizona	57	21
Arkansas	65	15
California	13	46
Colorado	14	45
Connecticut	87	8
Delaware	142	4
Florida	64	16
Georgia	34	27
Hawaii	157	1
Idaho	29	31
Illinois	17	44
Indiana	22	40
Iowa	94	7
Kansas	76	10
Kentucky	26	37
Louisiana	58	20
Maine	27	36
Maryland	39	26
Massachusetts	20	41
Michigan	29	31
Minnesota	61	18
Mississippi	70	13
Missouri	28	33
Montana	19	42
Nebraska	49	25
Nevada	11	47
New Hampshire	11	47
New Jersey	50	24
New Mexico	152	2
New York	74	11
North Carolina	28	33
North Dakota	25	38
Ohio	52	23
Oklahoma	32	28
Oregon	0	50
Pennsylvania	61	18
Rhode Island	28	33
South Carolina	32	28
South Dakota	141	5
Tennessee	71	12
Texas	78	9
Utah	54	22
Vermont	23	39
Virginia	18	43
Washington	152	2
West Virginia	110	6
Wisconsin	69	14
Wyoming	63	17
50 States	n/a	
DC	63	
United States	n/a	

By #

1. Hawaii
2. New Mexico
2. Washington
4. Delaware
5. South Dakota
6. West Virginia
7. Iowa
8. Connecticut
9. Texas
10. Kansas
11. New York
12. Tennessee
13. Mississippi
14. Wisconsin
15. Arkansas
16. Florida
17. Wyoming
18. Minnesota
18. Pennsylvania
20. Louisiana
21. Arizona
22. Utah
23. Ohio
24. New Jersey
25. Nebraska
26. Maryland
27. Georgia
28. Alabama
28. Oklahoma
28. South Carolina
31. Idaho
31. Michigan
33. Missouri
33. North Carolina
33. Rhode Island
36. Maine
37. Kentucky
38. North Dakota
39. Vermont
40. Indiana
41. Massachusetts
42. Montana
43. Virginia
44. Illinois
45. Colorado
46. California
47. Nevada
47. New Hampshire
49. Alaska
50. Oregon

State	Individual income tax $(millions)	Income tax as percent of personal income %	Rank by %
Alabama	1,431	2.00	36
Alaska	0	n/a	n/a
Arizona	1,409	1.98	37
Arkansas	959	2.47	26
California	17,548	2.57	21
Colorado	1,926	2.51	23
Connecticut	2,237	2.44	27
Delaware	576	3.78	8
Florida	0	n/a	n/a
Georgia	3,581	2.70	18
Hawaii	962	3.51	7
Idaho	564	2.93	15
Illinois	5,054	1.92	38
Indiana	3,394	3.10	13
Iowa	1,528	2.96	14
Kansas	1,194	2.37	30
Kentucky	2,152	3.35	9
Louisiana	978	1.37	40
Maine	615	2.64	16
Maryland	4,908	4.13	3
Massachusetts	5,690	3.87	4
Michigan	4,866	2.50	24
Minnesota	3,449	3.63	6
Mississippi	638	1.64	39
Missouri	2,381	2.33	31
Montana	346	2.36	29
Nebraska	716	2.25	33
Nevada	0	n/a	n/a
New Hampshire	36	0.14	42
New Jersey	4,500	2.14	35
New Mexico	577	2.19	34
New York	20,121	4.46	1
North Carolina	4,288	3.30	11
North Dakota	137	1.26	41
Ohio	7,316	3.36	10
Oklahoma	1,315	2.39	28
Oregon	2,584	4.38	2
Pennsylvania	6,696	2.62	19
Rhode Island	528	2.49	25
South Carolina	1,531	2.50	22
South Dakota	0	0.00	44
Tennessee	99	0.11	43
Texas	0	n/a	n/a
Utah	925	3.08	12
Vermont	286	2.56	20
Virginia	3,812	2.73	17
Washington	0	n/a	n/a
West Virginia	670	2.28	32
Wisconsin	3,639	3.64	5
Wyoming	0	n/a	n/a
50 States	128,159	2.40	
DC	651	3.77	
United States	128,810	2.40	

Rank in order

By %

1. New York
2. Oregon
3. Maryland
4. Massachusetts
5. Wisconsin
6. Minnesota
7. Hawaii
8. Delaware
9. Kentucky
10. Ohio
11. North Carolina
12. Utah
13. Indiana
14. Iowa
15. Idaho
16. Maine
17. Virginia
18. Georgia
19. Pennsylvania
20. Vermont
21. California
22. South Carolina
23. Colorado
24. Michigan
25. Rhode Island
26. Arkansas
27. Connecticut
28. Oklahoma
29. Montana
30. Kansas
31. Missouri
32. West Virginia
33. Nebraska
34. New Mexico
35. New Jersey
36. Alabama
37. Arizona
38. Illinois
39. Mississippi
40. Louisiana
41. North Dakota
42. New Hampshire
43. Tennessee
44. South Dakota

State	Income taxes per capita $	Rank
Alabama	339	38
Alaska	0	n/a
Arizona	346	37
Arkansas	391	34
California	558	16
Colorado	527	20
Connecticut	683	9
Delaware	816	6
Florida	0	n/a
Georgia	508	22
Hawaii	816	5
Idaho	498	24
Illinois	430	30
Indiana	590	12
Iowa	540	18
Kansas	468	27
Kentucky	562	15
Louisiana	227	40
Maine	496	23
Maryland	980	2
Massachusetts	942	3
Michigan	512	21
Minnesota	755	7
Mississippi	239	39
Missouri	448	28
Montana	404	33
Nebraska	441	29
Nevada	0	n/a
New Hampshire	32	42
New Jersey	569	14
New Mexico	349	36
New York	1,107	1
North Carolina	607	11
North Dakota	215	41
Ohio	659	10
Oklahoma	404	32
Oregon	837	4
Pennsylvania	556	17
Rhode Island	530	19
South Carolina	418	31
South Dakota	0	44
Tennessee	19	43
Texas	0	n/a
Utah	485	26
Vermont	493	25
Virginia	582	13
Washington	0	n/a
West Virginia	368	35
Wisconsin	716	8
Wyoming	0	n/a
50 States	493	
DC	1,142	
United States	495	

Rank in order

By $

1. New York
2. Maryland
3. Massachusetts
4. Oregon
5. Hawaii
6. Delaware
7. Minnesota
8. Wisconsin
9. Connecticut
10. Ohio
11. North Carolina
12. Indiana
13. Virginia
14. New Jersey
15. Kentucky
16. California
17. Pennsylvania
18. Iowa
19. Rhode Island
20. Colorado
21. Michigan
22. Georgia
23. Maine
24. Idaho
25. Vermont
26. Utah
27. Kansas
28. Missouri
29. Nebraska
30. Illinois
31. South Carolina
32. Oklahoma
33. Montana
34. Arkansas
35. West Virginia
36. New Mexico
37. Arizona
38. Alabama
39. Mississippi
40. Louisiana
41. North Dakota
42. New Hampshire
43. Tennessee
44. South Dakota

State	Income tax as percent of three-tax revenues %	Rank
Alabama	24.8	26
Alaska	0.0	n/a
Arizona	17.4	38
Arkansas	26.1	24
California	26.7	19
Colorado	25.3	25
Connecticut	22.5	32
Delaware	54.8	1
Florida	0.0	n/a
Georgia	26.1	23
Hawaii	27.3	16
Idaho	29.5	12
Illinois	19.2	37
Indiana	30.7	10
Iowa	26.3	21
Kansas	22.9	31
Kentucky	34.5	5
Louisiana	15.7	40
Maine	22.9	30
Maryland	40.8	3
Massachusetts	37.3	4
Michigan	23.2	28
Minnesota	31.3	9
Mississippi	16.1	39
Missouri	26.9	17
Montana	26.5	20
Nebraska	21.1	34
Nevada	0.0	n/a
New Hampshire	1.7	42
New Jersey	19.4	36
New Mexico	20.3	35
New York	32.8	7
North Carolina	32.3	8
North Dakota	13.2	41
Ohio	32.9	6
Oklahoma	26.7	18
Oregon	44.8	2
Pennsylvania	28.9	14
Rhode Island	23.0	29
South Carolina	26.3	22
South Dakota	0.0	44
Tennessee	1.3	43
Texas	0.0	n/a
Utah	27.4	15
Vermont	22.0	33
Virginia	30.2	11
Washington	0.0	n/a
West Virginia	24.4	27
Wisconsin	29.0	13
Wyoming	0.0	n/a
50 States	23.4	
DC	28.7	
United States	23.4	

Rank in order

By %

1. Delaware
2. Oregon
3. Maryland
4. Massachusetts
5. Kentucky
6. Ohio
7. New York
8. North Carolina
9. Minnesota
10. Indiana
11. Virginia
12. Idaho
13. Wisconsin
14. Pennsylvania
15. Utah
16. Hawaii
17. Missouri
18. Oklahoma
19. California
20. Montana
21. Iowa
22. South Carolina
23. Georgia
24. Arkansas
25. Colorado
26. Alabama
27. West Virginia
28. Michigan
29. Rhode Island
30. Maine
31. Kansas
32. Connecticut
33. Vermont
34. Nebraska
35. New Mexico
36. New Jersey
37. Illinois
38. Arizona
39. Mississippi
40. Louisiana
41. North Dakota
42. New Hampshire
43. Tennessee
44. South Dakota

State	Highest rate %	Rank	By %
Alabama	3.0	39	1. Rhode Island
Alaska	No Tax	n/a	2. Hawaii
Arizona	5.6	30	3. Vermont
Arkansas	7.0	14	4. California
California	9.3	4	5. Oregon
Colorado	5.0	32	6. Maine
Connecticut	4.5	35	6. Minnesota
Delaware	7.1	13	6. New Mexico
Florida	No Tax	n/a	9. Idaho
Georgia	6.0	24	10. Kansas
Hawaii	10.0	2	10. North Carolina
Idaho	8.2	9	12. New York
Illinois	3.0	40	13. Delaware
Indiana	3.4	38	14. Ohio
Iowa	6.0	23	14. Arkansas
Kansas	7.8	10	14. South Carolina
Kentucky	6.0	24	17. Nebraska
Louisiana	3.6	37	18. Wisconsin
Maine	8.5	6	19. Montana
Maryland	5.0	32	20. West Virginia
Massachusetts	6.0	27	21. New Jersey
Michigan	4.4	36	22. Oklahoma
Minnesota	8.5	6	23. Iowa
Mississippi	5.0	32	24. Georgia
Missouri	6.0	24	24. Kentucky
Montana	6.6	19	24. Missouri
Nebraska	7.0	17	27. Massachusetts
Nevada	No Tax	n/a	28. Virginia
New Hampshire	No Tax	n/a	29. Utah
New Jersey	6.4	21	30. Arizona
New Mexico	8.5	6	31. North Dakota
New York	7.1	12	32. Colorado
North Carolina	7.8	10	32. Maryland
North Dakota	5.4	31	32. Mississippi
Ohio	7.0	14	35. Connecticut
Oklahoma	6.0	22	36. Michigan
Oregon	9.0	5	37. Louisiana
Pennsylvania	2.8	41	38. Indiana
Rhode Island	10.9	1	39. Alabama
South Carolina	7.0	14	40. Illinois
South Dakota	No Tax	n/a	41. Pennsylvania
Tennessee	No Tax	n/a	
Texas	No Tax	n/a	
Utah	5.6	29	
Vermont	9.9	3	
Virginia	5.8	28	
Washington	No Tax	n/a	
West Virginia	6.5	20	
Wisconsin	6.9	18	
Wyoming	No Tax	n/a	
50 States	n/a		
DC	9.5		
United States	n/a		

State	Corporate income taxes $(millions)	Corporate income taxes per capita $	Rank by per capita
Alabama	218	52	40
Alaska	176	291	2
Arizona	303	74	26
Arkansas	184	75	24
California	4,633	147	7
Colorado	146	40	46
Connecticut	702	214	5
Delaware	155	220	4
Florida	950	68	31
Georgia	521	74	28
Hawaii	68	58	39
Idaho	90	79	23
Illinois	1,229	105	15
Indiana	799	139	8
Iowa	174	62	35
Kansas	255	100	18
Kentucky	269	70	29
Louisiana	219	51	41
Maine	92	74	25
Maryland	320	64	33
Massachusetts	1,063	176	6
Michigan	2,175	229	3
Minnesota	552	121	12
Mississippi	168	63	34
Missouri	252	47	44
Montana	69	80	21
Nebraska	113	70	30
Nevada	0	n/a	n/a
New Hampshire	144	127	10
New Jersey	1,085	137	9
New Mexico	123	74	27
New York	5,597	308	1
North Carolina	737	104	16
North Dakota	71	112	13
Ohio	653	59	38
Oklahoma	162	50	43
Oregon	264	85	19
Pennsylvania	1,486	123	11
Rhode Island	79	80	22
South Carolina	219	60	37
South Dakota	37	51	42
Tennessee	422	82	20
Texas	0	n/a	n/a
Utah	125	66	32
Vermont	35	60	36
Virginia	307	47	45
Washington	0	n/a	n/a
West Virginia	185	101	17
Wisconsin	541	107	14
Wyoming	0	n/a	n/a
50 States	28,169	108	
DC	150	264	
United States	28,320	109	

Rank in order

By per capita

1. New York
2. Alaska
3. Michigan
4. Delaware
5. Connecticut
6. Massachusetts
7. California
8. Indiana
9. New Jersey
10. New Hampshire
11. Pennsylvania
12. Minnesota
13. North Dakota
14. Wisconsin
15. Illinois
16. North Carolina
17. West Virginia
18. Kansas
19. Oregon
20. Tennessee
21. Montana
22. Rhode Island
23. Idaho
24. Arkansas
25. Maine
26. Arizona
27. New Mexico
28. Georgia
29. Kentucky
30. Nebraska
31. Florida
32. Utah
33. Maryland
34. Mississippi
35. Iowa
36. Vermont
37. South Carolina
38. Ohio
39. Hawaii
40. Alabama
41. Louisiana
42. South Dakota
43. Oklahoma
44. Missouri
45. Virginia
46. Colorado

F-18 MOTOR FUEL TAXES

State	Gasoline tax 1997 cents/gal.	Motor fuel taxes FY 1994 $(millions)	Fuel taxes as % of personal income %	Rank by gas tax
Alabama	18	485	0.68	34
Alaska	8	41	0.29	49
Arizona	19	423	0.59	26
Arkansas	19	321	0.83	30
California	18	2,526	0.37	34
Colorado	22	406	0.53	15
Connecticut	39	406	0.44	1
Delaware	23	76	0.50	11
Florida	13	1,593	0.56	46
Georgia	8	491	0.37	50
Hawaii	16	136	0.50	41
Idaho	26	147	0.76	4
Illinois	19	1,264	0.48	26
Indiana	15	599	0.55	44
Iowa	21	354	0.69	18
Kansas	18	284	0.57	33
Kentucky	16	380	0.59	40
Louisiana	20	466	0.65	21
Maine	19	150	0.64	26
Maryland	24	588	0.49	10
Massachusetts	21	563	0.38	18
Michigan	15	795	0.41	44
Minnesota	20	487	0.51	21
Mississippi	18	347	0.89	32
Missouri	17	473	0.46	38
Montana	28	158	1.08	3
Nebraska	26	256	0.81	5
Nevada	24	225	0.71	8
New Hampshire	19	98	0.39	30
New Jersey	11	446	0.21	47
New Mexico	19	197	0.75	29
New York	22	490	0.11	17
North Carolina	23	909	0.70	13
North Dakota	20	83	0.76	21
Ohio	22	1,242	0.57	15
Oklahoma	17	353	0.64	39
Oregon	24	362	0.61	7
Pennsylvania	22	751	0.29	14
Rhode Island	29	120	0.56	2
South Carolina	16	304	0.50	41
South Dakota	18	88	0.68	34
Tennessee	21	684	0.73	18
Texas	20	2,171	0.63	21
Utah	20	187	0.62	25
Vermont	16	60	0.53	41
Virginia	18	671	0.48	37
Washington	23	632	0.55	11
West Virginia	25	205	0.70	6
Wisconsin	24	635	0.64	9
Wyoming	9	40	0.43	48
50 States	n/a	25,167	0.47	
DC	20	36	0.21	
United States	n/a	25,203	0.47	

State	Cigarette tax rate 1997 cents/pack	Tobacco taxes FY 1994 $(millions)	Tobacco taxes as % of personal income %	Rank by tax rate
Alabama	17	83.2	0.12	42
Alaska	29	16.8	0.12	27
Arizona	58	53.1	0.07	6
Arkansas	32	89.1	0.23	25
California	37	622.3	0.09	17
Colorado	20	62.8	0.08	36
Connecticut	50	124.8	0.14	8
Delaware	24	20.7	0.14	31
Florida	34	438.9	0.15	23
Georgia	12	80.6	0.06	45
Hawaii	60	32.7	0.12	5
Idaho	28	19.1	0.10	28
Illinois	44	479.6	0.18	10
Indiana	16	79.7	0.07	43
Iowa	36	96.2	0.19	19
Kansas	24	54.1	0.11	31
Kentucky	3	17.2	0.03	49
Louisiana	20	82.4	0.12	36
Maine	37	46.1	0.20	17
Maryland	36	139.8	0.12	19
Massachusetts	76	237.3	0.16	2
Michigan	75	395.8	0.20	3
Minnesota	48	169.7	0.18	9
Mississippi	18	54.2	0.14	38
Missouri	17	117.5	0.11	40
Montana	18	13.8	0.09	38
Nebraska	34	46.3	0.15	22
Nevada	35	47.9	0.15	21
New Hampshire	25	42.9	0.17	30
New Jersey	40	255.6	0.12	15
New Mexico	21	23.9	0.09	35
New York	56	742.5	0.16	7
North Carolina	5	37.9	0.03	48
North Dakota	44	24.0	0.22	10
Ohio	24	287.1	0.13	31
Oklahoma	23	73.1	0.13	34
Oregon	38	104.7	0.18	16
Pennsylvania	31	307.7	0.12	26
Rhode Island	61	41.1	0.19	4
South Carolina	7	29.2	0.05	47
South Dakota	33	14.2	0.11	24
Tennessee	13	81.4	0.09	44
Texas	41	573.5	0.17	14
Utah	27	27.6	0.09	29
Vermont	44	14.2	0.13	10
Virginia	3	44.4	0.03	50
Washington	83	215.3	0.19	1
West Virginia	17	33.6	0.11	40
Wisconsin	44	180.2	0.18	10
Wyoming	12	5.7	0.06	45
50 States	n/a	6,881.3	0.13	
DC	65	21.7	0.13	
United States	32	6,903.0	0.13	

Rank in order

By tax rate

1. Washington
2. Massachusetts
3. Michigan
4. Rhode Island
5. Hawaii
6. Arizona
7. New York
8. Connecticut
9. Minnesota
10. Illinois
10. North Dakota
10. Vermont
10. Wisconsin
14. Texas
15. New Jersey
16. Oregon
17. California
17. Maine
19. Iowa
19. Maryland
21. Nevada
22. Nebraska
23. Florida
24. South Dakota
25. Arkansas
26. Pennsylvania
27. Alaska
28. Idaho
29. Utah
30. New Hampshire
31. Delaware
31. Kansas
31. Ohio
34. Oklahoma
35. New Mexico
36. Colorado
36. Louisiana
38. Mississippi
38. Montana
40. Missouri
40. West Virginia
42. Alabama
43. Indiana
44. Tennessee
45. Georgia
45. Wyoming
47. South Carolina
48. North Carolina
49. Kentucky
50. Virginia

F-20 TAX BURDEN ON HIGH INCOME FAMILY, 1996

State	Tax burden $	Rank
Alabama	6,146	44
Alaska	2,982	50
Arizona	7,271	37
Arkansas	8,687	24
California	10,269	13
Colorado	7,639	34
Connecticut	10,174	14
Delaware	6,393	41
Florida	6,363	42
Georgia	8,480	26
Hawaii	10,304	12
Idaho	9,398	21
Illinois	10,937	9
Indiana	7,782	31
Iowa	10,589	10
Kansas	8,710	23
Kentucky	9,475	18
Louisiana	5,942	45
Maine	11,680	5
Maryland	10,349	11
Massachusetts	11,586	6
Michigan	9,421	20
Minnesota	12,424	3
Mississippi	7,004	38
Missouri	8,446	27
Montana	7,693	32
Nebraska	11,397	8
Nevada	5,246	46
New Hampshire	4,638	48
New Jersey	10,013	15
New Mexico	6,964	39
New York	14,005	1
North Carolina	8,860	22
North Dakota	8,218	29
Ohio	11,466	7
Oklahoma	8,317	28
Oregon	9,654	16
Pennsylvania	9,423	19
Rhode Island	12,398	4
South Carolina	7,690	33
South Dakota	7,337	36
Tennessee	4,877	47
Texas	6,435	40
Utah	8,590	25
Vermont	9,482	17
Virginia	7,431	35
Washington	6,319	43
West Virginia	8,113	30
Wisconsin	12,911	2
Wyoming	3,063	49
50 States	8,580	
DC	13,552	
United States	8,677	

By $

1. New York
2. Wisconsin
3. Minnesota
4. Rhode Island
5. Maine
6. Massachusetts
7. Ohio
8. Nebraska
9. Illinois
10. Iowa
11. Maryland
12. Hawaii
13. California
14. Connecticut
15. New Jersey
16. Oregon
17. Vermont
18. Kentucky
19. Pennsylvania
20. Michigan
21. Idaho
22. North Carolina
23. Kansas
24. Arkansas
25. Utah
26. Georgia
27. Missouri
28. Oklahoma
29. North Dakota
30. West Virginia
31. Indiana
32. Montana
33. South Carolina
34. Colorado
35. Virginia
36. South Dakota
37. Arizona
38. Mississippi
39. New Mexico
40. Texas
41. Delaware
42. Florida
43. Washington
44. Alabama
45. Louisiana
46. Nevada
47. Tennessee
48. New Hampshire
49. Wyoming
50. Alaska

State	Taxes for family with $50,000/year income $	Percent of income %	Rank by $	Rank in order By $
Alabama	3,899	7.8	31	1. Connecticut
Alaska	1,372	2.7	50	2. New Jersey
Arizona	4,048	8.1	25	3. New York
Arkansas	3,832	7.7	32	4. Maine
California	3,942	7.9	30	5. Wisconsin
Colorado	3,727	7.5	37	6. Pennsylvania
Connecticut	11,175	22.4	1	7. Maryland
Delaware	3,808	7.6	34	8. Kentucky
Florida	2,409	4.8	47	8. New Hampshire
Georgia	4,027	8.1	27	10. Massachusetts
Hawaii	4,525	9.1	16	11. Michigan
Idaho	4,143	8.3	23	12. Rhode Island
Illinois	4,017	8.0	28	13. Nebraska
Indiana	4,070	8.1	24	14. Ohio
Iowa	4,251	8.5	20	15. Oregon
Kansas	3,805	7.6	35	16. Hawaii
Kentucky	5,226	10.5	8	17. North Carolina
Louisiana	3,514	7.0	42	18. Utah
Maine	6,252	12.5	4	19. Virginia
Maryland	5,446	10.9	7	20. Iowa
Massachusetts	5,211	10.4	10	21. Minnesota
Michigan	5,205	10.4	11	22. Vermont
Minnesota	4,226	8.5	21	23. Idaho
Mississippi	3,654	7.3	40	24. Indiana
Missouri	3,822	7.6	33	25. Arizona
Montana	3,516	7.0	41	26. Oklahoma
Nebraska	4,816	9.6	13	27. Georgia
Nevada	2,301	4.6	48	28. Illinois
New Hampshire	5,226	10.5	8	29. South Carolina
New Jersey	6,860	13.7	2	30. California
New Mexico	3,723	7.4	38	31. Alabama
New York	6,514	13.0	3	32. Arkansas
North Carolina	4,395	8.8	17	33. Missouri
North Dakota	3,460	6.9	43	34. Delaware
Ohio	4,594	9.2	14	35. Kansas
Oklahoma	4,038	8.1	26	36. West Virginia
Oregon	4,561	9.1	15	37. Colorado
Pennsylvania	5,924	11.8	6	38. New Mexico
Rhode Island	5,180	10.4	12	39. South Dakota
South Carolina	3,992	8.0	29	40. Mississippi
South Dakota	3,702	7.4	39	41. Montana
Tennessee	2,529	5.1	46	42. Louisiana
Texas	2,758	5.5	45	43. North Dakota
Utah	4,262	8.5	18	44. Washington
Vermont	4,182	8.4	22	45. Texas
Virginia	4,256	8.5	19	46. Tennessee
Washington	2,978	6.0	44	47. Florida
West Virginia	3,747	7.5	36	48. Nevada
Wisconsin	6,075	12.2	5	49. Wyoming
Wyoming	1,777	3.6	49	50. Alaska
50 States	n/a	n/a		
DC	4,592	9.2		
United States	4,305	8.6		

State	Progressivity index %	Rank
Alabama	101.5	10
Alaska	116.7	3
Arizona	89.1	18
Arkansas	76.1	38
California	61.2	47
Colorado	85.8	22
Connecticut	89.3	17
Delaware	75.2	40
Florida	84.3	24
Georgia	64.2	46
Hawaii	77.6	36
Idaho	61.1	48
Illinois	97.7	12
Indiana	101.1	11
Iowa	84.5	23
Kansas	82.9	29
Kentucky	87.3	19
Louisiana	73.7	42
Maine	77.0	37
Maryland	86.1	21
Massachusetts	82.7	30
Michigan	90.2	16
Minnesota	59.5	50
Mississippi	67.5	44
Missouri	84.2	25
Montana	74.0	41
Nebraska	83.8	27
Nevada	121.2	1
New Hampshire	110.6	7
New Jersey	94.0	13
New Mexico	73.0	43
New York	67.3	45
North Carolina	82.5	31
North Dakota	93.9	14
Ohio	83.4	28
Oklahoma	81.5	33
Oregon	81.3	34
Pennsylvania	107.6	8
Rhode Island	84.1	26
South Carolina	59.6	49
South Dakota	114.1	5
Tennessee	117.0	2
Texas	111.9	6
Utah	75.5	39
Vermont	82.2	32
Virginia	90.9	15
Washington	114.8	4
West Virginia	79.5	35
Wisconsin	86.3	20
Wyoming	105.7	9
50 States	n/a	
DC	76.8	
United States	86.4	

Rank in order

By %

1. Nevada
2. Tennessee
3. Alaska
4. Washington
5. South Dakota
6. Texas
7. New Hampshire
8. Pennsylvania
9. Wyoming
10. Alabama
11. Indiana
12. Illinois
13. New Jersey
14. North Dakota
15. Virginia
16. Michigan
17. Connecticut
18. Arizona
19. Kentucky
20. Wisconsin
21. Maryland
22. Colorado
23. Iowa
24. Florida
25. Missouri
26. Rhode Island
27. Nebraska
28. Ohio
29. Kansas
30. Massachusetts
31. North Carolina
32. Vermont
33. Oklahoma
34. Oregon
35. West Virginia
36. Hawaii
37. Maine
38. Arkansas
39. Utah
40. Delaware
41. Montana
42. Louisiana
43. New Mexico
44. Mississippi
45. New York
46. Georgia
47. California
48. Idaho
49. South Carolina
50. Minnesota

State	Estate taxes above federal credit level	Inheritance taxes above federal credit level
Alabama		
Alaska		
Arizona		
Arkansas		
California		
Colorado		
Connecticut		Inheritance
Delaware		Inheritance
Florida		
Georgia		
Hawaii		
Idaho		
Illinois		
Indiana		Inheritance
Iowa		Inheritance
Kansas		Inheritance
Kentucky		Inheritance
Louisiana		Inheritance
Maine		
Maryland		Inheritance
Massachusetts	Estate	
Michigan		
Minnesota		
Mississippi	Estate	
Missouri		
Montana		Inheritance
Nebraska		Inheritance
Nevada		
New Hampshire		Inheritance
New Jersey		Inheritance
New Mexico		
New York	Estate	
North Carolina		Inheritance
North Dakota		
Ohio	Estate	
Oklahoma	Estate	
Oregon		
Pennsylvania		Inheritance
Rhode Island		
South Carolina		
South Dakota		Inheritance
Tennessee		Inheritance
Texas		
Utah		
Vermont		
Virginia		
Washington		
West Virginia		
Wisconsin		
Wyoming		
50 States		
DC		
United States		

Source Notes for Taxes (Section F)

F-1 State and Local Tax Revenue, Total and as Percent of Personal Income, FY 1994: This is the most common definition of the tax burdens of state and local governments. It is the tax component of "general revenue" used by the Census Bureau in its annual survey of government finances. It excludes taxes used to finance certain trust funds, such as Unemployment Insurance taxes, but includes other earmarked revenues, such as gasoline tax revenues for highway construction. Tax revenues are related to personal income as a common proxy for tax base or "ability to pay."

For decades, state officials, media, scholars, taxpayer groups, and others have been comparing tax burdens and spending patterns of states using data published by the Bureau of the Census in its annual volume *Governmental Finances In [year]*. These data were also republished in many secondary sources such as *Significant Features Of Fiscal Federalism*, published by the Advisory Commission on Intergovernmental Relations, the *Statistical Abstract Of The United States*, published by the Census Bureau and U.S. Government Printing Office, and other secondary sources.

The Census Bureau and other federal statistical agencies have been responding to tight budgets by limiting the number of their printed publications and analyses, both statistical and narrative, of the data they produce. This has allowed them to concentrate their resources on what only they can do — collecting and refining the underlying data. Beginning with the data for 1993, the Census Bureau has stopped publishing state and local fiscal data in printed reports such as *Governmental Finances*, making it available only electronically. Also the Bureau has discontinued making popular analytical calculations such as those comparing taxes and spending with personal income and population. This change and budget restrictions have eliminated some secondary sources, such as *Significant Features*.

Anyone with access to the Internet, computer capability, and the ability to "unzip" and download the Census data can make calculations such as taxes as a percentage of personal income and per capita spending on particular state and/or local functions. However, not everyone has these capabilities and those that do can produce different data from each other unless they are careful to follow particular complex conventions covering such matters as which concepts of taxing and spending to use, which revision of often-revised government data to use, and which years of population and personal income estimates to use.

No government agency, including the Census Bureau, will certify the resulting differing numbers as the appropriate ones nor vouch for their accuracy in applying past concepts for calculating them. However, many users will demand that comparative numbers be consistent from user to user, from year to year, and from state to state. As a result, some publications are becoming more authoritative than others. Congressional Quarterly, Inc., in conjunction with State Policy Research, Inc., is committed to publishing these comparative data annually in such widely used publications as *State Fact Finder*, *State Policy Reports*, and *Governing* magazine. It is likely that these sources, which are using identical data, will become the standard sources for most users.

All of the tables in *State Fact Finder* which rely on Census Bureau data covering government finances in 1994 use the same conventions, based on past practices of the Census Bureau. The underlying data on tax revenues and spending come from the Census Bureau Internet web site (http://www.census.gov) where they appear as "State and Local Government Finance Estimates, by State." These data reflect fiscal information for varying government fiscal years ending in 1994 which for most states is a fiscal year ending on June 30, 1994 and for many local governments is a fiscal year ending on December 31, 1994.

Following the historical practice of the Census Bureau not to use revised personal income and population numbers , the personal income numbers used for comparison with these fiscal data are calendar year data for 1993 representing the original 1993 estimates released by the Bureau of Economic Analysis. The population data used to calculate per capita amounts are estimates for July 1 of 1994, as originally released by the Census Bureau in 1995.

The data on tax burdens and spending in relation to personal income and per capita are comparable with those of prior years, as published by the Census Bureau and secondary sources, to exactly the degree that Census data for earlier years have been comparable. Data for any year are not recalculated. While underlying data on government revenues and spending are not normally revised, the Census Bureau and Bureau of Economic Analysis do re-estimate historical estimates of population and personal income.

F-2 Per Capita State and Local Tax Revenue, FY 1994: This table relates total tax revenue to population, providing another measure of relative tax burdens (see Table F-1). It also shows the division of tax revenues between state and local governments in each state.

F-3 State and Local Tax Effort, 1991: The revenue-raising ability of states and their local governments varies markedly among the states. For example, Alaska and Texas get massive revenues by taxing oil and gas and Nevada gets large revenues from taxing casino gambling, but most states get no revenue from these sources. What states will collect from particular tax rates applied to property, sales, and income is higher in states with more affluent citizens. Because of these differences, the revenue collected (see Tables F-1 and F-2) is not a good indicator of how high tax rates are in each state.

A more appropriate way to compare the relative burden of state and local taxes, or what is often called "tax effort," is to consider what each state would raise if it and its local governments applied national average tax rates to their own tax bases. This approach, known as the "representative tax system," has been pioneered by the Advisory Commission on Intergovernmental Relations. Its most recent publication, *State Revenue Capacity and Tax Effort*, was based on Census data for 1991.

The values reflect differences in tax effort. For example, New York state and local governments have taxes that raise 56 percent more than would be raised if tax rates in that state were equal to the national average.

Gradually since about 1980, the federal government has been reducing its support of analyses of state and local finances such as the calculation of the representative tax system. The resulting void has only been partly filled by associations of officials of state and local governments, foundations, individual university-based scholars, and organizations such as State Policy Research, Inc. The Advisory Commission on Intergovernmental Relations was phased out of existence during 1996. As a result, certain analytic statistics, such as the representative tax system, have not recently been recalculated.

The result is a large and growing gap between information that users would like to have and information available. For example, because of lags in the collection and publication of the underlying Census Bureau data, the representative tax system values shown in this table could not have been calculated for 1994 until the spring of 1997. But no one has made the calculations, which are expensive to make, for 1992 or 1993, and no one is making them for 1993.

While the best available data on tax effort and tax capacity are those appearing in Tables F-3 and F-4, they must be used with caution. Since 1991 there have been dramatic differences in the economic growth rates, and thus tax-raising capacity, of individual states. Key elements of tax capacity — such as property values, sales, and personal incomes — have risen much more rapidly in many Southern and Western states than in the Northeast. Within regions, some states (e.g., California and Hawaii in the West) have seen their tax bases grow more slowly than others (e.g., Oregon and Utah). So, currently, relative tax capacity in the fast-growing states was somewhat greater and in slow-growing states somewhat smaller than shown on Table F-4. Tax effort, as shown in this table, has changed both in response to changes in capacity and locally initiated changes in tax rates, but no one can calculate by how much.

F-4 State and Local Tax Capacity, 1991: The representative tax system (see Table F-3) also permits a comparison of the tax base, or fiscal capacity, of individual states.

This is presented in what can be viewed either as percentages of the national average or as index numbers. Either way, the table indicates, for example, that if it applied national average tax rates, Alabama would raise only 81 percent of the amount that those same rates would in the average state. For reasons indicated in the notes to Table F-3, these data are not available for any year more recent than 1991.

F-5 Change in State and Local Taxes, FY 1989-1994: In the five years covered by the table, the Census Bureau reports for each year indicate that state and local tax revenues have increased by about 34 percent. However, growth has been much faster in some states than others. See Table F-1 for source for 1994 figures, 1989 numbers come from Census publication GF-89-5 (*Government Finances in 1988-1989*)

The table shows increases in state and local taxes as would be expected because the nation's population has been growing and prices have increased due to inflation. Predictably, the increases tend to be largest in states where population and government workloads, such as children in public schools, have grown most rapidly, such as Nevada. However, tax burdens (taxes in relation to personal income) did not grow during the five years and actually declined in many states.

F-6 Property Taxes, Total and as Percent of Personal Income, FY 1994: This and subsequent tables deal with the total revenues raised by particular state and local taxes. They start with the revenues from that tax as indicated by Census Bureau date (see notes to Table F-1). That revenue is then related to both population and personal income to provide the two most common measures of the level, or burdens, of that tax in each state.

F-7 Property Taxes, Per Capita, FY 1994: See notes to Table F-6.

F-8 Property Tax Revenue as Percent of Three-Tax Revenues, FY 1994: Some people feel that their total state and local taxes are too high while others may not be sure about total tax burdens but feel that a particular revenue source, such as property taxes, is too heavily used in their state. This table, using Census data (see notes to Table F-1), relates the amount raised from taxing property with the amounts raised from the other two major tax bases — sales and income.

F-9 Sales Taxes, Total and as Percent of Personal Income, FY 1994: All states, including those which do not have state sales taxes, show some sales tax revenues. The Census Bureau counts as sales tax revenues both revenues from sales taxes levied on sales of most goods and special excise taxes on particular goods, such as tobacco and alcoholic beverages. See notes to Table F-6.

F-10 Sales Taxes Per Capita, FY 1994: See notes to Tables F-6 and F-9.

F-11 Sales Tax Revenue as Percent of Three-Tax Revenues, FY 1994: See notes to Tables F-8 and F-9.

F-12 Number of Services Reached by Sales Tax, 1996: Sales taxes of state and local governments typically apply to goods, such as cars and clothing, but not to services, such as barbering and landscaping. Many experts suggest that the sales tax would be fairer and a more productive revenue source if it applied equally to both sales and services. This table shows the number of services covered in 1996 by the sales tax in each state. It was compiled by the Federation of Tax Administrators and is available on their web site (http://sso.org/fta/fta.html). The table includes states, such as Oregon, that have no general sales tax and ones, such as Alaska, that may have special excise taxes on a few services.

F-13 Individual Income Taxes, Total and as Percent of Personal Income, FY 1994: Some states which do not tax personal income from wages and salaries do have taxes based on income from other sources, such as dividends, interest, rent, and capital gains. Revenues from these taxes appear in the table. For source see notes to Table F-6.

F-14 Individual Income Taxes Per Capita, FY 1994: See notes to Table F-6 and F-13.

F-15 Individual Income Tax Revenue as Percent of Three-Tax Revenues, FY 1994: See notes to Table F-8.

F-16 Highest Personal Income Tax Rate, 1997: While some states have no income tax at all, the rates paid by high-income households can go as high as 10 percent in a few. This table, developed by State Policy Research from compilations of state tax laws, shows the highest state personal income tax rates. A few states use low flat rate income taxes with few deductions and exemptions, so the same rate is applicable to all taxable income. Most states use a graduated rate schedule. In most of the states showing the highest rates in the table, this "marginal" or "top bracket" rate is paid only on income exceeding a threshold of $100,000 or more. The rates shown were those in effect in December of 1997 on income earned in 1997 to be reported on tax returns filed in early 1998. Some states, including Maryland and Ohio, lowered their rates on income during their 1997 legislative sessions. Others, such as Oregon, have made large income tax rebates.

F-17 Corporate Income Taxes, Total and Per Capita, FY 1994: See notes to Table F-6. This table is now the best of many unsatisfactory ways of comparing corporate income taxes in the 50 states. However, since 1994 states have made more changes in corporate income taxes (tax base, tax rates, tax credits) than in any other single tax affecting business.

Because of the widespread use of special tax credits for investment, research and development, job expansion and other purposes and differences among states in how much income of multi-state corporations is attributed to the taxing state, comparisons of corporate income tax rates are not particularly meaningful. Because of rapid changes in the location of business activity since 1991 as well as changes in tax laws, the representative tax system calculations of tax effort which appeared in the 1996 edition of *State Fact Finder* are no longer useful and have not been updated (see notes to Table F-3).

The most appropriate way to compare corporate income taxes of states is to make calculations of tax liability for individual hypothetical corporations. Such calculations reflect the different state definitions of the tax base, different tax rates, and different tax credits as well as different characteristics of firms in particularly industries which affect tax liability. These calculations are complex because taxes levied by one state depend in part on taxes levied by other states. Such calculations have been made in special studies prepared for individual states, but are typically made only for those 10 to 20 states that the requesting state considers to be its major competitors in economic development.

F-18 Motor Fuel Taxes: States tax motor fuels, such as gasoline and diesel fuel, mostly to provide funds for road construction and maintenance. The table shows the tax rate on gasoline from a special compilation prepared by the Federation of Tax Administrators, covering rates in effect at the beginning of 1997 (http://sso.org/fta/fta.html). It also includes total state and local revenues from motor fuel taxes in fiscal 1994 compiled by the Census Bureau and available on their website (see notes to Table F-1). *State Fact Finder* related those revenues to personal income.

F-19 Tobacco Taxes: These data come from the same sources as those of Table F-18 but cover cigarette and related tobacco taxes.

F-20 Tax Burden on High Income Family, 1996: The amounts shown are the liability to be faced by a typical higher income family for state and local income, sales, property, and gasoline taxes in 1996. The calculation was made by *Money* magazine from a variety of sources, including state-by-state calculations of income tax liability by the accounting firm of Ernst & Young. The tax liability reflects the average income of readers of the magazine ($88,764). *Money* published these results in its January 1997 issue.

F-21 State and Local Taxes in the Largest City in Each State, 1995: These data show the costs of state and local taxes in the largest city in each state to typical families with incomes of $50,000, as calculated by the District of Columbia Department of Finance and Revenue in *Tax Rates and Tax Burdens in the District of Columbia: A Nationwide Comparison* dated June, 1996. The calculations for each state's largest city are not necessarily representative of statewide averages.

F-22 Progressivity of Major State and Local Taxes, 1995: These data compare the tax burdens as a percentage of income on households of two income levels ($25,000 and $100,000), using data from the analysis described in the notes to Table F-21. Low numbers indicate that the percentage paid by higher income households is significantly higher than the percentage paid by low-income households, making the state and local tax structure "progressive." States with no personal income tax and high reliance on sales and property taxes, such as Nevada, have tax systems that can be called regressive. Their progressivity percentages over one hundred indicate that poorer households pay a larger percentage of their income on state and local taxes than do higher income households.

F-23 Estate and Inheritance Taxes Above Federal Credit Level, 1995: The federal government levies taxes on the estates of persons when they die. State governments also tax estates either directly by taxing the amount left to heirs (estate taxes) or by taxing the amounts received by particular heirs (inheritance taxes). Some of the state tax liability is allowed by the federal government as a 100 percent credit against federal taxes owed. This means that states can levy taxes up to the amount of the credit without making taxpayers pay more, so all states levy such "pick-up" taxes. Some states levy additional taxes, though the trend has been to eliminate the extra taxes out of fear that they encourage affluent older residents to take up residence in other states. The table shows which states levy these extra taxes and the type of tax they use. The information comes from a special compilation of the National Conference of State Legislatures.

Revenues and Finances

G-1 STATE AND LOCAL TOTAL REVENUE, FY 1994

State	Total revenue $(millions)	Per capita total revenue $	Total revenue as % of personal income %	Rank by per capita
Alabama	17,648	4,186	24.6	44
Alaska	7,824	12,911	56.8	1
Arizona	18,941	4,648	26.6	30
Arkansas	9,151	3,731	23.6	50
California	179,279	5,704	26.2	7
Colorado	18,387	5,029	24.0	18
Connecticut	18,045	5,510	19.7	12
Delaware	4,021	5,696	26.4	8
Florida	64,401	4,616	22.7	32
Georgia	32,099	4,550	24.2	35
Hawaii	7,075	6,001	25.8	4
Idaho	4,957	4,375	25.7	39
Illinois	55,660	4,736	21.1	29
Indiana	24,816	4,314	22.7	41
Iowa	13,530	4,783	26.2	27
Kansas	12,105	4,740	24.1	28
Kentucky	15,778	4,123	24.6	46
Louisiana	19,851	4,600	27.9	33
Maine	5,741	4,630	24.7	31
Maryland	24,350	4,864	20.5	22
Massachusetts	33,048	5,471	22.5	13
Michigan	48,191	5,075	24.8	17
Minnesota	26,314	5,762	27.7	6
Mississippi	10,831	4,058	27.9	48
Missouri	20,696	3,894	20.2	49
Montana	4,125	4,819	28.2	25
Nebraska	8,716	5,370	27.4	15
Nevada	7,248	4,975	22.9	19
New Hampshire	4,946	4,350	19.8	40
New Jersey	45,675	5,779	21.7	5
New Mexico	8,214	4,966	31.1	20
New York	135,266	7,445	30.0	2
North Carolina	31,708	4,485	24.4	37
North Dakota	3,081	4,829	28.3	24
Ohio	58,171	5,240	26.7	16
Oklahoma	13,235	4,062	24.0	47
Oregon	16,603	5,380	28.2	14
Pennsylvania	57,970	4,810	22.7	26
Rhode Island	5,561	5,578	26.2	10
South Carolina	16,581	4,525	27.1	36
South Dakota	3,093	4,290	24.1	42
Tennessee	23,807	4,600	25.4	34
Texas	78,821	4,289	22.8	43
Utah	9,229	4,837	30.8	23
Vermont	2,872	4,953	25.7	21
Virginia	27,279	4,163	19.5	45
Washington	30,381	5,686	26.6	9
West Virginia	8,108	4,450	27.6	38
Wisconsin	28,281	5,565	28.3	11
Wyoming	3,300	6,934	35.6	3
50 States	1,325,010	5,100	24.8	
DC	6,432	11,284	37.3	
United States	1,331,442	5,114	24.8	

Rank in order

By per capita

1. Alaska
2. New York
3. Wyoming
4. Hawaii
5. New Jersey
6. Minnesota
7. California
8. Delaware
9. Washington
10. Rhode Island
11. Wisconsin
12. Connecticut
13. Massachusetts
14. Oregon
15. Nebraska
16. Ohio
17. Michigan
18. Colorado
19. Nevada
20. New Mexico
21. Vermont
22. Maryland
23. Utah
24. North Dakota
25. Montana
26. Pennsylvania
27. Iowa
28. Kansas
29. Illinois
30. Arizona
31. Maine
32. Florida
33. Louisiana
34. Tennessee
35. Georgia
36. South Carolina
37. North Carolina
38. West Virginia
39. Idaho
40. New Hampshire
41. Indiana
42. South Dakota
43. Texas
44. Alabama
45. Virginia
46. Kentucky
47. Oklahoma
48. Mississippi
49. Missouri
50. Arkansas

State	General revenue $millions)	Per capita $	As % of personal income %	Rank by per capita		By per capita
Alabama	14,581	3,459	20.4	46		1. Alaska
Alaska	6,670	11,006	48.4	1		2. New York
Arizona	14,903	3,657	20.9	40		3. Wyoming
Arkansas	7,869	3,208	20.3	50		4. Hawaii
California	140,940	4,484	20.6	10		5. Connecticut
Colorado	14,693	4,019	19.2	25		6. New Jersey
Connecticut	16,771	5,121	18.3	5		7. Delaware
Delaware	3,459	4,899	22.7	7		8. Minnesota
Florida	54,516	3,907	19.2	31		9. Massachusetts
Georgia	26,961	3,821	20.3	35		10. California
Hawaii	6,292	5,336	23.0	4		11. Washington
Idaho	4,082	3,603	21.2	41		12. Rhode Island
Illinois	46,373	3,946	17.6	28		13. Oregon
Indiana	22,318	3,880	20.4	32		14. Wisconsin
Iowa	11,731	4,147	22.8	20		15. Michigan
Kansas	10,277	4,024	20.4	24		16. Vermont
Kentucky	13,488	3,525	21.0	44		17. North Dakota
Louisiana	17,400	4,032	24.4	23		18. New Mexico
Maine	5,098	4,112	21.9	21		19. Maryland
Maryland	20,858	4,167	17.6	19		20. Iowa
Massachusetts	28,747	4,759	19.5	9		21. Maine
Michigan	41,259	4,345	21.2	15		22. Nebraska
Minnesota	21,998	4,817	23.2	8		23. Louisiana
Mississippi	9,337	3,498	24.0	45		24. Kansas
Missouri	17,448	3,283	17.0	49		25. Colorado
Montana	3,434	4,012	23.5	26		26. Montana
Nebraska	6,553	4,038	20.6	22		27. Pennsylvania
Nevada	5,746	3,944	18.2	29		28. Illinois
New Hampshire	4,457	3,920	17.9	30		29. Nevada
New Jersey	39,278	4,969	18.6	6		30. New Hampshire
New Mexico	7,075	4,277	26.8	18		31. Florida
New York	113,354	6,239	25.1	2		32. Indiana
North Carolina	25,892	3,662	19.9	39		33. Ohio
North Dakota	2,740	4,294	25.2	17		34. West Virginia
Ohio	42,820	3,857	19.7	33		35. Georgia
Oklahoma	10,977	3,369	19.9	47		36. Utah
Oregon	13,566	4,396	23.0	13		37. South Dakota
Pennsylvania	47,849	3,970	18.7	27		38. South Carolina
Rhode Island	4,428	4,441	20.9	12		39. North Carolina
South Carolina	13,469	3,676	22.0	38		40. Arizona
South Dakota	2,655	3,683	20.6	37		41. Idaho
Tennessee	17,394	3,361	18.5	48		42. Texas
Texas	66,108	3,597	19.2	42		43. Virginia
Utah	7,032	3,686	23.4	36		44. Kentucky
Vermont	2,513	4,333	22.5	16		45. Mississippi
Virginia	23,497	3,586	16.8	43		46. Alabama
Washington	23,821	4,458	20.8	11		47. Oklahoma
West Virginia	6,974	3,828	23.7	34		48. Tennessee
Wisconsin	22,182	4,365	22.2	14		49. Missouri
Wyoming	2,928	6,151	31.6	3		50. Arkansas
50 States	1,094,812	4,214	20.5			
DC	5,629	9,876	32.6			
United States	1,100,441	4,227	20.5			

State	State & local "own-source" general revenue $(millions)	Per capita $	As % of personal income %	Rank by per capita	Rank in order — By per capita
Alabama	11,281	2,676	15.8	46	1. Alaska
Alaska	5,667	9,351	41.1	1	2. New York
Arizona	12,078	2,964	16.9	35	3. Wyoming
Arkansas	5,868	2,392	15.1	50	4. Hawaii
California	110,469	3,515	16.2	13	5. New Jersey
Colorado	12,239	3,348	16.0	20	6. Connecticut
Connecticut	13,939	4,256	15.2	6	7. Delaware
Delaware	2,930	4,150	19.3	7	8. Minnesota
Florida	46,389	3,325	16.4	21	9. Massachusetts
Georgia	22,039	3,124	16.6	29	10. Washington
Hawaii	5,080	4,308	18.5	4	11. Wisconsin
Idaho	3,316	2,927	17.2	36	12. Michigan
Illinois	38,312	3,260	14.5	24	13. California
Indiana	17,946	3,120	16.4	30	14. Maryland
Iowa	9,549	3,375	18.5	18	15. Oregon
Kansas	8,484	3,322	16.9	22	16. New Mexico
Kentucky	10,413	2,721	16.2	44	17. Nevada
Louisiana	12,365	2,865	17.4	41	18. Iowa
Maine	3,923	3,163	16.9	28	19. Rhode Island
Maryland	17,533	3,502	14.8	14	20. Colorado
Massachusetts	23,046	3,815	15.7	9	21. Florida
Michigan	33,720	3,551	17.3	12	22. Kansas
Minnesota	18,386	4,026	19.4	8	23. Nebraska
Mississippi	6,726	2,520	17.3	49	24. Illinois
Missouri	13,554	2,550	13.2	48	25. Vermont
Montana	2,540	2,968	17.4	34	26. Pennsylvania
Nebraska	5,373	3,311	16.9	23	27. North Dakota
Nevada	4,941	3,391	15.6	17	28. Maine
New Hampshire	3,508	3,085	14.1	32	29. Georgia
New Jersey	34,037	4,306	16.2	5	30. Indiana
New Mexico	5,628	3,403	21.3	16	31. Virginia
New York	90,892	5,003	20.2	2	32. New Hampshire
North Carolina	20,596	2,913	15.9	38	33. Ohio
North Dakota	2,023	3,171	18.6	27	34. Montana
Ohio	33,915	3,055	15.6	33	35. Arizona
Oklahoma	8,866	2,721	16.1	43	36. Idaho
Oregon	10,517	3,408	17.8	15	37. Utah
Pennsylvania	38,271	3,175	15.0	26	38. North Carolina
Rhode Island	3,348	3,358	15.8	19	39. Texas
South Carolina	10,543	2,878	17.2	40	40. South Carolina
South Dakota	1,945	2,698	15.1	45	41. Louisiana
Tennessee	13,397	2,589	14.3	47	42. West Virginia
Texas	53,528	2,913	15.5	39	43. Oklahoma
Utah	5,574	2,921	18.6	37	44. Kentucky
Vermont	1,879	3,240	16.8	25	45. South Dakota
Virginia	20,239	3,089	14.5	31	46. Alabama
Washington	19,663	3,680	17.2	10	47. Tennessee
West Virginia	4,980	2,733	16.9	42	48. Missouri
Wisconsin	18,374	3,616	18.4	11	49. Mississippi
Wyoming	2,106	4,425	22.7	3	50. Arkansas
50 States	881,933	3,395	16.5		
DC	3,062	5,373	17.7		
United States	884,996	3,399	16.5		

State	State & local non-tax "own-source" revenue $(millions)	Per capita $	As % of personal income %	Rank by per capita
Alabama	4,526	1,073	6.3	18
Alaska	3,713	6,127	26.9	1
Arizona	3,205	786	4.5	46
Arkansas	1,749	713	4.5	49
California	34,898	1,110	5.1	12
Colorado	4,031	1,103	5.3	13
Connecticut	2,670	815	2.9	42
Delaware	1,169	1,656	7.7	3
Florida	15,890	1,139	5.6	10
Georgia	7,116	1,009	5.4	23
Hawaii	1,324	1,123	4.8	11
Idaho	1,096	968	5.7	28
Illinois	9,232	786	3.5	47
Indiana	5,757	1,001	5.3	25
Iowa	3,052	1,079	5.9	16
Kansas	2,584	1,012	5.1	22
Kentucky	3,027	791	4.7	45
Louisiana	4,942	1,145	6.9	7
Maine	1,008	813	4.3	43
Maryland	4,232	845	3.6	39
Massachusetts	5,920	980	4.0	27
Michigan	9,485	999	4.9	26
Minnesota	5,905	1,293	6.2	5
Mississippi	2,314	867	6.0	36
Missouri	3,710	698	3.6	50
Montana	870	1,016	5.9	21
Nebraska	1,656	1,020	5.2	20
Nevada	1,511	1,037	4.8	19
New Hampshire	1,018	896	4.1	31
New Jersey	8,615	1,090	4.1	14
New Mexico	2,151	1,301	8.1	4
New York	20,863	1,148	4.6	6
North Carolina	5,677	803	4.4	44
North Dakota	728	1,141	6.7	9
Ohio	9,442	850	4.3	38
Oklahoma	2,851	875	5.2	35
Oregon	3,524	1,142	6.0	8
Pennsylvania	10,044	833	3.9	40
Rhode Island	858	860	4.0	37
South Carolina	3,945	1,077	6.4	17
South Dakota	634	879	4.9	34
Tennessee	4,293	830	4.6	41
Texas	16,280	886	4.7	33
Utah	1,911	1,001	6.4	24
Vermont	440	758	3.9	48
Virginia	6,076	927	4.3	29
Washington	5,790	1,084	5.1	15
West Virginia	1,629	894	5.5	32
Wisconsin	4,659	917	4.7	30
Wyoming	910	1,912	9.8	2
50 States	258,930	997	4.8	
DC	539	946	3.1	
United States	259,469	997	4.8	

Rank in order

By per capita

1. Alaska
2. Wyoming
3. Delaware
4. New Mexico
5. Minnesota
6. New York
7. Louisiana
8. Oregon
9. North Dakota
10. Florida
11. Hawaii
12. California
13. Colorado
14. New Jersey
15. Washington
16. Iowa
17. South Carolina
18. Alabama
19. Nevada
20. Nebraska
21. Montana
22. Kansas
23. Georgia
24. Utah
25. Indiana
26. Michigan
27. Massachusetts
28. Idaho
29. Virginia
30. Wisconsin
31. New Hampshire
32. West Virginia
33. Texas
34. South Dakota
35. Oklahoma
36. Mississippi
37. Rhode Island
38. Ohio
39. Maryland
40. Pennsylvania
41. Tennessee
42. Connecticut
43. Maine
44. North Carolina
45. Kentucky
46. Arizona
47. Illinois
48. Vermont
49. Arkansas
50. Missouri

State	State & local total expenditures $(millions)	Per capita $	As % of personal income %	Rank by per capita
Alabama	17,218	4,084	24.0	40
Alaska	7,040	11,617	51.1	1
Arizona	17,825	4,374	25.0	31
Arkansas	8,263	3,368	21.3	50
California	173,876	5,532	25.5	9
Colorado	17,722	4,847	23.1	16
Connecticut	18,926	5,779	20.7	6
Delaware	3,511	4,973	23.1	14
Florida	59,026	4,230	20.8	38
Georgia	29,927	4,242	22.5	37
Hawaii	7,460	6,328	27.2	3
Idaho	4,207	3,713	21.8	47
Illinois	52,345	4,454	19.9	26
Indiana	23,334	4,057	21.3	41
Iowa	12,298	4,347	23.9	33
Kansas	11,030	4,319	21.9	35
Kentucky	14,473	3,782	22.5	46
Louisiana	18,902	4,380	26.5	29
Maine	5,494	4,431	23.6	28
Maryland	22,687	4,532	19.1	23
Massachusetts	33,703	5,579	22.9	7
Michigan	44,809	4,719	23.0	18
Minnesota	24,903	5,453	26.2	10
Mississippi	9,634	3,609	24.8	48
Missouri	18,301	3,443	17.9	49
Montana	3,729	4,356	25.5	32
Nebraska	8,189	5,046	25.8	12
Nevada	7,305	5,014	23.1	13
New Hampshire	4,882	4,294	19.6	36
New Jersey	43,928	5,558	20.9	8
New Mexico	7,577	4,581	28.7	21
New York	135,591	7,463	30.1	2
North Carolina	29,203	4,131	22.5	39
North Dakota	2,845	4,460	26.2	25
Ohio	50,518	4,550	23.2	22
Oklahoma	12,401	3,806	22.5	45
Oregon	15,126	4,902	25.7	15
Pennsylvania	55,500	4,605	21.7	20
Rhode Island	5,288	5,304	24.9	11
South Carolina	16,375	4,469	26.7	24
South Dakota	2,883	3,999	22.4	43
Tennessee	22,377	4,324	23.8	34
Texas	73,907	4,021	21.4	42
Utah	8,459	4,433	28.2	27
Vermont	2,699	4,654	24.1	19
Virginia	26,169	3,994	18.7	44
Washington	31,074	5,816	27.2	5
West Virginia	7,977	4,378	27.1	30
Wisconsin	24,482	4,817	24.5	17
Wyoming	2,837	5,960	30.6	4
50 States	1,258,237	4,843	23.6	
DC	6,052	10,618	35.1	
United States	1,264,289	4,856	23.6	

C-5 STATE AND LOCAL TOTAL EXPENDITURES, FY 1994

Rank in order

By per capita

1. Alaska
2. New York
3. Hawaii
4. Wyoming
5. Washington
6. Connecticut
7. Massachusetts
8. New Jersey
9. California
10. Minnesota
11. Rhode Island
12. Nebraska
13. Nevada
14. Delaware
15. Oregon
16. Colorado
17. Wisconsin
18. Michigan
19. Vermont
20. Pennsylvania
21. New Mexico
22. Ohio
23. Maryland
24. South Carolina
25. North Dakota
26. Illinois
27. Utah
28. Maine
29. Louisiana
30. West Virginia
31. Arizona
32. Montana
33. Iowa
34. Tennessee
35. Kansas
36. New Hampshire
37. Georgia
38. Florida
39. North Carolina
40. Alabama
41. Indiana
42. Texas
43. South Dakota
44. Virginia
45. Oklahoma
46. Kentucky
47. Idaho
48. Mississippi
49. Missouri
50. Arkansas

State	State & local general expenditures $(millions)	As percent of personal income %	Rank by %	Rank in order By %
Alabama	14,782	20.6	24	1. Alaska
Alaska	6,161	44.7	1	2. Wyoming
Arizona	15,033	21.1	21	3. New Mexico
Arkansas	7,449	19.2	36	4. New York
California	138,528	20.3	25	5. Hawaii
Colorado	15,004	19.6	31	6. North Dakota
Connecticut	16,656	18.2	44	7. Louisiana
Delaware	3,163	20.8	22	8. West Virginia
Florida	52,193	18.4	41	9. Minnesota
Georgia	26,084	19.6	29	10. Utah
Hawaii	6,650	24.3	5	11. Montana
Idaho	3,769	19.5	32	12. South Carolina
Illinois	44,325	16.8	47	13. Mississippi
Indiana	21,290	19.4	33	14. Wisconsin
Iowa	11,179	21.7	16	15. Oregon
Kansas	9,715	19.3	34	16. Iowa
Kentucky	12,710	19.8	28	17. Vermont
Louisiana	16,852	23.7	7	18. Rhode Island
Maine	4,925	21.2	19	19. Maine
Maryland	19,595	16.5	49	20. Washington
Massachusetts	28,142	19.1	39	21. Arizona
Michigan	39,370	20.2	26	22. Delaware
Minnesota	22,089	23.3	9	23. South Dakota
Mississippi	8,622	22.2	13	24. Alabama
Missouri	16,132	15.8	50	25. California
Montana	3,300	22.6	11	26. Michigan
Nebraska	6,236	19.6	30	27. Nevada
Nevada	6,280	19.9	27	28. Kentucky
New Hampshire	4,442	17.8	46	29. Georgia
New Jersey	38,137	18.1	45	30. Nebraska
New Mexico	6,895	26.1	3	31. Colorado
New York	113,412	25.2	4	32. Idaho
North Carolina	24,917	19.2	38	33. Indiana
North Dakota	2,585	23.8	6	34. Kansas
Ohio	42,039	19.3	35	35. Ohio
Oklahoma	10,571	19.2	37	36. Arkansas
Oregon	12,898	21.9	15	37. Oklahoma
Pennsylvania	46,833	18.3	43	38. North Carolina
Rhode Island	4,534	21.4	18	39. Massachusetts
South Carolina	13,821	22.6	12	40. Texas
South Dakota	2,662	20.7	23	41. Florida
Tennessee	17,211	18.3	42	42. Tennessee
Texas	63,906	18.5	40	43. Pennsylvania
Utah	6,897	23.0	10	44. Connecticut
Vermont	2,425	21.7	17	45. New Jersey
Virginia	23,493	16.8	48	46. New Hampshire
Washington	24,198	21.1	20	47. Illinois
West Virginia	6,857	23.3	8	48. Virginia
Wisconsin	21,932	22.0	14	49. Maryland
Wyoming	2,542	27.4	2	50. Missouri
50 States	1,069,441	20.0		
DC	4,576	26.5		
United States	1,074,017	20.0		

	State & local general exp. per capita	State general exp. per capita	Local general exp. per capita	Rank by state & local per capita
State	$	$	$	$
Alabama	3,506	1,796	1,710	42
Alaska	10,166	6,616	3,550	1
Arizona	3,689	1,461	2,228	38
Arkansas	3,037	1,669	1,367	49
California	4,407	1,486	2,921	12
Colorado	4,104	1,395	2,709	19
Connecticut	5,086	2,733	2,353	5
Delaware	4,481	2,789	1,692	11
Florida	3,741	1,357	2,384	34
Georgia	3,697	1,583	2,114	36
Hawaii	5,640	4,341	1,299	3
Idaho	3,326	1,581	1,746	44
Illinois	3,772	1,587	2,185	32
Indiana	3,701	1,694	2,008	35
Iowa	3,952	1,795	2,157	22
Kansas	3,804	1,557	2,246	29
Kentucky	3,321	1,823	1,498	46
Louisiana	3,905	2,072	1,833	25
Maine	3,972	2,186	1,786	21
Maryland	3,914	1,797	2,117	23
Massachusetts	4,659	2,645	2,014	8
Michigan	4,146	1,790	2,356	18
Minnesota	4,837	1,877	2,959	6
Mississippi	3,230	1,526	1,705	48
Missouri	3,035	1,381	1,654	50
Montana	3,855	2,006	1,848	27
Nebraska	3,842	1,725	2,117	28
Nevada	4,310	1,460	2,850	14
New Hampshire	3,907	2,136	1,771	24
New Jersey	4,825	2,045	2,780	7
New Mexico	4,169	2,266	1,903	17
New York	6,242	2,210	4,032	2
North Carolina	3,524	1,563	1,961	41
North Dakota	4,052	2,294	1,758	20
Ohio	3,787	1,652	2,135	30
Oklahoma	3,245	1,483	1,761	47
Oregon	4,179	1,800	2,379	16
Pennsylvania	3,886	1,824	2,062	26
Rhode Island	4,548	2,770	1,778	9
South Carolina	3,772	2,007	1,765	31
South Dakota	3,692	1,996	1,696	37
Tennessee	3,326	1,584	1,742	45
Texas	3,477	1,427	2,050	43
Utah	3,615	1,775	1,840	39
Vermont	4,181	2,532	1,649	15
Virginia	3,586	1,588	1,998	40
Washington	4,529	2,114	2,415	10
West Virginia	3,763	2,196	1,568	33
Wisconsin	4,316	1,672	2,644	13
Wyoming	5,340	2,244	3,096	4
50 States	4,116	1,762	2,354	
DC	8,029	0	8,029	
United States	4,125	1,759	2,367	

G-7 STATE AND LOCAL GENERAL EXPENDITURES PER CAPITA, FY 1994

Rank in order

By per capita

1. Alaska
2. New York
3. Hawaii
4. Wyoming
5. Connecticut
6. Minnesota
7. New Jersey
8. Massachusetts
9. Rhode Island
10. Washington
11. Delaware
12. California
13. Wisconsin
14. Nevada
15. Vermont
16. Oregon
17. New Mexico
18. Michigan
19. Colorado
20. North Dakota
21. Maine
22. Iowa
23. Maryland
24. New Hampshire
25. Louisiana
26. Pennsylvania
27. Montana
28. Nebraska
29. Kansas
30. Ohio
31. South Carolina
32. Illinois
33. West Virginia
34. Florida
35. Indiana
36. Georgia
37. South Dakota
38. Arizona
39. Utah
40. Virginia
41. North Carolina
42. Alabama
43. Texas
44. Idaho
45. Tennessee
46. Kentucky
47. Oklahoma
48. Mississippi
49. Arkansas
50. Missouri

State	Percent change %	Rank	Rank in order By %
Alabama	48.8	12	1. Nevada
Alaska	18.8	50	2. Hawaii
Arizona	31.6	46	3. Washington
Arkansas	51.3	9	4. South Carolina
California	42.0	25	5. West Virginia
Colorado	52.0	7	6. Idaho
Connecticut	34.4	38	7. Colorado
Delaware	32.3	42	8. Indiana
Florida	45.4	19	9. Arkansas
Georgia	45.6	18	10. North Carolina
Hawaii	79.4	2	11. Utah
Idaho	55.6	6	12. Alabama
Illinois	40.2	28	13. New Mexico
Indiana	51.4	8	14. South Dakota
Iowa	34.6	37	15. New Hampshire
Kansas	41.3	26	16. Texas
Kentucky	39.0	29	17. Tennessee
Louisiana	42.2	24	18. Georgia
Maine	33.7	39	19. Florida
Maryland	32.7	41	20. Oregon
Massachusetts	30.5	47	21. Wisconsin
Michigan	32.2	43	22. Ohio
Minnesota	36.9	33	23. Pennsylvania
Mississippi	36.3	35	24. Louisiana
Missouri	36.4	34	25. California
Montana	40.3	27	26. Kansas
Nebraska	38.8	30	27. Montana
Nevada	82.6	1	28. Illinois
New Hampshire	46.6	15	29. Kentucky
New Jersey	36.3	36	30. Nebraska
New Mexico	48.4	13	31. Rhode Island
New York	37.1	32	32. New York
North Carolina	50.7	10	33. Minnesota
North Dakota	21.5	49	34. Missouri
Ohio	42.6	22	35. Mississippi
Oklahoma	32.0	45	36. New Jersey
Oregon	45.1	20	37. Iowa
Pennsylvania	42.4	23	38. Connecticut
Rhode Island	37.6	31	39. Maine
South Carolina	59.9	4	40. Vermont
South Dakota	48.3	14	41. Maryland
Tennessee	45.8	17	42. Delaware
Texas	46.0	16	43. Michigan
Utah	48.9	11	44. Virginia
Vermont	33.6	40	45. Oklahoma
Virginia	32.2	44	46. Arizona
Washington	67.9	3	47. Massachusetts
West Virginia	58.2	5	48. Wyoming
Wisconsin	44.0	21	49. North Dakota
Wyoming	22.1	48	50. Alaska
50 States	41.5		
DC	25.0		
United States	41.4		

State	State government general revenue $(millions)	State government general revenue per capita $	Rank by per capita		By per capita
Alabama	10,894	2,550	40		1. Alaska
Alaska	6,819	11,234	1		2. Delaware
Arizona	10,867	2,454	45		3. Hawaii
Arkansas	7,023	2,798	25		4. Wyoming
California	98,185	3,080	21		5. New York
Colorado	9,461	2,475	43		6. Connecticut
Connecticut	12,357	3,774	6		7. Massachusetts
Delaware	3,303	4,556	2		8. New Mexico
Florida	32,994	2,291	49		9. Minnesota
Georgia	18,345	2,495	41		10. Rhode Island
Hawaii	5,379	4,544	3		11. Michigan
Idaho	3,305	2,779	27		12. North Dakota
Illinois	30,306	2,558	39		13. New Jersey
Indiana	15,065	2,579	37		14. Vermont
Iowa	8,133	2,852	24		15. Wisconsin
Kansas	6,892	2,679	34		16. Montana
Kentucky	11,571	2,979	22		17. West Virginia
Louisiana	11,833	2,720	33		18. Oregon
Maine	3,836	3,085	20		19. Washington
Maryland	14,011	2,763	29		20. Maine
Massachusetts	22,845	3,750	7		21. California
Michigan	32,129	3,349	11		22. Kentucky
Minnesota	16,192	3,476	9		23. Utah
Mississippi	7,461	2,747	30		24. Iowa
Missouri	13,022	2,430	46		25. Arkansas
Montana	2,831	3,219	16		26. Pennsylvania
Nebraska	4,536	2,746	31		27. Idaho
Nevada	4,146	2,586	36		28. South Carolina
New Hampshire	2,706	2,328	48		29. Maryland
New Jersey	26,615	3,332	13		30. Mississippi
New Mexico	6,318	3,688	8		31. Nebraska
New York	71,219	3,916	5		32. North Carolina
North Carolina	20,047	2,738	32		33. Louisiana
North Dakota	2,144	3,332	12		34. Kansas
Ohio	29,467	2,637	35		35. Ohio
Oklahoma	8,156	2,471	44		36. Nevada
Oregon	9,958	3,108	18		37. Indiana
Pennsylvania	33,512	2,780	26		38. South Dakota
Rhode Island	3,346	3,379	10		39. Illinois
South Carolina	10,261	2,774	28		40. Alabama
South Dakota	1,886	2,575	38		41. Georgia
Tennessee	12,510	2,352	47		42. Virginia
Texas	42,616	2,228	50		43. Colorado
Utah	5,831	2,915	23		44. Oklahoma
Vermont	1,950	3,313	14		45. Arizona
Virginia	16,617	2,489	42		46. Missouri
Washington	17,195	3,108	19		47. Tennessee
West Virginia	5,836	3,196	17		48. New Hampshire
Wisconsin	16,778	3,252	15		49. Florida
Wyoming	2,004	4,163	4		50. Texas
50 States	770,713	2,911			
DC	n/a	n/a			
United States	770,713	2,905			

Rank in order

State	State government general spending $(millions)	State government general spending per capita $	Rank by per capita		By per capita
Alabama	9,050	2,118	32		1. Alaska
Alaska	4,572	7,532	1		2. Hawaii
Arizona	7,643	1,726	50		3. Delaware
Arkansas	5,414	2,157	31		4. Rhode Island
California	64,603	2,027	37		5. Connecticut
Colorado	7,462	1,952	43		6. Massachusetts
Connecticut	11,105	3,392	5		7. New York
Delaware	2,737	3,776	3		8. West Virginia
Florida	25,314	1,758	48		9. New Jersey
Georgia	14,728	2,003	39		10. Vermont
Hawaii	5,802	4,902	2		11. Wyoming
Idaho	2,502	2,104	33		12. Washington
Illinois	25,562	2,158	30		13. Maine
Indiana	10,277	1,760	47		14. Montana
Iowa	6,181	2,167	29		15. New Mexico
Kansas	5,013	1,949	44		16. Oregon
Kentucky	9,017	2,322	25		17. South Carolina
Louisiana	11,004	2,529	19		18. North Dakota
Maine	3,497	2,812	13		19. Louisiana
Maryland	12,316	2,428	21		20. New Hampshire
Massachusetts	19,790	3,248	6		21. Maryland
Michigan	21,781	2,270	27		22. Minnesota
Minnesota	11,257	2,417	22		23. Pennsylvania
Mississippi	5,710	2,102	34		24. Utah
Missouri	9,407	1,755	49		25. Kentucky
Montana	2,437	2,771	14		26. Ohio
Nebraska	3,314	2,006	38		27. Michigan
Nevada	3,207	2,000	40		28. South Dakota
New Hampshire	2,848	2,450	20		29. Iowa
New Jersey	24,544	3,073	9		30. Illinois
New Mexico	4,685	2,734	15		31. Arkansas
New York	57,003	3,135	7		32. Alabama
North Carolina	14,568	1,989	41		33. Idaho
North Dakota	1,652	2,567	18		34. Mississippi
Ohio	25,464	2,279	26		35. Wisconsin
Oklahoma	6,729	2,038	36		36. Oklahoma
Oregon	8,748	2,731	16		37. California
Pennsylvania	29,023	2,407	23		38. Nebraska
Rhode Island	3,556	3,591	4		39. Georgia
South Carolina	9,679	2,617	17		40. Nevada
South Dakota	1,605	2,192	28		41. North Carolina
Tennessee	10,312	1,938	45		42. Virginia
Texas	33,717	1,763	46		43. Colorado
Utah	4,645	2,322	24		44. Kansas
Vermont	1,748	2,969	10		45. Tennessee
Virginia	13,254	1,986	42		46. Texas
Washington	15,656	2,830	12		47. Indiana
West Virginia	5,644	3,092	8		48. Florida
Wisconsin	10,700	2,074	35		49. Missouri
Wyoming	1,375	2,857	11		50. Arizona
50 States	607,856	2,296			
DC	n/a	n/a			
United States	607,856	2,291			

State	State government general fund spending $(millions)	As percent of personal income %	Rank by %	Rank in order By %
Alabama	11,664	13.6	18	1. Hawaii
Alaska	n/a	n/a	n/a	2. New Mexico
Arizona	12,763	13.7	16	3. Delaware
Arkansas	7,609	16.0	7	4. Wyoming
California	94,082	11.7	29	5. Kentucky
Colorado	8,775	9.2	46	6. Louisiana
Connecticut	13,104	12.1	28	7. Arkansas
Delaware	3,743	18.7	3	8. Maine
Florida	39,441	11.4	32	9. Mississippi
Georgia	18,825	11.3	34	10. Oregon
Hawaii	6,310	21.2	1	11. South Carolina
Idaho	2,870	12.4	25	12. West Virginia
Illinois	27,131	8.6	47	13. Rhode Island
Indiana	13,220	10.1	43	14. Wisconsin
Iowa	8,762	13.6	17	15. Montana
Kansas	7,905	13.2	21	16. Arizona
Kentucky	12,589	16.5	5	17. Iowa
Louisiana	14,089	16.3	6	18. Alabama
Maine	4,086	15.8	8	19. North Dakota
Maryland	14,556	10.5	39	20. Utah
Massachusetts	19,837	11.1	36	21. Kansas
Michigan	27,698	11.6	30	22. New York
Minnesota	14,622	12.3	26	23. Oklahoma
Mississippi	7,307	15.4	9	24. Vermont
Missouri	12,492	10.2	42	25. Idaho
Montana	2,306	13.8	15	26. Minnesota
Nebraska	4,247	11.2	35	27. Washington
Nevada	n/a	n/a	n/a	28. Connecticut
New Hampshire	2,312	7.5	48	29. California
New Jersey	23,872	9.6	44	30. Michigan
New Mexico	6,161	19.2	2	31. Ohio
New York	68,688	13.1	22	32. Florida
North Carolina	18,194	11.3	33	33. North Carolina
North Dakota	1,789	13.4	19	34. Georgia
Ohio	30,515	11.6	31	35. Nebraska
Oklahoma	8,175	12.8	23	36. Massachusetts
Oregon	11,067	15.2	10	37. Pennsylvania
Pennsylvania	32,771	11.0	37	38. Tennessee
Rhode Island	3,487	14.2	13	39. Maryland
South Carolina	10,912	14.9	11	40. South Dakota
South Dakota	1,657	10.5	40	41. Virginia
Tennessee	12,534	10.8	38	42. Missouri
Texas	39,987	9.5	45	43. Indiana
Utah	5,080	13.3	20	44. New Jersey
Vermont	1,609	12.4	24	45. Texas
Virginia	17,181	10.3	41	46. Colorado
Washington	16,689	12.1	27	47. Illinois
West Virginia	4,915	14.6	12	48. New Hampshire
Wisconsin	16,678	13.9	14	
Wyoming	1,885	18.4	4	
50 States	746,191	11.6		
DC	n/a	n/a		
United States	746,191	11.6		

G-12 STATE AND LOCAL DEBT, FY 1994

State	State & local debt $(millions)	Per capita $	As percent of personal income %	Rank by per capita
Alabama	11,293	2,679	15.8	42
Alaska	7,380	12,178	53.5	1
Arizona	19,181	4,707	26.9	15
Arkansas	4,983	2,031	12.9	49
California	140,939	4,484	20.6	18
Colorado	17,930	4,904	23.4	12
Connecticut	17,962	5,485	19.6	9
Delaware	4,574	6,478	30.1	3
Florida	60,467	4,334	21.3	19
Georgia	20,716	2,936	15.6	37
Hawaii	7,093	6,016	25.9	5
Idaho	2,148	1,895	11.1	50
Illinois	46,434	3,951	17.6	21
Indiana	13,249	2,303	12.1	46
Iowa	5,880	2,078	11.4	48
Kansas	7,982	3,125	15.9	35
Kentucky	18,736	4,896	29.2	13
Louisiana	16,982	3,936	23.8	22
Maine	4,557	3,675	19.6	26
Maryland	21,062	4,207	17.7	20
Massachusetts	35,898	5,942	24.4	6
Michigan	28,121	2,961	14.4	36
Minnesota	21,973	4,811	23.1	14
Mississippi	5,794	2,171	14.9	47
Missouri	12,721	2,393	12.4	45
Montana	2,955	3,452	20.2	30
Nebraska	6,168	3,800	19.4	23
Nevada	6,648	4,563	21.0	17
New Hampshire	6,693	5,887	26.8	7
New Jersey	39,350	4,978	18.7	11
New Mexico	4,679	2,829	17.7	39
New York	133,402	7,342	29.6	2
North Carolina	20,186	2,855	15.6	38
North Dakota	1,721	2,697	15.8	40
Ohio	27,485	2,476	12.6	43
Oklahoma	8,740	2,683	15.9	41
Oregon	10,984	3,559	18.6	28
Pennsylvania	55,270	4,586	21.6	16
Rhode Island	6,307	6,326	29.7	4
South Carolina	12,157	3,318	19.9	33
South Dakota	2,314	3,209	18.0	34
Tennessee	12,474	2,410	13.3	44
Texas	69,706	3,793	20.2	24
Utah	10,595	5,553	35.3	8
Vermont	2,076	3,580	18.6	27
Virginia	22,039	3,364	15.8	32
Washington	28,761	5,383	25.1	10
West Virginia	6,321	3,469	21.5	29
Wisconsin	17,353	3,415	17.4	31
Wyoming	1,786	3,752	19.3	25
50 States	1,070,223	4,119	20.0	
DC	4,437	7,785	25.7	
United States	1,074,660	4,128	20.1	

By per capita

1. Alaska
2. New York
3. Delaware
4. Rhode Island
5. Hawaii
6. Massachusetts
7. New Hampshire
8. Utah
9. Connecticut
10. Washington
11. New Jersey
12. Colorado
13. Kentucky
14. Minnesota
15. Arizona
16. Pennsylvania
17. Nevada
18. California
19. Florida
20. Maryland
21. Illinois
22. Louisiana
23. Nebraska
24. Texas
25. Wyoming
26. Maine
27. Vermont
28. Oregon
29. West Virginia
30. Montana
31. Wisconsin
32. Virginia
33. South Carolina
34. South Dakota
35. Kansas
36. Michigan
37. Georgia
38. North Carolina
39. New Mexico
40. North Dakota
41. Oklahoma
42. Alabama
43. Ohio
44. Tennessee
45. Missouri
46. Indiana
47. Mississippi
48. Iowa
49. Arkansas
50. Idaho

State	State & local debt as percent of general revenue %	Rank
Alabama	64.0	37
Alaska	94.3	15
Arizona	101.3	6
Arkansas	54.5	44
California	78.6	21
Colorado	97.5	8
Connecticut	99.5	16
Delaware	113.7	5
Florida	93.9	14
Georgia	64.5	38
Hawaii	100.2	13
Idaho	43.3	49
Illinois	83.4	20
Indiana	53.4	48
Iowa	43.5	50
Kansas	65.9	36
Kentucky	118.7	4
Louisiana	85.6	23
Maine	79.4	28
Maryland	86.5	18
Massachusetts	108.6	7
Michigan	58.4	41
Minnesota	83.5	22
Mississippi	53.5	46
Missouri	61.5	39
Montana	71.6	30
Nebraska	70.8	24
Nevada	91.7	11
New Hampshire	135.3	2
New Jersey	86.2	19
New Mexico	57.0	42
New York	98.6	10
North Carolina	63.7	35
North Dakota	55.9	45
Ohio	47.2	43
Oklahoma	66.0	33
Oregon	66.2	32
Pennsylvania	95.3	12
Rhode Island	113.4	3
South Carolina	73.3	27
South Dakota	74.8	29
Tennessee	52.4	40
Texas	88.4	17
Utah	114.8	1
Vermont	72.3	31
Virginia	80.8	25
Washington	94.7	9
West Virginia	78.0	26
Wisconsin	61.4	34
Wyoming	54.1	47
50 States	80.8	
DC	69.0	
United States	80.7	

Rank in order

By %

1. Utah
2. New Hampshire
3. Rhode Island
4. Kentucky
5. Delaware
6. Arizona
7. Massachusetts
8. Colorado
9. Washington
10. New York
11. Nevada
12. Pennsylvania
13. Hawaii
14. Florida
15. Alaska
16. Connecticut
17. Texas
18. Maryland
19. New Jersey
20. Illinois
21. California
22. Minnesota
23. Louisiana
24. Nebraska
25. Virginia
26. West Virginia
27. South Carolina
28. Maine
29. South Dakota
30. Montana
31. Vermont
32. Oregon
33. Oklahoma
34. Wisconsin
35. North Carolina
36. Kansas
37. Alabama
38. Georgia
39. Missouri
40. Tennessee
41. Michigan
42. New Mexico
43. Ohio
44. Arkansas
45. North Dakota
46. Mississippi
47. Wyoming
48. Indiana
49. Idaho
50. Iowa

G-14 STATE AND LOCAL FULL FAITH AND CREDIT DEBT, FY 1994

State	State & local full faith and credit debt $(millions)	Pe capita $	As percent of personal income %	Rank by per capita
Alabama	4,311	1,022	6.0	25
Alaska	2,066	3,409	15.0	3
Arizona	5,853	1,436	8.2	19
Arkansas	1,181	481	3.0	43
California	28,982	922	4.2	29
Colorado	3,795	1,038	5.0	23
Connecticut	12,349	3,771	13.5	2
Delaware	1,066	1,510	7.0	17
Florida	7,674	550	2.7	40
Georgia	6,227	883	4.7	32
Hawaii	4,596	3,898	16.8	1
Idaho	510	450	2.6	46
Illinois	19,391	1,650	7.4	13
Indiana	1,879	327	1.7	49
Iowa	1,819	643	3.5	36
Kansas	2,327	911	4.6	30
Kentucky	1,304	341	2.0	48
Louisiana	6,287	1,457	8.8	18
Maine	1,536	1,239	6.6	21
Maryland	9,567	1,911	8.1	11
Massachusetts	15,726	2,603	10.7	5
Michigan	9,567	1,008	4.9	26
Minnesota	8,811	1,929	9.3	10
Mississippi	2,280	854	5.9	34
Missouri	2,948	555	2.9	39
Montana	481	562	3.3	38
Nebraska	924	569	2.9	37
Nevada	3,627	2,490	11.5	6
New Hampshire	1,719	1,512	6.9	16
New Jersey	12,630	1,598	6.0	14
New Mexico	903	546	3.4	41
New York	48,742	2,683	10.8	4
North Carolina	6,296	891	4.9	31
North Dakota	311	487	2.9	42
Ohio	9,556	861	4.4	33
Oklahoma	1,329	408	2.4	47
Oregon	7,084	2,295	12.0	7
Pennsylvania	19,244	1,597	7.5	15
Rhode Island	1,983	1,989	9.4	9
South Carolina	3,490	952	5.7	28
South Dakota	338	469	2.6	44
Tennessee	5,030	972	5.4	27
Texas	25,844	1,406	7.5	20
Utah	1,431	750	4.8	35
Vermont	706	1,218	6.3	22
Virginia	6,740	1,029	4.8	24
Washington	11,550	2,162	10.1	8
West Virginia	539	296	1.8	50
Wisconsin	9,112	1,793	9.1	12
Wyoming	221	464	2.4	45
50 States	341,881	1,316	6.4	
DC	3,637	6,381	21.1	
United States	345,518	1,327	6.4	

Rank in order

By per capita

1. Hawaii
2. Connecticut
3. Alaska
4. New York
5. Massachusetts
6. Nevada
7. Oregon
8. Washington
9. Rhode Island
10. Minnesota
11. Maryland
12. Wisconsin
13. Illinois
14. New Jersey
15. Pennsylvania
16. New Hampshire
17. Delaware
18. Louisiana
19. Arizona
20. Texas
21. Maine
22. Vermont
23. Colorado
24. Virginia
25. Alabama
26. Michigan
27. Tennessee
28. South Carolina
29. California
30. Kansas
31. North Carolina
32. Georgia
33. Ohio
34. Mississippi
35. Utah
36. Iowa
37. Nebraska
38. Montana
39. Missouri
40. Florida
41. New Mexico
42. North Dakota
43. Arkansas
44. South Dakota
45. Wyoming
46. Idaho
47. Oklahoma
48. Kentucky
49. Indiana
50. West Virginia

G-15 STATE GOVERNMENT BOND RATINGS, 1997

State	State bond ratings	Rank
Alabama	Aa	3
Alaska	Aa	3
Arizona	n/a	n/a
Arkansas	Aa3	5
California	A1	6
Colorado	n/a	n/a
Connecticut	Aa3	5
Delaware	Aa1	2
Florida	Aa2	4
Georgia	Aaa	1
Hawaii	Aa3	5
Idaho	n/a	n/a
Illinois	Aa3	5
Indiana	n/a	n/a
Iowa	n/a	n/a
Kansas	n/a	n/a
Kentucky	n/a	n/a
Louisiana	A3	8
Maine	Aa3	5
Maryland	Aaa	1
Massachusetts	A1	6
Michigan	Aa2	4
Minnesota	Aaa	1
Mississippi	Aa3	5
Missouri	Aaa	1
Montana	Aa3	5
Nebraska	n/a	n/a
Nevada	Aa2	4
New Hampshire	Aa2	4
New Jersey	Aa1	2
New Mexico	Aa1	2
New York	A2	7
North Carolina	Aaa	1
North Dakota	Aa3	5
Ohio	Aa1	2
Oklahoma	Aa3	5
Oregon	Aa2	4
Pennsylvania	Aa3	5
Rhode Island	A1	6
South Carolina	Aaa	1
South Dakota	n/a	n/a
Tennessee	Aaa	1
Texas	Aa2	4
Utah	Aaa	1
Vermont	Aa2	4
Virginia	Aaa	1
Washington	Aa1	2
West Virginia	A1	6
Wisconsin	Aa2	4
Wyoming	n/a	n/a
50 States	n/a	
DC	n/a	
United States	n/a	

Rank in order

By rating

1. Georgia
1. Maryland
1. Minnesota
1. Missouri
1. North Carolina
1. South Carolina
1. Tennessee
1. Utah
1. Virginia
2. Delaware
2. New Jersey
2. New Mexico
2. Ohio
2. Washington
3. Alabama
3. Alaska
4. Florida
4. Michigan
4. Nevada
4. New Hampshire
4. Oregon
4. Texas
4. Vermont
4. Wisconsin
5. Arkansas
5. Connecticut
5. Hawaii
5. Illinois
5. Maine
5. Mississippi
5. Montana
5. North Dakota
5. Oklahoma
5. Pennsylvania
6. California
6. Massachusetts
6. Rhode Island
6. West Virginia
7. New York
8. Louisiana

State	State solvency index	Rank
Alabama	46	23
Alaska	21,344	1
Arizona	97	22
Arkansas	483	12
California	-512	34
Colorado	784	6
Connecticut	-2,895	49
Delaware	200	17
Florida	-424	32
Georgia	139	20
Hawaii	-1,119	44
Idaho	137	21
Illinois	-854	38
Indiana	-233	27
Iowa	723	7
Kansas	582	8
Kentucky	-339	31
Louisiana	-2,206	48
Maine	-1,802	47
Maryland	-951	41
Massachusetts	-2,943	50
Michigan	-1,097	43
Minnesota	179	18
Mississippi	-256	28
Missouri	-19	24
Montana	259	15
Nebraska	498	11
Nevada	-319	30
New Hampshire	-624	35
New Jersey	-886	40
New Mexico	2,812	3
New York	-134	25
North Carolina	545	9
North Dakota	1,018	5
Ohio	-178	26
Oklahoma	-782	37
Oregon	1,138	4
Pennsylvania	-474	33
Rhode Island	-1,649	45
South Carolina	-877	39
South Dakota	527	10
Tennessee	142	19
Texas	352	14
Utah	359	13
Vermont	-1,061	42
Virginia	-292	29
Washington	-767	36
West Virginia	-1,657	46
Wisconsin	251	16
Wyoming	5,572	2
50 States	-304	
DC	n/a	
United States	-304	

Rank in order

By index

1. Alaska
2. Wyoming
3. New Mexico
4. Oregon
5. North Dakota
6. Colorado
7. Iowa
8. Kansas
9. North Carolina
10. South Dakota
11. Nebraska
12. Arkansas
13. Utah
14. Texas
15. Montana
16. Wisconsin
17. Delaware
18. Minnesota
19. Tennessee
20. Georgia
21. Idaho
22. Arizona
23. Alabama
24. Missouri
25. New York
26. Ohio
27. Indiana
28. Mississippi
29. Virginia
30. Nevada
31. Kentucky
32. Florida
33. Pennsylvania
34. California
35. New Hampshire
36. Washington
37. Oklahoma
38. Illinois
39. South Carolina
40. New Jersey
41. Maryland
42. Vermont
43. Michigan
44. Hawaii
45. Rhode Island
46. West Virginia
47. Maine
48. Louisiana
49. Connecticut
50. Massachusetts

State	Total assets $(millions)	Total membership #	Average assets per member $	Rank by average
Alabama	12,855	266,051	48,317	24
Alaska	6,553	69,420	94,393	3
Arizona	13,416	101,644	131,985	1
Arkansas	5,838	171,711	34,000	40
California	174,114	2,135,016	81,551	5
Colorado	15,786	233,324	67,656	8
Connecticut	11,752	191,620	61,329	13
Delaware	2,498	51,093	48,888	21
Florida	39,546	821,963	48,111	25
Georgia	21,715	413,845	52,473	18
Hawaii	5,528	89,962	61,450	12
Idaho	2,590	79,554	32,562	42
Illinois	44,777	867,726	51,603	19
Indiana	9,298	333,320	27,896	46
Iowa	7,919	223,986	35,353	37
Kansas	4,905	194,435	25,227	47
Kentucky	10,460	261,463	40,004	33
Louisiana	12,944	319,718	40,486	32
Maine	2,514	115,598	21,750	48
Maryland	20,285	290,937	69,722	7
Massachusetts	15,258	442,363	34,491	38
Michigan	35,113	663,054	52,957	16
Minnesota	21,195	712,870	29,732	44
Mississippi	4,231	241,633	17,509	50
Missouri	17,143	272,375	62,940	11
Montana	2,370	81,635	29,030	45
Nebraska	3,149	64,728	48,655	23
Nevada	5,216	80,640	64,682	10
New Hampshire	567	12,136	46,741	26
New Jersey	28,877	588,152	49,099	20
New Mexico	6,023	151,405	39,781	34
New York	139,288	1,674,863	83,164	4
North Carolina	23,436	536,940	43,647	29
North Dakota	1,268	37,078	34,193	39
Ohio	69,366	1,036,524	66,921	9
Oklahoma	6,313	198,556	31,793	43
Oregon	9,174	236,181	38,842	35
Pennsylvania	42,600	709,535	60,040	14
Rhode Island	3,211	53,925	59,547	15
South Carolina	11,906	262,203	45,409	28
South Dakota	2,210	51,791	42,663	31
Tennessee	11,952	116,171	102,883	2
Texas	55,029	1,130,301	48,686	22
Utah	5,117	139,691	36,628	36
Vermont	1,095	32,399	33,803	41
Virginia	18,880	410,498	45,994	27
Washington	20,609	392,331	52,530	17
West Virginia	2,318	114,311	20,282	49
Wisconsin	32,500	428,745	75,802	6
Wyoming	2,162	50,340	42,949	30
50 States	1,022,869	18,155,760	56,339	
DC	2,512	23,659	106,174	
United States	1,025,381	18,179,419	56,403	

Rank in order

By average

1. Arizona
2. Tennessee
3. Alaska
4. New York
5. California
6. Wisconsin
7. Maryland
8. Colorado
9. Ohio
10. Nevada
11. Missouri
12. Hawaii
13. Connecticut
14. Pennsylvania
15. Rhode Island
16. Michigan
17. Washington
18. Georgia
19. Illinois
20. New Jersey
21. Delaware
22. Texas
23. Nebraska
24. Alabama
25. Florida
26. New Hampshire
27. Virginia
28. South Carolina
29. North Carolina
30. Wyoming
31. South Dakota
32. Louisiana
33. Kentucky
34. New Mexico
35. Oregon
36. Utah
37. Iowa
38. Massachusetts
39. North Dakota
40. Arkansas
41. Vermont
42. Idaho
43. Oklahoma
44. Minnesota
45. Montana
46. Indiana
47. Kansas
48. Maine
49. West Virginia
50. Mississippi

State	Balances as a percent of expenditures %	Rank
Alabama	0.7	47
Alaska	137.9	1
Arizona	16.2	7
Arkansas	0.0	48
California	1.8	45
Colorado	8.3	22
Connecticut	6.4	28
Delaware	22.3	2
Florida	7.8	23
Georgia	9.1	19
Hawaii	4.3	37
Idaho	2.9	42
Illinois	4.4	36
Indiana	15.3	8
Iowa	19.8	4
Kansas	13.0	12
Kentucky	8.6	21
Louisiana	0.0	48
Maine	3.6	40
Maryland	9.5	18
Massachusetts	6.7	27
Michigan	13.8	10
Minnesota	16.9	5
Mississippi	9.8	16
Missouri	3.7	39
Montana	2.3	44
Nebraska	16.6	6
Nevada	15.3	8
New Hampshire	2.2	50
New Jersey	7.0	26
New Mexico	7.1	25
New York	1.3	46
North Carolina	7.8	23
North Dakota	12.0	15
Ohio	6.2	30
Oklahoma	13.8	10
Oregon	20.8	3
Pennsylvania	4.9	33
Rhode Island	6.3	29
South Carolina	12.4	13
South Dakota	3.9	38
Tennessee	2.7	43
Texas	9.6	17
Utah	5.0	32
Vermont	4.9	33
Virginia	4.9	33
Washington	5.5	31
West Virginia	8.9	20
Wisconsin	3.5	41
Wyoming	12.3	14
50 States	n/a	
DC	n/a	
United States	7.5	

Rank in order

By %

1. Alaska
2. Delaware
3. Oregon
4. Iowa
5. Minnesota
6. Nebraska
7. Arizona
8. Indiana
8. Nevada
10. Michigan
10. Oklahoma
12. Kansas
13. South Carolina
14. Wyoming
15. North Dakota
16. Mississippi
17. Texas
18. Maryland
19. Georgia
20. West Virginia
21. Kentucky
22. Colorado
23. Florida
23. North Carolina
25. New Mexico
26. New Jersey
27. Massachusetts
28. Connecticut
29. Rhode Island
30. Ohio
31. Washington
32. Utah
33. Pennsylvania
33. Vermont
33. Virginia
36. Illinois
37. Hawaii
38. South Dakota
39. Missouri
40. Maine
41. Wisconsin
42. Idaho
43. Tennessee
44. Montana
45. New Hampshire
46. California
47. New York
48. Alabama
48. Arkansas
50. Louisiana

State	Outlays and interest per capita $	Capital outlay per capita $	Interest per capita $	Rank by outlay and interest per capita
Alabama	585	411	173	43
Alaska	2,535	1,519	1,015	1
Arizona	900	605	295	12
Arkansas	475	342	133	50
California	827	593	234	14
Colorado	1,200	857	342	6
Connecticut	822	519	303	15
Delaware	960	556	404	9
Florida	761	477	283	18
Georgia	715	519	196	26
Hawaii	1,695	1,358	337	2
Idaho	636	519	117	37
Illinois	735	497	238	21
Indiana	577	446	131	45
Iowa	673	535	137	36
Kansas	678	468	209	32
Kentucky	724	439	285	24
Louisiana	675	402	273	34
Maine	585	358	228	42
Maryland	703	475	229	28
Massachusetts	940	608	332	10
Michigan	530	368	162	47
Minnesota	893	608	285	13
Mississippi	482	351	130	49
Missouri	516	370	145	48
Montana	689	497	192	31
Nebraska	933	695	238	11
Nevada	1,276	1,005	271	3
New Hampshire	636	264	372	38
New Jersey	736	449	287	20
New Mexico	699	515	184	29
New York	1,202	779	423	5
North Carolina	627	456	172	39
North Dakota	753	558	195	19
Ohio	579	425	154	44
Oklahoma	544	354	190	46
Oregon	723	511	212	25
Pennsylvania	673	379	294	35
Rhode Island	772	433	339	17
South Carolina	728	512	216	22
South Dakota	807	584	223	16
Tennessee	622	479	143	40
Texas	727	483	244	23
Utah	991	639	352	8
Vermont	619	411	209	41
Virginia	694	494	200	30
Washington	1,125	819	306	7
West Virginia	677	450	227	33
Wisconsin	715	502	213	27
Wyoming	1,202	925	277	4
50 States	774	527	247	
DC	1,571	941	629	
United States	776	528	248	

By per capita

1. Alaska
2. Hawaii
3. Nevada
4. Wyoming
5. New York
6. Colorado
7. Washington
8. Utah
9. Delaware
10. Massachusetts
11. Nebraska
12. Arizona
13. Minnesota
14. California
15. Connecticut
16. South Dakota
17. Rhode Island
18. Florida
19. North Dakota
20. New Jersey
21. Illinois
22. South Carolina
23. Texas
24. Kentucky
25. Oregon
26. Georgia
27. Wisconsin
28. Maryland
29. New Mexico
30. Virginia
31. Montana
32. Kansas
33. West Virginia
34. Louisiana
35. Pennsylvania
36. Iowa
37. Idaho
38. New Hampshire
39. North Carolina
40. Tennessee
41. Vermont
42. Maine
43. Alabama
44. Ohio
45. Indiana
46. Oklahoma
47. Michigan
48. Missouri
49. Mississippi
50. Arkansas

State	Index	Rank	By index
Alabama	59.3	32	1. Colorado
Alaska	64.0	25	2. Michigan
Arizona	73.0	13	3. New Jersey
Arkansas	47.0	43	4. Massachusetts
California	46.7	44	5. Missouri
Colorado	98.0	1	6. Oregon
Connecticut	76.4	10	7. Georgia
Delaware	72.0	15	8. Iowa
Florida	70.9	17	9. Rhode Island
Georgia	79.4	7	10. Connecticut
Hawaii	72.0	16	11. South Carolina
Idaho	58.0	35	12. Utah
Illinois	45.4	46	13. Arizona
Indiana	39.0	47	14. Tennessee
Iowa	79.1	8	15. Delaware
Kansas	54.0	38	16. Hawaii
Kentucky	60.0	31	17. Florida
Louisiana	62.0	28	18. North Dakota
Maine	35.6	49	19. Minnesota
Maryland	58.2	33	20. Oklahoma
Massachusetts	82.3	4	21. Ohio
Michigan	88.0	2	22. Pennsylvania
Minnesota	68.0	19	23. Montana
Mississippi	63.0	26	24. South Dakota
Missouri	80.5	5	25. Alaska
Montana	66.0	23	26. Mississippi
Nebraska	50.0	39	27. Texas
Nevada	56.0	37	28. Louisiana
New Hampshire	37.7	48	29. New York
New Jersey	87.0	3	30. West Virginia
New Mexico	58.1	34	31. Kentucky
New York	61.6	29	32. Alabama
North Carolina	49.8	40	33. Maryland
North Dakota	68.8	18	34. New Mexico
Ohio	66.7	21	35. Idaho
Oklahoma	67.0	20	36. Wyoming
Oregon	80.0	6	37. Nevada
Pennsylvania	66.6	22	38. Kansas
Rhode Island	77.3	9	39. Nebraska
South Carolina	75.0	11	40. North Carolina
South Dakota	65.5	24	41. Virginia
Tennessee	73.0	14	42. Washington
Texas	63.0	27	43. Arkansas
Utah	73.5	12	44. California
Vermont	18.6	50	45. Wisconsin
Virginia	48.4	41	46. Illinois
Washington	48.0	42	47. Indiana
West Virginia	60.9	30	48. New Hampshire
Wisconsin	45.6	45	49. Maine
Wyoming	58.0	36	50. Vermont
50 States	63.2		
DC	n/a		
United States	63.2		

G-21 RELATIVE STATE SPENDING "NEEDS"

State	Per capita additional spending needed to meet national average %	Rank by least "needed" spending to most "needed"
Alabama	10.8	41
Alaska	-0.3	27
Arizona	7.5	38
Arkansas	14.3	46
California	0.1	28
Colorado	-4.5	20
Connecticut	-16.0	2
Delaware	-13.3	7
Florida	-8.5	12
Georgia	4.2	33
Hawaii	-13.2	8
Idaho	7.2	37
Illinois	-1.4	26
Indiana	-5.7	16
Iowa	-4.3	21
Kansas	-2.5	23
Kentucky	11.7	43
Louisiana	34.9	49
Maine	-7.2	14
Maryland	-14.2	4
Massachusetts	-14.1	5
Michigan	3.7	32
Minnesota	-5.1	19
Mississippi	37.7	50
Missouri	0.7	30
Montana	10.5	40
Nebraska	-2.4	25
Nevada	-13.3	6
New Hampshire	-17.5	1
New Jersey	-15.6	3
New Mexico	26.8	48
New York	-2.6	22
North Carolina	-5.5	17
North Dakota	5.2	35
Ohio	0.6	29
Oklahoma	10.0	39
Oregon	-5.2	18
Pennsylvania	-7.8	13
Rhode Island	-12.1	9
South Carolina	5.5	36
South Dakota	13.5	45
Tennessee	2.1	31
Texas	16.8	47
Utah	12.5	44
Vermont	-9.8	11
Virginia	-11.9	10
Washington	-6.2	15
West Virginia	11.2	42
Wisconsin	-2.4	24
Wyoming	4.3	34
50 States	0.0	
DC	-6.3	
United States	0.0	

Rank in order

By %
low to high

1. New Hampshire
2. Connecticut
3. New Jersey
4. Maryland
5. Massachusetts
6. Nevada
7. Delaware
8. Hawaii
9. Rhode Island
10. Virginia
11. Vermont
12. Florida
13. Pennsylvania
14. Maine
15. Washington
16. Indiana
17. North Carolina
18. Oregon
19. Minnesota
20. Colorado
21. Iowa
22. New York
23. Kansas
24. Wisconsin
25. Nebraska
26. Illinois
27. Alaska
28. California
29. Ohio
30. Missouri
31. Tennessee
32. Michigan
33. Georgia
34. Wyoming
35. North Dakota
36. South Carolina
37. Idaho
38. Arizona
39. Oklahoma
40. Montana
41. Alabama
42. West Virginia
43. Kentucky
44. Utah
45. South Dakota
46. Arkansas
47. Texas
48. New Mexico
49. Louisiana
50. Mississippi

Source Notes for Revenues and Finances (Section G)

G-1 State and Local Total Revenue, FY 1994: This table and many others in this section of *State Fact Finder* rely on analysis of data collected by the Census Bureau for FY 1994, the latest information available when *State Fact Finder* went to press in late 1997. For sources of the fiscal data and the population and personal income estimates used to build the tables see the extensive note associated with Table F-1. Total revenue, shown in this table, is the most inclusive definition of the financial size of state and local governments used by the Census Bureau in its annual survey of government finances. It includes utilities run by state and local governments and many categories of trust funds. Such funds typically collect revenues, such as Unemployment Insurance taxes, for a particular purpose, such as paying Unemployment Compensation benefits, and are not commingled with other public funds. The revenues included come from state and local taxes, fees such as hospital charges and university tuition, and from the federal government.

G-2 State and Local General Revenue, FY 1994: From the same source as Table F-1, this table relates general revenue to population and personal income in each state. It excludes utility and trust fund revenues.

G-3 State and Local "Own-Source" General Revenue, FY 1994: These data reflect the concept often used to measure the fiscal burdens associated with state and local activity. Revenues from federal aid are excluded, along with the revenues of trust funds and utilities. See source for Table F-1.

G-4 State And Local Non-Tax "Own-Source" Revenue, FY 1994: The principal sources of non-tax revenues are (1) fees related to use of state facilities and services, such as those charged by public hospitals and universities, and (2) interest earned on money held by governments in anticipation of spending. See source for Table F-1.

G-5 State and Local Total Expenditures, FY 1994: This is the spending counterpart of the revenues shown on Table G-1. See source for Table F-1.

G-6 State and Local General Expenditures, FY 1994: This concept of "general" spending (see notes to Table G-2) is the most appropriate for comparing spending among states. See source for Table F-1.

G-7 State and Local General Expenditures Per Capita, FY 1994: This table relates general expenditure to population with separate totals for state governments and local governments. State aid to local governments is included only when local officials spend the resources, to avoid double counting. See source for Table F-1.

G-8 Percentage Change in State and Local General Expenditures, FY 1989-1994: This statistic shows the differences among states in the five-year growth of state and local spending. The changes shown are not adjusted for factors that might account for some of the differences in growth rates, such as growth in population and other factors affecting needs for government service. FY 1989 data come from Census publication GF-89-5, *Government Finances in 1988-1989*. See source for Table F-1 for FY 1994 data.

G-9 State Government General Revenue, FY 1996: Unlike Tables G-1 through G-8, these data deal with state governments alone, not state and local governments combined. Unlike data in those tables, these data cover fiscal year 1996. They are from the 1996 version of State Government Finances available on the Census web page (http://www.census.gov) and were retrieved by *State Fact Finder* on September 29, 1997. The corresponding data for 1996 for local governments are not yet available.

For most purposes, comparisons of finances among states need to include state and local revenues and spending because of major differences in the division of state and local responsibilities between states. For example, New York local governments pay nearly half of all state and local welfare costs, but local governments in most states have almost no responsibility for paying these costs. Comparisons of states alone would make New York spending look artificially small. In Hawaii, the state alone pays for schools, while in other states local governments pay half these costs. Comparisons of states alone would make Hawaii's spending look artificially large.

However, comparisons of state governments alone are useful for those attempting to evaluate state office holders and aspirants and for discussions of state government spending priorities and tax burdens.

This table and Table G-10 show "general" revenues and expenditures, a less inclusive measure than "total" expenditures. The difference is primarily associated with enterprises run by some state governments and not others, particularly liquor sales monopolies run by about a third of the states and the electric power marketing operations run by a few states. State impacts on utility services and liquor prices and sales are similar from state to state but some states achieve them by their direct management of these functions. Because huge amounts of money are involved, inclusion of these operations in state comparisons would artificially distort the spending comparisons, so the concepts of general expenditures and general revenues exclude them.

G-10 State Government General Spending, FY 1996: See notes to Table G-9.

G-11 State Government General Fund Spending, FY 1996: These data reflect other estimates of state government spending. They come from a survey of state executive branch budget offices reported in the *1997 State*

Expenditure Report by the National Association of State Budget Officers (NASBO). They reflect state fiscal 1996 definitions. The year ended on June 30, 1996, for forty-six states, while one state ended the fiscal year in the spring and three ended in the fall.

The NASBO report differs from Census reports in many ways. The Census Bureau reports include all funds, while the NASBO report covers primarily funds subject to appropriation by legislatures and therefore for most states excludes funds of quasi-independent entities such as toll highway authorities. The Census Bureau does not distinguish among funds within state government, while the NASBO report presents data separately for state general funds, federal funds, and other state funds. The data shown in the table reflect the total of all reported funds. The NASBO data use different definitions of spending categories than the Census Bureau data. See the notes for Table G-9 on the hazards of considering state spending without also considering local spending.

G-12 State and Local Debt, FY 1994: These data, from the Census Bureau (see notes to Table F-1), reflect the total debt of all state and local governments at the end of fiscal 1994, including debt of special authorities.

G-13 State and Local Debt Related to Revenue, FY 1994: This table relates total debt (see Table G-12) to total revenue (see Table G-1). Consequently, it offers a measure of how state and local budgets are strained by the costs of paying principal and interest on past obligations.

G-14 State and Local Full Faith and Credit Debt, FY 1994: These data reflect the component of total debt (see Table G-12) that is backed by the "full faith and credit" of the governments that issued the debt. This debt, commonly known as "general obligation" debt, is backed by all revenue sources of the issuing government. The debt not included in these totals, often known as revenue bonds, is backed only by specified revenues, not general taxes.

G-15 State Government Bond Ratings, 1997: Because thousands of individual state and local governments issue bonds, purchasers such as individuals and mutual funds find it difficult to analyze the risks associated with each individual issue. As a result, three rating agencies (Fitch, Moody's, and Standard & Poor's) evaluate the quality of individual bond issues. The ratings of revenue bonds are unique to the bonds and the revenue sources that back them. The ratings of general obligation bonds shown in this table are reflections of the fiscal soundness of state governments overall. As a result, they affect perceptions of fiscal soundness of states by voters as well as by potential bond purchasers.

The ratings shown come from Moody's and are dated October 24, 1997. Ratings from the other two agencies would show about the same ranking of states. Moody's system considers Aaa highest, followed by Aa1, Aa, Aa2, Aa3, A1, etc., down to lower ratings, which are awarded

some local governments but no states that are generally considered good credit risks. Some states have so little general obligation debt that they have no recent ratings and therefore are not ranked in this table. While there is no clearly appropriate way to insert them in the rankings, many of these states have strong credit and would rank above many of the states shown in the rankings.

G-16 State Solvency Index, 1993: While state financial reports and Census Bureau data provide substantial detail about state finances, they do not provide answers to some common sense questions about state financial status. One of these questions is equivalent to "net worth," a fundamental concept in viewing the finances of individuals and companies. This table reflects a special study by State Policy Research, reported in its *State Policy Reports* (September 1993), using data from a variety of dates as close to late 1993 as possible.

Conceptually, the number shown is an answer to the question: If each state were to cease operations tomorrow and pay off all debts (including pension promises to employees), how much money would be left over? For most states, the answer is that nothing would be left. Instead, they would have to levy a special assessment on each citizen (the amounts shown as negative numbers) in order to cease operations. Some states, particularly Alaska with its large reserves built from oil revenues, would have money left over that could be distributed to taxpayers. The calculations exclude the value of physical assets, such as state park lands, trucks and computers.

The solvency index has not been revised by State Policy Research, Inc. by replacing 1992 Census data on debt and assets with 1994 data and by updating estimates of unfunded pension liabilities. Such an update would show little change in the rankings. At the end of 1997, state solvency was substantially improved from the situation shown in this table because state balances and rainy day funds have grown substantially and rising stock and bond markets have increased the value of investments by state-administered employee pension funds. But Census data that will reflect these changes and also show how great the changes are will not be available until about 1999.

G-17 Assets of State-Administered Pension Plans, 1994: States run pension plans for their own employees and, in most states, for teachers, city workers, and other local employees as well. To be considered actuarially sound, these plans must have built up enough assets from contributions of employees and their government employers to be able to cover the amounts needed to pay retired workers plus current workers when they retire. How much this amounts to depends on many factors, such as the exact benefits promised and the life expectancy of workers. There is no substitute for actuarial studies of each plan for determining the right amount each plan should have to cover future obligations.

This table shows the assets of state-administered plans and the persons who are considered members of these plans—retirees and active workers accruing retirement benefits. Dividing these two numbers produces average assets per member, which is a rough measure of the relative solvency of the public pension plans in each state. The data come from a special computer run of 1994 state and local retirement statistics from Donna Hirsch of the Census Bureau's Governments division in October of 1996.

G-18 State Reserves at the End of FY 1997: These data reflect the cash reserves of state governments as they finished fiscal year 1997, generally in the summer of 1997. These reserves come in two primary forms—balances (equivalent to the balances people show in their checkbooks) and "rainy day" or stabilization funds (formal reserves, somewhat akin to the savings accounts maintained by individuals). The data come from a survey of state budget officers by the National Association of State Budget Officers published in late 1997, titled *The Fiscal Survey of States*.

Relating balances to spending provides a basis for comparisons among states of different size and financial responsibilities. Nationwide, this table indicates that states have enough in reserve to pay their normal bills for about 7.5 percent of their fiscal years, or roughly 27 working days, with no additional revenue coming in.

G-19 State and Local Capital Outlays and Interest, FY 1994: This table, from the same source as Table F-1, shows the total spending of state and local governments for capital outlays and interest and per capita amounts of spending in fiscal 1994 for interest and capital outlays. The outlays reflect the pace of activity in financing new facilities, such as roads and schools. The interest reflects the extent to which taxpayers of each state are seeing their tax funds used to pay interest on past spending, normally borrowing to finance capital outlays.

G-20 Index of State Budget Process Quality, 1994: Experts in public administration and budgeting generally agree on criteria of best budgeting practices, such as considering the impacts of spending and tax decisions over a longer period than one year. The numbers shown in the table are scores, with a perfect score being 100, developed by State Policy Research by comparing these criteria with actual state budget practices, as reported by the National Association of State Budget Officers in its special report, *Budget Processes in the States*. This special study appeared in *State Policy Reports* (Volume 13, Issue 5, 1995).

G-21 Relative State Spending "Needs": Individual states have quite different population characteristics, as shown by many of the tables in *State Fact Finder*. For example, school-age children are an extraordinarily large proportion of the population of Utah, but a smaller-than-average proportion of Pennsylvania's population. As a result, some states would have higher per capita spending than others, even if all states spent identical amounts per pupil, had identical welfare payments, and identical levels of other services. These differences are important to consider in viewing differences in per capita spending among states.

A special study by State Policy Research, which appeared in *State Policy Reports* (Vol. 13, Issue 20, 1995), calculated what state and local governments in each state would have to spend if they applied national average spending (for example, spending per pupil) to their own particular mix of population using government services. The study, sometimes called the "representative expenditure system," can be expressed as differences in per capita amounts like those shown in the table. For example, to match national average spending patterns, Mississippi would have to spend 37.7 percent more per capita than the national average. Why? Because the state has extra burdens associated with large percentages of welfare recipients and school children.

These data are conceptually similar to concepts of tax capacity shown in Table F-4. Together, these data reflect a consistent pattern of strains that circumstances put on taxpayers and decision makers of individual states. More affluent states, such as Connecticut, often combine above average tax bases with below average spending needs while less affluent states, like Mississippi, show the reverse.

Education

State	Average math score	Rank
Alabama	257	38
Alaska	278	10
Arizona	268	25
Arkansas	262	33
California	263	31
Colorado	276	14
Connecticut	280	8
Delaware	267	27
Florida	264	30
Georgia	262	33
Hawaii	262	33
Idaho	n/a	n/a
Illinois	n/a	n/a
Indiana	276	14
Iowa	284	1
Kansas	n/a	n/a
Kentucky	267	27
Louisiana	252	39
Maine	284	1
Maryland	270	20
Massachusetts	278	10
Michigan	277	12
Minnesota	284	1
Mississippi	250	40
Missouri	273	19
Montana	283	5
Nebraska	283	5
Nevada	n/a	n/a
New Hampshire	n/a	n/a
New Jersey	n/a	n/a
New Mexico	262	33
New York	270	20
North Carolina	268	25
North Dakota	284	1
Ohio	n/a	n/a
Oklahoma	n/a	n/a
Oregon	276	14
Pennsylvania	n/a	n/a
Rhode Island	269	24
South Carolina	261	37
South Dakota	n/a	n/a
Tennessee	263	31
Texas	270	20
Utah	277	12
Vermont	279	9
Virginia	270	20
Washington	276	14
West Virginia	265	29
Wisconsin	283	5
Wyoming	275	18
50 States	n/a	
DC	233	
United States	271	

Rank in order

By score

1. Iowa
1. Maine
1. Minnesota
1. North Dakota
5. Montana
5. Nebraska
5. Wisconsin
8. Connecticut
9. Vermont
10. Alaska
10. Massachusetts
12. Michigan
12. Utah
14. Colorado
14. Indiana
14. Oregon
14. Washington
18. Wyoming
19. Missouri
20. Maryland
20. New York
20. Texas
20. Virginia
24. Rhode Island
25. Arizona
25. North Carolina
27. Delaware
27. Kentucky
29. West Virginia
30. Florida
31. California
31. Tennessee
33. Arkansas
33. Georgia
33. Hawaii
33. New Mexico
37. South Carolina
38. Alabama
39. Louisiana
40. Mississippi

H-2 AVERAGE PROFICIENCY IN SCIENCE, EIGHTH GRADE, 1996

State	Science score	Rank
Alabama	139	35
Alaska	153	15
Arizona	145	26
Arkansas	144	29
California	138	37
Colorado	155	12
Connecticut	155	13
Delaware	142	31
Florida	142	32
Georgia	142	33
Hawaii	135	38
Idaho	n/a	n/a
Illinois	n/a	n/a
Indiana	153	16
Iowa	158	6
Kansas	n/a	n/a
Kentucky	147	22
Louisiana	132	40
Maine	163	1
Maryland	145	27
Massachusetts	157	8
Michigan	153	17
Minnesota	159	5
Mississippi	133	39
Missouri	151	18
Montana	162	2
Nebraska	157	9
Nevada	n/a	n/a
New Hampshire	n/a	n/a
New Jersey	n/a	n/a
New Mexico	141	34
New York	146	25
North Carolina	147	23
North Dakota	162	3
Ohio	n/a	n/a
Oklahoma	n/a	n/a
Oregon	155	14
Pennsylvania	n/a	n/a
Rhode Island	149	20
South Carolina	139	36
South Dakota	n/a	n/a
Tennessee	143	30
Texas	145	28
Utah	156	11
Vermont	157	10
Virginia	149	21
Washington	150	19
West Virginia	147	24
Wisconsin	160	4
Wyoming	158	7
50 States	n/a	
DC	113	
United States	148	

Rank in order

By score

1. Maine
2. Montana
3. North Dakota
4. Wisconsin
5. Minnesota
6. Iowa
7. Wyoming
8. Massachusetts
9. Nebraska
10. Vermont
11. Utah
12. Colorado
13. Connecticut
14. Oregon
15. Alaska
16. Indiana
17. Michigan
18. Missouri
19. Washington
20. Rhode Island
21. Virginia
22. Kentucky
23. North Carolina
24. West Virginia
25. New York
26. Arizona
27. Maryland
28. Texas
29. Arkansas
30. Tennessee
31. Delaware
32. Florida
33. Georgia
34. New Mexico
35. Alabama
36. South Carolina
37. California
38. Hawaii
39. Mississippi
40. Louisiana

State	AFQT rank	Rank
Alabama	57.1	48
Alaska	65.0	8
Arizona	62.8	19
Arkansas	58.5	43
California	60.3	39
Colorado	62.9	18
Connecticut	61.6	25
Delaware	60.3	39
Florida	61.3	29
Georgia	58.1	46
Hawaii	58.4	44
Idaho	66.0	2
Illinois	61.4	28
Indiana	63.7	16
Iowa	64.7	10
Kansas	64.4	12
Kentucky	60.1	41
Louisiana	57.0	49
Maine	62.5	20
Maryland	60.8	32
Massachusetts	61.6	25
Michigan	62.2	22
Minnesota	65.8	4
Mississippi	54.8	50
Missouri	61.9	24
Montana	65.3	6
Nebraska	64.2	15
Nevada	64.3	13
New Hampshire	65.3	6
New Jersey	60.4	38
New Mexico	60.6	35
New York	61.1	30
North Carolina	59.1	42
North Dakota	66.4	1
Ohio	61.6	25
Oklahoma	60.8	32
Oregon	65.8	4
Pennsylvania	62.2	22
Rhode Island	60.8	32
South Carolina	58.0	47
South Dakota	62.3	21
Tennessee	60.6	35
Texas	61.1	30
Utah	63.0	17
Vermont	64.8	9
Virginia	60.5	37
Washington	64.7	10
West Virginia	58.4	44
Wisconsin	65.9	3
Wyoming	64.3	13
50 States	n/a	
DC	55.6	
United States	61.1	

Rank in order

By rank

1. North Dakota
2. Idaho
3. Wisconsin
4. Minnesota
4. Oregon
6. Montana
6. New Hampshire
8. Alaska
9. Vermont
10. Iowa
10. Washington
12. Kansas
13. Nevada
13. Wyoming
15. Nebraska
16. Indiana
17. Utah
18. Colorado
19. Arizona
20. Maine
21. South Dakota
22. Michigan
22. Pennsylvania
24. Missouri
25. Connecticut
25. Massachusetts
25. Ohio
28. Illinois
29. Florida
30. New York
30. Texas
32. Maryland
32. Oklahoma
32. Rhode Island
35. New Mexico
35. Tennessee
37. Virginia
38. New Jersey
39. California
39. Delaware
41. Kentucky
42. North Carolina
43. Arkansas
44. Hawaii
44. West Virginia
46. Georgia
47. South Carolina
48. Alabama
49. Louisiana
50. Mississippi

H-4 SCHOLASTIC APTITUDE TEST SCORES, 1997

State	Average SAT score	Percent graduates tested %	Rank by score
Alabama	n/a	n/a	n/a
Alaska	1,037	48	4
Arizona	n/a	n/a	n/a
Arkansas	n/a	n/a	n/a
California	1,010	45	9
Colorado	n/a	n/a	n/a
Connecticut	1,016	79	5
Delaware	1,003	65	12
Florida	998	50	14
Georgia	967	63	22
Hawaii	995	54	16
Idaho	n/a	n/a	n/a
Illinois	n/a	n/a	n/a
Indiana	991	57	20
Iowa	n/a	n/a	n/a
Kansas	n/a	n/a	n/a
Kentucky	n/a	n/a	n/a
Louisiana	n/a	n/a	n/a
Maine	1,011	67	8
Maryland	1,014	64	7
Massachusetts	1,016	80	5
Michigan	n/a	n/a	n/a
Minnesota	n/a	n/a	n/a
Mississippi	n/a	n/a	n/a
Missouri	n/a	n/a	n/a
Montana	n/a	n/a	n/a
Nebraska	n/a	n/a	n/a
Nevada	n/a	n/a	n/a
New Hampshire	1,039	70	3
New Jersey	1,005	69	11
New Mexico	n/a	n/a	n/a
New York	997	74	15
North Carolina	978	59	21
North Dakota	n/a	n/a	n/a
Ohio	n/a	n/a	n/a
Oklahoma	n/a	n/a	n/a
Oregon	1,049	50	1
Pennsylvania	993	72	18
Rhode Island	992	70	19
South Carolina	953	56	23
South Dakota	n/a	n/a	n/a
Tennessee	n/a	n/a	n/a
Texas	995	49	16
Utah	n/a	n/a	n/a
Vermont	1,010	69	9
Virginia	1,003	69	12
Washington	1,046	46	2
West Virginia	n/a	n/a	n/a
Wisconsin	n/a	n/a	n/a
Wyoming	n/a	n/a	n/a
50 States	n/a	n/a	
DC	965	60	
United States	1,016	42	

Rank in order

By score

1. Oregon
2. Washington
3. New Hampshire
4. Alaska
5. Connecticut
5. Massachusetts
7. Maryland
8. Maine
9. California
9. Vermont
11. New Jersey
12. Delaware
12. Virginia
14. Florida
15. New York
16. Hawaii
16. Texas
18. Pennsylvania
19. Rhode Island
20. Indiana
21. North Carolina
22. Georgia
23. South Carolina

H-5 ACT SCORES, 1997

State	ACT composite scores	Percent graduates tested %	Rank by score
Alabama	20	61	22
Alaska	n/a	n/a	n/a
Arizona	21	27	18
Arkansas	20	66	20
California	n/a	n/a	n/a
Colorado	22	62	7
Connecticut	n/a	n/a	n/a
Delaware	n/a	n/a	n/a
Florida	n/a	n/a	n/a
Georgia	n/a	n/a	n/a
Hawaii	n/a	n/a	n/a
Idaho	21	62	10
Illinois	21	69	17
Indiana	n/a	n/a	n/a
Iowa	22	64	2
Kansas	22	74	5
Kentucky	20	65	23
Louisiana	19	80	26
Maine	n/a	n/a	n/a
Maryland	n/a	n/a	n/a
Massachusetts	n/a	n/a	n/a
Michigan	21	68	13
Minnesota	22	60	2
Mississippi	19	79	27
Missouri	22	64	7
Montana	22	55	4
Nebraska	22	73	5
Nevada	21	39	13
New Hampshire	n/a	n/a	n/a
New Jersey	n/a	n/a	n/a
New Mexico	20	59	20
New York	n/a	n/a	n/a
North Carolina	n/a	n/a	n/a
North Dakota	21	78	10
Ohio	21	60	13
Oklahoma	21	66	19
Oregon	n/a	n/a	n/a
Pennsylvania	n/a	n/a	n/a
Rhode Island	n/a	n/a	n/a
South Carolina	n/a	n/a	n/a
South Dakota	21	68	13
Tennessee	20	83	25
Texas	n/a	n/a	n/a
Utah	22	69	7
Vermont	n/a	n/a	n/a
Virginia	n/a	n/a	n/a
Washington	n/a	n/a	n/a
West Virginia	20	57	24
Wisconsin	22	64	1
Wyoming	21	70	10
50 States	n/a	n/a	
DC	n/a	n/a	
United States	21	36	

Rank in order

By score

1. Wisconsin
2. Iowa
2. Minnesota
4. Montana
5. Kansas
5. Nebraska
7. Colorado
7. Missouri
7. Utah
10. Idaho
10. North Dakota
10. Wyoming
13. Michigan
13. Nevada
13. Ohio
13. South Dakota
17. Illinois
18. Arizona
19. Oklahoma
20. Arkansas
20. New Mexico
22. Alabama
23. Kentucky
24. West Virginia
25. Tennessee
26. Louisiana
27. Mississippi

H-6 PERCENT OF POPULATION OVER 25 WITH A HIGH SCHOOL DIPLOMA, 1996

State	High school graduates %	Rank
Alabama	75.7	45
Alaska	91.4	1
Arizona	83.5	28
Arkansas	76.2	43
California	79.8	37
Colorado	89.1	5
Connecticut	85.3	17
Delaware	82.7	30
Florida	81.5	35
Georgia	76.5	41
Hawaii	84.4	22
Idaho	85.9	13
Illinois	83.2	29
Indiana	83.7	27
Iowa	87.4	10
Kansas	87.7	8
Kentucky	74.0	49
Louisiana	74.5	48
Maine	84.7	20
Maryland	84.6	21
Massachusetts	84.9	18
Michigan	84.2	23
Minnesota	87.9	7
Mississippi	75.2	46
Missouri	83.9	25
Montana	85.6	14
Nebraska	87.4	10
Nevada	85.4	15
New Hampshire	85.4	15
New Jersey	84.9	18
New Mexico	77.1	40
New York	81.6	33
North Carolina	76.0	44
North Dakota	80.2	36
Ohio	84.0	24
Oklahoma	83.8	26
Oregon	87.5	9
Pennsylvania	81.6	33
Rhode Island	78.6	39
South Carolina	73.8	50
South Dakota	82.4	31
Tennessee	79.0	38
Texas	76.4	42
Utah	90.7	2
Vermont	86.9	12
Virginia	82.0	32
Washington	90.2	3
West Virginia	74.7	47
Wisconsin	88.7	6
Wyoming	90.2	3
50 States	n/a	
DC	79.1	
United States	81.7	

By %

1. Alaska
2. Utah
3. Washington
3. Wyoming
5. Colorado
6. Wisconsin
7. Minnesota
8. Kansas
9. Oregon
10. Iowa
10. Nebraska
12. Vermont
13. Idaho
14. Montana
15. Nevada
15. New Hampshire
17. Connecticut
18. Massachusetts
18. New Jersey
20. Maine
21. Maryland
22. Hawaii
23. Michigan
24. Ohio
25. Missouri
26. Oklahoma
27. Indiana
28. Arizona
29. Illinois
30. Delaware
31. South Dakota
32. Virginia
33. New York
33. Pennsylvania
35. Florida
36. North Dakota
37. California
38. Tennessee
39. Rhode Island
40. New Mexico
41. Georgia
42. Texas
43. Arkansas
44. North Carolina
45. Alabama
46. Mississippi
47. West Virginia
48. Louisiana
49. Kentucky
50. South Carolina

H-7 STUDENTS IN PRIVATE SCHOOLS, 1993

State	Private school enrollment #	As percent of total enrollment %	Rank by %
Alabama	72,630	9.0	23
Alaska	5,884	4.5	44
Arizona	41,957	5.6	41
Arkansas	29,011	6.1	37
California	569,062	9.6	19
Colorado	53,732	7.9	28
Connecticut	70,198	12.4	12
Delaware	22,308	17.4	1
Florida	233,743	10.3	18
Georgia	97,726	7.3	32
Hawaii	30,537	14.5	6
Idaho	8,019	3.3	48
Illinois	293,038	13.4	9
Indiana	91,986	8.7	25
Iowa	50,602	9.2	21
Kansas	37,045	7.5	29
Kentucky	58,058	8.1	27
Louisiana	145,512	15.4	3
Maine	16,999	7.3	33
Maryland	112,481	12.7	10
Massachusetts	126,744	12.6	11
Michigan	187,741	10.5	16
Minnesota	86,051	9.6	20
Mississippi	58,655	10.4	17
Missouri	117,466	11.8	15
Montana	9,111	5.3	43
Nebraska	39,564	12.2	13
Nevada	10,723	4.3	45
New Hampshire	18,386	9.0	22
New Jersey	195,921	14.5	5
New Mexico	20,007	5.8	39
New York	473,119	14.8	4
North Carolina	69,000	5.7	40
North Dakota	7,577	6.0	38
Ohio	246,805	12.0	14
Oklahoma	25,837	4.1	47
Oregon	34,092	6.2	36
Pennsylvania	342,298	16.4	2
Rhode Island	23,153	13.7	8
South Carolina	51,600	7.4	31
South Dakota	9,575	6.3	35
Tennessee	84,538	8.9	24
Texas	211,337	5.5	42
Utah	9,793	2.0	49
Vermont	9,107	8.1	26
Virginia	84,438	7.5	30
Washington	70,205	7.1	34
West Virginia	13,539	4.1	46
Wisconsin	141,762	14.4	7
Wyoming	1,919	1.9	50
50 States	4,820,591	10.0	
DC	15,854	16.4	
United States	4,836,442	10.0	

Rank in order

By %

1. Delaware
2. Pennsylvania
3. Louisiana
4. New York
5. New Jersey
6. Hawaii
7. Wisconsin
8. Rhode Island
9. Illinois
10. Maryland
11. Massachusetts
12. Connecticut
13. Nebraska
14. Ohio
15. Missouri
16. Michigan
17. Mississippi
18. Florida
19. California
20. Minnesota
21. Iowa
22. New Hampshire
23. Alabama
24. Tennessee
25. Indiana
26. Vermont
27. Kentucky
28. Colorado
29. Kansas
30. Virginia
31. South Carolina
32. Georgia
33. Maine
34. Washington
35. South Dakota
36. Oregon
37. Arkansas
38. North Dakota
39. New Mexico
40. North Carolina
41. Arizona
42. Texas
43. Montana
44. Alaska
45. Nevada
46. West Virginia
47. Oklahoma
48. Idaho
49. Utah
50. Wyoming

H-8 HIGH SCHOOL COMPLETION RATES, 1993-1995

State	Percent of 18 to 24 year olds completing high school %	Rank
Alabama	84.0	39
Alaska	90.5	17
Arizona	84.0	39
Arkansas	88.4	24
California	78.9	50
Colorado	88.4	24
Connecticut	94.7	2
Delaware	93.3	7
Florida	80.7	46
Georgia	80.3	48
Hawaii	92.0	12
Idaho	86.4	35
Illinois	86.7	34
Indiana	88.5	23
Iowa	93.2	9
Kansas	90.9	15
Kentucky	82.4	43
Louisiana	80.5	47
Maine	92.9	10
Maryland	93.6	5
Massachusetts	92.5	11
Michigan	88.7	22
Minnesota	93.3	7
Mississippi	83.9	41
Missouri	90.3	18
Montana	89.8	19
Nebraska	94.5	3
Nevada	81.9	45
New Hampshire	86.9	32
New Jersey	91.8	13
New Mexico	82.4	43
New York	87.1	30
North Carolina	85.5	37
North Dakota	96.6	1
Ohio	88.4	24
Oklahoma	87.0	31
Oregon	82.7	42
Pennsylvania	89.5	20
Rhode Island	89.4	21
South Carolina	88.0	28
South Dakota	91.5	14
Tennessee	84.6	38
Texas	79.5	49
Utah	93.6	5
Vermont	88.1	27
Virginia	87.7	29
Washington	85.7	36
West Virginia	86.8	33
Wisconsin	93.7	4
Wyoming	90.8	16
50 States	n/a	
DC	87.7	
United States	85.3	

Rank in order

By %

1. North Dakota
2. Connecticut
3. Nebraska
4. Wisconsin
5. Maryland
5. Utah
7. Delaware
7. Minnesota
9. Iowa
10. Maine
11. Massachusetts
12. Hawaii
13. New Jersey
14. South Dakota
15. Kansas
16. Wyoming
17. Alaska
18. Missouri
19. Montana
20. Pennsylvania
21. Rhode Island
22. Michigan
23. Indiana
24. Arkansas
24. Colorado
24. Ohio
27. Vermont
28. South Carolina
29. Virginia
30. New York
31. Oklahoma
32. New Hampshire
33. West Virginia
34. Illinois
35. Idaho
36. Washington
37. North Carolina
38. Tennessee
39. Alabama
39. Arizona
41. Mississippi
42. Oregon
43. Kentucky
43. New Mexico
45. Nevada
46. Florida
47. Louisiana
48. Georgia
49. Texas
50. California

H-9 PUPIL-TEACHER RATIO, 1994

State	Pupil-teacher ratio	Rank low to high	By ratio
Alabama	17.2	32	1. Maine
Alaska	17.6	38	1. New Jersey
Arizona	19.3	45	1. Vermont
Arkansas	17.1	30	4. Connecticut
California	24.0	49	4. South Dakota
Colorado	18.4	40	6. Nebraska
Connecticut	14.4	4	7. Virginia
Delaware	16.6	25	8. Rhode Island
Florida	19.1	43	9. Massachusetts
Georgia	16.3	22	9. West Virginia
Hawaii	17.9	39	11. Wyoming
Idaho	19.1	43	12. Kansas
Illinois	17.3	34	13. New York
Indiana	17.5	35	14. North Dakota
Iowa	15.7	18	15. Missouri
Kansas	15.1	12	15. Oklahoma
Kentucky	17.0	28	17. New Hampshire
Louisiana	16.6	25	18. Iowa
Maine	13.8	1	18. Texas
Maryland	17.0	28	20. Wisconsin
Massachusetts	14.8	9	21. North Carolina
Michigan	20.1	47	22. Georgia
Minnesota	17.5	35	22. Montana
Mississippi	17.5	35	24. South Carolina
Missouri	15.5	15	25. Delaware
Montana	16.3	22	25. Louisiana
Nebraska	14.5	6	25. Ohio
Nevada	18.7	42	28. Kentucky
New Hampshire	15.6	17	28. Maryland
New Jersey	13.8	1	30. Arkansas
New Mexico	17.2	32	30. Pennsylvania
New York	15.2	13	32. Alabama
North Carolina	16.2	21	32. New Mexico
North Dakota	15.3	14	34. Illinois
Ohio	16.6	25	35. Indiana
Oklahoma	15.5	15	35. Minnesota
Oregon	19.9	46	35. Mississippi
Pennsylvania	17.1	30	38. Alaska
Rhode Island	14.7	8	39. Hawaii
South Carolina	16.4	24	40. Colorado
South Dakota	14.4	4	41. Tennessee
Tennessee	18.6	41	42. Nevada
Texas	15.7	18	43. Florida
Utah	24.3	50	43. Idaho
Vermont	13.8	1	45. Arizona
Virginia	14.6	7	46. Oregon
Washington	20.2	48	47. Michigan
West Virginia	14.8	9	48. Washington
Wisconsin	15.9	20	49. California
Wyoming	15.0	11	50. Utah
50 States	n/a		
DC	13.2		
United States	17.3		

State	Enrollment (000)	As percent of total population %	Rank by %		Rank in order By %
Alabama	741	17.3	26		1. Utah
Alaska	131	21.6	2		2. Alaska
Arizona	790	17.8	18		3. Idaho
Arkansas	456	18.2	13		4. Wyoming
California	5,535	17.4	25		5. Texas
Colorado	673	17.6	21		6. Oklahoma
Connecticut	528	16.1	42		7. Montana
Delaware	111	15.3	48		8. Mississippi
Florida	2,241	15.6	45		9. South Dakota
Georgia	1,321	18.0	17		10. North Dakota
Hawaii	188	15.9	43		11. Minnesota
Idaho	245	20.6	3		12. Vermont
Illinois	1,961	16.6	35		13. Arkansas
Indiana	981	16.8	31		14. Kansas
Iowa	504	17.7	19		15. Louisiana
Kansas	466	18.1	14		16. New Mexico
Kentucky	629	16.2	40		17. Georgia
Louisiana	786	18.1	15		18. Arizona
Maine	214	17.2	28		19. Iowa
Maryland	819	16.1	41		20. Washington
Massachusetts	930	15.3	47		21. Colorado
Michigan	1,660	17.3	27		22. Nebraska
Minnesota	854	18.3	11		23. Nevada
Mississippi	504	18.6	8		24. South Carolina
Missouri	883	16.5	37		25. California
Montana	165	18.7	7		26. Alabama
Nebraska	291	17.6	22		27. Michigan
Nevada	282	17.6	23		28. Maine
New Hampshire	198	17.0	30		29. Wisconsin
New Jersey	1,215	15.2	49		30. New Hampshire
New Mexico	309	18.0	16		31. Indiana
New York	2,865	15.8	44		32. Oregon
North Carolina	1,189	16.2	39		33. Tennessee
North Dakota	118	18.4	10		34. West Virginia
Ohio	1,843	16.5	36		35. Illinois
Oklahoma	621	18.8	6		36. Ohio
Oregon	537	16.8	32		37. Missouri
Pennsylvania	1,807	15.0	50		38. Virginia
Rhode Island	152	15.3	46		39. North Carolina
South Carolina	644	17.4	24		40. Kentucky
South Dakota	135	18.4	9		41. Maryland
Tennessee	892	16.8	33		42. Connecticut
Texas	3,807	19.9	5		43. Hawaii
Utah	478	23.9	1		44. New York
Vermont	108	18.3	12		45. Florida
Virginia	1,096	16.4	38		46. Rhode Island
Washington	977	17.7	20		47. Massachusetts
West Virginia	303	16.6	34		48. Delaware
Wisconsin	886	17.2	29		49. New Jersey
Wyoming	99	20.5	4		50. Pennsylvania
50 States	45,171	17.1			
DC	80	14.7			
United States	45,251	17.1			

State	Holdings per capita	Rank
Alabama	2.0	38
Alaska	3.1	22
Arizona	2.0	38
Arkansas	2.1	36
California	1.9	45
Colorado	2.6	29
Connecticut	4.3	7
Delaware	1.9	45
Florida	1.7	48
Georgia	1.8	47
Hawaii	2.3	33
Idaho	3.3	19
Illinois	3.4	17
Indiana	3.7	14
Iowa	3.9	11
Kansas	4.4	5
Kentucky	2.0	38
Louisiana	2.2	34
Maine	4.9	1
Maryland	2.7	27
Massachusetts	4.7	3
Michigan	2.9	24
Minnesota	2.8	25
Mississippi	2.0	38
Missouri	4.0	10
Montana	3.1	22
Nebraska	3.8	12
Nevada	2.0	38
New Hampshire	4.4	5
New Jersey	3.8	12
New Mexico	3.3	19
New York	4.2	8
North Carolina	2.0	38
North Dakota	3.5	16
Ohio	3.6	15
Oklahoma	2.2	34
Oregon	2.4	32
Pennsylvania	2.1	36
Rhode Island	4.1	9
South Carolina	1.7	48
South Dakota	3.4	17
Tennessee	1.7	48
Texas	2.0	38
Utah	2.7	27
Vermont	4.8	2
Virginia	2.5	30
Washington	2.8	25
West Virginia	2.5	30
Wisconsin	3.2	21
Wyoming	4.7	3
50 States	n/a	
DC	3.6	
United States	2.7	

Rank in order

By per capita

1. Maine
2. Vermont
3. Massachusetts
3. Wyoming
5. Kansas
5. New Hampshire
7. Connecticut
8. New York
9. Rhode Island
10. Missouri
11. Iowa
12. Nebraska
12. New Jersey
14. Indiana
15. Ohio
16. North Dakota
17. Illinois
17. South Dakota
19. Idaho
19. New Mexico
21. Wisconsin
22. Alaska
22. Montana
24. Michigan
25. Minnesota
25. Washington
27. Maryland
27. Utah
29. Colorado
30. Virginia
30. West Virginia
32. Oregon
33. Hawaii
34. Louisiana
34. Oklahoma
36. Arkansas
36. Pennsylvania
38. Alabama
38. Arizona
38. Kentucky
38. Mississippi
38. Nevada
38. North Carolina
38. Texas
45. California
45. Delaware
47. Georgia
48. Florida
48. South Carolina
48. Tennessee

State	Children with disabilities #	Percent of public school enrollment %	Rank by %		Rank in order By %
Alabama	99,760	13.6	11		1. Massachusetts
Alaska	18,006	14.3	6		2. New Jersey
Arizona	69,530	9.8	49		3. Rhode Island
Arkansas	53,187	12.0	32		4. Connecticut
California	533,807	10.0	46		5. Delaware
Colorado	66,595	10.7	43		6. Alaska
Connecticut	71,863	14.5	4		7. Florida
Delaware	15,196	14.4	5		8. West Virginia
Florida	289,539	14.2	7		9. Tennessee
Georgia	123,143	10.0	47		10. Illinois
Hawaii	15,248	8.5	50		11. Alabama
Idaho	23,536	9.9	48		12. Maine
Illinois	257,986	13.6	10		13. New Mexico
Indiana	127,961	13.3	15		14. New York
Iowa	63,373	12.7	19		15. Indiana
Kansas	50,438	11.0	39		16. Missouri
Kentucky	80,539	12.3	25		17. Nebraska
Louisiana	86,931	10.9	41		18. South Carolina
Maine	29,350	13.5	12		19. Iowa
Maryland	97,998	12.7	20		20. Maryland
Massachusetts	160,275	18.3	1		21. Mississippi
Michigan	181,251	11.3	34		22. New Hampshire
Minnesota	90,918	11.2	36		23. Virginia
Mississippi	64,153	12.7	21		24. Wyoming
Missouri	114,008	13.2	16		25. Kentucky
Montana	18,401	11.3	35		26. Oregon
Nebraska	37,112	13.0	17		27. Ohio
Nevada	25,242	10.7	42		28. Wisconsin
New Hampshire	23,354	12.6	22		29. Oklahoma
New Jersey	190,003	16.5	2		30. Pennsylvania
New Mexico	43,474	13.5	13		31. North Carolina
New York	365,697	13.4	14		32. Arkansas
North Carolina	136,513	12.0	31		33. Texas
North Dakota	12,440	10.4	44		34. Michigan
Ohio	219,875	12.2	27		35. Montana
Oklahoma	73,130	12.1	29		36. Minnesota
Oregon	63,212	12.2	26		37. South Dakota
Pennsylvania	210,826	12.1	30		38. Washington
Rhode Island	23,582	16.2	3		39. Kansas
South Carolina	81,930	12.7	18		40. Utah
South Dakota	15,907	11.1	37		41. Louisiana
Tennessee	119,146	13.7	9		42. Nevada
Texas	411,917	11.4	33		43. Colorado
Utah	51,950	11.0	40		44. North Dakota
Vermont	10,452	10.2	45		45. Vermont
Virginia	131,599	12.6	23		46. California
Washington	101,254	11.1	38		47. Georgia
West Virginia	44,528	14.2	8		48. Idaho
Wisconsin	102,412	12.1	28		49. Arizona
Wyoming	12,480	12.4	24		50. Hawaii
50 States	5,311,027	12.2			
DC	6,994	8.7			
United States	5,318,021	12.2			

State	Total spending $(millions)	Per capita $	As percent of personal income %	Rank by per capita
Alabama	4,857	1,152	6.8	45
Alaska	1,471	2,427	10.7	1
Arizona	5,283	1,297	7.4	31
Arkansas	2,761	1,126	7.1	47
California	38,829	1,235	5.7	39
Colorado	5,017	1,372	6.6	23
Connecticut	4,903	1,497	5.4	16
Delaware	1,216	1,723	8.0	4
Florida	14,984	1,074	5.3	50
Georgia	8,886	1,259	6.7	36
Hawaii	1,496	1,269	5.5	34
Idaho	1,415	1,249	7.3	37
Illinois	14,480	1,232	5.5	40
Indiana	8,138	1,415	7.4	20
Iowa	4,245	1,500	8.2	15
Kansas	3,802	1,489	7.6	18
Kentucky	4,412	1,153	6.9	44
Louisiana	5,097	1,181	7.2	42
Maine	1,643	1,325	7.1	27
Maryland	7,064	1,411	5.9	21
Massachusetts	7,376	1,221	5.0	41
Michigan	15,020	1,582	7.7	10
Minnesota	7,441	1,629	7.8	8
Mississippi	3,050	1,143	7.8	46
Missouri	5,873	1,105	5.7	48
Montana	1,280	1,495	8.8	17
Nebraska	2,539	1,564	8.0	12
Nevada	1,713	1,176	5.4	43
New Hampshire	1,415	1,244	5.7	38
New Jersey	13,525	1,711	6.4	5
New Mexico	2,316	1,400	8.8	22
New York	31,674	1,743	7.0	3
North Carolina	9,031	1,277	7.0	33
North Dakota	1,000	1,567	9.2	11
Ohio	14,590	1,314	6.7	28
Oklahoma	4,199	1,289	7.6	32
Oregon	4,651	1,507	7.9	14
Pennsylvania	15,784	1,310	6.2	29
Rhode Island	1,420	1,425	6.7	19
South Carolina	4,622	1,261	7.5	35
South Dakota	937	1,299	7.3	30
Tennessee	5,561	1,075	5.9	49
Texas	24,500	1,333	7.1	26
Utah	2,948	1,545	9.8	13
Vermont	949	1,637	8.5	6
Virginia	8,813	1,345	6.3	24
Washington	8,711	1,630	7.6	7
West Virginia	2,443	1,341	8.3	25
Wisconsin	8,231	1,620	8.2	9
Wyoming	933	1,961	10.1	2
50 States	352,546	1,357	6.6	
DC	741	1,300	4.3	
United States	353,287	1,357	6.6	

Rank in order

By per capita

1. Alaska
2. Wyoming
3. New York
4. Delaware
5. New Jersey
6. Vermont
7. Washington
8. Minnesota
9. Wisconsin
10. Michigan
11. North Dakota
12. Nebraska
13. Utah
14. Oregon
15. Iowa
16. Connecticut
17. Montana
18. Kansas
19. Rhode Island
20. Indiana
21. Maryland
22. New Mexico
23. Colorado
24. Virginia
25. West Virginia
26. Texas
27. Maine
28. Ohio
29. Pennsylvania
30. South Dakota
31. Arizona
32. Oklahoma
33. North Carolina
34. Hawaii
35. South Carolina
36. Georgia
37. Idaho
38. New Hampshire
39. California
40. Illinois
41. Massachusetts
42. Louisiana
43. Nevada
44. Kentucky
45. Alabama
46. Mississippi
47. Arkansas
48. Missouri
49. Tennessee
50. Florida

State	As percent of general spending %	Rank
Alabama	32.9	37
Alaska	23.9	49
Arizona	35.1	27
Arkansas	37.1	16
California	28.0	45
Colorado	33.4	34
Connecticut	29.4	43
Delaware	38.4	8
Florida	28.7	44
Georgia	34.1	30
Hawaii	22.5	50
Idaho	37.5	13
Illinois	32.7	38
Indiana	38.2	10
Iowa	38.0	12
Kansas	39.1	4
Kentucky	34.7	28
Louisiana	30.2	42
Maine	33.4	36
Maryland	36.0	21
Massachusetts	26.2	48
Michigan	38.2	11
Minnesota	33.7	32
Mississippi	35.4	25
Missouri	36.4	18
Montana	38.8	6
Nebraska	40.7	2
Nevada	27.3	47
New Hampshire	31.8	40
New Jersey	35.5	24
New Mexico	33.6	33
New York	27.9	46
North Carolina	36.2	19
North Dakota	38.7	7
Ohio	34.7	29
Oklahoma	39.7	3
Oregon	36.1	20
Pennsylvania	33.7	31
Rhode Island	31.3	41
South Carolina	33.4	35
South Dakota	35.2	26
Tennessee	32.3	39
Texas	38.3	9
Utah	42.7	1
Vermont	39.1	5
Virginia	37.5	15
Washington	36.0	22
West Virginia	35.6	23
Wisconsin	37.5	14
Wyoming	36.7	17
50 States	33.0	
DC	16.2	
United States	32.9	

1. Utah
2. Nebraska
3. Oklahoma
4. Kansas
5. Vermont
6. Montana
7. North Dakota
8. Delaware
9. Texas
10. Indiana
11. Michigan
12. Iowa
13. Idaho
14. Wisconsin
15. Virginia
16. Arkansas
17. Wyoming
18. Missouri
19. North Carolina
20. Oregon
21. Maryland
22. Washington
23. West Virginia
24. New Jersey
25. Mississippi
26. South Dakota
27. Arizona
28. Kentucky
29. Ohio
30. Georgia
31. Pennsylvania
32. Minnesota
33. New Mexico
34. Colorado
35. South Carolina
36. Maine
37. Alabama
38. Illinois
39. Tennessee
40. New Hampshire
41. Rhode Island
42. Louisiana
43. Connecticut
44. Florida
45. California
46. New York
47. Nevada
48. Massachusetts
49. Alaska
50. Hawaii

State	Spending per pupil $	Rank	By $
Alabama	4,544	43	1. New Jersey
Alaska	8,813	2	2. Alaska
Arizona	4,048	49	3. New York
Arkansas	4,172	48	4. Connecticut
California	5,336	32	5. Rhode Island
Colorado	5,147	36	6. Delaware
Connecticut	8,376	4	7. Massachusetts
Delaware	7,086	6	8. Pennsylvania
Florida	5,429	30	9. Michigan
Georgia	5,585	25	10. Wisconsin
Hawaii	5,720	22	11. Maryland
Idaho	4,500	45	12. West Virginia
Illinois	5,455	29	13. Vermont
Indiana	5,893	18	14. Maine
Iowa	5,705	23	15. Oregon
Kansas	5,528	26	16. New Hampshire
Kentucky	5,675	24	17. Virginia
Louisiana	4,527	44	18. Indiana
Maine	6,369	14	19. Minnesota
Maryland	6,547	11	20. Wyoming
Massachusetts	7,069	7	21. Washington
Michigan	6,750	9	22. Hawaii
Minnesota	5,877	19	23. Iowa
Mississippi	4,269	46	24. Kentucky
Missouri	4,949	38	25. Georgia
Montana	5,381	31	26. Kansas
Nebraska	5,286	34	27. Ohio
Nevada	4,977	37	28. Texas
New Hampshire	5,974	16	29. Illinois
New Jersey	9,455	1	30. Florida
New Mexico	5,310	33	31. Montana
New York	8,564	3	32. California
North Carolina	4,902	39	33. New Mexico
North Dakota	4,667	42	34. Nebraska
Ohio	5,527	27	35. South Carolina
Oklahoma	4,187	47	36. Colorado
Oregon	5,988	15	37. Nevada
Pennsylvania	6,955	8	38. Missouri
Rhode Island	7,284	5	39. North Carolina
South Carolina	5,172	35	40. Tennessee
South Dakota	4,682	41	41. South Dakota
Tennessee	4,898	40	42. North Dakota
Texas	5,466	28	43. Alabama
Utah	3,837	50	44. Louisiana
Vermont	6,503	13	45. Idaho
Virginia	5,920	17	46. Mississippi
Washington	5,805	21	47. Oklahoma
West Virginia	6,522	12	48. Arkansas
Wisconsin	6,701	10	49. Arizona
Wyoming	5,872	20	50. Utah
50 States	n/a		
DC	7,175		
United States	5,885		

H-16 AVERAGE TEACHER SALARY, 1996-1997

State	Average teacher salary $	Rank
Alabama	32,549	37
Alaska	50,647	1
Arizona	33,350	32
Arkansas	29,975	43
California	43,474	8
Colorado	36,175	22
Connecticut	50,426	2
Delaware	41,436	11
Florida	33,881	29
Georgia	36,042	23
Hawaii	35,842	24
Idaho	31,818	38
Illinois	42,679	10
Indiana	38,575	16
Iowa	33,275	33
Kansas	35,837	25
Kentucky	33,950	28
Louisiana	28,347	47
Maine	33,800	30
Maryland	41,148	12
Massachusetts	43,806	7
Michigan	44,251	6
Minnesota	37,975	17
Mississippi	27,720	48
Missouri	34,342	27
Montana	29,950	44
Nebraska	31,768	39
Nevada	37,340	19
New Hampshire	36,867	21
New Jersey	49,349	4
New Mexico	29,715	45
New York	49,560	3
North Carolina	31,225	42
North Dakota	27,711	49
Ohio	38,831	15
Oklahoma	29,270	46
Oregon	40,900	13
Pennsylvania	47,429	5
Rhode Island	43,019	9
South Carolina	32,659	35
South Dakota	26,764	50
Tennessee	33,789	31
Texas	32,644	36
Utah	31,750	40
Vermont	37,200	20
Virginia	35,837	26
Washington	37,860	18
West Virginia	33,159	34
Wisconsin	38,950	14
Wyoming	31,721	41
50 States	n/a	
DC	45,012	
United States	38,509	

Rank in order

By $

1. Alaska
2. Connecticut
3. New York
4. New Jersey
5. Pennsylvania
6. Michigan
7. Massachusetts
8. California
9. Rhode Island
10. Illinois
11. Delaware
12. Maryland
13. Oregon
14. Wisconsin
15. Ohio
16. Indiana
17. Minnesota
18. Washington
19. Nevada
20. Vermont
21. New Hampshire
22. Colorado
23. Georgia
24. Hawaii
25. Kansas
26. Virginia
27. Missouri
28. Kentucky
29. Florida
30. Maine
31. Tennessee
32. Arizona
33. Iowa
34. West Virginia
35. South Carolina
36. Texas
37. Alabama
38. Idaho
39. Nebraska
40. Utah
41. Wyoming
42. North Carolina
43. Arkansas
44. Montana
45. New Mexico
46. Oklahoma
47. Louisiana
48. Mississippi
49. North Dakota
50. South Dakota

H-17 SOURCES OF SCHOOL FUNDS, 1995-1996

State	Percent from federal %	Percent from state %	Percent from local %	Rank by percent local
Alabama	10.0	70.9	19.1	48
Alaska	12.6	63.6	23.9	46
Arizona	8.7	42.0	49.3	19
Arkansas	8.5	65.4	26.1	43
California	8.8	57.0	34.2	36
Colorado	5.5	44.2	50.3	18
Connecticut	4.4	39.1	56.5	9
Delaware	8.2	65.2	26.7	42
Florida	7.2	49.5	43.3	27
Georgia	6.7	52.6	40.7	30
Hawaii	8.4	89.5	2.0	50
Idaho	7.7	61.2	31.1	39
Illinois	8.8	29.9	61.3	4
Indiana	5.2	52.3	42.5	28
Iowa	5.1	49.5	45.4	23
Kansas	5.3	57.4	37.3	32
Kentucky	8.9	67.2	23.9	47
Louisiana	13.2	54.4	32.5	38
Maine	6.9	47.5	45.5	22
Maryland	5.8	39.3	54.9	13
Massachusetts	5.3	35.5	59.2	6
Michigan	6.5	57.9	35.6	34
Minnesota	4.5	51.7	43.8	26
Mississippi	15.3	55.6	29.1	40
Missouri	6.8	37.3	55.8	11
Montana	10.0	49.6	40.4	31
Nebraska	4.2	38.4	57.3	8
Nevada	4.7	34.4	60.9	5
New Hampshire	3.0	7.0	90.0	1
New Jersey	3.6	40.3	56.0	10
New Mexico	10.7	74.3	14.9	49
New York	6.1	39.3	54.6	14
North Carolina	8.6	66.5	24.9	44
North Dakota	11.0	42.5	46.5	21
Ohio	6.3	41.7	52.0	16
Oklahoma	8.9	63.5	27.6	41
Oregon	7.1	56.5	36.4	33
Pennsylvania	5.6	41.8	52.6	15
Rhode Island	4.0	41.0	55.0	12
South Carolina	8.7	46.1	45.2	24
South Dakota	10.1	26.1	63.7	3
Tennessee	8.7	50.3	40.9	29
Texas	8.8	43.5	47.7	20
Utah	6.4	58.4	35.2	35
Vermont	5.1	29.7	65.2	2
Virginia	5.3	36.3	58.4	7
Washington	6.3	69.4	24.3	45
West Virginia	7.8	58.5	33.7	37
Wisconsin	4.4	44.1	51.5	17
Wyoming	6.5	49.0	44.5	25
50 States	n/a	n/a	n/a	
DC	14.7	n/a	85.3	
United States	7.1	47.9	45.0	

Rank in order

By % local

1. New Hampshire
2. Vermont
3. South Dakota
4. Illinois
5. Nevada
6. Massachusetts
7. Virginia
8. Nebraska
9. Connecticut
10. New Jersey
11. Missouri
12. Rhode Island
13. Maryland
14. New York
15. Pennsylvania
16. Ohio
17. Wisconsin
18. Colorado
19. Arizona
20. Texas
21. North Dakota
22. Maine
23. Iowa
24. South Carolina
25. Wyoming
26. Minnesota
27. Florida
28. Indiana
29. Tennessee
30. Georgia
31. Montana
32. Kansas
33. Oregon
34. Michigan
35. Utah
36. California
37. West Virginia
38. Louisiana
39. Idaho
40. Mississippi
41. Oklahoma
42. Delaware
43. Arkansas
44. North Carolina
45. Washington
46. Alaska
47. Kentucky
48. Alabama
49. New Mexico
50. Hawaii

State	State aid per pupil $(000)	Rank		By $
Alabama	3,588	20		1. Hawaii
Alaska	6,530	2		2. Alaska
Arizona	2,341	44		3. Delaware
Arkansas	3,531	21		4. Michigan
California	3,757	17		5. New Mexico
Colorado	2,840	38		6. Washington
Connecticut	3,735	18		7. West Virginia
Delaware	5,877	3		8. Wisconsin
Florida	3,362	27		9. New Jersey
Georgia	3,458	25		10. Kentucky
Hawaii	6,829	1		11. Minnesota
Idaho	3,398	26		12. Kansas
Illinois	1,986	48		13. New York
Indiana	4,007	14		14. Indiana
Iowa	3,517	22		15. North Carolina
Kansas	4,142	12		16. Oregon
Kentucky	4,327	10		17. California
Louisiana	2,791	39		18. Connecticut
Maine	3,274	28		19. Pennsylvania
Maryland	3,046	31		20. Alabama
Massachusetts	2,984	33		21. Arkansas
Michigan	5,671	4		22. Iowa
Minnesota	4,236	11		23. Rhode Island
Mississippi	2,948	34		24. Wyoming
Missouri	2,614	40		25. Georgia
Montana	3,175	30		26. Idaho
Nebraska	2,272	46		27. Florida
Nevada	2,149	47		28. Maine
New Hampshire	479	50		29. Oklahoma
New Jersey	4,336	9		30. Montana
New Mexico	5,129	5		31. Maryland
New York	4,115	13		32. Utah
North Carolina	3,841	15		33. Massachusetts
North Dakota	2,375	43		34. Mississippi
Ohio	2,859	36		35. South Carolina
Oklahoma	3,273	29		36. Ohio
Oregon	3,835	16		37. Texas
Pennsylvania	3,680	19		38. Colorado
Rhode Island	3,514	23		39. Louisiana
South Carolina	2,884	35		40. Missouri
South Dakota	1,873	49		41. Tennessee
Tennessee	2,599	41		42. Vermont
Texas	2,843	37		43. North Dakota
Utah	3,003	32		44. Arizona
Vermont	2,452	42		45. Virginia
Virginia	2,273	45		46. Nebraska
Washington	4,881	6		47. Nevada
West Virginia	4,642	7		48. Illinois
Wisconsin	4,519	8		49. South Dakota
Wyoming	3,501	24		50. New Hampshire
50 States	3,491			
DC	n/a			
United States	3,485			

H-19 STATE AND LOCAL HIGHER EDUCATION SPENDING, FY 1994

State	Higher education spending $(millions)	Per capita $	As percent of personal income %	Rank by per capita
Alabama	1,709	405	2.39	19
Alaska	300	496	2.18	8
Arizona	1,569	385	2.20	22
Arkansas	733	299	1.89	43
California	10,126	322	1.48	36
Colorado	1,652	452	2.16	13
Connecticut	831	254	0.91	47
Delaware	413	585	2.71	3
Florida	3,474	249	1.23	48
Georgia	1,990	282	1.50	45
Hawaii	589	500	2.15	7
Idaho	447	395	2.32	21
Illinois	3,516	299	1.33	42
Indiana	2,448	426	2.24	16
Iowa	1,490	527	2.89	5
Kansas	1,168	457	2.32	12
Kentucky	1,281	335	1.99	30
Louisiana	1,351	313	1.90	38
Maine	371	299	1.59	41
Maryland	1,924	384	1.62	23
Massachusetts	1,365	226	0.93	50
Michigan	4,473	471	2.30	10
Minnesota	1,821	399	1.92	20
Mississippi	976	366	2.51	25
Missouri	1,284	241	1.25	49
Montana	290	339	1.99	29
Nebraska	730	450	2.30	14
Nevada	408	280	1.29	46
New Hampshire	333	293	1.34	44
New Jersey	2,521	319	1.20	37
New Mexico	841	508	3.19	6
New York	5,878	324	1.30	35
North Carolina	2,975	421	2.29	18
North Dakota	386	605	3.55	1
Ohio	3,693	333	1.70	31
Oklahoma	1,120	344	2.03	28
Oregon	1,308	424	2.22	17
Pennsylvania	3,636	302	1.42	40
Rhode Island	308	309	1.45	39
South Carolina	1,341	366	2.19	24
South Dakota	237	329	1.84	33
Tennessee	1,695	328	1.81	34
Texas	6,499	354	1.88	27
Utah	1,028	539	3.42	4
Vermont	279	481	2.49	9
Virginia	2,369	362	1.69	26
Washington	2,341	438	2.05	15
West Virginia	602	330	2.05	32
Wisconsin	2,363	465	2.37	11
Wyoming	285	599	3.07	2
50 States	90,769	349	1.70	
DC	102	178	0.59	
United States	90,871	349	1.70	

By per capita

1. North Dakota
2. Wyoming
3. Delaware
4. Utah
5. Iowa
6. New Mexico
7. Hawaii
8. Alaska
9. Vermont
10. Michigan
11. Wisconsin
12. Kansas
13. Colorado
14. Nebraska
15. Washington
16. Indiana
17. Oregon
18. North Carolina
19. Alabama
20. Minnesota
21. Idaho
22. Arizona
23. Maryland
24. South Carolina
25. Mississippi
26. Virginia
27. Texas
28. Oklahoma
29. Montana
30. Kentucky
31. Ohio
32. West Virginia
33. South Dakota
34. Tennessee
35. New York
36. California
37. New Jersey
38. Louisiana
39. Rhode Island
40. Pennsylvania
41. Maine
42. Illinois
43. Arkansas
44. New Hampshire
45. Georgia
46. Nevada
47. Connecticut
48. Florida
49. Missouri
50. Massachusetts

H-20 HIGHER EDUCATION SPENDING AS PERCENT OF GENERAL SPENDING, FY 1994

State	Higher education spending as percent of general spending %	Rank
Alabama	11.6	10
Alaska	4.9	49
Arizona	10.4	19
Arkansas	9.8	25
California	7.3	42
Colorado	11.0	16
Connecticut	5.0	48
Delaware	13.1	4
Florida	6.7	44
Georgia	7.6	39
Hawaii	8.9	30
Idaho	11.9	8
Illinois	7.9	37
Indiana	11.5	12
Iowa	13.3	3
Kansas	12.0	6
Kentucky	10.1	23
Louisiana	8.0	35
Maine	7.5	40
Maryland	9.8	26
Massachusetts	4.9	50
Michigan	11.4	13
Minnesota	8.2	34
Mississippi	11.3	14
Missouri	8.0	36
Montana	8.8	31
Nebraska	11.7	9
Nevada	6.5	46
New Hampshire	7.5	41
New Jersey	6.6	45
New Mexico	12.2	5
New York	5.2	47
North Carolina	11.9	7
North Dakota	14.9	1
Ohio	8.8	32
Oklahoma	10.6	18
Oregon	10.1	21
Pennsylvania	7.8	38
Rhode Island	6.8	43
South Carolina	9.7	27
South Dakota	8.9	29
Tennessee	9.8	24
Texas	10.2	20
Utah	14.9	2
Vermont	11.5	11
Virginia	10.1	22
Washington	9.7	28
West Virginia	8.8	33
Wisconsin	10.8	17
Wyoming	11.2	15
50 States	8.5	
DC	2.2	
United States	8.5	

Rank in order

By %

1. North Dakota
2. Utah
3. Iowa
4. Delaware
5. New Mexico
6. Kansas
7. North Carolina
8. Idaho
9. Nebraska
10. Alabama
11. Vermont
12. Indiana
13. Michigan
14. Mississippi
15. Wyoming
16. Colorado
17. Wisconsin
18. Oklahoma
19. Arizona
20. Texas
21. Oregon
22. Virginia
23. Kentucky
24. Tennessee
25. Arkansas
26. Maryland
27. South Carolina
28. Washington
29. South Dakota
30. Hawaii
31. Montana
32. Ohio
33. West Virginia
34. Minnesota
35. Louisiana
36. Missouri
37. Illinois
38. Pennsylvania
39. Georgia
40. Maine
41. New Hampshire
42. California
43. Rhode Island
44. Florida
45. New Jersey
46. Nevada
47. New York
48. Connecticut
49. Alaska
50. Massachusetts

H-21 PUBLIC HIGHER EDUCATION ENROLLMENT, 1995

State	Higher education enrollment #	As percent of total population %	Rank by %	Rank in order By %
Alabama	203,165	4.8	14	1. Kansas
Alaska	28,368	4.7	15	2. Wyoming
Arizona	254,530	5.9	3	3. Arizona
Arkansas	87,067	3.5	41	4. Nebraska
California	1,564,230	5.0	10	5. New Mexico
Colorado	210,312	5.6	8	6. North Dakota
Connecticut	100,539	3.1	48	7. Utah
Delaware	36,204	5.0	9	8. Colorado
Florida	530,607	3.7	37	9. Delaware
Georgia	248,682	3.4	43	10. California
Hawaii	50,198	4.3	26	11. Michigan
Idaho	48,986	4.2	28	12. Oklahoma
Illinois	530,248	4.5	19	13. Wisconsin
Indiana	224,795	3.9	35	14. Alabama
Iowa	122,396	4.3	24	15. Alaska
Kansas	160,449	6.3	1	16. Minnesota
Kentucky	148,808	3.9	36	17. Oregon
Louisiana	174,873	4.0	33	18. Washington
Maine	38,195	3.1	47	19. Illinois
Maryland	222,857	4.4	22	20. Texas
Massachusetts	176,777	2.9	49	21. Virginia
Michigan	462,390	4.8	11	22. Maryland
Minnesota	217,249	4.7	16	23. Nevada
Mississippi	110,600	4.1	29	24. Iowa
Missouri	189,993	3.6	40	25. Montana
Montana	37,435	4.3	25	26. Hawaii
Nebraska	95,599	5.8	4	27. North Carolina
Nevada	66,683	4.3	23	28. Idaho
New Hampshire	36,069	3.1	46	29. Mississippi
New Jersey	271,069	3.4	44	30. West Virginia
New Mexico	97,220	5.8	5	31. South Dakota
New York	588,491	3.2	45	32. South Carolina
North Carolina	303,099	4.2	27	33. Louisiana
North Dakota	36,810	5.7	6	34. Rhode Island
Ohio	409,818	3.7	39	35. Indiana
Oklahoma	158,026	4.8	12	36. Kentucky
Oregon	143,617	4.6	17	37. Florida
Pennsylvania	339,928	2.8	50	38. Tennessee
Rhode Island	38,653	3.9	34	39. Ohio
South Carolina	148,706	4.1	32	40. Missouri
South Dakota	29,693	4.1	31	41. Arkansas
Tennessee	193,136	3.7	38	42. Vermont
Texas	836,851	4.5	20	43. Georgia
Utah	110,560	5.6	7	44. New Jersey
Vermont	20,470	3.5	42	45. New York
Virginia	293,127	4.4	21	46. New Hampshire
Washington	246,635	4.5	18	47. Maine
West Virginia	74,857	4.1	30	48. Connecticut
Wisconsin	245,770	4.8	13	49. Massachusetts
Wyoming	29,420	6.1	2	50. Pennsylvania
50 States	10,994,260	4.2		
DC	9,663	1.7		
United States	11,092,374	4.2		

State	Per pupil support $	Rank
Alabama	4,799	20
Alaska	5,944	5
Arizona	3,095	48
Arkansas	5,938	6
California	4,078	37
Colorado	3,097	47
Connecticut	5,744	7
Delaware	4,285	30
Florida	4,237	34
Georgia	5,564	8
Hawaii	6,941	1
Idaho	5,068	11
Illinois	4,244	33
Indiana	4,857	17
Iowa	6,072	4
Kansas	3,506	45
Kentucky	4,819	19
Louisiana	4,152	36
Maine	4,868	16
Maryland	3,928	42
Massachusetts	5,129	10
Michigan	3,953	40
Minnesota	5,434	9
Mississippi	6,582	3
Missouri	4,414	27
Montana	3,385	46
Nebraska	4,350	29
Nevada	4,375	28
New Hampshire	2,462	50
New Jersey	4,988	14
New Mexico	4,987	15
New York	4,846	18
North Carolina	6,622	2
North Dakota	4,664	23
Ohio	4,547	25
Oklahoma	4,215	35
Oregon	3,838	43
Pennsylvania	5,047	12
Rhode Island	3,591	44
South Carolina	5,005	13
South Dakota	4,063	39
Tennessee	4,684	22
Texas	4,254	31
Utah	4,251	32
Vermont	2,784	49
Virginia	3,935	41
Washington	4,476	26
West Virginia	4,712	21
Wisconsin	4,074	38
Wyoming	4,590	24
50 States	4,493	
DC	n/a	
United States	4,454	

By $

1. Hawaii
2. North Carolina
3. Mississippi
4. Iowa
5. Alaska
6. Arkansas
7. Connecticut
8. Georgia
9. Minnesota
10. Massachusetts
11. Idaho
12. Pennsylvania
13. South Carolina
14. New Jersey
15. New Mexico
16. Maine
17. Indiana
18. New York
19. Kentucky
20. Alabama
21. West Virginia
22. Tennessee
23. North Dakota
24. Wyoming
25. Ohio
26. Washington
27. Missouri
28. Nevada
29. Nebraska
30. Delaware
31. Texas
32. Utah
33. Illinois
34. Florida
35. Oklahoma
36. Louisiana
37. California
38. Wisconsin
39. South Dakota
40. Michigan
41. Virginia
42. Maryland
43. Oregon
44. Rhode Island
45. Kansas
46. Montana
47. Colorado
48. Arizona
49. Vermont
50. New Hampshire

State	Average tuition $	Rank
Alabama	2,363	31
Alaska	2,552	27
Arizona	2,009	45
Arkansas	2,255	34
California	2,731	23
Colorado	2,562	26
Connecticut	4,105	7
Delaware	4,180	6
Florida	1,789	50
Georgia	2,244	35
Hawaii	2,298	32
Idaho	1,973	46
Illinois	3,525	16
Indiana	3,200	20
Iowa	2,655	25
Kansas	2,223	38
Kentucky	2,241	36
Louisiana	2,230	37
Maine	3,639	14
Maryland	3,848	11
Massachusetts	4,266	5
Michigan	3,986	8
Minnesota	3,539	15
Mississippi	2,497	28
Missouri	3,230	18
Montana	2,488	29
Nebraska	2,269	33
Nevada	1,814	49
New Hampshire	4,644	3
New Jersey	4,269	4
New Mexico	2,016	43
New York	3,797	13
North Carolina	1,841	48
North Dakota	2,381	30
Ohio	3,834	12
Oklahoma	1,936	47
Oregon	3,407	17
Pennsylvania	4,994	2
Rhode Island	3,907	10
South Carolina	3,206	19
South Dakota	2,727	24
Tennessee	2,051	41
Texas	2,022	42
Utah	2,010	44
Vermont	6,538	1
Virginia	3,962	9
Washington	2,928	21
West Virginia	2,088	40
Wisconsin	2,747	22
Wyoming	2,144	39
50 States	n/a	
DC	1,502	
United States	2,986	

Rank in order

By $

1. Vermont
2. Pennsylvania
3. New Hampshire
4. New Jersey
5. Massachusetts
6. Delaware
7. Connecticut
8. Michigan
9. Virginia
10. Rhode Island
11. Maryland
12. Ohio
13. New York
14. Maine
15. Minnesota
16. Illinois
17. Oregon
18. Missouri
19. South Carolina
20. Indiana
21. Washington
22. Wisconsin
23. California
24. South Dakota
25. Iowa
26. Colorado
27. Alaska
28. Mississippi
29. Montana
30. North Dakota
31. Alabama
32. Hawaii
33. Nebraska
34. Arkansas
35. Georgia
36. Kentucky
37. Louisiana
38. Kansas
39. Wyoming
40. West Virginia
41. Tennessee
42. Texas
43. New Mexico
44. Utah
45. Arizona
46. Idaho
47. Oklahoma
48. North Carolina
49. Nevada
50. Florida

State	Average salary $(000)	Rank
Alabama	48.0	35
Alaska	55.1	10
Arizona	51.6	24
Arkansas	48.0	35
California	56.9	6
Colorado	54.0	18
Connecticut	63.3	2
Delaware	58.7	4
Florida	50.4	30
Georgia	51.8	22
Hawaii	55.4	9
Idaho	46.1	44
Illinois	46.9	41
Indiana	53.1	20
Iowa	55.0	11
Kansas	46.9	41
Kentucky	51.7	23
Louisiana	47.4	40
Maine	47.9	37
Maryland	54.7	14
Massachusetts	57.1	5
Michigan	54.1	17
Minnesota	52.6	21
Mississippi	47.5	39
Missouri	54.7	14
Montana	42.6	47
Nebraska	50.7	29
Nevada	54.9	12
New Hampshire	n/a	n/a
New Jersey	64.2	1
New Mexico	48.6	34
New York	54.6	16
North Carolina	59.0	3
North Dakota	41.1	48
Ohio	55.6	8
Oklahoma	46.3	43
Oregon	45.2	45
Pennsylvania	54.9	12
Rhode Island	51.0	27
South Carolina	51.0	27
South Dakota	39.1	49
Tennessee	51.2	26
Texas	51.6	24
Utah	49.3	33
Vermont	49.4	32
Virginia	56.4	7
Washington	49.9	31
West Virginia	47.9	37
Wisconsin	53.5	19
Wyoming	44.8	46
50 States	50.4	
DC	60.9	
United States	50.6	

Rank in order

By $

1. New Jersey
2. Connecticut
3. North Carolina
4. Delaware
5. Massachusetts
6. California
7. Virginia
8. Ohio
9. Hawaii
10. Alaska
11. Iowa
12. Nevada
12. Pennsylvania
14. Maryland
14. Missouri
16. New York
17. Michigan
18. Colorado
19. Wisconsin
20. Indiana
21. Minnesota
22. Georgia
23. Kentucky
24. Arizona
24. Texas
26. Tennessee
27. Rhode Island
27. South Carolina
29. Nebraska
30. Florida
31. Washington
32. Vermont
33. Utah
34. New Mexico
35. Alabama
35. Arkansas
37. Maine
37. West Virginia
39. Mississippi
40. Louisiana
41. Illinois
41. Kansas
43. Oklahoma
44. Idaho
45. Oregon
46. Wyoming
47. Montana
48. North Dakota
49. South Dakota

H-25 STATE AND LOCAL EDUCATION EMPLOYEES, 1995

State	Education employees	Per 10,000 employees	Rank by per 10,000
Alabama	90,597	213	30
Alaska	14,776	245	13
Arizona	85,974	200	36
Arkansas	61,417	247	11
California	495,587	157	50
Colorado	77,245	206	34
Connecticut	69,792	213	29
Delaware	14,008	195	40
Florida	255,627	180	46
Georgia	186,396	259	6
Hawaii	23,365	198	37
Idaho	26,706	229	22
Illinois	215,474	183	45
Indiana	127,817	220	24
Iowa	67,764	238	16
Kansas	65,575	256	8
Kentucky	94,715	246	12
Louisiana	105,840	244	14
Maine	32,259	260	5
Maryland	98,057	195	41
Massachusetts	130,278	215	28
Michigan	184,756	194	42
Minnesota	107,641	233	19
Mississippi	65,400	243	15
Missouri	114,866	216	27
Montana	27,225	313	1
Nebraska	41,964	256	7
Nevada	27,427	179	47
New Hampshire	24,987	218	26
New Jersey	187,442	236	18
New Mexico	41,809	247	10
New York	380,411	209	32
North Carolina	152,039	211	31
North Dakota	14,045	219	25
Ohio	209,908	189	44
Oklahoma	81,669	249	9
Oregon	61,922	197	38
Pennsylvania	203,093	168	48
Rhode Island	19,209	194	43
South Carolina	83,245	227	23
South Dakota	17,273	237	17
Tennessee	102,810	196	39
Texas	521,993	278	4
Utah	39,915	204	35
Vermont	16,947	290	3
Virginia	151,882	230	21
Washington	87,730	161	49
West Virginia	42,406	232	20
Wisconsin	106,434	208	33
Wyoming	14,558	304	2
50 States	5,470,275	209	
DC	8,819	159	
United States	5,479,094	208	

Rank in order

By per 10,000

1. Montana
2. Wyoming
3. Vermont
4. Texas
5. Maine
6. Georgia
7. Nebraska
8. Kansas
9. Oklahoma
10. New Mexico
11. Arkansas
12. Kentucky
13. Alaska
14. Louisiana
15. Mississippi
16. Iowa
17. South Dakota
18. New Jersey
19. Minnesota
20. West Virginia
21. Virginia
22. Idaho
23. South Carolina
24. Indiana
25. North Dakota
26. New Hampshire
27. Missouri
28. Massachusetts
29. Connecticut
30. Alabama
31. North Carolina
32. New York
33. Wisconsin
34. Colorado
35. Utah
36. Arizona
37. Hawaii
38. Oregon
39. Tennessee
40. Delaware
41. Maryland
42. Michigan
43. Rhode Island
44. Ohio
45. Illinois
46. Florida
47. Nevada
48. Pennsylvania
49. Washington
50. California

State	Federal R&D spending $(000)	Per capita $	Rank by per capita
Alabama	2,016,252	475	7
Alaska	96,915	161	25
Arizona	915,087	213	15
Arkansas	97,724	39	48
California	12,703,572	402	9
Colorado	965,060	258	12
Connecticut	902,334	276	11
Delaware	56,381	79	34
Florida	2,403,899	169	21
Georgia	4,365,770	606	3
Hawaii	480,428	407	8
Idaho	211,063	181	20
Illinois	1,116,137	95	30
Indiana	426,192	74	38
Iowa	214,316	75	35
Kansas	120,846	47	45
Kentucky	75,670	20	50
Louisiana	176,253	41	47
Maine	54,476	44	46
Maryland	7,039,183	1,397	1
Massachusetts	3,339,532	550	4
Michigan	688,376	72	40
Minnesota	571,128	124	27
Mississippi	212,739	79	33
Missouri	1,613,322	303	10
Montana	64,821	74	36
Nebraska	86,762	53	42
Nevada	372,570	243	13
New Hampshire	213,647	186	19
New Jersey	1,325,902	167	22
New Mexico	1,987,076	1,176	2
New York	2,581,383	142	26
North Carolina	825,433	115	28
North Dakota	47,313	74	37
Ohio	1,811,413	163	23
Oklahoma	159,395	49	43
Oregon	277,229	88	32
Pennsylvania	2,414,250	200	17
Rhode Island	515,425	520	6
South Carolina	177,962	49	44
South Dakota	26,492	36	49
Tennessee	581,956	111	29
Texas	4,062,175	216	14
Utah	371,208	190	18
Vermont	53,590	92	31
Virginia	3,603,023	545	5
Washington	1,127,750	207	16
West Virginia	296,347	162	24
Wisconsin	347,089	68	41
Wyoming	35,151	73	39
50 States	64,228,017	245	
DC	2,805,093	5,059	
United States	67,246,794	256	

Rank in order

By per capita

1. Maryland
2. New Mexico
3. Georgia
4. Massachusetts
5. Virginia
6. Rhode Island
7. Alabama
8. Hawaii
9. California
10. Missouri
11. Connecticut
12. Colorado
13. Nevada
14. Texas
15. Arizona
16. Washington
17. Pennsylvania
18. Utah
19. New Hampshire
20. Idaho
21. Florida
22. New Jersey
23. Ohio
24. West Virginia
25. Alaska
26. New York
27. Minnesota
28. North Carolina
29. Tennessee
30. Illinois
31. Vermont
32. Oregon
33. Mississippi
34. Delaware
35. Iowa
36. Montana
37. North Dakota
38. Indiana
39. Wyoming
40. Michigan
41. Wisconsin
42. Nebraska
43. Oklahoma
44. South Carolina
45. Kansas
46. Maine
47. Louisiana
48. Arkansas
49. South Dakota
50. Kentucky

State	Library spending $(000)	Library spending per capita $	Rank by per capita
Alabama	44,836	10.6	42
Alaska	18,047	30.0	3
Arizona	66,374	16.2	27
Arkansas	19,895	8.1	50
California	529,629	16.9	24
Colorado	80,111	21.9	13
Connecticut	89,620	27.4	5
Delaware	8,541	12.1	39
Florida	216,022	15.5	28
Georgia	98,455	13.9	32
Hawaii	24,819	21.2	15
Idaho	14,489	12.7	37
Illinois	294,894	25.1	8
Indiana	146,199	25.4	7
Iowa	47,253	16.7	25
Kansas	43,895	17.2	22
Kentucky	41,600	10.9	41
Louisiana	62,547	14.5	30
Maine	17,670	14.3	31
Maryland	122,100	24.4	9
Massachusetts	135,636	22.4	11
Michigan	172,274	18.2	20
Minnesota	104,429	22.8	10
Mississippi	21,750	8.2	49
Missouri	90,037	17.1	23
Montana	9,064	10.6	43
Nebraska	23,894	14.7	29
Nevada	23,988	16.4	26
New Hampshire	21,690	19.1	18
New Jersey	234,665	29.7	4
New Mexico	19,645	11.8	40
New York	588,274	32.3	2
North Carolina	92,431	13.1	35
North Dakota	6,108	9.5	48
Ohio	368,829	33.2	1
Oklahoma	33,005	10.1	44
Oregon	57,411	18.6	19
Pennsylvania	162,205	13.5	34
Rhode Island	19,743	19.8	16
South Carolina	44,482	12.2	38
South Dakota	9,252	12.8	36
Tennessee	51,851	10.0	45
Texas	183,734	10.0	46
Utah	33,384	17.5	21
Vermont	8,074	13.9	33
Virginia	125,772	19.2	17
Washington	140,634	26.3	6
West Virginia	17,421	9.6	47
Wisconsin	111,472	21.9	12
Wyoming	10,359	21.8	14
50 States	4,908,509	18.9	
DC	22,340	39.3	
United States	4,930,847	18.9	

Rank in order

By per capita

1. Ohio
2. New York
3. Alaska
4. New Jersey
5. Connecticut
6. Washington
7. Indiana
8. Illinois
9. Maryland
10. Minnesota
11. Massachusetts
12. Wisconsin
13. Colorado
14. Wyoming
15. Hawaii
16. Rhode Island
17. Virginia
18. New Hampshire
19. Oregon
20. Michigan
21. Utah
22. Kansas
23. Missouri
24. California
25. Iowa
26. Nevada
27. Arizona
28. Florida
29. Nebraska
30. Louisiana
31. Maine
32. Georgia
33. Vermont
34. Pennsylvania
35. North Carolina
36. South Dakota
37. Idaho
38. South Carolina
39. Delaware
40. New Mexico
41. Kentucky
42. Alabama
43. Montana
44. Oklahoma
45. Tennessee
46. Texas
47. West Virginia
48. North Dakota
49. Mississippi
50. Arkansas

Source Notes for Education (Section H)

H-1 Average Proficiency in Math, Eighth Grade, 1996: These statistics reflect scores on national tests administered to eighth graders to determine their ability to deal with basic concepts of mathematics. Because some states choose different assessment methods, only 40 states participated in this study. The statistics are representative of those being developed through the National Assessment of Educational Progress, as administered by the U.S. Department of Education and cooperating states. They were printed in the *NAEP 1996 Mathematics Report Card.*

Statistics comparing the educational achievements of students in individual states, school districts, and schools are a response to the widespread criticism that taxpayers and parents have few ways to assess how well schools are educating children. Many states have established their own tests and print comparisons, often called "report cards," among school districts and schools within the state. Supporters of these statistics and tests argue that it is much more appropriate to compare results in education programs than the common statistics that just compare costs, such as how much is spent per pupil. Statistics on test results measure achievement of pupils, not that of teachers or school systems. Experts disagree on the relative influence of factors affecting student achievement, but all agree that it is heavily influenced by such out-of-school factors as early childhood training in the home, children's physical and mental health, and participation of parents in the educational process.

H-2 Average Proficiency in Science, Eighth Grade, 1996: These data are comparable to those shown in Table H-1, except they cover science. Through the National Assessment of Educational Assessment, the U.S. Department of Education conducts mathematics, reading and science assessments every other year on different timelines. *State Fact Finder* will publish the most recent assessment statistic available. These statistics, while not available for all states (see notes to Table H-1) come from the *NAEP 1996 Science Report Card.*

H-3 Armed Forces Qualification Test Ranks, FY 1995: Many employers test potential employees to determine their suitability for work, as indicated by such factors as ability to read and understand instructions and perform simple calculations. One of the most widely used tests is offered nationwide to persons seeking to enlist in the armed forces. These data reflect average scores of test-takers in the period from October 1994 to the end of September 1995. These data are prepared by the Department of Defense and published annually, along with other information about persons in uniform, in *Population Representation in the Military Services.* The Defense Department, which does not want to become an arbitrator of which states prepare students best for jobs, tries to

discourage the use of these results to rank states. Regardless, the results provide the best single measure of performance of high school graduates being tested by an employer using criteria approximating aptitude for work.

H-4 Scholastic Aptitude Test Scores, 1997: College-bound students are generally required to take an achievement test to gain admission to the college or university of their choice. There are two major tests used for this purpose, the Scholastic Aptitude Test (SAT), which is administered by the College Board (212-713-8000), and the ACT test, which is administered by the American College Testing Program (319-337-1028). Both organizations seek to discourage the use of their test scores as a way to compare education systems of states, but they are commonly used for lack of other comparisons indicating how well states and individual school districts and schools compare in meeting these standards for college admissions. The test scores are presented here and in Table H-5, with neither table including all states. Each state's results are for the test that is most often taken in that state. Failure to do this would produce highly misleading results. For example, many southern states rely primarily on the ACT, but their students who seek admission to exclusive private universities in the Northeast and California must take the SAT to gain admission. As a result, the SAT test is taken by a small fraction of high school graduates, but those who take it score extraordinarily high.

H-5 ACT Scores, 1997: See notes to Table H-4.

H-6 Percentage of Population Over 25 with a High School Diploma, 1996: These data reflect the percentage of the total population over age twenty-five that has a high school degree. Because each generation of Americans has, on average, attended school longer than its predecessors, the states with the highest ranks tend to be those with the fastest growth and thus youngest population. The data was provided by the Census Bureau's population division by fax on September 12, 1997.

H-7 Students in Private Schools, 1993: Almost five million students in kindergarten through the twelfth grade attend private schools. The enrollment statistics (both public and private) are gathered by the Department of Education and published in the *Digest of Education Statistics 1996* available on the Internet (http://www.ed.gov).

H-8 High School Completion Rates, 1993-1995: An average over a three year period shows that, nationwide, 85 percent of 18 to 25 year olds have graduated from high school. Subtracting this figure from a 100 percent graduation rate suggests a "dropout" rate of 15 percent. This approach is one of several ways of comparing dropout rates among the states. The Department of Education has produced a dropout rate statistic that relies on a count of dropouts. Currently only 17 states have reliable data that use this concept. The data printed here is from the Census Bureau and are available on their web site (http://www.census.gov).

H-9 Pupil-Teacher Ratio, 1994: Small classes are generally believed to be more beneficial to students than large ones, so pupil-teacher ratios are commonly used as a proxy measure of educational quality. The statistic shows a lower ratio than typical class sizes because some specialized teachers, such as those teaching art or special education, are included. These data come from the same source as Table H-7.

For these and other commonly used educational statistics comparing states, there are three primary sources: the Department of Education, the National Education Association (NEA), and the American Federation of Teachers (which, like the NEA, represents teachers). These organizations produce somewhat different data, using different concepts and different schedules. However, the rankings of states on any particular indicator are about the same regardless of the source used.

H-10 Public School Enrollment, 1996-1997: These statistics show how the nation's 45.2 million public school pupils are distributed among the states. The comparison with each state's population is a rough indicator of the differences among states in the financial burdens of providing free public education. The data come from the National Education Association's report *1996-97 Estimates of School Statistics.*

H-11 Public Library Holdings Per Capita, FY 1994: These data, from *Public Libraries in the United States: FY 1994* published by the National Center of Educational Statistics, relate the holdings of books (and related materials) to the population of each state. Nationally, public libraries hold about three books for every person. The reports exclude significant sources of reading materials not in public libraries, such as collections of private and university libraries and certain public school systems.

H-12 Children with Disabilities, 1993: A substantial percentage of the nation's public school students are given special financing by state and federal programs because of something unique about them. The table reflects a Department of Education count of students in the 1993-1994 school year classified as disabled or receiving extra school money because of poverty. These data and the enrollment data used to calculate a percentage come from the 1996 *Digest of Education Statistics* available on the Internet (http://www.ed.gov).

H-13 State and Local Education Spending, FY 1994: This table relates spending data to population and personal income in each state. The data come from the Census Bureau's electronic publication, *State and Local Government Finance Estimates, by State* available on the Internet (http://www.census.gov) in April of 1997. Population

numbers, also from the Census, are as of July 1, 1994 and personal income numbers are from the Department of Commerce. Based on Census historical practices, State Fact Finder used CY 1993 numbers. See notes to Table F-1 for more extensive information on the source of the data.

H-14 State and Local Education Spending as Percent of General Spending, FY 1994: This table, from the same source as Table H-13, shows the relative importance of education spending in state and local budgets. It is derived by comparing this spending with total "general" spending. General spending includes essentially all other spending, except municipal electric and other utilities and trust funds, such as those for Workers' Compensation.

H-15 Spending Per Pupil, 1996-1997: This table, from the same source as Table H-10, shows spending in public schools for operations (excluding capital outlays) in relation to the number of pupils enrolled.

H-16 Average Teacher Salary, 1996-1997: These average salary calculations, from the same source as Table H-10, show the average gross wage of teachers, not including special pay for leading student activities or teaching in summer sessions.

H-17 Sources of School Funds, 1995-1996: Except in a few states, federal aid covers less than 10 percent of public school costs. State and local governments divide the remainder in proportions that vary considerably from state to state, as shown in the table. The data come from the National Education Association's *Rankings of the States, 1996.*

H-18 State Aid Per Pupil in Average Daily Attendance, 1996-1997: These data, calculated from statistics in the National Education Association's *1996-97 Estimates of School Statistics,* show the amount each state government spends on supporting local public schools, expressed in relation to the number of pupils attending school.

H-19 State and Local Spending for Higher Education, FY 1994: This table relates spending data to population and personal income in each state. For source see notes to Table H-13

H-20 State and Local Spending for Higher Education as Percent of General Spending, FY 1994: This table, from the same source as H-13, shows the relative importance of higher education in state and local budgets. It is derived by comparing this spending with total "general" spending. General spending includes essentially all other spending excepting municipal electric and other utilities and trust funds, such as those for Workers' Compensation.

H-21 Public Higher Education Enrollment, 1995: This table shows the total number of students enrolled in public universities and colleges in the fall of 1995 and relates this number to the total population of each state. This percentage is an indicator of the relative costs of supporting public higher education in each state. The enrollment data are from the Department of Education and appear annually in the *Digest of Education Statistics*. These numbers will appear in the 1997 Digest and were provided to *State Fact Finder* in an early release.

H-22 Per Pupil State Support of Higher Education, 1997-1998: There are a variety of different statistics seeking to measure state outlays for higher education on a per pupil basis. None are totally satisfactory for complex reasons, such as difficulty in classifying pupils as private or public in institutions that receive public support for some of their programs but are truly private in financing other programs. This table relates state government spending for fiscal year 1996-1997 to fall 1995 enrollment. The enrollment data are from the U.S. Department of Education (see Table H-21). The amount of state support comes from a survey of Fiscal Year 1998 state appropriations for higher education conducted by the Center for Higher Education at Illinois State University as reported in *Chronicle of Higher Education* (November 14, 1997).

H-23 Average Tuition and Fees at Public Universities, 1996-1997: These data, from the same source as H-21 reflect a composite of average tuition and general fees charged by public four-year institutions of higher education in the 1996-1997 academic year.

H-24 Average Salary of Associate Professors at "Flagship" State Universities, 1996-1997: These statistics were developed for *State Fact Finder* based on detailed salary surveys by the American Association of University Professors as printed in its magazine *Academe*

(March/April 1997). To make the comparisons, the "flagship" university salary for an associate professor was used. Usually the "flagship" is the largest, oldest state university, but in some states several institutions can be considered flagships, such as the University of Michigan and Michigan State. In those cases, State Fact Finder generally selected the university originally constituted as the general land-grant institution (e.g., the University of Michigan) rather than the one initially designated as an agricultural and mechanical school (e.g., Michigan State). N/A reflects flagship state universities that did not report salary statistics to the AAUP.

H-25 State and Local Education Employees, 1995: This statistic comes from a Census Bureau survey of state and local government employment, available on the Internet (http://www.census.gov, "Public Employment"). It covers employees of public schools, from janitors to principals, but it does not include higher education employees.

H-26 Federal Research and Development Spending, FY 1995: The federal government is a major supplier of funds for research and development of new products and processes. This federally supported research provides an important source of income for state and private universities and a base from which state economies can develop in high technology industries. The table shows how federal R&D spending in fiscal 1995 was distributed among the states and relates that spending to the population of each state. The data were developed by the National Science Foundation in its *Survey of Federal Funds for Research and Development*.

H-27 Total Library Operating Expenditures, FY 1994: These data are from the same source as Table H-11.

Health

State	Vaccination coverage %	Rank by %	By %
Alabama	78	27	1. Connecticut
Alaska	73	43	2. Maine
Arizona	72	45	2. Massachusetts
Arkansas	75	39	4. South Carolina
California	78	27	4. Vermont
Colorado	79	21	6. Minnesota
Connecticut	88	1	6. Rhode Island
Delaware	81	15	8. New Hampshire
Florida	78	27	9. Georgia
Georgia	83	9	9. North Dakota
Hawaii	78	27	11. Iowa
Idaho	68	49	11. Nebraska
Illinois	76	36	11. New York
Indiana	73	43	11. South Dakota
Iowa	82	11	15. Delaware
Kansas	76	36	15. Mississippi
Kentucky	79	21	15. Pennsylvania
Louisiana	80	18	18. Louisiana
Maine	87	2	18. Maryland
Maryland	80	18	18. New Mexico
Massachusetts	87	2	21. Colorado
Michigan	76	36	21. Kentucky
Minnesota	85	6	21. Ohio
Mississippi	81	15	21. Tennessee
Missouri	75	39	21. Washington
Montana	78	27	21. Wyoming
Nebraska	82	11	27. Alabama
Nevada	71	48	27. California
New Hampshire	84	8	27. Florida
New Jersey	78	27	27. Hawaii
New Mexico	80	18	27. Montana
New York	82	11	27. New Jersey
North Carolina	78	27	27. North Carolina
North Dakota	83	9	27. Virginia
Ohio	79	21	27. Wisconsin
Oklahoma	75	39	36. Illinois
Oregon	72	45	36. Kansas
Pennsylvania	81	15	36. Michigan
Rhode Island	85	6	39. Arkansas
South Carolina	86	4	39. Missouri
South Dakota	82	11	39. Oklahoma
Tennessee	79	21	42. Texas
Texas	74	42	43. Alaska
Utah	64	50	43. Indiana
Vermont	86	4	45. Arizona
Virginia	78	27	45. Oregon
Washington	79	21	45. West Virginia
West Virginia	72	45	48. Nevada
Wisconsin	78	27	49. Idaho
Wyoming	79	21	50. Utah
50 States	n/a		
DC	80		
United States	78		

State	Infant deaths per 1,000 live births	Rank
Alabama	10.3	1
Alaska	7.9	16
Arizona	7.6	21
Arkansas	8.0	15
California	6.0	38
Colorado	7.6	21
Connecticut	6.2	35
Delaware	7.7	19
Florida	7.5	24
Georgia	9.0	5
Hawaii	5.8	42
Idaho	7.1	31
Illinois	8.1	13
Indiana	7.5	24
Iowa	6.5	33
Kansas	8.9	6
Kentucky	7.6	21
Louisiana	9.2	3
Maine	4.4	49
Maryland	8.4	10
Massachusetts	4.9	48
Michigan	7.9	16
Minnesota	6.4	34
Mississippi	9.7	2
Missouri	8.1	13
Montana	7.3	29
Nebraska	8.7	9
Nevada	6.2	35
New Hampshire	5.7	43
New Jersey	7.3	29
New Mexico	5.9	40
New York	6.7	32
North Carolina	9.2	3
North Dakota	4.3	50
Ohio	7.7	19
Oklahoma	8.9	6
Oregon	5.6	44
Pennsylvania	7.4	27
Rhode Island	5.2	47
South Carolina	7.9	16
South Dakota	5.4	45
Tennessee	8.4	10
Texas	6.1	37
Utah	5.9	40
Vermont	8.9	6
Virginia	7.4	27
Washington	5.3	46
West Virginia	8.2	12
Wisconsin	7.5	24
Wyoming	6.0	38
50 States	n/a	
DC	14.9	
United States	7.2	

By rate

1. Alabama
2. Mississippi
3. Louisiana
3. North Carolina
5. Georgia
6. Kansas
6. Oklahoma
6. Vermont
9. Nebraska
10. Maryland
10. Tennessee
12. West Virginia
13. Illinois
13. Missouri
15. Arkansas
16. Alaska
16. Michigan
16. South Carolina
19. Delaware
19. Ohio
21. Arizona
21. Colorado
21. Kentucky
24. Florida
24. Indiana
24. Wisconsin
27. Pennsylvania
27. Virginia
29. Montana
29. New Jersey
31. Idaho
32. New York
33. Iowa
34. Minnesota
35. Connecticut
35. Nevada
37. Texas
38. California
38. Wyoming
40. New Mexico
40. Utah
42. Hawaii
43. New Hampshire
44. Oregon
45. South Dakota
46. Washington
47. Rhode Island
48. Massachusetts
49. Maine
50. North Dakota

I-3 STATE HEALTH RANKINGS, 1996

State	State health rankings	Rank		By ranking
Alabama	-10	42		1. Minnesota
Alaska	-13	44		2. Utah
Arizona	-2	31		2. West Virginia
Arkansas	-13	44		4. Hawaii
California	4	21		5. New Hampshire
Colorado	11	10		6. Massachusetts
Connecticut	12	8		7. Wisconsin
Delaware	-7	37		8. Connecticut
Florida	-7	37		8. Iowa
Georgia	1	25		10. Colorado
Hawaii	16	4		11. Virginia
Idaho	-2	31		12. Maryland
Illinois	1	25		12. Nebraska
Indiana	5	19		12. Washington
Iowa	12	8		15. Kansas
Kansas	6	15		15. New Jersey
Kentucky	-9	41		15. Ohio
Louisiana	-19	50		15. Pennsylvania
Maine	2	23		19. Indiana
Maryland	8	12		19. Vermont
Massachusetts	14	6		21. California
Michigan	0	28		21. Oregon
Minnesota	22	1		23. Maine
Mississippi	-18	48		23. North Dakota
Missouri	-4	35		25. Georgia
Montana	-3	34		25. Illinois
Nebraska	8	12		25. Texas
Nevada	-18	48		28. Michigan
New Hampshire	15	5		29. North Carolina
New Jersey	6	15		29. Rhode Island
New Mexico	-15	46		31. Arizona
New York	-7	37		31. Idaho
North Carolina	-1	29		31. South Dakota
North Dakota	2	23		34. Montana
Ohio	6	15		35. Missouri
Oklahoma	-6	36		36. Oklahoma
Oregon	4	21		37. Delaware
Pennsylvania	6	15		37. Florida
Rhode Island	-1	29		37. New York
South Carolina	-15	46		37. Wyoming
South Dakota	-2	31		41. Kentucky
Tennessee	-11	43		42. Alabama
Texas	1	25		43. Tennessee
Utah	17	2		44. Alaska
Vermont	5	19		44. Arkansas
Virginia	9	11		46. New Mexico
Washington	8	12		46. South Carolina
West Virginia	17	2		48. Mississippi
Wisconsin	13	7		48. Nevada
Wyoming	-7	37		50. Louisiana
50 States	n/a			
DC	n/a			
United States	n/a			

State	Percent of non-elderly population without health insurance %	Rank
Alabama	14.9	25
Alaska	13.8	30
Arizona	27.5	1
Arkansas	24.8	3
California	22.2	7
Colorado	17.8	17
Connecticut	12.4	39
Delaware	14.8	26
Florida	22.7	6
Georgia	19.6	9
Hawaii	9.7	49
Idaho	18.6	14
Illinois	12.5	38
Indiana	12.2	41
Iowa	13.1	33
Kansas	13.1	33
Kentucky	17.6	18
Louisiana	23.2	5
Maine	13.9	29
Maryland	12.8	37
Massachusetts	14.1	28
Michigan	10.1	48
Minnesota	11.2	43
Mississippi	20.5	8
Missouri	15.3	23
Montana	15.4	22
Nebraska	12.9	36
Nevada	17.6	18
New Hampshire	10.9	47
New Jersey	19.1	11
New Mexico	24.7	4
New York	19.1	11
North Carolina	18.0	15
North Dakota	11.2	43
Ohio	13.1	33
Oklahoma	19.6	9
Oregon	17.4	20
Pennsylvania	11.1	45
Rhode Island	12.0	42
South Carolina	18.7	13
South Dakota	11.1	45
Tennessee	17.1	21
Texas	26.7	2
Utah	13.3	32
Vermont	12.4	39
Virginia	13.8	30
Washington	14.8	26
West Virginia	17.9	16
Wisconsin	9.5	50
Wyoming	15.0	24
50 States	n/a	
DC	16.8	
United States	17.6	

Rank in order

By %

1. Arizona
2. Texas
3. Arkansas
4. New Mexico
5. Louisiana
6. Florida
7. California
8. Mississippi
9. Georgia
9. Oklahoma
11. New Jersey
11. New York
13. South Carolina
14. Idaho
15. North Carolina
16. West Virginia
17. Colorado
18. Kentucky
18. Nevada
20. Oregon
21. Tennessee
22. Montana
23. Missouri
24. Wyoming
25. Alabama
26. Delaware
26. Washington
28. Massachusetts
29. Maine
30. Alaska
30. Virginia
32. Utah
33. Iowa
33. Kansas
33. Ohio
36. Nebraska
37. Maryland
38. Illinois
39. Connecticut
39. Vermont
41. Indiana
42. Rhode Island
43. Minnesota
43. North Dakota
45. Pennsylvania
45. South Dakota
47. New Hampshire
48. Michigan
49. Hawaii
50. Wisconsin

State	Abortions #	Per 1,000 births ratio	Rank by ratio
Alabama	14,825	244	22
Alaska	1,585	148	44
Arizona	13,930	196	32
Arkansas	5,885	169	37
California	308,564	544	2
Colorado	9,584	177	36
Connecticut	14,757	323	10
Delaware	5,637	543	3
Florida	73,394	385	5
Georgia	36,374	328	9
Hawaii	5,783	298	13
Idaho	1,047	60	49
Illinois	55,050	291	14
Indiana	12,499	151	42
Iowa	5,914	160	39
Kansas	10,468	281	17
Kentucky	8,145	154	40
Louisiana	12,154	179	34
Maine	3,089	215	29
Maryland	17,627	238	25
Massachusetts	32,195	384	6
Michigan	33,061	240	24
Minnesota	14,027	218	28
Mississippi	3,979	95	46
Missouri	11,879	162	38
Montana	2,761	250	21
Nebraska	5,324	230	26
Nevada	6,736	282	16
New Hampshire	3,008	199	31
New Jersey	33,286	283	15
New Mexico	4,929	179	34
New York	149,598	549	1
North Carolina	35,088	346	7
North Dakota	1,301	152	41
Ohio	37,742	242	23
Oklahoma	6,774	149	43
Oregon	13,392	320	11
Pennsylvania	41,645	266	20
Rhode Island	6,092	452	4
South Carolina	10,922	210	30
South Dakota	987	94	47
Tennessee	16,837	230	26
Texas	89,185	278	19
Utah	3,609	94	47
Vermont	2,321	314	12
Virginia	26,369	279	18
Washington	25,965	336	8
West Virginia	2,085	98	45
Wisconsin	13,396	196	32
Wyoming	174	27	50
50 States	1,250,978	n/a	
DC	16,437	n/a	
United States	1,267,415	321	

By ratio

1. New York
2. California
3. Delaware
4. Rhode Island
5. Florida
6. Massachusetts
7. North Carolina
8. Washington
9. Georgia
10. Connecticut
11. Oregon
12. Vermont
13. Hawaii
14. Illinois
15. New Jersey
16. Nevada
17. Kansas
18. Virginia
19. Texas
20. Pennsylvania
21. Montana
22. Alabama
23. Ohio
24. Michigan
25. Maryland
26. Nebraska
26. Tennessee
28. Minnesota
29. Maine
30. South Carolina
31. New Hampshire
32. Arizona
32. Wisconsin
34. Louisiana
34. New Mexico
36. Colorado
37. Arkansas
38. Missouri
39. Iowa
40. Kentucky
41. North Dakota
42. Indiana
43. Oklahoma
44. Alaska
45. West Virginia
46. Mississippi
47. South Dakota
47. Utah
49. Idaho
50. Wyoming

I-6 ALCOHOL CONSUMPTION PER CAPITA, 1994

State	Per capita consumption in gallons	Rank
Alabama	1.88	41
Alaska	3.03	3
Arizona	2.65	7
Arkansas	1.68	48
California	2.24	24
Colorado	2.61	8
Connecticut	2.22	28
Delaware	2.79	4
Florida	2.66	6
Georgia	2.18	29
Hawaii	2.48	11
Idaho	2.14	33
Illinois	2.38	15
Indiana	1.95	38
Iowa	1.86	43
Kansas	1.75	46
Kentucky	1.74	47
Louisiana	2.41	13
Maine	2.17	30
Maryland	2.15	32
Massachusetts	2.40	14
Michigan	2.13	34
Minnesota	2.38	15
Mississippi	2.01	35
Missouri	2.24	24
Montana	2.53	9
Nebraska	2.17	30
Nevada	4.15	1
New Hampshire	4.14	2
New Jersey	2.30	21
New Mexico	2.30	21
New York	1.96	37
North Carolina	1.94	39
North Dakota	2.35	17
Ohio	1.85	44
Oklahoma	1.80	45
Oregon	2.24	24
Pennsylvania	1.94	39
Rhode Island	2.33	19
South Carolina	2.31	20
South Dakota	2.28	23
Tennessee	1.88	41
Texas	2.34	18
Utah	1.28	50
Vermont	2.49	10
Virginia	2.00	36
Washington	2.24	24
West Virginia	1.64	49
Wisconsin	2.75	5
Wyoming	2.46	12
50 States	n/a	
DC	3.89	
United States	2.21	

Rank in order

By per capita

1. Nevada
2. New Hampshire
3. Alaska
4. Delaware
5. Wisconsin
6. Florida
7. Arizona
8. Colorado
9. Montana
10. Vermont
11. Hawaii
12. Wyoming
13. Louisiana
14. Massachusetts
15. Illinois
15. Minnesota
17. North Dakota
18. Texas
19. Rhode Island
20. South Carolina
21. New Jersey
21. New Mexico
23. South Dakota
24. California
24. Missouri
24. Oregon
24. Washington
28. Connecticut
29. Georgia
30. Maine
30. Nebraska
32. Maryland
33. Idaho
34. Michigan
35. Mississippi
36. Virginia
37. New York
38. Indiana
39. North Carolina
39. Pennsylvania
41. Alabama
41. Tennessee
43. Iowa
44. Ohio
45. Oklahoma
46. Kansas
47. Kentucky
48. Arkansas
49. West Virginia
50. Utah

State	Adult smokers %	Rank	By %
Alabama	24.5	15	1. Kentucky
Alaska	25.0	12	2. Indiana
Arizona	22.9	24	3. Tennessee
Arkansas	25.2	10	4. Nevada
California	15.5	49	5. Ohio
Colorado	21.8	31	6. North Carolina
Connecticut	20.8	42	7. Michigan
Delaware	25.5	9	7. West Virginia
Florida	23.1	22	9. Delaware
Georgia	20.5	43	10. Arkansas
Hawaii	17.8	48	10. Louisiana
Idaho	19.8	46	12. Alaska
Illinois	23.1	22	12. Maine
Indiana	27.2	2	14. Rhode Island
Iowa	23.2	21	15. Alabama
Kansas	22.0	27	16. Missouri
Kentucky	27.8	1	17. Pennsylvania
Louisiana	25.2	10	18. Mississippi
Maine	25.0	12	19. South Carolina
Maryland	21.2	39	19. Texas
Massachusetts	21.7	35	21. Iowa
Michigan	25.7	7	22. Florida
Minnesota	20.5	43	22. Illinois
Mississippi	24.0	18	24. Arizona
Missouri	24.3	16	25. North Dakota
Montana	21.1	41	26. Vermont
Nebraska	21.9	30	27. Kansas
Nevada	26.3	4	27. Virginia
New Hampshire	21.4	38	27. Wyoming
New Jersey	19.2	47	30. Nebraska
New Mexico	21.2	39	31. Colorado
New York	21.5	37	31. Oregon
North Carolina	25.8	6	31. South Dakota
North Dakota	22.7	25	31. Wisconsin
Ohio	26.0	5	35. Massachusetts
Oklahoma	21.7	35	35. Oklahoma
Oregon	21.8	31	37. New York
Pennsylvania	24.2	17	38. New Hampshire
Rhode Island	24.7	14	39. Maryland
South Carolina	23.7	19	39. New Mexico
South Dakota	21.8	31	41. Montana
Tennessee	26.5	3	42. Connecticut
Texas	23.7	19	43. Georgia
Utah	13.2	50	43. Minnesota
Vermont	22.1	26	45. Washington
Virginia	22.0	27	46. Idaho
Washington	20.2	45	47. New Jersey
West Virginia	25.7	7	48. Hawaii
Wisconsin	21.8	31	49. California
Wyoming	22.0	27	50. Utah
50 States	n/a		
DC	n/a		
United States	22.4		

State	Overweight population %	Rank by %		Rank in order By %
Alabama	35.8	10		1. Indiana
Alaska	36.9	2		2. Alaska
Arizona	29.0	45		3. Missouri
Arkansas	34.8	15		4. Michigan
California	30.7	38		5. West Virginia
Colorado	26.3	48		6. Mississippi
Connecticut	29.4	43		7. Iowa
Delaware	33.8	19		8. Ohio
Florida	33.5	21		9. North Dakota
Georgia	34.7	16		10. Alabama
Hawaii	26.0	50		11. Tennessee
Idaho	31.3	34		12. Wisconsin
Illinois	34.7	17		13. Pennsylvania
Indiana	38.8	1		14. Louisiana
Iowa	36.4	7		15. Arkansas
Kansas	32.1	31		16. Georgia
Kentucky	33.0	24		17. Illinois
Louisiana	35.0	14		18. Maryland
Maine	32.1	32		19. Delaware
Maryland	33.8	18		20. Oregon
Massachusetts	26.3	49		21. Florida
Michigan	36.7	4		22. Virginia
Minnesota	32.6	27		23. Nebraska
Mississippi	36.5	6		24. Kentucky
Missouri	36.8	3		25. North Carolina
Montana	30.8	35		26. New York
Nebraska	33.0	23		27. Minnesota
Nevada	30.7	36		28. South Dakota
New Hampshire	30.6	39		29. South Carolina
New Jersey	29.8	42		30. Texas
New Mexico	28.6	46		31. Kansas
New York	32.6	26		32. Maine
North Carolina	32.8	25		33. Wyoming
North Dakota	36.1	9		34. Idaho
Ohio	36.4	8		35. Montana
Oklahoma	28.5	47		36. Nevada
Oregon	33.6	20		36. Rhode Island
Pennsylvania	35.3	13		38. California
Rhode Island	30.7	36		39. New Hampshire
South Carolina	32.4	29		40. Washington
South Dakota	32.5	28		41. Utah
Tennessee	35.4	11		42. New Jersey
Texas	32.3	30		43. Connecticut
Utah	29.9	41		44. Vermont
Vermont	29.2	44		45. Arizona
Virginia	33.4	22		46. New Mexico
Washington	30.2	40		47. Oklahoma
West Virginia	36.6	5		48. Colorado
Wisconsin	35.3	12		49. Massachusetts
Wyoming	32.0	33		50. Hawaii
50 States	n/a			
DC	n/a			
United States	32.7			

State	AIDS cases #	Per 100,000 residents rate	Rank by rate
I-9 AIDS CASES, 1996			
Alabama	607	14.2	24
Alaska	36	5.9	41
Arizona	594	13.4	26
Arkansas	269	10.7	29
California	9,610	30.1	9
Colorado	522	13.7	25
Connecticut	1,112	34.0	6
Delaware	285	39.3	5
Florida	7,330	50.9	2
Georgia	2,411	32.8	8
Hawaii	198	16.7	18
Idaho	39	3.3	47
Illinois	2,199	18.6	15
Indiana	596	10.2	32
Iowa	112	3.9	45
Kansas	239	9.3	35
Kentucky	401	10.3	31
Louisiana	1,470	33.8	7
Maine	50	4.0	44
Maryland	2,253	44.4	4
Massachusetts	1,307	21.5	13
Michigan	965	10.1	33
Minnesota	304	6.5	39
Mississippi	450	16.6	19
Missouri	858	16.0	20
Montana	34	3.9	45
Nebraska	100	6.1	40
Nevada	427	26.6	10
New Hampshire	93	8.0	37
New Jersey	3,613	45.2	3
New Mexico	205	12.0	28
New York	12,379	68.1	1
North Carolina	895	12.2	27
North Dakota	12	1.9	48
Ohio	1,161	10.4	30
Oklahoma	272	8.2	36
Oregon	463	14.5	22
Pennsylvania	2,348	19.5	14
Rhode Island	178	18.0	16
South Carolina	869	23.5	12
South Dakota	14	1.9	48
Tennessee	826	15.5	21
Texas	4,830	25.3	11
Utah	196	9.8	34
Vermont	25	4.2	43
Virginia	1,195	17.9	17
Washington	804	14.5	22
West Virginia	121	6.8	38
Wisconsin	270	5.2	42
Wyoming	7	1.5	50
50 States	65,554	25.2	
DC	1,262	232.2	
United States	69,151	25.6	

Rank in order

By rate

1. New York
2. Florida
3. New Jersey
4. Maryland
5. Delaware
6. Connecticut
7. Louisiana
8. Georgia
9. California
10. Nevada
11. Texas
12. South Carolina
13. Massachusetts
14. Pennsylvania
15. Illinois
16. Rhode Island
17. Virginia
18. Hawaii
19. Mississippi
20. Missouri
21. Tennessee
22. Oregon
22. Washington
24. Alabama
25. Colorado
26. Arizona
27. North Carolina
28. New Mexico
29. Arkansas
30. Ohio
31. Kentucky
32. Indiana
33. Michigan
34. Utah
35. Kansas
36. Oklahoma
37. New Hampshire
38. West Virginia
39. Minnesota
40. Nebraska
41. Alaska
42. Wisconsin
43. Vermont
44. Maine
45. Iowa
45. Montana
47. Idaho
48. North Dakota
48. South Dakota
50. Wyoming

I-10 PHYSICIANS PER 100,000 POPULATION, 1996

State	Physicians per 100,000 population	Rank
Alabama	212	22
Alaska	189	48
Arizona	244	23
Arkansas	204	33
California	282	1
Colorado	267	25
Connecticut	379	27
Delaware	255	46
Florida	281	4
Georgia	228	11
Hawaii	309	40
Idaho	171	42
Illinois	277	6
Indiana	207	14
Iowa	195	30
Kansas	232	32
Kentucky	220	24
Louisiana	254	21
Maine	248	39
Maryland	424	19
Massachusetts	431	13
Michigan	239	8
Minnesota	274	20
Mississippi	174	31
Missouri	245	16
Montana	222	44
Nebraska	231	37
Nevada	189	38
New Hampshire	262	41
New Jersey	310	9
New Mexico	243	36
New York	399	3
North Carolina	251	10
North Dakota	234	47
Ohio	250	7
Oklahoma	184	28
Oregon	259	29
Pennsylvania	306	5
Rhode Island	342	43
South Carolina	224	26
South Dakota	205	45
Tennessee	260	17
Texas	218	2
Utah	221	34
Vermont	326	49
Virginia	267	12
Washington	270	15
West Virginia	227	35
Wisconsin	246	18
Wyoming	192	50
50 States	273	
DC	790	
United States	278	

Rank in order

By per 100,000

1. California
2. Texas
3. New York
4. Florida
5. Pennsylvania
6. Illinois
7. Ohio
8. Michigan
9. New Jersey
10. North Carolina
11. Georgia
12. Virginia
13. Massachusetts
14. Indiana
15. Washington
16. Missouri
17. Tennessee
18. Wisconsin
19. Maryland
20. Minnesota
21. Louisiana
22. Alabama
23. Arizona
24. Kentucky
25. Colorado
26. South Carolina
27. Connecticut
28. Oklahoma
29. Oregon
30. Iowa
31. Mississippi
32. Kansas
33. Arkansas
34. Utah
35. West Virginia
36. New Mexico
37. Nebraska
38. Nevada
39. Maine
40. Hawaii
41. New Hampshire
42. Idaho
43. Rhode Island
44. Montana
45. South Dakota
46. Delaware
47. North Dakota
48. Alaska
49. Vermont
50. Wyoming

I-11 HOSPITAL BEDS PER 1,000 POPULATION, 1995

State	Hospital beds per 1,000 population	Rank
Alabama	5.3	9
Alaska	3.0	44
Arizona	3.0	45
Arkansas	4.8	16
California	2.9	46
Colorado	3.2	42
Connecticut	3.4	40
Delaware	3.6	36
Florida	4.1	24
Georgia	4.6	17
Hawaii	3.1	43
Idaho	3.3	41
Illinois	4.3	22
Indiana	4.0	28
Iowa	5.2	10
Kansas	5.5	5
Kentucky	4.6	18
Louisiana	5.3	8
Maine	4.0	26
Maryland	3.5	38
Massachusetts	4.4	21
Michigan	3.6	37
Minnesota	4.5	20
Mississippi	6.0	3
Missouri	4.9	14
Montana	5.2	11
Nebraska	5.7	4
Nevada	2.7	48
New Hampshire	3.8	33
New Jersey	4.5	19
New Mexico	3.4	39
New York	5.1	12
North Carolina	4.1	25
North Dakota	7.5	2
Ohio	3.9	31
Oklahoma	4.2	23
Oregon	2.9	47
Pennsylvania	5.1	13
Rhode Island	3.9	29
South Carolina	3.7	34
South Dakota	7.7	1
Tennessee	4.9	15
Texas	3.8	32
Utah	2.6	49
Vermont	3.6	35
Virginia	3.9	30
Washington	2.5	50
West Virginia	5.4	7
Wisconsin	4.0	27
Wyoming	5.4	6
50 States	4.1	
DC	11.3	
United States	4.1	

Rank in order

By per 1,000

1. South Dakota
2. North Dakota
3. Mississippi
4. Nebraska
5. Kansas
6. Wyoming
7. West Virginia
8. Louisiana
9. Alabama
10. Iowa
11. Montana
12. New York
13. Pennsylvania
14. Missouri
15. Tennessee
16. Arkansas
17. Georgia
18. Kentucky
19. New Jersey
20. Minnesota
21. Massachusetts
22. Illinois
23. Oklahoma
24. Florida
25. North Carolina
26. Maine
27. Wisconsin
28. Indiana
29. Rhode Island
30. Virginia
31. Ohio
32. Texas
33. New Hampshire
34. South Carolina
35. Vermont
36. Delaware
37. Michigan
38. Maryland
39. New Mexico
40. Connecticut
41. Idaho
42. Colorado
43. Hawaii
44. Alaska
45. Arizona
46. California
47. Oregon
48. Nevada
49. Utah
50. Washington

State	Recipients (000)	As percent of population %	Rank by %
Alabama	546	12.8	19
Alaska	69	11.4	27
Arizona	528	11.9	22
Arkansas	363	14.4	12
California	5,107	16.0	10
Colorado	271	7.1	48
Connecticut	329	10.0	36
Delaware	82	11.3	29
Florida	1,638	11.4	28
Georgia	1,185	16.1	9
Hawaii	41	3.4	50
Idaho	119	10.0	37
Illinois	1,454	12.3	20
Indiana	594	10.2	35
Iowa	308	10.8	32
Kansas	251	9.8	39
Kentucky	641	16.5	8
Louisiana	778	17.9	6
Maine	167	13.5	15
Maryland	399	7.9	46
Massachusetts	715	11.7	24
Michigan	1,172	12.2	21
Minnesota	455	9.8	38
Mississippi	510	18.8	3
Missouri	636	11.9	23
Montana	101	11.5	26
Nebraska	191	11.6	25
Nevada	109	6.8	49
New Hampshire	100	8.6	44
New Jersey	714	8.9	43
New Mexico	318	18.6	4
New York	3,281	18.0	5
North Carolina	1,130	15.4	11
North Dakota	61	9.5	41
Ohio	1,478	13.2	17
Oklahoma	358	10.8	31
Oregon	450	14.1	13
Pennsylvania	1,168	9.7	40
Rhode Island	130	13.1	18
South Carolina	503	13.6	14
South Dakota	77	10.5	34
Tennessee	1,409	26.5	1
Texas	2,572	13.4	16
Utah	152	7.6	47
Vermont	102	17.4	7
Virginia	623	9.3	42
Washington	621	11.2	30
West Virginia	395	21.6	2
Wisconsin	434	8.4	45
Wyoming	51	10.6	33
50 States	34,884	13.2	
DC	143	26.4	
United States	36,118	13.6	

By %

1. Tennessee
2. West Virginia
3. Mississippi
4. New Mexico
5. New York
6. Louisiana
7. Vermont
8. Kentucky
9. Georgia
10. California
11. North Carolina
12. Arkansas
13. Oregon
14. South Carolina
15. Maine
16. Texas
17. Ohio
18. Rhode Island
19. Alabama
20. Illinois
21. Michigan
22. Arizona
23. Missouri
24. Massachusetts
25. Nebraska
26. Montana
27. Alaska
28. Florida
29. Delaware
30. Washington
31. Oklahoma
32. Iowa
33. Wyoming
34. South Dakota
35. Indiana
36. Connecticut
37. Idaho
38. Minnesota
39. Kansas
40. Pennsylvania
41. North Dakota
42. Virginia
43. New Jersey
44. New Hampshire
45. Wisconsin
46. Maryland
47. Utah
48. Colorado
49. Nevada
50. Hawaii

State	Recipients as percent of poverty population %	Rank	Rank in order By %
Alabama	91.8	30	1. Tennessee
Alaska	128.0	6	2. Indiana
Arizona	53.9	49	3. Vermont
Arkansas	80.8	41	4. New Hampshire
California	93.3	28	5. Delaware
Colorado	65.7	46	6. Alaska
Connecticut	83.8	38	7. North Carolina
Delaware	129.8	5	8. Missouri
Florida	80.4	42	9. Rhode Island
Georgia	108.0	17	10. Maine
Hawaii	28.5	50	11. West Virginia
Idaho	85.1	36	12. Oregon
Illinois	101.8	21	13. Massachusetts
Indiana	138.7	2	14. Nebraska
Iowa	110.4	15	15. Iowa
Kansas	87.5	35	16. Michigan
Kentucky	97.3	25	17. Georgia
Louisiana	89.1	31	18. New York
Maine	123.9	10	19. South Carolina
Maryland	76.3	44	20. Ohio
Massachusetts	114.9	13	21. Illinois
Michigan	109.7	16	22. Utah
Minnesota	99.3	23	23. Minnesota
Mississippi	88.6	32	24. New Jersey
Missouri	127.2	8	25. Kentucky
Montana	65.3	47	26. Wisconsin
Nebraska	113.1	14	27. South Dakota
Nevada	81.7	39	28. California
New Hampshire	136.4	4	29. Washington
New Jersey	98.4	24	30. Alabama
New Mexico	67.4	45	31. Louisiana
New York	107.3	18	32. Mississippi
North Carolina	127.7	7	33. North Dakota
North Dakota	88.4	33	34. Wyoming
Ohio	103.8	20	35. Kansas
Oklahoma	64.4	48	36. Idaho
Oregon	117.9	12	37. Pennsylvania
Pennsylvania	85.0	37	38. Connecticut
Rhode Island	124.6	9	39. Nevada
South Carolina	104.4	19	40. Texas
South Dakota	93.6	27	41. Arkansas
Tennessee	160.5	1	42. Florida
Texas	80.9	40	43. Virginia
Utah	99.4	22	44. Maryland
Vermont	138.1	3	45. New Mexico
Virginia	78.4	43	46. Colorado
Washington	93.3	29	47. Montana
West Virginia	122.3	11	48. Oklahoma
Wisconsin	94.4	26	49. Arizona
Wyoming	88.3	34	50. Hawaii
50 States	95.8		
DC	110.3		
United States	98.9		

I-14 STATE AND LOCAL SPENDING FOR HEALTH AND HOSPITALS, FY 1994

State	Total spending $(millions)	Per capita $	As percent of personal income %	Rank by per capita
Alabama	2,782	660	3.9	3
Alaska	237	391	1.7	18
Arizona	827	203	1.2	44
Arkansas	760	310	2.0	30
California	14,263	454	2.1	9
Colorado	1,006	275	1.3	33
Connecticut	1,256	383	1.4	20
Delaware	174	247	1.1	37
Florida	5,387	386	1.9	19
Georgia	3,718	527	2.8	6
Hawaii	515	437	1.9	11
Idaho	352	311	1.8	29
Illinois	3,068	261	1.2	36
Indiana	2,194	381	2.0	21
Iowa	1,217	430	2.4	13
Kansas	901	353	1.8	22
Kentucky	872	228	1.4	42
Louisiana	2,412	559	3.4	5
Maine	234	189	1.0	46
Maryland	949	190	0.8	45
Massachusetts	2,489	412	1.7	16
Michigan	3,958	417	2.0	15
Minnesota	2,144	469	2.3	8
Mississippi	1,289	483	3.3	7
Missouri	1,453	273	1.4	34
Montana	185	216	1.3	43
Nebraska	548	338	1.7	25
Nevada	479	329	1.5	28
New Hampshire	111	97	0.4	50
New Jersey	1,898	240	0.9	38
New Mexico	690	417	2.6	14
New York	11,226	618	2.5	4
North Carolina	3,204	453	2.5	10
North Dakota	88	138	0.8	48
Ohio	3,665	330	1.7	27
Oklahoma	1,144	351	2.1	23
Oregon	1,020	331	1.7	26
Pennsylvania	2,854	237	1.1	39
Rhode Island	232	232	1.1	41
South Carolina	2,589	707	4.2	2
South Dakota	135	187	1.1	47
Tennessee	2,236	432	2.4	12
Texas	6,225	339	1.8	24
Utah	512	269	1.7	35
Vermont	69	119	0.6	49
Virginia	2,010	307	1.4	31
Washington	2,149	402	1.9	17
West Virginia	431	236	1.5	40
Wisconsin	1,405	276	1.4	32
Wyoming	343	721	3.7	1
50 States	99,903	385	1.9	
DC	527	924	3.1	
United States	100,429	386	1.9	

By per capita

1. Wyoming
2. South Carolina
3. Alabama
4. New York
5. Louisiana
6. Georgia
7. Mississippi
8. Minnesota
9. California
10. North Carolina
11. Hawaii
12. Tennessee
13. Iowa
14. New Mexico
15. Michigan
16. Massachusetts
17. Washington
18. Alaska
19. Florida
20. Connecticut
21. Indiana
22. Kansas
23. Oklahoma
24. Texas
25. Nebraska
26. Oregon
27. Ohio
28. Nevada
29. Idaho
30. Arkansas
31. Virginia
32. Wisconsin
33. Colorado
34. Missouri
35. Utah
36. Illinois
37. Delaware
38. New Jersey
39. Pennsylvania
40. West Virginia
41. Rhode Island
42. Kentucky
43. Montana
44. Arizona
45. Maryland
46. Maine
47. South Dakota
48. North Dakota
49. Vermont
50. New Hampshire

State	Health & hospital spending as percent of general spending %	Rank	Rank in order By %
Alabama	18.8	1	1. Alabama
Alaska	3.8	47	2. South Carolina
Arizona	5.5	41	3. Mississippi
Arkansas	10.2	14	4. Louisiana
California	10.3	13	5. Georgia
Colorado	6.7	35	6. Wyoming
Connecticut	7.5	31	7. Tennessee
Delaware	5.5	40	8. North Carolina
Florida	10.3	11	9. Iowa
Georgia	14.3	5	10. Oklahoma
Hawaii	7.7	29	11. Florida
Idaho	9.3	20	12. Indiana
Illinois	6.9	33	13. California
Indiana	10.3	12	14. Arkansas
Iowa	10.9	9	15. Michigan
Kansas	9.3	21	16. New Mexico
Kentucky	6.9	34	17. New York
Louisiana	14.3	4	18. Texas
Maine	4.7	46	19. Minnesota
Maryland	4.8	45	20. Idaho
Massachusetts	8.8	24	21. Kansas
Michigan	10.1	15	22. Missouri
Minnesota	9.7	19	23. Washington
Mississippi	15.0	3	24. Massachusetts
Missouri	9.0	22	25. Nebraska
Montana	5.6	39	26. Ohio
Nebraska	8.8	25	27. Virginia
Nevada	7.6	30	28. Oregon
New Hampshire	2.5	50	29. Hawaii
New Jersey	5.0	44	30. Nevada
New Mexico	10.0	16	31. Connecticut
New York	9.9	17	32. Utah
North Carolina	12.9	8	33. Illinois
North Dakota	3.4	48	34. Kentucky
Ohio	8.7	26	35. Colorado
Oklahoma	10.8	10	36. Wisconsin
Oregon	7.9	28	37. West Virginia
Pennsylvania	6.1	38	38. Pennsylvania
Rhode Island	5.1	42	39. Montana
South Carolina	18.7	2	40. Delaware
South Dakota	5.1	43	41. Arizona
Tennessee	13.0	7	42. Rhode Island
Texas	9.7	18	43. South Dakota
Utah	7.4	32	44. New Jersey
Vermont	2.8	49	45. Maryland
Virginia	8.6	27	46. Maine
Washington	8.9	23	47. Alaska
West Virginia	6.3	37	48. North Dakota
Wisconsin	6.4	36	49. Vermont
Wyoming	13.5	6	50. New Hampshire
50 States	9.3		
DC	11.5		
United States	9.4		

State	Per capita Medicaid spending $	Rank
Alabama	342	39
Alaska	459	20
Arizona	48	50
Arkansas	488	16
California	349	38
Colorado	270	44
Connecticut	620	3
Delaware	426	23
Florida	324	42
Georgia	420	25
Hawaii	225	48
Idaho	341	40
Illinois	453	21
Indiana	420	24
Iowa	382	32
Kansas	334	41
Kentucky	497	13
Louisiana	564	7
Maine	581	6
Maryland	404	29
Massachusetts	620	4
Michigan	350	37
Minnesota	522	9
Mississippi	494	14
Missouri	377	34
Montana	401	30
Nebraska	411	27
Nevada	228	47
New Hampshire	471	17
New Jersey	466	18
New Mexico	512	11
New York	1,229	1
North Carolina	502	12
North Dakota	463	19
Ohio	493	15
Oklahoma	309	43
Oregon	410	28
Pennsylvania	387	31
Rhode Island	691	2
South Carolina	412	26
South Dakota	431	22
Tennessee	543	8
Texas	359	36
Utah	211	49
Vermont	513	10
Virginia	266	45
Washington	252	46
West Virginia	618	5
Wisconsin	369	35
Wyoming	380	33
50 States	456	
DC	1,307	
United States	459	

Rank in order

By $

1. New York
2. Rhode Island
3. Connecticut
4. Massachusetts
5. West Virginia
6. Maine
7. Louisiana
8. Tennessee
9. Minnesota
10. Vermont
11. New Mexico
12. North Carolina
13. Kentucky
14. Mississippi
15. Ohio
16. Arkansas
17. New Hampshire
18. New Jersey
19. North Dakota
20. Alaska
21. Illinois
22. South Dakota
23. Delaware
24. Indiana
25. Georgia
26. South Carolina
27. Nebraska
28. Oregon
29. Maryland
30. Montana
31. Pennsylvania
32. Iowa
33. Wyoming
34. Missouri
35. Wisconsin
36. Texas
37. Michigan
38. California
39. Alabama
40. Idaho
41. Kansas
42. Florida
43. Oklahoma
44. Colorado
45. Virginia
46. Washington
47. Nevada
48. Hawaii
49. Utah
50. Arizona

I-17 AVERAGE MEDICAID SPENDING PER AGED RECIPIENT, FY 1996

State	Average spending per aged recipient $	Rank	Rank in order By $
Alabama	6,663	41	1. New Hampshire
Alaska	10,579	19	2. Minnesota
Arizona	567	50	3. Connecticut
Arkansas	7,089	35	4. Rhode Island
California	5,141	49	5. New York
Colorado	9,492	22	6. New Jersey
Connecticut	15,190	3	7. Delaware
Delaware	13,121	7	8. Massachusetts
Florida	6,893	38	9. Wisconsin
Georgia	5,363	48	10. Montana
Hawaii	8,908	28	11. Indiana
Idaho	10,908	17	12. Pennsylvania
Illinois	9,012	27	13. North Dakota
Indiana	11,982	11	14. South Dakota
Iowa	8,248	30	15. Maryland
Kansas	10,247	21	16. Ohio
Kentucky	7,480	34	17. Idaho
Louisiana	6,639	42	18. Nebraska
Maine	10,279	20	19. Alaska
Maryland	11,045	15	20. Maine
Massachusetts	13,083	8	21. Kansas
Michigan	9,407	24	22. Colorado
Minnesota	15,392	2	23. Washington
Mississippi	5,686	46	24. Michigan
Missouri	8,177	32	25. Wyoming
Montana	12,097	10	26. Utah
Nebraska	10,810	18	27. Illinois
Nevada	6,833	39	28. Hawaii
New Hampshire	17,935	1	29. Vermont
New Jersey	13,318	6	30. Iowa
New Mexico	7,054	36	31. West Virginia
New York	13,983	5	32. Missouri
North Carolina	6,942	37	33. Oregon
North Dakota	11,420	13	34. Kentucky
Ohio	10,923	16	35. Arkansas
Oklahoma	6,518	43	36. New Mexico
Oregon	7,511	33	37. North Carolina
Pennsylvania	11,480	12	38. Florida
Rhode Island	14,174	4	39. Nevada
South Carolina	5,485	47	40. Virginia
South Dakota	11,384	14	41. Alabama
Tennessee	5,892	45	42. Louisiana
Texas	6,327	44	43. Oklahoma
Utah	9,145	26	44. Texas
Vermont	8,638	29	45. Tennessee
Virginia	6,809	40	46. Mississippi
Washington	9,435	23	47. South Carolina
West Virginia	8,177	31	48. Georgia
Wisconsin	12,458	9	49. California
Wyoming	9,165	25	50. Arizona
50 States	9,035		
DC	13,991		
United States	8,622		

State	Average spending per AFDC child $	Rank
Alabama	503	48
Alaska	1,929	2
Arizona	154	49
Arkansas	974	25
California	566	46
Colorado	806	42
Connecticut	963	26
Delaware	927	29
Florida	1,063	20
Georgia	948	27
Hawaii	0	50
Idaho	894	33
Illinois	1,156	15
Indiana	1,017	23
Iowa	1,086	17
Kansas	844	40
Kentucky	1,069	19
Louisiana	912	32
Maine	1,571	4
Maryland	1,383	7
Massachusetts	886	34
Michigan	785	43
Minnesota	1,393	6
Mississippi	856	39
Missouri	868	37
Montana	884	35
Nebraska	1,026	22
Nevada	1,093	16
New Hampshire	1,343	8
New Jersey	1,169	13
New Mexico	1,224	11
New York	1,919	3
North Carolina	922	30
North Dakota	1,249	10
Ohio	1,075	18
Oklahoma	915	31
Oregon	1,962	1
Pennsylvania	1,307	9
Rhode Island	624	45
South Carolina	1,060	21
South Dakota	1,160	14
Tennessee	871	36
Texas	928	28
Utah	808	41
Vermont	1,399	5
Virginia	671	44
Washington	552	47
West Virginia	1,015	24
Wisconsin	868	38
Wyoming	1,202	12
50 States	1,038	
DC	1,710	
United States	1,032	

Rank in order

By $

1. Oregon
2. Alaska
3. New York
4. Maine
5. Vermont
6. Minnesota
7. Maryland
8. New Hampshire
9. Pennsylvania
10. North Dakota
11. New Mexico
12. Wyoming
13. New Jersey
14. South Dakota
15. Illinois
16. Nevada
17. Iowa
18. Ohio
19. Kentucky
20. Florida
21. South Carolina
22. Nebraska
23. Indiana
24. West Virginia
25. Arkansas
26. Connecticut
27. Georgia
28. Texas
29. Delaware
30. North Carolina
31. Oklahoma
32. Louisiana
33. Idaho
34. Massachusetts
35. Montana
36. Tennessee
37. Missouri
38. Wisconsin
39. Mississippi
40. Kansas
41. Utah
42. Colorado
43. Michigan
44. Virginia
45. Rhode Island
46. California
47. Washington
48. Alabama
49. Arizona
50. Hawaii

I-19 MEDICARE PAYMENT PER HOSPITAL-DAY, FY 1996

State	Average payment per hospital-day $	Rank		By $
Alabama	2,052	12		1. California
Alaska	2,135	7		2. Nevada
Arizona	2,590	3		3. Arizona
Arkansas	1,371	47		4. Florida
California	3,176	1		5. Colorado
Colorado	2,235	5		6. Illinois
Connecticut	1,994	14		7. Alaska
Delaware	1,705	30		8. Pennsylvania
Florida	2,386	4		9. Texas
Georgia	1,679	34		10. Utah
Hawaii	2,078	11		11. Hawaii
Idaho	1,885	16		12. Alabama
Illinois	2,176	6		13. Missouri
Indiana	1,682	33		14. Connecticut
Iowa	1,562	40		15. Oregon
Kansas	1,765	25		16. Idaho
Kentucky	1,633	37		17. Michigan
Louisiana	1,850	19		18. Minnesota
Maine	1,675	35		19. Louisiana
Maryland	1,054	50		20. Wyoming
Massachusetts	1,541	41		21. Nebraska
Michigan	1,883	17		22. Montana
Minnesota	1,855	18		23. New Jersey
Mississippi	1,423	45		24. New Mexico
Missouri	2,006	13		25. Kansas
Montana	1,818	22		26. Ohio
Nebraska	1,826	21		27. Tennessee
Nevada	2,980	2		28. Virginia
New Hampshire	1,528	44		29. Wisconsin
New Jersey	1,816	23		30. Delaware
New Mexico	1,773	24		31. Washington
New York	1,225	49		32. South Carolina
North Carolina	1,567	39		33. Indiana
North Dakota	1,531	43		34. Georgia
Ohio	1,736	26		35. Maine
Oklahoma	1,569	38		36. Rhode Island
Oregon	1,988	15		37. Kentucky
Pennsylvania	2,130	8		38. Oklahoma
Rhode Island	1,641	36		39. North Carolina
South Carolina	1,683	32		40. Iowa
South Dakota	1,532	42		41. Massachusetts
Tennessee	1,727	27		42. South Dakota
Texas	2,127	9		43. North Dakota
Utah	2,120	10		44. New Hampshire
Vermont	1,413	46		45. Mississippi
Virginia	1,713	28		46. Vermont
Washington	1,705	31		47. Arkansas
West Virginia	1,370	48		48. West Virginia
Wisconsin	1,710	29		49. New York
Wyoming	1,829	20		50. Maryland
50 States	1,884			
DC	2,485			
United States	1,870			

State	Expense per inpatient-day $	Rank	By $
Alabama	819	35	1. Alaska
Alaska	1,341	1	2. Washington
Arizona	1,191	6	3. California
Arkansas	704	43	4. Connecticut
California	1,315	3	5. Utah
Colorado	1,069	12	6. Arizona
Connecticut	1,264	4	7. Massachusetts
Delaware	1,058	16	8. Oregon
Florida	1,004	18	9. Rhode Island
Georgia	836	33	10. New Mexico
Hawaii	956	24	11. Nevada
Idaho	719	41	12. Colorado
Illinois	1,050	17	13. Maryland
Indiana	963	22	14. Texas
Iowa	702	44	15. Ohio
Kansas	732	40	16. Delaware
Kentucky	795	36	17. Illinois
Louisiana	902	29	18. Florida
Maine	916	26	19. Michigan
Maryland	1,064	13	20. Missouri
Massachusetts	1,157	7	21. Pennsylvania
Michigan	994	19	22. Indiana
Minnesota	736	39	23. New Jersey
Mississippi	584	46	24. Hawaii
Missouri	967	20	25. South Carolina
Montana	493	49	26. Maine
Nebraska	661	45	27. New Hampshire
Nevada	1,072	11	28. New York
New Hampshire	915	27	29. Louisiana
New Jersey	962	23	30. Virginia
New Mexico	1,073	10	31. Tennessee
New York	909	28	32. Oklahoma
North Carolina	832	34	33. Georgia
North Dakota	521	48	34. North Carolina
Ohio	1,061	15	35. Alabama
Oklahoma	861	32	36. Kentucky
Oregon	1,141	8	37. Wisconsin
Pennsylvania	963	21	38. West Virginia
Rhode Island	1,092	9	39. Minnesota
South Carolina	923	25	40. Kansas
South Dakota	476	50	41. Idaho
Tennessee	871	31	42. Vermont
Texas	1,063	14	43. Arkansas
Utah	1,213	5	44. Iowa
Vermont	714	42	45. Nebraska
Virginia	901	30	46. Mississippi
Washington	1,318	2	47. Wyoming
West Virginia	763	38	48. North Dakota
Wisconsin	794	37	49. Montana
Wyoming	545	47	50. South Dakota
50 States	n/a		
DC	1,346		
United States	968		

State	Percent of population in HMOs %	Rank
Alabama	9.8	38
Alaska	n/a	n/a
Arizona	28.8	14
Arkansas	8.7	40
California	43.8	3
Colorado	31.1	10
Connecticut	34.7	8
Delaware	38.8	5
Florida	29.0	13
Georgia	12.7	33
Hawaii	25.0	18
Idaho	4.3	43
Illinois	17.1	25
Indiana	11.9	35
Iowa	4.6	42
Kansas	11.5	37
Kentucky	27.4	16
Louisiana	14.7	31
Maine	15.9	26
Maryland	38.0	6
Massachusetts	44.6	2
Michigan	23.5	21
Minnesota	32.7	9
Mississippi	2.4	46
Missouri	30.2	11
Montana	3.1	45
Nebraska	15.4	28
Nevada	20.8	23
New Hampshire	23.9	20
New Jersey	27.5	15
New Mexico	21.0	22
New York	35.7	7
North Carolina	14.6	32
North Dakota	1.7	47
Ohio	17.6	24
Oklahoma	12.4	34
Oregon	47.2	1
Pennsylvania	29.9	12
Rhode Island	11.8	36
South Carolina	8.4	41
South Dakota	3.5	44
Tennessee	15.3	29
Texas	15.3	29
Utah	40.7	4
Vermont	0.0	49
Virginia	15.7	27
Washington	25.1	17
West Virginia	9.4	39
Wisconsin	24.9	19
Wyoming	0.4	48
50 States	n/a	
DC	34.1	
United States	26.7	

By %

1. Oregon
2. Massachusetts
3. California
4. Utah
5. Delaware
6. Maryland
7. New York
8. Connecticut
9. Minnesota
10. Colorado
11. Missouri
12. Pennsylvania
13. Florida
14. Arizona
15. New Jersey
16. Kentucky
17. Washington
18. Hawaii
19. Wisconsin
20. New Hampshire
21. Michigan
22. New Mexico
23. Nevada
24. Ohio
25. Illinois
26. Maine
27. Virginia
28. Nebraska
29. Tennessee
29. Texas
31. Louisiana
32. North Carolina
33. Georgia
34. Oklahoma
35. Indiana
36. Rhode Island
37. Kansas
38. Alabama
39. West Virginia
40. Arkansas
41. South Carolina
42. Iowa
43. Idaho
44. South Dakota
45. Montana
46. Mississippi
47. North Dakota
48. Wyoming
49. Vermont

Source Notes for Health (Section I)

I-1 Immunization Rates, 1996: The data were collected by the Department of Health and Human Services and reported in *Morbidity and Mortality Weekly Report* (July 25, 1997, Volume 46, Number 29).

I-2 Infant Mortality Rates, 1996: These data are collected by the Centers for Disease Control and Prevention (CDC) and are published in *Monthly Vital Statistics Report* (Vol. 45, No. 12, July 17, 1997). They cover deaths of all children under one year of age, expressed in relation to each 1,000 live births. This statistic is considered one of the best indicators with which to compare health among states and local areas. Higher death rates are associated with poor health of the mother, absence of medical care during pregnancy, and lack of medical treatment for infants.

I-3 State Health Rankings, 1996: These scores and rankings are developed annually for Reliastar (formally known as Northwestern National Life Insurance Company) by T. E. Eckstein & Associates, Inc. (1926 Fairmouth Ave., St. Paul, Minnesota 55105). The results are from *An Analysis of the Relative Healthiness of the Population in All Fifty States*. They reflect a composite of indicators, including unemployment, health practices (such as smoking), the availability of health services, and outcomes (such as death rates). Probably no two researchers would use identical lists to produce such rankings, but the state rankings would likely be similar. While decisions by states have some impact on health rankings, decisions on health practices by individual citizens have more of an impact.

I-4 Percent of Non-Elderly Population Without Health Insurance, 1996: Most Americans get health insurance coverage through their employers. All Americans over age sixty-four are covered by Medicare. About 12 percent of the non-elderly, including all welfare recipients, get coverage paid for by state and federal governments through Medicaid. About 17.6 percent of non-elderly citizens have no health insurance. These data come from the Housing and Household Economic Statistics Division of the Census Bureau by fax on November 12, 1997.

I-5 Abortions, 1994: There are about 1.3 million legal abortions performed each year. The numbers in each state are collected by the Department of Health and Human Services (Centers for Disease Control), which furnished the data to *State Fact Finder* in a fax dated September 17, 1997. The abortion ratio shown compares the number of abortions with the number of live births.

I-6 Alcohol Consumption Per Capita, 1994: Some public health authorities consider high levels of alcoholic beverage consumption an indicator of poor health of a state's population. The data show the number of gallons of pure ethanol (typical liquor is about 43 percent ethanol or ethanol alcohol, wine 14 percent, and beer about 6 percent) consumed per resident age fourteen and over.

The data are derived by dividing sales of alcoholic beverages by population. Those shown were developed by the Department of Health and Human Services (National Institute on Alcohol Abuse and Alcoholism) and published in *Surveillance Report # 39*, December 1996. They are called "apparent" alcohol consumption because some alcoholic beverages are bought in one state for consumption by residents of another. This raises the apparent consumption of tourist-destination states, like Nevada, and states with low prices, like New Hampshire, that draw purchasers from other states.

I-7 Percent Adult Smokers, 1995: These estimates are developed by the Office on Smoking and Health Department, a division of the Centers for Disease Control and Prevention. They were provided to *State Fact Finder* in a fax dated July 21, 1997.

I-8 Percent of Population Overweight, 1995: These data were developed as part of the Centers for Disease Control behavioral risk factor surveillance system. Different definitions of how much people can weigh without being considered to have health risks would produce different percentages for every state, but not appreciably affect the rankings. *State Fact Finder* received these statistics by fax on July 16, 1997 from CDC's Division of Nutrition and Physical Activity.

I-9 AIDS Cases, 1996: These data are developed by the Centers for Disease Control and reported in the *HIV/AIDS Surveillance Report*. They cover cases newly reported in CY 1996. The rate shown is cases per 100,000 residents. Because persons at most risk of contracting AIDS are predominately found in larger metropolitan areas, states containing those areas typically show the highest rates.

I-10 Physicians Per 100,000 Population, 1996: This table shows the number of physicians in relation to population. Rural states will show below-average numbers in part because intensive medical care, such as that received from major hospitals, is often sought in nearby states with large metropolitan areas. The statistics are based on data from the American Medical Association (Chicago, Illinois), supplied to *State Fact Finder* by fax on July 16, 1997.

I-11 Hospital Beds Per 1,000 Population, 1995: This table shows the number of hospital beds in relation to population. The data come from *Hospital Stat 96/7* a publication of the American Hospital Association.

I-12 Medicaid Recipients, FY 1996: Over 36 million people receive health care through the Medicaid program each year. The federal government sets minimum standards for this program and pays about 57 percent of the costs nationwide through a formula that provides 50 percent of the costs in the most affluent states and up to 80 percent in the poorest states. Within federal guidelines, states set the rules for eligibility, the health services covered, and the amount of reimbursements to the providers of care.

The primary recipients are families that receive cash assistance from states through Aid to Families with Dependent Children or from the federal government through Supplemental Security Income. These data come from tabulations of the Department of Health and Human Services Health Care Financing Administration furnished to *State Fact Finder* in a special computer run dated October 7, 1997.

I-13 Medicaid Recipients as Percent of Poverty Population, FY 1996: These data, from the same source as Table I-12, relate the number of Medicaid recipients to the number of persons in households with income below federally defined poverty levels (see Table A-11). The differences among states are a good indication of how inclusive are the eligibility criteria set by the individual states.

I-14 State and Local Spending for Health and Hospitals, FY 1994: This table relates spending data to population and personal income in each state. The data come from the Census Bureau and is available on the Internet (http://www.census.gov). See notes to Table F-1 for more information. The spending includes public health activities plus the gross outlays of hospitals and nursing homes run by state and local governments, including costs defrayed by the charges such hospitals make to patients and their health insurance providers. The largest outlays appear in states that rely heavily on government-owned hospitals.

I-15 State and Local Health and Hospital Spending as Percent of General Spending, FY 1994: This table shows the relative importance of health and hospitals outlays in state and local budgets. It is derived by comparing this spending (see Table I-14) with total "general" spending. General spending includes essentially all other spending except municipal electric and other utilities and trust funds, such as those for Workers' Compensation.

I-16 Per Capita Medicaid Spending, FY 1996: These data, from the same source as the number of recipients in Table I-12, reflect the major impact that Medicaid costs are having on government budgets. The amounts shown reflect primarily federal grants spent by states, about 57 percent of the total with differences among the states, and state government matching funds. In a few states, particularly New York, some of the federally required state match is provided by local governments.

I-17 Average Medicaid Spending Per Aged Recipient, FY 1996: These data, from the same source as Table I-12, illustrate differences among the states in this component of Medicaid costs. They relate total spending on all Medicaid recipients age sixty-five and over to the number of recipients. Over half of the nursing home residents in the United States are having their bills paid by Medicaid. States differ in the extent and success of programs designed to encourage people to live at home and with relatives rather than enter nursing homes. Those programs typically provide visiting nurses and homemakers who assist frail elderly persons in their homes, thereby reducing the need for institutionalization.

I-18 Average Medicaid Spending Per AFDC Child, FY 1996: These data reflect the same concepts and come from the same source as those shown in Table I-17. Differences among states primarily reflect differences in how much doctors and other providers of health care are compensated for providing services.

I-19 Medicare Payment Per Hospital- Day, FY 1996: These data are one way to measure health care cost differences among states. They reflect the cost of a day in short-stay hospitals as reimbursed by the federal Medicare program. The data come from the Health Care Financing Administration and were furnished to *State Fact Finder* by fax on November 13, 1997. These data include both the basic rate for staying in the hospital (see Table I-20) and charges for specific services.

I-20 Hospital Expense Per Inpatient-Day, 1995: See source for Table I-11.

I-21 Percentage of Population in Health Maintenance Organizations, 1997: Most Americans receive their health care by purchasing it from individual doctors, hospitals, pharmacies, and others. However, a growing percentage are served by health maintenance organizations that provide complete packages of care for one monthly fee. Many people believe that this approach to buying care will reduce health care costs because the service providers cannot increase their incomes by providing additional services. Many companies providing health insurance to their employees and government programs have been shifting to this approach.

The statistics, reflecting enrollment in January 1997 as a percentage of population, come from Interstudy (Saint Paul, Minnesota) and are published in the Interstudy's *HMO Industry Report 7.2*.

Crime and Law Enforcement

J-1 TOTAL CRIME RATE, 1995

State	Crime rate (per 100,000 population)	Rank
Alabama	4,848	26
Alaska	5,754	14
Arizona	8,214	1
Arkansas	4,691	28
California	5,831	13
Colorado	5,396	19
Connecticut	4,503	33
Delaware	5,159	23
Florida	7,702	2
Georgia	6,004	12
Hawaii	7,199	3
Idaho	4,401	36
Illinois	5,456	18
Indiana	4,632	29
Iowa	4,102	40
Kansas	4,887	25
Kentucky	3,352	45
Louisiana	6,676	4
Maine	3,285	46
Maryland	6,295	8
Massachusetts	4,342	37
Michigan	5,183	22
Minnesota	4,497	34
Mississippi	4,514	32
Missouri	5,121	24
Montana	5,305	21
Nebraska	4,544	31
Nevada	6,579	5
New Hampshire	2,655	49
New Jersey	4,704	27
New Mexico	6,428	7
New York	4,560	30
North Carolina	5,640	16
North Dakota	2,866	48
Ohio	4,405	35
Oklahoma	5,597	17
Oregon	6,564	6
Pennsylvania	3,365	44
Rhode Island	4,245	39
South Carolina	6,064	11
South Dakota	3,061	47
Tennessee	5,363	20
Texas	5,684	15
Utah	6,091	10
Vermont	3,434	43
Virginia	3,989	41
Washington	6,270	9
West Virginia	2,458	50
Wisconsin	3,886	42
Wyoming	4,320	38
50 States	n/a	
DC	12,173	
United States	5,278	

Rank in order

By rate

1. Arizona
2. Florida
3. Hawaii
4. Louisiana
5. Nevada
6. Oregon
7. New Mexico
8. Maryland
9. Washington
10. Utah
11. South Carolina
12. Georgia
13. California
14. Alaska
15. Texas
16. North Carolina
17. Oklahoma
18. Illinois
19. Colorado
20. Tennessee
21. Montana
22. Michigan
23. Delaware
24. Missouri
25. Kansas
26. Alabama
27. New Jersey
28. Arkansas
29. Indiana
30. New York
31. Nebraska
32. Mississippi
33. Connecticut
34. Minnesota
35. Ohio
36. Idaho
37. Massachusetts
38. Wyoming
39. Rhode Island
40. Iowa
41. Virginia
42. Wisconsin
43. Vermont
44. Pennsylvania
45. Kentucky
46. Maine
47. South Dakota
48. North Dakota
49. New Hampshire
50. West Virginia

State	Violent crime rate (per 100,000 population)	Rank
Alabama	632	21
Alaska	771	11
Arizona	713	13
Arkansas	553	23
California	966	6
Colorado	440	29
Connecticut	406	32
Delaware	725	12
Florida	1,071	1
Georgia	657	19
Hawaii	296	41
Idaho	322	40
Illinois	996	3
Indiana	525	24
Iowa	354	38
Kansas	421	31
Kentucky	365	35
Louisiana	1,007	2
Maine	131	47
Maryland	987	4
Massachusetts	687	15
Michigan	688	14
Minnesota	356	37
Mississippi	503	26
Missouri	664	18
Montana	171	46
Nebraska	382	33
Nevada	945	7
New Hampshire	114	49
New Jersey	600	22
New Mexico	819	9
New York	842	8
North Carolina	646	20
North Dakota	87	50
Ohio	482	28
Oklahoma	664	16
Oregon	522	25
Pennsylvania	427	30
Rhode Island	368	34
South Carolina	982	5
South Dakota	208	45
Tennessee	772	10
Texas	664	17
Utah	329	39
Vermont	118	48
Virginia	361	36
Washington	484	27
West Virginia	210	44
Wisconsin	281	42
Wyoming	254	43
50 States	n/a	
DC	2,661	
United States	685	

Rank in order

By rate

1. Florida
2. Louisiana
3. Illinois
4. Maryland
5. South Carolina
6. California
7. Nevada
8. New York
9. New Mexico
10. Tennessee
11. Alaska
12. Delaware
13. Arizona
14. Michigan
15. Massachusetts
16. Oklahoma
17. Texas
18. Missouri
19. Georgia
20. North Carolina
21. Alabama
22. New Jersey
23. Arkansas
24. Indiana
25. Oregon
26. Mississippi
27. Washington
28. Ohio
29. Colorado
30. Pennsylvania
31. Kansas
32. Connecticut
33. Nebraska
34. Rhode Island
35. Kentucky
36. Virginia
37. Minnesota
38. Iowa
39. Utah
40. Idaho
41. Hawaii
42. Wisconsin
43. Wyoming
44. West Virginia
45. South Dakota
46. Montana
47. Maine
48. Vermont
49. New Hampshire
50. North Dakota

State	Murder rate (per 100,000 population)	Rape rate (per 100,000 population)	Rank by murder rate	By murder rate
Alabama	11	32	6	1. Louisiana
Alaska	9	80	14	2. Mississippi
Arizona	10	34	10	3. Oklahoma
Arkansas	10	37	9	4. Maryland
California	11	33	5	5. California
Colorado	6	39	27	6. Alabama
Connecticut	5	24	33	7. Nevada
Delaware	3	80	40	8. Tennessee
Florida	7	49	23	9. Arkansas
Georgia	9	35	12	10. Arizona
Hawaii	5	28	32	11. Illinois
Idaho	4	28	35	12. Georgia
Illinois	10	36	11	13. North Carolina
Indiana	8	33	20	14. Alaska
Iowa	2	22	49	15. Texas
Kansas	6	37	26	16. Missouri
Kentucky	7	32	24	17. New Mexico
Louisiana	17	43	1	18. New York
Maine	2	21	46	19. Michigan
Maryland	12	42	4	20. Indiana
Massachusetts	4	29	39	21. South Carolina
Michigan	8	62	19	22. Virginia
Minnesota	4	56	37	23. Florida
Mississippi	13	39	2	24. Kentucky
Missouri	9	32	16	25. Pennsylvania
Montana	3	26	42	26. Kansas
Nebraska	3	19	43	27. Colorado
Nevada	11	61	7	28. Ohio
New Hampshire	2	29	47	29. New Jersey
New Jersey	5	24	29	30. Washington
New Mexico	9	57	17	31. West Virginia
New York	9	24	18	32. Hawaii
North Carolina	9	32	13	33. Connecticut
North Dakota	1	23	50	34. Wisconsin
Ohio	5	43	28	35. Idaho
Oklahoma	12	45	3	36. Oregon
Oregon	4	42	36	37. Minnesota
Pennsylvania	6	25	25	38. Utah
Rhode Island	3	27	41	39. Massachusetts
South Carolina	8	47	21	40. Delaware
South Dakota	2	41	48	41. Rhode Island
Tennessee	11	47	8	42. Montana
Texas	9	46	15	43. Nebraska
Utah	4	43	38	44. Vermont
Vermont	2	28	44	45. Wyoming
Virginia	8	27	22	46. Maine
Washington	5	59	30	47. New Hampshire
West Virginia	5	21	31	48. South Dakota
Wisconsin	4	23	34	49. Iowa
Wyoming	2	34	45	50. North Dakota
50 States	n/a	n/a		
DC	65	53		
United States	8	37		

State	Property crime rate (per 100,000 population)	Rank
Alabama	4,216	26
Alaska	4,983	16
Arizona	7,500	1
Arkansas	4,138	29
California	4,865	19
Colorado	4,956	17
Connecticut	4,097	32
Delaware	4,434	25
Florida	6,631	3
Georgia	5,347	10
Hawaii	6,903	2
Idaho	4,079	33
Illinois	4,460	23
Indiana	4,107	30
Iowa	3,748	38
Kansas	4,466	22
Kentucky	2,987	45
Louisiana	5,669	7
Maine	3,153	44
Maryland	5,308	11
Massachusetts	3,654	40
Michigan	4,495	21
Minnesota	4,141	28
Mississippi	4,012	35
Missouri	4,457	24
Montana	5,134	12
Nebraska	4,162	27
Nevada	5,634	8
New Hampshire	2,541	49
New Jersey	4,104	31
New Mexico	5,609	9
New York	3,718	39
North Carolina	4,993	15
North Dakota	2,780	48
Ohio	3,923	36
Oklahoma	4,933	18
Oregon	6,042	4
Pennsylvania	2,938	46
Rhode Island	3,877	37
South Carolina	5,082	13
South Dakota	2,853	47
Tennessee	4,591	20
Texas	5,020	14
Utah	5,762	6
Vermont	3,315	43
Virginia	3,628	41
Washington	5,786	5
West Virginia	2,248	50
Wisconsin	3,605	42
Wyoming	4,066	34
50 States	n/a	
DC	9,512	
United States	4,593	

Rank in order

By rate

1. Arizona
2. Hawaii
3. Florida
4. Oregon
5. Washington
6. Utah
7. Louisiana
8. Nevada
9. New Mexico
10. Georgia
11. Maryland
12. Montana
13. South Carolina
14. Texas
15. North Carolina
16. Alaska
17. Colorado
18. Oklahoma
19. California
20. Tennessee
21. Michigan
22. Kansas
23. Illinois
24. Missouri
25. Delaware
26. Alabama
27. Nebraska
28. Minnesota
29. Arkansas
30. Indiana
31. New Jersey
32. Connecticut
33. Idaho
34. Wyoming
35. Mississippi
36. Ohio
37. Rhode Island
38. Iowa
39. New York
40. Massachusetts
41. Virginia
42. Wisconsin
43. Vermont
44. Maine
45. Kentucky
46. Pennsylvania
47. South Dakota
48. North Dakota
49. New Hampshire
50. West Virginia

State	Motor vehicle theft rate (per 100,000 population)	Rank
Alabama	347	34
Alaska	522	19
Arizona	1,158	1
Arkansas	325	36
California	888	2
Colorado	388	29
Connecticut	540	17
Delaware	414	26
Florida	786	3
Georgia	608	11
Hawaii	691	7
Idaho	242	42
Illinois	523	18
Indiana	466	23
Iowa	223	43
Kansas	324	37
Kentucky	259	41
Louisiana	598	13
Maine	135	49
Maryland	718	5
Massachusetts	604	12
Michigan	646	9
Minnesota	341	35
Mississippi	361	32
Missouri	473	22
Montana	308	39
Nebraska	351	33
Nevada	745	4
New Hampshire	145	47
New Jersey	632	10
New Mexico	513	20
New York	566	14
North Carolina	311	38
North Dakota	179	44
Ohio	415	25
Oklahoma	496	21
Oregon	702	6
Pennsylvania	413	27
Rhode Island	441	24
South Carolina	385	30
South Dakota	121	50
Tennessee	649	8
Texas	560	15
Utah	389	28
Vermont	136	48
Virginia	293	40
Washington	554	16
West Virginia	166	46
Wisconsin	364	31
Wyoming	168	45
50 States	n/a	
DC	1,840	
United States	561	

Rank in order

By rate

1. Arizona
2. California
3. Florida
4. Nevada
5. Maryland
6. Oregon
7. Hawaii
8. Tennessee
9. Michigan
10. New Jersey
11. Georgia
12. Massachusetts
13. Louisiana
14. New York
15. Texas
16. Washington
17. Connecticut
18. Illinois
19. Alaska
20. New Mexico
21. Oklahoma
22. Missouri
23. Indiana
24. Rhode Island
25. Ohio
26. Delaware
27. Pennsylvania
28. Utah
29. Colorado
30. South Carolina
31. Wisconsin
32. Mississippi
33. Nebraska
34. Alabama
35. Minnesota
36. Arkansas
37. Kansas
38. North Carolina
39. Montana
40. Virginia
41. Kentucky
42. Idaho
43. Iowa
44. North Dakota
45. Wyoming
46. West Virginia
47. New Hampshire
48. Vermont
49. Maine
50. South Dakota

J-6 VIOLENT CRIME RATE CHANGE, 1990-1995

State	1990 violent crime rate (per 100,000)	Percent change in violent crime 1990-95 %	Rank by %
Alabama	591	7.0	29
Alaska	498	54.8	2
Arizona	600	18.9	20
Arkansas	474	16.7	23
California	978	-1.2	38
Colorado	471	-6.5	45
Connecticut	512	-20.7	48
Delaware	557	30.2	12
Florida	1,109	-3.4	43
Georgia	736	-10.7	46
Hawaii	270	9.5	28
Idaho	255	26.3	16
Illinois	846	17.7	22
Indiana	407	28.9	13
Iowa	266	33.2	11
Kansas	401	4.9	30
Kentucky	357	2.2	34
Louisiana	782	28.8	14
Maine	137	-4.1	44
Maryland	855	15.4	26
Massachusetts	675	1.8	35
Michigan	709	-3.0	42
Minnesota	288	23.6	18
Mississippi	311	61.7	1
Missouri	633	4.9	31
Montana	116	47.0	5
Nebraska	280	36.4	9
Nevada	625	51.2	4
New Hampshire	169	-32.3	50
New Jersey	609	-1.5	40
New Mexico	704	16.4	24
New York	1,131	-25.6	49
North Carolina	546	18.4	21
North Dakota	63	37.7	8
Ohio	469	2.9	32
Oklahoma	492	35.0	10
Oregon	519	0.7	37
Pennsylvania	379	12.7	27
Rhode Island	378	-2.7	41
South Carolina	814	20.6	19
South Dakota	136	52.6	3
Tennessee	549	40.5	7
Texas	659	0.7	36
Utah	259	27.0	15
Vermont	133	-11.1	47
Virginia	313	15.5	25
Washington	472	2.6	33
West Virginia	147	43.0	6
Wisconsin	223	26.0	17
Wyoming	258	-1.5	39
50 States	n/a	n/a	
DC	2,458	8.3	
United States	663	3.3	

Rank in order

By %

1. Mississippi
2. Alaska
3. South Dakota
4. Nevada
5. Montana
6. West Virginia
7. Tennessee
8. North Dakota
9. Nebraska
10. Oklahoma
11. Iowa
12. Delaware
13. Indiana
14. Louisiana
15. Utah
16. Idaho
17. Wisconsin
18. Minnesota
19. South Carolina
20. Arizona
21. North Carolina
22. Illinois
23. Arkansas
24. New Mexico
25. Virginia
26. Maryland
27. Pennsylvania
28. Hawaii
29. Alabama
30. Kansas
31. Missouri
32. Ohio
33. Washington
34. Kentucky
35. Massachusetts
36. Texas
37. Oregon
38. California
39. Wyoming
40. New Jersey
41. Rhode Island
42. Michigan
43. Florida
44. Maine
45. Colorado
46. Georgia
47. Vermont
48. Connecticut
49. New York
50. New Hampshire

State	Prisoners #	Rank
Alabama	21,760	17
Alaska	3,706	40
Arizona	22,573	14
Arkansas	9,407	29
California	147,712	1
Colorado	12,438	27
Connecticut	15,007	22
Delaware	5,110	35
Florida	63,763	4
Georgia	35,139	8
Hawaii	4,011	37
Idaho	3,834	39
Illinois	38,852	7
Indiana	16,960	20
Iowa	6,342	33
Kansas	7,756	32
Kentucky	12,910	24
Louisiana	26,779	13
Maine	1,476	48
Maryland	22,050	15
Massachusetts	11,790	28
Michigan	42,349	6
Minnesota	5,158	34
Mississippi	14,292	23
Missouri	22,003	16
Montana	2,073	44
Nebraska	3,275	41
Nevada	8,215	31
New Hampshire	2,071	45
New Jersey	27,490	12
New Mexico	4,724	36
New York	69,709	3
North Carolina	30,701	10
North Dakota	722	50
Ohio	46,174	5
Oklahoma	19,593	19
Oregon	8,661	30
Pennsylvania	34,537	9
Rhode Island	3,271	42
South Carolina	20,446	18
South Dakota	2,064	46
Tennessee	15,626	21
Texas	132,383	2
Utah	3,939	38
Vermont	1,125	49
Virginia	27,655	11
Washington	12,527	26
West Virginia	2,754	43
Wisconsin	12,854	25
Wyoming	1,483	47
50 States	1,067,249	
DC	9,376	
United States	1,076,625	

1. California
2. Texas
3. New York
4. Florida
5. Ohio
6. Michigan
7. Illinois
8. Georgia
9. Pennsylvania
10. North Carolina
11. Virginia
12. New Jersey
13. Louisiana
14. Arizona
15. Maryland
16. Missouri
17. Alabama
18. South Carolina
19. Oklahoma
20. Indiana
21. Tennessee
22. Connecticut
23. Mississippi
24. Kentucky
25. Wisconsin
26. Washington
27. Colorado
28. Massachusetts
29. Arkansas
30. Oregon
31. Nevada
32. Kansas
33. Iowa
34. Minnesota
35. Delaware
36. New Mexico
37. Hawaii
38. Utah
39. Idaho
40. Alaska
41. Nebraska
42. Rhode Island
43. West Virginia
44. Montana
45. New Hampshire
46. South Dakota
47. Wyoming
48. Maine
49. Vermont
50. North Dakota

State	Percent change in prisoners %	Rank
Alabama	28.7	33
Alaska	n/a	n/a
Arizona	45.5	16
Arkansas	16.4	40
California	n/a	n/a
Colorado	48.2	12
Connecticut	20.0	37
Delaware	26.1	34
Florida	37.0	21
Georgia	49.2	10
Hawaii	67.3	2
Idaho	n/a	n/a
Illinois	33.4	28
Indiana	23.8	35
Iowa	53.0	5
Kansas	31.4	30
Kentucky	31.7	29
Louisiana	33.9	26
Maine	-10.1	44
Maryland	17.7	38
Massachusetts	n/a	n/a
Michigan	16.3	41
Minnesota	48.6	11
Mississippi	56.4	3
Missouri	38.4	19
Montana	40.3	18
Nebraska	33.5	27
Nevada	41.1	17
New Hampshire	35.1	24
New Jersey	17.1	39
New Mexico	49.4	9
New York	20.5	36
North Carolina	52.9	6
North Dakota	47.4	14
Ohio	29.2	32
Oklahoma	46.9	15
Oregon	31.2	31
Pennsylvania	47.7	13
Rhode Island	16.1	42
South Carolina	14.8	43
South Dakota	50.2	7
Tennessee	36.2	23
Texas	156.2	1
Utah	50.2	7
Vermont	n/a	n/a
Virginia	37.7	20
Washington	36.7	22
West Virginia	n/a	n/a
Wisconsin	53.4	4
Wyoming	34.9	25
50 States	n/a	
DC	21.9	
United States	43.2	

Rank in order

By %

1. Texas
2. Hawaii
3. Mississippi
4. Wisconsin
5. Iowa
6. North Carolina
7. South Dakota
7. Utah
9. New Mexico
10. Georgia
11. Minnesota
12. Colorado
13. Pennsylvania
14. North Dakota
15. Oklahoma
16. Arizona
17. Nevada
18. Montana
19. Missouri
20. Virginia
21. Florida
22. Washington
23. Tennessee
24. New Hampshire
25. Wyoming
26. Louisiana
27. Nebraska
28. Illinois
29. Kentucky
30. Kansas
31. Oregon
32. Ohio
33. Alabama
34. Delaware
35. Indiana
36. New York
37. Connecticut
38. Maryland
39. New Jersey
40. Arkansas
41. Michigan
42. Rhode Island
43. South Carolina
44. Maine

State	Incarceration rate (per 100,000 population)	Rank		By rate
Alabama	492	7		1. Texas
Alaska	379	19		2. Louisiana
Arizona	481	8		3. Oklahoma
Arkansas	357	21		4. South Carolina
California	451	10		5. Nevada
Colorado	322	25		6. Mississippi
Connecticut	314	27		7. Alabama
Delaware	428	13		8. Arizona
Florida	439	12		9. Georgia
Georgia	462	9		10. California
Hawaii	249	36		11. Michigan
Idaho	319	26		12. Florida
Illinois	327	24		13. Delaware
Indiana	287	32		14. Ohio
Iowa	222	41		15. Maryland
Kansas	301	30		16. Missouri
Kentucky	331	23		17. Virginia
Louisiana	615	2		18. New York
Maine	112	48		19. Alaska
Maryland	412	15		20. North Carolina
Massachusetts	302	29		21. Arkansas
Michigan	440	11		22. New Jersey
Minnesota	110	49		23. Kentucky
Mississippi	498	6		24. Illinois
Missouri	409	16		25. Colorado
Montana	235	37		26. Idaho
Nebraska	194	43		27. Connecticut
Nevada	502	5		28. Wyoming
New Hampshire	177	45		29. Massachusetts
New Jersey	343	22		30. Kansas
New Mexico	261	35		31. Tennessee
New York	383	18		32. Indiana
North Carolina	379	20		33. Pennsylvania
North Dakota	101	50		34. South Dakota
Ohio	413	14		35. New Mexico
Oklahoma	591	3		36. Hawaii
Oregon	226	39		37. Montana
Pennsylvania	286	33		38. Wisconsin
Rhode Island	205	42		39. Oregon
South Carolina	532	4		40. Washington
South Dakota	281	34		41. Iowa
Tennessee	292	31		42. Rhode Island
Texas	686	1		43. Nebraska
Utah	194	44		44. Utah
Vermont	137	47		45. New Hampshire
Virginia	404	17		46. West Virginia
Washington	224	40		47. Vermont
West Virginia	150	46		48. Maine
Wisconsin	230	38		49. Minnesota
Wyoming	307	28		50. North Dakota
50 States	n/a			
DC	1,609			
United States	394			

State	Juvenile violent crime rate (per 100,000 youths)	Rank
Alabama	236	33
Alaska	414	16
Arizona	505	10
Arkansas	286	28
California	787	3
Colorado	296	27
Connecticut	577	7
Delaware	n/a	n/a
Florida	799	2
Georgia	384	20
Hawaii	285	30
Idaho	286	28
Illinois	n/a	n/a
Indiana	494	12
Iowa	273	31
Kansas	n/a	n/a
Kentucky	n/a	n/a
Louisiana	535	8
Maine	143	36
Maryland	689	5
Massachusetts	590	6
Michigan	387	19
Minnesota	409	18
Mississippi	n/a	n/a
Missouri	515	9
Montana	n/a	n/a
Nebraska	184	34
Nevada	421	15
New Hampshire	n/a	n/a
New Jersey	697	4
New Mexico	n/a	n/a
New York	979	1
North Carolina	413	17
North Dakota	159	35
Ohio	n/a	n/a
Oklahoma	380	21
Oregon	349	24
Pennsylvania	n/a	n/a
Rhode Island	504	11
South Carolina	378	22
South Dakota	305	26
Tennessee	n/a	n/a
Texas	377	23
Utah	307	25
Vermont	30	39
Virginia	267	32
Washington	426	14
West Virginia	80	38
Wisconsin	427	13
Wyoming	106	37
50 States	n/a	
DC	1,418	
United States	517	

By rate

1. New York
2. Florida
3. California
4. New Jersey
5. Maryland
6. Massachusetts
7. Connecticut
8. Louisiana
9. Missouri
10. Arizona
11. Rhode Island
12. Indiana
13. Wisconsin
14. Washington
15. Nevada
16. Alaska
17. North Carolina
18. Minnesota
19. Michigan
20. Georgia
21. Oklahoma
22. South Carolina
23. Texas
24. Oregon
25. Utah
26. South Dakota
27. Colorado
28. Arkansas
28. Idaho
30. Hawaii
31. Iowa
32. Virginia
33. Alabama
34. Nebraska
35. North Dakota
36. Maine
37. Wyoming
38. West Virginia
39. Vermont

State	Proportion of sentence served %	Rank	Rank in order By %
Alabama	n/a	n/a	1. California
Alaska	65	7	2. Arizona
Arizona	82	2	3. Massachusetts
Arkansas	36	34	4. Minnesota
California	86	1	5. Idaho
Colorado	52	14	5. Washington
Connecticut	n/a	n/a	7. Alaska
Delaware	59	8	8. Delaware
Florida	47	18	9. Louisiana
Georgia	48	17	10. Vermont
Hawaii	42	24	11. Maryland
Idaho	67	5	11. New York
Illinois	43	23	11. West Virginia
Indiana	n/a	n/a	14. Colorado
Iowa	32	37	15. Missouri
Kansas	n/a	n/a	16. Pennsylvania
Kentucky	38	29	17. Georgia
Louisiana	57	9	18. Florida
Maine	n/a	n/a	18. Wyoming
Maryland	54	11	20. North Dakota
Massachusetts	77	3	21. Nebraska
Michigan	n/a	n/a	21. Utah
Minnesota	73	4	23. Illinois
Mississippi	40	27	24. Hawaii
Missouri	51	15	24. Oregon
Montana	37	31	26. New Hampshire
Nebraska	45	21	27. Mississippi
Nevada	n/a	n/a	28. Texas
New Hampshire	41	26	29. Kentucky
New Jersey	37	31	29. Wisconsin
New Mexico	n/a	n/a	31. Montana
New York	54	11	31. New Jersey
North Carolina	30	38	31. South Carolina
North Dakota	46	20	34. Arkansas
Ohio	17	39	34. Oklahoma
Oklahoma	36	34	36. Tennessee
Oregon	42	24	37. Iowa
Pennsylvania	49	16	38. North Carolina
Rhode Island	n/a	n/a	39. Ohio
South Carolina	37	31	
South Dakota	n/a	n/a	
Tennessee	35	36	
Texas	39	28	
Utah	45	21	
Vermont	56	10	
Virginia	n/a	n/a	
Washington	67	5	
West Virginia	54	11	
Wisconsin	38	29	
Wyoming	47	18	
50 States	n/a		
DC	67		
United States	46		

State	Law enforcement employees	Per 10,000 employees	Rank by per 10,000
Alabama	10,891	25.6	33
Alaska	1,772	29.4	15
Arizona	12,751	29.6	12
Arkansas	6,293	25.3	34
California	90,484	28.7	21
Colorado	10,608	28.3	23
Connecticut	9,625	29.4	14
Delaware	2,000	27.9	25
Florida	48,669	34.3	4
Georgia	21,151	29.3	17
Hawaii	3,291	27.9	24
Idaho	3,334	28.6	22
Illinois	43,120	36.6	3
Indiana	14,440	24.9	37
Iowa	6,633	23.3	42
Kansas	7,552	29.5	13
Kentucky	7,706	20.0	49
Louisiana	13,436	31.0	7
Maine	2,818	22.8	44
Maryland	15,728	31.2	6
Massachusetts	18,320	30.2	11
Michigan	23,338	24.5	39
Minnesota	9,869	21.4	47
Mississippi	7,514	27.9	26
Missouri	16,283	30.6	8
Montana	2,130	24.5	38
Nebraska	4,140	25.3	36
Nevada	4,672	30.5	9
New Hampshire	3,043	26.5	30
New Jersey	32,185	40.5	2
New Mexico	4,955	29.3	18
New York	76,593	42.1	1
North Carolina	19,827	27.5	28
North Dakota	1,338	20.9	48
Ohio	29,635	26.6	29
Oklahoma	9,548	29.2	19
Oregon	7,397	23.5	41
Pennsylvania	31,486	26.1	31
Rhode Island	2,879	29.0	20
South Carolina	10,770	29.4	16
South Dakota	1,574	21.6	46
Tennessee	13,562	25.8	32
Texas	56,794	30.2	10
Utah	4,663	23.8	40
Vermont	1,278	21.9	45
Virginia	16,710	25.3	35
Washington	12,410	22.8	43
West Virginia	3,240	17.8	50
Wisconsin	14,201	27.7	27
Wyoming	1,610	33.6	5
50 States	774,266	29.5	
DC	4,490	81.0	
United States	778,756	29.6	

By per 10,000

1. New York
2. New Jersey
3. Illinois
4. Florida
5. Wyoming
6. Maryland
7. Louisiana
8. Missouri
9. Nevada
10. Texas
11. Massachusetts
12. Arizona
13. Kansas
14. Connecticut
15. Alaska
16. South Carolina
17. Georgia
18. New Mexico
19. Oklahoma
20. Rhode Island
21. California
22. Idaho
23. Colorado
24. Hawaii
25. Delaware
26. Mississippi
27. Wisconsin
28. North Carolina
29. Ohio
30. New Hampshire
31. Pennsylvania
32. Tennessee
33. Alabama
34. Arkansas
35. Virginia
36. Nebraska
37. Indiana
38. Montana
39. Michigan
40. Utah
41. Oregon
42. Iowa
43. Washington
44. Maine
45. Vermont
46. South Dakota
47. Minnesota
48. North Dakota
49. Kentucky
50. West Virginia

State	Corrections employees	Per 10,000 population	Rank by per 10,000	Rank in order By per 10,000
Alabama	6,760	15.9	41	1. Georgia
Alaska	1,296	21.5	19	2. Texas
Arizona	12,324	28.6	6	3. New York
Arkansas	4,627	18.6	28	4. Florida
California	70,854	22.4	14	5. New Mexico
Colorado	7,108	19.0	27	6. Arizona
Connecticut	7,443	22.8	13	7. Virginia
Delaware	1,840	25.7	12	8. South Carolina
Florida	44,315	31.2	4	9. Nevada
Georgia	25,355	35.2	1	10. Oklahoma
Hawaii	2,131	18.1	32	11. Maryland
Idaho	2,342	20.1	23	12. Delaware
Illinois	21,757	18.5	29	13. Connecticut
Indiana	10,116	17.5	34	14. California
Iowa	3,234	11.4	48	15. Michigan
Kansas	5,510	21.5	20	16. North Carolina
Kentucky	7,507	19.5	26	17. Louisiana
Louisiana	9,377	21.6	17	18. Tennessee
Maine	1,818	14.7	44	19. Alaska
Maryland	13,125	26.0	11	20. Kansas
Massachusetts	11,097	18.3	30	21. New Jersey
Michigan	21,226	22.3	15	22. Washington
Minnesota	7,161	15.5	42	23. Idaho
Mississippi	4,731	17.5	33	24. Ohio
Missouri	8,984	16.9	37	25. Pennsylvania
Montana	1,170	13.4	46	26. Kentucky
Nebraska	2,728	16.6	39	27. Colorado
Nevada	4,181	27.3	9	28. Arkansas
New Hampshire	1,543	13.4	47	29. Illinois
New Jersey	16,125	20.3	21	30. Massachusetts
New Mexico	5,187	30.7	5	31. Oregon
New York	58,067	31.9	3	32. Hawaii
North Carolina	15,922	22.1	16	33. Mississippi
North Dakota	717	11.2	49	34. Indiana
Ohio	22,215	20.0	24	35. Wisconsin
Oklahoma	8,875	27.1	10	36. Wyoming
Oregon	5,708	18.1	31	37. Missouri
Pennsylvania	23,498	19.5	25	38. Rhode Island
Rhode Island	1,655	16.7	38	39. Nebraska
South Carolina	10,075	27.5	8	40. Utah
South Dakota	1,001	13.7	45	41. Alabama
Tennessee	11,332	21.6	18	42. Minnesota
Texas	63,917	34.0	2	43. Vermont
Utah	3,196	16.3	40	44. Maine
Vermont	868	14.8	43	45. South Dakota
Virginia	18,926	28.6	7	46. Montana
Washington	10,944	20.1	22	47. New Hampshire
West Virginia	1,204	6.6	50	48. Iowa
Wisconsin	8,888	17.4	35	49. North Dakota
Wyoming	810	16.9	36	50. West Virginia
50 States	610,790	23.3		
DC	4,185	75.5		
United States	614,975	23.4		

State	Average cost per inmate per day $	Rank		Rank in order By $
Alabama	25.10	50		1. Alaska
Alaska	106.63	1		2. Maine
Arizona	44.79	34		3. Minnesota
Arkansas	34.84	46		4. Massachusetts
California	59.26	15		5. Rhode Island
Colorado	58.64	16		6. Hawaii
Connecticut	63.19	13		7. New Mexico
Delaware	51.46	21		8. New York
Florida	42.51	38		9. Vermont
Georgia	48.91	27		10. New Jersey
Hawaii	78.56	6		11. North Carolina
Idaho	48.31	29		11. Washington
Illinois	43.18	37		13. Connecticut
Indiana	45.17	33		14. Pennsylvania
Iowa	48.40	28		15. California
Kansas	51.17	22		16. Colorado
Kentucky	37.30	43		17. Wisconsin
Louisiana	34.52	47		18. Utah
Maine	83.15	2		19. Oregon
Maryland	50.00	25		20. Michigan
Massachusetts	81.37	4		21. Delaware
Michigan	51.74	20		22. Kansas
Minnesota	82.24	3		23. Tennessee
Mississippi	33.28	48		24. North Dakota
Missouri	28.18	49		25. Maryland
Montana	41.29	39		26. Wyoming
Nebraska	45.64	32		27. Georgia
Nevada	38.76	41		28. Iowa
New Hampshire	47.00	30		29. Idaho
New Jersey	70.15	10		30. New Hampshire
New Mexico	76.89	7		31. Virginia
New York	76.57	8		32. Nebraska
North Carolina	63.53	11		33. Indiana
North Dakota	50.60	24		34. Arizona
Ohio	40.70	40		35. Texas
Oklahoma	37.19	44		36. West Virginia
Oregon	53.73	19		37. Illinois
Pennsylvania	60.46	14		38. Florida
Rhode Island	79.00	5		39. Montana
South Carolina	36.00	45		40. Ohio
South Dakota	37.47	42		41. Nevada
Tennessee	50.80	23		42. South Dakota
Texas	44.40	35		43. Kentucky
Utah	54.22	18		44. Oklahoma
Vermont	74.38	9		45. South Carolina
Virginia	46.39	31		46. Arkansas
Washington	63.53	11		47. Louisiana
West Virginia	43.84	36		48. Mississippi
Wisconsin	55.24	17		49. Missouri
Wyoming	49.40	26		50. Alabama
50 States	n/a			
DC	68.16			
United States	53.85			

J-14 AVERAGE COST PER INMATE-DAY, 1996

Source: Criminal Justice Institute's *Corrections Yearbook, 1996* (South Salem, NY 10590)

State	Corrections spending $(millions)	Per prisoner $	Rank by per prisoner	By per prisoner
Alabama	213	9,789	48	1. Minnesota
Alaska	n/a	n/a	n/a	2. Maine
Arizona	464	20,556	33	3. Utah
Arkansas	110	11,693	45	4. Vermont
California	3,395	22,984	26	5. New York
Colorado	301	24,200	23	6. Rhode Island
Connecticut	373	24,855	19	7. Oregon
Delaware	99	19,374	36	8. Washington
Florida	1,378	21,611	28	9. Maryland
Georgia	692	19,693	35	10. Wisconsin
Hawaii	97	24,183	24	11. Michigan
Idaho	79	20,605	32	12. Pennsylvania
Illinois	773	19,896	34	13. Montana
Indiana	354	20,873	30	14. Tennessee
Iowa	156	24,598	21	15. Massachusetts
Kansas	191	24,626	20	16. New Jersey
Kentucky	207	16,034	40	17. New Mexico
Louisiana	429	16,020	41	18. North Carolina
Maine	65	44,038	2	19. Connecticut
Maryland	632	28,662	9	20. Kansas
Massachusetts	307	26,039	15	21. Iowa
Michigan	1,198	28,289	11	22. Virginia
Minnesota	263	50,989	1	23. Colorado
Mississippi	158	11,055	46	24. Hawaii
Missouri	319	14,498	44	25. Ohio
Montana	56	27,014	13	26. California
Nebraska	69	21,069	29	27. New Hampshire
Nevada	n/a	n/a	n/a	28. Florida
New Hampshire	45	21,729	27	29. Nebraska
New Jersey	705	25,646	16	30. Indiana
New Mexico	121	25,614	17	31. North Dakota
New York	2,481	35,591	5	32. Idaho
North Carolina	768	25,015	18	33. Arizona
North Dakota	15	20,776	31	34. Illinois
Ohio	1,064	23,043	25	35. Georgia
Oklahoma	207	10,565	47	36. Delaware
Oregon	287	33,137	7	37. Texas
Pennsylvania	966	27,970	12	38. West Virginia
Rhode Island	114	34,852	6	39. Wyoming
South Carolina	311	15,211	42	40. Kentucky
South Dakota	31	15,019	43	41. Louisiana
Tennessee	412	26,366	14	42. South Carolina
Texas	2,516	19,005	37	43. South Dakota
Utah	155	39,350	3	44. Missouri
Vermont	44	39,111	4	45. Arkansas
Virginia	670	24,227	22	46. Mississippi
Washington	366	29,217	8	47. Oklahoma
West Virginia	49	17,792	38	48. Alabama
Wisconsin	368	28,629	10	
Wyoming	26	17,532	39	
50 States	24,099	22,580		
DC	n/a	n/a		
United States	24,099	22,384		

Rank in order

State	Percent increase in state corrections spending %	Rank	Rank in order By %
Alabama	8.7	40	1. Missouri
Alaska	n/a	n/a	2. Mississippi
Arizona	48.7	4	3. Montana
Arkansas	18.3	23	4. Arizona
California	10.7	36	5. West Virginia
Colorado	-19.3	48	6. Idaho
Connecticut	7.8	42	7. Pennsylvania
Delaware	16.5	27	8. Oregon
Florida	23.0	17	9. Utah
Georgia	20.8	18	10. Texas
Hawaii	7.8	43	11. Louisiana
Idaho	43.6	6	12. New York
Illinois	15.5	29	13. Ohio
Indiana	14.9	31	14. Minnesota
Iowa	12.2	35	15. North Carolina
Kansas	7.3	45	16. Wisconsin
Kentucky	18.3	22	17. Florida
Louisiana	33.6	11	18. Georgia
Maine	8.3	41	19. New Mexico
Maryland	14.9	32	20. Oklahoma
Massachusetts	9.3	39	21. Vermont
Michigan	14.4	33	22. Kentucky
Minnesota	32.2	14	23. Arkansas
Mississippi	66.3	2	24. Wyoming
Missouri	73.4	1	25. South Carolina
Montana	60.0	3	26. Nebraska
Nebraska	16.9	26	27. Delaware
Nevada	n/a	n/a	28. Virginia
New Hampshire	15.4	30	29. Illinois
New Jersey	10.7	38	30. New Hampshire
New Mexico	19.8	19	31. Indiana
New York	33.1	12	32. Maryland
North Carolina	30.8	15	33. Michigan
North Dakota	7.1	46	34. Rhode Island
Ohio	33.0	13	35. Iowa
Oklahoma	19.0	20	36. California
Oregon	38.6	8	37. South Dakota
Pennsylvania	39.0	7	38. New Jersey
Rhode Island	12.9	34	39. Massachusetts
South Carolina	17.8	25	40. Alabama
South Dakota	10.7	37	41. Maine
Tennessee	7.6	44	42. Connecticut
Texas	35.6	10	43. Hawaii
Utah	37.2	9	44. Tennessee
Vermont	18.9	21	45. Kansas
Virginia	15.7	28	46. North Dakota
Washington	-3.2	47	47. Washington
West Virginia	44.1	5	48. Colorado
Wisconsin	26.0	16	
Wyoming	18.2	24	
50 States	20.1		
DC	n/a		
United States	20.1		

State	Law enforcement spending $(millions)	Per capita $	Rank by per capita
Alabama	753	179	36
Alaska	283	467	1
Arizona	1,183	290	9
Arkansas	372	151	46
California	11,609	369	3
Colorado	937	256	17
Connecticut	971	297	8
Delaware	187	265	12
Florida	4,648	333	5
Georgia	1,760	250	20
Hawaii	291	246	23
Idaho	223	197	33
Illinois	3,079	262	13
Indiana	967	168	40
Iowa	460	163	42
Kansas	528	207	31
Kentucky	594	155	45
Louisiana	1,003	233	26
Maine	196	158	44
Maryland	1,553	310	7
Massachusetts	1,560	258	16
Michigan	2,644	278	10
Minnesota	956	209	30
Mississippi	337	126	48
Missouri	947	178	37
Montana	137	160	43
Nebraska	273	168	39
Nevada	529	363	4
New Hampshire	213	188	35
New Jersey	2,611	330	6
New Mexico	433	262	14
New York	7,483	412	2
North Carolina	1,750	248	22
North Dakota	71	111	49
Ohio	2,573	232	27
Oklahoma	554	170	38
Oregon	777	252	18
Pennsylvania	2,599	216	28
Rhode Island	251	252	19
South Carolina	788	215	29
South Dakota	120	166	41
Tennessee	1,024	198	32
Texas	5,093	277	11
Utah	366	192	34
Vermont	86	148	47
Virginia	1,597	244	24
Washington	1,384	259	15
West Virginia	194	106	50
Wisconsin	1,265	249	21
Wyoming	111	234	25
50 States	70,326	271	
DC	589	1,034	
United States	70,915	272	

Rank in order

By per capita

1. Alaska
2. New York
3. California
4. Nevada
5. Florida
6. New Jersey
7. Maryland
8. Connecticut
9. Arizona
10. Michigan
11. Texas
12. Delaware
13. Illinois
14. New Mexico
15. Washington
16. Massachusetts
17. Colorado
18. Oregon
19. Rhode Island
20. Georgia
21. Wisconsin
22. North Carolina
23. Hawaii
24. Virginia
25. Wyoming
26. Louisiana
27. Ohio
28. Pennsylvania
29. South Carolina
30. Minnesota
31. Kansas
32. Tennessee
33. Idaho
34. Utah
35. New Hampshire
36. Alabama
37. Missouri
38. Oklahoma
39. Nebraska
40. Indiana
41. South Dakota
42. Iowa
43. Montana
44. Maine
45. Kentucky
46. Arkansas
47. Vermont
48. Mississippi
49. North Dakota
50. West Virginia

State	Law enforcement spending as percent of general spending %	Rank
Alabama	5.10	33
Alaska	4.59	37
Arizona	7.87	6
Arkansas	4.99	34
California	8.38	3
Colorado	6.25	15
Connecticut	5.83	23
Delaware	5.91	21
Florida	8.91	1
Georgia	6.75	11
Hawaii	4.37	42
Idaho	5.91	20
Illinois	6.95	8
Indiana	4.54	38
Iowa	4.12	45
Kansas	5.44	30
Kentucky	4.67	36
Louisiana	5.95	18
Maine	3.98	46
Maryland	7.93	5
Massachusetts	5.54	28
Michigan	6.72	12
Minnesota	4.33	43
Mississippi	3.91	47
Missouri	5.87	22
Montana	4.15	44
Nebraska	4.38	41
Nevada	8.43	2
New Hampshire	4.80	35
New Jersey	6.85	9
New Mexico	6.29	14
New York	6.60	13
North Carolina	7.02	7
North Dakota	2.74	50
Ohio	6.12	16
Oklahoma	5.24	32
Oregon	6.02	17
Pennsylvania	5.55	27
Rhode Island	5.53	29
South Carolina	5.70	26
South Dakota	4.51	39
Tennessee	5.95	19
Texas	7.97	4
Utah	5.31	31
Vermont	3.53	48
Virginia	6.80	10
Washington	5.72	25
West Virginia	2.82	49
Wisconsin	5.77	24
Wyoming	4.38	40
50 States	6.58	
DC	12.88	
United States	6.60	

Rank in order

By %

1. Florida
2. Nevada
3. California
4. Texas
5. Maryland
6. Arizona
7. North Carolina
8. Illinois
9. New Jersey
10. Virginia
11. Georgia
12. Michigan
13. New York
14. New Mexico
15. Colorado
16. Ohio
17. Oregon
18. Louisiana
19. Tennessee
20. Idaho
21. Delaware
22. Missouri
23. Connecticut
24. Wisconsin
25. Washington
26. South Carolina
27. Pennsylvania
28. Massachusetts
29. Rhode Island
30. Kansas
31. Utah
32. Oklahoma
33. Alabama
34. Arkansas
35. New Hampshire
36. Kentucky
37. Alaska
38. Indiana
39. South Dakota
40. Wyoming
41. Nebraska
42. Hawaii
43. Minnesota
44. Montana
45. Iowa
46. Maine
47. Mississippi
48. Vermont
49. West Virginia
50. North Dakota

Source Notes for Crime and Law Enforcement (Section J)

J-1 Total Crime Rate, 1995: This table reflects the total crime rate as defined by the uniform crime reporting system of the U.S. Department of Justice (Federal Bureau of Investigation). The reports are compiled by individual law enforcement agencies throughout the nation and summarized in the Justice Department publication *Crime in the United States, 1995.*

These statistics inherently cover only crime known to law enforcement agencies, so they are often cited as "crime reported to the police." Certain crimes, such as murder and thefts where victims seek insurance reimbursement, are almost always reported to police. Victims often fail to report other categories of crime, ranging from rape to thefts of small items. To capture information on crimes actually committed, the Justice Department does a survey of households known as the "victimization survey." Because that survey is based on nationwide samples, data from it are not available on a state-by-state basis.

The FBI has worked for years to make the statistics reported from different states and cities more comparable. However, some significant differences remain. Some reflect differences among states in their criminal laws and crime reporting systems. Some reflect inherent differences among citizens in reporting crime that are in turn related to differences in perceptions of whether law enforcement authorities will be able to solve the crimes. Small thefts, for example, are often not reported in large cities but are commonly reported in some smaller communities.

J-2 Violent Crime Rate, 1995: Crimes fall into two major classes. Some, such as murder and assault, involve violence or the threat of violence. Others, such as auto theft and burglary, do not. This table, from the same source as Table J-1, shows the rates for all violent crimes combined.

J-3 Murder and Rape Rates, 1995: This table, from the same source as Table J-1, shows the rates for two specific crimes.

J-4 Property Crime, 1995: This table, from the same source as Table J-1, shows the rates for crimes against property, such as burglary and auto theft.

J-5 Motor Vehicle Theft Rate, 1995: This table combines auto theft with theft of other vehicles, such as pickup trucks, using the same source as Table J-1.

J-6 Violent Crime Rate Change, 1990-1995: Although there have recently been signs that the crime rate is decreasing, there was a nationwide increase in the crime rate (crimes per 100,000 people) from 1990 to 1995. The data come from the 1990 and 1995 editions of *Crime in the United States.*

J-7 Prisoners, 1996: This table shows the total number of prisoners held in state penal institutions at the end of 1996. These data are developed by the Department of Justice from statistical reports of state and federal corrections agencies. The data shown come from the Department's website (http://www.ojp.usdoj.gov). They reflect state prisoners only. Federal prisoners constitute about 9 percent of all prisoners. The count of total state prisoners covers only those sentenced for more than a year and thus excludes persons who are being held for short periods in local jails.

J-8 Change in Prisoners, 1991-1996: This table, from the same source as Table J-7, shows the percentage change in the number of prisoners, reflecting an increase of about 43 percent over this five-year period. States shown as not having data available did know how many prisoners they had, but the Department of Justice concluded that changes in methods of counting between 1991 and 1996 made comparisons inappropriate.

J-9 Incarceration Rate, 1996: This table measures the relationship between state prison populations (see Table J-7) and total population. While the national rate is equivalent to having 0.4 percent of the population in prison, the percentages are much higher for certain age and ethnic groups and for males.

J-10 Juvenile Violent Crime Index, 1995: This table is from the February 1997 issue of *Juvenile Justice Bulletin*, a publication of the Office of Juvenile Justice and Delinquency Prevention of the U.S. Department of Justice. It reflects the number of violent crime arrests during 1995 of youths between the ages of ten and seventeen per 100,000 youths in the population of each state.

J-11 Proportion of Sentence Served, 1994: Because of parole and time off for good behavior, violent offenders typically serve only about half of the time they are sentenced to serve. These statistics, not available for all states, show the proportion of time served based on data reported in the Department of Justice publication *Violent Offenders in State Prison: Sentences and Time Served*. The United States total reflects only the states participating in the survey. The states with high percentages are not necessarily the toughest on criminals. They may have shorter sentences but force prisoners to serve a longer percentage of their sentences.

J-12 State and Local Law Enforcement Employees, 1995: This statistic comes from a Census Bureau survey of state and local government employment, *Public Employment in 1995*. It is available only on the Census Bureau website (http://www.census.gov).

J-13 State and Local Corrections Employees, 1995: This statistic comes from the same source as Table J-12.

J-14 Average Cost Per Inmate-Day, 1996: These estimates of daily costs of keeping an inmate in prison for a day were developed by the Criminal Justice Institute, Inc. (South Salem, New York 10590) for its publication *The Corrections Yearbook 1996*. The data are reprinted with the permission of the Institute. Copies or other use of the data in this table may not be made without the written permission of the Institute. This table is reprinted from the 1997 version of State Fact Finder. The Criminal Justice Institute will provide more recent estimates for a fee.

These data primarily reflect variable costs of holding an inmate, such as food, clothing, and health care, as well as categories of operating costs known to the corrections agencies that supply the data. These include, for example, the salaries of prison guards. However, the data understate substantially the full costs, which include constructing and rehabilitating prisons as well as operating them and certain overhead costs often not included in corrections agency budgets (insurance, employee retirement benefits, and central operations, such as personnel and purchasing management).

J-15 State Corrections Spending, FY 1996: These data provide another approach to the costs of maintaining prison systems in each state. The total spending shown is the general fund spending reported by state budget offices in the National Association of State Budget Officers' *1996 State Expenditure Report*. These general fund data showing about $22.4 billion for the 50 states exclude about $3.3 billion financed outside state general funds, primarily by bond funds used to finance prison construction.

The per-inmate spending is the result of dividing the spending in fiscal 1996 by the number of inmates in prison at the end of 1996.

The resulting calculation is somewhat arbitrary as it does not separately account for the supervision of inmates on parole, which is another major function of corrections agencies not associated directly with inmates in prison. However, it provides a useful contrast with the comparisons shown in Table J-14.

J-16 Percent Increase in State Corrections Spending, 1994-1996: These data, from the same source as Table J-15, reflect the major impact that growing prison populations are having on state government budgets. Large deviations from one year to the next are often associated with large one-time expenditures for capital outlays in one of the years being compared. *State Fact Finder* has accounted for this by comparing spending over a two year interval.

J-17 State and Local Spending for Law Enforcement, FY 1994: This table relates spending on police and corrections to population in each state. The spending data come from the Census Bureau web site (http://www.census.gov, "State and Local Government Finance Estimates, by State"). The population numbers are from the Census Bureau and are as of July 1, 1994.

J-18 State and Local Law Enforcement Spending as Percent of General Spending, FY 1994: This table shows the relative importance of law enforcement outlays in state and local budgets. It is derived by comparing this spending (see Table J-17) with total "general" spending. General spending includes essentially all other spending except municipal electric and other utilities and trust funds, such as those for Workers' Compensation.

Transportation

K-1 TRAVEL ON INTERSTATE HIGHWAYS, 1996

State	Annual vehicle-miles interstate (millions)	Percent of travel on interstates %	Rank by %	Rank in order By %
Alabama	10,111	19.7	42	1. Utah
Alaska	1,277	31.0	3	2. Wyoming
Arizona	9,762	23.2	26	3. Alaska
Arkansas	5,803	20.8	36	4. Connecticut
California	70,868	25.5	19	5. Maryland
Colorado	9,032	25.0	20	6. Illinois
Connecticut	8,642	30.7	4	7. Virginia
Delaware	1,273	16.6	50	8. Rhode Island
Florida	25,610	19.7	41	9. New Mexico
Georgia	23,384	26.2	17	10. Massachusetts
Hawaii	1,583	19.7	40	11. Tennessee
Idaho	2,729	21.1	35	12. Washington
Illinois	27,200	28.1	6	13. Missouri
Indiana	14,495	21.9	31	14. West Virginia
Iowa	5,967	22.2	29	15. Nevada
Kansas	5,584	21.5	32	16. Ohio
Kentucky	10,521	24.7	23	17. Georgia
Louisiana	9,191	24.1	25	18. South Dakota
Maine	2,395	18.7	46	19. California
Maryland	13,726	29.7	5	20. Colorado
Massachusetts	13,662	27.3	10	21. South Carolina
Michigan	19,388	21.5	33	22. Oregon
Minnesota	10,241	23.0	27	23. Kentucky
Mississippi	5,526	18.1	48	24. Montana
Missouri	16,434	26.9	13	25. Louisiana
Montana	2,315	24.5	24	26. Arizona
Nebraska	3,098	19.1	43	27. Minnesota
Nevada	3,790	26.8	15	28. Texas
New Hampshire	2,345	21.3	34	29. Iowa
New Jersey	11,666	18.7	45	30. Vermont
New Mexico	5,934	27.6	9	31. Indiana
New York	21,467	18.1	47	32. Kansas
North Carolina	14,832	18.8	44	33. Michigan
North Dakota	1,380	20.5	39	34. New Hampshire
Ohio	27,595	26.8	16	35. Idaho
Oklahoma	8,199	20.8	37	36. Arkansas
Oregon	7,532	24.8	22	37. Oklahoma
Pennsylvania	19,804	20.5	38	38. Pennsylvania
Rhode Island	1,973	27.7	8	39. North Dakota
South Carolina	9,927	25.0	21	40. Hawaii
South Dakota	2,042	26.1	18	41. Florida
Tennessee	15,883	27.2	11	42. Alabama
Texas	42,111	22.7	28	43. Nebraska
Utah	6,945	35.5	1	44. North Carolina
Vermont	1,399	21.9	30	45. New Jersey
Virginia	19,913	27.9	7	46. Maine
Washington	13,422	27.2	12	47. New York
West Virginia	4,738	26.8	14	48. Mississippi
Wisconsin	8,873	16.8	49	49. Wisconsin
Wyoming	2,338	31.8	2	50. Delaware
50 States	583,925	23.6		
DC	459	13.8		
United States	584,384	23.5		

State	Interstate mileage in poor or mediocre condition %	Rank by %
Alabama	4.3	45
Alaska	56.4	7
Arizona	10.8	36
Arkansas	77.2	4
California	7.6	38
Colorado	47.4	12
Connecticut	57.4	6
Delaware	n/a	n/a
Florida	14.0	32
Georgia	0.0	48
Hawaii	n/a	n/a
Idaho	47.7	11
Illinois	16.1	29
Indiana	11.0	35
Iowa	5.0	42
Kansas	34.5	17
Kentucky	34.3	18
Louisiana	22.2	26
Maine	16.0	30
Maryland	25.1	25
Massachusetts	4.9	43
Michigan	44.0	13
Minnesota	78.9	3
Mississippi	93.0	1
Missouri	6.1	39
Montana	40.3	16
Nebraska	53.3	9
Nevada	4.3	46
New Hampshire	5.1	40
New Jersey	17.7	27
New Mexico	28.6	22
New York	15.5	31
North Carolina	28.0	23
North Dakota	33.0	19
Ohio	10.6	37
Oklahoma	13.6	33
Oregon	4.8	44
Pennsylvania	41.9	15
Rhode Island	28.6	21
South Carolina	17.5	28
South Dakota	60.7	5
Tennessee	11.6	34
Texas	53.7	8
Utah	5.1	41
Vermont	3.2	47
Virginia	25.4	24
Washington	43.7	14
West Virginia	52.0	10
Wisconsin	29.3	20
Wyoming	80.7	2
50 States	31.4	
DC	n/a	
United States	31.4	

By %

1. Mississippi
2. Wyoming
3. Minnesota
4. Arkansas
5. South Dakota
6. Connecticut
7. Alaska
8. Texas
9. Nebraska
10. West Virginia
11. Idaho
12. Colorado
13. Michigan
14. Washington
15. Pennsylvania
16. Montana
17. Kansas
18. Kentucky
19. North Dakota
20. Wisconsin
21. Rhode Island
22. New Mexico
23. North Carolina
24. Virginia
25. Maryland
26. Louisiana
27. New Jersey
28. South Carolina
29. Illinois
30. Maine
31. New York
32. Florida
33. Oklahoma
34. Tennessee
35. Indiana
36. Arizona
37. Ohio
38. California
39. Missouri
40. New Hampshire
41. Utah
42. Iowa
43. Massachusetts
44. Oregon
45. Alabama
46. Nevada
47. Vermont
48. Georgia

K-3 DEFICIENT BRIDGES, 1996

State	Total deficient bridges #	Percent of bridges deficient %	Rank by %
Alabama	2,182	27.8	19
Alaska	133	19.4	40
Arizona	458	9.2	49
Arkansas	1,501	19.5	39
California	4,332	26.5	25
Colorado	862	20.6	36
Connecticut	796	27.6	21
Delaware	118	22.0	32
Florida	1,854	25.1	28
Georgia	1,884	22.6	31
Hawaii	422	52.1	3
Idaho	388	20.3	37
Illinois	2,701	24.0	29
Indiana	1,548	20.1	38
Iowa	1,590	21.7	33
Kansas	2,024	18.2	42
Kentucky	1,578	29.8	15
Louisiana	2,035	32.0	14
Maine	445	34.6	9
Maryland	738	26.8	23
Massachusetts	2,234	58.4	2
Michigan	2,202	33.5	11
Minnesota	766	13.8	46
Mississippi	2,077	28.5	16
Missouri	3,079	33.6	10
Montana	542	21.5	34
Nebraska	713	13.6	47
Nevada	207	21.3	35
New Hampshire	331	27.7	20
New Jersey	1,879	41.3	6
New Mexico	399	14.7	45
New York	5,509	58.8	1
North Carolina	2,027	32.3	12
North Dakota	146	8.3	50
Ohio	3,099	25.8	27
Oklahoma	3,210	26.8	24
Oregon	1,159	26.9	22
Pennsylvania	4,641	40.5	7
Rhode Island	282	46.3	4
South Carolina	1,047	22.7	30
South Dakota	338	12.4	48
Tennessee	2,435	26.2	26
Texas	5,404	18.1	43
Utah	477	28.4	17
Vermont	492	37.2	8
Virginia	2,010	28.0	18
Washington	1,392	32.3	13
West Virginia	1,480	44.1	5
Wisconsin	1,273	18.7	41
Wyoming	342	17.6	44
50 States	78,781	26.5	
DC	118	58.7	
United States	79,542	26.6	

Rank in order

By %

1. New York
2. Massachusetts
3. Hawaii
4. Rhode Island
5. West Virginia
6. New Jersey
7. Pennsylvania
8. Vermont
9. Maine
10. Missouri
11. Michigan
12. North Carolina
13. Washington
14. Louisiana
15. Kentucky
16. Mississippi
17. Utah
18. Virginia
19. Alabama
20. New Hampshire
21. Connecticut
22. Oregon
23. Maryland
24. Oklahoma
25. California
26. Tennessee
27. Ohio
28. Florida
29. Illinois
30. South Carolina
31. Georgia
32. Delaware
33. Iowa
34. Montana
35. Nevada
36. Colorado
37. Idaho
38. Indiana
39. Arkansas
40. Alaska
41. Wisconsin
42. Kansas
43. Texas
44. Wyoming
45. New Mexico
46. Minnesota
47. Nebraska
48. South Dakota
49. Arizona
50. North Dakota

State	Traffic deaths rate	Rank
Alabama	2.22	18
Alaska	1.94	35
Arizona	2.36	17
Arkansas	2.21	35
California	1.43	46
Colorado	1.71	38
Connecticut	1.10	30
Delaware	1.51	13
Florida	2.12	9
Georgia	1.77	5
Hawaii	1.84	4
Idaho	1.99	49
Illinois	1.53	32
Indiana	1.49	26
Iowa	1.73	16
Kansas	1.89	39
Kentucky	1.97	45
Louisiana	2.05	20
Maine	1.32	40
Maryland	1.32	5
Massachusetts	0.83	43
Michigan	1.67	47
Minnesota	1.30	2
Mississippi	2.65	24
Missouri	1.88	9
Montana	2.12	22
Nebraska	1.80	1
Nevada	2.46	44
New Hampshire	1.22	29
New Jersey	1.31	50
New Mexico	2.24	40
New York	1.32	40
North Carolina	1.89	12
North Dakota	1.26	15
Ohio	1.35	20
Oklahoma	1.96	26
Oregon	1.73	34
Pennsylvania	1.52	31
Rhode Island	0.97	14
South Carolina	2.34	23
South Dakota	2.24	25
Tennessee	2.12	9
Texas	2.02	33
Utah	1.64	48
Vermont	1.38	28
Virginia	1.23	37
Washington	1.44	8
West Virginia	1.95	3
Wisconsin	1.44	18
Wyoming	1.94	7
50 States	n/a	
DC	1.87	
United States	1.69	

Rank in order

By rate

1. Mississippi
2. Nevada
3. Arizona
4. South Carolina
5. New Mexico
5. South Dakota
7. Alabama
8. Arkansas
9. Florida
9. Montana
9. Tennessee
12. Louisiana
13. Texas
14. Idaho
15. Kentucky
16. Oklahoma
17. West Virginia
18. Alaska
18. Wyoming
20. Kansas
20. North Carolina
22. Missouri
23. Hawaii
24. Nebraska
25. Georgia
26. Iowa
26. Oregon
28. Colorado
29. Michigan
30. Utah
31. Illinois
32. Pennsylvania
33. Delaware
34. Indiana
35. Washington
35. Wisconsin
37. California
38. Vermont
39. Ohio
40. Maine
40. Maryland
40. New York
43. New Jersey
44. Minnesota
45. North Dakota
46. Virginia
47. New Hampshire
48. Connecticut
49. Rhode Island
50. Massachusetts

K-5 PERCENT OF DRIVERS USING SEAT BELTS, 1997

State	Drivers using seatbelts %	Rank by %
Alabama	54	40
Alaska	69	17
Arizona	56	37
Arkansas	48	45
California	87	1
Colorado	56	37
Connecticut	62	26
Delaware	68	19
Florida	64	22
Georgia	62	26
Hawaii	80	6
Idaho	54	40
Illinois	64	22
Indiana	62	26
Iowa	75	7
Kansas	54	40
Kentucky	55	39
Louisiana	68	19
Maine	50	44
Maryland	70	15
Massachusetts	54	40
Michigan	71	12
Minnesota	64	22
Mississippi	46	48
Missouri	62	26
Montana	73	10
Nebraska	65	21
Nevada	71	12
New Hampshire	n/a	n/a
New Jersey	60	33
New Mexico	85	2
New York	74	8
North Carolina	82	4
North Dakota	43	49
Ohio	62	26
Oklahoma	48	45
Oregon	82	4
Pennsylvania	71	12
Rhode Island	58	35
South Carolina	61	31
South Dakota	47	47
Tennessee	63	25
Texas	74	8
Utah	60	33
Vermont	69	17
Virginia	70	15
Washington	84	3
West Virginia	58	35
Wisconsin	61	31
Wyoming	72	11
50 States	n/a	
DC	58	
United States	68	

Rank in order

By %

1. California
2. New Mexico
3. Washington
4. North Carolina
4. Oregon
6. Hawaii
7. Iowa
8. New York
8. Texas
10. Montana
11. Wyoming
12. Michigan
12. Nevada
12. Pennsylvania
15. Maryland
15. Virginia
17. Alaska
17. Vermont
19. Delaware
19. Louisiana
21. Nebraska
22. Florida
22. Illinois
22. Minnesota
25. Tennessee
26. Connecticut
26. Georgia
26. Indiana
26. Missouri
26. Ohio
31. South Carolina
31. Wisconsin
33. New Jersey
33. Utah
35. Rhode Island
35. West Virginia
37. Arizona
37. Colorado
39. Kentucky
40. Alabama
40. Idaho
40. Kansas
40. Massachusetts
44. Maine
45. Arkansas
45. Oklahoma
47. South Dakota
48. Mississippi
49. North Dakota

State	Vehicle-miles traveled (millions)	Vehicle-miles traveled per capita	Rank by per capita	By per capita
Alabama	51,433	12,037	4	1. Wyoming
Alaska	4,115	6,779	49	2. New Mexico
Arizona	42,123	9,513	29	3. Georgia
Arkansas	27,840	11,093	9	4. Alabama
California	278,043	8,722	41	5. Oklahoma
Colorado	36,141	9,454	31	6. Missouri
Connecticut	28,135	8,593	42	7. Indiana
Delaware	7,666	10,576	19	8. Mississippi
Florida	130,004	9,028	37	9. Arkansas
Georgia	89,132	12,121	3	10. Tennessee
Hawaii	8,030	6,784	48	11. Kentucky
Idaho	12,961	10,898	12	12. Idaho
Illinois	96,730	8,165	44	13. Vermont
Indiana	66,220	11,338	7	14. North Carolina
Iowa	26,880	9,426	33	15. South Carolina
Kansas	25,942	10,086	23	16. Montana
Kentucky	42,586	10,965	11	17. Virginia
Louisiana	38,095	8,756	40	18. South Dakota
Maine	12,819	10,310	21	19. Delaware
Maryland	46,187	9,107	36	20. North Dakota
Massachusetts	49,956	8,200	43	21. Maine
Michigan	90,215	9,403	34	22. Wisconsin
Minnesota	44,465	9,546	28	23. Kansas
Mississippi	30,562	11,252	8	24. Nebraska
Missouri	61,162	11,414	6	25. Utah
Montana	9,446	10,742	16	26. Texas
Nebraska	16,238	9,829	24	27. West Virginia
Nevada	14,158	8,831	39	28. Minnesota
New Hampshire	10,987	9,451	32	29. Arizona
New Jersey	62,334	7,804	46	30. Oregon
New Mexico	21,510	12,554	2	31. Colorado
New York	118,641	6,524	50	32. New Hampshire
North Carolina	78,935	10,779	14	33. Iowa
North Dakota	6,741	10,475	20	34. Michigan
Ohio	103,090	9,227	35	35. Ohio
Oklahoma	39,427	11,944	5	36. Maryland
Oregon	30,319	9,464	30	37. Florida
Pennsylvania	96,646	8,016	45	38. Washington
Rhode Island	7,120	7,190	47	39. Nevada
South Carolina	39,756	10,749	15	40. Louisiana
South Dakota	7,817	10,673	18	41. California
Tennessee	58,435	10,985	10	42. Connecticut
Texas	185,386	9,692	26	43. Massachusetts
Utah	19,539	9,767	25	44. Illinois
Vermont	6,377	10,833	13	45. Pennsylvania
Virginia	71,302	10,681	17	46. New Jersey
Washington	49,405	8,929	38	47. Rhode Island
West Virginia	17,693	9,691	27	48. Hawaii
Wisconsin	52,782	10,229	22	49. Alaska
Wyoming	7,360	15,289	1	50. New York
50 States	2,478,886	9,363		
DC	3,316	6,104		
United States	2,482,202	9,357		

State	Workers using public transportation %	Rank by %
Alabama	0.8	41
Alaska	2.4	21
Arizona	2.1	25
Arkansas	0.5	49
California	4.9	8
Colorado	2.9	15
Connecticut	3.9	11
Delaware	2.4	21
Florida	2.0	26
Georgia	2.8	16
Hawaii	7.4	6
Idaho	1.9	28
Illinois	10.1	2
Indiana	1.3	32
Iowa	1.2	34
Kansas	0.7	43
Kentucky	1.6	29
Louisiana	3.0	14
Maine	0.9	40
Maryland	8.1	5
Massachusetts	8.3	4
Michigan	1.6	29
Minnesota	3.6	12
Mississippi	0.8	41
Missouri	2.0	26
Montana	0.6	46
Nebraska	1.2	34
Nevada	2.7	17
New Hampshire	0.7	43
New Jersey	8.8	3
New Mexico	1.0	38
New York	24.8	1
North Carolina	1.0	38
North Dakota	0.6	46
Ohio	2.5	18
Oklahoma	0.6	46
Oregon	3.4	13
Pennsylvania	6.4	7
Rhode Island	2.5	18
South Carolina	1.1	36
South Dakota	0.3	50
Tennessee	1.3	32
Texas	2.2	24
Utah	2.3	23
Vermont	0.7	43
Virginia	4.0	10
Washington	4.5	9
West Virginia	1.1	36
Wisconsin	2.5	18
Wyoming	1.4	31
50 States	3.1	
DC	36.6	
United States	5.3	

Rank in order

By %

1. New York
2. Illinois
3. New Jersey
4. Massachusetts
5. Maryland
6. Hawaii
7. Pennsylvania
8. California
9. Washington
10. Virginia
11. Connecticut
12. Minnesota
13. Oregon
14. Louisiana
15. Colorado
16. Georgia
17. Nevada
18. Ohio
18. Rhode Island
18. Wisconsin
21. Alaska
21. Delaware
23. Utah
24. Texas
25. Arizona
26. Florida
26. Missouri
28. Idaho
29. Kentucky
29. Michigan
31. Wyoming
32. Indiana
32. Tennessee
34. Iowa
34. Nebraska
36. South Carolina
36. West Virginia
38. New Mexico
38. North Carolina
40. Maine
41. Alabama
41. Mississippi
43. Kansas
43. New Hampshire
43. Vermont
46. Montana
46. North Dakota
46. Oklahoma
49. Arkansas
50. South Dakota

K-8 ROAD AND STREET MILES, 1996

State	Total road & street miles #	Total miles under state control #	Percent under state control %	Rank
Alabama	93,340	11,012	11.8	32
Alaska	13,255	6,089	45.9	6
Arizona	54,895	6,143	11.2	36
Arkansas	77,746	16,294	21.0	16
California	170,506	18,252	10.7	40
Colorado	84,797	9,237	10.9	38
Connecticut	20,600	3,977	19.3	20
Delaware	5,715	5,045	88.3	2
Florida	114,422	11,925	10.4	41
Georgia	111,746	17,917	16.0	25
Hawaii	4,142	1,135	27.4	11
Idaho	59,674	5,106	8.6	47
Illinois	137,577	17,134	12.5	30
Indiana	92,970	11,293	12.1	31
Iowa	112,708	10,117	9.0	46
Kansas	133,386	10,659	8.0	50
Kentucky	73,158	27,498	37.6	8
Louisiana	60,667	16,675	27.5	10
Maine	22,577	8,533	37.8	7
Maryland	29,680	5,410	18.2	22
Massachusetts	34,725	3,609	10.4	42
Michigan	117,620	9,622	8.2	49
Minnesota	130,613	13,274	10.2	43
Mississippi	73,202	10,688	14.6	26
Missouri	122,748	32,385	26.4	14
Montana	69,809	8,185	11.7	33
Nebraska	92,805	10,282	11.1	37
Nevada	45,039	5,270	11.7	34
New Hampshire	15,106	4,017	26.6	12
New Jersey	35,924	3,289	9.2	45
New Mexico	59,455	11,552	19.4	19
New York	112,347	16,321	14.5	27
North Carolina	97,509	78,400	80.4	4
North Dakota	86,808	7,399	8.5	48
Ohio	114,642	20,518	17.9	23
Oklahoma	112,664	13,104	11.6	35
Oregon	83,190	11,095	13.3	29
Pennsylvania	118,952	44,148	37.1	9
Rhode Island	6,001	1,156	19.3	21
South Carolina	64,359	41,692	64.8	5
South Dakota	83,375	7,874	9.4	44
Tennessee	85,795	14,056	16.4	24
Texas	296,259	78,628	26.5	13
Utah	41,718	5,795	13.9	28
Vermont	14,192	2,839	20.0	17
Virginia	69,384	57,128	82.3	3
Washington	79,555	18,932	23.8	15
West Virginia	35,130	32,151	91.5	1
Wisconsin	111,435	12,021	10.8	39
Wyoming	34,115	6,809	20.0	18
50 States	3,918,037	801,690	20.5	
DC	1,413	1,371	97.0	
United States	3,919,450	803,061	20.5	

Rank in order

By %

1. West Virginia
2. Delaware
3. Virginia
4. North Carolina
5. South Carolina
6. Alaska
7. Maine
8. Kentucky
9. Pennsylvania
10. Louisiana
11. Hawaii
12. New Hampshire
13. Texas
14. Missouri
15. Washington
16. Arkansas
17. Vermont
18. Wyoming
19. New Mexico
20. Connecticut
21. Rhode Island
22. Maryland
23. Ohio
24. Tennessee
25. Georgia
26. Mississippi
27. New York
28. Utah
29. Oregon
30. Illinois
31. Indiana
32. Alabama
33. Montana
34. Nevada
35. Oklahoma
36. Arizona
37. Nebraska
38. Colorado
39. Wisconsin
40. California
41. Florida
42. Massachusetts
43. Minnesota
44. South Dakota
45. New Jersey
46. Iowa
47. Idaho
48. North Dakota
49. Michigan
50. Kansas

K-9 STATE AND LOCAL HIGHWAY EMPLOYEES, 1995

State	Highway employees	Per 10,000 population	Rank by per 10,000	Rank in order By per 10,000
Alabama	10,874	25.6	20	1. Alaska
Alaska	3,724	61.8	1	2. Wyoming
Arizona	6,904	16.0	47	3. South Dakota
Arkansas	7,232	29.1	14	4. West Virginia
California	38,877	12.3	50	5. Kansas
Colorado	8,356	22.3	29	6. Vermont
Connecticut	7,808	23.9	24	7. Montana
Delaware	2,111	29.4	13	8. Maine
Florida	24,143	17.0	45	9. Nebraska
Georgia	13,870	19.2	38	10. North Dakota
Hawaii	1,799	15.3	48	11. Mississippi
Idaho	3,364	28.8	16	12. Oklahoma
Illinois	19,951	16.9	46	13. Delaware
Indiana	10,926	18.8	40	14. Arkansas
Iowa	8,206	28.9	15	15. Iowa
Kansas	9,357	36.5	5	16. Idaho
Kentucky	8,452	21.9	31	17. New Hampshire
Louisiana	10,511	24.2	22	18. Minnesota
Maine	4,351	35.1	8	19. New Mexico
Maryland	9,666	19.2	39	20. Alabama
Massachusetts	10,445	17.2	43	21. New York
Michigan	13,921	14.6	49	22. Louisiana
Minnesota	12,395	26.9	18	23. Virginia
Mississippi	8,726	32.4	11	24. Connecticut
Missouri	11,961	22.5	28	25. Washington
Montana	3,105	35.7	7	26. New Jersey
Nebraska	5,473	33.4	9	27. Oregon
Nevada	2,747	17.9	41	28. Missouri
New Hampshire	3,308	28.8	17	29. Colorado
New Jersey	18,761	23.6	26	30. North Carolina
New Mexico	4,347	25.7	19	31. Kentucky
New York	44,185	24.3	21	32. Wisconsin
North Carolina	15,966	22.2	30	33. Tennessee
North Dakota	2,096	32.7	10	34. South Carolina
Ohio	21,921	19.7	36	35. Pennsylvania
Oklahoma	9,661	29.5	12	36. Ohio
Oregon	7,426	23.6	27	37. Rhode Island
Pennsylvania	24,237	20.1	35	38. Georgia
Rhode Island	1,917	19.3	37	39. Maryland
South Carolina	7,429	20.3	34	40. Indiana
South Dakota	2,810	38.5	3	41. Nevada
Tennessee	11,388	21.7	33	42. Texas
Texas	32,902	17.5	42	43. Massachusetts
Utah	3,351	17.1	44	44. Utah
Vermont	2,089	35.7	6	45. Florida
Virginia	15,974	24.1	23	46. Illinois
Washington	12,894	23.7	25	47. Arizona
West Virginia	6,862	37.6	4	48. Hawaii
Wisconsin	11,144	21.8	32	49. Michigan
Wyoming	2,434	50.8	2	50. California
50 States	542,357	20.7		
DC	786	14.2		
United States	543,143	20.7		

K-10 STATE AND LOCAL PUBLIC TRANSIT EMPLOYEES, 1995

State	Transit employees	Per 10,000 employees	Rank by per 10,000		By per 10,000
Alabama	379	0.9	37		1. New York
Alaska	819	13.6	4		2. Washington
Arizona	110	0.3	49		3. Illinois
Arkansas	195	0.8	39		4. Alaska
California	29,453	9.3	7		5. Pennsylvania
Colorado	2,443	6.5	9		6. Massachusetts
Connecticut	448	1.4	32		7. California
Delaware	467	6.5	10		8. Oregon
Florida	5,927	4.2	21		9. Colorado
Georgia	4,407	6.1	11		10. Delaware
Hawaii	91	0.8	40		11. Georgia
Idaho	23	0.2	50		12. Utah
Illinois	16,726	14.2	3		13. Maryland
Indiana	1,372	2.4	24		14. Ohio
Iowa	665	2.3	25		15. Rhode Island
Kansas	208	0.8	38		16. Missouri
Kentucky	852	2.2	26		17. Minnesota
Louisiana	330	0.8	41		18. Texas
Maine	92	0.7	42		19. Wisconsin
Maryland	2,979	5.9	13		20. Michigan
Massachusetts	6,412	10.6	6		21. Florida
Michigan	4,139	4.3	20		22. New Mexico
Minnesota	2,377	5.2	17		23. Nebraska
Mississippi	131	0.5	47		24. Indiana
Missouri	2,788	5.2	16		25. Iowa
Montana	132	1.5	30		26. Kentucky
Nebraska	402	2.5	23		27. West Virginia
Nevada	92	0.6	46		28. Virginia
New Hampshire	104	0.9	35		29. Vermont
New Jersey	924	1.2	33		30. Montana
New Mexico	535	3.2	22		31. Oklahoma
New York	60,354	33.2	1		32. Connecticut
North Carolina	651	0.9	36		33. New Jersey
North Dakota	41	0.6	44		34. South Carolina
Ohio	6,175	5.5	14		35. New Hampshire
Oklahoma	470	1.4	31		36. North Carolina
Oregon	2,567	8.2	8		37. Alabama
Pennsylvania	12,873	10.7	5		38. Kansas
Rhode Island	538	5.4	15		39. Arkansas
South Carolina	407	1.1	34		40. Hawaii
South Dakota	25	0.3	48		41. Louisiana
Tennessee	331	0.6	45		42. Maine
Texas	9,379	5.0	18		43. Wyoming
Utah	1,160	5.9	12		44. North Dakota
Vermont	94	1.6	29		45. Tennessee
Virginia	1,362	2.1	28		46. Nevada
Washington	13,757	25.3	2		47. Mississippi
West Virginia	389	2.1	27		48. South Dakota
Wisconsin	2,478	4.8	19		49. Arizona
Wyoming	34	0.7	43		50. Idaho
50 States	199,107	7.6			
DC	8,313	149.9			
United States	207,420	7.9			

K-11 STATE AND LOCAL SPENDING FOR HIGHWAYS, FY 1994

State	Highway spending $(millions)	Per capita $	As percent of personal income %	Rank by per capita	By per capita
Alabama	1,132	268	1.58	33	1. Alaska
Alaska	649	1,072	4.71	1	2. Wyoming
Arizona	1,089	267	1.53	34	3. New Mexico
Arkansas	690	281	1.78	29	4. South Dakota
California	6,175	196	0.90	49	5. Vermont
Colorado	1,127	308	1.47	25	6. North Dakota
Connecticut	1,069	326	1.17	19	7. Montana
Delaware	297	421	1.95	10	8. Iowa
Florida	3,949	283	1.39	28	9. Kansas
Georgia	1,526	216	1.15	48	10. Delaware
Hawaii	430	365	1.57	15	11. Nevada
Idaho	372	329	1.93	18	12. West Virginia
Illinois	3,444	293	1.31	26	13. Nebraska
Indiana	1,335	232	1.22	45	14. Minnesota
Iowa	1,228	434	2.38	8	15. Hawaii
Kansas	1,094	428	2.18	9	16. Wisconsin
Kentucky	984	257	1.53	39	17. Washington
Louisiana	1,166	270	1.64	31	18. Idaho
Maine	395	319	1.70	20	19. Connecticut
Maryland	1,142	228	0.96	46	20. Maine
Massachusetts	1,902	315	1.29	21	21. Massachusetts
Michigan	2,156	227	1.11	47	22. New York
Minnesota	1,716	376	1.81	14	23. New Jersey
Mississippi	730	273	1.88	30	24. Oregon
Missouri	1,412	266	1.38	35	25. Colorado
Montana	378	442	2.59	7	26. Illinois
Nebraska	641	395	2.02	13	27. Virginia
Nevada	593	407	1.88	11	28. Florida
New Hampshire	306	269	1.23	32	29. Arkansas
New Jersey	2,444	309	1.16	23	30. Mississippi
New Mexico	897	542	3.40	3	31. Louisiana
New York	5,690	313	1.26	22	32. New Hampshire
North Carolina	1,834	259	1.41	38	33. Alabama
North Dakota	294	460	2.70	6	34. Arizona
Ohio	2,650	239	1.22	43	35. Missouri
Oklahoma	785	241	1.43	42	36. Utah
Oregon	954	309	1.62	24	37. Rhode Island
Pennsylvania	2,829	235	1.11	44	38. North Carolina
Rhode Island	259	260	1.22	37	39. Kentucky
South Carolina	711	194	1.16	50	40. Tennessee
South Dakota	371	515	2.89	4	41. Texas
Tennessee	1,293	250	1.38	40	42. Oklahoma
Texas	4,490	244	1.30	41	43. Ohio
Utah	497	260	1.65	36	44. Pennsylvania
Vermont	267	461	2.39	5	45. Indiana
Virginia	1,873	286	1.34	27	46. Maryland
Washington	1,810	339	1.58	17	47. Michigan
West Virginia	740	406	2.52	12	48. Georgia
Wisconsin	1,784	351	1.79	16	49. California
Wyoming	309	650	3.33	2	50. South Carolina
50 States	71,909	277	1.35		
DC	158	277	0.92		
United States	72,067	277	1.34		

K-12 STATE & LOCAL HIGHWAY SPENDING AS % OF GENERAL SPENDING, FY 1994

State	Highway spending as percent of general spending %	Rank by %
Alabama	7.66	24
Alaska	10.54	10
Arizona	7.24	32
Arkansas	9.26	15
California	4.46	50
Colorado	7.51	27
Connecticut	6.42	39
Delaware	9.39	14
Florida	7.57	25
Georgia	5.85	44
Hawaii	6.47	38
Idaho	9.88	12
Illinois	7.77	22
Indiana	6.27	42
Iowa	10.99	8
Kansas	11.26	6
Kentucky	7.74	23
Louisiana	6.92	35
Maine	8.03	19
Maryland	5.83	45
Massachusetts	6.76	37
Michigan	5.48	47
Minnesota	7.77	21
Mississippi	8.46	17
Missouri	8.75	16
Montana	11.47	4
Nebraska	10.28	11
Nevada	9.44	13
New Hampshire	6.89	36
New Jersey	6.41	40
New Mexico	13.00	2
New York	5.02	49
North Carolina	7.36	31
North Dakota	11.36	5
Ohio	6.30	41
Oklahoma	7.42	29
Oregon	7.40	30
Pennsylvania	6.04	43
Rhode Island	5.71	46
South Carolina	5.14	48
South Dakota	13.94	1
Tennessee	7.51	26
Texas	7.03	34
Utah	7.20	33
Vermont	11.03	7
Virginia	7.97	20
Washington	7.48	28
West Virginia	10.80	9
Wisconsin	8.13	18
Wyoming	12.17	3
50 States	6.72	
DC	3.45	
United States	6.71	

Rank in order

By %

1. South Dakota
2. New Mexico
3. Wyoming
4. Montana
5. North Dakota
6. Kansas
7. Vermont
8. Iowa
9. West Virginia
10. Alaska
11. Nebraska
12. Idaho
13. Nevada
14. Delaware
15. Arkansas
16. Missouri
17. Mississippi
18. Wisconsin
19. Maine
20. Virginia
21. Minnesota
22. Illinois
23. Kentucky
24. Alabama
25. Florida
26. Tennessee
27. Colorado
28. Washington
29. Oklahoma
30. Oregon
31. North Carolina
32. Arizona
33. Utah
34. Texas
35. Louisiana
36. New Hampshire
37. Massachusetts
38. Hawaii
39. Connecticut
40. New Jersey
41. Ohio
42. Indiana
43. Pennsylvania
44. Georgia
45. Maryland
46. Rhode Island
47. Michigan
48. South Carolina
49. New York
50. California

Source Notes for Transportation (Section K)

K-1 Travel on Interstate Highways, 1996: Use of highways is measured by vehicle-miles (travel by one vehicle for one mile). By this measure, interstate highways account for nearly one-fourth of the nation's highway travel, according to calculations based on the U.S. Department of Transportation's 1996 *Highway Statistics*. The federal government provides 90 percent of the money used to build interstates, but lower percentages for other highways. Having a large percentage of travel on interstates is good fiscal news as well as an indication of highway quality.

K-2 Percent of Mileage on Interstates in Poor or Mediocre Condition, 1993: The Federal Highway Administration (FHwA) and the states, which are responsible for highway maintenance, maintain a rating system for interstate highways. This table, from *1993 Highway Statistics*, shows the percentage of interstates in the worst two categories of conditions. As of the end of 1997 the FHwA has not updated this statistic.

K-3 Deficient Bridges, 1996: This table shows the total number of deficient bridges on major highways in each state. Details appear in the complete inventory, *The Status of the Nation's Highway Bridges*, published by the Department of Transportation in 1996. Bridges can be classified as deficient as a result of deterioration, poor maintenance, or by original design (for example, too narrow for modern traffic).

K-4 Traffic Deaths Per 100 Million Vehicle Miles, 1996: Relating deaths to total miles traveled is a common way of measuring the safety of highways. Many factors could affect the totals, including weather conditions, highway designs, congestion, and traffic law enforcement by the states. The figures come from the Department of Transportation (see notes to Table K-1).

K-5 Percentage of Drivers Using Seat Belts, 1997: These data come from periodic checks of safety belt usage, as reported by the Department of Transportation. *State Fact Finder* received the information from an unpublished tabulation furnished by the National Highway Traffic Safety Administration on September 17, 1997.

K-6 Vehicle-Miles Traveled Per Capita, 1996: Vehicle-miles of travel, as reported by the U.S. Department of Transportation in *1996 Highway Statistics*, show the intensity of use of state highway systems. Vehicle miles per capita show that the average American travels over 9,000 miles a year. Short distances between homes, shopping, and offices plus mass transit make usage lowest in northern urban areas.

K-7 Percent of Workers Using Public Transportation, 1990: This table shows the percentage of workers who used public transportation systems for their journey to work in 1990. The data come from questions about transportation usage from the 1990 Census, so the next update will not come until the next Census is taken in the year 2000.

K-8 Road and Street Miles, 1996: These data, from the same source as Table K-1, reflect total road and street (as distinct from highway) miles. They show the percentage of these miles that are controlled and maintained by state governments. Some states, such as Delaware and Virginia, maintain many local service roads that are controlled and maintained by counties and municipalities in other states.

K-9 State and Local Highway Employees, 1995: This statistic comes from a Census Bureau survey of state and local government employment, *Public Employment in 1995*. It is available on the Internet at the Census Bureau website (http://www.census.gov). It shows the higher levels of employees, and thus costs, associated with maintaining highways in rural states.

K-10 State and Local Public Transit Employees, 1995: This statistic, from the same source as Table K-9, shows the higher levels of employees, and thus costs, associated with transit in urbanized states.

K-11 State and Local Spending for Highways, FY 1994: This table relates spending data to population and personal income in each state. The spending data, which cover local streets as well as state highways, come from the Census Bureau web site (http://www.census.gov, *State and Local Government Finance Estimates, by State*). Population numbers are from the Census Bureau and are as of July 1, 1994 and personal income numbers for CY 1993 are from the Department of Commerce (see notes to Table F-1).

K-12 State and Local Highway Spending as Percent of General Spending, FY 1994: This table shows the relative importance of highway outlays in state and local budgets. It is derived by comparing highway spending with total "general" spending (see notes to Table K-11). General spending includes essentially all other spending excepting municipal electric and other utilities and trust funds, such as those for Workers' Compensation.

Welfare

State	Percent of births %	Rank by %
Alabama	33.5	14
Alaska	31.3	25
Arizona	39.0	5
Arkansas	33.9	11
California	31.6	23
Colorado	24.8	45
Connecticut	31.3	25
Delaware	35.5	9
Florida	36.0	8
Georgia	35.0	10
Hawaii	30.2	29
Idaho	21.3	49
Illinois	33.7	13
Indiana	32.6	20
Iowa	26.3	42
Kansas	26.9	40
Kentucky	29.8	30
Louisiana	43.4	2
Maine	28.7	34
Maryland	33.4	15
Massachusetts	25.6	43
Michigan	33.8	12
Minnesota	24.4	47
Mississippi	45.1	1
Missouri	33.1	17
Montana	27.8	36
Nebraska	24.7	46
Nevada	42.7	3
New Hampshire	23.4	48
New Jersey	27.9	35
New Mexico	42.1	4
New York	38.8	6
North Carolina	32.0	22
North Dakota	25.2	44
Ohio	32.9	18
Oklahoma	30.9	27
Oregon	29.7	31
Pennsylvania	32.3	21
Rhode Island	32.9	18
South Carolina	37.2	7
South Dakota	29.5	32
Tennessee	33.4	15
Texas	30.5	28
Utah	16.0	50
Vermont	26.4	41
Virginia	28.8	33
Washington	27.3	38
West Virginia	31.4	24
Wisconsin	27.4	37
Wyoming	27.0	39
50 States	n/a	
DC	66.0	
United States	32.4	

Rank in order

By %

1. Mississippi
2. Louisiana
3. Nevada
4. New Mexico
5. Arizona
6. New York
7. South Carolina
8. Florida
9. Delaware
10. Georgia
11. Arkansas
12. Michigan
13. Illinois
14. Alabama
15. Maryland
15. Tennessee
17. Missouri
18. Ohio
18. Rhode Island
20. Indiana
21. Pennsylvania
22. North Carolina
23. California
24. West Virginia
25. Alaska
25. Connecticut
27. Oklahoma
28. Texas
29. Hawaii
30. Kentucky
31. Oregon
32. South Dakota
33. Virginia
34. Maine
35. New Jersey
36. Montana
37. Wisconsin
38. Washington
39. Wyoming
40. Kansas
41. Vermont
42. Iowa
43. Massachusetts
44. North Dakota
45. Colorado
46. Nebraska
47. Minnesota
48. New Hampshire
49. Idaho
50. Utah

State	Average monthly number of recipients #	Recipients as percent of population %	Rank by %	Rank in order By %
Alabama	105,204	2.5	41	1. California
Alaska	36,192	6.0	3	2. New York
Arizona	171,533	3.9	25	3. Alaska
Arkansas	58,166	2.3	45	4. New Mexico
California	2,625,833	8.2	1	5. Rhode Island
Colorado	98,525	2.6	39	6. Hawaii
Connecticut	161,733	4.9	11	7. Illinois
Delaware	23,367	3.2	32	8. Michigan
Florida	560,561	3.9	23	9. West Virginia
Georgia	352,607	4.8	14	10. Washington
Hawaii	66,539	5.6	6	11. Connecticut
Idaho	22,926	1.9	50	12. Tennessee
Illinois	655,396	5.5	7	13. Ohio
Indiana	147,995	2.5	40	14. Georgia
Iowa	89,208	3.1	35	15. Mississippi
Kansas	68,497	2.7	38	16. Pennsylvania
Kentucky	174,882	4.5	17	17. Kentucky
Louisiana	235,551	4.0	22	18. Maine
Maine	55,878	4.5	18	19. Missouri
Maryland	204,105	4.0	21	20. Vermont
Massachusetts	236,842	3.9	24	21. Maryland
Michigan	527,110	5.5	8	22. Louisiana
Minnesota	171,109	3.7	27	23. Florida
Mississippi	129,052	4.8	15	24. Massachusetts
Missouri	231,891	4.3	19	25. Arizona
Montana	31,192	3.5	30	26. North Carolina
Nebraska	38,724	2.3	43	27. Minnesota
Nevada	37,561	2.3	44	28. New Jersey
New Hampshire	24,200	2.1	48	29. Texas
New Jersey	288,486	3.6	28	30. Montana
New Mexico	101,123	5.9	4	31. Wisconsin
New York	1,188,532	6.5	2	32. Delaware
North Carolina	277,841	3.8	26	33. South Carolina
North Dakota	13,399	2.1	47	34. Oklahoma
Ohio	545,918	4.9	13	35. Iowa
Oklahoma	104,845	3.2	34	36. Oregon
Oregon	86,940	2.7	36	37. Wyoming
Pennsylvania	543,502	4.5	16	38. Kansas
Rhode Island	58,397	5.9	5	39. Colorado
South Carolina	119,184	3.2	33	40. Indiana
South Dakota	16,282	2.2	46	41. Alabama
Tennessee	260,257	4.9	12	42. Virginia
Texas	684,020	3.6	29	43. Nebraska
Utah	40,330	2.0	49	44. Nevada
Vermont	25,294	4.3	20	45. Arkansas
Virginia	161,928	2.4	42	46. South Dakota
Washington	274,160	5.0	10	47. North Dakota
West Virginia	95,085	5.2	9	48. New Hampshire
Wisconsin	170,224	3.3	31	49. Utah
Wyoming	12,839	2.7	37	50. Idaho
50 States	12,410,965	4.7		
DC	70,201	12.9		
United States	12,648,859	4.8		

State	Food stamp recipients $	Recipients as percent of population %	Rank by %	Rank in order By %
Alabama	509,214	11.9	8	1. Mississippi
Alaska	46,233	7.6	32	2. West Virginia
Arizona	427,481	9.7	19	3. Louisiana
Arkansas	273,900	10.9	11	4. New Mexico
California	3,143,390	9.9	16	5. Texas
Colorado	243,692	6.4	41	6. Kentucky
Connecticut	222,758	6.8	35	7. Tennessee
Delaware	57,836	8.0	31	8. Alabama
Florida	1,371,352	9.5	21	9. New York
Georgia	792,502	10.8	12	10. Hawaii
Hawaii	130,344	11.0	10	11. Arkansas
Idaho	79,855	6.7	37	12. Georgia
Illinois	1,105,160	9.3	23	13. Oklahoma
Indiana	389,537	6.7	39	14. Maine
Iowa	177,283	6.2	43	15. Missouri
Kansas	171,831	6.7	38	16. California
Kentucky	478,425	12.3	6	17. Michigan
Louisiana	670,034	15.4	3	18. South Carolina
Maine	130,872	10.5	14	19. Arizona
Maryland	374,512	7.4	33	20. Vermont
Massachusetts	373,599	6.1	46	21. Florida
Michigan	935,416	9.7	17	22. Ohio
Minnesota	294,825	6.3	42	23. Illinois
Mississippi	457,106	16.8	1	24. Pennsylvania
Missouri	553,930	10.3	15	25. Rhode Island
Montana	70,754	8.0	30	26. Oregon
Nebraska	101,625	6.2	45	27. North Carolina
Nevada	96,712	6.0	47	28. Washington
New Hampshire	52,809	4.5	50	29. Virginia
New Jersey	540,626	6.8	36	30. Montana
New Mexico	235,060	13.7	4	31. Delaware
New York	2,098,561	11.5	9	32. Alaska
North Carolina	631,061	8.6	27	33. Maryland
North Dakota	39,825	6.2	44	34. Wyoming
Ohio	1,045,066	9.4	22	35. Connecticut
Oklahoma	353,790	10.7	13	36. New Jersey
Oregon	287,607	9.0	26	37. Idaho
Pennsylvania	1,123,541	9.3	24	38. Kansas
Rhode Island	90,873	9.2	25	39. Indiana
South Carolina	358,341	9.7	18	40. South Dakota
South Dakota	48,843	6.7	40	41. Colorado
Tennessee	637,773	12.0	7	42. Minnesota
Texas	2,371,958	12.4	5	43. Iowa
Utah	110,011	5.5	48	44. North Dakota
Vermont	56,459	9.6	20	45. Nebraska
Virginia	537,531	8.1	29	46. Massachusetts
Washington	476,391	8.6	28	47. Nevada
West Virginia	299,719	16.4	2	48. Utah
Wisconsin	283,255	5.5	49	49. Wisconsin
Wyoming	33,013	6.9	34	50. New Hampshire
50 States	25,392,291	9.6		
DC	92,751	17.1		
United States	25,533,302	9.6		

L-4 SSI RECIPIENTS, TOTAL AND AS PERCENT OF POPULATION, 1997

State	SSI recipients #	Recipients as percent of population %	Rank by %
Alabama	165,982	3.9	4
Alaska	7,255	1.2	48
Arizona	74,968	1.7	31
Arkansas	93,993	3.7	6
California	1,027,571	3.2	9
Colorado	57,424	1.5	37
Connecticut	45,947	1.4	42
Delaware	11,429	1.6	35
Florida	351,966	2.4	16
Georgia	200,012	2.7	11
Hawaii	19,366	1.6	33
Idaho	17,317	1.5	41
Illinois	259,490	2.2	21
Indiana	89,843	1.5	36
Iowa	41,950	1.5	40
Kansas	37,926	1.5	39
Kentucky	168,242	4.3	2
Louisiana	181,754	4.2	3
Maine	27,720	2.2	19
Maryland	84,145	1.7	32
Massachusetts	163,944	2.7	12
Michigan	210,075	2.2	22
Minnesota	62,713	1.3	45
Mississippi	140,544	5.2	1
Missouri	115,963	2.2	24
Montana	14,106	1.6	34
Nebraska	21,723	1.3	46
Nevada	21,614	1.3	44
New Hampshire	11,061	1.0	50
New Jersey	145,171	1.8	28
New Mexico	45,465	2.7	13
New York	603,689	3.3	7
North Carolina	194,292	2.7	14
North Dakota	8,891	1.4	43
Ohio	251,212	2.2	18
Oklahoma	74,859	2.3	17
Oregon	47,806	1.5	38
Pennsylvania	268,310	2.2	20
Rhode Island	25,107	2.5	15
South Carolina	111,565	3.0	10
South Dakota	13,661	1.9	27
Tennessee	175,210	3.3	8
Texas	411,368	2.2	25
Utah	20,836	1.0	49
Vermont	12,830	2.2	23
Virginia	132,868	2.0	26
Washington	94,054	1.7	30
West Virginia	68,813	3.8	5
Wisconsin	93,757	1.8	29
Wyoming	5,871	1.2	47
50 States	6,531,678	2.5	
DC	20,084	3.7	
United States	6,552,397	2.5	

Rank in order

By %

1. Mississippi
2. Kentucky
3. Louisiana
4. Alabama
5. West Virginia
6. Arkansas
7. New York
8. Tennessee
9. California
10. South Carolina
11. Georgia
12. Massachusetts
13. New Mexico
14. North Carolina
15. Rhode Island
16. Florida
17. Oklahoma
18. Ohio
19. Maine
20. Pennsylvania
21. Illinois
22. Michigan
23. Vermont
24. Missouri
25. Texas
26. Virginia
27. South Dakota
28. New Jersey
29. Wisconsin
30. Washington
31. Arizona
32. Maryland
33. Hawaii
34. Montana
35. Delaware
36. Indiana
37. Colorado
38. Oregon
39. Kansas
40. Iowa
41. Idaho
42. Connecticut
43. North Dakota
44. Nevada
45. Minnesota
46. Nebraska
47. Wyoming
48. Alaska
49. Utah
50. New Hampshire

L-5 CHANGE IN AFDC RECIPIENTS, FY 1991-1996

State	Average monthly AFDC recipients 1991	Percent change 1991-1996 %	Rank by %	By %
Alabama	135,440	-22.3	46	1. Hawaii
Alaska	26,424	37.0	4	2. Nevada
Arizona	150,435	14.0	8	3. New Mexico
Arkansas	74,567	-22.0	45	4. Alaska
California	2,110,168	24.4	6	5. Idaho
Colorado	112,273	-12.2	29	6. California
Connecticut	142,707	13.3	9	7. Florida
Delaware	23,639	-1.2	20	8. Arizona
Florida	452,045	24.0	7	9. Connecticut
Georgia	342,439	3.0	15	10. New York
Hawaii	45,555	46.1	1	11. Washington
Idaho	18,394	24.6	5	12. Tennessee
Illinois	671,802	-2.4	22	13. Rhode Island
Indiana	175,844	-15.8	36	14. New Hampshire
Iowa	99,045	-9.9	28	15. Georgia
Kansas	79,405	-13.7	31	16. Montana
Kentucky	214,936	-18.6	41	17. North Carolina
Louisiana	278,587	-15.4	35	18. Missouri
Maine	64,249	-13.0	30	19. Maryland
Maryland	205,243	-0.6	19	20. Delaware
Massachusetts	292,187	-18.9	43	21. Texas
Michigan	685,457	-23.1	47	22. Illinois
Minnesota	179,749	-4.8	26	23. Virginia
Mississippi	177,390	-27.2	49	24. Pennsylvania
Missouri	228,134	1.6	18	25. Vermont
Montana	30,420	2.5	16	26. Minnesota
Nebraska	45,310	-14.5	33	27. South Carolina
Nevada	26,611	41.1	2	28. Iowa
New Hampshire	23,393	3.4	14	29. Colorado
New Jersey	336,055	-14.2	32	30. Maine
New Mexico	73,095	38.3	3	31. Kansas
New York	1,053,433	12.8	10	32. New Jersey
North Carolina	272,245	2.1	17	33. Nebraska
North Dakota	16,521	-18.9	42	34. Oklahoma
Ohio	678,810	-19.6	44	35. Louisiana
Oklahoma	123,892	-15.4	34	36. Indiana
Oregon	105,664	-17.7	39	37. West Virginia
Pennsylvania	562,830	-3.4	24	38. Utah
Rhode Island	54,389	7.4	13	39. Oregon
South Carolina	125,667	-5.2	27	40. South Dakota
South Dakota	19,998	-18.6	40	41. Kentucky
Tennessee	240,901	8.0	12	42. North Dakota
Texas	697,343	-1.9	21	43. Massachusetts
Utah	48,338	-16.6	38	44. Ohio
Vermont	26,518	-4.6	25	45. Arkansas
Virginia	167,083	-3.1	23	46. Alabama
Washington	249,306	10.0	11	47. Michigan
West Virginia	113,622	-16.3	37	48. Wyoming
Wisconsin	240,326	-29.2	50	49. Mississippi
Wyoming	17,072	-24.8	48	50. Wisconsin
50 States	12,334,956	0.6		
DC	55,739	25.9		
United States	12,592,268	0.4		

Condition of Children Index
"child well-being" ranked from 1 (highest) to 51 (lowest)

State	Condition of Children Index		Rank in order
Alabama	46		1. New Hampshire
Alaska	24		2. Maine
Arizona	41		3. North Dakota
Arkansas	40		4. Vermont
California	32		5. Iowa
Colorado	28		6. Nebraska
Connecticut	12		7. Utah
Delaware	20		8. Massachusetts
Florida	47		9. Wisconsin
Georgia	45		10. Hawaii
Hawaii	10		11. Minnesota
Idaho	23		12. Connecticut
Illinois	35		13. Montana
Indiana	26		14. Rhode Island
Iowa	5		15. Kansas
Kansas	15		16. Washington
Kentucky	38		17. New Jersey
Louisiana	50		18. South Dakota
Maine	2		19. Wyoming
Maryland	30		20. Delaware
Massachusetts	8		21. Oregon
Michigan	29		22. Virginia
Minnesota	11		23. Idaho
Mississippi	49		24. Alaska
Missouri	33		25. Ohio
Montana	13		26. Indiana
Nebraska	6		27. Pennsylvania
Nevada	34		28. Colorado
New Hampshire	1		29. Michigan
New Jersey	17		30. Maryland
New Mexico	44		31. Oklahoma
New York	36		32. California
North Carolina	42		33. Missouri
North Dakota	3		34. Nevada
Ohio	25		35. Illinois
Oklahoma	31		36. New York
Oregon	21		37. West Virginia
Pennsylvania	27		38. Kentucky
Rhode Island	14		39. Texas
South Carolina	48		40. Arkansas
South Dakota	18		41. Arizona
Tennessee	43		42. North Carolina
Texas	39		43. Tennessee
Utah	7		44. New Mexico
Vermont	4		45. Georgia
Virginia	22		46. Alabama
Washington	16		47. Florida
West Virginia	37		48. South Carolina
Wisconsin	9		49. Mississippi
Wyoming	19		50. Louisiana
50 States	n/a		
DC	51		
United States	n/a		

State	Percent of families %	Rank		Rank in order By %
Alabama	27	11		1. Louisiana
Alaska	25	21		2. Mississippi
Arizona	26	14		3. Florida
Arkansas	24	26		3. New York
California	26	14		5. Georgia
Colorado	24	26		5. South Carolina
Connecticut	24	26		5. Tennessee
Delaware	28	8		8. Delaware
Florida	30	3		8. Michigan
Georgia	29	5		8. Rhode Island
Hawaii	22	40		11. Alabama
Idaho	17	49		11. New Mexico
Illinois	26	14		11. North Carolina
Indiana	24	26		14. Arizona
Iowa	21	45		14. California
Kansas	23	37		14. Illinois
Kentucky	24	26		14. Maryland
Louisiana	33	1		14. Massachusetts
Maine	25	21		14. Missouri
Maryland	26	14		14. Nevada
Massachusetts	26	14		21. Alaska
Michigan	28	8		21. Maine
Minnesota	25	21		21. Minnesota
Mississippi	32	2		21. Ohio
Missouri	26	14		21. West Virginia
Montana	24	26		26. Arkansas
Nebraska	19	47		26. Colorado
Nevada	26	14		26. Connecticut
New Hampshire	22	40		26. Indiana
New Jersey	24	26		26. Kentucky
New Mexico	27	11		26. Montana
New York	30	3		26. New Jersey
North Carolina	27	11		26. Oklahoma
North Dakota	19	47		26. Oregon
Ohio	25	21		26. Texas
Oklahoma	24	26		26. Washington
Oregon	24	26		37. Kansas
Pennsylvania	22	40		37. Virginia
Rhode Island	28	8		37. Wisconsin
South Carolina	29	5		40. Hawaii
South Dakota	20	46		40. New Hampshire
Tennessee	29	5		40. Pennsylvania
Texas	24	26		40. Vermont
Utah	14	50		40. Wyoming
Vermont	22	40		45. Iowa
Virginia	23	37		46. South Dakota
Washington	24	26		47. Nebraska
West Virginia	25	21		47. North Dakota
Wisconsin	23	37		49. Idaho
Wyoming	22	40		50. Utah
50 States	n/a			
DC	58			
United States	27			

State	Typical monthly AFDC payment $	Rank	Rank in order By $
Alabama	148	49	1. Alaska
Alaska	770	1	2. Hawaii
Arizona	294	32	3. California
Arkansas	184	45	4. Massachusetts
California	557	3	5. Washington
Colorado	312	27	6. Rhode Island
Connecticut	483	9	7. New York
Delaware	311	28	8. New Hampshire
Florida	256	38	9. Connecticut
Georgia	249	40	10. Minnesota
Hawaii	648	2	11. Vermont
Idaho	282	34	12. Wisconsin
Illinois	307	29	13. Maine
Indiana	251	39	14. Michigan
Iowa	365	19	15. Pennsylvania
Kansas	336	23	16. New Jersey
Kentucky	228	43	17. North Dakota
Louisiana	158	47	18. Oregon
Maine	429	13	19. Iowa
Maryland	325	24	20. Utah
Massachusetts	539	4	21. Montana
Michigan	413	14	22. New Mexico
Minnesota	472	10	23. Kansas
Mississippi	116	50	24. Maryland
Missouri	269	37	25. Nebraska
Montana	360	21	26. Ohio
Nebraska	319	25	27. Colorado
Nevada	286	33	28. Delaware
New Hampshire	503	8	29. Illinois
New Jersey	382	16	30. Wyoming
New Mexico	354	22	31. South Dakota
New York	506	7	32. Arizona
North Carolina	236	42	33. Nevada
North Dakota	381	17	34. Idaho
Ohio	318	26	35. Oklahoma
Oklahoma	272	35	36. Virginia
Oregon	366	18	37. Missouri
Pennsylvania	382	15	38. Florida
Rhode Island	515	6	39. Indiana
South Carolina	185	44	40. Georgia
South Dakota	297	31	41. West Virginia
Tennessee	181	46	42. North Carolina
Texas	156	48	43. Kentucky
Utah	362	20	44. South Carolina
Vermont	468	11	45. Arkansas
Virginia	271	36	46. Tennessee
Washington	519	5	47. Louisiana
West Virginia	242	41	48. Texas
Wisconsin	446	12	49. Alabama
Wyoming	306	30	50. Mississippi
50 States	n/a		
DC	415		
United States	377		

L-9 WELFARE AS PERCENTAGE OF POVERTY LEVEL INCOME, 1996

State	Welfare as percentage of poverty level income %	Rank		Rank in order By %
Alabama	44	49		1 Hawaii
Alaska	92	2		2 Alaska
Arizona	61	31		3 New York
Arkansas	48	44		4 Vermont
California	79	6		5 Connecticut
Colorado	67	17		6 California
Connecticut	81	5		6 Rhode Island
Delaware	60	33		8 Washington
Florida	57	36		9 Massachusetts
Georgia	55	40		10 New Hampshire
Hawaii	95	1		11 Minnesota
Idaho	58	35		12 Wisconsin
Illinois	64	26		13 Oregon
Indiana	56	38		14 Kansas
Iowa	67	17		14 Michigan
Kansas	69	14		16 New Jersey
Kentucky	53	42		17 Colorado
Louisiana	47	45		17 Iowa
Maine	66	24		17 Montana
Maryland	63	27		17 North Dakota
Massachusetts	76	9		17 Pennsylvania
Michigan	69	14		17 South Dakota
Minnesota	74	11		17 Utah
Mississippi	40	50		24 Maine
Missouri	56	38		25 New Mexico
Montana	67	17		26 Illinois
Nebraska	63	27		27 Maryland
Nevada	61	31		27 Nebraska
New Hampshire	75	10		29 Virginia
New Jersey	68	16		29 Wyoming
New Mexico	65	25		31 Arizona
New York	86	3		31 Nevada
North Carolina	54	41		33 Delaware
North Dakota	67	17		33 Ohio
Ohio	60	33		35 Idaho
Oklahoma	57	36		36 Florida
Oregon	71	13		36 Oklahoma
Pennsylvania	67	17		38 Indiana
Rhode Island	79	6		38 Missouri
South Carolina	47	45		40 Georgia
South Dakota	67	17		41 North Carolina
Tennessee	46	47		42 Kentucky
Texas	46	47		43 West Virginia
Utah	67	17		44 Arkansas
Vermont	82	4		45 Louisiana
Virginia	62	29		45 South Carolina
Washington	77	8		47 Tennessee
West Virginia	52	43		47 Texas
Wisconsin	73	12		49 Alabama
Wyoming	62	29		50 Mississippi
50 States	n/a			
DC	67			
United States	65			

State	SSI state supplements per recipient $	Rank	By $
Alabama	5.9	38	1. Idaho
Alaska	1,788.0	4	2. Connecticut
Arizona	4.5	39	3. California
Arkansas	0.1	43	4. Alaska
California	1,907.0	3	5. Delaware
Colorado	1,162.9	6	6. Colorado
Connecticut	1,982.3	2	7. Massachusetts
Delaware	1,684.1	5	8. New Hampshire
Florida	52.3	34	9. New York
Georgia	0.1	47	10. Minnesota
Hawaii	596.1	13	11. Rhode Island
Idaho	2,042.8	1	12. Vermont
Illinois	114.6	29	13. Hawaii
Indiana	39.4	35	14. New Jersey
Iowa	73.5	32	15. Oklahoma
Kansas	0.3	42	16. Pennsylvania
Kentucky	93.2	30	17. North Carolina
Louisiana	0.1	45	18. Oregon
Maine	1.7	41	19. Washington
Maryland	78.3	31	20. Nebraska
Massachusetts	980.2	7	21. Missouri
Michigan	139.3	26	22. North Dakota
Minnesota	863.6	10	23. Nevada
Mississippi	0.1	44	24. South Dakota
Missouri	218.2	21	25. Virginia
Montana	63.0	33	26. Michigan
Nebraska	286.7	20	27. South Carolina
Nevada	192.1	23	28. Wyoming
New Hampshire	910.2	8	29. Illinois
New Jersey	545.5	14	30. Kentucky
New Mexico	6.3	37	31. Maryland
New York	886.1	9	32. Iowa
North Carolina	464.3	17	33. Montana
North Dakota	215.9	22	34. Florida
Ohio	0.0	48	35. Indiana
Oklahoma	539.3	15	36. Wisconsin
Oregon	422.0	18	37. New Mexico
Pennsylvania	475.6	16	38. Alabama
Rhode Island	790.1	11	39. Arizona
South Carolina	118.7	27	40. Utah
South Dakota	155.5	24	41. Maine
Tennessee	0.1	46	42. Kansas
Texas	0.0	49	43. Arkansas
Utah	3.5	40	44. Mississippi
Vermont	768.8	12	45. Louisiana
Virginia	154.2	25	46. Tennessee
Washington	319.0	19	47. Georgia
West Virginia	0.0	49	48. Ohio
Wisconsin	6.4	36	49. Texas
Wyoming	118.5	28	49. West Virginia
50 States	541.8		
DC	149.4		
United States	540.6		

L-11 STATE INCOME TAX LIABILITY OF TYPICAL FAMILY IN POVERTY, 1996

State	Income tax liability $	Rank
Alabama	308	4
Alaska	n/a	n/a
Arizona	0	23
Arkansas	137	11
California	0	23
Colorado	0	23
Connecticut	0	23
Delaware	120	12
Florida	n/a	n/a
Georgia	72	17
Hawaii	384	1
Idaho	0	23
Illinois	285	5
Indiana	323	3
Iowa	0	23
Kansas	6	22
Kentucky	338	2
Louisiana	65	18
Maine	7	21
Maryland	0	23
Massachusetts	0	23
Michigan	234	6
Minnesota	-505	39
Mississippi	0	23
Missouri	86	16
Montana	160	10
Nebraska	0	23
Nevada	n/a	n/a
New Hampshire	n/a	n/a
New Jersey	119	13
New Mexico	-15	37
New York	-652	40
North Carolina	0	23
North Dakota	0	23
Ohio	46	19
Oklahoma	94	15
Oregon	233	7
Pennsylvania	105	14
Rhode Island	0	23
South Carolina	0	23
South Dakota	n/a	n/a
Tennessee	n/a	n/a
Texas	n/a	n/a
Utah	22	20
Vermont	-842	41
Virginia	225	8
Washington	n/a	n/a
West Virginia	197	9
Wisconsin	-246	38
Wyoming	n/a	n/a
50 States	n/a	
DC	0	
United States	n/a	

By $

1. Hawaii
2. Kentucky
3. Indiana
4. Alabama
5. Illinois
6. Michigan
7. Oregon
8. Virginia
9. West Virginia
10. Montana
11. Arkansas
12. Delaware
13. New Jersey
14. Pennsylvania
15. Oklahoma
16. Missouri
17. Georgia
18. Louisiana
19. Ohio
20. Utah
21. Maine
22. Kansas
23. Arizona
23. California
23. Colorado
23. Connecticut
23. Idaho
23. Iowa
23. Maryland
23. Massachusetts
23. Mississippi
23. Nebraska
23. North Carolina
23. North Dakota
23. Rhode Island
23. South Carolina
37. New Mexico
38. Wisconsin
39. Minnesota
40. New York
41. Vermont

State	Total collections $(000)	Per capita collections $	Rank by per capita	By per capita
Alabama	113,096	26.6	27	1. Michigan
Alaska	49,692	82.5	2	2. Alaska
Arizona	79,009	18.4	43	3. Wisconsin
Arkansas	55,073	22.2	34	4. Ohio
California	599,056	19.0	41	5. Pennsylvania
Colorado	80,747	21.5	35	6. New Jersey
Connecticut	109,903	33.6	16	7. Washington
Delaware	32,273	45.0	10	8. Minnesota
Florida	n/a	n/a	n/a	9. Hawaii
Georgia	199,303	27.6	24	10. Delaware
Hawaii	53,800	45.6	9	11. Nebraska
Idaho	31,504	27.0	26	12. Maryland
Illinois	244,306	20.7	38	13. Maine
Indiana	n/a	n/a	n/a	14. New Hampshire
Iowa	43,402	15.3	45	15. Oregon
Kansas	70,716	27.6	25	16. Connecticut
Kentucky	108,921	28.2	22	17. Massachusetts
Louisiana	29,526	6.8	47	18. Nevada
Maine	48,835	39.4	13	19. South Dakota
Maryland	215,097	42.7	12	20. North Carolina
Massachusetts	190,951	31.5	17	21. Vermont
Michigan	810,169	84.9	1	22. Kentucky
Minnesota	241,000	52.2	8	23. Missouri
Mississippi	52,860	19.6	40	24. Georgia
Missouri	148,929	28.0	23	25. Kansas
Montana	19,811	22.8	32	26. Idaho
Nebraska	70,150	42.8	11	27. Alabama
Nevada	48,186	31.4	18	28. Utah
New Hampshire	42,669	37.2	14	29. South Carolina
New Jersey	441,750	55.6	6	30. Tennessee
New Mexico	16,740	9.9	46	31. New York
New York	437,158	24.0	31	32. Montana
North Carolina	217,892	30.3	20	33. Wyoming
North Dakota	10,896	17.0	44	34. Arkansas
Ohio	730,131	65.6	4	35. Colorado
Oklahoma	14,387	4.4	48	36. Rhode Island
Oregon	116,680	37.1	15	37. West Virginia
Pennsylvania	731,527	60.7	5	38. Illinois
Rhode Island	21,106	21.3	36	39. Virginia
South Carolina	93,937	25.6	29	40. Mississippi
South Dakota	22,857	31.3	19	41. California
Tennessee	133,994	25.5	30	42. Texas
Texas	348,181	18.5	42	43. Arizona
Utah	50,826	26.0	28	44. North Dakota
Vermont	17,527	30.0	21	45. Iowa
Virginia	132,191	20.0	39	46. New Mexico
Washington	299,857	55.0	7	47. Louisiana
West Virginia	38,661	21.2	37	48. Oklahoma
Wisconsin	402,484	78.6	3	
Wyoming	10,704	22.3	33	
50 States	8,078,469	30.8		
DC	28,950	52.2		
United States	8,214,402	31.2		

L-13 CHILD SUPPORT COLLECTIONS PER $ OF ADMINISTRATIVE COSTS, FY 1995

State	Collections per dollar of costs $	Rank
Alabama	2.24	39
Alaska	2.93	27
Arizona	1.48	49
Arkansas	2.75	31
California	2.17	42
Colorado	2.54	34
Connecticut	2.78	30
Delaware	2.23	40
Florida	3.53	17
Georgia	3.50	18
Hawaii	2.36	38
Idaho	2.39	37
Illinois	2.23	40
Indiana	5.18	6
Iowa	4.72	9
Kansas	1.69	47
Kentucky	3.21	25
Louisiana	n/a	n/a
Maine	4.28	10
Maryland	4.07	12
Massachusetts	3.54	16
Michigan	7.82	2
Minnesota	3.96	13
Mississippi	2.16	43
Missouri	3.41	21
Montana	2.87	28
Nebraska	3.44	20
Nevada	2.08	44
New Hampshire	2.50	35
New Jersey	4.75	8
New Mexico	1.54	48
New York	3.39	22
North Carolina	2.40	36
North Dakota	4.13	11
Ohio	5.63	4
Oklahoma	2.70	32
Oregon	4.81	7
Pennsylvania	8.20	1
Rhode Island	3.45	19
South Carolina	2.84	29
South Dakota	5.27	5
Tennessee	3.75	14
Texas	3.01	26
Utah	1.96	45
Vermont	2.69	33
Virginia	3.63	15
Washington	3.35	23
West Virginia	3.24	24
Wisconsin	6.09	3
Wyoming	1.76	46
50 States	n/a	
DC	2.03	
United States	3.59	

Rank in order

By $

1. Pennsylvania
2. Michigan
3. Wisconsin
4. Ohio
5. South Dakota
6. Indiana
7. Oregon
8. New Jersey
9. Iowa
10. Maine
11. North Dakota
12. Maryland
13. Minnesota
14. Tennessee
15. Virginia
16. Massachusetts
17. Florida
18. Georgia
19. Rhode Island
20. Nebraska
21. Missouri
22. New York
23. Washington
24. West Virginia
25. Kentucky
26. Texas
27. Alaska
28. Montana
29. South Carolina
30. Connecticut
31. Arkansas
32. Oklahoma
33. Vermont
34. Colorado
35. New Hampshire
36. North Carolina
37. Idaho
38. Hawaii
39. Alabama
40. Delaware
40. Illinois
42. California
43. Mississippi
44. Nevada
45. Utah
46. Wyoming
47. Kansas
48. New Mexico
49. Arizona

L-14 CHILDREN IN FOSTER CARE, FY 1995				Rank in order
State	Children in foster care #	Children in foster care per 10,000 children	Rank by per 10,000	By per 10,000
Alabama	3,590	33.3	45	1. Wyoming
Alaska	1,783	95.6	8	2. Illinois
Arizona	5,640	49.5	33	3. Rhode Island
Arkansas	2,374	36.4	43	4. New York
California	96,617	110.2	5	5. California
Colorado	7,258	74.1	13	6. Vermont
Connecticut	7,045	89.0	10	7. Massachusetts
Delaware	843	47.9	35	8. Alaska
Florida	9,002	26.8	49	9. Georgia
Georgia	17,876	93.0	9	10. Connecticut
Hawaii	2,454	80.4	12	11. Maine
Idaho	1,058	30.7	47	12. Hawaii
Illinois	47,852	153.1	2	13. Colorado
Indiana	10,145	68.1	21	14. Nebraska
Iowa	3,952	54.6	29	15. Montana
Kansas	4,744	69.1	18	16. Pennsylvania
Kentucky	3,760	38.7	42	17. North Carolina
Louisiana	5,962	48.3	34	18. Kansas
Maine	2,473	81.8	11	19. Washington
Maryland	7,399	58.2	27	20. Minnesota
Massachusetts	13,591	95.7	7	21. Indiana
Michigan	10,889	43.0	37	22. West Virginia
Minnesota	8,452	68.2	20	23. Missouri
Mississippi	2,940	38.8	41	24. Oregon
Missouri	9,331	67.4	23	25. Ohio
Montana	1,695	72.6	15	26. Wisconsin
Nebraska	3,213	72.8	14	27. Maryland
Nevada	1,823	45.9	36	28. South Carolina
New Hampshire	1,477	50.3	31	29. Iowa
New Jersey	8,014	40.8	40	30. North Dakota
New Mexico	2,050	41.3	39	31. New Hampshire
New York	52,395	115.7	4	32. Tennessee
North Carolina	12,760	70.9	17	33. Arizona
North Dakota	887	52.3	30	34. Louisiana
Ohio	17,800	62.5	25	35. Delaware
Oklahoma	3,017	34.5	44	36. Nevada
Oregon	5,138	64.4	24	37. Michigan
Pennsylvania	20,559	71.1	16	38. Virginia
Rhode Island	3,309	140.7	3	39. New Mexico
South Carolina	5,234	55.6	28	40. New Jersey
South Dakota	665	32.4	46	41. Mississippi
Tennessee	6,520	49.8	32	42. Kentucky
Texas	11,700	21.8	50	43. Arkansas
Utah	1,936	28.7	48	44. Oklahoma
Vermont	1,430	97.5	6	45. Alabama
Virginia	6,844	42.3	38	46. South Dakota
Washington	9,715	68.5	19	47. Idaho
West Virginia	2,877	67.6	22	48. Utah
Wisconsin	7,832	58.3	26	49. Florida
Wyoming	2,241	166.1	1	50. Texas
50 States	478,161	69.9		
DC	2,088	185.1		
United States	482,733	70.5		

State	Welfare spending $(millions)	Per capita $	As percent of personal income %	Rank by per capita	Rank in order By per capita
Alabama	2,214	525	3.1	36	1. New York
Alaska	545	899	4.0	7	2. New Hampshire
Arizona	2,412	592	3.4	27	3. Maine
Arkansas	1,394	568	3.6	29	4. Massachusetts
California	23,401	745	3.4	13	5. Connecticut
Colorado	1,693	463	2.2	44	6. Minnesota
Connecticut	3,014	920	3.3	5	7. Alaska
Delaware	352	499	2.3	39	8. Rhode Island
Florida	5,949	426	2.1	49	9. West Virginia
Georgia	4,239	601	3.2	26	10. Pennsylvania
Hawaii	720	610	2.6	23	11. Vermont
Idaho	484	427	2.5	48	12. Ohio
Illinois	7,088	603	2.7	25	13. California
Indiana	3,975	691	3.6	17	14. Wisconsin
Iowa	1,583	559	3.1	31	15. Michigan
Kansas	1,120	438	2.2	45	16. New Jersey
Kentucky	2,542	664	4.0	19	17. Indiana
Louisiana	2,851	661	4.0	20	18. Washington
Maine	1,184	955	5.1	3	19. Kentucky
Maryland	2,788	557	2.3	32	20. Louisiana
Massachusetts	5,663	937	3.8	4	21. South Carolina
Michigan	6,951	732	3.6	15	22. North Dakota
Minnesota	4,147	908	4.4	6	23. Hawaii
Mississippi	1,463	548	3.8	33	24. Tennessee
Missouri	2,713	511	2.7	38	25. Illinois
Montana	426	498	2.9	41	26. Georgia
Nebraska	910	561	2.9	30	27. Arizona
Nevada	596	409	1.9	50	28. New Mexico
New Hampshire	1,136	999	4.6	2	29. Arkansas
New Jersey	5,753	728	2.7	16	30. Nebraska
New Mexico	951	575	3.6	28	31. Iowa
New York	23,932	1,317	5.3	1	32. Maryland
North Carolina	3,761	532	2.9	35	33. Mississippi
North Dakota	396	620	3.6	22	34. Oregon
Ohio	8,440	760	3.9	12	35. North Carolina
Oklahoma	1,526	468	2.8	43	36. Alabama
Oregon	1,672	542	2.8	34	37. South Dakota
Pennsylvania	9,672	803	3.8	10	38. Missouri
Rhode Island	869	871	4.1	8	39. Delaware
South Carolina	2,310	630	3.8	21	40. Texas
South Dakota	371	514	2.9	37	41. Montana
Tennessee	3,127	604	3.3	24	42. Wyoming
Texas	9,151	498	2.7	40	43. Oklahoma
Utah	831	436	2.8	47	44. Colorado
Vermont	444	766	4.0	11	45. Kansas
Virginia	2,863	437	2.0	46	46. Virginia
Washington	3,602	674	3.1	18	47. Utah
West Virginia	1,545	848	5.3	9	48. Idaho
Wisconsin	3,757	739	3.8	14	49. Florida
Wyoming	226	475	2.4	42	50. Nevada
50 States	178,749	688	3.2		
DC	1,080	1,895	6.3		
United States	179,829	691	3.4		

State	Welfare spending as percent of general spending %	Rank	By %
Alabama	15.0	29	1. New Hampshire
Alaska	8.8	50	2. Maine
Arizona	16.0	24	3. West Virginia
Arkansas	18.7	11	4. New York
California	16.9	20	5. Pennsylvania
Colorado	11.3	45	6. Massachusetts
Connecticut	18.1	15	7. Ohio
Delaware	11.1	46	8. Kentucky
Florida	11.4	44	9. Rhode Island
Georgia	16.3	23	10. Minnesota
Hawaii	10.8	47	11. Arkansas
Idaho	12.8	40	12. Indiana
Illinois	16.0	25	13. Vermont
Indiana	18.7	12	14. Tennessee
Iowa	14.2	35	15. Connecticut
Kansas	11.5	43	16. Michigan
Kentucky	20.0	8	17. Wisconsin
Louisiana	16.9	19	18. Mississippi
Maine	24.0	2	19. Louisiana
Maryland	14.2	34	20. California
Massachusetts	20.1	6	21. Missouri
Michigan	17.7	16	22. South Carolina
Minnesota	18.8	10	23. Georgia
Mississippi	17.0	18	24. Arizona
Missouri	16.8	21	25. Illinois
Montana	12.9	39	26. North Dakota
Nebraska	14.6	31	27. North Carolina
Nevada	9.5	48	28. New Jersey
New Hampshire	25.6	1	29. Alabama
New Jersey	15.1	28	30. Washington
New Mexico	13.8	37	31. Nebraska
New York	21.1	4	32. Oklahoma
North Carolina	15.1	27	33. Texas
North Dakota	15.3	26	34. Maryland
Ohio	20.1	7	35. Iowa
Oklahoma	14.4	32	36. South Dakota
Oregon	13.0	38	37. New Mexico
Pennsylvania	20.7	5	38. Oregon
Rhode Island	19.2	9	39. Montana
South Carolina	16.7	22	40. Idaho
South Dakota	13.9	36	41. Virginia
Tennessee	18.2	14	42. Utah
Texas	14.3	33	43. Kansas
Utah	12.1	42	44. Florida
Vermont	18.3	13	45. Colorado
Virginia	12.2	41	46. Delaware
Washington	14.9	30	47. Hawaii
West Virginia	22.5	3	48. Nevada
Wisconsin	17.1	17	49. Wyoming
Wyoming	8.9	49	50. Alaska

50 States	16.7	
DC	23.6	
United States	16.7	

L-17 AVERAGE MONTHLY ADMINISTRATIVE COSTS PER AFDC CASE, FY 1996

State	Costs per case $	Rank
Alabama	38.08	38
Alaska	64.81	18
Arizona	57.49	20
Arkansas	48.29	29
California	49.46	27
Colorado	50.64	26
Connecticut	45.23	31
Delaware	90.36	6
Florida	43.03	32
Georgia	32.53	43
Hawaii	35.38	41
Idaho	74.40	14
Illinois	42.01	33
Indiana	40.79	35
Iowa	49.03	28
Kansas	78.26	11
Kentucky	36.37	39
Louisiana	17.19	49
Maine	25.31	46
Maryland	85.82	8
Massachusetts	80.26	10
Michigan	71.51	15
Minnesota	77.68	12
Mississippi	26.63	44
Missouri	18.13	48
Montana	39.74	36
Nebraska	83.67	9
Nevada	68.20	17
New Hampshire	104.30	5
New Jersey	75.35	13
New Mexico	36.27	40
New York	105.91	4
North Carolina	47.43	30
North Dakota	70.07	16
Ohio	35.08	42
Oklahoma	86.80	7
Oregon	128.02	1
Pennsylvania	41.86	34
Rhode Island	39.23	37
South Carolina	52.22	24
South Dakota	57.39	21
Tennessee	25.71	45
Texas	24.22	47
Utah	110.89	2
Vermont	52.36	23
Virginia	52.84	22
Washington	62.16	19
West Virginia	12.95	50
Wisconsin	109.93	3
Wyoming	52.06	25
50 States	n/a	
DC	71.08	
United States	54.23	

Rank in order

By $

1. Oregon
2. Utah
3. Wisconsin
4. New York
5. New Hampshire
6. Delaware
7. Oklahoma
8. Maryland
9. Nebraska
10. Massachusetts
11. Kansas
12. Minnesota
13. New Jersey
14. Idaho
15. Michigan
16. North Dakota
17. Nevada
18. Alaska
19. Washington
20. Arizona
21. South Dakota
22. Virginia
23. Vermont
24. South Carolina
25. Wyoming
26. Colorado
27. California
28. Iowa
29. Arkansas
30. North Carolina
31. Connecticut
32. Florida
33. Illinois
34. Pennsylvania
35. Indiana
36. Montana
37. Rhode Island
38. Alabama
39. Kentucky
40. New Mexico
41. Hawaii
42. Ohio
43. Georgia
44. Mississippi
45. Tennessee
46. Maine
47. Texas
48. Missouri
49. Louisiana
50. West Virginia

Source Notes for Welfare (Section L)

L-1 Percent of Births to Unwed Mothers, 1996: These data come from state reports summarized by the National Center for Health Statistics in its *Monthly Vital Statistics Report* (Vol. 46, No. 1, Supplement 2, September 11, 1997). The birth data, which come from hospitals, are highly reliable, but some states report the marital status of mothers somewhat differently.

L-2 AFDC Recipients, Total and as a Percent of Population, FY 1996: The primary federal welfare program has been Aid to Families with Dependent Children (AFDC) for households with children and income below stipulated levels. During 1997 states were making the transition to new programs under federal welfare reform legislation passed in 1996. The table, calculated from a special tabulation of data the U.S. Department of Health and Human Services provided to *State Fact Finder* on September 23, 1997, expresses the total number of people in households receiving AFDC during fiscal year 1996 as a percentage of population on July 1, 1996. Because states set their own eligibility standards, states with high percentages of persons in poverty do not necessarily have a larger-than-average percentage.

L-3 Food Stamp Recipients, Total and as Percent of Population, FY 1996: Unlike Aid to Families with Dependent Children, Food Stamp standards of eligibility are uniform nationwide, so participation in this program tends to resemble closely the percentage of state population in poverty. The data are from a special Department of Agriculture Division of Food and Consumer Division tabulation provided to *State Fact Finder* on September 4, 1997.

L-4 SSI Recipients, Total and as Percent of Population, 1997: The Supplemental Security Income (SSI) program provides federal cash payments to persons eligible by reason of a combination of low incomes and disability, blindness, or age over sixty-five. The eligibility standards are uniform nationwide, as are the cash payments, except in about half the states that supplement the federal payments with state money (see Table L-10). The data, reflecting recipients in January 1997, were calculated from information on recipients published in *Social Security Bulletin* (Volume 60, No. 2, 1997).

L-5 Change in AFDC Recipients, FY 1991-1996: This table compares the FY 1991 average monthly number of recipients in each state with the FY 1996 average to show growth in welfare recipients over the past five years. The data come from the same source as Table L-2. Since 1996 there has been a dramatic reduction in welfare caseloads as the result of a strong national economy and implementation of welfare reform.

L-6 Condition of Children Index, 1997: This is a ranking of states (1 highest, 50 lowest) prepared by the Annie E. Casey Foundation based on 10 indicators of health, income, education, and other factors. The details behind the rankings are found in *Kids Count Data Book* for 1997, the foundation's annual comprehensive publication.

L-7 Percent of Families with Children Headed by Single Parent, 1994: A large and growing number of American children do not live in households with two parents. These statistics (from *Kids Count*; see notes to Table L-6) include only children in households with a single parent present.

L-8 Typical Monthly AFDC Payments, Family of Three, FY 1996: These data (reflecting the situation over the year ending in September of 1996) show what a welfare family with two children would receive in cash each month. Each state sets its own level of benefits. A few states have cut their benefits recently, while a few have raised them. In addition to these cash payments, a typical welfare household would receive Food Stamps, assistance in paying heating and cooling bills, and free medical care under the Medicaid program. Some households would also receive additional cash as "emergency assistance" and reduced rents under various federal housing subsidy programs. For source see Table L-2.

L-9 Welfare as Percentage of Poverty Level Income, 1996: These data are from a special compilation of the Congressional Research Service and are included in the 1996 "Green Book" of the Ways and Means Committee of the U.S. House of Representatives. The data compare the combined value of AFDC cash payments and Food Stamps of a typical welfare family with the poverty level for that family. The AFDC cash payments are set by the states (see notes to Table L-8). Federally determined Food Stamp values differ from state to state, as greater amounts are provided in states with low cash welfare payments. The poverty level is uniform nationwide. CRS provides two numbers for the states of Michigan and New York. *State Fact Finder* included the data for Wayne County, Michigan rather than Washtenaw Co. (71%) and New York City rather than Suffolk Co. (86%).

The table indicates that the typical welfare family receives enough in cash and the cash-equivalent of Food Stamps to bring it up to 65 percent of the poverty level, assuming no income from any other sources and not counting non-cash benefits, such as housing and Medicaid care.

L-10 SSI State Supplements, 1997: These data compare the extent to which states supplement benefits under the federal SSI program. For a description of the program and for the source of the data, see the notes to Table L-4. The complex rules for determining who receives supplements and how large they are mean that the averages shown are not necessarily indicative of the average supplement received by those receiving and by supplement. Some states provide relatively large supplements to some beneficiaries and none to the rest. However, the extreme differences among states show marked differences in their willingness to add to federally funded benefits using their own funds. These annual data were calculated by multiplying monthly averages by twelve.

L-11 State Income Tax Liability of Typical Family in Poverty, 1996: States have quite different approaches toward taxes on poor working families. The table illustrates these by showing how much state income tax a family of three making the poverty level income ($12,511) would have to pay in tax on their 1996 income. A few states, like the federal government, supplement their income with a refundable credit indicated by the minus amounts shown in the table. Some states do not have income taxes (n/a on the table) or have a tax but do not make such families pay it (shown as zeroes on the table). The others charge the taxes shown. The calculations were performed by the Center on Budget and Policy Priorities and provided to *State Fact Finder* in a fax dated September 3, 1997.

L-12 Child Support Collections, FY 1995: Because large numbers of families on welfare consist of mothers and children who receive little or no child support from fathers, state and federal officials are intensifying efforts to ensure that fathers pay the support amounts they owe. The table provides an indication of the relative significance of the resulting child support payments in each state. The collections are those reported by the Department of Health and Human Services in the *Child Support Enforcement Twentieth Annual Report to Congress* for fiscal year 1995. The per capita amounts are those collections divided by each states' population on July 1, 1995. While most differences among states are real, some reflect the different degrees to which individual states enforce child support requirements through centralized systems.

L-13 Child Support Collections Per Dollar of Administrative Costs, FY 1995: Nationwide, it costs about 36 cents to collect every dollar of child support. These data, from the same source as Table L-12, indicate that the effec-

tiveness of collections efforts shows considerable variation among the states.

L-14 Children in Foster Care, FY 1995: At the end of FY 1995, over 480,000 children were in "substitute care" (foster care). Most commonly, these are children who have been removed from their natural parent(s) because of suspected abuse or neglect. The count is from a special calculation furnished by the American Public Welfare Association (APWA) on September 9, 1997.

High rankings are not necessarily good or bad. Having large numbers of children in foster care for long periods is generally viewed as undesirable because the alternatives (adoption, return to natural parents) provide more stability for the child than temporary homes with strangers. However, having small numbers may indicate that child welfare authorities are leaving abused and neglected children in homes where they should not be left.

L-15 State and Local Welfare Spending, FY 1994: This data are from the Census Bureau web site (http://www.census.gov, "State and Local Government Finance Estimates, by State"). See notes to Table F-1. Each state's state and local spending (including spending of federal funds) is expressed in relation to population and personal income. In addition to cash payments, the Bureau's definition of welfare spending includes Medicaid, and other payments to vendors, administrative costs, and welfare-related social services.

L-16 State and Local Welfare Spending as Percent of General Spending, FY 1994: These data (see notes to Table L-15) show the importance of welfare spending relative to total spending of state and local governments for "general" activities, a category that excludes spending for certain trust funds such as Unemployment Compensation and municipal utilities.

L-17 Average Monthly Administrative Costs Per AFDC Case, FY 1996: The average monthly costs of administering welfare run about $54 per case, with substantial variation among the states. The information comes from unpublished tabulations by the Department of Health and Human Services (see notes to Table L-2).

State Rankings

Alabama

Revenues & Finances - Section G

Per Capita General Revenue	46
Per Capita Non-Tax Revenue	18
Per Capita General Spending	42
Change in General Expenditures	12
State Government General Spending	32
Debt As Percent of Revenue	37
Per Capita Full Faith and Credit Debt	25
State Solvency Index	23
Pension Plan Assets	24
State Reserves	47
State Budget Process Quality	32
Relative State Spending "Needs"	41

Education - Section H

Math Proficiency, Eighth Grade	38
AFQT Ranks	48
SAT Scores	n/a
ACT Scores	22
Over-25 Population With High School Diploma	45
Students in Private Schools	23
High School Completion Rates	39
Pupil-Teacher Ratio	32
Public School Enrollment	26
Library Holdings Per Capita	38
Education Spending As Percent of Total	37
Spending Per Pupil	43
Average Teacher Salary	37
State Aid Per Pupil	20
Higher Education Spending As Percent of Total	10
Public Higher Education Enrollment	14
State Per Pupil Support of Higher Education	20
Tuition and Fees	31
Average Professor Salary	35
Education Employees	30

Health - Section I

Infant Mortality Rates	1
State Health Rankings	42
Population Without Health Insurance	25
Abortions	22
Alcohol Consumption	41
Percent Smokers	15
Percent Overweight	10
AIDS Cases	24
Health And Hospital Spending As Percent Of Total	1
Per Capita Medicaid Spending	39
Medicaid Spending Per Aged Recipient	41
Medicaid Spending Per AFDC Child	48
Medicare Payment Per Hospital -Day	12
Population in HMOs	38

Crime - Section J

Crime Rate	26
Violent Crime Rate	21
Murder Rate	6
Property Crime Rate	26
Motor Vehicle Theft Rate	34
Violent Crime Rate Change	29
Change in Prisoners	33
Incarceration Rate	7
Juvenile Violent Crime Rate	33
Corrections Employees	41
State Corrections Spending	48
Law Enforcement Spending As Percent of Total	33

Transportation - Section K

Percent of Travel on Interstates	42
Interstate Mileage In Poor Condition	45
Deficient Bridges	19
Traffic Deaths Per 100 Million Vehicle Miles	18
Seat Belt Use	40
Vehicle Miles Traveled Per Capita	4
Workers Using Public Transportation	41
Road and Street Miles Under State Control	32
Highway Employees	20
Public Transit Employees	37
Highway Spending As Percent of Total	24

Welfare - Section L

Percent of Births To Unwed Mothers	14
AFDC Recipients As Percent of Population	41
Food Stamp Recipients As Percent of Population	8
SSI Recipients As Percent Of Population	4
Change in AFDC Recipients	46
Condition of Children Index	46
Percent of Families With Single Parent	11
Typical Monthly AFDC Payments	49
Welfare as Percent Of Poverty Level Income	49
Average SSI State Supplements Per Recipient	38
State Income Tax Liability Of Typical Family in Poverty	4
Child Support Collections Per $ of Administrative Costs	39
Children In Foster Care	45
State and Local Welfare Spending Per Capita	36
Welfare Spending As Percent of Total	29
Administrative Costs Per AFDC Case	38

Alaska

Population - Section A

Population 1996	48
Percent Change in Population	25
Population 2000	48
Median Age	49
Percent Population African-American	32
Percent Population In Poverty	46
Percent Population Female	50
Birth Rates	5
Death Rates	28
Illegal Immigrant Population	40

Economies - Section B

Personal Income	47
Per Capita Personal Income	19
Percent Personal Income From Wages and Salaries	2
Average Annual Pay	9
Cost Of Living	3
Average Annual Pay in Manufacturing	42
Average Annual Pay in Retailing	2
Unemployment Rate	1
Government Employment	1
Manufacturing Employment	47
Fortune 500 Companies	n/a
Tourism Spending Per Capita	5
Exports Per Capita	4
Percent Change in Home Prices	33
Net Farm Income	49
Financial Institution Assets	46
Bankruptcy Filings	50
Patents Issued	45
WC Disability Payment	4
UC Average Weekly Benefit	4
Economic Momentum	50
Employment Change	48
Manufacturing Employment Change	50
Home Ownership	41
Gambling	42

Electricity Use Per Residential Customer	36
Revenue Per Kwh	47
New Companies	20

Geography - Section C

Total Land Area	1
Federally-Owned Land	1
State Park Acreage	1
State Park Visitors	5
Population Not Active	28
Hunters With Firearms	n/a
Registered Boats	48
State Spending For The Arts	22
Energy Consumption and Per Capita	1
Toxic Chemical Release Per Capita	15
Hazardous Waste Sites	43
Polluted Rivers	12
Air Pollution Emissions	44

Government - Section D

Members of US House	44
Legislators Per Million Population	9
Units of Government	29
Female Legislators	43
Turnover in Legislatures	12
Democrats in State Legislatures	43
Governor's Power Rating	14
Number of Statewide Elected Officials	45
State and Local Government Employees	2
State and Local Average Salaries	1
Local Employment	48
Local Spending Accountability	31
Registered Voters	1
Statewide Initiatives	n/a

Federal - Section E

Per Capita Federal Spending	3
Increase In Federal Spending	44
Per Capita Federal Grant Spending	1
Per Capita Federal Spending On Procurement	5
Per Capita Federal Spending on Social Security and Medicare	50
Social Security Benefits	37
Federal Spending On Employee Wages and Salaries	1
Federal Grant Spending Per $ of State Tax Revenue	12
General Revenue From Federal Government	46
Federal Tax Burden Per Capita	8
Highway Charges Returned to States	1
Terms of Trade	2
Per Capita Federal Income Tax Liability	7

Taxes - Section F

Tax Revenue	2
Per Capita Tax Revenue	3
Tax Effort	2
Tax Capacity	1
Percent Change In Taxes	50
Property Taxes Per Capita	5
Property Tax Revenue as Percent of Three-Tax Revenues	2
Sales Taxes Per Capita	47
Sales Tax Revenue as Percent of Three-Tax Revenues	45
Services With Sales Tax	49
Income Taxes Per Capita	n/a
Income Tax Revenue as Percent of Three-Tax Revenues	n/a
Motor Fuel Taxes	49
Tobacco Taxes	27
Tax Burden on High Income Family	50
Progressivity of Taxes	3

Alaska

Revenues & Finances - Section G

Per Capita General Revenue	1
Per Capita Non-Tax Revenue	1
Per Capita General Spending	1
Change in General Expenditures	50
State Government General Spending	1
Debt As Percent of Revenue	15
Per Capita Full Faith and Credit Debt	3
State Solvency Index	1
Pension Plan Assets	3
State Reserves	1
State Budget Process Quality	25
Relative State Spending "Needs"	27

Education - Section H

Math Proficiency, Eighth Grade	10
AFQT Ranks	8
SAT Scores	3
ACT Scores	n/a
Over-25 Population With High School Diploma	1
Students in Private Schools	44
High School Completion Rates	17
Pupil-Teacher Ratio	38
Public School Enrollment	2
Library Holdings Per Capita	22
Education Spending As Percent of Total	49
Spending Per Pupil	2
Average Teacher Salary	1
State Aid Per Pupil	2
Higher Education Spending As Percent of Total	49
Public Higher Education Enrollment	15
State Per Pupil Support of Higher Education	5
Tuition and Fees	27
Average Professor Salary	10
Education Employees	13

Health - Section I

Infant Mortality Rates	16
State Health Rankings	44
Population Without Health Insurance	30
Abortions	44
Alcohol Consumption	3
Percent Smokers	12
Percent Overweight	2
AIDS Cases	41
Health And Hospital Spending As Percent Of Total	47
Per Capita Medicaid Spending	20
Medicaid Spending Per Aged Recipient	19
Medicaid Spending Per AFDC Child	2
Medicare Payment Per Hospital -Day	7
Population in HMOs	n/a

Crime - Section J

Crime Rate	14
Violent Crime Rate	11
Murder Rate	14
Property Crime Rate	16
Motor Vehicle Theft Rate	19
Violent Crime Rate Change	2
Change in Prisoners	n/a
Incarceration Rate	19
Juvenile Violent Crime Rate	16
Corrections Employees	19
State Corrections Spending	n/a
Law Enforcement Spending As Percent of Total	37

Transportation - Section K

Percent of Travel on Interstates	3
Interstate Mileage In Poor Condition	7
Deficient Bridges	40
Traffic Deaths Per 100 Million Vehicle Miles	35
Seat Belt Use	17
Vehicle Miles Traveled Per Capita	49
Workers Using Public Transportation	21
Road and Street Miles Under State Control	6
Highway Employees	1
Public Transit Employees	4
Highway Spending As Percent of Total	10

Welfare - Section L

Percent of Births To Unwed Mothers	25
AFDC Recipients As Percent of Population	3
Food Stamp Recipients As Percent of Population	32
SSI Recipients As Percent Of Population	48
Change in AFDC Recipients	4
Condition of Children Index	24
Percent of Families With Single Parent	21
Typical Monthly AFDC Payments	1
Welfare as Percent Of Poverty Level Income	2
Average SSI State Supplements Per Recipient	4
State Income Tax Liability Of Typical Family in Poverty	n/a
Child Support Collections Per $ of Administrative Costs	27
Children In Foster Care	8
State and Local Welfare Spending Per Capita	7
Welfare Spending As Percent of Total	50
Administrative Costs Per AFDC Case	18

Arizona

Revenues & Finances - Section G

Per Capita General Revenue	40
Per Capita Non-Tax Revenue	46
Per Capita General Spending	38
Change in General Expenditures	46
State Government General Spending	50
Debt As Percent of Revenue	6
Per Capita Full Faith and Credit Debt	19
State Solvency Index	22
Pension Plan Assets	1
State Reserves	7
State Budget Process Quality	13
Relative State Spending "Needs"	38

Education - Section H

Math Proficiency, Eighth Grade	25
AFQT Ranks	19
SAT Scores	n/a
ACT Scores	18
Over-25 Population With High School Diploma	28
Students in Private Schools	41
High School Completion Rates	39
Pupil-Teacher Ratio	45
Public School Enrollment	18
Library Holdings Per Capita	38
Education Spending As Percent of Total	27
Spending Per Pupil	49
Average Teacher Salary	32
State Aid Per Pupil	44
Higher Education Spending As Percent of Total	19
Public Higher Education Enrollment	3
State Per Pupil Support of Higher Education	48
Tuition and Fees	45
Average Professor Salary	24
Education Employees	36

Health - Section I

Infant Mortality Rates	21
State Health Rankings	31
Population Without Health Insurance	1
Abortions	32
Alcohol Consumption	7
Percent Smokers	24
Percent Overweight	45
AIDS Cases	26
Health And Hospital Spending As Percent Of Total	41
Per Capita Medicaid Spending	50
Medicaid Spending Per Aged Recipient	50
Medicaid Spending Per AFDC Child	49
Medicare Payment Per Hospital -Day	3
Population in HMOs	14

Crime - Section J

Crime Rate	1
Violent Crime Rate	13
Murder Rate	10
Property Crime Rate	1
Motor Vehicle Theft Rate	1
Violent Crime Rate Change	20
Change in Prisoners	16
Incarceration Rate	8
Juvenile Violent Crime Rate	10
Corrections Employees	6
State Corrections Spending	33
Law Enforcement Spending As Percent of Total	6

Transportation - Section K

Percent of Travel on Interstates	26
Interstate Mileage In Poor Condition	36
Deficient Bridges	49
Traffic Deaths Per 100 Million Vehicle Miles	17
Seat Belt Use	37
Vehicle Miles Traveled Per Capita	29
Workers Using Public Transportation	25
Road and Street Miles Under State Control	36
Highway Employees	47
Public Transit Employees	49
Highway Spending As Percent of Total	32

Welfare - Section L

Percent of Births To Unwed Mothers	5
AFDC Recipients As Percent of Population	25
Food Stamp Recipients As Percent of Population	19
SSI Recipients As Percent Of Population	31
Change in AFDC Recipients	8
Condition of Children Index	41
Percent of Families With Single Parent	14
Typical Monthly AFDC Payments	32
Welfare as Percent Of Poverty Level Income	31
Average SSI State Supplements Per Recipient	39
State Income Tax Liability Of Typical Family in Poverty	23
Child Support Collections Per $ of Administrative Costs	49
Children In Foster Care	33
State and Local Welfare Spending Per Capita	27
Welfare Spending As Percent of Total	24
Administrative Costs Per AFDC Case	20

Revenues & Finances - Section G

Per Capita General Revenue	50
Per Capita Non-Tax Revenue	49
Per Capita General Spending	49
Change in General Expenditures	9
State Government General Spending	31
Debt As Percent of Revenue	44
Per Capita Full Faith and Credit Debt	43
State Solvency Index	12
Pension Plan Assets	40
State Reserves	48
State Budget Process Quality	43
Relative State Spending "Needs"	46

Education - Section H

Math Proficiency, Eighth Grade	33
AFQT Ranks	43
SAT Scores	n/a
ACT Scores	20
Over-25 Population With High School Diploma	43
Students in Private Schools	37
High School Completion Rates	24
Pupil-Teacher Ratio	30
Public School Enrollment	13
Library Holdings Per Capita	36
Education Spending As Percent of Total	16
Spending Per Pupil	48
Average Teacher Salary	43
State Aid Per Pupil	21
Higher Education Spending As Percent of Total	25
Public Higher Education Enrollment	41
State Per Pupil Support of Higher Education	6
Tuition and Fees	34
Average Professor Salary	35
Education Employees	11

Health - Section I

Infant Mortality Rates	15
State Health Rankings	44
Population Without Health Insurance	3
Abortions	37
Alcohol Consumption	48
Percent Smokers	10
Percent Overweight	15
AIDS Cases	29
Health And Hospital Spending As Percent Of Total	14
Per Capita Medicaid Spending	16
Medicaid Spending Per Aged Recipient	35
Medicaid Spending Per AFDC Child	25
Medicare Payment Per Hospital -Day	47
Population in HMOs	40

Crime - Section J

Crime Rate	28
Violent Crime Rate	23
Murder Rate	9
Property Crime Rate	29
Motor Vehicle Theft Rate	36
Violent Crime Rate Change	23
Change in Prisoners	40
Incarceration Rate	21
Juvenile Violent Crime Rate	28
Corrections Employees	28
State Corrections Spending	45
Law Enforcement Spending As Percent of Total	34

Transportation - Section K

Percent of Travel on Interstates	36
Interstate Mileage In Poor Condition	4
Deficient Bridges	39
Traffic Deaths Per 100 Million Vehicle Miles	35
Seat Belt Use	45
Vehicle Miles Traveled Per Capita	9
Workers Using Public Transportation	49
Road and Street Miles Under State Control	16
Highway Employees	14
Public Transit Employees	39
Highway Spending As Percent of Total	15

Welfare - Section L

Percent of Births To Unwed Mothers	11
AFDC Recipients As Percent of Population	45
Food Stamp Recipients As Percent of Population	11
SSI Recipients As Percent Of Population	6
Change in AFDC Recipients	45
Condition of Children Index	40
Percent of Families With Single Parent	26
Typical Monthly AFDC Payments	45
Welfare as Percent Of Poverty Level Income	44
Average SSI State Supplements Per Recipient	43
State Income Tax Liability Of Typical Family in Poverty	11
Child Support Collections Per $ of Administrative Costs	31
Children In Foster Care	43
State and Local Welfare Spending Per Capita	29
Welfare Spending As Percent of Total	11
Administrative Costs Per AFDC Case	29

California

Population - Section A

Population 1996	1
Percent Change in Population	18
Population 2000	1
Median Age	47
Percent Population African-American	24
Percent Population In Poverty	9
Percent Population Female	46
Birth Rates	4
Death Rates	31
Illegal Immigrant Population	1

Economies - Section B

Personal Income	1
Per Capita Personal Income	12
Percent Personal Income From Wages and Salaries	28
Average Annual Pay	6
Cost Of Living	14
Average Annual Pay in Manufacturing	7
Average Annual Pay in Retailing	5
Unemployment Rate	7
Government Employment	27
Manufacturing Employment	28
Fortune 500 Companies	18
Tourism Spending Per Capita	16
Exports Per Capita	6
Percent Change in Home Prices	49
Net Farm Income	1
Financial Institution Assets	12
Bankruptcy Filings	6
Patents Issued	8
WC Disability Payment	24
UC Average Weekly Benefit	24
Economic Momentum	12
Employment Change	8
Manufacturing Employment Change	13
Home Ownership	47
Gambling	4

Electricity Use Per Residential Customer	47
Revenue Per Kwh	37
New Companies	7

Geography - Section C

Total Land Area	3
Federally-Owned Land	3
State Park Acreage	2
State Park Visitors	34
Population Not Active	39
Hunters With Firearms	44
Registered Boats	2
State Spending For The Arts	46
Energy Consumption and Per Capita	47
Toxic Chemical Release Per Capita	46
Hazardous Waste Sites	3
Polluted Rivers	10
Air Pollution Emissions	2

Government - Section D

Members of US House	1
Legislators Per Million Population	50
Units of Government	42
Female Legislators	24
Turnover in Legislatures	2
Democrats in State Legislatures	19
Governor's Power Rating	32
Number of Statewide Elected Officials	7
State and Local Government Employees	49
State and Local Average Salaries	3
Local Employment	1
Local Spending Accountability	45
Registered Voters	45
Statewide Initiatives	2

Federal - Section E

Per Capita Federal Spending	28
Increase In Federal Spending	36
Per Capita Federal Grant Spending	22
Per Capita Federal Spending On Procurement	10
Per Capita Federal Spending on Social Security and Medicare	40
Social Security Benefits	18
Federal Spending On Employee Wages and Salaries	28
Federal Grant Spending Per $ of State Tax Revenue	30
General Revenue From Federal Government	18
Federal Tax Burden Per Capita	17
Highway Charges Returned to States	34
Terms of Trade	32
Per Capita Federal Income Tax Liability	17

Taxes - Section F

Tax Revenue	35
Per Capita Tax Revenue	17
Tax Effort	24
Tax Capacity	9
Percent Change In Taxes	47
Property Taxes Per Capita	30
Property Tax Revenue as Percent of Three-Tax Revenues	32
Sales Taxes Per Capita	13
Sales Tax Revenue as Percent of Three-Tax Revenues	22
Services With Sales Tax	46
Income Taxes Per Capita	16
Income Tax Revenue as Percent of Three-Tax Revenues	19
Motor Fuel Taxes	34
Tobacco Taxes	17
Tax Burden on High Income Family	13
Progressivity of Taxes	47

Revenues & Finances - Section G

Per Capita General Revenue	10
Per Capita Non-Tax Revenue	12
Per Capita General Spending	12
Change in General Expenditures	25
State Government General Spending	37
Debt As Percent of Revenue	21
Per Capita Full Faith and Credit Debt	29
State Solvency Index	34
Pension Plan Assets	5
State Reserves	45
State Budget Process Quality	44
Relative State Spending "Needs"	28

Education - Section H

Math Proficiency, Eighth Grade	31
AFQT Ranks	39
SAT Scores	8
ACT Scores	n/a
Over-25 Population With High School Diploma	37
Students in Private Schools	19
High School Completion Rates	50
Pupil-Teacher Ratio	49
Public School Enrollment	25
Library Holdings Per Capita	45
Education Spending As Percent of Total	45
Spending Per Pupil	32
Average Teacher Salary	8
State Aid Per Pupil	17
Higher Education Spending As Percent of Total	42
Public Higher Education Enrollment	10
State Per Pupil Support of Higher Education	37
Tuition and Fees	23
Average Professor Salary	6
Education Employees	50

Health - Section I

Infant Mortality Rates	38
State Health Rankings	21
Population Without Health Insurance	7
Abortions	2
Alcohol Consumption	24
Percent Smokers	49
Percent Overweight	38
AIDS Cases	9
Health And Hospital Spending As Percent Of Total	13
Per Capita Medicaid Spending	38
Medicaid Spending Per Aged Recipient	49
Medicaid Spending Per AFDC Child	46
Medicare Payment Per Hospital -Day	1
Population in HMOs	3

Crime - Section J

Crime Rate	13
Violent Crime Rate	6
Murder Rate	5
Property Crime Rate	19
Motor Vehicle Theft Rate	2
Violent Crime Rate Change	38
Change in Prisoners	n/a
Incarceration Rate	10
Juvenile Violent Crime Rate	3
Corrections Employees	14
State Corrections Spending	26
Law Enforcement Spending As Percent of Total	3

Transportation - Section K

Percent of Travel on Interstates	19
Interstate Mileage In Poor Condition	38
Deficient Bridges	25
Traffic Deaths Per 100 Million Vehicle Miles	46
Seat Belt Use	1
Vehicle Miles Traveled Per Capita	41
Workers Using Public Transportation	8
Road and Street Miles Under State Control	40
Highway Employees	50
Public Transit Employees	7
Highway Spending As Percent of Total	50

Welfare - Section L

Percent of Births To Unwed Mothers	23
AFDC Recipients As Percent of Population	1
Food Stamp Recipients As Percent of Population	16
SSI Recipients As Percent Of Population	9
Change in AFDC Recipients	6
Condition of Children Index	32
Percent of Families With Single Parent	14
Typical Monthly AFDC Payments	3
Welfare as Percent Of Poverty Level Income	6
Average SSI State Supplements Per Recipient	3
State Income Tax Liability Of Typical Family in Poverty	23
Child Support Collections Per $ of Administrative Costs	42
Children In Foster Care	5
State and Local Welfare Spending Per Capita	13
Welfare Spending As Percent of Total	20
Administrative Costs Per AFDC Case	27

Colorado

Population - Section A

Population 1996	25
Percent Change in Population	5
Population 2000	24
Median Age	22
Percent Population African-American	31
Percent Population In Poverty	36
Percent Population Female	40
Birth Rates	16
Death Rates	43
Illegal Immigrant Population	11

Economies - Section B

Personal Income	22
Per Capita Personal Income	13
Percent Personal Income From Wages and Salaries	8
Average Annual Pay	15
Cost Of Living	19
Average Annual Pay in Manufacturing	14
Average Annual Pay in Retailing	16
Unemployment Rate	44
Government Employment	31
Manufacturing Employment	41
Fortune 500 Companies	34
Tourism Spending Per Capita	7
Exports Per Capita	31
Percent Change in Home Prices	3
Net Farm Income	22
Financial Institution Assets	43
Bankruptcy Filings	23
Patents Issued	10
WC Disability Payment	26
UC Average Weekly Benefit	26
Economic Momentum	7
Employment Change	22
Manufacturing Employment Change	20
Home Ownership	38
Gambling	19

Electricity Use Per Residential Customer	42
Revenue Per Kwh	30
New Companies	2

Geography - Section C

Total Land Area	8
Federally-Owned Land	11
State Park Acreage	6
State Park Visitors	22
Population Not Active	49
Hunters With Firearms	34
Registered Boats	34
State Spending For The Arts	40
Energy Consumption and Per Capita	39
Toxic Chemical Release Per Capita	48
Hazardous Waste Sites	22
Polluted Rivers	44
Air Pollution Emissions	31

Government - Section D

Members of US House	23
Legislators Per Million Population	35
Units of Government	18
Female Legislators	3
Turnover in Legislatures	12
Democrats in State Legislatures	38
Governor's Power Rating	32
Number of Statewide Elected Officials	30
State and Local Government Employees	27
State and Local Average Salaries	18
Local Employment	13
Local Spending Accountability	27
Registered Voters	15
Statewide Initiatives	3

Federal - Section E

Per Capita Federal Spending	20
Increase In Federal Spending	42
Per Capita Federal Grant Spending	46
Per Capita Federal Spending On Procurement	6
Per Capita Federal Spending on Social Security and Medicare	48
Social Security Benefits	31
Federal Spending On Employee Wages and Salaries	7
Federal Grant Spending Per $ of State Tax Revenue	22
General Revenue From Federal Government	42
Federal Tax Burden Per Capita	12
Highway Charges Returned to States	26
Terms of Trade	47
Per Capita Federal Income Tax Liability	10

Taxes - Section F

Tax Revenue	42
Per Capita Tax Revenue	25
Tax Effort	39
Tax Capacity	11
Percent Change In Taxes	19
Property Taxes Per Capita	24
Property Tax Revenue as Percent of Three-Tax Revenues	25
Sales Taxes Per Capita	21
Sales Tax Revenue as Percent of Three-Tax Revenues	27
Services With Sales Tax	45
Income Taxes Per Capita	20
Income Tax Revenue as Percent of Three-Tax Revenues	25
Motor Fuel Taxes	15
Tobacco Taxes	36
Tax Burden on High Income Family	34
Progressivity of Taxes	22

Revenues & Finances - Section G

Per Capita General Revenue	25
Per Capita Non-Tax Revenue	13
Per Capita General Spending	19
Change in General Expenditures	7
State Government General Spending	43
Debt As Percent of Revenue	8
Per Capita Full Faith and Credit Debt	23
State Solvency Index	6
Pension Plan Assets	8
State Reserves	22
State Budget Process Quality	1
Relative State Spending "Needs"	20

Education - Section H

Math Proficiency, Eighth Grade	14
AFQT Ranks	18
SAT Scores	n/a
ACT Scores	7
Over-25 Population With High School Diploma	5
Students in Private Schools	28
High School Completion Rates	24
Pupil-Teacher Ratio	40
Public School Enrollment	21
Library Holdings Per Capita	29
Education Spending As Percent of Total	34
Spending Per Pupil	36
Average Teacher Salary	22
State Aid Per Pupil	38
Higher Education Spending As Percent of Total	16
Public Higher Education Enrollment	8
State Per Pupil Support of Higher Education	47
Tuition and Fees	26
Average Professor Salary	18
Education Employees	34

Health - Section I

Infant Mortality Rates	21
State Health Rankings	10
Population Without Health Insurance	17
Abortions	36
Alcohol Consumption	8
Percent Smokers	31
Percent Overweight	48
AIDS Cases	25
Health And Hospital Spending As Percent Of Total	35
Per Capita Medicaid Spending	44
Medicaid Spending Per Aged Recipient	22
Medicaid Spending Per AFDC Child	42
Medicare Payment Per Hospital -Day	5
Population in HMOs	10

Crime - Section J

Crime Rate	19
Violent Crime Rate	29
Murder Rate	27
Property Crime Rate	17
Motor Vehicle Theft Rate	29
Violent Crime Rate Change	45
Change in Prisoners	12
Incarceration Rate	25
Juvenile Violent Crime Rate	27
Corrections Employees	27
State Corrections Spending	23
Law Enforcement Spending As Percent of Total	15

Transportation - Section K

Percent of Travel on Interstates	20
Interstate Mileage In Poor Condition	12
Deficient Bridges	36
Traffic Deaths Per 100 Million Vehicle Miles	38
Seat Belt Use	37
Vehicle Miles Traveled Per Capita	31
Workers Using Public Transportation	15
Road and Street Miles Under State Control	38
Highway Employees	29
Public Transit Employees	9
Highway Spending As Percent of Total	27

Welfare - Section L

Percent of Births To Unwed Mothers	45
AFDC Recipients As Percent of Population	39
Food Stamp Recipients As Percent of Population	41
SSI Recipients As Percent Of Population	37
Change in AFDC Recipients	29
Condition of Children Index	28
Percent of Families With Single Parent	26
Typical Monthly AFDC Payments	27
Welfare as Percent Of Poverty Level Income	17
Average SSI State Supplements Per Recipient	6
State Income Tax Liability Of Typical Family in Poverty	23
Child Support Collections Per $ of Administrative Costs	34
Children In Foster Care	13
State and Local Welfare Spending Per Capita	44
Welfare Spending As Percent of Total	45
Administrative Costs Per AFDC Case	26

Connecticut

Population - Section A

Population 1996	28
Percent Change in Population	46
Population 2000	29
Median Age	7
Percent Population African-American	21
Percent Population In Poverty	29
Percent Population Female	18
Birth Rates	37
Death Rates	38
Illegal Immigrant Population	18

Economies - Section B

Personal Income	21
Per Capita Personal Income	1
Percent Personal Income From Wages and Salaries	29
Average Annual Pay	2
Cost Of Living	6
Average Annual Pay in Manufacturing	2
Average Annual Pay in Retailing	3
Unemployment Rate	21
Government Employment	43
Manufacturing Employment	17
Fortune 500 Companies	1
Tourism Spending Per Capita	36
Exports Per Capita	18
Percent Change in Home Prices	48
Net Farm Income	39
Financial Institution Assets	23
Bankruptcy Filings	31
Patents Issued	2
WC Disability Payment	5
UC Average Weekly Benefit	5
Economic Momentum	30
Employment Change	21
Manufacturing Employment Change	31
Home Ownership	20
Gambling	26

Electricity Use Per Residential Customer	37
Revenue Per Kwh	40
New Companies	30

Geography - Section C

Total Land Area	48
Federally-Owned Land	49
State Park Acreage	18
State Park Visitors	28
Population Not Active	40
Hunters With Firearms	45
Registered Boats	33
State Spending For The Arts	12
Energy Consumption and Per Capita	46
Toxic Chemical Release Per Capita	39
Hazardous Waste Sites	28
Polluted Rivers	32
Air Pollution Emissions	41

Government - Section D

Members of US House	23
Legislators Per Million Population	17
Units of Government	39
Female Legislators	10
Turnover in Legislatures	46
Democrats in State Legislatures	11
Governor's Power Rating	8
Number of Statewide Elected Officials	18
State and Local Government Employees	40
State and Local Average Salaries	5
Local Employment	43
Local Spending Accountability	13
Registered Voters	15
Statewide Initiatives	n/a

Federal - Section E

Per Capita Federal Spending	16
Increase In Federal Spending	50
Per Capita Federal Grant Spending	16
Per Capita Federal Spending On Procurement	8
Per Capita Federal Spending on Social Security and Medicare	5
Social Security Benefits	1
Federal Spending On Employee Wages and Salaries	41
Federal Grant Spending Per $ of State Tax Revenue	47
General Revenue From Federal Government	41
Federal Tax Burden Per Capita	1
Highway Charges Returned to States	6
Terms of Trade	44
Per Capita Federal Income Tax Liability	1

Taxes - Section F

Tax Revenue	16
Per Capita Tax Revenue	2
Tax Effort	17
Tax Capacity	4
Percent Change In Taxes	17
Property Taxes Per Capita	3
Property Tax Revenue as Percent of Three-Tax Revenues	10
Sales Taxes Per Capita	9
Sales Tax Revenue as Percent of Three-Tax Revenues	35
Services With Sales Tax	8
Income Taxes Per Capita	9
Income Tax Revenue as Percent of Three-Tax Revenues	32
Motor Fuel Taxes	1
Tobacco Taxes	8
Tax Burden on High Income Family	14
Progressivity of Taxes	17

Connecticut

Revenues & Finances - Section G

Per Capita General Revenue	5
Per Capita Non-Tax Revenue	42
Per Capita General Spending	5
Change in General Expenditures	38
State Government General Spending	5
Debt As Percent of Revenue	16
Per Capita Full Faith and Credit Debt	2
State Solvency Index	49
Pension Plan Assets	13
State Reserves	28
State Budget Process Quality	10
Relative State Spending "Needs"	2

Education - Section H

Math Proficiency, Eighth Grade	8
AFQT Ranks	25
SAT Scores	5
ACT Scores	n/a
Over-25 Population With High School Diploma	17
Students in Private Schools	12
High School Completion Rates	2
Pupil-Teacher Ratio	4
Public School Enrollment	42
Library Holdings Per Capita	7
Education Spending As Percent of Total	43
Spending Per Pupil	4
Average Teacher Salary	2
State Aid Per Pupil	18
Higher Education Spending As Percent of Total	48
Public Higher Education Enrollment	48
State Per Pupil Support of Higher Education	7
Tuition and Fees	7
Average Professor Salary	2
Education Employees	29

Health - Section I

Infant Mortality Rates	35
State Health Rankings	8
Population Without Health Insurance	39
Abortions	10
Alcohol Consumption	28
Percent Smokers	42
Percent Overweight	43
AIDS Cases	6
Health And Hospital Spending As Percent Of Total	31
Per Capita Medicaid Spending	3
Medicaid Spending Per Aged Recipient	3
Medicaid Spending Per AFDC Child	26
Medicare Payment Per Hospital -Day	14
Population in HMOs	8

Crime - Section J

Crime Rate	33
Violent Crime Rate	32
Murder Rate	33
Property Crime Rate	32
Motor Vehicle Theft Rate	17
Violent Crime Rate Change	48
Change in Prisoners	37
Incarceration Rate	27
Juvenile Violent Crime Rate	7
Corrections Employees	13
State Corrections Spending	19
Law Enforcement Spending As Percent of Total	23

Transportation - Section K

Percent of Travel on Interstates	4
Interstate Mileage In Poor Condition	6
Deficient Bridges	21
Traffic Deaths Per 100 Million Vehicle Miles	30
Seat Belt Use	26
Vehicle Miles Traveled Per Capita	42
Workers Using Public Transportation	11
Road and Street Miles Under State Control	20
Highway Employees	24
Public Transit Employees	32
Highway Spending As Percent of Total	39

Welfare - Section L

Percent of Births To Unwed Mothers	25
AFDC Recipients As Percent of Population	11
Food Stamp Recipients As Percent of Population	35
SSI Recipients As Percent Of Population	42
Change in AFDC Recipients	9
Condition of Children Index	12
Percent of Families With Single Parent	26
Typical Monthly AFDC Payments	9
Welfare as Percent Of Poverty Level Income	5
Average SSI State Supplements Per Recipient	2
State Income Tax Liability Of Typical Family in Poverty	23
Child Support Collections Per $ of Administrative Costs	30
Children In Foster Care	10
State and Local Welfare Spending Per Capita	5
Welfare Spending As Percent of Total	15
Administrative Costs Per AFDC Case	31

Delaware

Population - Section A

Population 1996	46
Percent Change in Population	15
Population 2000	46
Median Age	22
Percent Population African-American	9
Percent Population In Poverty	45
Percent Population Female	23
Birth Rates	25
Death Rates	14
Illegal Immigrant Population	44

Economies - Section B

Personal Income	44
Per Capita Personal Income	5
Percent Personal Income From Wages and Salaries	6
Average Annual Pay	8
Cost Of Living	12
Average Annual Pay in Manufacturing	1
Average Annual Pay in Retailing	19
Unemployment Rate	30
Government Employment	45
Manufacturing Employment	25
Fortune 500 Companies	2
Tourism Spending Per Capita	26
Exports Per Capita	11
Percent Change in Home Prices	46
Net Farm Income	41
Financial Institution Assets	1
Bankruptcy Filings	42
Patents Issued	1
WC Disability Payment	43
UC Average Weekly Benefit	43
Economic Momentum	8
Employment Change	15
Manufacturing Employment Change	37
Home Ownership	12
Gambling	27

Electricity Use Per

Residential Customer	26
Revenue Per Kwh	8
New Companies	8

Geography - Section C

Total Land Area	49
Federally-Owned Land	48
State Park Acreage	49
State Park Visitors	11
Population Not Active	10
Hunters With Firearms	41
Registered Boats	44
State Spending For The Arts	2
Energy Consumption and Per Capita	21
Toxic Chemical Release Per Capita	31
Hazardous Waste Sites	19
Polluted Rivers	5
Air Pollution Emissions	47

Government - Section D

Members of US House	44
Legislators Per Million Population	11
Units of Government	22
Female Legislators	15
Turnover in Legislatures	48
Democrats in State Legislatures	36
Governor's Power Rating	28
Number of Statewide Elected Officials	18
State and Local Government Employees	19
State and Local Average Salaries	20
Local Employment	49
Local Spending Accountability	49
Registered Voters	20
Statewide Initiatives	n/a

Federal - Section E

Per Capita Federal Spending	36
Increase In Federal Spending	7
Per Capita Federal Grant Spending	23
Per Capita Federal Spending On Procurement	48
Per Capita Federal Spending on Social Security and Medicare	16
Social Security Benefits	6
Federal Spending On Employee Wages and Salaries	27
Federal Grant Spending Per $ of State Tax Revenue	45
General Revenue From Federal Government	45
Federal Tax Burden Per Capita	9
Highway Charges Returned to States	11
Terms of Trade	36
Per Capita Federal Income Tax Liability	12

Taxes - Section F

Tax Revenue	41
Per Capita Tax Revenue	14
Tax Effort	48
Tax Capacity	6
Percent Change In Taxes	40
Property Taxes Per Capita	43
Property Tax Revenue as Percent of Three-Tax Revenues	41
Sales Taxes Per Capita	48
Sales Tax Revenue as Percent of Three-Tax Revenues	48
Services With Sales Tax	4
Income Taxes Per Capita	6
Income Tax Revenue as Percent of Three-Tax Revenues	1
Motor Fuel Taxes	11
Tobacco Taxes	31
Tax Burden on High Income Family	41
Progressivity of Taxes	40

Revenues & Finances - Section G

Per Capita General Revenue	7
Per Capita Non-Tax Revenue	3
Per Capita General Spending	11
Change in General Expenditures	42
State Government General Spending	3
Debt As Percent of Revenue	5
Per Capita Full Faith and Credit Debt	17
State Solvency Index	17
Pension Plan Assets	21
State Reserves	2
State Budget Process Quality	15
Relative State Spending "Needs"	7

Education - Section H

Math Proficiency, Eighth Grade	27
AFQT Ranks	39
SAT Scores	10
ACT Scores	n/a
Over-25 Population With High School Diploma	30
Students in Private Schools	1
High School Completion Rates	7
Pupil-Teacher Ratio	25
Public School Enrollment	48
Library Holdings Per Capita	45
Education Spending As Percent of Total	8
Spending Per Pupil	6
Average Teacher Salary	11
State Aid Per Pupil	3
Higher Education Spending As Percent of Total	4
Public Higher Education Enrollment	9
State Per Pupil Support of Higher Education	30
Tuition and Fees	6
Average Professor Salary	4
Education Employees	40

Health - Section I

Infant Mortality Rates	19
State Health Rankings	37
Population Without Health Insurance	26
Abortions	3
Alcohol Consumption	4
Percent Smokers	9
Percent Overweight	19
AIDS Cases	5
Health And Hospital Spending As Percent Of Total	40
Per Capita Medicaid Spending	23
Medicaid Spending Per Aged Recipient	7
Medicaid Spending Per AFDC Child	29
Medicare Payment Per Hospital -Day	30
Population in HMOs	5

Crime - Section J

Crime Rate	23
Violent Crime Rate	12
Murder Rate	40
Property Crime Rate	25
Motor Vehicle Theft Rate	26
Violent Crime Rate Change	12
Change in Prisoners	34
Incarceration Rate	13
Juvenile Violent Crime Rate	n/a
Corrections Employees	12
State Corrections Spending	36
Law Enforcement Spending As Percent of Total	21

Transportation - Section K

Percent of Travel on Interstates	50
Interstate Mileage In Poor Condition	n/a
Deficient Bridges	32
Traffic Deaths Per 100 Million Vehicle Miles	13
Seat Belt Use	19
Vehicle Miles Traveled Per Capita	19
Workers Using Public Transportation	21
Road and Street Miles Under State Control	2
Highway Employees	13
Public Transit Employees	10
Highway Spending As Percent of Total	14

Welfare - Section L

Percent of Births To Unwed Mothers	9
AFDC Recipients As Percent of Population	32
Food Stamp Recipients As Percent of Population	31
SSI Recipients As Percent Of Population	35
Change in AFDC Recipients	20
Condition of Children Index	20
Percent of Families With Single Parent	8
Typical Monthly AFDC Payments	28
Welfare as Percent Of Poverty Level Income	33
Average SSI State Supplements Per Recipient	5
State Income Tax Liability Of Typical Family in Poverty	12
Child Support Collections Per $ of Administrative Costs	40
Children In Foster Care	35
State and Local Welfare Spending Per Capita	39
Welfare Spending As Percent of Total	46
Administrative Costs Per AFDC Case	6

Population - Section A

Population 1996	4
Percent Change in Population	11
Population 2000	4
Median Age	2
Percent Population African-American	14
Percent Population In Poverty	15
Percent Population Female	15
Birth Rates	38
Death Rates	25
Illegal Immigrant Population	4

Economies - Section B

Personal Income	4
Per Capita Personal Income	20
Percent Personal Income From Wages and Salaries	48
Average Annual Pay	30
Cost Of Living	30
Average Annual Pay in Manufacturing	28
Average Annual Pay in Retailing	14
Unemployment Rate	26
Government Employment	38
Manufacturing Employment	42
Fortune 500 Companies	32
Tourism Spending Per Capita	4
Exports Per Capita	29
Percent Change in Home Prices	35
Net Farm Income	10
Financial Institution Assets	38
Bankruptcy Filings	24
Patents Issued	26
WC Disability Payment	25
UC Average Weekly Benefit	25
Economic Momentum	11
Employment Change	6
Manufacturing Employment Change	23
Home Ownership	50
Gambling	9

Electricity Use Per Residential Customer	7
Revenue Per Kwh	39
New Companies	12

Geography - Section C

Total Land Area	26
Federally-Owned Land	16
State Park Acreage	4
State Park Visitors	47
Population Not Active	26
Hunters With Firearms	42
Registered Boats	4
State Spending For The Arts	5
Energy Consumption and Per Capita	42
Toxic Chemical Release Per Capita	33
Hazardous Waste Sites	6
Polluted Rivers	31
Air Pollution Emissions	3

Government - Section D

Members of US House	4
Legislators Per Million Population	48
Units of Government	48
Female Legislators	21
Turnover in Legislatures	42
Democrats in State Legislatures	33
Governor's Power Rating	28
Number of Statewide Elected Officials	7
State and Local Government Employees	42
State and Local Average Salaries	23
Local Employment	6
Local Spending Accountability	5
Registered Voters	29
Statewide Initiatives	7

Federal - Section E

Per Capita Federal Spending	13
Increase In Federal Spending	6
Per Capita Federal Grant Spending	48
Per Capita Federal Spending On Procurement	23
Per Capita Federal Spending on Social Security and Medicare	1
Social Security Benefits	20
Federal Spending On Employee Wages and Salaries	29
Federal Grant Spending Per $ of State Tax Revenue	40
General Revenue From Federal Government	47
Federal Tax Burden Per Capita	19
Highway Charges Returned to States	35
Terms of Trade	48
Per Capita Federal Income Tax Liability	14

Taxes - Section F

Tax Revenue	40
Per Capita Tax Revenue	28
Tax Effort	39
Tax Capacity	15
Percent Change In Taxes	5
Property Taxes Per Capita	19
Property Tax Revenue as Percent of Three-Tax Revenues	15
Sales Taxes Per Capita	4
Sales Tax Revenue as Percent of Three-Tax Revenues	7
Services With Sales Tax	16
Income Taxes Per Capita	n/a
Income Tax Revenue as Percent of Three-Tax Revenues	n/a
Motor Fuel Taxes	46
Tobacco Taxes	23
Tax Burden on High Income Family	42
Progressivity of Taxes	24

Florida

Georgia

Population - Section A

Population 1996	10
Percent Change in Population	4
Population 2000	10
Median Age	42
Percent Population African-American	4
Percent Population In Poverty	14
Percent Population Female	20
Birth Rates	9
Death Rates	5
Illegal Immigrant Population	17

Economies - Section B

Personal Income	11
Per Capita Personal Income	26
Percent Personal Income From Wages and Salaries	4
Average Annual Pay	17
Cost Of Living	45
Average Annual Pay in Manufacturing	34
Average Annual Pay in Retailing	20
Unemployment Rate	29
Government Employment	33
Manufacturing Employment	20
Fortune 500 Companies	19
Tourism Spending Per Capita	17
Exports Per Capita	27
Percent Change in Home Prices	29
Net Farm Income	8
Financial Institution Assets	13
Bankruptcy Filings	2
Patents Issued	30
WC Disability Payment	49
UC Average Weekly Benefit	49
Economic Momentum	16
Employment Change	33
Manufacturing Employment Change	27
Home Ownership	30
Gambling	14

Electricity Use Per Residential Customer	15
Revenue Per Kwh	20
New Companies	13

Geography - Section C

Total Land Area	21
Federally-Owned Land	24
State Park Acreage	34
State Park Visitors	31
Population Not Active	12
Hunters With Firearms	28
Registered Boats	15
State Spending For The Arts	30
Energy Consumption and Per Capita	26
Toxic Chemical Release Per Capita	26
Hazardous Waste Sites	24
Polluted Rivers	18
Air Pollution Emissions	8

Government - Section D

Members of US House	11
Legislators Per Million Population	31
Units of Government	36
Female Legislators	36
Turnover in Legislatures	24
Democrats in State Legislatures	17
Governor's Power Rating	38
Number of Statewide Elected Officials	3
State and Local Government Employees	8
State and Local Average Salaries	38
Local Employment	8
Local Spending Accountability	3
Registered Voters	36
Statewide Initiatives	n/a

Federal - Section E

Per Capita Federal Spending	33
Increase In Federal Spending	2
Per Capita Federal Grant Spending	37
Per Capita Federal Spending On Procurement	21
Per Capita Federal Spending on Social Security and Medicare	42
Social Security Benefits	42
Federal Spending On Employee Wages and Salaries	11
Federal Grant Spending Per $ of State Tax Revenue	24
General Revenue From Federal Government	35
Federal Tax Burden Per Capita	28
Highway Charges Returned to States	48
Terms of Trade	33
Per Capita Federal Income Tax Liability	23

Taxes - Section F

Tax Revenue	31
Per Capita Tax Revenue	32
Tax Effort	24
Tax Capacity	31
Percent Change In Taxes	10
Property Taxes Per Capita	32
Property Tax Revenue as Percent of Three-Tax Revenues	31
Sales Taxes Per Capita	23
Sales Tax Revenue as Percent of Three-Tax Revenues	23
Services With Sales Tax	27
Income Taxes Per Capita	22
Income Tax Revenue as Percent of Three-Tax Revenues	23
Motor Fuel Taxes	50
Tobacco Taxes	45
Tax Burden on High Income Family	26
Progressivity of Taxes	46

Georgia

Hawaii

Population - Section A

Population 1996	41
Percent Change in Population	38
Population 2000	41
Median Age	18
Percent Population African-American	38
Percent Population In Poverty	22
Percent Population Female	48
Birth Rates	11
Death Rates	50
Illegal Immigrant Population	31

Economies - Section B

Personal Income	40
Per Capita Personal Income	11
Percent Personal Income From Wages and Salaries	22
Average Annual Pay	24
Cost Of Living	1
Average Annual Pay in Manufacturing	38
Average Annual Pay in Retailing	8
Unemployment Rate	6
Government Employment	6
Manufacturing Employment	50
Fortune 500 Companies	n/a
Tourism Spending Per Capita	2
Exports Per Capita	50
Percent Change in Home Prices	50
Net Farm Income	50
Financial Institution Assets	7
Bankruptcy Filings	43
Patents Issued	44
WC Disability Payment	19
UC Average Weekly Benefit	19
Economic Momentum	49
Employment Change	50
Manufacturing Employment Change	44
Home Ownership	18
Gambling	n/a

Electricity Use Per Residential Customer	40
Revenue Per Kwh	42
New Companies	15

Geography - Section C

Total Land Area	47
Federally-Owned Land	36
State Park Acreage	45
State Park Visitors	1
Population Not Active	43
Hunters With Firearms	n/a
Registered Boats	50
State Spending For The Arts	1
Energy Consumption and Per Capita	49
Toxic Chemical Release Per Capita	50
Hazardous Waste Sites	45
Polluted Rivers	2
Air Pollution Emissions	49

Government - Section D

Members of US House	38
Legislators Per Million Population	14
Units of Government	50
Female Legislators	32
Turnover in Legislatures	30
Democrats in State Legislatures	3
Governor's Power Rating	1
Number of Statewide Elected Officials	45
State and Local Government Employees	23
State and Local Average Salaries	17
Local Employment	50
Local Spending Accountability	6
Registered Voters	45
Statewide Initiatives	n/a

Federal - Section E

Per Capita Federal Spending	5
Increase In Federal Spending	19
Per Capita Federal Grant Spending	15
Per Capita Federal Spending On Procurement	11
Per Capita Federal Spending on Social Security and Medicare	45
Social Security Benefits	24
Federal Spending On Employee Wages and Salaries	2
Federal Grant Spending Per $ of State Tax Revenue	41
General Revenue From Federal Government	28
Federal Tax Burden Per Capita	20
Highway Charges Returned to States	2
Terms of Trade	19
Per Capita Federal Income Tax Liability	28

Taxes - Section F

Tax Revenue	3
Per Capita Tax Revenue	5
Tax Effort	24
Tax Capacity	2
Percent Change In Taxes	15
Property Taxes Per Capita	34
Property Tax Revenue as Percent of Three-Tax Revenues	47
Sales Taxes Per Capita	1
Sales Tax Revenue as Percent of Three-Tax Revenues	11
Services With Sales Tax	1
Income Taxes Per Capita	5
Income Tax Revenue as Percent of Three-Tax Revenues	16
Motor Fuel Taxes	41
Tobacco Taxes	5
Tax Burden on High Income Family	12
Progressivity of Taxes	36

Hawaii

Revenues & Finances - Section G

Per Capita General Revenue	4
Per Capita Non-Tax Revenue	11
Per Capita General Spending	3
Change in General Expenditures	2
State Government General Spending	2
Debt As Percent of Revenue	13
Per Capita Full Faith and Credit Debt	1
State Solvency Index	44
Pension Plan Assets	12
State Reserves	37
State Budget Process Quality	16
Relative State Spending "Needs"	8

Education - Section H

Math Proficiency, Eighth Grade	33
AFQT Ranks	44
SAT Scores	15
ACT Scores	n/a
Over-25 Population With High School Diploma	22
Students in Private Schools	6
High School Completion Rates	12
Pupil-Teacher Ratio	39
Public School Enrollment	43
Library Holdings Per Capita	33
Education Spending As Percent of Total	50
Spending Per Pupil	22
Average Teacher Salary	24
State Aid Per Pupil	1
Higher Education Spending As Percent of Total	30
Public Higher Education Enrollment	26
State Per Pupil Support of Higher Education	1
Tuition and Fees	32
Average Professor Salary	9
Education Employees	37

Health - Section I

Infant Mortality Rates	42
State Health Rankings	4
Population Without Health Insurance	49
Abortions	13
Alcohol Consumption	11
Percent Smokers	48
Percent Overweight	50
AIDS Cases	18
Health And Hospital Spending As Percent Of Total	29
Per Capita Medicaid Spending	48
Medicaid Spending Per Aged Recipient	28
Medicaid Spending Per AFDC Child	50
Medicare Payment Per Hospital -Day	11
Population in HMOs	18

Crime - Section J

Crime Rate	3
Violent Crime Rate	41
Murder Rate	32
Property Crime Rate	2
Motor Vehicle Theft Rate	7
Violent Crime Rate Change	28
Change in Prisoners	2
Incarceration Rate	36
Juvenile Violent Crime Rate	30
Corrections Employees	32
State Corrections Spending	24
Law Enforcement Spending As Percent of Total	42

Transportation - Section K

Percent of Travel on Interstates	40
Interstate Mileage In Poor Condition	n/a
Deficient Bridges	3
Traffic Deaths Per 100 Million Vehicle Miles	4
Seat Belt Use	6
Vehicle Miles Traveled Per Capita	48
Workers Using Public Transportation	6
Road and Street Miles Under State Control	11
Highway Employees	48
Public Transit Employees	40
Highway Spending As Percent of Total	38

Welfare - Section L

Percent of Births To Unwed Mothers	29
AFDC Recipients As Percent of Population	6
Food Stamp Recipients As Percent of Population	10
SSI Recipients As Percent Of Population	33
Change in AFDC Recipients	1
Condition of Children Index	10
Percent of Families With Single Parent	40
Typical Monthly AFDC Payments	2
Welfare as Percent Of Poverty Level Income	1
Average SSI State Supplements Per Recipient	13
State Income Tax Liability Of Typical Family in Poverty	1
Child Support Collections Per $ of Administrative Costs	38
Children In Foster Care	12
State and Local Welfare Spending Per Capita	23
Welfare Spending As Percent of Total	47
Administrative Costs Per AFDC Case	41

Idaho

Revenues & Finances - Section G

Per Capita General Revenue	41
Per Capita Non-Tax Revenue	28
Per Capita General Spending	44
Change in General Expenditures	6
State Government General Spending	33
Debt As Percent of Revenue	49
Per Capita Full Faith and Credit Debt	46
State Solvency Index	21
Pension Plan Assets	42
State Reserves	42
State Budget Process Quality	35
Relative State Spending "Needs"	37

Education - Section H

Math Proficiency, Eighth Grade	n/a
AFQT Ranks	2
SAT Scores	n/a
ACT Scores	10
Over-25 Population With High School Diploma	13
Students in Private Schools	48
High School Completion Rates	35
Pupil-Teacher Ratio	43
Public School Enrollment	3
Library Holdings Per Capita	19
Education Spending As Percent of Total	13
Spending Per Pupil	45
Average Teacher Salary	38
State Aid Per Pupil	26
Higher Education Spending As Percent of Total	8
Public Higher Education Enrollment	28
State Per Pupil Support of Higher Education	11
Tuition and Fees	46
Average Professor Salary	44
Education Employees	22

Health - Section I

Infant Mortality Rates	31
State Health Rankings	31
Population Without Health Insurance	14
Abortions	49
Alcohol Consumption	33
Percent Smokers	46
Percent Overweight	34
AIDS Cases	47
Health And Hospital Spending As Percent Of Total	20
Per Capita Medicaid Spending	40
Medicaid Spending Per Aged Recipient	17
Medicaid Spending Per AFDC Child	33
Medicare Payment Per Hospital -Day	16
Population in HMOs	43

Crime - Section J

Crime Rate	36
Violent Crime Rate	40
Murder Rate	35
Property Crime Rate	33
Motor Vehicle Theft Rate	42
Violent Crime Rate Change	16
Change in Prisoners	n/a
Incarceration Rate	26
Juvenile Violent Crime Rate	28
Corrections Employees	23
State Corrections Spending	32
Law Enforcement Spending As Percent of Total	20

Transportation - Section K

Percent of Travel on Interstates	35
Interstate Mileage In Poor Condition	11
Deficient Bridges	37
Traffic Deaths Per 100 Million Vehicle Miles	49
Seat Belt Use	40
Vehicle Miles Traveled Per Capita	12
Workers Using Public Transportation	28
Road and Street Miles Under State Control	47
Highway Employees	16
Public Transit Employees	50
Highway Spending As Percent of Total	12

Welfare - Section L

Percent of Births To Unwed Mothers	49
AFDC Recipients As Percent of Population	50
Food Stamp Recipients As Percent of Population	37
SSI Recipients As Percent Of Population	41
Change in AFDC Recipients	5
Condition of Children Index	23
Percent of Families With Single Parent	49
Typical Monthly AFDC Payments	34
Welfare as Percent Of Poverty Level Income	35
Average SSI State Supplements Per Recipient	1
State Income Tax Liability Of Typical Family in Poverty	23
Child Support Collections Per $ of Administrative Costs	37
Children In Foster Care	47
State and Local Welfare Spending Per Capita	48
Welfare Spending As Percent of Total	40
Administrative Costs Per AFDC Case	14

Illinois

Population - Section A

Population 1996	6
Percent Change in Population	35
Population 2000	6
Median Age	41
Percent Population African-American	13
Percent Population In Poverty	22
Percent Population Female	25
Birth Rates	9
Death Rates	17
Illegal Immigrant Population	5

Economies - Section B

Personal Income	5
Per Capita Personal Income	7
Percent Personal Income From Wages and Salaries	13
Average Annual Pay	7
Cost Of Living	16
Average Annual Pay in Manufacturing	10
Average Annual Pay in Retailing	13
Unemployment Rate	25
Government Employment	42
Manufacturing Employment	18
Fortune 500 Companies	5
Tourism Spending Per Capita	24
Exports Per Capita	13
Percent Change in Home Prices	30
Net Farm Income	6
Financial Institution Assets	6
Bankruptcy Filings	18
Patents Issued	11
WC Disability Payment	2
UC Average Weekly Benefit	2
Economic Momentum	40
Employment Change	41
Manufacturing Employment Change	22
Home Ownership	13
Gambling	5

Electricity Use Per Residential Customer	35
Revenue Per Kwh	6
New Companies	44

Geography - Section C

Total Land Area	24
Federally-Owned Land	30
State Park Acreage	5
State Park Visitors	17
Population Not Active	15
Hunters With Firearms	39
Registered Boats	10
State Spending For The Arts	28
Energy Consumption and Per Capita	34
Toxic Chemical Release Per Capita	21
Hazardous Waste Sites	8
Polluted Rivers	24
Air Pollution Emissions	6

Government - Section D

Members of US House	6
Legislators Per Million Population	45
Units of Government	14
Female Legislators	13
Turnover in Legislatures	38
Democrats in State Legislatures	27
Governor's Power Rating	8
Number of Statewide Elected Officials	13
State and Local Government Employees	44
State and Local Average Salaries	12
Local Employment	4
Local Spending Accountability	4
Registered Voters	23
Statewide Initiatives	n/a

Federal - Section E

Per Capita Federal Spending	44
Increase In Federal Spending	30
Per Capita Federal Grant Spending	27
Per Capita Federal Spending On Procurement	45
Per Capita Federal Spending on Social Security and Medicare	23
Social Security Benefits	5
Federal Spending On Employee Wages and Salaries	36
Federal Grant Spending Per $ of State Tax Revenue	32
General Revenue From Federal Government	39
Federal Tax Burden Per Capita	5
Highway Charges Returned to States	23
Terms of Trade	42
Per Capita Federal Income Tax Liability	5

Taxes - Section F

Tax Revenue	34
Per Capita Tax Revenue	16
Tax Effort	13
Tax Capacity	18
Percent Change In Taxes	29
Property Taxes Per Capita	11
Property Tax Revenue as Percent of Three-Tax Revenues	14
Sales Taxes Per Capita	14
Sales Tax Revenue as Percent of Three-Tax Revenues	29
Services With Sales Tax	44
Income Taxes Per Capita	30
Income Tax Revenue as Percent of Three-Tax Revenues	37
Motor Fuel Taxes	26
Tobacco Taxes	10
Tax Burden on High Income Family	9
Progressivity of Taxes	12

Revenues & Finances - Section G

Per Capita General Revenue	28
Per Capita Non-Tax Revenue	47
Per Capita General Spending	32
Change in General Expenditures	28
State Government General Spending	30
Debt As Percent of Revenue	20
Per Capita Full Faith and Credit Debt	13
State Solvency Index	38
Pension Plan Assets	19
State Reserves	36
State Budget Process Quality	46
Relative State Spending "Needs"	26

Education - Section H

Math Proficiency, Eighth Grade	n/a
AFQT Ranks	28
SAT Scores	n/a
ACT Scores	17
Over-25 Population With High School Diploma	29
Students in Private Schools	9
High School Completion Rates	34
Pupil-Teacher Ratio	34
Public School Enrollment	35
Library Holdings Per Capita	17
Education Spending As Percent of Total	38
Spending Per Pupil	29
Average Teacher Salary	10
State Aid Per Pupil	48
Higher Education Spending As Percent of Total	37
Public Higher Education Enrollment	19
State Per Pupil Support of Higher Education	33
Tuition and Fees	16
Average Professor Salary	41
Education Employees	45

Health - Section I

Infant Mortality Rates	13
State Health Rankings	25
Population Without Health Insurance	38
Abortions	14
Alcohol Consumption	15
Percent Smokers	22
Percent Overweight	17
AIDS Cases	15
Health And Hospital Spending As Percent Of Total	33
Per Capita Medicaid Spending	21
Medicaid Spending Per Aged Recipient	27
Medicaid Spending Per AFDC Child	15
Medicare Payment Per Hospital -Day	6
Population in HMOs	25

Crime - Section J

Crime Rate	18
Violent Crime Rate	3
Murder Rate	11
Property Crime Rate	23
Motor Vehicle Theft Rate	18
Violent Crime Rate Change	22
Change in Prisoners	28
Incarceration Rate	24
Juvenile Violent Crime Rate	n/a
Corrections Employees	29
State Corrections Spending	34
Law Enforcement Spending As Percent of Total	8

Transportation - Section K

Percent of Travel on Interstates	6
Interstate Mileage In Poor Condition	29
Deficient Bridges	29
Traffic Deaths Per 100 Million Vehicle Miles	32
Seat Belt Use	22
Vehicle Miles Traveled Per Capita	44
Workers Using Public Transportation	2
Road and Street Miles Under State Control	30
Highway Employees	46
Public Transit Employees	3
Highway Spending As Percent of Total	22

Welfare - Section L

Percent of Births To Unwed Mothers	13
AFDC Recipients As Percent of Population	7
Food Stamp Recipients As Percent of Population	23
SSI Recipients As Percent Of Population	21
Change in AFDC Recipients	22
Condition of Children Index	35
Percent of Families With Single Parent	14
Typical Monthly AFDC Payments	29
Welfare as Percent Of Poverty Level Income	26
Average SSI State Supplements Per Recipient	29
State Income Tax Liability Of Typical Family in Poverty	5
Child Support Collections Per $ of Administrative Costs	40
Children In Foster Care	2
State and Local Welfare Spending Per Capita	25
Welfare Spending As Percent of Total	25
Administrative Costs Per AFDC Case	33

Indiana

Revenues & Finances - Section G

Education - Section H

Health - Section I

Crime - Section J

Transportation - Section K

Welfare - Section L

Iowa

Revenues & Finances - Section G

Per Capita General Revenue	20
Per Capita Non-Tax Revenue	16
Per Capita General Spending	22
Change in General Expenditures	37
State Government General Spending	29
Debt As Percent of Revenue	50
Per Capita Full Faith and Credit Debt	36
State Solvency Index	7
Pension Plan Assets	37
State Reserves	4
State Budget Process Quality	8
Relative State Spending "Needs"	21

Education - Section H

Math Proficiency, Eighth Grade	1
AFQT Ranks	10
SAT Scores	n/a
ACT Scores	2
Over-25 Population With High School Diploma	10
Students in Private Schools	21
High School Completion Rates	9
Pupil-Teacher Ratio	18
Public School Enrollment	19
Library Holdings Per Capita	11
Education Spending As Percent of Total	12
Spending Per Pupil	23
Average Teacher Salary	33
State Aid Per Pupil	22
Higher Education Spending As Percent of Total	3
Public Higher Education Enrollment	24
State Per Pupil Support of Higher Education	4
Tuition and Fees	25
Average Professor Salary	11
Education Employees	16

Health - Section I

Infant Mortality Rates	33
State Health Rankings	8
Population Without Health Insurance	33
Abortions	39
Alcohol Consumption	43
Percent Smokers	21
Percent Overweight	7
AIDS Cases	45
Health And Hospital Spending As Percent Of Total	9
Per Capita Medicaid Spending	32
Medicaid Spending Per Aged Recipient	30
Medicaid Spending Per AFDC Child	17
Medicare Payment Per Hospital -Day	40
Population in HMOs	42

Crime - Section J

Crime Rate	40
Violent Crime Rate	38
Murder Rate	49
Property Crime Rate	38
Motor Vehicle Theft Rate	43
Violent Crime Rate Change	11
Change in Prisoners	5
Incarceration Rate	41
Juvenile Violent Crime Rate	31
Corrections Employees	48
State Corrections Spending	21
Law Enforcement Spending As Percent of Total	45

Transportation - Section K

Percent of Travel on Interstates	29
Interstate Mileage In Poor Condition	42
Deficient Bridges	33
Traffic Deaths Per 100 Million Vehicle Miles	16
Seat Belt Use	7
Vehicle Miles Traveled Per Capita	33
Workers Using Public Transportation	34
Road and Street Miles Under State Control	46
Highway Employees	15
Public Transit Employees	25
Highway Spending As Percent of Total	8

Welfare - Section L

Percent of Births To Unwed Mothers	42
AFDC Recipients As Percent of Population	35
Food Stamp Recipients As Percent of Population	43
SSI Recipients As Percent Of Population	40
Change in AFDC Recipients	28
Condition of Children Index	5
Percent of Families With Single Parent	45
Typical Monthly AFDC Payments	19
Welfare as Percent Of Poverty Level Income	17
Average SSI State Supplements Per Recipient	32
State Income Tax Liability Of Typical Family in Poverty	23
Child Support Collections Per $ of Administrative Costs	9
Children In Foster Care	29
State and Local Welfare Spending Per Capita	31
Welfare Spending As Percent of Total	35
Administrative Costs Per AFDC Case	28

Kansas

Kansas

Revenues & Finances - Section G

Per Capita General Revenue	24
Per Capita Non-Tax Revenue	22
Per Capita General Spending	29
Change in General Expenditures	26
State Government General Spending	44
Debt As Percent of Revenue	36
Per Capita Full Faith and Credit Debt	30
State Solvency Index	8
Pension Plan Assets	47
State Reserves	12
State Budget Process Quality	38
Relative State Spending "Needs"	23

Education - Section H

Math Proficiency, Eighth Grade	n/a
AFQT Ranks	12
SAT Scores	n/a
ACT Scores	5
Over-25 Population With High School Diploma	8
Students in Private Schools	29
High School Completion Rates	15
Pupil-Teacher Ratio	12
Public School Enrollment	14
Library Holdings Per Capita	5
Education Spending As Percent of Total	4
Spending Per Pupil	26
Average Teacher Salary	25
State Aid Per Pupil	12
Higher Education Spending As Percent of Total	6
Public Higher Education Enrollment	1
State Per Pupil Support of Higher Education	45
Tuition and Fees	38
Average Professor Salary	41
Education Employees	8

Health - Section I

Infant Mortality Rates	6
State Health Rankings	15
Population Without Health Insurance	33
Abortions	17
Alcohol Consumption	46
Percent Smokers	27
Percent Overweight	31
AIDS Cases	35
Health And Hospital Spending As Percent Of Total	21
Per Capita Medicaid Spending	41
Medicaid Spending Per Aged Recipient	21
Medicaid Spending Per AFDC Child	40
Medicare Payment Per Hospital -Day	25
Population in HMOs	37

Crime - Section J

Crime Rate	25
Violent Crime Rate	31
Murder Rate	26
Property Crime Rate	22
Motor Vehicle Theft Rate	37
Violent Crime Rate Change	30
Change in Prisoners	30
Incarceration Rate	30
Juvenile Violent Crime Rate	n/a
Corrections Employees	20
State Corrections Spending	20
Law Enforcement Spending As Percent of Total	30

Transportation - Section K

Percent of Travel on Interstates	32
Interstate Mileage In Poor Condition	17
Deficient Bridges	42
Traffic Deaths Per 100 Million Vehicle Miles	39
Seat Belt Use	40
Vehicle Miles Traveled Per Capita	23
Workers Using Public Transportation	43
Road and Street Miles Under State Control	50
Highway Employees	5
Public Transit Employees	38
Highway Spending As Percent of Total	6

Welfare - Section L

Percent of Births To Unwed Mothers	40
AFDC Recipients As Percent of Population	38
Food Stamp Recipients As Percent of Population	38
SSI Recipients As Percent Of Population	39
Change in AFDC Recipients	31
Condition of Children Index	15
Percent of Families With Single Parent	37
Typical Monthly AFDC Payments	23
Welfare as Percent Of Poverty Level Income	14
Average SSI State Supplements Per Recipient	42
State Income Tax Liability Of Typical Family in Poverty	22
Child Support Collections Per $ of Administrative Costs	47
Children In Foster Care	18
State and Local Welfare Spending Per Capita	45
Welfare Spending As Percent of Total	43
Administrative Costs Per AFDC Case	11

Kentucky

Revenues & Finances - Section G

Per Capita General Revenue	44
Per Capita Non-Tax Revenue	45
Per Capita General Spending	46
Change in General Expenditures	29
State Government General Spending	25
Debt As Percent of Revenue	4
Per Capita Full Faith and Credit Debt	48
State Solvency Index	31
Pension Plan Assets	33
State Reserves	21
State Budget Process Quality	31
Relative State Spending "Needs"	43

Education - Section H

Math Proficiency, Eighth Grade	27
AFQT Ranks	41
SAT Scores	n/a
ACT Scores	23
Over-25 Population With High School Diploma	49
Students in Private Schools	27
High School Completion Rates	43
Pupil-Teacher Ratio	28
Public School Enrollment	40
Library Holdings Per Capita	38
Education Spending As Percent of Total	28
Spending Per Pupil	24
Average Teacher Salary	28
State Aid Per Pupil	10
Higher Education Spending As Percent of Total	23
Public Higher Education Enrollment	36
State Per Pupil Support of Higher Education	19
Tuition and Fees	36
Average Professor Salary	23
Education Employees	12

Health - Section I

Infant Mortality Rates	21
State Health Rankings	41
Population Without Health Insurance	18
Abortions	40
Alcohol Consumption	47
Percent Smokers	1
Percent Overweight	24
AIDS Cases	31
Health And Hospital Spending As Percent Of Total	34
Per Capita Medicaid Spending	13
Medicaid Spending Per Aged Recipient	34
Medicaid Spending Per AFDC Child	19
Medicare Payment Per Hospital -Day	37
Population in HMOs	16

Crime - Section J

Crime Rate	45
Violent Crime Rate	35
Murder Rate	24
Property Crime Rate	45
Motor Vehicle Theft Rate	41
Violent Crime Rate Change	34
Change in Prisoners	29
Incarceration Rate	23
Juvenile Violent Crime Rate	n/a
Corrections Employees	26
State Corrections Spending	40
Law Enforcement Spending As Percent of Total	36

Transportation - Section K

Percent of Travel on Interstates	23
Interstate Mileage In Poor Condition	18
Deficient Bridges	15
Traffic Deaths Per 100 Million Vehicle Miles	45
Seat Belt Use	39
Vehicle Miles Traveled Per Capita	11
Workers Using Public Transportation	29
Road and Street Miles Under State Control	8
Highway Employees	31
Public Transit Employees	26
Highway Spending As Percent of Total	23

Welfare - Section L

Percent of Births To Unwed Mothers	30
AFDC Recipients As Percent of Population	17
Food Stamp Recipients As Percent of Population	6
SSI Recipients As Percent Of Population	2
Change in AFDC Recipients	41
Condition of Children Index	38
Percent of Families With Single Parent	26
Typical Monthly AFDC Payments	43
Welfare as Percent Of Poverty Level Income	42
Average SSI State Supplements Per Recipient	30
State Income Tax Liability Of Typical Family in Poverty	2
Child Support Collections Per $ of Administrative Costs	25
Children In Foster Care	42
State and Local Welfare Spending Per Capita	19
Welfare Spending As Percent of Total	8
Administrative Costs Per AFDC Case	39

Population - Section A

Population 1996	22
Percent Change in Population	45
Population 2000	23
Median Age	44
Percent Population African-American	2
Percent Population In Poverty	3
Percent Population Female	6
Birth Rates	14
Death Rates	2
Illegal Immigrant Population	21

Economies - Section B

Personal Income	24
Per Capita Personal Income	40
Percent Personal Income From Wages and Salaries	32
Average Annual Pay	31
Cost Of Living	38
Average Annual Pay in Manufacturing	19
Average Annual Pay in Retailing	40
Unemployment Rate	5
Government Employment	11
Manufacturing Employment	40
Fortune 500 Companies	41
Tourism Spending Per Capita	21
Exports Per Capita	2
Percent Change in Home Prices	14
Net Farm Income	25
Financial Institution Assets	41
Bankruptcy Filings	16
Patents Issued	41
WC Disability Payment	45
UC Average Weekly Benefit	45
Economic Momentum	39
Employment Change	37
Manufacturing Employment Change	24
Home Ownership	6
Gambling	6

Electricity Use Per Residential Customer	2
Revenue Per Kwh	16
New Companies	34

Geography - Section C

Total Land Area	33
Federally-Owned Land	31
State Park Acreage	44
State Park Visitors	50
Population Not Active	14
Hunters With Firearms	20
Registered Boats	12
State Spending For The Arts	17
Energy Consumption and Per Capita	2
Toxic Chemical Release Per Capita	2
Hazardous Waste Sites	19
Polluted Rivers	26
Air Pollution Emissions	13

Government - Section D

Members of US House	21
Legislators Per Million Population	28
Units of Government	46
Female Legislators	47
Turnover in Legislatures	6
Democrats in State Legislatures	6
Governor's Power Rating	45
Number of Statewide Elected Officials	7
State and Local Government Employees	10
State and Local Average Salaries	48
Local Employment	38
Local Spending Accountability	21
Registered Voters	12
Statewide Initiatives	n/a

Federal - Section E

Per Capita Federal Spending	24
Increase In Federal Spending	8
Per Capita Federal Grant Spending	12
Per Capita Federal Spending On Procurement	27
Per Capita Federal Spending on Social Security and Medicare	19
Social Security Benefits	49
Federal Spending On Employee Wages and Salaries	33
Federal Grant Spending Per $ of State Tax Revenue	4
General Revenue From Federal Government	1
Federal Tax Burden Per Capita	44
Highway Charges Returned to States	46
Terms of Trade	7
Per Capita Federal Income Tax Liability	43

Taxes - Section F

Tax Revenue	45
Per Capita Tax Revenue	47
Tax Effort	36
Tax Capacity	37
Percent Change In Taxes	49
Property Taxes Per Capita	47
Property Tax Revenue as Percent of Three-Tax Revenues	44
Sales Taxes Per Capita	11
Sales Tax Revenue as Percent of Three-Tax Revenues	5
Services With Sales Tax	20
Income Taxes Per Capita	40
Income Tax Revenue as Percent of Three-Tax Revenues	40
Motor Fuel Taxes	21
Tobacco Taxes	36
Tax Burden on High Income Family	45
Progressivity of Taxes	42

Maine

Maine

Maryland

Population - Section A

Population 1996	19
Percent Change in Population	31
Population 2000	19
Median Age	24
Percent Population African-American	5
Percent Population In Poverty	37
Percent Population Female	19
Birth Rates	31
Death Rates	16
Illegal Immigrant Population	12

Economies - Section B

Personal Income	14
Per Capita Personal Income	6
Percent Personal Income From Wages and Salaries	44
Average Annual Pay	10
Cost Of Living	20
Average Annual Pay in Manufacturing	11
Average Annual Pay in Retailing	9
Unemployment Rate	23
Government Employment	13
Manufacturing Employment	43
Fortune 500 Companies	27
Tourism Spending Per Capita	35
Exports Per Capita	41
Percent Change in Home Prices	43
Net Farm Income	34
Financial Institution Assets	48
Bankruptcy Filings	13
Patents Issued	24
WC Disability Payment	10
UC Average Weekly Benefit	10
Economic Momentum	29
Employment Change	28
Manufacturing Employment Change	43
Home Ownership	1
Gambling	18

Electricity Use Per Residential Customer	16
Revenue Per Kwh	5
New Companies	38

Geography - Section C

Total Land Area	42
Federally-Owned Land	44
State Park Acreage	14
State Park Visitors	32
Population Not Active	19
Hunters With Firearms	40
Registered Boats	25
State Spending For The Arts	8
Energy Consumption and Per Capita	40
Toxic Chemical Release Per Capita	40
Hazardous Waste Sites	24
Polluted Rivers	35
Air Pollution Emissions	33

Government - Section D

Members of US House	19
Legislators Per Million Population	25
Units of Government	47
Female Legislators	8
Turnover in Legislatures	49
Democrats in State Legislatures	7
Governor's Power Rating	1
Number of Statewide Elected Officials	30
State and Local Government Employees	41
State and Local Average Salaries	9
Local Employment	30
Local Spending Accountability	8
Registered Voters	39
Statewide Initiatives	n/a

Federal - Section E

Per Capita Federal Spending	2
Increase In Federal Spending	31
Per Capita Federal Grant Spending	43
Per Capita Federal Spending On Procurement	4
Per Capita Federal Spending on Social Security and Medicare	36
Social Security Benefits	21
Federal Spending On Employee Wages and Salaries	4
Federal Grant Spending Per $ of State Tax Revenue	42
General Revenue From Federal Government	44
Federal Tax Burden Per Capita	6
Highway Charges Returned to States	30
Terms of Trade	45
Per Capita Federal Income Tax Liability	9

Taxes - Section F

Tax Revenue	30
Per Capita Tax Revenue	9
Tax Effort	8
Tax Capacity	13
Percent Change In Taxes	41
Property Taxes Per Capita	25
Property Tax Revenue as Percent of Three-Tax Revenues	35
Sales Taxes Per Capita	37
Sales Tax Revenue as Percent of Three-Tax Revenues	44
Services With Sales Tax	26
Income Taxes Per Capita	2
Income Tax Revenue as Percent of Three-Tax Revenues	3
Motor Fuel Taxes	10
Tobacco Taxes	19
Tax Burden on High Income Family	11
Progressivity of Taxes	21

Revenues & Finances - Section G

Per Capita General Revenue	19
Per Capita Non-Tax Revenue	39
Per Capita General Spending	23
Change in General Expenditures	41
State Government General Spending	21
Debt As Percent of Revenue	18
Per Capita Full Faith and Credit Debt	11
State Solvency Index	41
Pension Plan Assets	7
State Reserves	18
State Budget Process Quality	33
Relative State Spending "Needs"	4

Education - Section H

Math Proficiency, Eighth Grade	20
AFQT Ranks	32
SAT Scores	5
ACT Scores	n/a
Over-25 Population With High School Diploma	21
Students in Private Schools	10
High School Completion Rates	5
Pupil-Teacher Ratio	28
Public School Enrollment	41
Library Holdings Per Capita	27
Education Spending As Percent of Total	21
Spending Per Pupil	11
Average Teacher Salary	12
State Aid Per Pupil	31
Higher Education Spending As Percent of Total	26
Public Higher Education Enrollment	22
State Per Pupil Support of Higher Education	42
Tuition and Fees	11
Average Professor Salary	14
Education Employees	41

Health - Section I

Infant Mortality Rates	10
State Health Rankings	12
Population Without Health Insurance	37
Abortions	25
Alcohol Consumption	32
Percent Smokers	39
Percent Overweight	18
AIDS Cases	4
Health And Hospital Spending As Percent Of Total	45
Per Capita Medicaid Spending	29
Medicaid Spending Per Aged Recipient	15
Medicaid Spending Per AFDC Child	7
Medicare Payment Per Hospital -Day	50
Population in HMOs	6

Crime - Section J

Crime Rate	8
Violent Crime Rate	4
Murder Rate	4
Property Crime Rate	11
Motor Vehicle Theft Rate	5
Violent Crime Rate Change	26
Change in Prisoners	38
Incarceration Rate	15
Juvenile Violent Crime Rate	5
Corrections Employees	11
State Corrections Spending	9
Law Enforcement Spending As Percent of Total	5

Transportation - Section K

Percent of Travel on Interstates	5
Interstate Mileage In Poor Condition	25
Deficient Bridges	23
Traffic Deaths Per 100 Million Vehicle Miles	5
Seat Belt Use	15
Vehicle Miles Traveled Per Capita	36
Workers Using Public Transportation	5
Road and Street Miles Under State Control	22
Highway Employees	39
Public Transit Employees	13
Highway Spending As Percent of Total	45

Welfare - Section L

Percent of Births To Unwed Mothers	15
AFDC Recipients As Percent of Population	21
Food Stamp Recipients As Percent of Population	33
SSI Recipients As Percent Of Population	32
Change in AFDC Recipients	19
Condition of Children Index	30
Percent of Families With Single Parent	14
Typical Monthly AFDC Payments	24
Welfare as Percent Of Poverty Level Income	27
Average SSI State Supplements Per Recipient	31
State Income Tax Liability Of Typical Family in Poverty	23
Child Support Collections Per $ of Administrative Costs	12
Children In Foster Care	27
State and Local Welfare Spending Per Capita	32
Welfare Spending As Percent of Total	34
Administrative Costs Per AFDC Case	8

Massachusetts

Revenues & Finances - Section G

Per Capita General Revenue	9
Per Capita Non-Tax Revenue	27
Per Capita General Spending	8
Change in General Expenditures	47
State Government General Spending	6
Debt As Percent of Revenue	7
Per Capita Full Faith and Credit Debt	5
State Solvency Index	50
Pension Plan Assets	38
State Reserves	27
State Budget Process Quality	4
Relative State Spending "Needs"	5

Education - Section H

Math Proficiency, Eighth Grade	10
AFQT Ranks	25
SAT Scores	5
ACT Scores	n/a
Over-25 Population With High School Diploma	18
Students in Private Schools	11
High School Completion Rates	11
Pupil-Teacher Ratio	9
Public School Enrollment	47
Library Holdings Per Capita	3
Education Spending As Percent of Total	48
Spending Per Pupil	7
Average Teacher Salary	7
State Aid Per Pupil	33
Higher Education Spending As Percent of Total	50
Public Higher Education Enrollment	49
State Per Pupil Support of Higher Education	10
Tuition and Fees	5
Average Professor Salary	5
Education Employees	28

Health - Section I

Infant Mortality Rates	48
State Health Rankings	6
Population Without Health Insurance	28
Abortions	6
Alcohol Consumption	14
Percent Smokers	35
Percent Overweight	49
AIDS Cases	13
Health And Hospital Spending As Percent Of Total	24
Per Capita Medicaid Spending	4
Medicaid Spending Per Aged Recipient	8
Medicaid Spending Per AFDC Child	34
Medicare Payment Per Hospital -Day	41
Population in HMOs	2

Crime - Section J

Crime Rate	37
Violent Crime Rate	15
Murder Rate	39
Property Crime Rate	40
Motor Vehicle Theft Rate	12
Violent Crime Rate Change	35
Change in Prisoners	n/a
Incarceration Rate	29
Juvenile Violent Crime Rate	6
Corrections Employees	30
State Corrections Spending	15
Law Enforcement Spending As Percent of Total	28

Transportation - Section K

Percent of Travel on Interstates	10
Interstate Mileage In Poor Condition	43
Deficient Bridges	2
Traffic Deaths Per 100 Million Vehicle Miles	43
Seat Belt Use	40
Vehicle Miles Traveled Per Capita	43
Workers Using Public Transportation	4
Road and Street Miles Under State Control	42
Highway Employees	43
Public Transit Employees	6
Highway Spending As Percent of Total	37

Welfare - Section L

Percent of Births To Unwed Mothers	43
AFDC Recipients As Percent of Population	24
Food Stamp Recipients As Percent of Population	46
SSI Recipients As Percent Of Population	12
Change in AFDC Recipients	43
Condition of Children Index	8
Percent of Families With Single Parent	14
Typical Monthly AFDC Payments	4
Welfare as Percent Of Poverty Level Income	9
Average SSI State Supplements Per Recipient	7
State Income Tax Liability Of Typical Family in Poverty	23
Child Support Collections Per $ of Administrative Costs	16
Children In Foster Care	7
State and Local Welfare Spending Per Capita	4
Welfare Spending As Percent of Total	6
Administrative Costs Per AFDC Case	10

Michigan

Michigan

Revenues & Finances - Section G

Per Capita General Revenue	15
Per Capita Non-Tax Revenue	26
Per Capita General Spending	18
Change in General Expenditures	43
State Government General Spending	27
Debt As Percent of Revenue	41
Per Capita Full Faith and Credit Debt	26
State Solvency Index	43
Pension Plan Assets	16
State Reserves	10
State Budget Process Quality	2
Relative State Spending "Needs"	32

Education - Section H

Math Proficiency, Eighth Grade	12
AFQT Ranks	22
SAT Scores	n/a
ACT Scores	13
Over-25 Population With High School Diploma	23
Students in Private Schools	16
High School Completion Rates	22
Pupil-Teacher Ratio	47
Public School Enrollment	27
Library Holdings Per Capita	24
Education Spending As Percent of Total	11
Spending Per Pupil	9
Average Teacher Salary	6
State Aid Per Pupil	4
Higher Education Spending As Percent of Total	13
Public Higher Education Enrollment	11
State Per Pupil Support of Higher Education	40
Tuition and Fees	8
Average Professor Salary	17
Education Employees	42

Health - Section I

Infant Mortality Rates	16
State Health Rankings	28
Population Without Health Insurance	48
Abortions	24
Alcohol Consumption	34
Percent Smokers	7
Percent Overweight	4
AIDS Cases	33
Health And Hospital Spending As Percent Of Total	15
Per Capita Medicaid Spending	37
Medicaid Spending Per Aged Recipient	24
Medicaid Spending Per AFDC Child	43
Medicare Payment Per Hospital -Day	17
Population in HMOs	21

Crime - Section J

Crime Rate	22
Violent Crime Rate	14
Murder Rate	19
Property Crime Rate	21
Motor Vehicle Theft Rate	9
Violent Crime Rate Change	42
Change in Prisoners	41
Incarceration Rate	11
Juvenile Violent Crime Rate	19
Corrections Employees	15
State Corrections Spending	11
Law Enforcement Spending As Percent of Total	12

Transportation - Section K

Percent of Travel on Interstates	33
Interstate Mileage In Poor Condition	13
Deficient Bridges	11
Traffic Deaths Per 100 Million Vehicle Miles	47
Seat Belt Use	12
Vehicle Miles Traveled Per Capita	34
Workers Using Public Transportation	29
Road and Street Miles Under State Control	49
Highway Employees	49
Public Transit Employees	20
Highway Spending As Percent of Total	47

Welfare - Section L

Percent of Births To Unwed Mothers	12
AFDC Recipients As Percent of Population	8
Food Stamp Recipients As Percent of Population	17
SSI Recipients As Percent Of Population	22
Change in AFDC Recipients	47
Condition of Children Index	29
Percent of Families With Single Parent	8
Typical Monthly AFDC Payments	14
Welfare as Percent Of Poverty Level Income	14
Average SSI State Supplements Per Recipient	26
State Income Tax Liability Of Typical Family in Poverty	6
Child Support Collections Per $ of Administrative Costs	2
Children In Foster Care	37
State and Local Welfare Spending Per Capita	15
Welfare Spending As Percent of Total	16
Administrative Costs Per AFDC Case	15

Minnesota

Population - Section A

Population 1996	20
Percent Change in Population	19
Population 2000	20
Median Age	35
Percent Population African-American	37
Percent Population In Poverty	40
Percent Population Female	35
Birth Rates	31
Death Rates	48
Illegal Immigrant Population	34

Economies - Section B

Personal Income	19
Per Capita Personal Income	9
Percent Personal Income From Wages and Salaries	5
Average Annual Pay	11
Cost Of Living	31
Average Annual Pay in Manufacturing	12
Average Annual Pay in Retailing	25
Unemployment Rate	43
Government Employment	35
Manufacturing Employment	15
Fortune 500 Companies	6
Tourism Spending Per Capita	39
Exports Per Capita	15
Percent Change in Home Prices	21
Net Farm Income	7
Financial Institution Assets	21
Bankruptcy Filings	27
Patents Issued	4
WC Disability Payment	9
UC Average Weekly Benefit	9
Economic Momentum	20
Employment Change	14
Manufacturing Employment Change	16
Home Ownership	5
Gambling	25

Electricity Use Per Residential Customer	32
Revenue Per Kwh	25
New Companies	35

Geography - Section C

Total Land Area	14
Federally-Owned Land	13
State Park Acreage	15
State Park Visitors	37
Population Not Active	38
Hunters With Firearms	11
Registered Boats	3
State Spending For The Arts	9
Energy Consumption and Per Capita	24
Toxic Chemical Release Per Capita	34
Hazardous Waste Sites	12
Polluted Rivers	20
Air Pollution Emissions	21

Government - Section D

Members of US House	19
Legislators Per Million Population	23
Units of Government	9
Female Legislators	7
Turnover in Legislatures	24
Democrats in State Legislatures	18
Governor's Power Rating	21
Number of Statewide Elected Officials	30
State and Local Government Employees	16
State and Local Average Salaries	16
Local Employment	10
Local Spending Accountability	42
Registered Voters	15
Statewide Initiatives	n/a

Federal - Section E

Per Capita Federal Spending	49
Increase In Federal Spending	48
Per Capita Federal Grant Spending	31
Per Capita Federal Spending On Procurement	38
Per Capita Federal Spending on Social Security and Medicare	38
Social Security Benefits	25
Federal Spending On Employee Wages and Salaries	46
Federal Grant Spending Per $ of State Tax Revenue	49
General Revenue From Federal Government	43
Federal Tax Burden Per Capita	15
Highway Charges Returned to States	20
Terms of Trade	37
Per Capita Federal Income Tax Liability	16

Taxes - Section F

Tax Revenue	8
Per Capita Tax Revenue	7
Tax Effort	5
Tax Capacity	19
Percent Change In Taxes	32
Property Taxes Per Capita	17
Property Tax Revenue as Percent of Three-Tax Revenues	29
Sales Taxes Per Capita	15
Sales Tax Revenue as Percent of Three-Tax Revenues	32
Services With Sales Tax	18
Income Taxes Per Capita	7
Income Tax Revenue as Percent of Three-Tax Revenues	9
Motor Fuel Taxes	21
Tobacco Taxes	9
Tax Burden on High Income Family	3
Progressivity of Taxes	50

Revenues & Finances - Section G

Per Capita General Revenue	8
Per Capita Non-Tax Revenue	5
Per Capita General Spending	6
Change in General Expenditures	33
State Government General Spending	22
Debt As Percent of Revenue	22
Per Capita Full Faith and Credit Debt	10
State Solvency Index	18
Pension Plan Assets	44
State Reserves	5
State Budget Process Quality	19
Relative State Spending "Needs"	19

Education - Section H

Math Proficiency, Eighth Grade	1
AFQT Ranks	4
SAT Scores	n/a
ACT Scores	2
Over-25 Population With High School Diploma	7
Students in Private Schools	20
High School Completion Rates	7
Pupil-Teacher Ratio	35
Public School Enrollment	11
Library Holdings Per Capita	25
Education Spending As Percent of Total	32
Spending Per Pupil	19
Average Teacher Salary	17
State Aid Per Pupil	11
Higher Education Spending As Percent of Total	34
Public Higher Education Enrollment	16
State Per Pupil Support of Higher Education	9
Tuition and Fees	15
Average Professor Salary	21
Education Employees	19

Health - Section I

Infant Mortality Rates	34
State Health Rankings	1
Population Without Health Insurance	43
Abortions	28
Alcohol Consumption	15
Percent Smokers	43
Percent Overweight	27
AIDS Cases	39
Health And Hospital Spending As Percent Of Total	19
Per Capita Medicaid Spending	9
Medicaid Spending Per Aged Recipient	2
Medicaid Spending Per AFDC Child	6
Medicare Payment Per Hospital -Day	18
Population in HMOs	9

Crime - Section J

Crime Rate	34
Violent Crime Rate	37
Murder Rate	37
Property Crime Rate	28
Motor Vehicle Theft Rate	35
Violent Crime Rate Change	18
Change in Prisoners	11
Incarceration Rate	49
Juvenile Violent Crime Rate	18
Corrections Employees	42
State Corrections Spending	1
Law Enforcement Spending As Percent of Total	43

Transportation - Section K

Percent of Travel on Interstates	27
Interstate Mileage In Poor Condition	3
Deficient Bridges	46
Traffic Deaths Per 100 Million Vehicle Miles	2
Seat Belt Use	22
Vehicle Miles Traveled Per Capita	28
Workers Using Public Transportation	12
Road and Street Miles Under State Control	43
Highway Employees	18
Public Transit Employees	17
Highway Spending As Percent of Total	21

Welfare - Section L

Percent of Births To Unwed Mothers	47
AFDC Recipients As Percent of Population	27
Food Stamp Recipients As Percent of Population	42
SSI Recipients As Percent Of Population	45
Change in AFDC Recipients	26
Condition of Children Index	11
Percent of Families With Single Parent	21
Typical Monthly AFDC Payments	10
Welfare as Percent Of Poverty Level Income	11
Average SSI State Supplements Per Recipient	10
State Income Tax Liability Of Typical Family in Poverty	39
Child Support Collections Per $ of Administrative Costs	13
Children In Foster Care	20
State and Local Welfare Spending Per Capita	6
Welfare Spending As Percent of Total	10
Administrative Costs Per AFDC Case	12

Mississippi

Population - Section A

Population 1996	31
Percent Change in Population	27
Population 2000	31
Median Age	46
Percent Population African-American	1
Percent Population In Poverty	2
Percent Population Female	1
Birth Rates	13
Death Rates	1
Illegal Immigrant Population	41

Economies - Section B

Personal Income	33
Per Capita Personal Income	50
Percent Personal Income From Wages and Salaries	35
Average Annual Pay	47
Cost Of Living	50
Average Annual Pay in Manufacturing	50
Average Annual Pay in Retailing	43
Unemployment Rate	18
Government Employment	7
Manufacturing Employment	5
Fortune 500 Companies	39
Tourism Spending Per Capita	34
Exports Per Capita	42
Percent Change in Home Prices	26
Net Farm Income	20
Financial Institution Assets	42
Bankruptcy Filings	5
Patents Issued	50
WC Disability Payment	50
UC Average Weekly Benefit	50
Economic Momentum	44
Employment Change	47
Manufacturing Employment Change	47
Home Ownership	2
Gambling	7

Electricity Use Per Residential Customer	9
Revenue Per Kwh	38
New Companies	40

Geography - Section C

Total Land Area	31
Federally-Owned Land	25
State Park Acreage	46
State Park Visitors	42
Population Not Active	7
Hunters With Firearms	12
Registered Boats	19
State Spending For The Arts	32
Energy Consumption and Per Capita	16
Toxic Chemical Release Per Capita	7
Hazardous Waste Sites	46
Polluted Rivers	6
Air Pollution Emissions	22

Government - Section D

Members of US House	29
Legislators Per Million Population	16
Units of Government	27
Female Legislators	46
Turnover in Legislatures	26
Democrats in State Legislatures	8
Governor's Power Rating	32
Number of Statewide Elected Officials	3
State and Local Government Employees	7
State and Local Average Salaries	50
Local Employment	20
Local Spending Accountability	38
Registered Voters	4
Statewide Initiatives	n/a

Federal - Section E

Per Capita Federal Spending	10
Increase In Federal Spending	11
Per Capita Federal Grant Spending	14
Per Capita Federal Spending On Procurement	12
Per Capita Federal Spending on Social Security and Medicare	24
Social Security Benefits	50
Federal Spending On Employee Wages and Salaries	25
Federal Grant Spending Per $ of State Tax Revenue	11
General Revenue From Federal Government	4
Federal Tax Burden Per Capita	50
Highway Charges Returned to States	42
Terms of Trade	3
Per Capita Federal Income Tax Liability	50

Taxes - Section F

Tax Revenue	26
Per Capita Tax Revenue	49
Tax Effort	32
Tax Capacity	50
Percent Change In Taxes	11
Property Taxes Per Capita	42
Property Tax Revenue as Percent of Three-Tax Revenues	38
Sales Taxes Per Capita	16
Sales Tax Revenue as Percent of Three-Tax Revenues	8
Services With Sales Tax	13
Income Taxes Per Capita	39
Income Tax Revenue as Percent of Three-Tax Revenues	39
Motor Fuel Taxes	32
Tobacco Taxes	38
Tax Burden on High Income Family	38
Progressivity of Taxes	44

Revenues & Finances - Section G

Per Capita General Revenue	45
Per Capita Non-Tax Revenue	36
Per Capita General Spending	48
Change in General Expenditures	35
State Government General Spending	34
Debt As Percent of Revenue	46
Per Capita Full Faith and Credit Debt	34
State Solvency Index	28
Pension Plan Assets	50
State Reserves	16
State Budget Process Quality	26
Relative State Spending "Needs"	50

Education - Section H

Math Proficiency, Eighth Grade	40
AFQT Ranks	50
SAT Scores	n/a
ACT Scores	27
Over-25 Population With High School Diploma	46
Students in Private Schools	17
High School Completion Rates	41
Pupil-Teacher Ratio	35
Public School Enrollment	8
Library Holdings Per Capita	38
Education Spending As Percent of Total	25
Spending Per Pupil	46
Average Teacher Salary	48
State Aid Per Pupil	34
Higher Education Spending As Percent of Total	14
Public Higher Education Enrollment	29
State Per Pupil Support of Higher Education	3
Tuition and Fees	28
Average Professor Salary	39
Education Employees	15

Health - Section I

Infant Mortality Rates	2
State Health Rankings	48
Population Without Health Insurance	8
Abortions	46
Alcohol Consumption	35
Percent Smokers	18
Percent Overweight	6
AIDS Cases	19
Health And Hospital Spending As Percent Of Total	3
Per Capita Medicaid Spending	14
Medicaid Spending Per Aged Recipient	46
Medicaid Spending Per AFDC Child	39
Medicare Payment Per Hospital -Day	45
Population in HMOs	46

Crime - Section J

Crime Rate	32
Violent Crime Rate	26
Murder Rate	2
Property Crime Rate	35
Motor Vehicle Theft Rate	32
Violent Crime Rate Change	1
Change in Prisoners	3
Incarceration Rate	6
Juvenile Violent Crime Rate	n/a
Corrections Employees	33
State Corrections Spending	46
Law Enforcement Spending As Percent of Total	47

Transportation - Section K

Percent of Travel on Interstates	48
Interstate Mileage In Poor Condition	1
Deficient Bridges	16
Traffic Deaths Per 100 Million Vehicle Miles	24
Seat Belt Use	48
Vehicle Miles Traveled Per Capita	8
Workers Using Public Transportation	41
Road and Street Miles Under State Control	26
Highway Employees	11
Public Transit Employees	47
Highway Spending As Percent of Total	17

Welfare - Section L

Percent of Births To Unwed Mothers	1
AFDC Recipients As Percent of Population	15
Food Stamp Recipients As Percent of Population	1
SSI Recipients As Percent Of Population	1
Change in AFDC Recipients	49
Condition of Children Index	49
Percent of Families With Single Parent	2
Typical Monthly AFDC Payments	50
Welfare as Percent Of Poverty Level Income	50
Average SSI State Supplements Per Recipient	44
State Income Tax Liability Of Typical Family in Poverty	23
Child Support Collections Per $ of Administrative Costs	43
Children In Foster Care	41
State and Local Welfare Spending Per Capita	33
Welfare Spending As Percent of Total	18
Administrative Costs Per AFDC Case	44

Missouri

Revenues & Finances - Section G

Per Capita General Revenue	49
Per Capita Non-Tax Revenue	50
Per Capita General Spending	50
Change in General Expenditures	34
State Government General Spending	49
Debt As Percent of Revenue	39
Per Capita Full Faith and Credit Debt	39
State Solvency Index	24
Pension Plan Assets	11
State Reserves	39
State Budget Process Quality	5
Relative State Spending "Needs"	30

Education - Section H

Math Proficiency, Eighth Grade	19
AFQT Ranks	24
SAT Scores	n/a
ACT Scores	7
Over-25 Population With High School Diploma	25
Students in Private Schools	15
High School Completion Rates	18
Pupil-Teacher Ratio	15
Public School Enrollment	37
Library Holdings Per Capita	10
Education Spending As Percent of Total	18
Spending Per Pupil	38
Average Teacher Salary	27
State Aid Per Pupil	40
Higher Education Spending As Percent of Total	36
Public Higher Education Enrollment	40
State Per Pupil Support of Higher Education	27
Tuition and Fees	18
Average Professor Salary	14
Education Employees	27

Health - Section I

Infant Mortality Rates	13
State Health Rankings	35
Population Without Health Insurance	23
Abortions	38
Alcohol Consumption	24
Percent Smokers	16
Percent Overweight	3
AIDS Cases	20
Health And Hospital Spending As Percent Of Total	22
Per Capita Medicaid Spending	34
Medicaid Spending Per Aged Recipient	32
Medicaid Spending Per AFDC Child	37
Medicare Payment Per Hospital -Day	13
Population in HMOs	11

Crime - Section J

Crime Rate	24
Violent Crime Rate	18
Murder Rate	16
Property Crime Rate	24
Motor Vehicle Theft Rate	22
Violent Crime Rate Change	31
Change in Prisoners	19
Incarceration Rate	16
Juvenile Violent Crime Rate	9
Corrections Employees	37
State Corrections Spending	44
Law Enforcement Spending As Percent of Total	22

Transportation - Section K

Percent of Travel on Interstates	13
Interstate Mileage In Poor Condition	39
Deficient Bridges	10
Traffic Deaths Per 100 Million Vehicle Miles	9
Seat Belt Use	26
Vehicle Miles Traveled Per Capita	6
Workers Using Public Transportation	26
Road and Street Miles Under State Control	14
Highway Employees	28
Public Transit Employees	16
Highway Spending As Percent of Total	16

Welfare - Section L

Percent of Births To Unwed Mothers	17
AFDC Recipients As Percent of Population	19
Food Stamp Recipients As Percent of Population	15
SSI Recipients As Percent Of Population	24
Change in AFDC Recipients	18
Condition of Children Index	33
Percent of Families With Single Parent	14
Typical Monthly AFDC Payments	37
Welfare as Percent Of Poverty Level Income	38
Average SSI State Supplements Per Recipient	21
State Income Tax Liability Of Typical Family in Poverty	16
Child Support Collections Per $ of Administrative Costs	21
Children In Foster Care	23
State and Local Welfare Spending Per Capita	38
Welfare Spending As Percent of Total	21
Administrative Costs Per AFDC Case	48

Montana

Montana

Nebraska

Revenues & Finances - Section G

Per Capita General Revenue	22
Per Capita Non-Tax Revenue	20
Per Capita General Spending	28
Change in General Expenditures	30
State Government General Spending	38
Debt As Percent of Revenue	24
Per Capita Full Faith and Credit Debt	37
State Solvency Index	11
Pension Plan Assets	23
State Reserves	6
State Budget Process Quality	39
Relative State Spending "Needs"	25

Education - Section H

Math Proficiency, Eighth Grade	5
AFQT Ranks	15
SAT Scores	n/a
ACT Scores	5
Over-25 Population With High School Diploma	10
Students in Private Schools	13
High School Completion Rates	3
Pupil-Teacher Ratio	6
Public School Enrollment	22
Library Holdings Per Capita	12
Education Spending As Percent of Total	2
Spending Per Pupil	34
Average Teacher Salary	39
State Aid Per Pupil	46
Higher Education Spending As Percent of Total	9
Public Higher Education Enrollment	4
State Per Pupil Support of Higher Education	29
Tuition and Fees	33
Average Professor Salary	29
Education Employees	7

Health - Section I

Infant Mortality Rates	9
State Health Rankings	12
Population Without Health Insurance	36
Abortions	26
Alcohol Consumption	30
Percent Smokers	30
Percent Overweight	23
AIDS Cases	40
Health And Hospital Spending As Percent Of Total	25
Per Capita Medicaid Spending	27
Medicaid Spending Per Aged Recipient	18
Medicaid Spending Per AFDC Child	22
Medicare Payment Per Hospital -Day	21
Population in HMOs	28

Crime - Section J

Crime Rate	31
Violent Crime Rate	33
Murder Rate	43
Property Crime Rate	27
Motor Vehicle Theft Rate	33
Violent Crime Rate Change	9
Change in Prisoners	27
Incarceration Rate	43
Juvenile Violent Crime Rate	34
Corrections Employees	39
State Corrections Spending	29
Law Enforcement Spending As Percent of Total	41

Transportation - Section K

Percent of Travel on Interstates	43
Interstate Mileage In Poor Condition	9
Deficient Bridges	47
Traffic Deaths Per 100 Million Vehicle Miles	1
Seat Belt Use	21
Vehicle Miles Traveled Per Capita	24
Workers Using Public Transportation	34
Road and Street Miles Under State Control	37
Highway Employees	9
Public Transit Employees	23
Highway Spending As Percent of Total	11

Welfare - Section L

Percent of Births To Unwed Mothers	46
AFDC Recipients As Percent of Population	43
Food Stamp Recipients As Percent of Population	45
SSI Recipients As Percent Of Population	46
Change in AFDC Recipients	33
Condition of Children Index	6
Percent of Families With Single Parent	47
Typical Monthly AFDC Payments	25
Welfare as Percent Of Poverty Level Income	27
Average SSI State Supplements Per Recipient	20
State Income Tax Liability Of Typical Family in Poverty	23
Child Support Collections Per $ of Administrative Costs	20
Children In Foster Care	14
State and Local Welfare Spending Per Capita	30
Welfare Spending As Percent of Total	31
Administrative Costs Per AFDC Case	9

Nevada

Population - Section A

Population 1996	38
Percent Change in Population	1
Population 2000	35
Median Age	31
Percent Population African-American	26
Percent Population In Poverty	47
Percent Population Female	49
Birth Rates	6
Death Rates	7
Illegal Immigrant Population	19

Economies - Section B

Personal Income	34
Per Capita Personal Income	10
Percent Personal Income From Wages and Salaries	3
Average Annual Pay	20
Cost Of Living	15
Average Annual Pay in Manufacturing	29
Average Annual Pay in Retailing	4
Unemployment Rate	28
Government Employment	50
Manufacturing Employment	49
Fortune 500 Companies	n/a
Tourism Spending Per Capita	1
Exports Per Capita	45
Percent Change in Home Prices	34
Net Farm Income	45
Financial Institution Assets	10
Bankruptcy Filings	4
Patents Issued	36
WC Disability Payment	22
UC Average Weekly Benefit	22
Economic Momentum	1
Employment Change	1
Manufacturing Employment Change	7
Home Ownership	33
Gambling	1

Electricity Use Per Residential Customer	24
Revenue Per Kwh	44
New Companies	3

Geography - Section C

Total Land Area	7
Federally-Owned Land	2
State Park Acreage	20
State Park Visitors	35
Population Not Active	42
Hunters With Firearms	37
Registered Boats	40
State Spending For The Arts	44
Energy Consumption and Per Capita	25
Toxic Chemical Release Per Capita	42
Hazardous Waste Sites	49
Polluted Rivers	17
Air Pollution Emissions	43

Government - Section D

Members of US House	38
Legislators Per Million Population	24
Units of Government	40
Female Legislators	4
Turnover in Legislatures	18
Democrats in State Legislatures	20
Governor's Power Rating	42
Number of Statewide Elected Officials	18
State and Local Government Employees	48
State and Local Average Salaries	10
Local Employment	14
Local Spending Accountability	48
Registered Voters	42
Statewide Initiatives	4

Federal - Section E

Per Capita Federal Spending	37
Increase In Federal Spending	1
Per Capita Federal Grant Spending	49
Per Capita Federal Spending On Procurement	9
Per Capita Federal Spending on Social Security and Medicare	37
Social Security Benefits	11
Federal Spending On Employee Wages and Salaries	30
Federal Grant Spending Per $ of State Tax Revenue	50
General Revenue From Federal Government	48
Federal Tax Burden Per Capita	10
Highway Charges Returned to States	19
Terms of Trade	49
Per Capita Federal Income Tax Liability	4

Taxes - Section F

Tax Revenue	29
Per Capita Tax Revenue	19
Tax Effort	50
Tax Capacity	5
Percent Change In Taxes	1
Property Taxes Per Capita	36
Property Tax Revenue as Percent of Three-Tax Revenues	40
Sales Taxes Per Capita	3
Sales Tax Revenue as Percent of Three-Tax Revenues	1
Services With Sales Tax	47
Income Taxes Per Capita	n/a
Income Tax Revenue as Percent of Three-Tax Revenues	n/a
Motor Fuel Taxes	8
Tobacco Taxes	21
Tax Burden on High Income Family	46
Progressivity of Taxes	1

Nevada

New Hampshire

Revenues & Finances - Section G

Per Capita General Revenue	30
Per Capita Non-Tax Revenue	31
Per Capita General Spending	24
Change in General Expenditures	15
State Government General Spending	20
Debt As Percent of Revenue	2
Per Capita Full Faith and Credit Debt	16
State Solvency Index	35
Pension Plan Assets	26
State Reserves	50
State Budget Process Quality	48
Relative State Spending "Needs"	1

Education - Section H

Math Proficiency, Eighth Grade	n/a
AFQT Ranks	6
SAT Scores	3
ACT Scores	n/a
Over-25 Population With High School Diploma	15
Students in Private Schools	22
High School Completion Rates	32
Pupil-Teacher Ratio	17
Public School Enrollment	30
Library Holdings Per Capita	5
Education Spending As Percent of Total	40
Spending Per Pupil	16
Average Teacher Salary	21
State Aid Per Pupil	50
Higher Education Spending As Percent of Total	41
Public Higher Education Enrollment	46
State Per Pupil Support of Higher Education	50
Tuition and Fees	3
Average Professor Salary	n/a
Education Employees	26

Health - Section I

Infant Mortality Rates	43
State Health Rankings	5
Population Without Health Insurance	47
Abortions	31
Alcohol Consumption	2
Percent Smokers	38
Percent Overweight	39
AIDS Cases	37
Health And Hospital Spending As Percent Of Total	50
Per Capita Medicaid Spending	17
Medicaid Spending Per Aged Recipient	1
Medicaid Spending Per AFDC Child	8
Medicare Payment Per Hospital -Day	44
Population in HMOs	20

Crime - Section J

Crime Rate	49
Violent Crime Rate	49
Murder Rate	47
Property Crime Rate	49
Motor Vehicle Theft Rate	47
Violent Crime Rate Change	50
Change in Prisoners	24
Incarceration Rate	45
Juvenile Violent Crime Rate	n/a
Corrections Employees	47
State Corrections Spending	27
Law Enforcement Spending As Percent of Total	35

Transportation - Section K

Percent of Travel on Interstates	34
Interstate Mileage In Poor Condition	40
Deficient Bridges	20
Traffic Deaths Per 100 Million Vehicle Miles	29
Seat Belt Use	n/a
Vehicle Miles Traveled Per Capita	32
Workers Using Public Transportation	43
Road and Street Miles Under State Control	12
Highway Employees	17
Public Transit Employees	35
Highway Spending As Percent of Total	36

Welfare - Section L

Percent of Births To Unwed Mothers	48
AFDC Recipients As Percent of Population	48
Food Stamp Recipients As Percent of Population	50
SSI Recipients As Percent Of Population	50
Change in AFDC Recipients	14
Condition of Children Index	1
Percent of Families With Single Parent	40
Typical Monthly AFDC Payments	8
Welfare as Percent Of Poverty Level Income	10
Average SSI State Supplements Per Recipient	8
State Income Tax Liability Of Typical Family in Poverty	n/a
Child Support Collections Per $ of Administrative Costs	35
Children In Foster Care	31
State and Local Welfare Spending Per Capita	2
Welfare Spending As Percent of Total	1
Administrative Costs Per AFDC Case	5

New Jersey

Revenues & Finances - Section G

Per Capita General Revenue	6
Per Capita Non-Tax Revenue	14
Per Capita General Spending	7
Change in General Expenditures	36
State Government General Spending	9
Debt As Percent of Revenue	19
Per Capita Full Faith and Credit Debt	14
State Solvency Index	40
Pension Plan Assets	20
State Reserves	26
State Budget Process Quality	3
Relative State Spending "Needs"	3

Education - Section H

Math Proficiency, Eighth Grade	n/a
AFQT Ranks	38
SAT Scores	10
ACT Scores	n/a
Over-25 Population With High School Diploma	18
Students in Private Schools	5
High School Completion Rates	13
Pupil-Teacher Ratio	1
Public School Enrollment	49
Library Holdings Per Capita	12
Education Spending As Percent of Total	24
Spending Per Pupil	1
Average Teacher Salary	4
State Aid Per Pupil	9
Higher Education Spending As Percent of Total	45
Public Higher Education Enrollment	44
State Per Pupil Support of Higher Education	14
Tuition and Fees	4
Average Professor Salary	1
Education Employees	18

Health - Section I

Infant Mortality Rates	29
State Health Rankings	15
Population Without Health Insurance	11
Abortions	15
Alcohol Consumption	21
Percent Smokers	47
Percent Overweight	42
AIDS Cases	3
Health And Hospital Spending As Percent Of Total	44
Per Capita Medicaid Spending	18
Medicaid Spending Per Aged Recipient	6
Medicaid Spending Per AFDC Child	13
Medicare Payment Per Hospital -Day	23
Population in HMOs	15

Crime - Section J

Crime Rate	27
Violent Crime Rate	22
Murder Rate	29
Property Crime Rate	31
Motor Vehicle Theft Rate	10
Violent Crime Rate Change	40
Change in Prisoners	39
Incarceration Rate	22
Juvenile Violent Crime Rate	4
Corrections Employees	21
State Corrections Spending	16
Law Enforcement Spending As Percent of Total	9

Transportation - Section K

Percent of Travel on Interstates	45
Interstate Mileage In Poor Condition	27
Deficient Bridges	6
Traffic Deaths Per 100 Million Vehicle Miles	50
Seat Belt Use	33
Vehicle Miles Traveled Per Capita	46
Workers Using Public Transportation	3
Road and Street Miles Under State Control	45
Highway Employees	26
Public Transit Employees	33
Highway Spending As Percent of Total	40

Welfare - Section L

Percent of Births To Unwed Mothers	35
AFDC Recipients As Percent of Population	28
Food Stamp Recipients As Percent of Population	36
SSI Recipients As Percent Of Population	28
Change in AFDC Recipients	32
Condition of Children Index	17
Percent of Families With Single Parent	26
Typical Monthly AFDC Payments	16
Welfare as Percent Of Poverty Level Income	16
Average SSI State Supplements Per Recipient	14
State Income Tax Liability Of Typical Family in Poverty	13
Child Support Collections Per $ of Administrative Costs	8
Children In Foster Care	40
State and Local Welfare Spending Per Capita	16
Welfare Spending As Percent of Total	28
Administrative Costs Per AFDC Case	13

New Mexico

Revenues & Finances - Section G

Per Capita General Revenue	18
Per Capita Non-Tax Revenue	4
Per Capita General Spending	17
Change in General Expenditures	13
State Government General Spending	15
Debt As Percent of Revenue	42
Per Capita Full Faith and Credit Debt	41
State Solvency Index	3
Pension Plan Assets	34
State Reserves	25
State Budget Process Quality	34
Relative State Spending "Needs"	48

Education - Section H

Math Proficiency, Eighth Grade	33
AFQT Ranks	35
SAT Scores	n/a
ACT Scores	20
Over-25 Population With High School Diploma	40
Students in Private Schools	39
High School Completion Rates	43
Pupil-Teacher Ratio	32
Public School Enrollment	16
Library Holdings Per Capita	19
Education Spending As Percent of Total	33
Spending Per Pupil	33
Average Teacher Salary	45
State Aid Per Pupil	5
Higher Education Spending As Percent of Total	5
Public Higher Education Enrollment	5
State Per Pupil Support of Higher Education	15
Tuition and Fees	43
Average Professor Salary	34
Education Employees	10

Health - Section I

Infant Mortality Rates	40
State Health Rankings	46
Population Without Health Insurance	4
Abortions	34
Alcohol Consumption	21
Percent Smokers	39
Percent Overweight	46
AIDS Cases	28
Health And Hospital Spending As Percent Of Total	16
Per Capita Medicaid Spending	11
Medicaid Spending Per Aged Recipient	36
Medicaid Spending Per AFDC Child	11
Medicare Payment Per Hospital -Day	24
Population in HMOs	22

Crime - Section J

Crime Rate	7
Violent Crime Rate	9
Murder Rate	17
Property Crime Rate	9
Motor Vehicle Theft Rate	20
Violent Crime Rate Change	24
Change in Prisoners	9
Incarceration Rate	35
Juvenile Violent Crime Rate	n/a
Corrections Employees	5
State Corrections Spending	17
Law Enforcement Spending As Percent of Total	14

Transportation - Section K

Percent of Travel on Interstates	9
Interstate Mileage In Poor Condition	22
Deficient Bridges	45
Traffic Deaths Per 100 Million Vehicle Miles	40
Seat Belt Use	2
Vehicle Miles Traveled Per Capita	2
Workers Using Public Transportation	38
Road and Street Miles Under State Control	19
Highway Employees	19
Public Transit Employees	22
Highway Spending As Percent of Total	2

Welfare - Section L

Percent of Births To Unwed Mothers	4
AFDC Recipients As Percent of Population	4
Food Stamp Recipients As Percent of Population	4
SSI Recipients As Percent Of Population	13
Change in AFDC Recipients	3
Condition of Children Index	44
Percent of Families With Single Parent	11
Typical Monthly AFDC Payments	22
Welfare as Percent Of Poverty Level Income	25
Average SSI State Supplements Per Recipient	37
State Income Tax Liability Of Typical Family in Poverty	37
Child Support Collections Per $ of Administrative Costs	48
Children In Foster Care	39
State and Local Welfare Spending Per Capita	28
Welfare Spending As Percent of Total	37
Administrative Costs Per AFDC Case	40

New York

New York

Revenues & Finances - Section G

Per Capita General Revenue	2
Per Capita Non-Tax Revenue	6
Per Capita General Spending	2
Change in General Expenditures	32
State Government General Spending	7
Debt As Percent of Revenue	10
Per Capita Full Faith and Credit Debt	4
State Solvency Index	25
Pension Plan Assets	4
State Reserves	46
State Budget Process Quality	29
Relative State Spending "Needs"	22

Education - Section H

Math Proficiency, Eighth Grade	20
AFQT Ranks	30
SAT Scores	14
ACT Scores	n/a
Over-25 Population With High School Diploma	33
Students in Private Schools	4
High School Completion Rates	30
Pupil-Teacher Ratio	13
Public School Enrollment	44
Library Holdings Per Capita	8
Education Spending As Percent of Total	46
Spending Per Pupil	3
Average Teacher Salary	3
State Aid Per Pupil	13
Higher Education Spending As Percent of Total	47
Public Higher Education Enrollment	45
State Per Pupil Support of Higher Education	18
Tuition and Fees	13
Average Professor Salary	16
Education Employees	32

Health - Section I

Infant Mortality Rates	32
State Health Rankings	37
Population Without Health Insurance	11
Abortions	1
Alcohol Consumption	37
Percent Smokers	37
Percent Overweight	26
AIDS Cases	1
Health And Hospital Spending As Percent Of Total	17
Per Capita Medicaid Spending	1
Medicaid Spending Per Aged Recipient	5
Medicaid Spending Per AFDC Child	3
Medicare Payment Per Hospital -Day	49
Population in HMOs	7

Crime - Section J

Crime Rate	30
Violent Crime Rate	8
Murder Rate	18
Property Crime Rate	39
Motor Vehicle Theft Rate	14
Violent Crime Rate Change	49
Change in Prisoners	36
Incarceration Rate	18
Juvenile Violent Crime Rate	1
Corrections Employees	3
State Corrections Spending	5
Law Enforcement Spending As Percent of Total	13

Transportation - Section K

Percent of Travel on Interstates	47
Interstate Mileage In Poor Condition	31
Deficient Bridges	1
Traffic Deaths Per 100 Million Vehicle Miles	40
Seat Belt Use	8
Vehicle Miles Traveled Per Capita	50
Workers Using Public Transportation	1
Road and Street Miles Under State Control	27
Highway Employees	21
Public Transit Employees	1
Highway Spending As Percent of Total	49

Welfare - Section L

Percent of Births To Unwed Mothers	6
AFDC Recipients As Percent of Population	2
Food Stamp Recipients As Percent of Population	9
SSI Recipients As Percent Of Population	7
Change in AFDC Recipients	10
Condition of Children Index	36
Percent of Families With Single Parent	3
Typical Monthly AFDC Payments	7
Welfare as Percent Of Poverty Level Income	3
Average SSI State Supplements Per Recipient	9
State Income Tax Liability Of Typical Family in Poverty	40
Child Support Collections Per $ of Administrative Costs	22
Children In Foster Care	4
State and Local Welfare Spending Per Capita	1
Welfare Spending As Percent of Total	4
Administrative Costs Per AFDC Case	4

North Carolina

Revenues & Finances - Section G

Per Capita General Revenue	39
Per Capita Non-Tax Revenue	44
Per Capita General Spending	41
Change in General Expenditures	10
State Government General Spending	41
Debt As Percent of Revenue	35
Per Capita Full Faith and Credit Debt	31
State Solvency Index	9
Pension Plan Assets	29
State Reserves	23
State Budget Process Quality	40
Relative State Spending "Needs"	17

Education - Section H

Math Proficiency, Eighth Grade	25
AFQT Ranks	42
SAT Scores	21
ACT Scores	n/a
Over-25 Population With High School Diploma	44
Students in Private Schools	40
High School Completion Rates	37
Pupil-Teacher Ratio	21
Public School Enrollment	39
Library Holdings Per Capita	38
Education Spending As Percent of Total	19
Spending Per Pupil	39
Average Teacher Salary	42
State Aid Per Pupil	15
Higher Education Spending As Percent of Total	7
Public Higher Education Enrollment	27
State Per Pupil Support of Higher Education	2
Tuition and Fees	48
Average Professor Salary	3
Education Employees	31

Health - Section I

Infant Mortality Rates	3
State Health Rankings	29
Population Without Health Insurance	15
Abortions	7
Alcohol Consumption	39
Percent Smokers	6
Percent Overweight	25
AIDS Cases	27
Health And Hospital Spending As Percent Of Total	8
Per Capita Medicaid Spending	12
Medicaid Spending Per Aged Recipient	37
Medicaid Spending Per AFDC Child	30
Medicare Payment Per Hospital -Day	39
Population in HMOs	32

Crime - Section J

Crime Rate	16
Violent Crime Rate	20
Murder Rate	13
Property Crime Rate	15
Motor Vehicle Theft Rate	38
Violent Crime Rate Change	21
Change in Prisoners	6
Incarceration Rate	20
Juvenile Violent Crime Rate	17
Corrections Employees	16
State Corrections Spending	18
Law Enforcement Spending As Percent of Total	7

Transportation - Section K

Percent of Travel on Interstates	44
Interstate Mileage In Poor Condition	23
Deficient Bridges	12
Traffic Deaths Per 100 Million Vehicle Miles	12
Seat Belt Use	4
Vehicle Miles Traveled Per Capita	14
Workers Using Public Transportation	38
Road and Street Miles Under State Control	4
Highway Employees	30
Public Transit Employees	36
Highway Spending As Percent of Total	31

Welfare - Section L

Percent of Births To Unwed Mothers	22
AFDC Recipients As Percent of Population	26
Food Stamp Recipients As Percent of Population	27
SSI Recipients As Percent Of Population	14
Change in AFDC Recipients	17
Condition of Children Index	42
Percent of Families With Single Parent	11
Typical Monthly AFDC Payments	42
Welfare as Percent Of Poverty Level Income	41
Average SSI State Supplements Per Recipient	17
State Income Tax Liability Of Typical Family in Poverty	23
Child Support Collections Per $ of Administrative Costs	36
Children In Foster Care	17
State and Local Welfare Spending Per Capita	35
Welfare Spending As Percent of Total	27
Administrative Costs Per AFDC Case	30

North Dakota

Population - Section A

Population 1996	47
Percent Change in Population	43
Population 2000	47
Median Age	24
Percent Population African-American	45
Percent Population In Poverty	34
Percent Population Female	44
Birth Rates	41
Death Rates	47
Illegal Immigrant Population	49

Economies - Section B

Personal Income	48
Per Capita Personal Income	38
Percent Personal Income From Wages and Salaries	42
Average Annual Pay	48
Cost Of Living	36
Average Annual Pay in Manufacturing	47
Average Annual Pay in Retailing	50
Unemployment Rate	49
Government Employment	4
Manufacturing Employment	44
Fortune 500 Companies	n/a
Tourism Spending Per Capita	20
Exports Per Capita	38
Percent Change in Home Prices	24
Net Farm Income	19
Financial Institution Assets	11
Bankruptcy Filings	46
Patents Issued	42
WC Disability Payment	40
UC Average Weekly Benefit	40
Economic Momentum	22
Employment Change	9
Manufacturing Employment Change	1
Home Ownership	15
Gambling	38

Electricity Use Per Residential Customer	14
Revenue Per Kwh	45
New Companies	42

Geography - Section C

Total Land Area	17
Federally-Owned Land	22
State Park Acreage	47
State Park Visitors	40
Population Not Active	17
Hunters With Firearms	10
Registered Boats	46
State Spending For The Arts	41
Energy Consumption and Per Capita	5
Toxic Chemical Release Per Capita	37
Hazardous Waste Sites	50
Polluted Rivers	39
Air Pollution Emissions	40

Government - Section D

Members of US House	44
Legislators Per Million Population	3
Units of Government	1
Female Legislators	37
Turnover in Legislatures	26
Democrats in State Legislatures	46
Governor's Power Rating	8
Number of Statewide Elected Officials	1
State and Local Government Employees	13
State and Local Average Salaries	34
Local Employment	47
Local Spending Accountability	35
Registered Voters	n/a
Statewide Initiatives	11

Federal - Section E

Per Capita Federal Spending	11
Increase In Federal Spending	49
Per Capita Federal Grant Spending	7
Per Capita Federal Spending On Procurement	39
Per Capita Federal Spending on Social Security and Medicare	28
Social Security Benefits	40
Federal Spending On Employee Wages and Salaries	5
Federal Grant Spending Per $ of State Tax Revenue	15
General Revenue From Federal Government	6
Federal Tax Burden Per Capita	39
Highway Charges Returned to States	7
Terms of Trade	8
Per Capita Federal Income Tax Liability	40

Taxes - Section F

Tax Revenue	15
Per Capita Tax Revenue	35
Tax Effort	32
Tax Capacity	31
Percent Change In Taxes	30
Property Taxes Per Capita	33
Property Tax Revenue as Percent of Three-Tax Revenues	22
Sales Taxes Per Capita	22
Sales Tax Revenue as Percent of Three-Tax Revenues	15
Services With Sales Tax	38
Income Taxes Per Capita	41
Income Tax Revenue as Percent of Three-Tax Revenues	41
Motor Fuel Taxes	21
Tobacco Taxes	10
Tax Burden on High Income Family	29
Progressivity of Taxes	14

Revenues & Finances - Section G

Per Capita General Revenue	17
Per Capita Non-Tax Revenue	9
Per Capita General Spending	20
Change in General Expenditures	49
State Government General Spending	18
Debt As Percent of Revenue	45
Per Capita Full Faith and Credit Debt	42
State Solvency Index	5
Pension Plan Assets	39
State Reserves	15
State Budget Process Quality	18
Relative State Spending "Needs"	35

Education - Section H

Math Proficiency, Eighth Grade	1
AFQT Ranks	1
SAT Scores	n/a
ACT Scores	10
Over-25 Population With High School Diploma	36
Students in Private Schools	38
High School Completion Rates	1
Pupil-Teacher Ratio	14
Public School Enrollment	10
Library Holdings Per Capita	16
Education Spending As Percent of Total	7
Spending Per Pupil	42
Average Teacher Salary	49
State Aid Per Pupil	43
Higher Education Spending As Percent of Total	1
Public Higher Education Enrollment	6
State Per Pupil Support of Higher Education	23
Tuition and Fees	30
Average Professor Salary	48
Education Employees	25

Health - Section I

Infant Mortality Rates	50
State Health Rankings	23
Population Without Health Insurance	43
Abortions	41
Alcohol Consumption	17
Percent Smokers	25
Percent Overweight	9
AIDS Cases	48
Health And Hospital Spending As Percent Of Total	48
Per Capita Medicaid Spending	19
Medicaid Spending Per Aged Recipient	13
Medicaid Spending Per AFDC Child	10
Medicare Payment Per Hospital -Day	43
Population in HMOs	47

Crime - Section J

Crime Rate	48
Violent Crime Rate	50
Murder Rate	50
Property Crime Rate	48
Motor Vehicle Theft Rate	44
Violent Crime Rate Change	8
Change in Prisoners	14
Incarceration Rate	50
Juvenile Violent Crime Rate	35
Corrections Employees	49
State Corrections Spending	31
Law Enforcement Spending As Percent of Total	50

Transportation - Section K

Percent of Travel on Interstates	39
Interstate Mileage In Poor Condition	19
Deficient Bridges	50
Traffic Deaths Per 100 Million Vehicle Miles	15
Seat Belt Use	49
Vehicle Miles Traveled Per Capita	20
Workers Using Public Transportation	46
Road and Street Miles Under State Control	48
Highway Employees	10
Public Transit Employees	44
Highway Spending As Percent of Total	5

Welfare - Section L

Percent of Births To Unwed Mothers	44
AFDC Recipients As Percent of Population	47
Food Stamp Recipients As Percent of Population	44
SSI Recipients As Percent Of Population	43
Change in AFDC Recipients	42
Condition of Children Index	3
Percent of Families With Single Parent	47
Typical Monthly AFDC Payments	17
Welfare as Percent Of Poverty Level Income	17
Average SSI State Supplements Per Recipient	22
State Income Tax Liability Of Typical Family in Poverty	23
Child Support Collections Per $ of Administrative Costs	11
Children In Foster Care	30
State and Local Welfare Spending Per Capita	22
Welfare Spending As Percent of Total	26
Administrative Costs Per AFDC Case	16

Ohio

Population - Section A

Population 1996	27
Percent Change in Population	22
Population 2000	28
Median Age	24
Percent Population African-American	23
Percent Population In Poverty	11
Percent Population Female	27
Birth Rates	27
Death Rates	12
Illegal Immigrant Population	23

Economies - Section B

Personal Income	30
Per Capita Personal Income	44
Percent Personal Income From Wages and Salaries	41
Average Annual Pay	42
Cost Of Living	43
Average Annual Pay in Manufacturing	39
Average Annual Pay in Retailing	41
Unemployment Rate	39
Government Employment	9
Manufacturing Employment	34
Fortune 500 Companies	26
Tourism Spending Per Capita	45
Exports Per Capita	46
Percent Change in Home Prices	31
Net Farm Income	29
Financial Institution Assets	36
Bankruptcy Filings	7
Patents Issued	28
WC Disability Payment	37
UC Average Weekly Benefit	37
Economic Momentum	17
Employment Change	10
Manufacturing Employment Change	12
Home Ownership	19
Gambling	41

Electricity Use Per Residential Customer	18
Revenue Per Kwh	17
New Companies	28

Geography - Section C

Total Land Area	19
Federally-Owned Land	35
State Park Acreage	33
State Park Visitors	10
Population Not Active	22
Hunters With Firearms	25
Registered Boats	21
State Spending For The Arts	18
Energy Consumption and Per Capita	11
Toxic Chemical Release Per Capita	27
Hazardous Waste Sites	34
Polluted Rivers	3
Air Pollution Emissions	15

Government - Section D

Members of US House	23
Legislators Per Million Population	22
Units of Government	15
Female Legislators	48
Turnover in Legislatures	40
Democrats in State Legislatures	9
Governor's Power Rating	45
Number of Statewide Elected Officials	3
State and Local Government Employees	11
State and Local Average Salaries	47
Local Employment	35
Local Spending Accountability	37
Registered Voters	n/a
Statewide Initiatives	n/a

Federal - Section E

Per Capita Federal Spending	25
Increase In Federal Spending	27
Per Capita Federal Grant Spending	36
Per Capita Federal Spending On Procurement	33
Per Capita Federal Spending on Social Security and Medicare	17
Social Security Benefits	36
Federal Spending On Employee Wages and Salaries	9
Federal Grant Spending Per $ of State Tax Revenue	31
General Revenue From Federal Government	29
Federal Tax Burden Per Capita	46
Highway Charges Returned to States	38
Terms of Trade	17
Per Capita Federal Income Tax Liability	47

Taxes - Section F

Tax Revenue	37
Per Capita Tax Revenue	42
Tax Effort	30
Tax Capacity	39
Percent Change In Taxes	43
Property Taxes Per Capita	46
Property Tax Revenue as Percent of Three-Tax Revenues	45
Sales Taxes Per Capita	24
Sales Tax Revenue as Percent of Three-Tax Revenues	13
Services With Sales Tax	28
Income Taxes Per Capita	32
Income Tax Revenue as Percent of Three-Tax Revenues	18
Motor Fuel Taxes	39
Tobacco Taxes	34
Tax Burden on High Income Family	28
Progressivity of Taxes	33

Oregon

Population - Section A

Population 1996	29
Percent Change in Population	7
Population 2000	27
Median Age	6
Percent Population African-American	41
Percent Population In Poverty	27
Percent Population Female	38
Birth Rates	35
Death Rates	30
Illegal Immigrant Population	16

Economies - Section B

Personal Income	28
Per Capita Personal Income	27
Percent Personal Income From Wages and Salaries	21
Average Annual Pay	22
Cost Of Living	22
Average Annual Pay in Manufacturing	20
Average Annual Pay in Retailing	12
Unemployment Rate	14
Government Employment	28
Manufacturing Employment	22
Fortune 500 Companies	17
Tourism Spending Per Capita	22
Exports Per Capita	8
Percent Change in Home Prices	2
Net Farm Income	26
Financial Institution Assets	44
Bankruptcy Filings	11
Patents Issued	16
WC Disability Payment	14
UC Average Weekly Benefit	14
Economic Momentum	3
Employment Change	5
Manufacturing Employment Change	4
Home Ownership	24
Gambling	20

(continued)

Electricity Use Per Residential Customer	12
Revenue Per Kwh	36
New Companies	9

Geography - Section C

Total Land Area	10
Federally-Owned Land	7
State Park Acreage	30
State Park Visitors	2
Population Not Active	45
Hunters With Firearms	9
Registered Boats	24
State Spending For The Arts	48
Energy Consumption and Per Capita	29
Toxic Chemical Release Per Capita	29
Hazardous Waste Sites	34
Polluted Rivers	22
Air Pollution Emissions	28

Government - Section D

Members of US House	29
Legislators Per Million Population	33
Units of Government	19
Female Legislators	17
Turnover in Legislatures	5
Democrats in State Legislatures	35
Governor's Power Rating	28
Number of Statewide Elected Officials	18
State and Local Government Employees	31
State and Local Average Salaries	15
Local Employment	27
Local Spending Accountability	29
Registered Voters	8
Statewide Initiatives	1

Federal - Section E

Per Capita Federal Spending	43
Increase In Federal Spending	10
Per Capita Federal Grant Spending	17
Per Capita Federal Spending On Procurement	49
Per Capita Federal Spending on Social Security and Medicare	27
Social Security Benefits	13
Federal Spending On Employee Wages and Salaries	40
Federal Grant Spending Per $ of State Tax Revenue	9
General Revenue From Federal Government	15
Federal Tax Burden Per Capita	25
Highway Charges Returned to States	13
Terms of Trade	23
Per Capita Federal Income Tax Liability	29

Taxes - Section F

Tax Revenue	17
Per Capita Tax Revenue	24
Tax Effort	20
Tax Capacity	20
Percent Change In Taxes	21
Property Taxes Per Capita	16
Property Tax Revenue as Percent of Three-Tax Revenues	12
Sales Taxes Per Capita	50
Sales Tax Revenue as Percent of Three-Tax Revenues	50
Services With Sales Tax	50
Income Taxes Per Capita	4
Income Tax Revenue as Percent of Three-Tax Revenues	2
Motor Fuel Taxes	7
Tobacco Taxes	16
Tax Burden on High Income Family	16
Progressivity of Taxes	34

Revenues & Finances - Section G

Per Capita General Revenue	13
Per Capita Non-Tax Revenue	8
Per Capita General Spending	16
Change in General Expenditures	20
State Government General Spending	16
Debt As Percent of Revenue	32
Per Capita Full Faith and Credit Debt	7
State Solvency Index	4
Pension Plan Assets	35
State Reserves	3
State Budget Process Quality	6
Relative State Spending "Needs"	18

Education - Section H

Math Proficiency, Eighth Grade	14
AFQT Ranks	4
SAT Scores	1
ACT Scores	n/a
Over-25 Population With High School Diploma	9
Students in Private Schools	36
High School Completion Rates	42
Pupil-Teacher Ratio	46
Public School Enrollment	32
Library Holdings Per Capita	32
Education Spending As Percent of Total	20
Spending Per Pupil	15
Average Teacher Salary	13
State Aid Per Pupil	16
Higher Education Spending As Percent of Total	21
Public Higher Education Enrollment	17
State Per Pupil Support of Higher Education	43
Tuition and Fees	17
Average Professor Salary	45
Education Employees	38

Health - Section I

Infant Mortality Rates	44
State Health Rankings	21
Population Without Health Insurance	20
Abortions	11
Alcohol Consumption	24
Percent Smokers	31
Percent Overweight	20
AIDS Cases	22
Health And Hospital Spending As Percent Of Total	28
Per Capita Medicaid Spending	28
Medicaid Spending Per Aged Recipient	33
Medicaid Spending Per AFDC Child	1
Medicare Payment Per Hospital -Day	15
Population in HMOs	1

Crime - Section J

Crime Rate	6
Violent Crime Rate	25
Murder Rate	36
Property Crime Rate	4
Motor Vehicle Theft Rate	6
Violent Crime Rate Change	37
Change in Prisoners	31
Incarceration Rate	39
Juvenile Violent Crime Rate	24
Corrections Employees	31
State Corrections Spending	7
Law Enforcement Spending As Percent of Total	17

Transportation - Section K

Percent of Travel on Interstates	22
Interstate Mileage In Poor Condition	44
Deficient Bridges	22
Traffic Deaths Per 100 Million Vehicle Miles	34
Seat Belt Use	4
Vehicle Miles Traveled Per Capita	30
Workers Using Public Transportation	13
Road and Street Miles Under State Control	29
Highway Employees	27
Public Transit Employees	8
Highway Spending As Percent of Total	30

Welfare - Section L

Percent of Births To Unwed Mothers	31
AFDC Recipients As Percent of Population	36
Food Stamp Recipients As Percent of Population	26
SSI Recipients As Percent Of Population	38
Change in AFDC Recipients	39
Condition of Children Index	21
Percent of Families With Single Parent	26
Typical Monthly AFDC Payments	18
Welfare as Percent Of Poverty Level Income	13
Average SSI State Supplements Per Recipient	18
State Income Tax Liability Of Typical Family in Poverty	7
Child Support Collections Per $ of Administrative Costs	7
Children In Foster Care	24
State and Local Welfare Spending Per Capita	34
Welfare Spending As Percent of Total	38
Administrative Costs Per AFDC Case	1

Pennsylvania

Population - Section A

Population 1996	5
Percent Change in Population	49
Population 2000	5
Median Age	3
Percent Population African-American	20
Percent Population In Poverty	30
Percent Population Female	4
Birth Rates	46
Death Rates	20
Illegal Immigrant Population	13

Economies - Section B

Personal Income	6
Per Capita Personal Income	18
Percent Personal Income From Wages and Salaries	37
Average Annual Pay	13
Cost Of Living	10
Average Annual Pay in Manufacturing	17
Average Annual Pay in Retailing	24
Unemployment Rate	13
Government Employment	48
Manufacturing Employment	16
Fortune 500 Companies	9
Tourism Spending Per Capita	44
Exports Per Capita	34
Percent Change in Home Prices	39
Net Farm Income	21
Financial Institution Assets	8
Bankruptcy Filings	44
Patents Issued	19
WC Disability Payment	12
UC Average Weekly Benefit	12
Economic Momentum	33
Employment Change	16
Manufacturing Employment Change	29
Home Ownership	39
Gambling	11

Electricity Use Per Residential Customer	33
Revenue Per Kwh	29
New Companies	47

Geography - Section C

Total Land Area	32
Federally-Owned Land	37
State Park Acreage	10
State Park Visitors	18
Population Not Active	29
Hunters With Firearms	17
Registered Boats	11
State Spending For The Arts	21
Energy Consumption and Per Capita	35
Toxic Chemical Release Per Capita	36
Hazardous Waste Sites	2
Polluted Rivers	43
Air Pollution Emissions	5

Government - Section D

Members of US House	5
Legislators Per Million Population	40
Units of Government	21
Female Legislators	45
Turnover in Legislatures	42
Democrats in State Legislatures	29
Governor's Power Rating	1
Number of Statewide Elected Officials	30
State and Local Government Employees	50
State and Local Average Salaries	13
Local Employment	21
Local Spending Accountability	23
Registered Voters	32
Statewide Initiatives	n/a

Federal - Section E

Per Capita Federal Spending	17
Increase In Federal Spending	21
Per Capita Federal Grant Spending	21
Per Capita Federal Spending On Procurement	29
Per Capita Federal Spending on Social Security and Medicare	2
Social Security Benefits	8
Federal Spending On Employee Wages and Salaries	35
Federal Grant Spending Per $ of State Tax Revenue	26
General Revenue From Federal Government	24
Federal Tax Burden Per Capita	18
Highway Charges Returned to States	21
Terms of Trade	30
Per Capita Federal Income Tax Liability	18

Taxes - Section F

Tax Revenue	36
Per Capita Tax Revenue	20
Tax Effort	24
Tax Capacity	22
Percent Change In Taxes	27
Property Taxes Per Capita	27
Property Tax Revenue as Percent of Three-Tax Revenues	24
Sales Taxes Per Capita	38
Sales Tax Revenue as Percent of Three-Tax Revenues	30
Services With Sales Tax	18
Income Taxes Per Capita	17
Income Tax Revenue as Percent of Three-Tax Revenues	14
Motor Fuel Taxes	14
Tobacco Taxes	26
Tax Burden on High Income Family	19
Progressivity of Taxes	8

Population - Section A

Population 1996	43
Percent Change in Population	50
Population 2000	43
Median Age	10
Percent Population African-American	30
Percent Population In Poverty	34
Percent Population Female	3
Birth Rates	44
Death Rates	42
Illegal Immigrant Population	30

Economies - Section B

Personal Income	42
Per Capita Personal Income	17
Percent Personal Income From Wages and Salaries	45
Average Annual Pay	25
Cost Of Living	7
Average Annual Pay in Manufacturing	32
Average Annual Pay in Retailing	22
Unemployment Rate	8
Government Employment	46
Manufacturing Employment	13
Fortune 500 Companies	7
Tourism Spending Per Capita	50
Exports Per Capita	43
Percent Change in Home Prices	47
Net Farm Income	47
Financial Institution Assets	39
Bankruptcy Filings	20
Patents Issued	15
WC Disability Payment	18
UC Average Weekly Benefit	18
Economic Momentum	43
Employment Change	46
Manufacturing Employment Change	32
Home Ownership	11
Gambling	32

Electricity Use Per Residential Customer	49
Revenue Per Kwh	50
New Companies	14

Geography - Section C

Total Land Area	50
Federally-Owned Land	50
State Park Acreage	50
State Park Visitors	16
Population Not Active	n/a
Hunters With Firearms	n/a
Registered Boats	47
State Spending For The Arts	29
Energy Consumption and Per Capita	48
Toxic Chemical Release Per Capita	38
Hazardous Waste Sites	31
Polluted Rivers	38
Air Pollution Emissions	50

Government - Section D

Members of US House	38
Legislators Per Million Population	6
Units of Government	45
Female Legislators	13
Turnover in Legislatures	30
Democrats in State Legislatures	2
Governor's Power Rating	41
Number of Statewide Elected Officials	30
State and Local Government Employees	45
State and Local Average Salaries	6
Local Employment	46
Local Spending Accountability	14
Registered Voters	15
Statewide Initiatives	n/a

Federal - Section E

Per Capita Federal Spending	8
Increase In Federal Spending	38
Per Capita Federal Grant Spending	4
Per Capita Federal Spending On Procurement	31
Per Capita Federal Spending on Social Security and Medicare	4
Social Security Benefits	16
Federal Spending On Employee Wages and Salaries	18
Federal Grant Spending Per $ of State Tax Revenue	10
General Revenue From Federal Government	10
Federal Tax Burden Per Capita	16
Highway Charges Returned to States	3
Terms of Trade	13
Per Capita Federal Income Tax Liability	21

Taxes - Section F

Tax Revenue	22
Per Capita Tax Revenue	13
Tax Effort	4
Tax Capacity	37
Percent Change In Taxes	35
Property Taxes Per Capita	6
Property Tax Revenue as Percent of Three-Tax Revenues	9
Sales Taxes Per Capita	32
Sales Tax Revenue as Percent of Three-Tax Revenues	37
Services With Sales Tax	33
Income Taxes Per Capita	19
Income Tax Revenue as Percent of Three-Tax Revenues	29
Motor Fuel Taxes	2
Tobacco Taxes	4
Tax Burden on High Income Family	4
Progressivity of Taxes	26

Revenues & Finances - Section G

Per Capita General Revenue	12
Per Capita Non-Tax Revenue	37
Per Capita General Spending	9
Change in General Expenditures	31
State Government General Spending	4
Debt As Percent of Revenue	3
Per Capita Full Faith and Credit Debt	9
State Solvency Index	45
Pension Plan Assets	15
State Reserves	29
State Budget Process Quality	9
Relative State Spending "Needs"	9

Education - Section H

Math Proficiency, Eighth Grade	24
AFQT Ranks	32
SAT Scores	18
ACT Scores	n/a
Over-25 Population With High School Diploma	39
Students in Private Schools	8
High School Completion Rates	21
Pupil-Teacher Ratio	8
Public School Enrollment	46
Library Holdings Per Capita	9
Education Spending As Percent of Total	41
Spending Per Pupil	5
Average Teacher Salary	9
State Aid Per Pupil	23
Higher Education Spending As Percent of Total	43
Public Higher Education Enrollment	34
State Per Pupil Support of Higher Education	44
Tuition and Fees	10
Average Professor Salary	27
Education Employees	43

Health - Section I

Infant Mortality Rates	47
State Health Rankings	29
Population Without Health Insurance	42
Abortions	4
Alcohol Consumption	19
Percent Smokers	14
Percent Overweight	36
AIDS Cases	16
Health And Hospital Spending As Percent Of Total	42
Per Capita Medicaid Spending	2
Medicaid Spending Per Aged Recipient	4
Medicaid Spending Per AFDC Child	45
Medicare Payment Per Hospital -Day	36
Population in HMOs	36

Crime - Section J

Crime Rate	39
Violent Crime Rate	34
Murder Rate	41
Property Crime Rate	37
Motor Vehicle Theft Rate	24
Violent Crime Rate Change	41
Change in Prisoners	42
Incarceration Rate	42
Juvenile Violent Crime Rate	11
Corrections Employees	38
State Corrections Spending	6
Law Enforcement Spending As Percent of Total	29

Transportation - Section K

Percent of Travel on Interstates	8
Interstate Mileage In Poor Condition	21
Deficient Bridges	4
Traffic Deaths Per 100 Million Vehicle Miles	14
Seat Belt Use	35
Vehicle Miles Traveled Per Capita	47
Workers Using Public Transportation	18
Road and Street Miles Under State Control	21
Highway Employees	37
Public Transit Employees	15
Highway Spending As Percent of Total	46

Welfare - Section L

Percent of Births To Unwed Mothers	18
AFDC Recipients As Percent of Population	5
Food Stamp Recipients As Percent of Population	25
SSI Recipients As Percent Of Population	15
Change in AFDC Recipients	13
Condition of Children Index	14
Percent of Families With Single Parent	8
Typical Monthly AFDC Payments	6
Welfare as Percent Of Poverty Level Income	6
Average SSI State Supplements Per Recipient	11
State Income Tax Liability Of Typical Family in Poverty	23
Child Support Collections Per $ of Administrative Costs	19
Children In Foster Care	3
State and Local Welfare Spending Per Capita	8
Welfare Spending As Percent of Total	9
Administrative Costs Per AFDC Case	37

Revenues & Finances - Section G

Per Capita General Revenue	38
Per Capita Non-Tax Revenue	17
Per Capita General Spending	31
Change in General Expenditures	4
State Government General Spending	17
Debt As Percent of Revenue	27
Per Capita Full Faith and Credit Debt	28
State Solvency Index	39
Pension Plan Assets	28
State Reserves	13
State Budget Process Quality	11
Relative State Spending "Needs"	36

Education - Section H

Math Proficiency, Eighth Grade	37
AFQT Ranks	47
SAT Scores	23
ACT Scores	n/a
Over-25 Population With High School Diploma	50
Students in Private Schools	31
High School Completion Rates	28
Pupil-Teacher Ratio	24
Public School Enrollment	24
Library Holdings Per Capita	48
Education Spending As Percent of Total	35
Spending Per Pupil	35
Average Teacher Salary	35
State Aid Per Pupil	35
Higher Education Spending As Percent of Total	27
Public Higher Education Enrollment	32
State Per Pupil Support of Higher Education	13
Tuition and Fees	19
Average Professor Salary	27
Education Employees	23

Health - Section I

Infant Mortality Rates	16
State Health Rankings	46
Population Without Health Insurance	13
Abortions	30
Alcohol Consumption	20
Percent Smokers	19
Percent Overweight	29
AIDS Cases	12
Health And Hospital Spending As Percent Of Total	2
Per Capita Medicaid Spending	26
Medicaid Spending Per Aged Recipient	47
Medicaid Spending Per AFDC Child	21
Medicare Payment Per Hospital -Day	32
Population in HMOs	41

Crime - Section J

Crime Rate	11
Violent Crime Rate	5
Murder Rate	21
Property Crime Rate	13
Motor Vehicle Theft Rate	30
Violent Crime Rate Change	19
Change in Prisoners	43
Incarceration Rate	4
Juvenile Violent Crime Rate	22
Corrections Employees	8
State Corrections Spending	42
Law Enforcement Spending As Percent of Total	26

Transportation - Section K

Percent of Travel on Interstates	21
Interstate Mileage In Poor Condition	28
Deficient Bridges	30
Traffic Deaths Per 100 Million Vehicle Miles	23
Seat Belt Use	31
Vehicle Miles Traveled Per Capita	15
Workers Using Public Transportation	36
Road and Street Miles Under State Control	5
Highway Employees	34
Public Transit Employees	34
Highway Spending As Percent of Total	48

Welfare - Section L

Percent of Births To Unwed Mothers	7
AFDC Recipients As Percent of Population	33
Food Stamp Recipients As Percent of Population	18
SSI Recipients As Percent Of Population	10
Change in AFDC Recipients	27
Condition of Children Index	48
Percent of Families With Single Parent	5
Typical Monthly AFDC Payments	44
Welfare as Percent Of Poverty Level Income	45
Average SSI State Supplements Per Recipient	27
State Income Tax Liability Of Typical Family in Poverty	23
Child Support Collections Per $ of Administrative Costs	29
Children In Foster Care	28
State and Local Welfare Spending Per Capita	21
Welfare Spending As Percent of Total	22
Administrative Costs Per AFDC Case	24

South Dakota

Population - Section A

Population 1996	45
Percent Change in Population	37
Population 2000	45
Median Age	37
Percent Population African-American	46
Percent Population In Poverty	27
Percent Population Female	34
Birth Rates	21
Death Rates	36
Illegal Immigrant Population	49

Economies - Section B

Personal Income	46
Per Capita Personal Income	34
Percent Personal Income From Wages and Salaries	50
Average Annual Pay	49
Cost Of Living	41
Average Annual Pay in Manufacturing	48
Average Annual Pay in Retailing	49
Unemployment Rate	47
Government Employment	8
Manufacturing Employment	30
Fortune 500 Companies	24
Tourism Spending Per Capita	29
Exports Per Capita	47
Percent Change in Home Prices	7
Net Farm Income	13
Financial Institution Assets	3
Bankruptcy Filings	45
Patents Issued	48
WC Disability Payment	42
UC Average Weekly Benefit	42
Economic Momentum	24
Employment Change	35
Manufacturing Employment Change	3
Home Ownership	8
Gambling	30

Electricity Use Per Residential Customer	25
Revenue Per Kwh	35
New Companies	43

Geography - Section C

Total Land Area	16
Federally-Owned Land	17
State Park Acreage	29
State Park Visitors	3
Population Not Active	22
Hunters With Firearms	7
Registered Boats	42
State Spending For The Arts	33
Energy Consumption and Per Capita	33
Toxic Chemical Release Per Capita	41
Hazardous Waste Sites	48
Polluted Rivers	7
Air Pollution Emissions	42

Government - Section D

Members of US House	44
Legislators Per Million Population	8
Units of Government	2
Female Legislators	32
Turnover in Legislatures	3
Democrats in State Legislatures	45
Governor's Power Rating	8
Number of Statewide Elected Officials	18
State and Local Government Employees	21
State and Local Average Salaries	46
Local Employment	37
Local Spending Accountability	9
Registered Voters	5
Statewide Initiatives	18

Federal - Section E

Per Capita Federal Spending	18
Increase In Federal Spending	32
Per Capita Federal Grant Spending	5
Per Capita Federal Spending On Procurement	37
Per Capita Federal Spending on Social Security and Medicare	29
Social Security Benefits	44
Federal Spending On Employee Wages and Salaries	13
Federal Grant Spending Per $ of State Tax Revenue	3
General Revenue From Federal Government	5
Federal Tax Burden Per Capita	37
Highway Charges Returned to States	4
Terms of Trade	6
Per Capita Federal Income Tax Liability	36

Taxes - Section F

Tax Revenue	44
Per Capita Tax Revenue	45
Tax Effort	43
Tax Capacity	41
Percent Change In Taxes	18
Property Taxes Per Capita	26
Property Tax Revenue as Percent of Three-Tax Revenues	8
Sales Taxes Per Capita	18
Sales Tax Revenue as Percent of Three-Tax Revenues	12
Services With Sales Tax	5
Income Taxes Per Capita	44
Income Tax Revenue as Percent of Three-Tax Revenues	44
Motor Fuel Taxes	34
Tobacco Taxes	24
Tax Burden on High Income Family	36
Progressivity of Taxes	5

Revenues & Finances - Section G

Per Capita General Revenue	37
Per Capita Non-Tax Revenue	34
Per Capita General Spending	37
Change in General Expenditures	14
State Government General Spending	28
Debt As Percent of Revenue	29
Per Capita Full Faith and Credit Debt	44
State Solvency Index	10
Pension Plan Assets	31
State Reserves	38
State Budget Process Quality	24
Relative State Spending "Needs"	45

Education - Section H

Math Proficiency, Eighth Grade	n/a
AFQT Ranks	21
SAT Scores	n/a
ACT Scores	13
Over-25 Population With High School Diploma	31
Students in Private Schools	35
High School Completion Rates	14
Pupil-Teacher Ratio	4
Public School Enrollment	9
Library Holdings Per Capita	17
Education Spending As Percent of Total	26
Spending Per Pupil	41
Average Teacher Salary	50
State Aid Per Pupil	49
Higher Education Spending As Percent of Total	29
Public Higher Education Enrollment	31
State Per Pupil Support of Higher Education	39
Tuition and Fees	24
Average Professor Salary	49
Education Employees	17

Health - Section I

Infant Mortality Rates	45
State Health Rankings	31
Population Without Health Insurance	45
Abortions	47
Alcohol Consumption	23
Percent Smokers	31
Percent Overweight	28
AIDS Cases	48
Health And Hospital Spending As Percent Of Total	43
Per Capita Medicaid Spending	22
Medicaid Spending Per Aged Recipient	14
Medicaid Spending Per AFDC Child	14
Medicare Payment Per Hospital -Day	42
Population in HMOs	44

Crime - Section J

Crime Rate	47
Violent Crime Rate	45
Murder Rate	48
Property Crime Rate	47
Motor Vehicle Theft Rate	50
Violent Crime Rate Change	3
Change in Prisoners	7
Incarceration Rate	34
Juvenile Violent Crime Rate	26
Corrections Employees	45
State Corrections Spending	43
Law Enforcement Spending As Percent of Total	39

Transportation - Section K

Percent of Travel on Interstates	18
Interstate Mileage In Poor Condition	5
Deficient Bridges	48
Traffic Deaths Per 100 Million Vehicle Miles	25
Seat Belt Use	47
Vehicle Miles Traveled Per Capita	18
Workers Using Public Transportation	50
Road and Street Miles Under State Control	44
Highway Employees	3
Public Transit Employees	48
Highway Spending As Percent of Total	1

Welfare - Section L

Percent of Births To Unwed Mothers	32
AFDC Recipients As Percent of Population	46
Food Stamp Recipients As Percent of Population	40
SSI Recipients As Percent Of Population	27
Change in AFDC Recipients	40
Condition of Children Index	18
Percent of Families With Single Parent	46
Typical Monthly AFDC Payments	31
Welfare as Percent Of Poverty Level Income	17
Average SSI State Supplements Per Recipient	24
State Income Tax Liability Of Typical Family in Poverty	n/a
Child Support Collections Per $ of Administrative Costs	5
Children In Foster Care	46
State and Local Welfare Spending Per Capita	37
Welfare Spending As Percent of Total	36
Administrative Costs Per AFDC Case	21

Tennessee

Population - Section A

Population 1996	2
Percent Change in Population	8
Population 2000	2
Median Age	48
Percent Population African-American	17
Percent Population In Poverty	11
Percent Population Female	37
Birth Rates	3
Death Rates	23
Illegal Immigrant Population	2

Economies - Section B

Personal Income	3
Per Capita Personal Income	31
Percent Personal Income From Wages and Salaries	18
Average Annual Pay	12
Cost Of Living	47
Average Annual Pay in Manufacturing	18
Average Annual Pay in Retailing	17
Unemployment Rate	11
Government Employment	20
Manufacturing Employment	35
Fortune 500 Companies	16
Tourism Spending Per Capita	32
Exports Per Capita	5
Percent Change in Home Prices	36
Net Farm Income	5
Financial Institution Assets	33
Bankruptcy Filings	35
Patents Issued	23
WC Disability Payment	23
UC Average Weekly Benefit	23
Economic Momentum	9
Employment Change	11
Manufacturing Employment Change	17
Home Ownership	21
Gambling	8

Electricity Use Per Residential Customer	10
Revenue Per Kwh	7
New Companies	29

Geography - Section C

Total Land Area	2
Federally-Owned Land	19
State Park Acreage	3
State Park Visitors	45
Population Not Active	25
Hunters With Firearms	29
Registered Boats	5
State Spending For The Arts	49
Energy Consumption and Per Capita	4
Toxic Chemical Release Per Capita	8
Hazardous Waste Sites	14
Polluted Rivers	33
Air Pollution Emissions	1

Government - Section D

Members of US House	3
Legislators Per Million Population	49
Units of Government	31
Female Legislators	30
Turnover in Legislatures	30
Democrats in State Legislatures	23
Governor's Power Rating	49
Number of Statewide Elected Officials	30
State and Local Government Employees	12
State and Local Average Salaries	36
Local Employment	3
Local Spending Accountability	7
Registered Voters	20
Statewide Initiatives	n/a

Federal - Section E

Per Capita Federal Spending	40
Increase In Federal Spending	13
Per Capita Federal Grant Spending	44
Per Capita Federal Spending On Procurement	18
Per Capita Federal Spending on Social Security and Medicare	46
Social Security Benefits	35
Federal Spending On Employee Wages and Salaries	23
Federal Grant Spending Per $ of State Tax Revenue	18
General Revenue From Federal Government	30
Federal Tax Burden Per Capita	30
Highway Charges Returned to States	50
Terms of Trade	34
Per Capita Federal Income Tax Liability	25

Taxes - Section F

Tax Revenue	39
Per Capita Tax Revenue	36
Tax Effort	37
Tax Capacity	21
Percent Change In Taxes	13
Property Taxes Per Capita	21
Property Tax Revenue as Percent of Three-Tax Revenues	13
Sales Taxes Per Capita	8
Sales Tax Revenue as Percent of Three-Tax Revenues	9
Services With Sales Tax	9
Income Taxes Per Capita	n/a
Income Tax Revenue as Percent of Three-Tax Revenues	n/a
Motor Fuel Taxes	21
Tobacco Taxes	14
Tax Burden on High Income Family	40
Progressivity of Taxes	6

Texas

Utah

Revenues & Finances - Section G

Per Capita General Revenue	36
Per Capita Non-Tax Revenue	24
Per Capita General Spending	39
Change in General Expenditures	11
State Government General Spending	24
Debt As Percent of Revenue	1
Per Capita Full Faith and Credit Debt	35
State Solvency Index	13
Pension Plan Assets	36
State Reserves	32
State Budget Process Quality	12
Relative State Spending "Needs"	44

Education - Section H

Math Proficiency, Eighth Grade	12
AFQT Ranks	17
SAT Scores	n/a
ACT Scores	7
Over-25 Population With High School Diploma	2
Students in Private Schools	49
High School Completion Rates	5
Pupil-Teacher Ratio	50
Public School Enrollment	1
Library Holdings Per Capita	27
Education Spending As Percent of Total	1
Spending Per Pupil	50
Average Teacher Salary	40
State Aid Per Pupil	32
Higher Education Spending As Percent of Total	2
Public Higher Education Enrollment	7
State Per Pupil Support of Higher Education	32
Tuition and Fees	44
Average Professor Salary	33
Education Employees	35

Health - Section I

Infant Mortality Rates	40
State Health Rankings	2
Population Without Health Insurance	32
Abortions	47
Alcohol Consumption	50
Percent Smokers	50
Percent Overweight	41
AIDS Cases	34
Health And Hospital Spending As Percent Of Total	32
Per Capita Medicaid Spending	49
Medicaid Spending Per Aged Recipient	26
Medicaid Spending Per AFDC Child	41
Medicare Payment Per Hospital -Day	10
Population in HMOs	4

Crime - Section J

Crime Rate	10
Violent Crime Rate	39
Murder Rate	38
Property Crime Rate	6
Motor Vehicle Theft Rate	28
Violent Crime Rate Change	15
Change in Prisoners	7
Incarceration Rate	44
Juvenile Violent Crime Rate	25
Corrections Employees	40
State Corrections Spending	3
Law Enforcement Spending As Percent of Total	31

Transportation - Section K

Percent of Travel on Interstates	1
Interstate Mileage In Poor Condition	41
Deficient Bridges	17
Traffic Deaths Per 100 Million Vehicle Miles	48
Seat Belt Use	33
Vehicle Miles Traveled Per Capita	25
Workers Using Public Transportation	23
Road and Street Miles Under State Control	28
Highway Employees	44
Public Transit Employees	12
Highway Spending As Percent of Total	33

Welfare - Section L

Percent of Births To Unwed Mothers	50
AFDC Recipients As Percent of Population	49
Food Stamp Recipients As Percent of Population	48
SSI Recipients As Percent Of Population	49
Change in AFDC Recipients	38
Condition of Children Index	7
Percent of Families With Single Parent	50
Typical Monthly AFDC Payments	20
Welfare as Percent Of Poverty Level Income	17
Average SSI State Supplements Per Recipient	40
State Income Tax Liability Of Typical Family in Poverty	20
Child Support Collections Per $ of Administrative Costs	45
Children In Foster Care	48
State and Local Welfare Spending Per Capita	47
Welfare Spending As Percent of Total	42
Administrative Costs Per AFDC Case	2

Vermont

Revenues & Finances - Section G

Per Capita General Revenue	43
Per Capita Non-Tax Revenue	29
Per Capita General Spending	40
Change in General Expenditures	44
State Government General Spending	42
Debt As Percent of Revenue	25
Per Capita Full Faith and Credit Debt	24
State Solvency Index	29
Pension Plan Assets	27
State Reserves	33
State Budget Process Quality	41
Relative State Spending "Needs"	10

Education - Section H

Math Proficiency, Eighth Grade	20
AFQT Ranks	37
SAT Scores	10
ACT Scores	n/a
Over-25 Population With High School Diploma	32
Students in Private Schools	30
High School Completion Rates	29
Pupil-Teacher Ratio	7
Public School Enrollment	38
Library Holdings Per Capita	30
Education Spending As Percent of Total	15
Spending Per Pupil	17
Average Teacher Salary	26
State Aid Per Pupil	45
Higher Education Spending As Percent of Total	22
Public Higher Education Enrollment	21
State Per Pupil Support of Higher Education	41
Tuition and Fees	9
Average Professor Salary	7
Education Employees	21

Health - Section I

Infant Mortality Rates	27
State Health Rankings	11
Population Without Health Insurance	30
Abortions	18
Alcohol Consumption	36
Percent Smokers	27
Percent Overweight	22
AIDS Cases	17
Health And Hospital Spending As Percent Of Total	27
Per Capita Medicaid Spending	45
Medicaid Spending Per Aged Recipient	40
Medicaid Spending Per AFDC Child	44
Medicare Payment Per Hospital -Day	28
Population in HMOs	27

Crime - Section J

Crime Rate	41
Violent Crime Rate	36
Murder Rate	22
Property Crime Rate	41
Motor Vehicle Theft Rate	40
Violent Crime Rate Change	25
Change in Prisoners	20
Incarceration Rate	17
Juvenile Violent Crime Rate	32
Corrections Employees	7
State Corrections Spending	22
Law Enforcement Spending As Percent of Total	10

Transportation - Section K

Percent of Travel on Interstates	7
Interstate Mileage In Poor Condition	24
Deficient Bridges	18
Traffic Deaths Per 100 Million Vehicle Miles	37
Seat Belt Use	15
Vehicle Miles Traveled Per Capita	17
Workers Using Public Transportation	10
Road and Street Miles Under State Control	3
Highway Employees	23
Public Transit Employees	28
Highway Spending As Percent of Total	20

Welfare - Section L

Percent of Births To Unwed Mothers	33
AFDC Recipients As Percent of Population	42
Food Stamp Recipients As Percent of Population	29
SSI Recipients As Percent Of Population	26
Change in AFDC Recipients	23
Condition of Children Index	22
Percent of Families With Single Parent	37
Typical Monthly AFDC Payments	36
Welfare as Percent Of Poverty Level Income	29
Average SSI State Supplements Per Recipient	25
State Income Tax Liability Of Typical Family in Poverty	8
Child Support Collections Per $ of Administrative Costs	15
Children In Foster Care	38
State and Local Welfare Spending Per Capita	46
Welfare Spending As Percent of Total	41
Administrative Costs Per AFDC Case	22

Washington

Population - Section A

Population 1996	15
Percent Change in Population	10
Population 2000	15
Median Age	24
Percent Population African-American	35
Percent Population In Poverty	24
Percent Population Female	41
Birth Rates	17
Death Rates	41
Illegal Immigrant Population	10

Economies - Section B

Personal Income	15
Per Capita Personal Income	15
Percent Personal Income From Wages and Salaries	24
Average Annual Pay	14
Cost Of Living	13
Average Annual Pay in Manufacturing	8
Average Annual Pay in Retailing	10
Unemployment Rate	22
Government Employment	16
Manufacturing Employment	26
Fortune 500 Companies	23
Tourism Spending Per Capita	37
Exports Per Capita	3
Percent Change in Home Prices	28
Net Farm Income	12
Financial Institution Assets	28
Bankruptcy Filings	10
Patents Issued	21
WC Disability Payment	8
UC Average Weekly Benefit	8
Economic Momentum	4
Employment Change	4
Manufacturing Employment Change	2
Home Ownership	23
Gambling	23

Electricity Use Per Residential Customer	4
Revenue Per Kwh	24
New Companies	1

Geography - Section C

Total Land Area	20
Federally-Owned Land	12
State Park Acreage	13
State Park Visitors	4
Population Not Active	48
Hunters With Firearms	36
Registered Boats	18
State Spending For The Arts	47
Energy Consumption and Per Capita	15
Toxic Chemical Release Per Capita	35
Hazardous Waste Sites	7
Polluted Rivers	4
Air Pollution Emissions	18

Government - Section D

Members of US House	15
Legislators Per Million Population	34
Units of Government	26
Female Legislators	1
Turnover in Legislatures	19
Democrats in State Legislatures	34
Governor's Power Rating	38
Number of Statewide Elected Officials	7
State and Local Government Employees	34
State and Local Average Salaries	7
Local Employment	34
Local Spending Accountability	36
Registered Voters	29
Statewide Initiatives	4

Federal - Section E

Per Capita Federal Spending	19
Increase In Federal Spending	9
Per Capita Federal Grant Spending	32
Per Capita Federal Spending On Procurement	13
Per Capita Federal Spending on Social Security and Medicare	39
Social Security Benefits	7
Federal Spending On Employee Wages and Salaries	8
Federal Grant Spending Per $ of State Tax Revenue	46
General Revenue From Federal Government	37
Federal Tax Burden Per Capita	11
Highway Charges Returned to States	18
Terms of Trade	39
Per Capita Federal Income Tax Liability	11

Taxes - Section F

Tax Revenue	14
Per Capita Tax Revenue	10
Tax Effort	17
Tax Capacity	12
Percent Change In Taxes	3
Property Taxes Per Capita	20
Property Tax Revenue as Percent of Three-Tax Revenues	28
Sales Taxes Per Capita	2
Sales Tax Revenue as Percent of Three-Tax Revenues	3
Services With Sales Tax	2
Income Taxes Per Capita	n/a
Income Tax Revenue as Percent of Three-Tax Revenues	n/a
Motor Fuel Taxes	11
Tobacco Taxes	1
Tax Burden on High Income Family	43
Progressivity of Taxes	4

Washington

Revenues & Finances - Section G

Per Capita General Revenue	11
Per Capita Non-Tax Revenue	15
Per Capita General Spending	10
Change in General Expenditures	3
State Government General Spending	12
Debt As Percent of Revenue	9
Per Capita Full Faith and Credit Debt	8
State Solvency Index	36
Pension Plan Assets	17
State Reserves	31
State Budget Process Quality	42
Relative State Spending "Needs"	15

Education - Section H

Math Proficiency, Eighth Grade	14
AFQT Ranks	10
SAT Scores	2
ACT Scores	n/a
Over-25 Population With High School Diploma	3
Students in Private Schools	34
High School Completion Rates	36
Pupil-Teacher Ratio	48
Public School Enrollment	20
Library Holdings Per Capita	25
Education Spending As Percent of Total	22
Spending Per Pupil	21
Average Teacher Salary	18
State Aid Per Pupil	6
Higher Education Spending As Percent of Total	28
Public Higher Education Enrollment	18
State Per Pupil Support of Higher Education	26
Tuition and Fees	21
Average Professor Salary	31
Education Employees	49

Health - Section I

Infant Mortality Rates	46
State Health Rankings	12
Population Without Health Insurance	26
Abortions	8
Alcohol Consumption	24
Percent Smokers	45
Percent Overweight	40
AIDS Cases	22
Health And Hospital Spending As Percent Of Total	23
Per Capita Medicaid Spending	46
Medicaid Spending Per Aged Recipient	23
Medicaid Spending Per AFDC Child	47
Medicare Payment Per Hospital -Day	31
Population in HMOs	17

Crime - Section J

Crime Rate	9
Violent Crime Rate	27
Murder Rate	30
Property Crime Rate	5
Motor Vehicle Theft Rate	16
Violent Crime Rate Change	33
Change in Prisoners	22
Incarceration Rate	40
Juvenile Violent Crime Rate	14
Corrections Employees	22
State Corrections Spending	8
Law Enforcement Spending As Percent of Total	25

Transportation - Section K

Percent of Travel on Interstates	12
Interstate Mileage In Poor Condition	14
Deficient Bridges	13
Traffic Deaths Per 100 Million Vehicle Miles	8
Seat Belt Use	3
Vehicle Miles Traveled Per Capita	38
Workers Using Public Transportation	9
Road and Street Miles Under State Control	15
Highway Employees	25
Public Transit Employees	2
Highway Spending As Percent of Total	28

Welfare - Section L

Percent of Births To Unwed Mothers	38
AFDC Recipients As Percent of Population	10
Food Stamp Recipients As Percent of Population	28
SSI Recipients As Percent Of Population	30
Change in AFDC Recipients	11
Condition of Children Index	16
Percent of Families With Single Parent	26
Typical Monthly AFDC Payments	5
Welfare as Percent Of Poverty Level Income	8
Average SSI State Supplements Per Recipient	19
State Income Tax Liability Of Typical Family in Poverty	n/a
Child Support Collections Per $ of Administrative Costs	23
Children In Foster Care	19
State and Local Welfare Spending Per Capita	18
Welfare Spending As Percent of Total	30
Administrative Costs Per AFDC Case	19

West Virginia

Revenues & Finances - Section G

Per Capita General Revenue	34
Per Capita Non-Tax Revenue	32
Per Capita General Spending	33
Change in General Expenditures	5
State Government General Spending	8
Debt As Percent of Revenue	26
Per Capita Full Faith and Credit Debt	50
State Solvency Index	46
Pension Plan Assets	49
State Reserves	20
State Budget Process Quality	30
Relative State Spending "Needs"	42

Education - Section H

Math Proficiency, Eighth Grade	29
AFQT Ranks	44
SAT Scores	n/a
ACT Scores	24
Over-25 Population With High School Diploma	47
Students in Private Schools	46
High School Completion Rates	33
Pupil-Teacher Ratio	9
Public School Enrollment	34
Library Holdings Per Capita	30
Education Spending As Percent of Total	23
Spending Per Pupil	12
Average Teacher Salary	34
State Aid Per Pupil	7
Higher Education Spending As Percent of Total	33
Public Higher Education Enrollment	30
State Per Pupil Support of Higher Education	21
Tuition and Fees	40
Average Professor Salary	37
Education Employees	20

Health - Section I

Infant Mortality Rates	12
State Health Rankings	2
Population Without Health Insurance	16
Abortions	45
Alcohol Consumption	49
Percent Smokers	7
Percent Overweight	5
AIDS Cases	38
Health And Hospital Spending As Percent Of Total	37
Per Capita Medicaid Spending	5
Medicaid Spending Per Aged Recipient	31
Medicaid Spending Per AFDC Child	24
Medicare Payment Per Hospital -Day	48
Population in HMOs	39

Crime - Section J

Crime Rate	50
Violent Crime Rate	44
Murder Rate	31
Property Crime Rate	50
Motor Vehicle Theft Rate	46
Violent Crime Rate Change	6
Change in Prisoners	n/a
Incarceration Rate	46
Juvenile Violent Crime Rate	38
Corrections Employees	50
State Corrections Spending	38
Law Enforcement Spending As Percent of Total	49

Transportation - Section K

Percent of Travel on Interstates	14
Interstate Mileage In Poor Condition	10
Deficient Bridges	5
Traffic Deaths Per 100 Million Vehicle Miles	3
Seat Belt Use	35
Vehicle Miles Traveled Per Capita	27
Workers Using Public Transportation	36
Road and Street Miles Under State Control	1
Highway Employees	4
Public Transit Employees	27
Highway Spending As Percent of Total	9

Welfare - Section L

Percent of Births To Unwed Mothers	24
AFDC Recipients As Percent of Population	9
Food Stamp Recipients As Percent of Population	2
SSI Recipients As Percent Of Population	5
Change in AFDC Recipients	37
Condition of Children Index	37
Percent of Families With Single Parent	21
Typical Monthly AFDC Payments	41
Welfare as Percent Of Poverty Level Income	43
Average SSI State Supplements Per Recipient	49
State Income Tax Liability Of Typical Family in Poverty	9
Child Support Collections Per $ of Administrative Costs	24
Children In Foster Care	22
State and Local Welfare Spending Per Capita	9
Welfare Spending As Percent of Total	3
Administrative Costs Per AFDC Case	50

Wisconsin

Population - Section A

Population 1996	18
Percent Change in Population	28
Population 2000	18
Median Age	18
Percent Population African-American	29
Percent Population In Poverty	44
Percent Population Female	30
Birth Rates	41
Death Rates	39
Illegal Immigrant Population	32

Economies - Section B

Personal Income	18
Per Capita Personal Income	23
Percent Personal Income From Wages and Salaries	19
Average Annual Pay	28
Cost Of Living	27
Average Annual Pay in Manufacturing	23
Average Annual Pay in Retailing	42
Unemployment Rate	38
Government Employment	39
Manufacturing Employment	4
Fortune 500 Companies	21
Tourism Spending Per Capita	43
Exports Per Capita	19
Percent Change in Home Prices	10
Net Farm Income	28
Financial Institution Assets	18
Bankruptcy Filings	38
Patents Issued	17
WC Disability Payment	17
UC Average Weekly Benefit	17
Economic Momentum	36
Employment Change	20
Manufacturing Employment Change	26
Home Ownership	3
Gambling	29

Electricity Use Per Residential Customer	34
Revenue Per Kwh	15
New Companies	48

Geography - Section C

Total Land Area	25
Federally-Owned Land	15
State Park Acreage	25
State Park Visitors	25
Population Not Active	30
Hunters With Firearms	4
Registered Boats	6
State Spending For The Arts	39
Energy Consumption and Per Capita	27
Toxic Chemical Release Per Capita	32
Hazardous Waste Sites	9
Polluted Rivers	42
Air Pollution Emissions	20

Government - Section D

Members of US House	15
Legislators Per Million Population	37
Units of Government	16
Female Legislators	19
Turnover in Legislatures	46
Democrats in State Legislatures	28
Governor's Power Rating	14
Number of Statewide Elected Officials	18
State and Local Government Employees	35
State and Local Average Salaries	14
Local Employment	5
Local Spending Accountability	41
Registered Voters	39
Statewide Initiatives	n/a

Federal - Section E

Per Capita Federal Spending	50
Increase In Federal Spending	39
Per Capita Federal Grant Spending	40
Per Capita Federal Spending On Procurement	47
Per Capita Federal Spending on Social Security and Medicare	25
Social Security Benefits	10
Federal Spending On Employee Wages and Salaries	50
Federal Grant Spending Per $ of State Tax Revenue	48
General Revenue From Federal Government	40
Federal Tax Burden Per Capita	23
Highway Charges Returned to States	30
Terms of Trade	35
Per Capita Federal Income Tax Liability	20

Taxes - Section F

Tax Revenue	4
Per Capita Tax Revenue	8
Tax Effort	3
Tax Capacity	35
Percent Change In Taxes	14
Property Taxes Per Capita	9
Property Tax Revenue as Percent of Three-Tax Revenues	16
Sales Taxes Per Capita	30
Sales Tax Revenue as Percent of Three-Tax Revenues	40
Services With Sales Tax	14
Income Taxes Per Capita	8
Income Tax Revenue as Percent of Three-Tax Revenues	13
Motor Fuel Taxes	9
Tobacco Taxes	10
Tax Burden on High Income Family	2
Progressivity of Taxes	20

Wisconsin

Revenues & Finances - Section G

Per Capita General Revenue	14
Per Capita Non-Tax Revenue	30
Per Capita General Spending	13
Change in General Expenditures	21
State Government General Spending	35
Debt As Percent of Revenue	34
Per Capita Full Faith and Credit Debt	12
State Solvency Index	16
Pension Plan Assets	6
State Reserves	41
State Budget Process Quality	45
Relative State Spending "Needs"	24

Education - Section H

Math Proficiency, Eighth Grade	5
AFQT Ranks	3
SAT Scores	n/a
ACT Scores	1
Over-25 Population With High School Diploma	6
Students in Private Schools	7
High School Completion Rates	4
Pupil-Teacher Ratio	20
Public School Enrollment	29
Library Holdings Per Capita	21
Education Spending As Percent of Total	14
Spending Per Pupil	10
Average Teacher Salary	14
State Aid Per Pupil	8
Higher Education Spending As Percent of Total	17
Public Higher Education Enrollment	13
State Per Pupil Support of Higher Education	38
Tuition and Fees	22
Average Professor Salary	19
Education Employees	33

Health - Section I

Infant Mortality Rates	24
State Health Rankings	7
Population Without Health Insurance	50
Abortions	32
Alcohol Consumption	5
Percent Smokers	31
Percent Overweight	12
AIDS Cases	42
Health And Hospital Spending As Percent Of Total	36
Per Capita Medicaid Spending	35
Medicaid Spending Per Aged Recipient	9
Medicaid Spending Per AFDC Child	38
Medicare Payment Per Hospital -Day	29
Population in HMOs	19

Crime - Section J

Crime Rate	42
Violent Crime Rate	42
Murder Rate	34
Property Crime Rate	42
Motor Vehicle Theft Rate	31
Violent Crime Rate Change	17
Change in Prisoners	4
Incarceration Rate	38
Juvenile Violent Crime Rate	13
Corrections Employees	35
State Corrections Spending	10
Law Enforcement Spending As Percent of Total	24

Transportation - Section K

Percent of Travel on Interstates	49
Interstate Mileage In Poor Condition	20
Deficient Bridges	41
Traffic Deaths Per 100 Million Vehicle Miles	18
Seat Belt Use	31
Vehicle Miles Traveled Per Capita	22
Workers Using Public Transportation	18
Road and Street Miles Under State Control	39
Highway Employees	32
Public Transit Employees	19
Highway Spending As Percent of Total	18

Welfare - Section L

Percent of Births To Unwed Mothers	37
AFDC Recipients As Percent of Population	31
Food Stamp Recipients As Percent of Population	49
SSI Recipients As Percent Of Population	29
Change in AFDC Recipients	50
Condition of Children Index	9
Percent of Families With Single Parent	37
Typical Monthly AFDC Payments	12
Welfare as Percent Of Poverty Level Income	12
Average SSI State Supplements Per Recipient	36
State Income Tax Liability Of Typical Family in Poverty	38
Child Support Collections Per $ of Administrative Costs	3
Children In Foster Care	26
State and Local Welfare Spending Per Capita	14
Welfare Spending As Percent of Total	17
Administrative Costs Per AFDC Case	3

Wyoming

Population - Section A

Population 1996	50
Percent Change in Population	36
Population 2000	50
Median Age	24
Percent Population African-American	43
Percent Population In Poverty	24
Percent Population Female	47
Birth Rates	40
Death Rates	32
Illegal Immigrant Population	47

Economies - Section B

Personal Income	50
Per Capita Personal Income	35
Percent Personal Income From Wages and Salaries	38
Average Annual Pay	45
Cost Of Living	25
Average Annual Pay in Manufacturing	41
Average Annual Pay in Retailing	47
Unemployment Rate	20
Government Employment	2
Manufacturing Employment	48
Fortune 500 Companies	n/a
Tourism Spending Per Capita	3
Exports Per Capita	40
Percent Change in Home Prices	5
Net Farm Income	44
Financial Institution Assets	17
Bankruptcy Filings	28
Patents Issued	38
WC Disability Payment	34
UC Average Weekly Benefit	34
Economic Momentum	48
Employment Change	49
Manufacturing Employment Change	30
Home Ownership	25
Gambling	47

Electricity Use Per Residential Customer	31
Revenue Per Kwh	22
New Companies	6

Geography - Section C

Total Land Area	9
Federally-Owned Land	8
State Park Acreage	27
State Park Visitors	12
Population Not Active	44
Hunters With Firearms	2
Registered Boats	49
State Spending For The Arts	26
Energy Consumption and Per Capita	3
Toxic Chemical Release Per Capita	5
Hazardous Waste Sites	46
Polluted Rivers	15
Air Pollution Emissions	38

Government - Section D

Members of US House	44
Legislators Per Million Population	4
Units of Government	7
Female Legislators	31
Turnover in Legislatures	12
Democrats in State Legislatures	47
Governor's Power Rating	21
Number of Statewide Elected Officials	13
State and Local Government Employees	1
State and Local Average Salaries	42
Local Employment	16
Local Spending Accountability	30
Registered Voters	39
Statewide Initiatives	16

Federal - Section E

Per Capita Federal Spending	21
Increase In Federal Spending	24
Per Capita Federal Grant Spending	2
Per Capita Federal Spending On Procurement	40
Per Capita Federal Spending on Social Security and Medicare	41
Social Security Benefits	23
Federal Spending On Employee Wages and Salaries	10
Federal Grant Spending Per $ of State Tax Revenue	1
General Revenue From Federal Government	3
Federal Tax Burden Per Capita	21
Highway Charges Returned to States	10
Terms of Trade	4
Per Capita Federal Income Tax Liability	19

Taxes - Section F

Tax Revenue	6
Per Capita Tax Revenue	12
Tax Effort	46
Tax Capacity	3
Percent Change In Taxes	46
Property Taxes Per Capita	13
Property Tax Revenue as Percent of Three-Tax Revenues	3
Sales Taxes Per Capita	36
Sales Tax Revenue as Percent of Three-Tax Revenues	21
Services With Sales Tax	17
Income Taxes Per Capita	n/a
Income Tax Revenue as Percent of Three-Tax Revenues	n/a
Motor Fuel Taxes	48
Tobacco Taxes	45
Tax Burden on High Income Family	49
Progressivity of Taxes	9

Index

AARP. *See* American Association of Retired Persons

Abortions, 226

Acquired immunodeficiency syndrome (AIDS), 230. *See also* Health and health care

AFDC. *See* Aid to Families with Dependent Children

Age. *See* Population

Agriculture. *See* Farming and agriculture

AIDS. *See* Acquired immunodeficiency syndrome

Aid to Families with Dependent Children (AFDC), 131, 239, 285, 288, 291, 300

Alabama, 2, 5, 304-305

Alaska, 3, 4, 9, 11, 306-307

Alcohol consumption, 227

American Association of Retired Persons (AARP), 3

American Demographics, 6

Annie B. Casey Foundation, 2

Arizona, 308-309

Arkansas, 310-311

Armed forces qualification test, 192

Arts. *See* Cultural attractions and recreation

Banks. *See* Financial institution assets

Benefits
disability, 61
federal payments to individuals, 120
federal share of, 131
Medicare, 121
Social Security, 121-122
state pensions, 180

unemployment, 8, 62

Birth rates. *See* Social issues

Bridges. *See* Transportation

Bureau of Labor Statistics, 1, 8

"Business climate," 8

Business issues. *See also* Decisionmaking; Economic issues; Taxes; Trade
bankruptcy filings, 59
business location, 6, 7-8
Business Week 1000 companies, 52
costs, 6, 7
federal procurement, 119
Fortune 500 companies, 51
government regulation, 7-8
manufacturing, 4, 6, 7, 42, 50, 65
multistate firms, 7
new companies, 70
pro-business attitudes, 8
productivity, 6-7
retailing, 45
taxes, 7, 9
travel expenses, 5
utility costs, 69
wages and salaries, 39-41, 44-45

Business Week 1000 companies, 52

California, 4, 5, 312-313

Capital punishment, 4. *See also* Crime; Law enforcement

Center for Budget and Policy Priorities, 9

Children. *See also* Decisionmaking; Education; Social issues; Welfare
child support collections, 295-296
Condition of Children Index, 289
with disabilities, 201
environment for, 2

foster care, 297
infant mortality rates, 223
poverty rate, 27

Children's Defense Fund, 2

Colorado, 4, 314-315

Common Cause, 11

Connecticut, 11, 316-317

Construction industry, 1

Corporation for Enterprise Development, 8

Corrections. *See* Crime; Law enforcement

Cost of living index, 43

County Business Patterns, 1, 8

Crime. *See also* Decisionmaking
crime rates, 248-253
juvenile, 257
prisons and prisoners, 254-256, 261
safety from, 5
sentences, 258
spending on, 261-265

Cultural attractions and recreation. *See also* Decisionmaking; Environment
boats, 82
government support of, 8
hunting, 81
retirement and, 3
spending for the arts, 83
state parks, 78-79

Death rates. *See* Social issues

Decisionmaking. *See also* Information resources
business or home location, 1, 6, 7
children's issues, 2
commercial issues, 8
crime and law enforcement issues, 5